W9-AUV-529

תנ״ך

ArtScroll Tanach Series®

A traditional commentary on the Books of the Bible

Rabbis Nosson Scherman/Meir Zlotowitz
General Editors

Tehillim

Vol. 3

Tehillim

TEHILLIM / A NEW TRANSLATION WITH A COMMENTARY ANTHOLOGIZED FROM TALMUDIC, MIDRASHIC AND RABBINIC SOURCES.

Published by
Mesorah Publications, ltd.

Commentary by
Rabbi Avrohom Chaim Feuer

Translation by
Rabbi Avrohom Chaim Feuer
in collaboration with
Rabbi Nosson Scherman

FIRST EDITION
First Impression ... June, 1979

Published and Distributed by
MESORAH PUBLICATIONS, Ltd.
Brooklyn, New York 11223

Distributed in Israel by
MESORAH MAFITZIM
Rechov Bayit Vegan 90/5
Jerusalem, Israel

ISBN
TEHILLIM/PSALMS Volume 3
0-89906-054-4 (hard cover)
0-89906-055-2 (paperback)

סֻדַּר בִּמְסַדֶּרֶת
חֶבְרַת אַרְטְסְקְרוֹל בע״מ

Typography by Compuscribe at ArtScroll Studios, Ltd.
1969 Coney Island Ave. / Brooklyn, N.Y. 11223 / (212) 339-1700

מוקדש לזכר נשמת

מו״ר הרה״ג

ר׳ רפאל ברוך סורוצקין זצ״ל

ראש ישיבת טלז

נפטר לעולמו י״ג שבט תשל״ט

Dedicated to the memory of

Hagaon Harav Boruch Sorotzkin זצ״ל

Rosh Hayeshivah of Telshe

The blessed years of his life
were a constant psalm of joy
inspired by his burning love
of Torah and Klal Yisrael

תנצב״ה

Author's Preface

The Talmud (Bava Basra *16b) relates: Hanging from the neck of the Patriarch, Abraham, was a brilliant gem that cured the infirmities of all who gazed at it. When Abraham died, God took the gem and hung it on the fiery globe of the sun.*

Rabbeinu Bachya *(introduction to* Parshas Yisro) *gives an allegorical interpretation. Abraham was an eloquent orator who could convince even the most stubborn heretic of God's existence and power. This gem-like power of speech 'hung from his neck,' so to speak, in his throat and vocal chords. His luminous words cured the spiritually weak and the ailing in faith.*

When Abraham was gone, no man could replace him. Only the wonders of nature could so eloquently attest to God's Presence, and nothing could do so as well as the sun — the source of all energy and growth. The Psalmist says: The heavens declare the glory of God, and the expanse of the sky tells of His handiwork *(19:2).*

Tehillim, *perhaps more than any other part of* Tanach, *provides the means with which to see and hear the sun's message. Through the two years of research that have thus far gone into these* ARTSCROLL TEHILLIM *volumes, the author has been privileged to feel an intimate fellowship of the soul with all the countless Jews who have seen Abraham's gem and heard its message in every ray of the sun, every rumble of thunder, every breath of air and flash of intuition.*

The concluding stages of this work have coincided with our move to America's land of the sun to assume the position of dean of the Louis Merwitzer Mesivta of Greater Miami. Others came here earlier to show how the message of HASHEM *Yisborach can be found in every locale. May we be granted His help to continue and broaden their work.*

Finally, a feeble attempt to express the inexpressible. My wife, Luba תחי׳*, brings alive the tradition of love and sacrifice for Torah on which she was nurtured. Whatever she touches, she imbues with the message of Torah and faith. This* sefer *and the development of her home are the most eloquent testimony to her.*

May we be granted the privilege of helping build a community of Torah and completing the final volumes of the ARTSCROLL TEHILLIM.

Avrohom Chaim Feuer

Miami Beach, Florida
Erev Shavuos, 5739
May 1979

Author's Preface

מזמור נו 56

We first read of David's sojourn in the court of the Philistine king, Achish of Gath, in Psalm 34. There, speaking in retrospect, David exults over his miraculous escape from the Philistines. Here, however, his mood is somber as he records his initial shock and dismay upon realizing the terrible danger which faced him so unexpectedly in Achish's palace.

Hounded by Saul and his army, the fugitive could no longer evade his relentlessly determined pursuers. He was forced to flee to a hostile foreign kingdom in the hope that perhaps these gentiles would afford him the haven that was tragically unavailable to him in his own homeland.

How bitter was David's disappointment when he was recognized by the king's bodyguard, who was none other than the giant Yishbi, the brother of Goliath, David's most famous victim! David seemed to be on the very brink of death as Yishbi stormed before Achish and demanded the right to avenge the blood of his slain brother.

The holy spirit which enveloped David at that moment stirred him not only to bemoan his personal grief, but also to relate the woeful tale of his persecuted people, who were also fated to wander from land to land as hunted refugees. In this sense both the king and his people truly resembled יוֹנַת אֵלֶם רְחֹקִים, A silenced dove *in wandering, whose salvation is* far away *(v.1).*

נו
א־ג

א לַמְנַצֵּחַ | עַל־יוֹנַת אֵלֶם רְחֹקִים לְדָוִד
ב מִכְתָּם בֶּאֱחֹז אוֹתוֹ פְלִשְׁתִּים בְּגַת: חָנֵּנִי
אֱלֹהִים כִּי־שְׁאָפַנִי אֱנוֹשׁ כָּל־הַיּוֹם לֹחֵם
ג יִלְחָצֵנִי: שָׁאֲפוּ שׁוֹרְרַי כָּל־הַיּוֹם כִּי־רַבִּים

1. יוֹנַת אֵלֶם רְחֹקִים – *Upon* Yonas Eilem Rechokim.

Literally, this means *the silenced dove of those that are far away;* it refers to David, who was in the territory of the Philistines, outside of Israel, his native land. Threatened by Goliath's hostile brother Yishbi, David was helpless as a trapped dove, whose song is muted by fear (*Rashi*).

David saved himself by pretending to be a madman who could not possibly be the hero of Israel [See *comm.* to 34:1]. Thus, his characteristically intelligent speech became *silenced;* his hysterical raving resembled the cooing of the dove, which the prophet considers as a silly bird, as in the verse, כְּיוֹנָה פוֹתָה אֵין לֵב, *like a foolish dove without understanding (Hosea* 7:11*) (Radak).*

Meiri identifies the *Yonas Eilem Rechokim* as a musical instrument which reproduces the cooing of the dove. *Meiri* notes that the dove has two different calls. When this gentle bird is frightened, it repeats its moaning cry frantically, without respite. However, when at ease, the dove coos only at long intervals leaving a *silent* (אֵלֶם) pause between the cries which are *distant* (רְחֹקִים) from each other. [Thus, the musical accompaniment of this psalm underscores its theme, to suggest that David resembles a dove who is silenced for long intervals.]

The positioning of this psalm after the preceding one serves to emphsaize its theme. In the preceding psalm, David laments that the society in which he lives is corrupt and that no man can be trusted. Therefore, he yearns to abandon his land, saying *'O that I would have wings like the dove, then I would fly away and find a place of rest'* (55:7).

Now that sheer desperation has forced David to 'sprout' the wings of a *dove* and flee to Gath, he finds that there, too, he is betrayed and realizes that he resembles a helpless *silenced dove (Norah Tehillos; Tehillas Hashem).*

Even in the midst of this deep personal tragedy, David's thoughts transcended his individual situation to encompass the Jews who would be forced into exile throughout the centuries, for Israel resembles a flock of *doves* spread out רְחֹקִים, *far away (Tehillas Hashem).*

לְדָוִד מִכְתָּם – *By David, a* Michtam.

[See *comm.* to 16:1 for full discussion of the various definitions of *Michtam;* according to one opinion, it is a combination of two words, מָךְ and תָּם as follows:]

Midrash Shocher Tov comments that the threats of Goliath's brother rendered David אֵלֶם, *silent,* for he realized that he was helpless, since his own warriors were רְחֹקִים, *far away.* As a result of this sobering experience, David truly became מָךְ, *humble,* and תָּם, *perfect.*

בֶּאֱחֹז אוֹתוֹ פְלִשְׁתִּים בְּגַת – *When Philistines seized him in Gath.*

As explained in the Prefatory Remarks, most commentaries attribute this psalm to David's first encounter with Achish in Gath (I *Samuel* 21:11-16). However, *Be'er Avraham* maintains that it refers to David's second encounter with Achish.

When Saul first began to persecute him, David fled to Achish for the first time all alone. Many months later, weary of running from Saul, David again attempted to escape from the jealous king. Accompanied by six hundred great warriors and their

For the Conductor,
upon Yonas Eilem Rechokim,
By David, a Michtam
when Philistines seized him in Gath.
2 Favor me, O God,
for men yearn to swallow me,
Every day
the warrior oppresses me.
3 Every day my watchful foes
aspire to swallow me,

families, David pretended that he wished to enter into an alliance with Achish. This ruse enabled David to dwell safely in Philistia for more than four months (*I Samuel* 27).

Achish was firmly convinced that David despised his own people, Israel, and considered David to be a loyal vassal. David became filled with horror and dismay, however, when Achish appointed him to serve as his personal aide and bodyguard during a military campaign against Israel (*I Samuel* 28:1-2). David was trapped; he could never consent to wage war against his own people, but to refuse would mean certain death.

At that moment of crisis, God sent salvation: Achish's own generals refused to trust David, the Hebrew alien, to join them in their assaults against the Hebrew people (*I Samuel* 29:3-10). David now praises God for his miraculous escape.

2. חָנֵּנִי אֱלֹהִים — *Favor me, O God.*

Let Me find favor in Your eyes even though I have been forced to abandon Israel, Your favored country, and to flee to Philistia, a land which You despise (*Sforno*).

כִּי שְׁאָפַנִי אֱנוֹשׁ — *For men* [lit. *man*] *yearn to swallow me.*

I abandoned the Holy Land only under duress, when it became impossible for me to escape Saul's relentless pursuit (*Sforno*). Even here in Philistia, Achish and his men are eager to destroy me (*Radak*).

כָּל הַיּוֹם לֹחֵם יִלְחָצֵנִי — *Every day the warrior oppresses me.*

Saul's determination and persistence were incredible for he did not interrupt his pursuit of David even for a moment (*Radak; Sforno*).

3. שָׁאֲפוּ שׁוֹרְרַי כָּל הַיּוֹם — *Every day my watchful foes aspire to swallow me.*

Wherever I turn, in Israel or in foreign lands, I am confronted by *watchful foes* who do not let me out of their sight (*Radak*).

Norah Tehillos and *Yaavetz Hadoresh* render שׁוֹרְרַי as *my singers.* David traces the source of his woes back to the people who sang his praises after his triumph over Goliath by saying, *'Saul has slain his thousands and David his ten thousands.'* [Immediately, *Saul was very angry and the saying sorely displeased him . . . and Saul viewed David with enmity from that day onwards (I Samuel* 18:7-9).

It was this very song which endangered him when he fled to Achish! *And the servants of Achish said to him, 'Is this not David the King of the land? Did they not sing of him to one another in dances, saying, "Saul has slain his thousands and David his ten thousands"?' (I Samuel* 21:12) Achish's generals repeated this (ibid. 29:5) when

ד לְחֲמִים לִי מָרוֹם: יוֹם אִירָא אֲנִי אֵלֶיךָ
ה אֶבְטָח: בֵּאלֹהִים אֲהַלֵּל דְּבָרוֹ בֵּאלֹהִים
בָּטַחְתִּי לֹא אִירָא מַה־יַּעֲשֶׂה בָשָׂר לִי:
ו כָּל־הַיּוֹם דְּבָרַי יְעַצֵּבוּ עָלַי כָּל־מַחְשְׁבֹתָם
°יִצְפֹּנוּ ז לָרָע: יָגוּרוּ | °יצפינו הֵמָּה עֲקֵבַי יִשְׁמֹרוּ

they expressed their suspicions about David's facade of apparent loyalty *(Be'er Avraham).*

כִּי רַבִּים לֹחֲמִים לִי מָרוֹם — *For many war with me, O Most High!*

Although many yearn to swallow me, their aspirations will never be fulfilled, for You, O *Most High,* do battle for me *(Ibn Ezra).*

The words לֹחֲמִים לִי may also be translated: *they fight for me, on my behalf,* referring to the celestial (מָרוֹם) angels whom God has commanded to protect David from his foes *(Yaavetz HaDoresh).*

4. יוֹם אִירָא אֲנִי אֵלֶיךָ אֶבְטָח — *The day when I fear - I will trust in You.*

Midrash Shocher Tov (Psalm 34) comments: The Philistines and Goliath's brother demanded of Achish, 'Let us kill this man who killed our brother!'

Achish replied, 'Didn't David kill your brother in a fair fight? Had your brother Goliath killed David, instead, wouldn't that also have been in a fair fight? Furthermore, Goliath stipulated *"If he will be able to battle me, then we will all be your servants* " '(*I Samuel* 17:9).

Upon hearing this, the Philistines said to Achish, 'If this is true, get up from your throne, for your kingship rightfully belongs to David! In fact, since David is a subject of Saul, aren't we actually all servants of Saul?' Thus, they confounded Achish.

At that instant, David became afraid; but nevertheless, he declared, *'On the day when I fear I will trust in You.'* Then God saved him by giving him a touch of madness, which disguised his identity.

5. בֵּאלֹהִים אֲהַלֵּל דְּבָרוֹ — *In God['s strict justice]—I [still] praise His word.*

Even when He acts towards me as אֱלֹהִים, *the Dispenser of Strict Justice,* I appreciate His verdict and accept it gladly (*Rashi*) [see *v.* 11]. I rejoice in affliction, for thus do I repay the debt incurred through my sin (*Mikdash Me'at*).

Some interpret this as an oath: *'By God!* I swear to praise Him under all circumstances' (*Yaavetz HaDoresh; Ibn Yachya*).

בֵּאלֹהִים בָּטַחְתִּי לֹא אִירָא — *In God['s strict justice] I have trusted.*

God promised me through the prophet Samuel that I would someday be king. Since that promise was made, I have suffered terribly, yet my faith in God's word remains unshaken, for I console myself, saying: 'Just as אֱלֹהִים strictly and persistently adheres to His rules of Justice, so will He be unyielding in fulfilling His promise to me' (*Radak*).

כָּל הַיּוֹם דְּבָרַי יְעַצֵּבוּ — *Every day they turn my words sorrowful.*

Their relentless pursuit has transformed my normal conversation into an endless stream of sorrowful pleas for salvation (*Rashi*).

According to *Ibn Ezra* and *Radak,* it is the words of David which bring sorrow to his foes. David says: 'Because דְּבָרַי, *my words,* never fail to reiterate my faith in דְּבָרוֹ, *His word* (*v.* 5) [i.e., His promise to make me king], my enemies are sad.'

Alshich perceives in this the true cause for David's grave concern when he raved madly before Achish. As a man of deep faith, David realized that so long as he trained his thoughts upon God and incessantly expressed His

For many war with me,
O Most High!
4 *The day when I fear —*
I will trust in You.
5 *In God's strict justice —*
I still praise His word,
In God's strict justice I have trusted,
I shall not fear, what can flesh do to me?
6 *Every day they turn my words sorrowful,*
about me all their thoughts are for evil.
7 *They assemble,*
they lie in ambush,
they watch my every tread

praises, no man could possibly harm him. As he declared in the previous verse: *'In God... I praise His word'*, therefore, *'In God, I trusted, I shall not fear'*; for the man totally involved in praising God can boast, *'What can flesh do to me?'*

Now David laments that the very vehicle of his escape could become his undoing. Since his mind and mouth were filled with thoughts and words of madness, he lost his greatest merit for salvation. Thus instead of joyous praise, *they bring sorrow to my words*, by forcing me to feign madness.

עָלַי כָּל מַחְשְׁבֹתָם לָרָע — *About me all their thoughts are for evil.*

In the opinion of Saul and his cohorts, all of *my words* and my aspirations to be king are motivated exclusively by evil intentions *(Tehillas Hashem).*

Alshich interprets these words as a reference to Achish's hostile bodyguard. When David feigned madness, the king was inclined to fall for the ruse, but these sceptical men remained unconvinced. They were determined to prove that David's sole intention was to perpetrate an evil fraud.

According to *Be'er Avraham*, this refers to the Philistine generals who suspected David of evil in his alliance with Achish.

7. יָגוּרוּ — *They assemble.*

[This refers to Saul's three thousand men who searched for David.]

In order to carry out their aggressive intentions against me, they gather together their sympathizers and bring them to places where I will be vulnerable to attack *(Rashi; Radak; Metzudas David).*

יִצְפֹּנוּ — *They lie in ambush* [lit. *they wait*].

This translation follows the קְרִי, *pronunciation.* However, the כְּתִיב, *spelling*, is יַצְפִּינוּ, *they place in hiding*, i.e., not only do they lie in ambush themselves, but also they take the trouble to place other men in concealed vantage points *(Radak).*

The Philistines who suspect that my madness is a ruse hide spies everywhere to scrutinize my words and actions. They hope that during this intensive surveillance they will catch me acting sane and sober *(Alshich).*

הֵמָּה עֲקֵבַי יִשְׁמֹרוּ — *They watch my every tread* [lit. *my footsteps*].

The Philistines claim that close scrutiny of my footsteps will expose my

ח כַּאֲשֶׁר קִוּוּ נַפְשִׁי: עַל־אָוֶן פַּלֶּט־לָמוֹ בְּאַף
ט עַמִּים | הוֹרֵד אֱלֹהִים: נֹדִי סָפַרְתָּה אָתָּה
שִׂימָה דִמְעָתִי בְנֹאדֶךָ הֲלֹא בְּסִפְרָתֶךָ:
י אָז | יָשׁוּבוּ אוֹיְבַי אָחוֹר בְּיוֹם אֶקְרָא זֶה־
יא יָדַעְתִּי כִּי־אֱלֹהִים לִי: בֵּאלֹהִים אֲהַלֵּל
יב דָּבָר בַּיהוה אֲהַלֵּל דָּבָר: בֵּאלֹהִים

true mental status. If, upon being released from the palace of Achish, I walk straight back to *Eretz Yisrael,* this will prove my sanity; but if I aimlessly stumble and wander to and fro, this will lend credence to my claim of mental instability *(Alshich).*

כַּאֲשֶׁר קִוּוּ נַפְשִׁי — *Whenever they anticipate* [lit. *hope*] *my soul.*

They lay in ambush whenever they anticipate an opportunity to capture me and thereby take my life *(Rashi; Radak).*

8. עַל אָוֶן פַּלֶּט לָמוֹ — *For inquity shall rescue be theirs?*

Radak interprets this as a question: Is it possible that they should ever be *rescued* [i.e., absolved] from the terrible iniquity which they perpetrate?

Rashi, however, renders this as an indignant statement describing the baseness of David's pursuers: The men who follow Saul to assist in my pursuit are selfish. They desire פַּלֶּט, *to snatch* [lit. *rescue*] a handsome reward for their participation in this *iniquity.*

בְּאַף עַמִּים הוֹרֵד אֱלֹהִים — *In anger cast down the nations, O God!*

This Philistine nation has built up a scheme to trap me. Please, O God, *cast down* that evil design and shatter it *(Rashi).*

נֹדִי סָפַרְתָּה אָתָּה — *My wanderings have You Yourself counted.*

You are well aware of all the places in which I have been forced to seek refuge *(Rashi).* Since גָּלוּת, *exile,* atones for a person's sins, please erase my guilt according to the measure of my wanderings and suffering *(Chazah Zion).*

[Note the correspondence between verse 7 and verse 9. The Philistines *watch my every tread* for evil *as they anticipate for my soul* (*v.* 7). Therefore David now asks God to protect him by *counting* these very same steps of wandering in his merit.]

שִׂימָה דִמְעָתִי בְנֹאדֶךָ — *Place my tears in Your flask.*

When You assess my suffering, consider not only my wanderings, but also the many tears which I have shed. Surely You cannot neglect these, for the Sages say (*Bava Metzia* 59a): 'Even when all the gates of heaven are locked, the Gate of Tears is never shut' (*Sforno*).

[David was not moved to tears by his personal woes but by a larger, noble concern for *Eretz Yisrael.* As a devoted servant of God, David realized that he and God were inseparable. Thus, when David abandoned the land of Israel God 'accompanied' David and 'absented' Himself as well. David lamented this loss of sanctity in the Holy Land.]

From these words the *Talmud (Shabbos* 105a) derives that it is meritorious to shed tears over the loss of a worthy man. The tears shed for him are not forgotten. God counts them and safeguards them in His treasure room, as it says: *Place my tears into Your flask. Are they not in Your record?*

God preserves these holy tears because they will become the fresh dew which He will use to revive the dead at the time of תְּחִיַּת הַמֵּתִים, *Resurrection (Mahari Pinto).*

whenever they anticipate my soul.
8 *For iniquity shall rescue be theirs?*
In anger cast down the nations, O God!
9 *My wanderings have You Yourself counted;*
place my tears in Your flask.
Are they not in Your record?
10 *Then will my foes retreat on the day I cry out,*
thereby will I know that God is with me.
11 *In God's strict justice — I praise His word.*
In HASHEM's mercifulness — I praise His word.

הֲלֹא בְּסִפְרָתֶךָ — *Are they not in Your record?*

Radak explains that the word הֲלֹא is always used when there is a need for special emphasis [see *v.* 14].

According to *Rashi,* סִפְרָתֶךָ is derived from מִסְפָּר, *number, account;* but *Menachem* and *Radak* relate it to סֵפֶר, *book,* to imply, *Record all of my sufferings in Your ledger* so that they will never be forgotten.

10. אָז יָשׁוּבוּ אוֹיְבַי אָחוֹר בְּיוֹם אֶקְרָא — *Then will my foes retreat* [lit. *will return backward*] *on the day I cry out.*

[When You accept my prayers in the merit of my wandering and my tears (*v.* 9), then my foes will surely be routed.]

Furthermore, when I enter battle, I shall reinforce my merits *when I call out* (אֶקְרָא) the *Shema.* The *Talmud* (*Sotah* 42a) assures the armies of Israel: Even if you engage your enemies empty-handed, with nothing more than the merit of the *Shema* in your favor, you will overcome the foe! (*Sh'eiris Yaakov*).

זֶה יָדַעְתִּי כִּי אֱלֹהִים לִי — *Thereby will I know that God is with me.*

I.e., My victory will prove that God came to my aid *(Radak).*

Ibn Yachya prefers a different interpretation: זֶה יָדַעְתִּי, *This I know already,* i.e., that my triumph is assured, כִּי אֱלֹהִים לִי, *for I am for God,* i.e., my entire being is dedicated to His service, therefore He Shall not forsake me!

11. בֵּאלֹהִים אֲהַלֵּל דָּבָר — *In God*[*'s strict justice*] — *I praise His* [lit. *the*] *word.*

Even if God is strict and harsh with me, I joyously accept His decisions; and I will praise Him always *(Rashi; Midrash Shocher Tov).*

No matter what happens to me, I will remember the greatest kindness which You granted me: דָּבָר, *the word* i.e., the commitment You gave me when You promised to make me king *(Radak; Ibn Ezra;* see *v.* 5 דְּבָרוֹ).

בַּה׳ אֲהַלֵּל דָּבָר — *In HASHEM*[*'s mercifulness*] — *I praise His* [lit. *the*]

The Sages of the *Mishnah* taught that a person is obligated to bless God in the time of misfortune just as he blesses God in the time of good fortune. According to Rav Shmuel bar Nachmani, this obligation is derived from the verse: *As HASHEM* (i.e., the Name signifying the Divine Attribute of Mercy) — *I praise His word, As ELOHIM* (i.e., the Name signifying the Divine Attribute of Strict Justice) — *I praise His word,* to indicate that man's praise for God should remain unchanging and uninterrupted *(Berachos* 60a).

[In quoting this verse, the Sages reversed its actual order to emphasize that God's mercy is foremost and to teach that even when He is strict, His prime motivation is mercy and concern for His creations].

יג־יד
בָּטַחְתִּי לֹא אִירָא מַה־יַּעֲשֶׂה אָדָם לִי׃ עָלַי אֱלֹהִים נְדָרֶיךָ אֲשַׁלֵּם תּוֹדֹת לָךְ׃ כִּי הִצַּלְתָּ נַפְשִׁי מִמָּוֶת הֲלֹא רַגְלַי מִדֶּחִי לְהִתְהַלֵּךְ לִפְנֵי אֱלֹהִים בְּאוֹר הַחַיִּים׃

12. בֵּאלֹהִים בָּטַחְתִּי לֹא אִירָא — *In God I trust, I fear not.*

When *God* afflicts a person with *Strict Justice* it is possible that he will not be able to endure the pain and suffering. David therefore proclaims that he is completely confident that God Himself will reinforce his strength; thus he has no fear that he will collapse beneath the burden of his punishment *(Tehillas Hashem).*

מַה יַּעֲשֶׂה אָדָם לִי — *What can man do to me?*

This question is asked in verse 5 with one variation: there the word בָּשָׂר, *flesh,* is substituted for אָדָם, *man. Radak* defines these words as synonyms, but according to *Alshich,* אָדָם is a title of honor reserved for Jews [*Yevamos* 61a] and refers to David's Israelite enemies, whereas בָּשָׂר, *flesh,* is a derogatory reference to David's heathen enemies in general, and to Achish in particular.

13. עָלַי אֱלֹהִים נְדָרֶיךָ — *Uon me, O God, are Your vows.*

According to many commentaries *(Radak; Ibn Ezra; Sforno)* נְדָרֶיךָ, *Your vows,* refers to the vows which David made to God while he was in exile.

Alshich, however, maintains that *Your vows* refers to the vows which God made to the royal tribe of Judah, promising that the family of David would emanate from Judah and that its sovereignty would be unsurpassed. These Divine vows were expressed in the Patriarch Jacob's final blessing to his sons.

David declares that these *vows* buoyed his spirits even in the gloom of exile, for he realizes that 'Everything promised to the tribe of Judah really devolves עָלַי, *upon me,* and represents a special commitment to give me the throne.'

אֲשַׁלֵּם תּוֹדֹת לָךְ — *I shall render* [lit. *repay*] *thanksgiving offerings to You.*

When I was in danger, I promised that once rescued, I would sacrifice offerings of thanksgiving to God *(Radak).* [1]

14. כִּי הִצַּלְתָּ נַפְשִׁי מִמָּוֶת — *For You rescued my soul from death.*

1. *Midrash Shocher Tov* comments that this verse also alludes to Messianic times, because in the future, all forms of sacrifice are destined to become obsolete [since men will be righteous, no sacrifices will be required to atone for their sins *(Radak)*], with the exception of the thanksgiving offerings. [This will be retained so that men may show their appreciation to God for providing a utopian world *(Radak).*] Similarily, prayers of petition will be discontinued, (since God will provide men with all their requirements, they will no longer plead for their needs), but prayers of praise and thanks will still be recited (in recognition of God's kindness).

12 In God's strict justice have I trusted,
I shall not fear.
What can man do to me?
13 Upon me, O God, are Your vows,
I shall render thanksgiving offerings to You.
14 For You rescued my soul from death —
even my feet from stumbling —
To walk before God
in the light of life.

This refers to death at the hands of Saul *(Yalkut Shimoni)* and to the death reserved for sinners who forfeit their claim to life *(Targum).*

Yaavetz HaDoresh comments: Although the Torah usually discourages men from making vows (*Ecclesiastes* 5:4), the *Midrash (Bereishis Rabbah* 70:1) learns from the example of the Patriarch Jacob (*Genesis* 28:20) that it is advisable to make a vow to God in a time of mortal danger. [See *Tosafos Chullin* 2b s.v. אבל and *Ritva* and *Rashba* to *Nedarim* 9a.]

David now explains that he too has obligated himself to God with vows (*v.* 13), because God delivered him from death.

הֲלֹא רַגְלַי מִדֶּחִי — *Even my feet from stumbling.*

I.e., Not only did You save me from death, but You even prevented my feet from stumblinginto the snares set by the wily Achitophel *(Yalkut Shimoni);* and from being enmeshed in sin by the Evil Inclination *(Targum).*

Thus I am assured that I will not stumble into the fires of *Gehinnom (Alshich).*

Yaavetz HaDoresh continues: In addition to his human enemies, David was threatened by the terrible menace of a hostile environment. Often he was forced to take refuge in the inhospitable desert or in the forbidding wilderness. The *Talmud (Berachos* 54b) rules that surviving a trip across the uninhabited desert (or surviving any of three other dangerous situations) obligates a person to bring a קָרְבַּן תּוֹדָה, *a thanksgiving offering.*

Therefore David says: *I shall render thanksgiving offerings to You* (*v.* 13) because *You rescued ... my feet from stumbling* into the deadly pitfalls of the desert.

לְהִתְהַלֵּךְ לִפְנֵי אֱלֹהִים — *To walk before God.*

Before God means in the Land of Israel *(Midrash; Radak)* and in the *Beis Hamikdash (Metzudas David).*

There I will have the opportunity to study God's Torah in peace of mind, without harrassment by my enemies *(Sforno).*

בְּאוֹר הַחַיִּים — *In the light of life.*

This refers to the Garden of Eden *(Midrash; Radak). Sforno* identifies it as the World to Come.

This is congruent with the *Talmud's* statement (*Sanhedrin* 102a) that God said, 'Come, let us stroll together with [David] the son of Jesse in the Garden of Eden' *(Alshich).*

[This is the most sublime reward to which a man can aspire and it represents the goal of David's entire career.]

מזמור נז
57

The narrative of I Samuel, *chapter 24, serves as the background for this psalm. Saul and three thousand men search for David in the rocky caves of the wilderness of En-Gedi. All alone, Saul inadvertently entered the cave in which David and his men were hiding. Instead of yielding to his men's demands that he kill Saul, David contented himself with cutting off a corner from a garment, which Saul had momentarily removed. In this manner, David sought to impress upon Saul that he was not his enemy and that Saul was unjustified in hating and pursuing him.*

This highly dramatic moment, fraught with danger for both Saul and David, prompted David to compose this psalm.

This is the first of three psalms (57-59) which refer to Saul's pursuit of David; all begin with the plea Al Tashcheis — *Do not destroy!*

נז
א־ד

א לַמְנַצֵּחַ אַל־תַּשְׁחֵת לְדָוִד מִכְתָּם בְּבָרְחוֹ
ב מִפְּנֵי־שָׁאוּל בַּמְּעָרָה: חָנֵּנִי אֱלֹהִים | חָנֵּנִי
כִּי בְךָ חָסָיָה נַפְשִׁי וּבְצֵל־כְּנָפֶיךָ אֶחְסֶה
ג עַד יַעֲבֹר הַוּוֹת: אֶקְרָא לֵאלֹהִים עֶלְיוֹן
ד לָאֵל גֹּמֵר עָלָי: יִשְׁלַח מִשָּׁמַיִם | וְיוֹשִׁיעֵנִי
חֵרֵף שֹׁאֲפִי סֶלָה יִשְׁלַח אֱלֹהִים חַסְדּוֹ

1. לַמְנַצֵּחַ אַל תַּשְׁחֵת — *For the Conductor,* Al Tashcheis [lit. *do not destroy*].

This psalm is entitled *Al Tashcheis* because David composed it when he was on the brink of destruction and death; thus, he was pleading to God for salvation *(Rashi).*

David's righteousness and humility were truly astounding. Despite Saul's threat and his implacable hatred, David persisted in accepting him as his king and refused to injure his sovereign in any way. David's primary concern was not for his own life, but for Saul's. David's men forcefully insisted that it would be suicidal not to exploit this God-given opportunity to slay their pursuer, Saul; but David held them back, shouting, *Al Tashcheis — do not destroy!' (Alshich).*

[In a deeper sense, David implored his followers not to fall into the state of moral decay which had already corrupted a major portion of the nation under Saul's influence. David pleaded: 'Saul seeks to accomplish his desires through hatred, violence, and murder. Let us not allow ourselves to fall into this destructive syndrome. Rather, let us seize this opportunity to demonstrate to the nation that unity must be achieved through clemency, mercy, and pardon. Therefore, I beg you, *Do not destroy!'*]

בְּבָרְחוֹ מִפְּנֵי שָׁאוּל בַּמְּעָרָה — *When he fled from Saul, in the cave.*

Inside the cave it was Saul who was in danger, not David. Nevertheless, David is described as *fleeing* even while he was safe, because he *fled* from the temptation to kill his trapped, helpless enemy *(Alshich).*

The *Midrash (Bereishis Rabbah* 51:7) notes that centuries earlier, David's ancestor, Lot, was saved from the destruction of Sodom by hiding in a cave. Thus David prayed, 'Master of the Universe! Even before I entered this cave, You showed kindness to others for my sake and saved them in a cave! Therefore, now that I myself am in a cave, I beg of You, be kind and *do not destroy!'*

2. חָנֵּנִי אֱלֹהִים חָנֵּנִי — *Favor me, O God, favor me.*

A double request: 'Favor me by strengthening me not to kill others and by not allowing others to kill me!' *(Rashi).*

[Saul posed a double threat. Thus: 'Save me from both physical destruction and moral corruption.']

כִּי בְךָ חָסָיָה נַפְשִׁי — *For in You my soul took refuge.*

[In the past I have always sought to protect myself through You and not by means of violence and destruction.]

וּבְצֵל כְּנָפֶיךָ אֶחְסֶה — *And in the shadow of Your wings I shall take refuge.*

[Even now, as I am concealed in the shadowy depths of the dark cave, I realize that Your presence is my only true protection. By refusing to exploit this opportunity to slay Saul I will demonstrate that I reject the security of human might.]

עַד יַעֲבֹר הַוּוֹת — *Until treachery passes by.*

*F*or the Conductor, Al Tashcheis,
by David, a Michtam,
When he fled from Saul, in the cave.
2 *Favor me, O God, favor me,*
for in You my soul took refuge,
And in the shadow of Your wings I shall take refuge
until treachery passes by.
3 *I will call upon God, Most High,*
to the God Who fulfills for me.
4 *He will dispatch from heaven*
and save me;
From the disgrace of those
who desire to swallow me, Selah,
God will dispatch His mercy
and His truth.

I will continue to act in such a conciliatory fashion until I succeed in erasing the feelings of treachery and animosity which poison Saul's heart *(Meiri).*

3. אֶקְרָא לֵאלֹהִים עֶלְיוֹן – *I will call upon God, Most High.*

My situation seems hopeless. To whom can I appeal for justice if I am pursued by the king himself, since he is the supreme authority in the land? Nevertheless, I am not afraid; for I call upon God whose, authority is even higher! *(Radak).*

לָאֵל גֹּמֵר עָלָי – *To the God who fulfills for me.*

[The desperate man who feels compelled to resort to violence in order to achieve his goals is misled by a false conception. He is convinced that man is responsible for assuring his own success and that he must take matters into this own hands if he wishes to bring his schemes to completion.

David declares: 'I know differently! It is incumbent upon man to have the courage to take the first step to reach his goal, no matter how difficult that step may be. I firmly believe that a man need do no more, once he has taken this initiative. Upon recognizing a man's good intentions, God assumes responsibility for bringing his noble ideas to fruition.

'I call upon God to effect my salvation as He sees fit; I shall not end Saul's threat to me with an act of physical violence.']

4. יִשְׁלַח מִשָּׁמַיִם וְיוֹשִׁיעֵנִי – *He will dispatch from heaven and save me.*

The numerical superiority of the enemy forces does not intimidate me, for God will send down His ministering angels to rescue me *(Radak; Targum).*

חֵרֵף שֹׁאֲפִי – [*From*] *the disgrace of those who desire to swallow me.*

This punishment is appropriate because if Saul would respect the word of God, as transmitted through the prophet Samuel, he would recognize my Divinely ordained claim to the throne. By ignoring the word of God, he disgraces it; therefore, he himself deserves to be disgraced *(Radak).*

יִשְׁלַח אֱלֹהִים חַסְדּוֹ וַאֲמִתּוֹ – *God will dispatch His mercy and His truth.*

May He act with *mercy* towards me and with strict *truth* and justice towards my enemies *(Sforno).*

ה וַאֲמִתּוֹ: נַפְשִׁי | בְּתוֹךְ לְבָאִם אֶשְׁכְּבָה
לֹהֲטִים בְּנֵי־אָדָם שִׁנֵּיהֶם חֲנִית וְחִצִּים
ו וּלְשׁוֹנָם חֶרֶב חַדָּה: רוּמָה עַל־הַשָּׁמַיִם
ז אֱלֹהִים עַל כָּל־הָאָרֶץ כְּבוֹדֶךָ: רֶשֶׁת |
הֵכִינוּ לִפְעָמַי כָּפַף נַפְשִׁי כָּרוּ לְפָנַי שִׁיחָה
ח נָפְלוּ בְתוֹכָהּ סֶלָה: נָכוֹן לִבִּי אֱלֹהִים נָכוֹן

5. נַפְשִׁי בְּתוֹךְ לְבָאִם — *My soul is among lions.*

My soul is threatened by such heroic *lions* of Torah scholarship as Saul's generals Abner and Amassa, who make no protest against Saul's violent pursuit of an innocent man such as myself *(Rashi; Yerushalmi, Peah* 1:1).

Radak explains that although David was running away from these men he describes himself as בְּתוֹךְ, *among* them, because he never succeeded in eluding them; they were always following close behind him.

Alshich however, identifies these *lions* as David's own followers who were with him in the cave, for they resembled hungry, ferocious lions, roaring to tear Saul apart. David barely succeeded in restraining them.

אֶשְׁכְּבָה לֹהֲטִים — *I lie with fiery men.*

Once I sought refuge in the vicinity of the Ziphites, who proved to be vicious men, aflame with the desire to slander me to Saul *(Rashi).*

They sought to burn me alive with the fiery breath of their wicked mouths *(Radak).*

The malicious slanderer is far more dangerous than the hungriest lion *(Sforno).*

בְּנֵי אָדָם שִׁנֵּיהֶם חֲנִית וְחִצִּים — *People whose teeth are spears and arrows.*

These are the people of Keilah, who betrayed David to Saul *(Yerushalmi, Peah* 1:1).

Their scathing tales and evil reports were like *spears and arrows,* which kill even from a distance. Similarly, slander spoken in one place can injure someone far away *(Tanchuma Metzora* 2).

וּלְשׁוֹנָם חֶרֶב חַדָּה — *And whose tongue is a sharp sword.*

According to *Yerushalmi (Peah* 1:1), it is this description which refers to the Ziphites; the description *fiery men* (inflamed with a passion for slander) refers to Doeg and Achitophel. *Yerushalmi* concludes that because there were so many slanderers in the time of David, his armies would suffer many losses in battle.

6. רוּמָה עַל הַשָּׁמַיִם אֱלֹהִים — *Be exalted above the heavens, O God.*

Depart, O God, from this lowly world of men consumed by base passions and a lust for cheap slander. They do not deserve to have Your exalted, holy presence in their midst. Preserve Your glory in the heavens above where it belongs *(Rashi).*

עַל כָּל הָאָרֶץ כְּבוֹדֶךָ — *Above all the earth be Your glory.*

In heaven, where You rule over the many forces and angels *(Targum)* which control this world, please manipulate the universal order in such a way as to foil my enemies and to render me victorious so that *Your glory will be above all the earth (Radak; Sforno).*

7. רֶשֶׁת הֵכִינוּ לִפְעָמַי — *A snare they prepared for my footsteps.*

Saul said to the treacherous Ziphites *(I Samuel* 23:22), *'Go, I pray you; make yet even more sure, and know and observe the place where his foot treads and who has seen him there, for I am*

5 *My soul is among lions,*
I lie with fiery men,
People whose teeth are spears and arrows,
and whose tongue is a sharp sword.
6 *Be exalted above the heavens, O God,*
above all the earth be Your glory.
7 *A snare they prepared for my footsteps,*
they bent down my soul,
They dug a pit before me —
they fell into it, Selah.
8 *My heart is steadfast, O God, my heart is steadfast,*

told that he [*David*] *deals very subtly' (Radak).*

כָּפַף נַפְשִׁי — *They bent down my soul.*

[Saul sent messengers to all of the cities of Israel in his search for me. I was deeply depressed by the fact that so many of my countrymen responded readily to Saul's call and my soul was bent in shame.]

כָּרוּ לְפָנַי שִׁיחָה נָפְלוּ בְתוֹכָהּ — *They dug a pit before me, they* [*themselves*] *fell into it.*

[See 7:16, *He digs a pit, digs it deep, only to fall into his own trap.*]

Saul imagined that he had finally dug my grave when he surrounded me at the rock of division (*I Samuel* 23:28). In truth, he brought about his own downfall, because in order to stop Saul from pursuing me, God sent a murderous Philistine attack against him which diverted his attention and forced him to abandon me *(Sforno).*

Earlier, Saul had tried to bring about David's death by sending him on an impossibly hazardous mission: he ordered David to bring him the foreskins of no less than one hundred Philistines (*I Samuel* 18:25). With God's help, David succeeded and did not fall into Saul's pit. However, Saul eventually met his own final defeat at the hands of that same Philistine nation *(Rashbam).*

8. [The first seven verses of this psalm reflect David's anxiety and fear. However, once he has recounted the downfall of his enemies in the very trap which they had set for him (*v.* 7), he is imbued with a new spirit of confidence and ecstasy, which inspires the following rapturous verses of praise for God.]

נָכוֹן לִבִּי אֱלֹהִים נָכוֹן לִבִּי — *My heart is steadfast, O God, my heart is steadfast.*

[The final verses of this psalm are almost an exact replica of the opening verses of Psalm 108. Compare this verse with 108:2.]

My heart and faith are steadfast at all times *(Ibn Ezra),* both when You treat me with kind mercy and when You treat me with strict justice *(Rashi).*

I am confident of my ultimate success in this world and in the World to Come *(Ibn Yachya).*[1]

1. *Midrash Shocher Tov* observes that the episode in the cave convinced even Saul of the legitimacy of David's claim to the throne. According to one view cited by *Rashi* to *I Samuel* 15-27, after Samuel rebuked Saul for his sins, the prophet grasped Saul's cloak and tore it. Samuel told him, *'This symbolizes that God has torn the monarchy away from you' (ibid.* 15:28).

Saul asked, 'And who is my successor?'

Samuel replied, 'The man who will rip away the corner of your cloak (as I did) is the one

ט לִבִּי אָשִׁירָה וַאֲזַמֵּרָה: עוּרָה כְבוֹדִי עוּרָה
י הַנֵּבֶל וְכִנּוֹר אָעִירָה שָּׁחַר: אוֹדְךָ בָעַמִּים |
יא אֲדֹנָי אֲזַמֶּרְךָ בַּלְאֻמִּים: כִּי־גָדֹל עַד־
יב שָׁמַיִם חַסְדֶּךָ וְעַד־שְׁחָקִים אֲמִתֶּךָ: רוּמָה
עַל־שָׁמַיִם אֱלֹהִים עַל כָּל־הָאָרֶץ כְּבוֹדֶךָ:

אָשִׁירָה — *I will sing.*

[I will sing because I was delivered from the physical harm which Saul had intended to inflict on me.]

וַאֲזַמֵּרָה — *And I will make music.*

[See *comm.* to 30:1 מִזְמוֹר שִׁיר].

Not only was my body saved, but also my soul was rescued from ruination. I thank God for helping to restrain me from shedding Saul's blood. For this additional kindness I will add special musical accompaniment to my songs *(Malbim).*

9. עוּרָה כְבוֹדִי — *Awake, O my soul* [lit. *my honor*].

[The soul is the כָּבוֹד, *glory,* of man, as is explained in 8:6 and 30:13.]

Malbim explains that this verse vividly depicts the metamorphosis which took place within David's soul.

Saul's malicious jealousy and relentless pursuit had left a deep, dark blot on David's soul. As an innocent man condemned and vilified, as a helpless fugitive hunted and threatened, David suffered greatly and became withdrawn. The full radiance of David's brilliant personality went into eclipse. His senses and emotions were deadened by disgrace and pain; his lively talents became faded and dull.

David's primary fear had been that he might sink into a bitter melancholy similar to Saul's and that he might become a man obsessed with violence and revenge. This unexpected encounter with Saul instantly dissolved his fears. First, by refraining from harming Saul, David proved to himself that he had successfully preserved his own integrity, despite Saul's moral collapse. Second, Saul himself now publicly admitted his own folly and David's righteousness, thus restoring David's reputation.

David's soul now surged with renewed strength: *Awake, O my soul!* Once again David felt himself to be an instrument of God, dedicated to singing His praises *Awake, O Neivel and Kinnor!* He now anticipated a personal renaissance; his sun was rising, heralding a fresh morning of growth and success: *I shall awaken the dawn!*

עוּרָה הַנֵּבֶל וְכִנּוֹר — *Awake, O* Neivel *and* Kinnor.

[See *footnote* to 33:2 for a complete discussion of the precise nature and identity of these musical instruments, which were used more than any others to accompany David's psalms. Compare this verse with 108:3.]

Radak explains that David, speaking figuratively, calls upon these instruments to play by themselves, joining him in his moment of ecstatic release from sorrow.

[See *commentary* to 49:5 אֶפְתַּח בְּכִנּוֹר חִידָתִי.]

אָעִירָה שָּׁחַר — *I shall awaken the dawn.*[1]

10. אוֹדְךָ בָעַמִּים אֲדֹנָי — *I will thank You among the peoples, my Lord.*

I.e., among the tribes of Israel, who

destined to take away your kingdom.'

When David cut the corner of Saul's cloak in the cave, Saul immediately remembered Samuel's fateful prophecy and declared, 'וְעַתָּה הִנֵּה יָדַעְתִּי כִּי מָלֹךְ תִּמְלוֹךְ, *Behold now I know that you will indeed be king* [*I Samuel* 24:20]. You will be the monarch in This World and in the World to Come.'

I will sing and I will make music.
9 *Awake, O my soul, awake, O* Neivel *and* Kinnor;
I shall awaken the dawn.
10 *I will thank You among the peoples, my Lord.*
I will sing to You among the nations.
11 *For great until the very heavens is Your kindness,*
and until the upper heights is Your truth.
12 *Be exalted above heaven, O God,*
above all the earth be Your glory.

are called עַמִּים, *peoples,* (see *Deuteronomy* 33:19; *Ibn Ezra; Radak).* [Cf. 108:4.]

אֲזַמֶּרְךָ בַּלְאֻמִּים — *I will sing to You among the nations.*

I.e., the gentile nations of the world *(Ibn Ezra).*

[May the praises of God which spring forth from Israel overflow onto the lips of all the nations, who will learn from Israel's example.]

11. כִּי גָדֹל עַד שָׁמַיִם חַסְדֶּךָ — *For great until the very heavens is Your kindness.*

Malbim refers us to his comment on 36:6, where he explains in detail the two categories of heavenly order: חֶסֶד, *kindness,* and אֱמֶת, *truth.*

The *Talmud (Pesachim* 50b) notes an apparent contradiction between these words and those in 108:5, where it is written: כִּי גָדֹל מֵעַל שָׁמַיִם חַסְדֶּךָ, *for Your kindness is great even above the heavens.* The *Talmud* explains that for people who perform the *mitzvos* לִשְׁמָהּ, *for the sake of God,* God's kindness extends מֵעַל, even *beyond* the heavens. But for those who act שֶׁלֹּא לִשְׁמָהּ, *not* [completely] *for the sake of God,* God's kindness extends only עַד, *until* the heavens.[2]

וְעַד שְׁחָקִים אֲמִתֶּךָ — *And until the upper heights is Your truth.*

[שְׁחָקִים is the name of one of the seven heavenly spheres. See *Chagigah* 13a.]

12. רוּמָה עַל שָׁמַיִם אֱלֹהִים — *Be exalted above heaven, O God.*

This verse is practically a duplicate of

1. Based on this verse, the *Talmud (Berachos* 3b-4a) relates that David took only a short nap every night. Precisely at midnight the north wind would blow through the *Kinnor (harp)* over his bed, rousing him so that he could study Torah until the dawn.

Midrash (Eichah Rabbasi 2:27) adds: When the people of Israel heard their monarch studying Torah in the middle of the night, they said, 'If David, the [busy] king of Israel, is studying Torah, certainly we, too, must do so.' Immediately they engaged in Torah study [cf. *Overview* part IV].

Some commentaries interpret this story homiletically. Often the terrible tragedies of David's life would deaden his spirit to the extent that his faculties became dormant. Yet within the depths of his being, there remained a רוּחַ צְפוּנִית, *a hidden* (צָפוּן) *spirit* (רוּחַ), which never died. It was the spirit which awakened his soul to greet the dawn of spiritual renewal *(Yetev Lev).*

2. The *Chofetz Chaim* illustrates this Talmudic passage in *Ma'amar Toras Habayis,* ch. 8:

The performance of each and every *mitzvah* creates good angels and sacred forces which accompany a man to heaven when his soul departs from this earth. How fortunate the soul will feel when it sees itself surrounded by tens of thousands of angels of its own creation! However, to its utter dismay, as the soul enters the heavenly gates, it sees that the angels are left *v.* 6 and 108:6. However, in *v.* 6 we read עַל הַשָּׁמַיִם, *above* **the** *heavens.*

Hirsch explains that the definite article ה, *the,* is added there *(v.* 6) to indicate *the heavens,* par excellence. A devout servant of God merits special considerations in the workings of Divine Providence. Therefore, David first asked that God should arise and exalt Himself to act with the unique Divine Providence and control reserved for the chosen servants of God. This special celestial involvement is called הַשָּׁמַיִם, *the heavens.*

Now David concludes the psalm with a plea for the sake of all men — *Arise, O God,* and control this world from שָׁמַיִם, *heaven* above, and implement justice and order for the sake of all of humanity.

עַל כָּל הָאָרֶץ כְּבוֹדֶךָ — *Above all the earth be Your glory.*

May it become apparent when You overthrow all the monarchs of the earth that You are the Supreme Ruler above *(Sforno).*

[This is a most appropriate conclusion for this psalm dedicated to David's relationship with King Saul. David prays: At times it appears as if You are far removed from human affairs and events. But when You manipulated affairs so wondrously that Saul put himself into my hands in the cave, then Your special concern for me in *the heavens (v.* 6) became gloriously apparent on earth. Now I ask that even Your general supervision in *heaven (v.* 12) become a clear manifestation of Your presence over all the earth.]

behind, unable to enter the celestial paradise, for the myriads of *mitzvos* which created those angels were not done purely for the sake of God, but were motivated in part by mundane personal considerations. Therefore, these *mitzvos* must remain within the earthly sphere; they can rise no higher. Only those *mitzvos* performed purely 'for the sake of heaven,' soar above the heavens and accompany the soul for eternity.

מזמור נח 58

*T*his psalm is the second in the *Al Tashcheis* trilogy. It describes the abrupt end of Saul's short-lived benignity toward David.

Psalm 57 (based on the narrative of I Sam. 24*) told how David restrained his men from killing Saul. Instead, David cut off a corner of Saul's robe which he later showed the king as proof of his loyalty. Saul was convinced that he had misjudged David and his warm feelings of old returned.*

But Saul's underlings conspired to destroy this good will. They came to Saul and argued: 'Is David to be esteemed as a righteous man simply because he did not slay you in the cave? He knew that if he dared harm you, we would have torn him limb from limb. He was afraid to do you harm!' (Midrash Shocher Tov).

Abner, Saul's leading general, scorned David's claim, saying that Saul's garment had been torn by a thorn and that David found the severed piece of cloth and fabricated the claim that he had had Saul at his mercy (Yerushalmi Sotah *1:8*).

Abner's charge rekindled Saul's fury against David. The king resolved to hunt down his younger rival: And he [Saul] arose and went down to the Wilderness of Ziph with three thousand chosen men of Israel to seek David in the Wilderness of Ziph (I Sam. *26:3*). *This psalm is based on the events of that pursuit.*

א־ב לַמְנַצֵּחַ אַל־תַּשְׁחֵת לְדָוִד מִכְתָּם: הַאֻמְנָם
אֵלֶם צֶדֶק תְּדַבֵּרוּן מֵישָׁרִים תִּשְׁפְּטוּ בְּנֵי

1. אַל תַּשְׁחֵת — *Al Tashcheis* [lit. *do not destroy*].

While pursuing David, Saul and his men made camp in the desert. God cast a deep slumber on the company which enabled David and Avishai ben Zeruyah to enter the camp safely.

Saul lay sleeping with his spear thrust into the ground near his head. Avishai pleaded with David for permission to kill Saul with his own spear, but David restrained him, saying, 'אַל תַּשְׁחִיתֵהוּ, *do not destroy him — who can extend his hand against HASHEM's anointed and be pardoned?' (I Sam.* 26:9).

As he had done earlier when he cut off the corner of Saul's robe, David sought proof by which he could later show that he had not harmed the king even when he had the opportunity to do so.

He took the spear and the jug of water which were near Saul's head, and departed.[1]

מִכְתָּם — *A Michtam.*

Rashi (16:1) translates this as *a crown. Alshich* comments that this title is well deserved because David's noble conduct in all his dealings with Saul, especially in the incident of the spear and the jug, proved beyond any doubt that he was worthy of the royal *crown.*

[The incident of the spear and jug provided an unsurpassed glimpse into David's greatness of character, for after he cut Saul's robe, the king solemnly swore to cease his pursuit of David, but he went back on his word. Nevertheless, David did not lose faith in God's anointed, and he released Saul once again. This represents the *crown* of David's tolerance and magnanimity.]

2. הַאֻמְנָם — *Is it true?*

This word is derived from אָמֵן, *true,* and אֱמוּנָה, *belief.* With the addition of the suffix, מ, *mem,* it means *in truth.* (Similarly, the word חֵן, *grace, favor,* becomes *free of charge* when it is given the suffix, *mem).* When the interrogative prefix ה, *he,* is added, we have the question הַאֻמְנָם, *Is it true? (Hirsch).*

Rashi perceives this as the opening of a rhetorical question: David turns to his pursuers and asks incredulously, 'Can it be true that you are silent?'

The Sages, interpreting this verse homiletically, relate אֻמְנָם to אוּמָן, *craftsman*: 'Which craft should man pursue in this world? He should strive to emulate an אִלֵּם, *a mute* (in order to avoid evil talk). Should one refrain from speaking even words of Torah? Certainly not! For the verse continues: צֶדֶק תְּדַבֵּרוּן, *justice should you speak* [i.e., of Torah, which is the ultimate justice] *(Chullin* 89a).

אֵלֶם — [*That you are*] *silent?*

This translation follows *Rashi.* David

1. Psalms 56, 57, and 58 describe three incidents when David was saved from mortal danger. *Chazah David* relates the proximity of the three narratives to an incident cited in the *Midrash (Otzar Midrashim* I p. 47).

David sat in his garden and watched a flea attacking a spider. A madman came and chased both insects away with a stick. David asked of God, 'Master of the Universe, of what value are these three creatures? The flea only bites, but contribues nothing. The spider weaves and weaves all year, yet no one can wear its web. The madman causes damage to others, and he has no concept of Your greatness!'

God replied, 'David! The time will come when you will need all three and then you will realize their purpose!'

Psalms 56-58 demonstrate how David came to understand God's reply. Psalm 56 tells how David saved himself from Achish by feigning madness. Psalm 57 refers to David's attempt to elude Saul's pursuit by hiding in a cave. God sent a spider to spin a web across the cave's

For the Conductor, Al Tashcheis,
by David, a Michtam.
2 Is it true that you are silent?
Justice should you speak!
With fairness should you judge people!

demands of his antagonists: 'When you sought to convince Saul of my guilt, you spoke loudly and lengthily. Why have you suddenly fallen silent now that you can establish my innocence?'

However, *Ibn Ezra, Radak,* and *Meiri* relate אֵלֶם to אֲלֻמִּים, *sheaves, bundles.* In the context of this verse it means *an assembly* of the magistrates of the land. David calls upon them to live up to their responsibilities: 'Why do you allow innocent men like me to be unjustly persecuted? *Assemble* your courts. Evaluate my recent compassion towards Saul and declare me innocent of treachery.'

Meiri adds that אֵלֶם alludes to the אוּלָם, *chamber,* in which the court convenes.

צֶדֶק תְּדַבֵּרוּן — *Justice should you speak!*

Midrash Shocher Tov comments: After David took Saul's spear and jug, *he stood upon a distant mountain... and called...,* 'הֲלוֹא תַעֲנֶה אַבְנֵר, *will you not answer, Abner?... You are a man of valor* [charged with protecting the king, but now you deserve to die for] *you did not watch over God's anointed... Where are the king's spear and his jug?'* [ibid. v. 13-16].

But Abner could not answer. He was like a man struck dumb, and he refused to concede David's righteousness.

David asked further: 'Have you pursued me with צֶדֶק, *justice,* as the Torah says, צֶדֶק צֶדֶק תִּרְדֹּף, *Justice, justice shall you pursue (Deut.* 16:20)? [In that verse which is addressed to the courts, צֶדֶק has the connotation of justice. The verse to be cited next is addressed to the individual. There, the word צֶדֶק has the connotation of righteousness and fairness.] Have you judged me with righteousness, as the Torah says, בְּצֶדֶק תִּשְׁפֹּט עֲמִיתֶךָ, *In righteousness shall you judge your neighbor (Lev.* 19:15)?'

מֵישָׁרִים תִּשְׁפְּטוּ בְּנֵי אָדָם — *With fairness should you judge people* [lit. *the sons of man*]!

Abner was indeed unfair in his assessment of David's actions. When David offered the spear and jug as proof that Saul had been in his grasp, Abner refuted him by arguing that one of Saul's own men might have stolen the articles and delivered them to David; or Saul's armor bearer might have taken the spear and the jug down to a well to fetch water and forgotten them where David later found them.

When David heard these far-fetched arguments he challenged Abner, 'How

entrance. Seeing the unbroken web, Saul was convinced that no one could have entered. He went in to rest, giving David the opportunity to cut off a piece of the royal robe and flee undetected. Later David found the spider and kissed it, exclaiming, 'Blessed is your Creator Who fashioned such wondrous creatures for this world!'

Our psalm tells how David was saved thanks to a flea. When He and Avishai secretly entered Saul's camp, they saw the mighty Abner sleeping next to Saul's head. His legs surrounded the king protectively, but his knees were bent and elevated. David slipped beneath them and took Saul's spear and jug. Suddenly, the sleeping Abner stretched out his legs flat on the ground, trapping David beneath them. Had David attempted to move, he would have aroused Abner. David silently cried to God for mercy. God sent a flea which bit Abner's leg causing him to draw them up once again, allowing David to escape.

Thus, David's life was saved by the very creatures and conditions he had maligned. As a result, he perceived as never before the greatness of God's creation.

ג אָדָם: אַף־בְּלֵב עוֹלֹת תִּפְעָלוּן בָּאָרֶץ
ד חֲמַס יְדֵיכֶם תְּפַלֵּסוּן: זֹרוּ רְשָׁעִים מֵרָחֶם
ה תָּעוּ מִבֶּטֶן דֹּבְרֵי כָזָב: חֲמַת־לָמוֹ כִּדְמוּת
חֲמַת־נָחָשׁ כְּמוֹ־פֶתֶן חֵרֵשׁ יַאְטֵם אָזְנוֹ:
ו אֲשֶׁר לֹא־יִשְׁמַע לְקוֹל מְלַחֲשִׁים חוֹבֵר

do you explain the edge which I cut from the king's garment?'

Abner replied, 'The edge was ripped off by a thorn!'

Because Abner resorted to such tortured rationalizations rather than admit David's innocence and seek to heal the breach between David and Saul, he was condemned (by Heaven) to die. This incident is the source of the *Talmudic* saying: Abner died because of the well and the thorn (*Sanhedrin* 49a, *Rashi* and *Rabbeinu Chananel* ibid.).

3. אַף בְּלֵב עוֹלֹת תִּפְעָלוּן — *Even in your heart you do wrongs.*

Rashi and *Radak* explain that עולת is the plural of עַוְלָה, *offense, wrong.* The corrupt judges of Saul's kingdom never cease to think of new ways to commit *wrongs.* So intense was their concentration on these misdeeds that their thoughts had the force of deeds that were actually committed.

Chomas Anoch suggests that עולת may be interpreted in its literal sense as the plural of עוֹלָה, *a burnt sacrifice.* The Sages say that a person should bring such an offering to atone for הִרְהוּרֵי עֲבֵירָה, *sinful thoughts.* Therefore, the psalmist urges the corrupt foe not to minimize the power of an evil thought, for an obligation to atone with a burnt offering can be incurred *even in the heart.*

בָּאָרֶץ חֲמַס יְדֵיכֶם תְּפַלֵּסוּן — *In the land you weigh out the violence of your hands.*

According to *Rashi,* תְּפַלֵּסוּן bears the connotation of precise weighing and measuring. Saul's cunning magistrates cloak their crime in a robe of justice, claiming that their every verdict is based on the exact, precise weighing of the letter of the law.

[David's argument is that Abner and the rest of Saul's officers, judges, and advisors have perverted their minds to the point where they cannot differentiate between good and evil. Therefore it is no wonder that they distort David's clear-cut evidence of his peaceful intentions.]

4. זֹרוּ רְשָׁעִים מֵרָחֶם — *Estranged are the wicked from the womb.*

Even while still in their mother's womb, the evil are estranged from God. As our Sages tell us, while he was still an unborn fetus, Esau strained towards pagan temples *(Rashi).*

The opposite is true of the righteous. In the earliest stages of their development they are already inclined towards sanctity. Thus we find that when Rebeccah passed by the house of study, Jacob struggled to leave her womb. Of the righteous, the prophet says (*Jeremiah* 1:5), *Before I formed you in the belly I knew you, and before you came out of the womb I sanctified you (Midrash Shocher Tov).*

Alshich paraphrases David's argument: The difference between a robe ripped unevenly by a thorn and one cut clearly by a knife is readily apparent. How can anyone confuse a well planned act executed with smooth precision, with an accident? Such a distortion is the fruit of a mind *estranged* from truth and logic from the very moment of its conception.

תָּעוּ מִבֶּטֶן דֹּבְרֵי כָזָב — *Astray from birth* [lit. *from the belly*] *go the speakers of falsehood.*

The translation follows *Metzudas*

[3] *Even in your heart*
you do wrongs,
In the land you weigh out
the violence of your hands.
[4] *Estranged are the wicked from the womb,*
astray from birth go the speakers of falsehood.
[5] *They have venom like the venom of a snake,*
like a deaf viper that closes its ear.
[6] *So as not to hearken to the voice of charmers,*
of the most cunning spellbinder.

David, who perceives *from the belly* as a metaphor for the time of birth and onwards. *Malbim,* however, interprets מִבֶּטֶן literally, and stresses that these wicked people were perverted even before birth, while they were still embryos. Therefore they are permanently alienated from righteousness and integrity.

[This verse does not indicate a belief in a preordained fate which is beyond man's control. Although everyone is endowed with free will to choose between good and evil, he is also born with certain handicaps which hinder his ability to choose good. The challenge of life is to overcome these obstacles. Some have physical handicaps, others have social or economic ones. The people described here had mental and emotional tendencies toward evil which made it difficult for them to think objectively. Nevertheless, by applying themselves to the task of channeling their evil tendencies towards good, they could have achieved righteousness.]

5. חֲמַת לָמוֹ כִּדְמוּת חֲמַת נָחָשׁ - *They have venom like the* [lit. *image of*] *venom of a snake.*

When these evil men are incited to rage, their דְּמוּת, *image* [i.e., their facial features], is contorted with hate and their mouth seems to spit out poisonous venom *(Radak).*

When the serpent caused Eve to sin he injected into her and her seed a זוּהֲמָה, *defilement,* which pollutes mankind to this very day (*Shabbos* 146a). The righteous man neutralizes the negative effects of this *defilement,* but the wicked one allows this vile poison to numb his intellect so that the lessons of Torah and ethics leave no impression on him (*Sforno; Alshich).*

כְּמוֹ פֶתֶן חֵרֵשׁ יַאְטֵם אָזְנוֹ — *Like a deaf viper that closes its ear.*

As a serpent ages, it becomes deaf in one ear. Then it stuffs its other ear with dirt in order not to hear the incantations of the snake charmer who wishes to render it harmless (*Rashi).*

The passion for evil burns strongly within this man, compelling him to act criminally, even as the serpent is driven to bite because of its instinctive urge to do harm. Therefore this man deliberately deafens himself to reproach in order to foil any attempt to influence him to mend his ways (*Hirsch*).

אֲשֶׁר לֹא יִשְׁמַע לְקוֹל מְלַחֲשִׁים - *So as not to hearken* [lit. *hear*] *to the voice of charmers* [lit. *whisperers*].

David complains that no matter how convincing his arguments were, Abner adamantly refused to be swayed or *charmed* by them (*Alshich).*

חוֹבֵר חֲבָרִים מְחֻכָּם — *Of the most cunning spellbinder.*

This man refuses to listen to reason. He closes his ears so that logical arguments will not penetrate his mind, fear-

ז חֲבָרִים מְחֻכָּם: אֱלֹהִים הֲרָס־שִׁנֵּימוֹ
בְּפִימוֹ מַלְתְּעוֹת כְּפִירִים נְתֹץ | יהוה:
ח יִמָּאֲסוּ כְמוֹ־מַיִם יִתְהַלְּכוּ־לָמוֹ יִדְרֹךְ חִצָּו
ט כְּמוֹ יִתְמֹלָלוּ: כְּמוֹ שַׁבְּלוּל תֶּמֶס יַהֲלֹךְ
י נֵפֶל אֵשֶׁת בַּל־חָזוּ שָׁמֶשׁ: בְּטֶרֶם יָבִינוּ

ful lest he fall under the *spell* of truth and be stayed from the perpetration of evil. Just as the embryo is *estranged* from the outside world while *in the womb* (*v.*4), so does the wicked man seek to insulate himself from any benign outside influences (*Migdal David).*

7. אֱלֹהִים הֲרָס שִׁנֵּימוֹ בְּפִימוֹ – *O God, smash their teeth in their mouth.*

This verse continues to use the allegory of the snake charmers. After their spell has rendered the serpent temporarily harmless, they swiftly extract the snake's poisonous fangs (*Alshich).*

In the preceding psalm (57:6), David said of the wicked, *their teeth are spears and arrows,* i.e., their slanderous barbs are sharp and piercing. Now he calls to render them harmless by breaking the power of their slanderous bite *(Radak).*

[God hearkened to David's plea and Abner did become a victim of his own crime, as the Sages say (*Yerushalmi Peah* 1:1): In Saul's time four men died as a result of slander — Doeg, Saul, Achimelech, and Abner.]

מַלְתְּעוֹת כְּפִירִים – *The molars of the young lions.*

These are the large molars with which lions grind their food (*Rashi).*

The slanderer resembles the ferocious young lion which vigorously rips its prey apart and chews it to pieces (*Radak).*

Indeed, Abner with his legendary strength, resembled a mighty lion. The Sages teach that it was easier to move a massive wall six cubits wide than to move one of Abner's feet (*Koheles Rabbah* 9:11).

Yalkut Shimoni (Jeremiah 285) adds that Abner was the tallest man in the Israelite army. So confident was he of his strength, that he declared, 'If only the globe had a handle — I would grab the earth and shake it!'

8. יִמָּאֲסוּ – *Let them be despicable.*

Let them be so overcome by failure that anxiety and worry may plague their hearts and their lives become מָאוּס, *despicable (Rashi).*

However, *Radak* and *Ibn Ezra* render יִמָּאֲסוּ as a form of יִמַּסוּ, *let them melt;* the א, *aleph,* is added for extra emphasis, taking the place of the doubled consonant, the extra ס (יִמָּסְסוּ).

כְּמוֹ מַיִם יִתְהַלְּכוּ לָמוֹ – *As if in water, let them wade.*

Let them be inundated by a flood of sorrow and tears (*Rashi)*

Radak and *Ibn Ezra* render: [*Let them melt*] *and be as running water.*

יִדְרֹךְ חִצָּו – *Let Him* [*i.e., HASHEM*] *aim* [lit. *tread on*] *His arrows.*

Rashi comments that this plea is addressed directly to God, asking Him to attack the enemy and to *cut him down.*

According to *Radak,* this verse is a continuation of David's prayer for the failure of his foes: When any of them *treads on* his bow to prepare it for stringing and shooting, may the *arrows* crumble and fall apart as if *cut to pieces.*

9. כְּמוֹ שַׁבְּלוּל – *Like the snail.*

The meaning of שַׁבְּלוּל is uncertain. *Rashi* first suggests that it is a *snail. Hirsch* explains that as the snail moves, it leaves behind it a trail of mucous matter. Thus the name שַׁבְּלוּל may derive

58
7-9

7 *O God, smash their teeth*
in their mouth;
The molars of the young lions —
shatter, HASHEM.
8 *Let them be despicable,*
as if in water, let them wade,
Let Him aim His arrows
to cut him down.
9 *Like the snail that melts and slithers away,*
the stillbirth of a mole that never saw the sun.

from שְׁבִיל, *path. (Rashi* here renders שַׁבְּלוּל in Old French as a *limtza.* In *Leviticus* 11:30, *Rashi* applies the same term to the חֹמֶט, another creeping reptile.)

Alternatively *Rashi* explains שַׁבְּלוּל as שִׁבֹּלֶת מַיִם, *a great wave of water* (see 69:16), which washes away (*melts*) the foe.

תֶּמֶס יַהֲלֹךְ — *That melts and slithers* [lit. *goes*] *away.*

Because a slimy trail of mucous oozes from the snail, it appears to be melting away. David says, 'It is my prayer that my foes should continually melt away and disappear in similar fashion' *(Sforno).*

Midrash Shocher Tov observes that just as the snail disappears, yet leaves behind a visible trail, so too with evil slander; long after the actual sound of the words vanish, the damage which they caused still remains!

נֵפֶל אֵשֶׁת — *The stillbirth of a mole.*

The *Talmud (Moed Kattan* 6b) describes the אֵשֶׁת as a field pest which, together with mice and other rodents, damages crops. The most prominent feature of the אֵשֶׁת is that it cannot see. [Most translations identify אֵשֶׁת as the mole which lives mainly in the undergound darkness and has poor eyesight.]

Rashi here identifies the אֵשֶׁת as the תִּנְשֶׁמֶת which is listed among the unclean creeping animals (*Leviticus* 11:30) and which *Targum* (ibid.) renders as אֲשׁוּתָא.

Among the unclean birds, we also find the תִּנְשֶׁמֶת (ibid. 11:18) which *Rashi* identifies as the *bat* which flies blindly in the night and closely resembles the creeping rodent תִּנְשֶׁמֶת which has no eyes.

Hirsch comments: The stillborn animal never sees the light of the sun, nor does a mole, although born alive, ever behold the light because its habitat is underground. Similarly these evil men stray in darkness, for their minds were never illuminated by the brilliant light of Torah knowledge *(Sforno).*

Rashi also suggests that נֵפֶל אֵשֶׁת may be translated as *the stillborn child* of an אִשָּׁה, *woman.*

Radak observes that both the *stillborn child* in the mother's womb and the *snail* ensconced within its shell have *never seen the sun.*

בַּל חָזוּ שָׁמֶשׁ — *That never saw the sun.*

Midrash Shocher Tov interprets this homiletically with reference to the slanderers. They are destined to fall (נֵפֶל) into the fires (אֵשֶׁת) of *Gehinnom,* from which they shall never emerge to *see the sun* of the World to Come.

נח
יא־יב

סִירֹתֵיכֶם אָטָד כְּמוֹ־חַי כְּמוֹ־חָרוֹן
יא יִשְׂעָרֶנּוּ: יִשְׂמַח צַדִּיק כִּי־חָזָה נָקָם
יב פְּעָמָיו יִרְחַץ בְּדַם הָרָשָׁע: וְיֹאמַר אָדָם
אַךְ־פְּרִי לַצַּדִּיק אַךְ יֵשׁ־אֱלֹהִים שֹׁפְטִים
בָּאָרֶץ:

10. בְּטֶרֶם יָבִינוּ סִירֹתֵיכֶם אָטָד — *Before your tender briars develop into* [lit. *understand*] *hardened thorns.*

Rashi explains this as a simile: סִירָה is a young briar shoot which is still relatively soft; it symbolizes the young offspring of the wicked who still lack the בִּינָה, *understanding,* to be mature, hardened criminals who are symbolized by אָטָד, *hardened thorns.*

However, *Radak, Sforno,* and *Malbim* render סִירֹתֵיכֶם as *your cooking pots,* which are heated by a fire made of אָטָד, *dry thorns.* [Similarly we find כְקוֹל הַסִּירִים תַּחַת הַסִּיר, *Like the sound of crackling thorns under the pot (Koheles 7:6).*] By the use of the example of a pot, the psalmist alludes to the *swiftness* with which the wicked will be destroyed. Ordinarily, the fire burning beneath a pot heats the metal quickly; but the destruction of the wicked will occur with extraordinary dispatch, even before the pot *understands,* i.e., feels, the effect of the flames.

Sforno interprets this allegorically: God will not delay the punishment of the wicked until after they die and the flames of *Gehinnom* are felt by them. The punishment of the wicked will come much sooner — כְּמוֹ חַי, *even while they live,* כְּמוֹ חָרוֹן, *with unbridled wrath,* God will sweep them away.

Returning to *Rashi's* original translation of סִירוֹתֵיכֶם as *tender briars, Alshich* detects a special allusion to Abner's folly. David asks, 'בְּטֶרֶם יָבִינוּ, *Do you still fail to understand?* The *tender briar* which you claim ripped Saul's robe surely could not cut better than אָטָד, *a hardened thorn.* Thus, how do you explain the fact that the cut was straight, and neat כְּמוֹ חַי, *as if done by a live person?* If, indeed, a thorn tore the robe, then the rip should have been jagged, כְּמוֹ חָרוֹן, *resembling* [a cloth torn in] *anger!'*

כְּמוֹ חַי — *As if with might.*

חַי, *life,* is another term for גְּבוּרָה, *might (Rashi).*

Malbim observes that the prophets often compare the punishment of the wicked to cooking them in a pot, as in *Ezekiel* 24:3, שְׁפֹת הַסִּיר שְׁפֹת, *Set down the pot, set it down.* If God brings their suffering upon them only after patiently allowing them time to fill the measure of their evil, they are compared to well cooked flesh, but if their evil is so great that God is compelled to punish them sooner than anticipated, they are likened to בָּשָׂר חַי, *raw meat,* which has not had time to cook.

כְּמוֹ חָרוֹן יִשְׂעָרֶנּוּ — *As if with wrath He will storm at them* [i.e., He will sweep them away like a whirlwind].

God will not wait for these men to grow old and weak. Rather, while they are still חַי, *lively, robust,* and *mighty,* He will swoop down upon them in a turbulent burst of *wrath (Radak).*

11. יִשְׂמַח צַדִּיק כִּי חָזָה נָקָם — *The righteous one shall rejoice when he sees vengeance.*

I.e., when he witnesses God's wrath as He *sweeps them* [the wicked] *away in a storm (Radak).*

The Sages teach that often a person is saved from danger thanks to the merit of others who are more righteous than he. Such a person does not deserve to see the destruction of his enemies and God will prevent him from doing so. If someone is allowed to watch the down-

10 *Before your tender briars develop*
into hardened thorns,
As if with might, as if with wrath
He will storm at them.
11 *The righteous one shall rejoice*
when he sees vengeance,
His feet shall he bathe
in the blood of the wicked.
12 *And mankind shall say,*
'There is, indeed, a reward for the righteous;
there is, indeed, a God judging the land.'

fall of his adversaries, it proves that he is a truly righteous man. Therefore *The* [genuinely] *righteous one shall rejoice when he sees vengeance,* not because he gloats over the suffering of his enemy, but as a sign from God that he has been saved by virtue of his own merit (*Panim Yafos*).

פְּעָמָיו יִרְחַץ בְּדַם הָרָשָׁע — *His feet* [lit. *footsteps*] *shall he bathe in the blood of the wicked.*

Hirsch emphasizes that this phrase should not be understood literally, as a gruesome orgy of revenge. Rather the verse allegorically expresses the concept that righteous people should draw a lesson from the punishment of the wicked. When the wicked drown violently in their own blood, the righteous are inspired to avoid evil even more meticulously than before. Thus they *wash their own footsteps* because of the lesson they derive from *the blood of the wicked.*

[These words, which seem to make light of the blood of the wicked, allude to Abner. *Yerushalmi Peah* 1:1 lists the factors which sealed Abner's doom. Paramount was the accusation, 'He made the bloodshed of the youths into a game, therefore he forfeited his own blood.' This refers to the time when Abner met his rival general, Joab, who commanded David's army. Abner suggested, *'Let the young soldiers arise and play* (i.e., engage in swordplay) *before us' (II Samuel* 2:14). The duel resulted in fatalities, yet Abner considered it a sport. Because he was unconcerned with bloodshed, his own blood was spilled].

12. וְיֹאמַר אָדָם אַךְ פְּרִי לַצַּדִּיק — *And mankind shall say, 'There is, indeed, a reward* [lit. *fruit*] *for the righteous.'*

When the world will see that God avenges the righteous, all will admit that the good deeds of the devout do not go unrewarded (Rashi).

Sforno adds: They will see the truth of the *Mishnah (Peah* 1:1*)* which teaches that although the primary reward for good deeds is reserved for the World to Come, God benefits the righteous with פֵּירוֹת, *fruits,* of their labor in this world.

אַךְ יֵשׁ אֱלֹהִים שֹׁפְטִים בָּאָרֶץ — *'There is, indeed, a God judging the land.'*

The translation of אֱלֹהִים as God (in His role of Judge), follows *Targum* and *Radak. Radak* and *Ibn Ezra* also suggest that אֱלֹהִים are the *ministering angels* [see also *comm.* 27:6] whom God has appointed as His agents to supervise the world and administer justice to mankind. [Saul and his judges failed to do justice to David, but David informs them that they have no monopoly on justice. If human judges fail to discharge their duties, then the Supreme Judge has many agents through whom justice will be rendered ultimately.]

The Sages comment (*Avos d'Rabbi Nathan*, 29): He who diligently pursues his Torah studies is supplied with heavenly assistance in the form of angels who aid his diligence (by removing obstacles and difficulties from his path); but he who wastes his opportunity to study Torah is afflicted with many heaven-sent agents who interfere with his studies. Lions, wolves, leopards, tigers, snakes, soldiers, and bandits — all of these surround this man and punish him. As the verse states, *'Indeed there are ministering angels in the land.'*

[This is David's final message to Abner and the others who hunt him. They refused to acknowledge David's involvement in the cutting of the robe and the removal of the spear and jug. They attribute everything to chance. Probing deeper into their hearts, David reveals that they attribute all events to chance, and not to Divine intervention. Therefore their final punishment will come about in such a way as to demonstrate clearly that *there is a God who judges the land* and that nothing is left to chance.][1]

1. [Abner died a violent death and the events which led to it indicate that he was punished measure for measure.

Assael ben Zeruyah pursued Abner. Defending himself, Abner hurled his spear at Assael, striking him a mortal blow near the fifth rib where the bladder and the liver meet. Joab, Assael's brother, accused Abner of murder, arguing that Abner could have defended himself by wounding Assael. Abner protested his innocence, pleading that he killed Assael accidentally, that the spear struck the victim by chance.

Joab refuted this claim, saying, 'Only a skilled marksman who aims with unerring accuracy can hit this small, vulnerable spot. This did not happen by chance! Abner, you are a murderer!' The Sanhedrin condemned Abner, and Joab slew him.

As Abner lay dying, he conquered his own desire for revenge, in an act of strength that surpassed all his conquests on the battlefield. *Yalkut Shimoni, Jeremiah* 285, relates:

When Joab stabbed him, Abner grasped Joab and twisted his body around into a complete circle. Immediately, all the men of Israel pleaded with Abner, 'Sire, if you kill Joab, then we will be like orphans without a father to protect them, for the Philistines will surely attack and defeat us.'

Abner asked, 'But what shall I do! This man extinguished the bright candle of my life.'

The people replied, 'Bring your case before the דַּיַּין הָאֱמֶת, *The Judge of Truth*, and let Him decide.'

Abner released Joab from his death grip and fell. One man lived and the other went to his death.

Behold, Abner had finally learned that *Indeed there is a God who judges the land.*]

מזמור נט

59

This psalm is the third and last composition in the Al Tashcheis *series. It is based on the very first incident in which Saul pursued David (recorded in I Samuel 19).*

As David's star gained ascendancy, Saul's dark and troubled spirit sank to the lowest depths. Once, when David played music before the king in an attempt to soothe his anguish, a spirit of evil descended on Saul. He flung his deadly spear at David's head, barely missing his mark. David fled from the palace.

Saul sent soldiers to David's home to watch him that night and to slay him in the morning. David was Saul's son-in-law, for his wife was Saul's daughter Michal. She loved her noble husband more than she did her bitter father, so she helped David to escape through a side window.

Michal then placed a lifelike mannequin (teraphim) *in David's bed as a ruse. At first she was able to restrain Saul's men by claiming David was sick, but then Saul dispatched his messengers again, saying: 'Bring him back to me in his bed so that I myself can slay him.' By the time Saul's soldiers discovered the deception, David had disappeared, leaving only the mannequin in his place.*

David composed this psalm of entreaty and thanksgiving upon his narrow escape from Saul.

נט
א־ה

א לַמְנַצֵּחַ אַל־תַּשְׁחֵת לְדָוִד מִכְתָּם בִּשְׁלֹחַ
שָׁאוּל וַיִּשְׁמְרוּ אֶת־הַבַּיִת לַהֲמִיתוֹ׃
ב הַצִּילֵנִי מֵאֹיְבַי | אֱלֹהָי מִמִּתְקוֹמְמַי
ג תְּשַׂגְּבֵנִי׃ הַצִּילֵנִי מִפֹּעֲלֵי אָוֶן וּמֵאַנְשֵׁי
ד דָמִים הוֹשִׁיעֵנִי׃ כִּי הִנֵּה אָרְבוּ לְנַפְשִׁי
יָגוּרוּ עָלַי עַזִּים לֹא־פִשְׁעִי וְלֹא־חַטָּאתִי
ה יהוה׃ בְּלִי־עָוֺן יְרֻצוּן וְיִכּוֹנָנוּ עוּרָה

1. לַמְנַצֵּחַ — *For the Conductor.*

[We cannot fail to be amazed at David's awesome capacity to create music and song even in times of severe adversity. The *Talmud (Sotah* 48a) states that when the Sanhedrin, the High Court, was dissolved, song and music vanished from people's lips, as Scripture says (*Lamentations* 5:14) *The elders have gone from the gate* (where the court convened), *the young men* (have desisted) *from their music.*

The helpless victim of injustice is usually preoccupied with his own misery; he is oblivious to the joy which also exists in the world. Although David realized that there was not one honest magistrate to whom he could appeal and from whom he could demand justice, he would not allow the melody which always welled up in his heart to be stilled.

David appealed to the Supreme God of Justice, and sang of His fair verdict, which he awaited with perfect faith.]

אַל תַּשְׁחֵת — Al Tashcheis [lit. *Do not destroy*].

David composed this psalm while on the verge of death; therefore he pleaded with God, *'Do not destroy me' (Rashi).*

בִּשְׁלֹחַ שָׁאוּל וַיִּשְׁמְרוּ אֶת הַבַּיִת לַהֲמִיתוֹ — *When Saul dispatched, and they guarded the house to kill him.*

[I.e., when Saul dispatched troops to guard David's house to prevent his escape so that Saul could later have him killed (see *prefatory remarks).*]

Alshich observes that God inspired Saul to handle this affair in a most inefficient manner, thus affording David an opportunity to escape. Saul should have given immediate orders for his men to break into David's home and slay him. By waiting outside all night, Saul's men not only allowed David to escape but also enabled him to gain a substantial head start in his flight.

2. הַצִּילֵנִי מֵאֹיְבַי ... מִמִּתְקוֹמְמַי — *Rescue me from my foes... those who rise against me.*

Norah Tehillos observes that David was already plagued by his old *foes*, the marauding gentiles and Philistines who attacked Israel. He bemoans the fact that he must fight on two fronts — against the gentiles and against his own countrymen, former friends, who now *rise up against me.*

Hirsch attaches special significance to this description of David's enemies: David was completely innocent, for he had done absolutely nothing to offend Saul's supporters. His only 'crime' was that God was with him and had caused him to *rise* to spectacular success. Because David's star was rising, his jealous rivals sought *to rise up* themselves in order to engineer David's downfall.

3. הַצִּילֵנִי מִפֹּעֲלֵי אָוֶן — *Rescue me from evildoers.*

These are the men who lay in ambush outside the gates of David's home *(Radak).*

For the Conductor, Al Tashcheis,
by David, a Michtam
When Saul dispatched,
and they guarded the house to kill him.
2 Rescue me from my foes, O my God;
over those who rise against me, strengthen me.
3 Rescue me from evildoers;
and from bloody people, save me.
4 For, behold! they lie in ambush for my soul,
around me gather impudent ones —
Not for my transgression
and not for my sin, O HASHEM!
5 Without iniquity they run and prepare —

וּמֵאַנְשֵׁי דָמִים הוֹשִׁיעֵנִי — *And from bloody people, save me.*

The *evildoers* were appointed to capture David, whereas the *bloody people* were those who were assigned to kill him *(Radak).*

4. יָגוּרוּ עָלַי — *Around me* [lit. *upon me*] *gather.*

This translation follows *Rashi* and *Radak* [see 56:7]. *Ibn Ezra* suggests that it may be rendered *they settle around me* to suggest they establish a permanent guard post outside my house to ensure uninterrupted surveillance.

עַזִּים — *Impudent ones.*

Sforno identifies these impudent enemies of David as seven members of Saul's family who were later hung in order to appease the Gibeonites (II *Samuel* Chapter 21). [The reason that they were singled out for death is explained in *Yevamos* 79a.]

לֹא פִשְׁעִי וְלֹא חַטָּאתִי — *Not for my transgression and not for my sin.*

These killers do not stalk me because of any crime which I have committed *(Radak).* [They are spurred only by jealousy.]

ה׳ — *HASHEM!*

This is an exclamation. David cries out: 'HASHEM, save me — You know the truth!' *(Radak).*

5. בְּלִי עָוֹן — *Without iniquity.*

Not only am I innocent of any sin towards God (*v.* 4), but I am also guiltless of committing any iniquity against these foes which could justify the hatred they feel for me *(Radak).*

And yet they attack me without the slightest compunction. Even as they wrong me, they persistently declare 'בְּלִי עָוֹן, *We are without iniquity'* *(Malbim).*

יְרֻצוּן וְיִכּוֹנָנוּ — *They run and prepare.*

Their audacity has no limits! Even if they commit their crimes with cold-blooded indifference, one might expect them to be ashamed to perpetrate them publicly. Yet, they bustle about and make a tremendous public commotion while they prepare for the kill *(Norah Tehillos).*

Furthermore, as they spy on me, they hurry to run back to Saul with slanderous reports about my behavior *(Maharam Markado).*

נט ו־ח

ו לִקְרָאתִי וּרְאֵה: וְאַתָּה יהוה־אֱלֹהִים | צְבָאוֹת אֱלֹהֵי יִשְׂרָאֵל הָקִיצָה לִפְקֹד כָּל־ הַגּוֹיִם אַל־תָּחֹן כָּל־בֹּגְדֵי אָוֶן סֶלָה:
ז יָשׁוּבוּ לָעֶרֶב יֶהֱמוּ כַכָּלֶב וִיסוֹבְבוּ עִיר:
ח הִנֵּה | יַבִּיעוּן בְּפִיהֶם חֲרָבוֹת

עוּרָה לִקְרָאתִי וּרְאֵה — *Awaken towards me and see.*

[See 44:24 where we find that עוּרָה implies: Show that You are awake. Certainly, God's personal supervision over the righteous never ceases; however, when He does not react to the persecution which they suffer at the hands of their pursuers, it appears as if He slumbers and must be awakened.]

6. [In this verse, David abruptly shifts his attention from Saul to the gentiles, whom he now asks God to destroy. The commentaries attempt to explain this sudden change of theme.]

וְאַתָּה ה׳ אֱלֹהִים צְבָאוֹת אֱלֹהֵי יִשְׂרָאֵל — *And You, HASHEM, God of Legions, God of Israel.*

David seeks to arouse God in all of His vast glory; in all of His attributes which include kindness and justice; and in all of His power, which rules both the celestial forces above and the nation of Israel below *(Ibn Ezra)*.

According to *Radak,* David abandoned hope of receiving justice in his own time. He surveyed the society around him and saw only corruption and dishonesty. The land of Israel did not lack judges and sheriffs, yet none of them protested Saul's outrageous conduct. In despair, David trains his hopes on the future, when God will appear as the all-powerful אֱלֹהִים, *Judge,* of the entire world. Then God will mete out true justice to all men, including Saul and his bloodthirsty cohorts.

Malbim, however, views David's plea as a request for the present. David was the mighty champion of Israel, the foremost defender against the Philistine host. Here David displays a great sense of responsibility towards his people, for now that he must go into hiding, he can no longer publicly lead their defense against the foe. Therefore, he turns over his command to another General, *the God of Legions, the God of Israel,* and begs Him to continue the fight.

הָקִיצָה לִפְקֹד כָּל הַגּוֹיִם — *Arouse Yourself to remember all the nations.*

According to *Rashi, the nations* actually refers to Saul and his minions. *Yaavetz Hadoresh* explains that they resemble the gentiles, for just as *the nations* hate Israel, without any real reason, so do Saul and his men hate David without cause. Therefore, the verdict issued against them should resemble that of the gentile nations.

[The comparison of Saul and his supporters to *the nations* alludes to the basic defect which undermined the foundation of Saul's monarchy. When Israel first demanded that Samuel appoint a king for them, they were motivated by a sense of inferiority and by a desire to imitate the gentiles. They cried, *'Appoint for us a king who will rule us like all the nations'* (*I Samuel* 8:5). Saul's ill-conceived reign was doomed from its very inception (see *comm.* to 4:9). Consequently, this monarchy was plagued by the kinds of machinations, intrigues, and jealousies with which the royal palaces of the gentiles are rife. This jealousy was the source of David's woes and Saul's ultimate destruction.]

Malbim, following his previous comment, interprets: 'Now that I [David] must relinquish my command of Israel, please, God, take charge *and remember*

59
6-8

awaken towards me and see.
6 *And You, HASHEM, God of Legions,*
God of Israel,
Arouse Yourself to remember all the nations,
favor not any evil traitors, Selah.
7 *They return toward evening,*
they howl like the dog and go round about the city.
8 *Behold! they spew with their mouths,*

to wage war against *the nations* who threaten Israel.'

אַל תָּחֹן כָּל בֹּגְדֵי אָוֶן – *Favor not any evil traitors.*

David concludes his request: 'Although I ask You to combat the gentiles, I also ask You to remember that the *evil traitors* of Israel must also be punished without undeserved mercy' *(Malbim).*

7. יָשׁוּבוּ לָעֶרֶב – *They return toward evening.*

This alludes to the soldiers who stood guard around David's house from evening until the following morning *(Radak).*

יֶהֱמוּ כַכָּלֶב – *They howl like the dog.*

[Although there were many soldiers, David refers to them in the singular, as כֶּלֶב, *one dog,* for they all repeated the same slanderous tales in Saul's ears, so their voices were as one.]

Just as the dog tends to howl in the darkness of night, the cowardly talebearer slanders his foes in dark secrecy rather than denouncing them publicly *(Rashbam).*

[Moreover, the *Talmud (Bava Kama* 60b) states that when the Angel of Death comes to a city to claim someone's soul, the dogs sense his presence and howl. Saul's men played a dual role; they lurked in the night as agents of death, and they howled like dogs.]

[See *Chafetz Chaim, Shmiras HaLashon,* 1:4-9, for a detailed comparison of the talebearer and the dog.

וִיסוֹבְבוּ עִיר – *And go round about the city.*

The guards resembled a pack of hungry dogs, surrounding its prey.

In addition to the armed guards stationed outside David's house, Saul dispatched search parties to go around and comb the city in the event that David managed to slip through the cordon around his home *(Radak).*[1]

8. הִנֵּה יַבִּיעוּן בְּפִיהֶם – *Behold! they spew with their mouths.*

Rashi explains that this is a direct continuation of the preceding verse. Towards evening my foes assembled to besiege my home, but in truth, their wickedness had already begun by day, when they *spewed forth* evil tales about me in the ears of Saul and incited his wrath.

[Although common sense dictates

1. [This alludes to the *Talmud (Eruvin* 61a) which says that a killer is dangerous only in his own city, where his confidence is bolstered by the familiar environment. Put him in a strange city and he will feel too insecure and frightened to do much harm. As the folk saying goes: 'Take a dog away from his hometown and he won't bark even once in seven years!'

Therefore, David says, 'Because these killers roam around the city, their hometown, at will, they feel a sense of mastery, and howl menacingly like dogs!']

נט ט-יב

ט בְּשִׂפְתוֹתֵיהֶם כִּי־מִי שֹׁמֵעַ: וְאַתָּה יהוה
י תִּשְׂחַק־לָמוֹ תִּלְעַג לְכָל־גּוֹיִם: עֻזּוֹ אֵלֶיךָ
יא אֶשְׁמֹרָה כִּי־אֱלֹהִים מִשְׂגַּבִּי: אֱלֹהֵי
°חַסְדִּי °חסדו יְקַדְּמֵנִי אֱלֹהִים יַרְאֵנִי בְשֹׁרְרָי:
יב אַל־תַּהַרְגֵם | פֶּן־יִשְׁכְּחוּ עַמִּי הֲנִיעֵמוֹ

that men who are laying a trap should exercise the utmost caution and secrecy in order to catch their prey by surprise, Saul's men carelessly publicized their plot to every passer-by. They were so thrilled by the thought of David's impending doom that they could not contain their excitement, but spewed forth the details of their strategy.

In addition, they were proud that the king himself had appointed them to execute this mission. While they gloried in their great prestige, they failed to consider the enormity of their intended crime (see *Sforno*).]

חֲרָבוֹת בְּשִׂפְתוֹתֵיהֶם — *Swords are on their lips.*

Their razor-sharp words of slander are as murderous as the blade of a sword (*Targum*).

כִּי מִי שֹׁמֵעַ — *For 'Who listens?'*

They proudly boast of their 'courageous' campaign against David, but, in truth, they are cowards. They dare to speak so boldly only because they think that David does not hear. If they realized that he could overhear them, they would immediately fall silent, for fear that David might someday ascend to the throne and punish them (*Radak*).

9. וְאַתָּה ה׳ תִּשְׂחַק לָמוֹ — *But as for You, HASHEM — You laugh at them.*

David said: 'These men imagine that since I do not hear of their plots, I am defenseless and at their mercy. O God, foil their schemes and show them how greatly they err! For You, my Protector, hear every word they utter. You can ridicule them as no one else can, for You realize the emptiness of their threats' (*Radak*).

They strut about and boast that they have the entire city under the tightest security. You laugh at this presumption (*Sforno*).

תִּלְעַג לְכָל גּוֹיִם — *You mock all nations.*

Just as You mock all nations which threaten to harm Israel [see 2:4], so will You ridicule these enemies of mine [and undo their schemes] (*Rashi*).

10. עֻזּוֹ — *Power is his* [lit. *his power*].

The translation follows *Rashi*, who refers this to the enemy, who has the upper hand in this conflict with David; and *Radak* who applies this to Saul.

Hirsch perceives in these words the rule which influenced all of David's actions towards Saul: 'As long as all the royal might and power remain in the hands of Saul, I [David] shall refrain from any belligerent action against him. Patiently and faithfully I wait for You, O God, to take the initiative. It was You who invested Saul with his royal powers, and You alone will decide when to divest him of them.'

Ibn Ezra interprets עֻזּוֹ as a reference to God Himself, of whom we can say *Power is His* alone. Therefore, says David, *'For You* [*alone*] *do I wait.'*

אֵלֶיךָ אֶשְׁמֹרָה — *For You do I wait.*

I.e., to deliver me from the threat of my foes.

Patiently, I await the end of the time which You have destined for the duration of Saul's reign (*Hirsch*).

Until that time, not only will I not attack Saul but also אֶשְׁמֹרָה, *I shall guard*, him even from my own men who wish to slay him (*Sforno*). [See *I Samuel*, chapters 24 and 26.]

swords are on their lips — for 'Who listens?'
9 *But as for You, HASHEM — You laugh at them,*
You mock all nations.
10 *Power is his —*
for You do I wait, for God is my stronghold.
11 *The God of my kindness — He will anticipate me,*
God will show me my watchful foes.
12 *Slay them not,*
lest my nation forget.

כִּי אֱלֹהִים מִשְׂגַּבִּי — *For God is my stronghold.*

[David says: 'I am determined to defend myself from Saul only passively, despite the tremendous risk involved in such a dangerous course of action. I do not consider this to be suicidal because I firmly believe that I am well protected, *for God is my stronghold.*']

11. אֱלֹהֵי חַסְדִּי יְקַדְּמֵנִי — *The God of my kindness — He will anticipate me.*

God will *anticipate* my need and extend His help before my enemies can vanquish me *(Rashi).*

Sforno comments that God promised the kings of Israel special kindness in their struggles and wars. David says: 'Although I am not yet the king, I hope that God will *anticipate* my ascension to the throne by kindly granting me special power to emerge triumphant from conflicts, even before my coronation.'

[The word is spelled (כְּתִיב) חַסְדּוֹ, *His kindness,* but is pronounced (קְרִי) חַסְדִּי, *my kindness.* This duality suggests, 'Because I am assured of His [God's] protective kindness towards me, I can be kindly towards Saul.'

David's use of the Name אֱלֹהִים, denoting God as Dispenser of Justice indicates his confidence that if his pursuer deserves punishment, then יְקַדְּמֵנִי, *God will anticipate me,* by meting out justice so that I need not take action (see *Radak; Rashi; Ibn Ezra).*]

As *Hirsch* explains, the discrepancy between the spelling and pronunciation serves to emphasize that the actions of God and man are intertwined. The psalmist declares: God's actions towards me are a reflection of my own deeds. To the degree that I practice lovingkindness (חַסְדִּי) towards others, God will act kindly towards me (חַסְדּוֹ).

Olelos Yehudah points out that these words, *The God of my kindness — He will anticipate me,* teach a general rule of God's conduct with man: First, He displays kindness and showers a person with the means to perform the commandments. Only then, does God obligate man to respond. As the *Midrash* says, 'Did I [God] ever ask anyone to put up a *mezuzah* before giving him a house? Did I ever require a circumcision before blessing a person with a son? Did I ever demand tithes before supplying a man with fruits?'

אֱלֹהִים יַרְאֵנִי בְשֹׁרְרָי — *God will show me my watchful foes.*

Radak explains: God will show me the downfall of those who dog my steps and watch me with hatred, as Scripture says, *And Saul watched David with an evil eye (I Samuel* 18:9).

12. אַל תַּהַרְגֵם פֶּן יִשְׁכְּחוּ עַמִּי — *Slay them not, lest my nation forget.*

[David's prime concern was neither his own safety nor revenge; rather, he sought to counter the bad influence

יג בְּחֵילְךָ וְהוֹרִידֵמוֹ מָגִנֵּנוּ אֲדֹנָי: חַטַּאת־
פִּימוֹ דְּבַר־שְׂפָתֵימוֹ וְיִלָּכְדוּ בִגְאוֹנָם
יד וּמֵאָלָה וּמִכַּחַשׁ יְסַפֵּרוּ: כַּלֵּה בְחֵמָה כַּלֵּה
וְאֵינֵמוֹ וְיֵדְעוּ כִּי־אֱלֹהִים מֹשֵׁל בְּיַעֲקֹב
טו לְאַפְסֵי הָאָרֶץ סֶלָה: וְיָשֻׁבוּ לָעֶרֶב יֶהֱמוּ

which his foes exercised over the people of Israel. He desired that God publicize the downfall of the wicked as an object lesson for the benefit of those who harbored any wish to follow in their ways.]

David asked: 'Do not destroy them with one quick blow, which is hardly noticed and swiftly forgotten' *(Rashi, Radak).* [Instead, reduce their power gradually, so that people will marvel at their protracted and irreversible decline and will witness the utter helplessness of these once powerful men.]

הֲנִיעֵמוֹ בְחֵילְךָ — *Deprive them of Your wealth* [lit. *Impoverish them with Your might*].

This translation follows *Rashi,* who renders הֲנִיעֵמוֹ as *remove them* from their property, for it is truly *Your wealth* which You had graciously bestowed upon them. [Man's 'ownership' of goods is an illusion, for God actually owns everything. One's material goods should be viewed as a Divine trust which is to be properly disbursed.]

Radak, however, interprets הֲנִיעֵמוֹ as *make them wander about* (from נָעוּ) to search for their daily bread. *Ibn Ezra* adds that in this manner they will resemble the dog which strays around the city and sniffs for scraps of food. This punishment is particularly fitting, for *they howl like the dog and go round about the city (v. 7).*

[The dog is a symbol of extreme poverty, as the *Talmud (Shabbos* 155b) says: There is no creature as poor as the dog for his food supply is very scarce.]

The *Chafetz Chaim* in *Shmiras Halashon* 1:6 explains that arrogance is the root of the desire to slander and degrade one's fellow man. Therefore, poverty is its most appropriate punishment, for it serves to humble the proud. Even today, although the punishment of צָרַעַת, *leprous spots,* no longer strikes the arrogant slanderer, poverty still does!

Rashbam perceives yet another moral lesson here: The slanderer drifts around peddling his gossip (הוֹלֵךְ רָכִיל), and therefore, he is ultimately condemned to wander about in search of a livelihood.

וְהוֹרִידֵמוֹ — *And cast them down.*

[Let them descend not only from their financial position but also from their high level of social prestige.]

13. חַטַּאת פִּימוֹ דְּבַר שְׂפָתֵימוֹ — *The sin of their mouth is the word of their lips.*

Let their punishment be so clear that not only will others learn from it, but also they themselves will recognize the evil of their slanderous words *(Radak).*

Let them admit *with the words of their own lips* to the *sin of their mouth (Alshich).*

וְיִלָּכְדוּ בִגְאוֹנָם — *And they shall be ensnared by their pride.*

In their arrogance, they declared, *'Who listens?' (v.* 8) and disregarded the threat of Divine retribution. They will be trapped in this very arrogance, [for You, O God, *listen* closely to every proud word they utter] *(Ibn Ezra).*

וּמֵאָלָה וּמִכַּחַשׁ יְסַפֵּרוּ — *Because of curses and falsehoods which they recount.*

[The word כַּחַשׁ literally means *denial.* The slanderer is eventually rebuked by his victim for his vicious tales. If the slanderer fears the victim, he will feel

Deprive them of Your wealth, and cast them down,
O our Shield, my Master.
13 *The sin of their mouth is the word of their lips,*
and they shall be ensnared by their pride,
Because of curses and falsehoods
which they recount.
14 *Destroy them in wrath,*
destroy them until they are no more!
And then shall they know that God rules Jacob,
to the ends of the earth, Selah.
15 *And they return toward evening,*
they howl like the dog

compelled to resort to *falsehood* to deny that he had ever slandered him. If the slanderer has no fear of the man whom he wronged, he will contemptuously *curse* him in response to his accusation.]

14. כַּלֵּה בְחֵמָה כַּלֵּה – *Destroy them in wrath, destroy them.*

Eradicate them by degrees *(Radak).* The repeated use of the word כַּלֵּה implies the gradual process of their downfall *(Hirsch).*

Norah Tehillos perceives here an allusion to the suffering of Gehinnom, which is not limited to one isolated punishment. After the wicked are consumed by the flames, they are repeatedly re-created so that they can be returned to the fire again and again. [See *commentary* to 6:11 and 21:18.]

וְאֵינֵמוֹ – *Until they are no more.*

[Although it is desirable that their terrible fate should long be remembered, they themselves must be completely destroyed and obliterated.]

וְיֵדְעוּ כִּי אֱלֹהִים מֹשֵׁל בְּיַעֲקֹב לְאַפְסֵי הָאָרֶץ – *And then shall they know that God rules Jacob, to the ends of the earth.*

God pays more attention to His Chosen People, Israel, than He does to the other nations. Nevertheless, when the world sees the intensity of His exacting supervision over Jacob, they will recognize His ability to control mankind in general, even *to the ends of the earth (Radak).*

['Israel' is the title applied to our people when they are meritorious; the designation 'Jacob' is employed when the Jews are less deserving of Divine favor.

God is called מוֹשֵׁל, *ruler,* when He must force His sovereignty on His subjects against their will. He is referred to as מֶלֶךְ, *king,* when the people readily accept His dominion.

David addresses himself to the wicked Jews who pursue him; he refers to them as *Jacob* because of their evil ways. God will force His will upon them as their מוֹשֵׁל, *ruler,* which will be a lesson to all of the far-flung nations who are also estranged from God and refuse to recognize His authority.]

15. וְיָשֻׁבוּ לָעֶרֶב יֶהֱמוּ כַכָּלֶב – *And they return towards evening, they howl like the dog.*

This is a repetition of *v.* 7. There, however, David spoke only to his Jewish enemies, who were of his generation, whereas here he addresses himself to all the nations who will gather with Gog and Magog at the end of days, as the sun of history sets before the Mes-

נט
טז־יח

°יְנִיעוּן טז כַּכָּלֶב וִיסוֹבְבוּ עִיר: הֵמָּה °ינועון לֶאֱכֹל
יז אִם־לֹא יִשְׂבְּעוּ וַיָּלִינוּ: וַאֲנִי | אָשִׁיר עֻזֶּךָ
וַאֲרַנֵּן לַבֹּקֶר חַסְדֶּךָ כִּי־הָיִיתָ מִשְׂגָּב לִי
יח וּמָנוֹס בְּיוֹם צַר לִי: עֻזִּי אֵלֶיךָ אֲזַמֵּרָה כִּי־
אֱלֹהִים מִשְׂגַּבִּי אֱלֹהֵי חַסְדִּי:

sianic era. They will howl at Israel like mad dogs *(Sforno).*

[This alludes to the *Talmudic* statement (*Sotah* 49b) that in the era preceding the advent of Messiah 'the face of the generation will resemble the face of a dog.' Their deeds will resemble the treachery of Saul's cohorts, as will their ultimate punishment.]

וִיסוֹבְבוּ עִיר — *And go round about the city.*

The armies of Gog and Magog will encircle Jerusalem and besiege the Holy City *(Sforno).*

According to *Meiri,* both verses refer to Saul's men. However, verse 7 tells of their wicked deeds, while this verse describes their punishment, measure for measure. Since they roamed the city to find David, they are doomed to wander about the city forever as beggars and scavengers.

16. הֵמָּה יְנוּעוּן לֶאֱכֹל — *They wander about to eat.*

They resemble the starving dog, whose hunger does not let him sleep. Until he is sated, he wanders about in search of food *(Rashi).*

[Saul's men sought to satisfy their lust for power and revenge by 'feasting' on David's corpse, therefore they are doomed to eternal poverty and starvation.]

17. וַאֲנִי אָשִׁיר עֻזֶּךָ — *But as for me, I shall sing of Your might.*

This is a repetition of David's previous declaration, *Power is His (v.*

59
16-18 *and go round about the city.*
16 *They wander about to eat,*
if they are not sated that they may sleep.
17 *But as for me, I shall sing of Your might,*
and rejoice before dawn in Your kindness,
For You have been my stronghold
and a refuge in the day of my distress.
18 *My Power — to You shall I sing,*
for God is my stronghold, God of my kindness.

10); i.e., *Power* belongs to God alone, and He alone may be praised for it *(Ibn Ezra).*

Joy will return when God displays His *might* against the foe *(Radak)* and when He finally bestows His *might* upon David, by publicly crowning him king *(Sforno).*

וַאֲרַנֵּן לַבֹּקֶר חַסְדֶּךָ — *And rejoice before dawn in Your kindness.*

When dawn will begin to break and I see that my escape from Saul's men (last night) was successful, then I shall rejoice *(Rashi).*

18. עֻזִּי אֵלֶיךָ אֲזַמֵּרָה — *My Power — to You shall I sing.*

This concluding verse contrasts with *v.* 10, עֻזּוֹ אֵלֶיךָ אֶשְׁמֹרָה, *Power is his — for You do I wait. Rashi* to verse 10 translates עֻזּוֹ, *power is his,* and applies it to David's enemies. However, *Rashi* refers עֻזִּי, *my Power,* in this verse to God who is the source of my strength.

Radak, who refers עֻזּוֹ, *Power is his,* to Saul, here translates עֻזִּי as *power is mine.* As long as the royal power was in the hands of Saul, I could only wait in silence. However, now that עֻזִּי, *power is mine,* I can sing joyously.

כִּי אֱלֹהִים מִשְׂגַּבִּי אֱלֹהֵי חַסְדִּי — *For God is my stronghold, God of my kindness.*

[No matter how powerful I become, I shall never abuse my power and privileges as Saul did. I will never forget that I owe all that I am to Your *kindness,* for You alone are *my stronghold* and my strength.]

מזמור ס

60

This psalm presents David's inspired vision of a universal order of nations united in complete harmony. This was his dream. True, Scripture describes David as a mighty warrior endowed with extraordinary martial skills; nevertheless, he was not a belligerent man of war, but an ambassador of peace.

The concept of universal peace is a manifestation of monotheism, the belief in one Almighty God. Pagan mythology depicts a chaotic heaven torn asunder by jealous, warring 'gods' who are no more than an exaggerated reflection of their human creators. Struggle, conflict, and polarization are basic elements of the idolator's weltanschauung.

The Jew, who believes in one Creator, believes that all of the diverse elements of this universe are basically united to serve the purposes of the one God, Who gives order to the world. Israel is at the center of this world order, and the supreme tribunal of this nation, the Great Sanhedrin, convenes in the Temple, which is the spiritual center of the earth. Each of the seventy members of this august body is symbolic of one of the world's seventy nations and the seventy-first member, the chief justice, represents Israel, the nation which controls the order of all other peoples (Ramban, Numbers *11:16).*

David dedicated this psalm of war to Sanhedrin, because he fought only upon the advice and consent of this high court. He waged war only to establish Israel's mastery over the seventy nations and to establish a harmonious world order of nations dedicated to divine peace.

א לַמְנַצֵּחַ עַל־שׁוּשַׁן עֵדוּת מִכְתָּם לְדָוִד
ב לְלַמֵּד: בְּהַצּוֹתוֹ | אֶת אֲרַם נַהֲרַיִם וְאֶת־

1. לַמְנַצֵּחַ — *For the Conductor.*

[It is essential to be aware of the background and the setting of this composition. In *II Samuel,* Chapter 7 and again in *I Chronicles,* Chapter 17, Nathan, the prophet, informs David that his life's dream will indeed be realized, and that a Temple will be built to serve as the focal point of God's Holy Presence in the world. The actual construction of this edifice would be executed by David's son; nevertheless, David was charged with making all preparations necessary for this universal center of sanctity.

[In *II Samuel,* Chapter 8 and *I Chronicles,* Chapter 18, we read of David's preparations (see *Rashi, I Chronicles* 8:1). Until now, David's wars were purely defensive campaigns to counter foreign assaults. Henceforth David takes the offensive (*Malbim, I Samuel* 8:11), for now he must subjugate the nations in order to prepare for universal peace.

[First David smote the Philistines; then he subjugated Moab. Finally he was victorious over Hadadezer, the king of Aram Tzovah.]

עַל שׁוּשַׁן עֵדוּת — *Upon* Shushan Eidus [lit. *the rose of the testimony.*]

Many commentaries suggest that this is a special type of musical instrument shaped like a rose (*Metzudas Zion*). It produced exquisite music, and thus resembled the rose, which is the most lovely of flowers (*Meiri*). עֵדוּת, *Eidus,* is related to the word עֲדִי, *jewel, adornment* [see *Ezekiel* 16:7], and describes the beauty of this instrument (*Ibn Ezra; Meiri*).

Rashi, following *Midrash Shocher Tov,* renders עֵדוּת as *testimony,* an allusion to the Great Sanhedrin, which accepts testimony and has final jurisdiction over legal affairs.

Sanhedrin is also called שׁוּשַׁן as in בִּטְנֵךְ עֲרֵמַת חִטִּים סוּגָה בַּשּׁוֹשַׁנִּים, *Your belly is like a heap of wheat hedged about with roses* (*Songs* 7:3). [As the *Talmud* (*Sanhedrin* 37a) comments, 'Just as all men benefit from a heap of nutritious wheat, so do all benefit from the decisions of Sanhedrin. The Sanhedrin also protects Israel from sin, by erecting legal barriers and moral deterrents which safeguard Israel just as a thorny hedge protects the roses.][1]

מִכְתָּם — *A* Michtam.

Targum renders this as פַּרְשְׁגֶן, *an explanation;* i.e., Sanhedrin examined the terms of the covenant with Aram and explained that since Aram had initiated hostilities twice, the pact was void (*Targuma d'HaTargum*).

According to the *Midrash* (*Bereishis*

1. The *Midrash* relates that when Joab, David's general, went to wage war on Aram, the Arameans confronted him and asked, 'Are you not the descendant of Jacob, and therefore does not a covenant exist between us? For Laban, our forebear, said, *"Now come let us make a covenant, you* [Jacob] *and I"... And Jacob took a stone and set it up for a monument... and Laban said, "This stone is a testimony* (עֵד) *between me and you this day"'* (*Genesis* 31:44, 45, 48).

[This incident is the basis for the *Targum* on our verse, which translates שׁוּשַׁן as יָשָׁן, *the ancient,* עֵדוּת, *monument of testimony,* which was rerected by Jacob and Laban.]

Joab had no answer for this claim and so he returned to consult with David, who assembled the Sanhedrin. It ruled that Joab should reply: 'The Arameans themselves nullified this covenant of peace! Indeed, Bilaam [on his way to curse Israel] admitted, *"Balak, the King of Moab, brings me from Aram"* (*Numbers* 23:7). This was not the only time the Arameans betrayed their pact with the intent of harming Israel, for Scripture testifies, *The children of Israel served Cushan-Rishasaim the King of Aram-Naharaim* (*Judges* 3:8). Aram is guilty on two counts!'

For the Conductor, upon Shushan Eidus,
a Michtam by David, to instruct.
2 When he made war against
Aram Naharaim and Aram Tzovah,

Rabbah 74:15), מִכְתָּם is a contraction of two words: מַכּוֹת תַּמּוֹת, *total beatings*, referring to the license Sanhedrin gave David to wage a total war against Aram.

The *Midrash* also relates that when Joab informed David of the problem with Aram, David was determined to resolve this question immediately. He forsook the customary pomp and protocol befitting a king, removing the imperial robes from his shoulders and the royal crown from his head. He wrapped himself in a simple *talis* and came humbly before Sanhedrin with his halachic question concerning the interpretation of the covenant.

[This alludes to two other translations of מִכְתָּם discussed in the *commentary* to 16:1. First, the *Talmud (Sotah* 10b) says that even at the height of his imperial splendor, David remained מִכְתָּם, i.e., מָךְ, *humble*, and תָּם, *innocent*, to all. Second, although David removed his מִכְתָּם, *crown*, as a sign of submission to the court's ruling, nevertheless, his sterling character invested him with an aura of majesty which far surpassed that provided by his royal crown.]

לְלַמֵּד — *To instruct.*

Sanhedrin taught David that he was justified in fighting Aram, and David composed this work to make known this fact (see *Radak).*

In addition, David taught this composition to the Temple singers and instructed them to publicize it, for it speaks of God's mercy in aiding David's army to vanquish Aram despite Israel's relative weakness and military inferiority *(Ibn Ezra).*

Meiri concludes that this psalm has the power to instruct mankind and instill in them the faith and recognition that all human affairs and events are directed by a Divine order and with a purpose.

2. בְּהַצּוֹתוֹ — *When he made war.*

This translation follows *Rashi, Radak* and *Metzudos*, based on *Numbers* 26:9.

Ibn Ezra suggests that it means *when he destroyed.*

Midrash Shocher Tov here offers additional interpretations of בְּהַצּוֹתוֹ.

— It means that Joab set Aram on fire (לְהַצִּית אֶת הָאוּר).

— When the ה is *midrashically* interchanged with a ח, the word reads בְּחַצּוֹתוֹ, *when he split in two*, meaning that David divided and mixed up the nations, for he took the people of Aram-Naharaim and settled them in Aram-Tzovah, and placed the people of Aram-Tzovah in Aram-Naharaim [cf. *Radak*]. בְּחַצּוֹתוֹ also means that David riddled Aram with חִצִּים, *arrows.*

אֲרַם נַהֲרַיִם — *Aram Naharaim* [lit. *Aram of the pair of rivers.*]

[*Rashi (Genesis* 24:10) says that this city is situated on *two rivers*, one of which is פְּרָת, *the Euphrates* (cf. *Targum* here and in *Genesis* 24:10). This river is called *the great river (Genesis* 5:18) because it is the eastern border of *Eretz Yisrael*, the greatest of all lands (*Shavuos* 47b; *Rashi, Genesis* 2:14). Possibly the name נַהֲרַיִם (lit. *pair of rivers)* is an honorific title for the Euphrates River itself, indicating its distinguished status.]

Midrash Shocher Tov (on Psalm 1) relates this name to the preceding word [בְּהַצּוֹתוֹ =] בְּחַצּוֹתוֹ, *when he split in two*, stating, 'We find that whatever Moses did, David did as well... Moses split the sea and David split the river, as it says, *when he split Aram of the two*

אֲרַם צוֹבָה וַיָּשָׁב יוֹאָב וַיַּךְ אֶת־אֱדוֹם
ג בְּגֵיא־מֶלַח שְׁנֵים עָשָׂר אָלֶף: אֱלֹהִים
זְנַחְתָּנוּ פְרַצְתָּנוּ אָנַפְתָּ תְּשׁוֹבֵב לָנוּ:
ד הִרְעַשְׁתָּה אֶרֶץ פְּצַמְתָּהּ רְפָה שְׁבָרֶיהָ

rivers [i.e., he miraculously caused the Euphrates River to split into two so that it would not block his army when he went out to attack Aram.]

אֲרַם צוֹבָה – *Aram Tzovah.*

[There were two separate kingdoms of Aram, located in present-day Syria (see ArtScroll *Bereishis I* p. 328 for a description of the geographical locations referred to in our verse). First David smote Hadadezer, the king of Aram Tzovah (Aleppo), who was attempting to expand the boundaries of his own country by conquering and annexing land on the other side of the Euphrates River (*Rashi, I Chronicles* 18:3). The king of Aram-Damascus then came to aid Hadadezer; both met with disastrous defeat.]

וַיָּשָׁב יוֹאָב וַיַּךְ אֶת אֱדוֹם ... שְׁנֵים עָשָׂר אָלֶף – *And Joab returned and smote Edom ... twelve thousand* [*men.*]

Scripture records this event in three different places; the commentaries point out discrepancies among the three accounts in regard to (1) the victorious general, (2) the vanquished nation, and (3) the extent of the enemy's loss.

Here the victorious general is Joab ben Zeruyah; in *II Samuel* 8:13, it is David; in *I Chronicles* 18:12, it is Joab's brother, Avishai.

Both here and in *Chronicles* the defeated nation is described as Edom, but in *II Samuel* it is identified as Aram.

Here, the enemy loss is put at twelve thousand, but the other two sources recorded it as eighteen thousand.

From the commentaries of *Rashi* and *Radak*, we can develop the following reconciliation of the various sources:

Edom and Aram joined their armies in order to defend themselves against David; therefore their force is sometimes called Aram and sometimes Edom. First Avishai battled them and killed only six thousand men. Then his brother Joab *returned* (וַיָּשָׁב) and fought them again, killing an additional twelve thousand as recorded here. In *Chronicles*, Scripture credits Avishai with all eighteen thousand casualties; because he had the merit of beginning the campaign, the entire amount is attributed to him. In *II Samuel,* the victory is ascribed to David because, as king, he was commander-in-chief of *both* armies.

However, according to the *Midrash (Bereishis Rabbah* 74:15) Israel smote twelve thousand of Edom and set up a military government to rule the occupied land. Edom then rebelled against Israel and this uprising was put down at the cost of an additional eighteen thousand Edomite casualties [see *Alshich* and *Sforno* here and *Malbim (II Samuel* 18:13), based on *Midrash Tanchuma.*]

שְׁנֵים עָשָׂר אָלֶף – *Twelve thousand* [*men*].

[These words appear after the אתנחתא *separation* note, and thus appear not to refer back to the Edomite army, i.e., it is not a total of enemy losses. This justifies the opinion of the *Targum* that the reference is to the number of Jews who fell during the campaign against Edom and Aram. However, *Targuma d'HaTargum* says that our printed version of the *Targum* is erroneous and that it should read that David and Joab smote twelve thousand of the Edomites.]

3. אֱלֹהִים זְנַחְתָּנוּ פְרַצְתָּנוּ – *O God, You forsook us, You breached us.*

David said this at the very outset of the hostilities, when Hadadezer crossed the Euphrates and brazenly attempted

and Joab returned and smote Edom
in the Valley of Salt,
twelve thousand men.
3 *O God, You forsook us, You breached us,*
You were angry with us, O restore us!
4 *You made the land quake, You broke it;*

to annex part of the land of Israel. Initially Hadadezer's penetration was successful and he broke through Israel's defenses; thus, with God's help, Hadadezer had *breached our defenses* and it seemed as if he might conquer the entire land, showing that *You forsook us (Radak).* [1]

[According to our version of *Targum* (but see comment above), David's lament may refer to the twelve thousand lives his army had to pay for its triumph (see the *Targum* on the preceding verse).]

Rashi maintains that at his moment of victory over Edom, David was deeply troubled by his prophetic vision of the future. He foresaw that Edom would strike back and dominate Israel with tyranny and harsh oppression. Now David turned to God and asked for Divine mercy during the future Edomite-Roman persecution.

אָנַפְתָּ תְּשׁוֹבֵב לָנוּ – *You were angry [with us], O restore us!*

Do not forsake us forever. Once You have vented Your anger on us [as punishment for our sins], restore us to our former glory *(Rashi).*

☙ The *commentary* to the coming verses will follow two separate lines of thought: *Radak* traces David's feelings concerning the present campaign against Aram-Edom, whereas *Rashi* relates David's statements to the Roman conquest of the future.

4. הִרְעַשְׁתָּה אֶרֶץ – *You made the land quake.*

Midrash Tanchuma (Vayeitzei 3) contends that this refers to the miraculous assistance which God gave to Joab and Avishai in their campaign against Aram. He caused an earthquake (רַעַשׁ) to shatter (פְּצַמְתָּהּ) the earth into pieces; these pieces (שְׁבָרֶיהָ) were brought close to each other, thus shortening the road to Aram considerably. This is called קְפִיצַת הָאָרֶץ, *a leaping of the earth.* This miracle was

1. Many nations attacked Israel previously but their intentions had only been to plunder, tax, or enslave the Jews; therefore, in retaliation, David merely subjugated and taxed these nations. But David's treatment of Aram was unique, for only this country was annexed to the Land of Israel; it was known as *Surya.* David attempted to invest this territory with the halachic status of the Holy Land proper. He did this as a punishment *measure for measure,* since Aram had sought to lay claim to and annex Jewish land (see *Sotah* 44b, *Rashi* s.v. ומלחמת בית דוד and *Gittin* 8a *Rashi* s.v. סוריא).

However, the halachah does not officially recognize the annexation of Aram, because it was not done with the sanction and authority of the Great Sanhedrin. They argued with David, saying 'Near your own palace there are still large tracts of land which have not yet been conquered from the Canaanites; why do you go out to conquer foreign lands?' (See the *Ran*'s commentary on *Avodah Zarah* 21a).

Previously in this Psalm we saw that David's campaign against Aram was indeed officially sanctioned by Sanhedrin, who ruled that the ancient covenant with Laban was nullified. However, Sanhedrin had only authorized David to wage war against Aram, but not to conquer and annex it. David felt that the annexation was an integral part of the battle, for he wanted to punish them measure for measure for having dared to annex part of *Eretz Yisrael.* (עיין ויואל משה : מאמר ישוב א״י סימן י״ג ובמור וקציעה או״ח סימן ש״ו).

ה כִּי־מָטָה: הִרְאִיתָ עַמְּךָ קָשָׁה הִשְׁקִיתָנוּ
ו יַיִן תַּרְעֵלָה: נָתַתָּה לִּירֵאֶיךָ נֵּס לְהִתְנוֹסֵס
ז מִפְּנֵי קֹשֶׁט סֶלָה: לְמַעַן יֵחָלְצוּן יְדִידֶיךָ

granted to only three other individuals: Abraham, Eliezer, and Jacob.

According to *Rashi*, David foresaw the droves of Roman legions who were destined to march through the land, causing it to tremble beneath their feet.

פְּצַמְתָּה — *You broke it.*

The translation follows *Rashi*, who also offers as an alternative the rendering of *Rabbi Moshe HaDarshon: You tore it open* (see *Meiri*).

According to *Radak*, this alludes to the breaches which Hadadezer made in Israel's borders. Following *Rashi*'s interpretation, this foretells the time when Rome would establish colonies at strategic points throughout Israel in an effort to divide the Jewish populace, as the *Talmud* (*Megillah* 6a) states: The Roman city of Caesarea situated between the shores was like a sharp peg thrust into the midst of Israel [to fragment it] *(Rashi).* [1]

רְפָה שְׁבָרֶיהָ — *Heal its fragments.*

Although the word derives from רְפָא, *heal,* and should therefore be spelled with an א , *aleph,* we often find a ה, *he,* substitued for an א, *aleph (Rashi; Radak; Ibn Ezra).*

[The word רָפָה literally means *soft, weak.* This alludes to the request that the remedy for Israel's wounds be gentle rather than harsh.]

כִּי מָטָה — *For it totters.*

This alludes to the many *Talmudic* statements (*Sanhedrin* 97a) testifying that the Messianic redemption from the Roman exile will not come until Israel totters and falls to the lowest possible level of degradation. At that point, the Jewish nation will rise again *(Zera Yaakov).*

5. הִרְאִיתָ עַמְּךָ קָשָׁה — *You showed Your nation harshness.*

This occurred in the war with Edom, when so many men of Israel were killed *(Sforno).*

הִשְׁקִיתָנוּ יַיִן תַּרְעֵלָה — *You made us drink benumbing wine.*

Rashi explains that רַעַל literally means *an envelopment, an enclosure.* Wine deadens the sensitivity and emotion of the heart and seals it off from external stimuli. [Thus, 'the shocking tragedy of our nation has paralyzed us with fear and killed all the feelings of our heart.' The *Talmud (Shabbos* 13b) says that since Israel is constantly plagued with the cruel persecutions of the Romans, the Jews have become completely numb and insensitive to the pain, just as a dead man's flesh cannot feel the sharp point of the dagger.]

Midrash Shocher Tov interprets תַּרְעֵלָה as a contraction of two sets of two words, thus finding a double meaning to the word: This wine מְתַעֵר, *arouses,* the עוֹלָם, *world,* to מַתִּיר, *undo,* עוֹלָה, *the burden,* of Torah. This intimates that the yoke of Torah has been

1. This concept of the earth being *broken* alludes to the idea that the world is only considered to be united when Israel is recognized by all nations as the center of world affairs for it says: יַעֲקֹב חֶבֶל נַחֲלָתוֹ , *Jacob is the bond* (which keeps together all the nations) *of His estate (Deuteronomy* 32:9).

The *Zohar (Parshas Balak)* says that of all the gentile nations, Moab, in particular, denied this principle of a Divine universal order. Therefore David punished them (measure for measure) and *measured them according to the* חֶבֶל, *bond* [*line*] *(II Samuel* 8:2).

Two-thirds of the nation were found to have denied this 'bond' and were put to death. The remaining third were spared. (See *comm. v.* 10 מוֹאָב סִיר רַחְצִי.)

heal its fragments for it totters.
5 You showed Your nation harshness,
You made us drink benumbing wine.
6 You gave those who fear You
a banner to raise themselves,
for truth's sake, Selah!
7 So that Your beloved ones may be released —

torn away from Israel through the sin of drunkenness.

6. נָתַתָּה לִּירֵאֶיךָ נֵּס לְהִתְנוֹסֵס — *You gave those who fear You a banner to raise themselves.*

You have given us the power to vanquish our enemies [Aram and Edom] and to wave our battle standards over them in triumph (*Radak; Meiri*).

Rashi (based on *Bereishis Rabbah* 55:1) renders נֵס homiletically as נִסָּיוֹן, *trial,* to suggest, 'You have tested us in many trying and oppressive situations [such as the tyrannical persecution of Edom-Rome] in order to provide us with the opportunity לְהִתְנוֹסֵס, *to be proven,* faithful under all circumstances. Each time we successfully pass such a test we rise higher and higher, like the נֵס, *banner,* which is unfurled on the highest mast of the ship.[1]

מִפְּנֵי קֹשֶׁט — *For truth's sake.*

You granted us victory against the invaders in order to be *true* to Your promise to let us live peacefully in our land *(Radak).*

Furthermore, our victories were granted by virtue of the fact that we studied the *truth* of Your Torah. As the *Talmud* (*Sanhedrin* 49a) says: If not for the merit of David, who stayed behind the battle lines to study Torah, his general, Joab, would not have emerged triumphant from his wars *(Sforno).*

According to *Rashi,* these words explain that God constantly puts Israel through difficult trials in anticipation of His final judgment, in which they will be generously rewarded. God wants the gentiles to admit wholeheartedly the *truth* and equity of His verdict and to say, 'It is only fair that Israel should be rewarded, for they withstood so many difficult trials.'

Hirsch explains that קֹשֶׁט in Chaldean is synonymous with אֱמֶת, *truth,* in Hebrew (cf. *Proverbs* 22:21 לְהוֹדִיעֲךָ קֹשְׁטְ אִמְרֵי אֱמֶת, *To inform you of the truth of true words*). Also, in Aramaic the word קשט means *to adorn* (see *Bava Basra* 60b); it is obviously related to תַּכְשִׁיט, *jewel, adornment.* [The נִסָּיוֹן uncovers a person's *true* inner qualities and displays them to the world as the most glorious of *adornments,* for no quality is more precious than truth.]

Finally *Targum* observes that the psalmist is requesting Divine assistance in the merit of the Patriarchs [each of whom endured difficult *trials* and was found to be *true*]. *Targuma d'HaTragum* notes that this verse recalls the merit of Abraham's קֹשֶׁט, *truth,* for Scripture says, *You found his heart true to You (Nechemiah* 9:8).

7. לְמַעַן יֵחָלְצוּן יְדִידֶיךָ — *So that Your beloved ones may be released.*

Meiri comments that this is a form of blessed tranquility, a release from ten-

1. The comparison of a נִסָּיוֹן, *trial,* to an unfurled *banner* is most appropriate. *Ramban (Bereishis* 22:1) explains that God Himself harbors no doubt as to the successful outcome of every trial, because God only 'tests' righteous people who will survive the challenge. Why, then, does He bother to 'test' them at all, if the results are assured? The answer is that God

ס ח הוֹשִׁיעָה יְמִינְךָ °ועננו: אֱלֹהִים | דִּבֶּר
ח בְּקָדְשׁוֹ אֶעֱלֹזָה אֲחַלְּקָה שְׁכֶם וְעֵמֶק °וַעֲנֵנִי

sion and care. [The *Talmud* (*Yevamos* 102b) comments on וְעַצְמֹתֶיךָ יַחֲלִיץ, *He shall release your bones (Isaiah* 58:11), that this is the most sublime blessing]. On the Sabbath we pray רְצֵה וְהַחֲלִיצֵנוּ, *Favor us and release us (Bircas Hamazon)* from our weekday worries.]

Malbim notes that חָלוּץ also has a military connotation: *to be armed* [see *Rashi* on *Numbers* 31:3], i.e., 'fortify Your beloved nation of Israel to go forth well armed and prepared for battle.'

יְדִידֶיךָ — *Your beloved ones.*

Most commentators (*Radak, Metzudas David*) render this as a reference to righteous people in general, for whose success the psalmist prays.

Targum, however, renders it as a specific reference to Isaac. Thus, the psalmist prays that Israel be saved in the merit of Isaac.

[In the special benediction offered at the circumcision ceremony, Isaac is called יְדִיד, *beloved,* because he was the cherished son of Abraham. See *Rashi* on *Shabbos* 137b, *Targuma d'HaTargum.*]

According to *Midrash Shocher Tov (Psalm* 84), this refers to the Temple of which it says, מַה יְּדִידוֹת מִשְׁכְּנוֹתֶיךָ, *how beloved are Your Tabernacles* (84:2). The Temple was built by Solomon, who was called יְדִידְיָה, *beloved of HASHEM.* (II *Samuel* 12:25). He built it in the territory of Benjamin, whom Moses called יְדִיד ה׳, *Beloved of HASHEM (Deuteronomy* 33:12). Therefore, for the sake of the Temple, David prayed *that Your beloved ones may be released.*

[According to *Radak's* interpretation, this alludes to the fact that David waged these wars as a preparation for Solomon's construction of the Temple (as explained in *comm.* to *v.* 1). According to *Rashi,* this alludes to the destruction of the beloved Temple at the hands of Edom-Rome.]

הוֹשִׁיעָה יְמִינְךָ — *Save [with] Your right hand.*

Ibn Ezra and *Ibn Yachya* observe that this should be interpreted as בִּימִינְךָ, including the prepositional prefix ב, *with:* i.e., *save with Your right hand.*

Radak explains the literal reading of *save Your right hand:* When God ignores the atrocities perpetrated against Israel and refrains from protecting His nation, it appears as if He lacks the ability to react and as if His hands are 'tied'. The psalmist calls upon God to *release* His might against the foe in order to *save* His 'reputation.'

Norah Tehillos and *Malbim* note that David specifically asks for Divine action with the *right hand,* symbolizing God's attribute of Mercy, which performs miracles for those deserving of His grace.

The *Targum* adds, 'Save us by virtue of the חֲסִידוּת, *devotion,* of our Patriarch Jacob.'

Hirsch explains the request *save Your right hand* according to the verse עִמּוֹ אָנֹכִי בְצָרָה אֲחַלְּצֵהוּ, *I [God] am with him [Israel] in distress; I shall release him* (91:15). The Sages say that when Israel wanders in exile, God, is also considered to be in exile. God's true glory manifests itself in the world only when Israel dwells securely in its sovereign state, its homeland. Therefore, the psalmist

wishes to do a kindness to the righteous, extracting their hidden potential powers of faith and bringing them to fruition. The righteous will be fortified when the power of their faith is activated, and their example will serve as an inspiration for others [see *Ramban, Shaar HaGemul* and *comm.* to 12:5]. Thus, the נִסָּיוֹן truly resembles a banner which is unfurled on high in order to display the identity of its bearers. [See Overview to *Lech Lecha,* ArtScroll Bereishis, vol. II.]

60
8

save with your right hand and respond to me.
[8] *God said in His sanctity*
that I would exult, divide portions;
and the Valley of Succos
would I measure out.

urges God to release His beloved nation so that His own splendor can be *released* and revealed to all.

וַעֲנֵנִי — *And respond to me.*

[The כְּתִיב, *spelling,* is וַעֲנֵנוּ, *respond to us,* but the קְרִי, *pronunciation,* is וַעֲנֵנִי, *respond to me.* This teaches us that, as King of Israel, David transcended his individual personality and dedicated himself completely to the commonwealth. The requests which he made of God did not concern personal problems, but matters of general welfare. God's fulfillment of his wishes was not merely an *answer* to David, but an *answer* to all of Israel.

[108:7-14 is a repetition of this verse and of those immediately following. There, too, we have this discrepancy between the pronunciation and the spelling (see *Minchas Shai* (108:7-14) and *Hirsch.*]

8. אֱלֹהִים דִּבֶּר בְּקָדְשׁוֹ — *God said in His sanctity.*

Through His Holy Inspiration, God communicated to me that I would [now] rule over His nation, Israel (*Radak*) and that [in the future] all of the scattered exiles would be ingathered and placed once again under the rule of the House of David *(Rashi).* Scripture states, *For HASHEM has spoken of David saying, 'By the hand of My servant David I will save My people Israel from the hands of the Philistines and from the hands of all their enemies'* (II *Samuel* 3:18).

Targum renders בְּקָדְשׁוֹ, *from the holy Temple,* because God spoke to David there [concerning its construction and its future survival].

אֶעֱלֹזָה — *[That] I would exult.*

This would occur when He fulfilled His promises by giving monarchy and victory to David *(Radak; Rashi; Metzudas David).*

אֲחַלְּקָה שְׁכֶם — *(I would) divide portions.*

Portions refers to enemy property which would be apportioned to the Jewish exiles returning from the Diaspora *(Rashi).* [See *Targum* and *Ibn Ezra* on *Genesis* 48:22 שְׁכֶם אַחַד, *one portion.*]

Rashi also suggests that שְׁכֶם may refer to the city of *Shechem,* which symbolizes Jacob's territorial claim over the Holy Land. [The city's significance is derived from the fact that Shechem was the first place where Jacob camped when he returned to Israel from Aram, and it was there that he made his first purchase of land from the Canaanite inhabitants *(Ibn Yachya)*] Thus, the psalmist prophesies that all Jacob's territorial possessions are destined to be returned to the Jewish nation.

Radak and *Meiri* interpret these words as a reference to David's personal experiences. After Saul's death, his son Ish-Boshes, supported by the mighty Abner, set up a kingdom in the province of Ephraim. All the places mentioned in this and the following verses were part of that domain. David now declares that God was true to His promise to grant David complete sovereignty over *all* of Israel, including the rival province of Ephraim and its cities (including Shechem). [This encourages David to place his full trust in God during the present campaign against Aram.]

וְעֵמֶק סֻכּוֹת אֲמַדֵּד — *And the Valley of Succos would I measure out.*

Rashi and *Ibn Yachya* observe that

ט סֻכּוֹת אֲמַדֵּד: לִי גִלְעָד | וְלִי מְנַשֶּׁה
וְאֶפְרַיִם מָעוֹז רֹאשִׁי יְהוּדָה מְחֹקְקִי:
י מוֹאָב | סִיר רַחְצִי עַל־אֱדוֹם אַשְׁלִיךְ נַעֲלִי
יא עָלַי פְּלֶשֶׁת הִתְרוֹעָעִי: מִי יֹבִלֵנִי עִיר

this also alludes to Jacob's initial claim to the Holy Land, because even before he came to Shechem he spent eighteen months at *Succos* (see *Rashi* on *Genesis* 33:17). When this territory is divided among the returning Jewish exiles, it will first be *measured out.*

According to *Radak* and *Meiri, Succos* was part of the territory of Ish-Boshes, who first challenged David's ascension to the throne, but later submitted to his reign.

9. לִי גִלְעָד וְלִי מְנַשֶּׁה וְאֶפְרַיִם מָעוֹז רֹאשִׁי — *Mine is Gilead, and mine is Menasheh, Ephraim is the stronghold of my head.*

David mentions Gilead and Ephraim, which both belonged to Ish-Boshes, and includes Menashe too, thus incorporating both sons of Joseph. This alludes to all of the tribes of Israel—with the exception of Judah (David's own tribe) — which were initially hostile. All of these eventually submitted to David's rule *(Meiri; Radak).*

יְהוּדָה מְחֹקְקִי — *Judah is my lawgiver.*

My officers, who are my main support and who enforce my authority, come from Judah *(Rashi).*

מְחוֹקֵק literally means *lawgiver* who decides legislation and inscribes the rulings in the nation's law books [חֲקִיקָה means *to engrave or inscribe*]. This is the special privilege of the royal tribe of Judah, as we read, לֹא יָסוּר שֵׁבֶט מִיהוּדָה וּמְחֹקֵק מִבֵּין רַגְלָיו, *The scepter shall not depart from Judah nor the lawgiver's staff from between his feet (Genesis* 49:10).

10. מוֹאָב סִיר רַחְצִי — *Moab is my washbasin.*

I will treat Moab with contempt, like the putrid water of the chamber pot which is cast away in disgust *(Radak).*

[סִיר may also be translated as *cooking pot*]. God said, 'For Moab, I set down on the stove a pot full of punishments!' (*Devarim Rabbah* 3:2) or 'I will clean their land thoroughly as one who scours a *cooking pot' (Ibn Ezra).*

David had good cause to despise Moab, as the *Midrash (Bamidbar Rabbah* 14:1) explains: When Saul's pursuit forced David to flee from the land of Israel, he placed his father and mother under the protection of the king of Moab [*I Samuel* 22:3-4]. David had more confidence in the Moabites than he had in Saul, because his grandmother was Ruth the Moabite; but the king of Moab killed the entire family.[1]

Therefore, Moab is likened to a *cooking pot,* for just as a pot dissolves meat, so was the flesh of David's family devoured in Moab. Only one of David's brothers escaped to Nachash, king of Ammon, who refused to heed the king of Moab's demands that the refugee be returned.

1. *Alshich* perceives in the phrase *Moab is my washbasin* an allusion to the taint of Moabite ancestry on David's lineage. David spent his life *washing* his soul and cleansing it from any trace of gentile association.

[The *Talmud* (*Yoma* 22b) states that no leader should be appointed to a position of authority over the community unless he has a basketful of 'creeping reptiles' tied to his back, meaning that his family tree should have some lowly ancestry. Then, if he grows excessively proud, people can taunt him, 'Turn around and see from whence you came.' The proof of this is that since Saul's pedigree was perfect, he disregarded admonition and fell; but David's Moabite ancestry always haunted him and caused him to be more humble and cautious in his affairs (see *Rashi, Yoma* 22b).]

9 *Mine is Gilead,*
and mine is Menasheh,
Ephraim is the stronghold of my head,
Judah is my lawgiver.
10 *Moab is my washbasin,*
upon Edom will I cast my lock,
Philistia, join together with me.
11 *Who will bring me*

Later David punished Moab for their treachery, as we read (II *Samuel* 8:2), *And he smote Moab, and measured them with the line, making them lie down on the ground, and he measured out two lines* [two-thirds of the populace] *to be put to death and one full line* [one-third] *to keep alive.*[*See footnote v.*4 פְּצַמְתָּה].

עַל אֱדוֹם אַשְׁלִיךְ נַעֲלִי – *Upon Edom will I cast my lock.*

The translation of נַעֲלִי follows *Rashi*, implying, 'I will *lock* Edom into my tight grip.' *Metzudas David* renders, 'I will cast iron chains on their feet in order to fetter them.'

Sforno adds that Moab was near *Eretz Yisrael.* Because it was under David's constant surveillance, he could humiliate Moab without fearing a revolt. Since Edom was further away, the threat of an uprising was greater in that country. Therefore, David *cast his lock* on all of Edom's fortifications and strongholds, in anticipation of armed resistance.

Radak, however, translates נַעֲלִי as *my shoe*, to indicate that David's armies trampled and subjugated the forces of Aram and Edom.

The *Midrash (Shemos Rabbah* 15:16) adds that in the future God will also grind Edom underfoot, as the prophet (*Isaiah* 63:3) foretells: *I* [*God*] *trod the winepress alone . . . I trod them* [*Edom*] *in my anger, and trampled them in my fury.* God will stamp on the rulers of Edom with special fury, as the psalmist says, *Upon Edom I cast* נַעֲלִי, *my shoe.*

[It should be emphasized that the psalmist speaks of these enemies with contempt only because they are considered adversaries of God. As a matter of fact, from this very campaign against Edom we learn that the Jewish army accorded its foes great respect as human beings. Scripture states *And David made himself a great reputation when he returned from smiting Aram, in the Valley of Salt (II Samuel* 8:13). This refers to the fact that David buried all of the Edomite dead, which enhanced Israel's reputation. The Jews will also bury their fallen enemies in the future war of Gog and Magog *(Rashi; Radak; Kara;* II *Samuel* 8:13)]

עָלַי פְּלֶשֶׁת הִתְרוֹעָעִי – *Philistia, join together with me.*

This translation follows *Rashi*, who derives הִתְרוֹעָעִי from רֵעַ, *friend, companion.* [David calls upon Philistia to submit to his dominion voluntarily since it is destined to fall before David's conquering army anyway.]

Metzudas David interprets הִתְרוֹעָעִי to mean *blow the horn blast* (from תְּרוּעָה), i.e., 'Let Philisita recognize my sovereignty and blow a ceremonial blast on the trumpet to announce my coronation.'

Sforno however relates this word to תרע, *to smash* [see 2:9 תְּרֹעֵם], meaning, 'Philistia, be shattered and disintegrate before me!'

Hirsch translates this entire phrase as a taunt to this enemy of Israel *after* its

יב מָצוֹר מִי נָחַנִי עַד־אֱדוֹם: הֲלֹא־אַתָּה
אֱלֹהִים זְנַחְתָּנוּ וְלֹא־תֵצֵא אֱלֹהִים
יג בְּצִבְאוֹתֵינוּ: הָבָה־לָּנוּ עֶזְרָת מִצָּר וְשָׁוְא
יד תְּשׁוּעַת אָדָם: בֵּאלֹהִים נַעֲשֶׂה־חָיִל וְהוּא
יָבוּס צָרֵינוּ:

defeat: 'Now let Philistia dare to claim triumph over me' [see *Ibn Ezra* and *Radak*].

11. מִי יוֹבִלֵנִי עִיר מָצוֹר – *Who will bring me to the fortified* [lit. *besieged*] *city.*

Rashi views this rhetorical question as a plea for future victories: 'Who will help me to conquer the mighty metropolis of Rome if not You?'

According to *Radak*, however, this is a rhetorical question concerning David's past victories (even though it is worded in future tense): 'Who brought me to victory over the fortified cities of Philistia, Moab, and Aram, if not You, O God?'

Targum identifies מָצוֹר as the city צוֹר, which is synonymous with Rome (see *Rashi, Genesis* 25:23, *Targuma d'HaTargum*).

12. הֲלֹא אַתָּה אֱלֹהִים זְנַחְתָּנוּ – *Did not You, O God, forsake us?*

According to *Radak*, this is the psalmist's reply to the question posed in the preceding verse: 'Who brought us victory over the fortified city? It was none other than You, O God! It was also You who had forsaken us and who refused to go out with our legions; but when You decided to favor us, You granted us amazing success over enemy forces which vastly surpassed our small army both in numbers and in might.[1]

Sforno observes that David bemoans the great losses he suffered in his campaign against Edom [twelve thousand men (see *v.* 2,3)] and sees this as a sign of Divine displeasure and indifference.

וְלֹא תֵצֵא אֱלֹהִים בְּצִבְאוֹתֵינוּ – *And not go forth, O God, with our legions?*

[Under normal conditions, God *does* accompany our legions: *For HASHEM, Your God, walks in the midst of Your camp to deliver you and to give up your enemies before you; therefore your camp shall be holy (Deuteronomy* 23:15). *Ramban* equates the sanctity of the Jewish army camp to the holiness of the *Beis HaMikdash,* where God's *Shechinah* dwells.

[The Sages tell us (*Kiddushin* 70b) that God's holy spirit dwells only among the families of Israel who strive to preserve their pure lineage. *Sforno (Deuteronomy* 23:15) explains that since David wished to arouse God's presence in his camp, he demanded that any soldier who wished to join his army

1. The *Talmud* (*Gittin* 57a) describes Bar Deroma, a Jewish warrior whose great strength robbed the Romans of the courage to fight. Unfortunately, Bar Deroma's arrogance caused his own downfall, for he said to God: *'You, O God, have forsaken us; go forth no longer with our legions,'* as if to say that he could be victorious without God's help. God complied by abandoning Bar Deroma to the forces of nature. Soon afterwards, he was killed by a snake.

The *Talmud* explains that David was neither punished nor criticized when he uttered this very same verse, because his intention was different, for his question and answer were rhetorical as explained above in the commentary (see *Maharsha, Gittin* 57a).

Yerushalmi (Taanis 4:5) says that Bar Kochba was guilty of the same arrogance as Bar Deroma, for he proclaimed, 'O God, do not help us and do not hinder us!' i.e., Remove Yourself from this conflict, because we can fend for ourselves. In fact, Bar Kochba quoted our verse (60:12) in his request for Divine nonintervention.

60
12-14

to the fortified city,
who will lead me
unto Edom?
12 *Did not You, O God,*
forsake us,
And not go forth,
O God, with our legions?
13 *Grant us help against the oppressor;*
futile is the aid of man.
14 *Through God we shall form an army*
and He will trample our oppressors.

provide evidence of his untarnished ancestry (See *Kiddushin* 76b).

In addition, only the most devout men of faith were allowed to remain in the ranks, while sinners were dismissed. Thus these pure souls clung to the pure spirit of God, Whose presence permeated the camp with holiness (*Chinuch* 566).

13. הָבָה לָּנוּ עֶזְרָת מִצָּר – *Grant us help against* [lit. *from*] *the oppressor.*

Grant us a victory directly from Your hands, rather than through a human intermediary. Let this redemption resemble our liberation from Egypt, which You engineered without employing an angel or a celestial being (*Tehillos Hashem*).

וְשָׁוְא תְּשׁוּעַת אָדָם – *Futile is the aid* [lit. *salvation*] *of man.*

[David and his generals waged war guided by this principle. Joab arrayed his army against Aram, and Avishai pitted his forces against Ammon. Joab said: *If the Arameans be too strong for me, then you shall save me; but if the children of Ammon be too strong for you, then I will come and save you* (*II Samuel* 10:11). Joab realized, however, that, in the final analysis, one cannot rely on mere military strategies. Therefore, he continued (II *Samuel* 10:11): *Be of good courage and let us prove strong for our people . . . and HASHEM will do that which seems proper to Him,* i.e., although we will fight with all our might, we know that salvation is exclusively in God's hands (*Radak*, II *Samuel* 10:11).]

14. בֵּאלֹהִים נַעֲשֶׂה חָיִל – *Through God shall we form an army.*

This translation follows *Radak*, who explains that even if our numbers are few and our enemies are many, we will make God our army and He will defend us.

Rambam (Hilchos Melochim 7:15) offers the following words of encouragement to the Jewish soldier on the eve of battle: When the soldier is locked in combat, he should depend on none other than God, the Hope and Savior of Israel in times of distress. Let him recognize that he is fighting for the preservation of God's Name. Therefore, he must throw himself into mortal danger without fear or panic. Let him forget his wife and family and train his thoughts only on the battle.

The man who battles with all his heart without fear, solely for the sanctification of God's Name, is assured that he will not suffer any wound or harm. Furthermore, this man will establish a fine home in Israel. His merits will protect his descendants forever, and he is assured of a portion in the World to Come.

The *Midrash (Eichah Rabbosi* 1:33) renders בֵּאלֹהִים נַעֲשֶׂה חָיִל, *In God we shall produce strength,* to teach that when Israel complies with God's will, the Chosen People 'strengthens' the Almighty, but when Israel abandons God's will, the Jewish people 'weakens' God.

וְהוּא יָבוּס צָרֵינוּ — *And He will trample our oppressors.* [See 44:6.]

Be'er Moshe (II *Samuel* 8) explains that David sought to subdue his adversaries in order to prepare for the Messianic era of order and harmony. *Yerushalmi (Kiddushin* 1:8) explains that in its initial conquest of the Land, Israel inherited the territory of only the seven Canaanite nations, but that in the future, they will expand their possessions to the land of the three nations of Edom, Moab, and Ammon (see *Bereishis Rabbah* 44).

[David triumphed over these three peoples (*II Samuel* 8:2; 12:29), and now he prayed for their complete defeat in Messianic times, when the universal peace and order for which David yearned all his life will be realized.]

מזמור סא 61

This psalm demonstrates that no distance or danger could diminish David's fervent love for God. Even when Saul pursued him to the furthest reaches of the realm, David's heart remained rooted in the spiritual center of the land — the House of God — and he yearned for the opportunity to serve God in the holy precincts (Malbim).

Sforno *and* Metzudos David *maintain that this psalm was composed when David traveled to repel Aram, the nation which threatened to overrun and to annex the remote eastern boundaries of the land of Israel,* the end of the land (v. *3). [That threat is discussed in the preceding psalm, to which this chapter is a sequel.]*

Radak, *based on the Midrash,* adds that David's cries echo the col*lective prayers of Israel in exile. From the dismal loneliness and isolation of the Diaspora, the Jews cry out to their Redeemer to restore them to their national home.*

The psalm concludes with a request for the continuity of the Davidic line of kings. The kings of the House of David are the precursors of the Messiah, who will gather the scattered remnants of Israel into the land of their fathers.

סא א־ב לַמְנַצֵּחַ | עַל־נְגִינַת לְדָוִד: שִׁמְעָה אֱלֹהִים

א־ו ג רִנָּתִי הַקְשִׁיבָה תְּפִלָּתִי: מִקְצֵה הָאָרֶץ |

אֵלֶיךָ אֶקְרָא בַּעֲטֹף לִבִּי בְּצוּר־יָרוּם מִמֶּנִּי

ד תַנְחֵנִי: כִּי־הָיִיתָ מַחְסֶה לִי מִגְדַּל־עֹז

ה מִפְּנֵי אוֹיֵב: אָגוּרָה בְאָהָלְךָ עוֹלָמִים

ו אֶחֱסֶה בְסֵתֶר כְּנָפֶיךָ סֶּלָה: כִּי־אַתָּה

1. לַמְנַצֵּחַ עַל נְגִינַת — *For the Conductor, on* Neginnas.

This title לַמְנַצֵּחַ בִּנְגִינוֹת appears frequently in psalms; however, this specific variation, עַל נְגִינַת, is unique. *Meiri* maintains that the two terms are synonymous and refer to musical instruments in the Levite orchestra [see *comm.* 4:1]. Thus עַל means *on*, i.e., this psalm was composed to be played on the *Neginnas* instrument.

However, *Pesikta Rabbosi* (9:2) renders עַל נְגִינַת*: because of songs.* David said: 'Because God has kindly granted me the privilege of praising Him with songs, I now dedicate a נֶצַח, *an eternal tune,* to His benevolence!' [David is particularly pleased that despite the fact that he is so far removed from the center of God's Presence, he is still granted the inspiration to compose psalms (see Pref.).]

2. שִׁמְעָה אֱלֹהִים רִנָּתִי — *Hear, O God, my cry.*

This refers to the audible call which escapes from the lips *(Ibn Ezra).*

Israel pleads: 'Please hear me even though I am in exile and distant from You' *(Dorash Moshe).*

הַקְשִׁיבָה תְּפִלָּתִי — *Listen to my prayer.*

This indicates the unspoken yearning of the heart *(Ibn Ezra).*

I praised You aloud for Your past kindness and You heard *my cry.* Therefore, continue to heed *my prayer* for Your future assistance *(Sforno).*

3. מִקְצֵה הָאָרֶץ אֵלֶיךָ אֶקְרָא — *From the end of the land unto You I call.*

According to *Rashi,* David sent his armies out on distant foreign campaigns [while his royal duties forced him to stay behind]. When he grew concerned for their safety at the *end of the land,* he implored God to assist them.

Radak identifies *the end of the land* as Philistia, where David himself sought refuge from Saul.

Midrash Shocher Tov interprets these words as a reference to Israel in exile: Wherever and whenever Israel cries out to the Holy One, Blessed be He, He responds, as it says, *I called on Your name, HASHEM, from the depths of the pit. You heard my voice (Lamentations* 3:55,56). God replies [with regret], 'Now you begin to call upon Me *from the end of the land,* but when you were still in your land you neglected to call Me!' [This implies, had the nation only cried out then, it certainly would have been spared the misery of exile.]

בַּעֲטֹף לִבִּי — *When my heart grows faint.*

This translation follows the *Targum* בְּאִשְׁתַּלְהֲיוּת לִבִּי, *when my heart is drained and exhausted.*

Metzudos David however, relates the word to עֲטִיפָה, *to be enveloped,* i.e., when my heart is shrouded in misery and suffering.

Radak notes that incessant prayer at the time of a crisis is called עֲטִיפָה, as in תְּפִלָּה לְעָנִי כִי יַעֲטֹף, *a prayer of the afflicted when he is shrouded* (102:1).

בְּצוּר יָרוּם מִמֶּנִּי תַנְחֵנִי — *To a rock which is too high for me—lead me!*

Place me upon the rocky pinnacle which, because of its towering height, is inaccesible to me unaided *(Rashi).*

For the Conductor, on Neginnas,
by David.
2 *Hear, O God, my cry,*
listen to my prayer.
3 *From the end of the land unto You I call,*
when my heart grows faint.
To a rock which is too high for me —
lead me!
4 *For You have been a refuge for me,*
a tower of strength in the enemy's face.
5 *I shall dwell in Your tent forever,*
take refuge in the shelter of Your wings, Selah.

The rock symbolizes the much desired land of Israel, which lay beyond the reach of the fugitive, David, and which is still inaccessible to the far-flung exiles of Israel *(Radak).*

Sforno suggests that David's heart grew faint when he contemplated his invincible enemies. Therefore, he calls for Divine assistance against the adversaries who tower over him.

4. כִּי הָיִיתָ מַחְסֶה לִי — *For You have been a refuge for me.*

In the past, You brought glory to Your name by providing me with miraculous protection. Therefore, I beseech You to continue Your shelter as *a tower of strength in the face* [i.e., in the presence] *of the enemy;* for if You abandon me now, O God, I fear that the enemy will attempt to strip You of Your glory, saying, 'God's strength has failed Him!' *(Sforno).*

5. אָגוּרָה בְאָהָלְךָ עוֹלָמִים — *I shall dwell in Your tent forever.*

[Until now the psalmist primarily lamented his dismal situation in exile. Now he expresses his innermost wishes concerning the redemption and the return to God's presence.]

Radak comments that in reference to David, אָהָלְךָ, *Your tent,* indicates the מִשְׁכָּן, *Tabernacle* [which then represented the focal point of sanctity]. In reference to the exiles of Israel, *Your tent* means the *Beis HaMikdash* [which the exiled Jews yearn to see rebuilt].

עוֹלָמִים — *Forever* [lit. *worlds*].

Grant me the privilege [of dwelling in Your Presence] not only in This World but also in the World to Come *(Rashi).*

Tehillos Hashem points out that the World to Come is actually composed of many עוֹלָמִים, *worlds,* as the *Mishnah* teaches: The Holy One, Blessed be He, is destined to bequeath to each *tzaddik* three hundred and ten worlds *(Uktzin* 3:12). These worlds will exist *forever.*

The Sages ask, 'Is it possible for a man to live עוֹלָמִים, *forever?*' They explain that David actually requested of God that Torah lessons be taught in his name, even after his death. As Rabbi Yochanan said in the name of Rabbi Shimon bar Yochai: Whenever the words of a Torah scholar are repeated in this world, his lips move along in the grave! In this manner, David hoped to achieve immortality *(Rashi; Yevamos* 96b).

Pesikta Rabbosi (2:4) adds that the Holy One, Blessed be He, swore to David: Even after you pass on, your name will not depart from My House.

אֱלֹהִים שָׁמַעְתָּ לִנְדָרָי נָתַתָּ יְרֻשַּׁת יִרְאֵי
ז שְׁמֶךָ: יָמִים עַל־יְמֵי־מֶלֶךְ תּוֹסִיף שְׁנוֹתָיו
ח כְּמוֹ־דֹר וָדֹר: יֵשֵׁב עוֹלָם לִפְנֵי אֱלֹהִים
ט חֶסֶד וֶאֱמֶת מַן יִנְצְרֻהוּ: כֵּן אֲזַמְּרָה שִׁמְךָ
לָעַד לְשַׁלְּמִי נְדָרַי יוֹם | יוֹם:

At every Temple offering, your name will be mentioned and your psalms will be sung!

Indeed, to this very day we proclaim, *(Rosh Hashanah* 25a) דָּוִד מֶלֶךְ יִשְׂרָאֵל חַי וְקַיָּם, *David, King of Israel, lives on and endures (Yalkut Eliezer).*

6. כִּי אַתָּה אֱלֹהִים שָׁמַעְתָּ לִנְדָרָי — *For You, O God, have heard my vows.*

[During his lifetime, David made a number of vows.]

At the moment of my birth, the angel adjured me [as he does all infants], 'Be righteous, and do not be wicked' *(Niddah* 30a; *Klei Chemdah).*

While I was in exile, I vowed to do many things for the sake of God, if He would return me safely to the Holy Land.

Throughout the centuries of exile, Jews have made similar vows *(Radak).*

Furthermore, I vowed that I would not rest until I found the proper site for the Temple (see 132:2-5).

Since God sees that I have dedicated my life to the fulfillment of all these vows, He grants me Divine protection *(Alshich).*

נָתַתָּ יְרֻשַּׁת יִרְאֵי שְׁמֶךָ — *You have granted the heritage of those who fear Your Name.*

Radak notes that although David speaks in past tense saying, *'You ... have heard my vows,'* actually, God has not yet responded. The psalmist speaks this way to demonstrate his firm faith that his requests will be fulfilled.

Rashi and *Radak* advance different versions of the prayer to which David alludes here.

Grant my return to *Eretz Yisrael,* the homeland of the nation which fears Your Name! *(Rashi).*

Bless me with the privilege of dwelling in Your estate — the holy Tabernacle [or the *Beis HaMikdash,* where all who enter are awed by Your Name] *(Radak).*

Malbim points out that when David made his vows to God, the Almighty reciprocated with the promise that if David's descendants would fear His *Name,* then the monarchy would remain as their *heritage* forever (see 132:11, 12).

7. יָמִים עַל יְמֵי מֶלֶךְ תּוֹסִיף — *May You add days on to the days of the king.*

Kings usually die young for they are at the center of all dissension *(Sforno).* The Sages teach *(Pesachim* 87b) that the throne 'buries' its royal occupants, for Scripture relates that every prophet in Israel outlived four kings *(Otzar Nechmad).*

David requested, 'If it has been ordained that I should die young, please add to the predestined number of my days so that they reach at least seventy years, which is the customary lifespan for *generation after generation (Rashi).*

[See 90:10: *The days of our years are seventy years.*]

Radak observes that a similar incident occured when fifteen years were added to the life of King Chizkiyahu, who was initially destined to die young *(Isaiah* 38:5).

As *Radak* explains, this psalm echoes the cries of Israel in exile: The nation pleads that its redeemer, the Messiah, be granted long life.

שְׁנוֹתָיו כְּמוֹ דֹר וָדֹר — *May his years be like generation after generation.*

Pirkei d'Rabbi Eliezer (19) explains this as an allusion to the first man, *Adam HaRishon,* who donated seventy years of his life to David so that he

6 *For You, O God,*
have heard my vows,
You have granted the heritage
of those who fear Your Name.
7 *May You add days on to the days of the king,*
may his years be like generation
after generation.
8 *May he sit forever before God.*
Appoint kindness and truth,
that they may preserve him.
9 *Thus shall I praise Your Name forever,*
to fulfill my vows day after day.

could enjoy a normal lifespan. [See Overview in Vol. I].[1]

8. יֵשֵׁב עוֹלָם לִפְנֵי אֱלֹהִים — *May he sit forever before God.*

This refers to the king [David or Messiah] *(Rashi).*

May he spend his days in permanent pursuit of total wisdom and fear of God *(Radak; Sforno).*

May he remain in Your presence, in the *Beis HaMikdash,* and not be forced to go to distant places to fight the enemy *(Metzudas David).*

חֶסֶד וֶאֱמֶת מַן יִנְצְרֻהוּ — *Appoint kindness and truth, that they may preserve him.*

This translation follows *Rashi, Radak, Sforno,* and *Metzudos,* who relate מַן to זַמֵּן *appoint, prepare* (see *Jonah* 4:6), i.e., may God's *kindness* and the *truth* of His vow to guard the king preserve him from his foes, so that wars will be unnecessary *(Metzudas David).*

The *Midrash (Shemos Rabbah* 31:5) however, renders מַן as מִי, the interrogative pronoun *who.* David said to the Holy One, Blessed be He, יַשֵּׁב עוֹלָמְךָ, *equalize men in Your world.* [יַשֵּׁב is thus interpreted as יַשְׁווּ, *equalize,* i.e., David wanted all people to be equally wealthy *(Yefeh Toar).*] 'Why should there be such disparity between rich and poor?' God replied: 'If I make all men equal (שָׁוֶה), then מַן, *who,* will preserve חֶסֶד

1. *Otzar Nechmad* and *Eretz HaChaim* note that the *Zohar (Vayishlach)* attributes David's lifespan to a different source: [Abraham was allotted one hundred-eighty years (as was his son Isaac; see *Rashi, Genesis* 25:30), but lived only one hundred seventy-five. If Jacob was unworthy of a full allotment of his father's years, he should have at least lived as long as his grandfather, but he lived twenty-eight years less (147 years). Joseph also would have been expected to equal his father in lifespan, but he fell short by thirty-seven years (110 years).] Abraham contributed five years of his life to David; Jacob contributed twenty-eight years; and Joseph contributed thirty-seven years, for a total of seventy years. Why didn't the seventy years donated by Adam suffice?

Chida (Midbar Kedeimos 4:6) resolves this problem by explaining that since David was unique, he required a double measure of life. The *Talmud (Shabbos* 89b) teaches that in the average lifespan of seventy years, fifty percent of the time is expended on sleep and mundane pursuits; but David did not have a normal sleep schedule; he needed only brief naps *(Sukkah* 26b). Since David's days were completely dedicated to *full* life, he required *two* gifts of seventy 'normal' years; in combination, these provided David with his *full* years.

[This explains the repetition in the phrase, *May his years be as generation after generation.* This alludes to the fact that David's years resulted from a double contribution of lifespans.]

וֶאֱמֶת, the *mitzvah* of *kindness and true charity?'* [See *Kol Yaakov* on *Megillas Esther* 3:11.]

[*Rav Yerucham Levovitz* explained: God did not create the precept of charity because He saw that there were poor people in the world. Rather, God created poor people in order that there would be an opportunity to fulfill the *mitzvah* of charity. A world devoid of opportunities to show kindness to others is inconceivable, for compassion is the very purpose of This World.][1]

9. כֵּן אֲזַמְּרָה שִׁמְךָ לָעַד — *Thus shall I praise Your Name forever.*

Literally, כֵּן means *so.* Just as I praise You when You accord me victory in the battlefield, *so shall I sing praise of Your Name forever* when I no longer need to go out to battle *(Metzudas David).*

Rashi intepretс: Just as You reveal Your kindness to me, *so* shall I reciprocate with appropriate hymns of appreciation to fulfill my vows to You. I shall record these praises as a memorial for all time *(Sforno).*

לְשַׁלְּמִי נְדָרַי יוֹם יוֹם — *To fulfill my vows day after day.*

With the dawn of each new day, I shall add fresh praises to Your Name *(Sforno).*

This refers specifically to the *day* of Israel's salvation and to the *day* when the Messiah will be invested with his monarchy *(Targum).*

Then, in complete peace and tranquility, I will truly be able to fulfill my vow *(v.* 5): אָגוּרָה בְאָהָלְךָ עוֹלָמִים, *I shall dwell in Your tent forever (Sforno).*

1. The *Talmud (Eruvin* 85b) relates that R' Judah the Prince displayed great respect for the rich. R' Akiva also accorded the rich much honor, based on a homiletical interpretation of this verse, which is understood as a question followed by an answer.

יֵשֵׁב עוֹלָם לִפְנֵי אֱלֹהִים, *When is the world properly settled in the eyes of God?* חֶסֶד וֶאֱמֶת מַן יִנְצְרֻהוּ, *when the rich are kind and prepare ample provisions for the poor, thus preserving the world. (Rashi* explains that מַן means *provisions* [as in מָן, *manna*]. God Himself has honored the wealthy by appointing them as His agents for the preservation of the world. Therefore, the rich deserve respect).

מזמור סב 62

*A*lthough he is pursued by murderous enemies who are both powerful and rich, David's complete trust in God remains unshaken. Indeed, the persecution by his enemies elicits new foundations of faith from David's soul. He lashes out against the very forces which threaten him and reveals their* הֶבֶל, worthlessness.

Obviously, a mortal's might and money can never prevail against the decrees of the Almighty Master of the universe. All God asks of man is that he await the ultimate Divine victory with faith and patience.

Rashi *identifies this as the hymn of Israel in exile. It depicts the supreme test of the nation's endurance throughout a seemingly interminable* Golus. *This psalm is a source of strength and courage to the beleaguered nation, for it counsels, 'Wait patiently. If you will place your hopes in God and in God alone — if you will relinquish your infatuation with money and political influence — then your swift redemption is assured!'*

סב א־ב לַמְנַצֵּחַ עַל־יְדוּתוּן מִזְמוֹר לְדָוִד: אַךְ אֶל־
א־ד ג אֱלֹהִים דּוּמִיָּה נַפְשִׁי מִמֶּנּוּ יְשׁוּעָתִי: אַךְ־
הוּא צוּרִי וִישׁוּעָתִי מִשְׂגַּבִּי לֹא־אֶמּוֹט
ד רַבָּה: עַד־אָנָה | תְּהוֹתְתוּ עַל־אִישׁ
תְּרָצְּחוּ כֻלְּכֶם כְּקִיר נָטוּי גָּדֵר הַדְּחוּיָה:

1. עַל יְדוּתוּן — *On* Yedusun (cf. *Minchas Shai).*

[See *Prefatory Remarks* and *comm.* to 39:1.]

Rashi describes the *Yedusun* as a unique instrument in the Temple orchestra. Homiletically, the word is related to דָּתוֹת, *evil decrees*, suggesting that this psalm is the chant of the victim of persection and oppression.

According to *Radak, Yedusun* was a prominent Levite, a leader of the Temple singers.

2. אַךְ אֶל אֱלֹהִים דּוּמִיָּה נַפְשִׁי — *Only for God does my soul wait silently.*

This translation combines the opinions of a number of commentaries. *Targum, Radak* and *Meiri* render דּוּמִיָּה as *silence. Rashi* and *Metzudas David* translate it as *await* [see *comm.* to *Psalms* 37:7 'דּוֹם לַה and 39:3 נֶאֱלַמְתִּי דוּמִיָּה].

[In fact, these two interpretations are related, because the man who sincerely *awaits* the salvation of God makes no attempt to secure assistance from any other source. He is *silent* like a דּוֹמֵם, *inanimate object.*]

The word אַךְ, *alone, only*, serves to exclude all power except God's. It recurs throughout this psalm, for the composer extols that pure conviction and unadulterated faith which recognize none but the Almighty *(Yaavetz; Hirsch).*

Even when God appears as אֱלֹהִים, the Divine Name representing the Attribute of Strict Justice, the faith of the psalmist remains firm *(Divrei Sholom).*

3. אַךְ הוּא צוּרִי וִישׁוּעָתִי — *Only He is my Rock and my Salvation.*

[Cf. *v.* 7 and *comm.* ibid.]

God is my sole shield against any mishap; He is my protective *Rock*; and if [I deserve that] misfortune should befall me, God is also *my Salvation* from suffering *(Alshich).*

Lechem Shlomo observes that man is a synthesis of חוֹמֶר, *shapeless physical matter*, and צוּרָה, *intelligent form.* Man's spiritual ascent depends on the extent to which his heavenly צוּרָה dominates his mundane חוֹמֶר by placing a Divine imprint on every aspect of his being. God molds and sculpts the צוּרָה of man with צָרָה, *suffering*, which teaches man to spurn physical attractions for the sake of enhancing his Divine intellect. Therefore, David refers to God as צוּרִי, meaning *He Who fashions and molds my* צוּרָה.

מִשְׂגַּבִּי — *My Stronghold.*

God does not rescue me from suffering and then desert me. After assuring my salvation, He elevates me and strengthens me with success *(Alshich).*

לֹא אֶמּוֹט — *I shall not falter.*

Since God is *my Stronghold*, He certainly will prevent me from falling *(Ibn Ezra).*

רַבָּה — *Greatly.*

[This word does not appear in verse 7. Here the psalmist is not yet imbued with total confidence in God's complete salvation. Although he feels secure that no major catastrophe will destroy him, he does feel vulnerable to minor failures.]

Rashi, based on *Midrash Shocher Tov*, interprets רַבָּה homiletically as *Gehinnom*, the great, eternal punishment from which there is no escape. David is confident that with God's help

62
1-4

For the Conductor, on Yedusun
a song of David.
2 Only for God does my soul wait silently,
from Him comes my salvation.
3 Only He is my Rock and my Salvation;
my Stronghold,
I shall not falter greatly.
4 How long will you plot treacherously
against man?
May You all be slain —
like a leaning wall; like a toppled fence.

he will not sin so *greatly* as to deserve such a severe punishment *(Alshich).*

According to *Sforno's* unique interpretation of this psalm, it was composed as a threat to the nation of Ammon, who dared to act treacherously towards David and Israel. David has no fear of their might and he is confident that he *will not falter* when he attacks רַבָּה, *Rabbah*, the capital of Ammon.

4. [The psalmist now addresses himself to his tormentors and admonishes them.]

עַד אָנָה תְּהוֹתְתוּ עַל אִישׁ — *How long* [lit. *until when*] *will you plot treacherously against man?*

The translation of תְּהוֹתְתוּ follows *Rashi, Ibn Ezra, Ibn Yachya,* and *Metzudas David*, who identify its root as הַוּוֹת, *treachery*, [see 5:10]. However, *Targum* and *Menachem* (quoted in *Rashi*) relate the word to וַיֵּתֵא, *gather*, suggesting, 'How long will you persist in assembling for the sake of perpetrating evil?'

Rashi also cites commentaries which render this, 'How long will you speak slanderously — at great length?'

Finally, *Hirsch* derives תְּהוֹתְתוּ from חִתַּת, *frighten*, translating, 'How long will you strike terror into a man?'

תְּרָצְּחוּ כֻלְּכֶם — *May you all be slain.*

This statement may be understood as a curse which the psalmist hurls at his bloodthirsty adversaries *(Ibn Ezra; Radak; Metzudas David)* or as a revelation of the treacherous plots of the enemy; according to the latter, David is exclaiming, 'You all plan to murder me!' *(Rashbam; Ibn Yachya).*

כְּקִיר נָטוּי — *Like a leaning wall.*

According to *Ibn Ezra, Radak*, and *Metzudos David*, this is a continuation of the preceding curse. It means, 'You should be murdered, but not with a quick and easy death. Rather, you should live in perpetual terror, always tottering on the brink of destruction, as does a weak leaning wall.'

However, other commentaries understand this as a description of the enemy's treacherous plot: 'You are cold-blooded murderers who kill without any qualms. You kill nonchalantly and effortlessly, like a man who gives a slight push to a tottering wall in order to knock it over' *(Ibn Yachya).*

The very wall in whose shade I took refuge you desire to topple on me! *(Rashbam).*[1]

1. The *Talmud (Sanhedrin* 109a) identifies the people of Sodom as the personification of the evils enumerated in this verse. When a wealthy traveler visited their city, they would cast

ה אַךְ מִשְּׂאֵתוֹ | יָעֲצוּ לְהַדִּיחַ יִרְצוּ כָזָב בְּפִיו
ו יְבָרֵכוּ וּבְקִרְבָּם יְקַלְלוּ־סֶלָה: אַךְ
לֵאלֹהִים דּוֹמִּי נַפְשִׁי כִּי־מִמֶּנּוּ תִּקְוָתִי:
ז אַךְ־הוּא צוּרִי וִישׁוּעָתִי מִשְׂגַּבִּי לֹא
ח אֶמּוֹט: עַל־אֱלֹהִים יִשְׁעִי וּכְבוֹדִי צוּר־עֻזִּי
ט מַחְסִי בֵּאלֹהִים: בִּטְחוּ בוֹ בְכָל־עֵת | עָם

גָּדֵר הַדְּחוּיָה — *[Like] a toppled fence.*

The קִיר is the *wall* of the house, upon which the heavy קוֹרוֹת, *rafters*, rest. The גָּדֵר is a flimsy *fence* around the outer property. Since the קִיר is sturdier than the גָּדֵר, pressure that causes the *wall* to lean will knock the *fence* down *(Norah Tehillos).*

5. אַךְ מִשְּׂאֵתוֹ יָעֲצוּ לְהַדִּיחַ — *Only because of his loftiness have they plotted to topple him.*

These murderers are so extraordinarily vicious because they are terrified lest some man challenge them by rising to a position of authority which would enable him to administer the punishment they so justly deserve. Therefore, they devise rash acts of terror to destroy any potential opposition *(Rashi).*

Ohel Yaakov observes that as a person's station in life rises, he grows more and more vulnerable to the attacks of antagonists who seek out his most minute errors. Thus, the wily hypocrite first lavishes praise on his victim, to increase his prestige; when the hypocrite later slanders him, the victim's fall from glory is doubly disgraceful.

Radak interprets the entire verse as a reference to God; each of the wicked seeks לְהַדִּיחַ, *to lure away,* his associates from recognizing the towering Omnipotence of God. These evil men deny that God knows the inner thoughts of man; therefore, they seek to deceive with expressions of blessing, while cursing Him in their hearts.

6. אַךְ לֵאלֹהִים דּוֹמִּי נַפְשִׁי — *For God alone my soul waits silently.*

[Although David realizes that his enemies are scheming against him *(v.* 4-5), he remains completely unafraid, for he recognizes that there exists no power on earth except *God alone.* Therefore, David maintains a tranquil silence.]

כִּי מִמֶּנּוּ תִּקְוָתִי — *Because from Him is my hope.*

This verse is almost the same as verse 2. *Chovos Halevovos* and *Hirsch* explain that the differences between the verses serve to characterize two men on different levels of faith.

The first man retains his own private aims and desires and trusts that God will help him to achieve his goals. The second man, however, is so devoted to his Maker that he abandons all personal ambitions and preferences, accepting whatever lot God decides to grant him.

The first man is described in *v.* 2 as waiting אֶל אֱלֹהִים, *to God,* implying that God is distant from him. He looks forward to a particular event which he personally considers יְשׁוּעָתִי, *my salvation.* Since this person's faith is relatively weak, he may falter; he is only assured that (*v.* 3) he *will not falter greatly.*

In this verse, however, the man is

covetous eyes on his riches. They sat him beneath *a leaning wall* and toppled it over on him, so that they could seize his money.

Maharsha (ibid.) explains that they staged the 'accident' in such a way that it appeared as if the victim was responsible for tipping over the wall. Since the traveler was liable for the 'damage' he had caused, the Sodomites confiscated the dead man's money as 'payment.'

62
5-9

5 *Only because of his loftiness*
have they plotted to topple him
delighting in deceit.
With their mouth they bless;
inwardly they curse, Selah!
6 *For God alone my soul waits silently —*
because from Him is my hope.
7 *He alone is my Rock and Salvation;*
my Stronghold,
I shall not falter.
8 *Upon God rests my salvation*
and my glory,
the Rock of my strength —
my refuge is with God.
9 *Trust in Him at every moment,*
O Nation!

completely committed לֵאלֹהִים, *for God.* Since God Himself is the man's sole desire and תִּקְוָה, *hope,* he will not falter at all (*v.*8).

7. אַךְ הוּא צוּרִי וִישׁוּעָתִי — *He alone is my Rock and Salvation.*

The psalmist repeats this credo [cf. *v.* 3] in order to constantly reinforce his unswerving faith *(Radak).*

לֹא אֶמּוֹט — *I shall not falter.*

This verse means, 'I shall not be swayed in the least,' whereas in *v.* 3, the psalmist implied that he might falter slightly.

According to *Radak*, this psalm echoes the words of the Jews in exile. He comments that before Israel was redeemed (see *v.* 3), the Jews were in danger of suffering a decline. Once they leave the *golus* behind (*v.* 7), however, they are completely safe from any fall.

8. עַל אֱלֹהִים יִשְׁעִי וּכְבוֹדִי — *Upon God rests my salvation and my glory.*

God is so intimately involved with my affairs that there is no reason for me to be concerned with my personal welfare. He will surely determine *my salvation* and He will preserve *my glory,* i.e., my reputation *(Ibn Ezra).*

In exile, the *glory* of Israel is tarnished by disgrace; but when God provides the *salvation* of total redemption, Israel's renewed prestige is assured *(Radak).*

צוּר עֻזִּי מַחְסִי בֵּאלֹהִים — *The Rock of my strength — my refuge is with God.*

God will grant me this complete protection and concern only if I depend upon Him without reservations and without placing my trust in any other force. I must consider Him alone as *the Rock of my strength.* I may seek *refuge* only *in God (Alshich).*

9. בִּטְחוּ בוֹ בְכָל עֵת — *Trust in Him at every moment.*

After completing his admonition [which began in *v.*4] to the treacherous foes, the psalmist now addresses the masses, to fortify their faith *(Ibn Ezra).*

Radak notes that these inspiring

שִׁפְכוּ־לְפָנָיו לְבַבְכֶם אֱלֹהִים מַחֲסֶה־לָּנוּ
י סֶלָה: אַךְ | הֶבֶל בְּנֵי אָדָם כָּזָב בְּנֵי אִישׁ
יא בְּמֹאזְנַיִם לַעֲלוֹת הֵמָּה מֵהֶבֶל יָחַד: אַל־
תִּבְטְחוּ בְעֹשֶׁק וּבְגָזֵל אַל־תֶּהְבָּלוּ חַיִל |
יב כִּי־יָנוּב אַל־תָּשִׁיתוּ לֵב: אַחַת | דִּבֶּר
אֱלֹהִים שְׁתַּיִם־זוּ שָׁמָעְתִּי כִּי עֹז

words are especially appropriate for the Jews in exile, implying, 'No matter how long the bitter exile endures, never give up hope, for the redemption can come suddenly, at any time.'

Even in the darkest hour, when there appears to be no glimmer of hope, never forget the credo of faith handed down by the royal family of David *(Berachos* 10a): Even when a sharpened blade is poised at a person's neck [to kill him], he should not give up hope of deliverance and for God's mercy [which appears at all times] *(Tehillos Hashem).*

The *Midrash (Aggados Bereishis)* stresses that David was particularly fortunate. Other men pray and receive no response; God ignores them purposely, because He wants them to continue praying. However, since David's life was one of constant prayer, he was assured that he would be answered instantly, *at every moment.*

שִׁפְכוּ לְפָנָיו לְבַבְכֶם — *Pour out your hearts before Him.*

Repent before God with total sincerity [hide nothing from Him]. Then your redemption will be assured *(Radak).*

10. אַךְ הֶבֶל בְּנֵי אָדָם — *Naught but vanity are common men!*

Place no faith in their assistance *(Ibn Ezra)* and do not fear their threat, for *God* [alone] is a refuge for us *(Rashi).*

כָּזָב בְּנֵי אִישׁ — *Deceit are distinguished people.*

[Cf. *comm.* to 49:3 גַּם בְּנֵי אָדָם גַּם בְּנֵי אִישׁ.]

The בְּנֵי אָדָם are simple people who lack distinguished ancestry. Understandably, others place little faith in their ability to help. The בְּנֵי אִישׁ, however, are those who possess wealth and influence inherited from their prestigious forebears. The psalmist warns that even these apparently powerful and capable men are not worthy of our confidence, for they are כָּזָב, *deceitful* and *disappointing.*]

בְּמֹאזְנַיִם לַעֲלוֹת הֵמָּה מֵהֶבֶל יָחַד — *If they be lifted on the scales, they and vanity would be equal.*

This translation follows *Rashi.* However, *Ibn Ezra* and *Radak* explain that if all men were weighed, they would be found to be even *less* than vanity [מֵהֶבֶל], rather than *equal* to it.

According to *Metzudas David,* the psalmist claims that if the בִּטָּחוֹן, *divine faith,* professed by all mankind *(v.* 9) were weighed on a scale, it would amount to less than הֶבֶל, *nothing.*

The Rabbis *(Kallah Rabbosi* 8) emphasize that human calculations and appraisals are הֶבֶל, *worthless.* People presumptuously decide that a woman is suitable for a certain man, that riches befit a certain person, that a house is appropriate for a certain family, but God

1. *Midrash Shocher Tov* points out that man's very existence proves God's constant mercy. The soul of man is a celestial, spiritual force which spurns its union with the mundane body and struggles for release to escape heavenward. Only God's never-ending intervention *at all times* preserves this precarious union and keeps the breath of life interwoven with the coarse flesh.

Pour out your hearts before Him,
God is a refuge for us, Selah!
10 *Naught but vanity are common men!*
Deceit are distinguished people!
If they be lifted on the scales,
they and vanity would be equal.
11 *Trust not in oppression,*
and in robbery place not vain hope;
Though wealth flourishes,
pay it no heed.
12 *Once has God spoken;*
twice have I heard this

has already weighed these questions *and lifted them on a scale,* arriving at different conclusions and matching other people יַחַד, *together.*

11. אַל תִּבְטְחוּ בְעֹשֶׁק — *Trust not in oppression.*

Just as it is *vanity* to trust in man (*v.*10), it is foolish to rely on wealth *(Ibn Ezra),* particularly when it is ill-gotten gain *(Radak).*

To the extent that man finds security in his riches, he deprives himself of complete trust in God *(Alshich).*

עֹשֶׁק — *Oppression.*

This refers to property which a person unlawfully withholds from its true owner and to wages or debts which a man refuses to pay *(Radak).*

Ibn Ezra identifies עֹשֶׁק as the money gained through deception and fraud. This includes excessive markup.

גָזֵל — *Robbery.*

This refers to money openly taken by force *(Radak; Ibn Ezra)* [see *Bava Kama* 79b].

The psalmist here depicts the unlawful man's descent into crime: at first, he merely fails to pay what he owes to creditors and to employees; eventually, however, he engages in active, violent robbery *(Migdal David).*

אַל תֶּהְבָּלוּ — *Place not vain hope.*

Man himself is empty *vanity* (*v.* 10), but when he places his hopes in criminal gains then he is doubly *vain (Ibn Ezra).*

חַיִל כִּי יָנוּב — *Though wealth flourishes.*

When you notice evil men who enjoy financial success and whose wealth grows daily *(Rashi),* like a tree which produces abundant fruit with no effort on the part of its owner, *pay no heed (Radak).*

אַל תָּשִׁיתוּ לֵב — *Pay it no heed* [lit. *do not set your heart upon them.*]

Their wealth will not endure, and it will not protect them when tragedy strikes *(Radak).*

12. אַחַת דִּבֶּר אֱלֹהִים שְׁתַּיִם זוּ שָׁמָעְתִּי — *Once* [lit. *one thing*] *has God spoken, twice* [lit. *two things*] *have I heard this.*

God has taught the truths of the Torah not only once but many times, through the prophets who speak in His Name *(Radak).*

God proclaimed the laws of the one Torah, and Moses, the great teacher, repeated them twice *(Targum).* The first four books of the Pentateuch are the original lesson. The fifth book is known as מִשְׁנֵה תּוֹרָה, *the repetition of the Torah (Targum D'Matargum).*

סב יג לֵאלֹהִים: וּלְךָ־אֲדֹנָי חָסֶד כִּי־אַתָּה
יג תְשַׁלֵּם לְאִישׁ כְּמַעֲשֵׂהוּ:

Moreover, each statement in the Torah conveys more than one message for every word has a dual meaning, the נִגְלֶה, *revealed truth*, and the נִסְתָּר, *concealed truth*. Thus God pronounced אַחַת, *one word*, from which we heard שְׁתַּיִם, *two things (Rabbeinu Bachya, comm.* to *Exodus* 13:1).

Thus God fashioned the לֻחֹת, *tablets*, so that the script could be seen from both sides of the stones, alluding to the double dimension of the Torah (*Rabbeinu Bachya, ibid.* 32:16).

This is what the prophet *Jeremiah* (23:29) meant when he said that the word of God is וּכְפַטִּישׁ יְפֹצֵץ סָלַע — *like an anvil smashing a rock*. Just as a rock can be shattered into many fragments, each verse can be broken down into many lessons and interpretations (*Sanhedrin* 34a).

כִּי עֹז לֵאלֹהִים — *That strength belongs to God.*

From *one* of the Ten Commandments we heard and understood *two* Divine attributes. In the second commandment, God declared that פֹּקֵד עֲוֹן אָבֹת עַל בָּנִים — *He visits the sins of the fathers upon the children (Exodus* 20:5). This demonstrates God's מִדַּת הַדִּין, *the Divine Attribute of Strict Justice*, from which we realize *that strength belongs to God (Rashi).*

Radak stresses that once we realize that *strength belongs to God* alone, we must place faith in Him exclusively. Man must abandon his reliance on human power and wealth.

13. וּלְךָ אֲדֹנָי חָסֶד — *And Yours, my Lord, is kindness.*

Rashi continues to point out that the second commandment reveals another aspect of the Divine: מִדַּת הַחֶסֶד, the *Divine Attribute of Mercy.*

Scripture says וְעֹשֶׂה חֶסֶד לַאֲלָפִים — *And I act kindly unto the two thousandth generation of them that love me and keep my commandments (Exodus* 20:6).

Thus we heard of *two* Divine attributes from *one* commandment.

כִּי אַתָּה תְשַׁלֵּם לְאִישׁ כְּמַעֲשֵׂהוּ — *For You reward each man in accordance with his deeds.*

[This seems to contradict the preceding statement, for, if God repays in strict accordance with a person's deeds, where is His *kindness?*]

The Talmud (*Rosh Hashanah* 17a) explains that God first attempts to adhere to the letter of the law, but if He sees that man cannot withstand this, He exercises His חֶסֶד, *kindness* [see *Tosafos, ibid. s.v.* בִּתְחִלָּה].

Other commentators detect a glimmer of *kindness* even in the word כְּמַעֲשֵׂהוּ. *Rashi* translates this *similar to his deeds*, indicating that God mercifully minimizes and softens the punishment so that it is *not* in complete accordance with the sin. Nevertheless, the punishment does

62 *that strength belongs to God.*
13 13 *And Yours, my Lord,*
is kindness, for You reward
each man in accordance with his deeds.

bear a similarity to the sin, measure for measure.

Alshich and *Metzudas David* observe that this mode of punishment is really a great boon, for often a person is unaware of his error, but the punishment then spurs him to self-awareness, for it reflects the nature of the offense.

Alshich adds that we can detect compassion even in God's *reward in* (precise) *accordance with his deeds,* for God takes man to task only for the actual act of sin and not for the thought which accompanied it. [See *Kiddushin* 40a; see also *comm.* and footnote to 66:18.]

Also, although an apparently isolated transgression may indirectly cause much more evil, God does not punish the sinner for the inadvertent results of his sin.

Rashi notes, however, that when a person does a *mitzvah*, the opposite is true; then God does *reward each man in accordance with his deeds.*

[God's reward is complete; it extends even to the good thoughts which accompanied the good deed and to the indirect good which results from the *mitzvah.*][1]

Radak concludes that these final words echo the hymn of Israel in exile, proclaiming, 'Despite the seemingly endless duration of the bleak exile, we remain undaunted and completely confident in Your חֶסֶד, *kindness.* We recognize that our suffering is truly our salvation, for it clears our account in this world so that we can fully enjoy the bliss of future redemption and perfect reward for our *mitzvah* without disturbance.'

1. *Midrash Shocher Tov* teaches that a sinful action bears no fruit, in that the sinner is not taken to task for the indirect outgrowth of his deeds; but a *mitzvah* is fertile and prolific, for all good things which sprout from the original deed are generously rewarded.

Moreover, God is scrupulous in His system of accounting. If a man sins ten times and then performs ten *mitzvos*, God does not use up the merit of the *mitzvos* in an attempt to cancel out the damage of the sins. Rather, He administers the complete punishment due for the offenses and then bestows the proper reward.

Rambam (comm. to *Mishnah, Avos* 4:22) echoes this theme, noting that the dictum, 'God accepts no bribes' seems odd, for what possible interest could God have in any human gift? He explains that this means that God will not be swayed even by gifts of the spirit; i.e., if a man is condemned to suffer for his sin, every myriad *mitzvos* will not make God overlook the man's single transgression [cf. *Ramban, Deuteronomy 10:16*].

The only 'spiritual bribes' which can divert God's attention from sin are תְּשׁוּבָה תְּפִלָּה וּצְדָקָה, *penitence, prayer, and charity (Midrash Shocher Tov* 17:2).

[See *Margolios Hayam* to *Sanhedrin* 102b for a lengthy discussion of this entire theme.]

מזמור סג 63

David sought refuge from his pursuers, but he became stranded and trapped in the parched wasteland of the Judean desert.

Outside, Saul and his army surrounded him. From within, David was attacked by a terrible thirst which utterly drained his energy.

Oblivious to these dangers, David erected a massive fortress of faith which insulated him from the ravages of his hostile physical environment. His vast intellectual powers were completely preoccupied with the desire to draw even closer to God.

David's thirst in the wilderness was essentially spiritual. He longed to gaze upon God's splendor and he yearned to hear the teachings of Torah scholars, who reveal the ways of God.

Indeed, David's soul was ablaze with love for his Maker. This flaming thirst could be quenched only by closeness to Hashem, as David states: In the shadow of Your wings I shall joyously sing (v. *8*).

Midrash Shocher Tov *observes that this psalm foretells that the exiled children of Israel will cry out, 'Our souls are weary and parched; we yearn for the refreshing words of Torah, but the gentiles will not allow us this.' Thus will the words of the prophet* (Amos *8:11*) *be fulfilled:* Behold the days are coming, says my Lord HASHEM / ELOHIM, when I shall send a famine in the land, not a famine of bread, nor a thirst for water, but a thirst for hearing the words of HASHEM.

א מִזְמוֹר לְדָוִד בִּהְיוֹתוֹ בְּמִדְבַּר יְהוּדָה׃
ב אֱלֹהִים | אֵלִי אַתָּה אֲשַׁחֲרֶךָּ צָמְאָה לְךָ |
נַפְשִׁי כָּמַהּ לְךָ בְשָׂרִי בְּאֶרֶץ־צִיָּה וְעָיֵף

1. מִזְמוֹר לְדָוִד – *A song of David.*

The *Zohar (Parshas Terumah)* cites David's intense spiritual ecstasy and his special genius for composing hymns of praise even in situations of extreme danger and adversity.

Alshich adds that although David found himself in one of the most barren and desolate spots in Israel, he still rejoiced, for at least he was in the Holy Land rather than on alien soil.

The *Midrash* states that it is better to be in the wastelands of Israel than in the palaces of any foreign land. According to the *Talmud (Kesubos* 110b), a person who lives outside of the land of Israel is like a man without a God.

Therefore, in the next verse, David sings, *O God, You are* [still] *my God! (Dorash Moshe).*

בִּהְיוֹתוֹ בְּמִדְבַּר יְהוּדָה – *When he was in the wilderness of Judah.*

Radak identifies this as the wilderness of Ziph, where David was hiding from Saul.

Norah Tehillos notes that the setting of this psalm is not identical to that of Psalm 54, for the people of Ziph threatened David twice. David's first encounter in Ziph, recorded in *I Samuel* 23:19-29, took place when the Ziphites informed Saul of David's hiding place; then David narrowly escaped at the סֶלַע הַמַּחְלְקוֹת, *Rock of Division* [see *footnote,* 18:3]. Psalm 54 is dedicated to that incident; therefore, it begins (*v.*2), *When the Ziphites came and said to Saul, 'Indeed, David is hiding in our midst.'*

The Ziphites betrayed David a second time, as described in *I Samuel* 26:2-3. At that time, however, David was not as concerned about the physical threat which they posed; rather, he mourned the suffering of his soul, which was exiled in a spiritual wilderness, completely cut off from the spiritual centers of Israel.

Since our psalm is based on the latter incident, David here makes no direct mention of the Ziphites. Rather he expresses anguish over his isolated location, *the wilderness of Judah.*

2. אֱלֹהִים אֵלִי אַתָּה – *O God – You are my God.*

See footnote to 22:2; אֵל is defined as the name of God which gives strength and power in times of distress to those who are completely righteous. *Targum* here renders אֵלִי as תּוּקְפִּי, *my might.*

Radak explains that a fugitive is highly vulnerable; God is his sole support and protection.

Chozeh David observes that David was particularly disillusioned by the treachery of the Ziphites, for they were his close kinsmen of the royal tribe of Judah. Not only did they betray David, but their perfidy even took place in the tribal territory which they shared with David, *the wilderness of Judah.*

Now David realized more than ever before the futility of putting trust in any man, however close he may seem. He proclaimed that, henceforth, *O God – You* [alone] *are my God* [and savior].

אֲשַׁחֲרֶךָּ – *I seek You.*

This translation follows *Rashi* and *Metzudas David. Targum* and *Ibn Ezra* suggest that this word may be related to שַׁחַר, *dawn,* implying that David renewed his quest for God with every new dawn [see 27:4 וּלְבַקֵּר בְּהֵיכָלוֹ].

צָמְאָה לְךָ נַפְשִׁי – *My soul thirsts for You.*

The psalmist does not describe himself as רָעֵב, *starving,* because that word does not adequately indicate the intensity of his passionate yearning.

63
1-2

A song of David,
when he was in the wilderness of Judah.
2 O God — You are my God,
I seek You.
My soul thirsts for You,
my flesh longs for You;
In a land barren,
and weary with no water.

The agony of acute thirst far surpasses the pangs of hunger, for the need for water is the most intense and urgent of human needs *(Radak; Yaavetz HaDoresh)*.

[Although David literally lacked water in this parched and torturous wasteland, he makes no mention of it, for his soul was ablaze with an ecstatic yearning for God which rendered him oblivious to all other desires and physical needs.]

Where then was the fresh wellspring which would have provided David with spiritual refreshment? According to *Radak*, David desired to be either in Kiryat Yearim, where the Holy Ark was kept, or in Givon, where the Tabernacle stood. Men who sought the presence of God would gather in these two spiritual centers to hear the teachings of the great scholars of Israel. David sorely missed the company of Torah scholars, for the fighters who joined David's band were not of high intellectual caliber; rather, they were bitter and broken men who had fled from their troubles (*I Samuel* 22:2).

כָּמַהּ לְךָ בְשָׂרִי — *My flesh longs for You.*

Rabbi Asher of Stolin (based on the words of *Rashi* and *Ibn Ezra*) explained that in all of Scripture, no word expresses such intense desire as the word כָּמַהּ. It is a longing of unsurpassed intensity.

Malbim traces this word to כַּמָּה, *how much*, to suggest, 'O, how much does my flesh long for You!' The man overcome with such longing concentrates all of his senses on this one wish and becomes oblivious to all else. In the desert, the typical person would be preoccupied with his need for water, but David thought only of God *(Rabbeinu Bachya)*.

The *Midrash (Bereishis Rabbah* 69:1) relates כָּמַהּ to כְּמֵהִין, *mushrooms*, for these plants derive no nourishment from the soil and survive exclusively on the moisture they absorb from the atmosphere. [Similarly, David recognizes that his survival depends only on the inspiration which he draws from above, rather than any mundane, physical sustenance.]

Norah Tehillos points out that David's body and soul achieved total harmony. Just as David's 'soul thirsted' for God, so did his 'flesh long' for God; his entire being was suffused with sublime spirituality.

בְּאֶרֶץ צִיָּה — *In a land barren.*

[It should be noted that the wilderness of Judah is not only hot and dry, but also highly saline. To the east, it borders on the Dead Sea, whose high salt concentration renders the surrounding area especially arid and desolate. The air is saturated with salt, which increases thirst immensely.]

וְעָיֵף בְּלִי מָיִם — [*And*] *weary with no water.*

According to *Radak* and *Ibn Ezra*, this describes the utterly parched earth of this wilderness.

However, *Metzudas David* and

ג בְּלִי־מָיִם: כֵּן בַּקֹּדֶשׁ חֲזִיתִךָ לִרְאוֹת עֻזְּךָ
ד וּכְבוֹדֶךָ: כִּי־טוֹב חַסְדְּךָ מֵחַיִּים שְׂפָתַי
ה יְשַׁבְּחוּנְךָ: כֵּן אֲבָרֶכְךָ בְחַיָּי בְּשִׁמְךָ אֶשָּׂא
ו כַפָּי: כְּמוֹ חֵלֶב וָדֶשֶׁן תִּשְׂבַּע נַפְשִׁי
ז וְשִׂפְתֵי רְנָנוֹת יְהַלֶּל־פִּי: אִם־זְכַרְתִּיךָ

Hirsch maintain that this refers to the man traveling through *the barren land*. It is he who grows *weary with no water.*

3. כֵּן בַּקֹּדֶשׁ חֲזִיתִךָ — *Thus have I beheld You in the Sanctuary.*

Rashi translates כֵּן, *thus* or *just as*, implying, 'To the extent that I thirsted and longed to witness Your splendor *just as* I once beheld it in Your Sanctuary, I am ultimately destined to see *Your might and Your glory.*

Radak renders: *Just as* a man in the desert thirsts for water, כֵּן, *thus*, do I long to behold Your sacred Presence in the holy shrine.

חֲזִיתִךָ — *I beheld You.*

Malbim points out that the root חָזָה denotes the spiritual perception experienced by the prophets. Such insight is called חָזוֹן, *a prophetic vision.*

Hirsch adds that חָזָה is derived from חָזֶה, *the breast*, for it alludes to vision of the heart, rather than of the eyes. The word רָאָה, in contrast, refers to ordinary physical eyesight.

Thus, 'now, while I am isolated and geographically distant, my heart perceives Your Sanctuary, and I envision the day when I will be privileged *to see* (לִרְאוֹת) *Your glory* face to face.'

לִרְאוֹת עֻזְּךָ וּכְבוֹדֶךָ — *To see Your might and Your glory.*

God's *might*, עֹז, refers to the holy Torah, as in 29:11 *(Alshich)*, and to the Ark of the Law, called (132:8) אֲרוֹן עֻזֶּךָ *(Hirsch)*.

כָּבוֹד refers to the *glory* of God's Presence, which rests upon the Ark *(Metzudas David)*.

4. כִּי טוֹב חַסְדְּךָ מֵחַיִּים — *For better is Your kindness than life.*

The *kindness* which You will bestow upon the righteous in the World to Come far surpasses the good *life* which You grant the wicked in This World *(Targum)*.

Radak explains: You displayed Your *kindness* to mankind when You endowed humanity with intelligence, for this faculty elevates man's existence above the life devoid of higher intelligence experienced by animals and other living things.

Metzudas David adds: The entire purpose of my *life* is to utilize *Your kindness*, intelligent speech, so that *my lips shall praise You.* If I am deprived of this opportunity , my *life* is bereft of all purpose. Therefore, *my soul thirsts for You* and *my flesh longs for You*, for every intelligent person yearns to fulfill his mission in life.

Radak suggests another interpretation, in which חַיִּים refers to the rich and powerful men [who possess all of the benefits of *life*.] According to this view, David here declares, 'These men promise to do charity and favors, yet, O God, Your *kindness* outshines theirs. Saul showed me kindness by accepting me into his court and by making me his general; he gave me his daughter in marriage and was my benefactor in many ways. Yet after all this kindness, he now seeks to kill me. [To escape his pursuit, I am exiled to this barren wilderness.] Therefore, it is fitting that *my lips shall praise* only *Your kindness* and not that of any חַיִּים, *living*, mortal man.

שְׂפָתַי יְשַׁבְּחוּנְךָ — *My lips shall praise You.*

In this manner, I shall accomplish my purpose in life *(Metzudas David)*.

3 *Thus have I beheld You in the Sanctuary;*
to see Your might and Your glory.
4 *For better is Your kindness than life;*
my lips shall praise You.
5 *Then I shall bless You all my life;*
in Your Name I shall lift my hands.
6 *As with fat and abundance*
will my soul be sated;
And with joyous language
will my mouth give praise.

5. כֵּן אֲבָרֶכְךָ בְחַיָּי — *Then I shall bless You all* [lit. *with*] *my life.*

When I come before You in Your Sanctuary, כֵּן, *then* I shall dedicate my entire life to blessing Your Name *(Rashi).*

Radak translates כֵּן as *so* or *similarly,* suggesting 'just as *my lips praised You* (*v.*4) until now, so shall I continue to bless You forever.'

The *Talmud (Berachos* 16a) explains the declaration *I shall bless You with my life* to mean: I shall recite the *Shema* before You.

[When he recites the *Shema,* the Jew accepts the command to love God בְּכָל נַפְשְׁךָ, *with all your soul (Deuteronomy* 6:5); i.e., he vows to sacrifice his life, if necessary, for the love of God.]

The three sections which make up the *Shema* contain a sum of 248 words, alluding to the 248 organs of the human body (which form the basis for life). All of these organs are to be dedicated to the service of God *(Eretz HaChaim).*

בְּשִׁמְךָ אֶשָּׂא כַפָּי — *In Your Name I shall lift my hands.*

After spending a lifetime blessing You in This World, I shall lift up my hands to Your name, in the World to Come *(Targum).*

The *Talmud (Berachos* 16a) interprets this to mean, 'I shall pray to You.'

Yalkut Eliezer explains that the true purpose of prayer is to *lift,* i.e., to elevate and exalt God's Name. Although the bulk of the benedictions of *Shemoneh Esrei* are requests for the welfare of the supplicant, the supplicant's motive for seeking personal success should be to add glory to God's Name.

6. כְּמוֹ חֵלֶב וָדֶשֶׁן תִּשְׂבַּע נַפְשִׁי — *As with fat and abundance will my soul be sated.*

David said, 'If You will grant me the opportunity to bless You and to exalt Your Name (*v.*5), then my thirsty, parched soul will be totally *satisfied,* just as the body is content after a *fat and abundant* meal.'

The *Kuzari* notes that the soul is sustained by a regimen of prayer, just as the body is maintained by ample meals at regular intervals (*Malbim;* see *comm.* to *Psalms* 55:18).

וְשִׂפְתֵי רְנָנוֹת יְהַלֶּל פִּי — *And with joyous language* [lit., *lips*] *will my mouth give praise.*

Here the word שִׂפְתֵי [lit. *lips*] is rendered as *languages* [cf. *Genesis* 11:1] *(Rashi; Metzudas David)* to imply 'I will use any language I know to express Your praise' *(Ibn Ezra).*

The words will be as sweet and pleasant to my lips as fat and abundant delicacies *(Radak).*

This spiritual joy is illustrated in the

ח עַל־יְצוּעָי בְּאַשְׁמֻרוֹת אֶהְגֶּה־בָּךְ: כִּי־
הָיִיתָ עֶזְרָתָה לִּי וּבְצֵל כְּנָפֶיךָ אֲרַנֵּן:
ט דָּבְקָה נַפְשִׁי אַחֲרֶיךָ בִּי תָּמְכָה יְמִינֶךָ:
י וְהֵמָּה לְשׁוֹאָה יְבַקְשׁוּ נַפְשִׁי יָבֹאוּ
יא בְּתַחְתִּיּוֹת הָאָרֶץ: יַגִּירֻהוּ עַל־יְדֵי־חָרֶב

Talmud (*Berachos* 9b) by Rav Bruna, whose devotion during morning prayer filled him with such rapture that he was smiling in ecstacy the whole day *(Yaavetz HaDoresh).*

7. אִם זְכַרְתִּיךָ עַל יְצוּעָי — *When I remember You upon my couch* [lit. *couches*].

Radak proves from various sources that אִם may be translated as *when.* In this verse, it implies: At night, *when* my mind is free of daily concerns and distractions, I can concentrate my thoughts on You. At that time, *my soul becomes satisfied as with fat and abundance (Ibn Ezra).*

Formerly, I would remember You while reclining on my soft, luxurious royal couch; now, lying on the cold, hard rocks in the wilderness, my thoughts are concentrated on You. Whenever I think of You, You draw near and Your Presence provides me joy and comfort *(Hirsch).*

Radak notes that David uses the plural יְצוּעָי, *couches,* because while David was fleeing from Saul, he slept in a different place every night.

בְּאַשְׁמֻרוֹת אֶהְגֶּה בָּךְ — *In night watches meditating upon You.*

Radak cites the *Talmudic* dictum (*Berachos* 3a) that the night is divided into three equal watches. At the end of every watch, the Holy One, Blessed be He, mourns for His Temple, which lies in ruins, and for His sons, the children of Israel, who are dispersed in exile. The *Shulchan Aruch (Orach Chaim* 1:2-3) accepts the ruling of the *Rosh (Berachos* 3a) that all God-fearing men should arise at the end of each night watch to join God in His lamentation.

Even in David's times, before the destruction of the Temple and the exile of Israel, the king would lament the misfortunes and problems of his people at the night watches. With his prophetic vision, David foresaw the future suffering of his people. Although David was awake almost all night (*Berachos* 3b; *Succah* 26b), he prayed with special inspiration and fervor at the אַשְׁמֻרוֹת.[1]

8. כִּי הָיִיתָ עֶזְרָתָה לִּי — *For You were a help for me.*

It is fitting that I should think of You at all times (*v.* 7) because You help me constantly *(Radak).*

וּבְצֵל כְּנָפֶיךָ אֲרַנֵּן — *In the shadow of Your wings I shall joyously sing.*

I am especially grateful to God for providing me with a place of refuge in *Eretz Yisrael* rather than in a foreign land [see *comm. v.* 1]. I sing with extra

1. אַשְׁמֻרוֹת also refers to the crack of dawn, the אַשְׁמֹרֶת הַבֹּקֶר [see *Exodus* 14:24]. The very first *halachah* in the entire *Shulchan Aruch (Orach Chaim* 1:1) is: A person should arise just before dawn to commence his daily service of God. *Ramoh* (ibid.) maintains that the Jew's Divine service actually begins at night: At bedtime, a man should think of God, in Whose Presence he will sleep, and immediately upon awakening, he should arise from bed with vigor and alacrity.

This teaches that a person's conduct upon retiring at night determines how and when he will arise. This is the message of this verse: *'If I remember You* [when I lay down to sleep] *on my couch,* [then] *I shall think of You* [and arise quickly] *at the* אַשְׁמֻרוֹת *of dawn.'*

7 *When I remember You upon my couch;*
in night watches meditating upon You.
8 *For You were a help for me;*
in the shadow of Your wings
I shall joyously sing.
9 *My soul cleaves after You;*
to me, Your right arm lent support.
10 *But as for them,*
they seek desolation for my soul;
They shall enter
the lowest depths of the earth.
11 *He shall drag him by the sword;*

joy, because I am still *in the shadow of Your wings (Alshich).*

9. דָּבְקָה נַפְשִׁי אַחֲרֶיךָ — *My soul cleaves after You.*

My spirit knows no desire other than the yearning for You *(Radak).*

[Although man cannot physically cleave to God, he can attain closeness to Him with his intellect and soul, by studying God's ways. The *Targum* here paraphrases: 'My soul is drawn after the pursuit of Your Torah.']

When Moses begged to understand God, He responded: *You cannot see My face, for no man can see Me and live ... You shall see* אֲחֹרָי, *My back, but My face will not be seen (Exodus* 33:20, 23).

Here David says, 'I cannot see Your face directly; like Moses, I must approach You *from behind,* by cleaving *after You.* Moreover, You respond with kindness and *support me with Your right hand,* as if I were face to face with You *(Divrei Shlomo).*

בִּי תָּמְכָה יְמִינֶךָ — *To me, Your right arm lent support.*

I cleave to You tenaciously, just as the flame clings to the candlewick; my hold is strengthened by the Torah which You presented with Your right hand, as Scripture says (*Deuteronomy* 33:2): *From His right hand a fiery law was given to them (Zerah Yaakov).*

10. וְהֵמָּה לְשׁוֹאָה יְבַקְשׁוּ נַפְשִׁי — *But as for them, they seek desolation for my soul.*

[Cf. translation of שׁוֹאָה in *comm.* to 35:8, 17.]

According to *Radak,* this refers to the pursuers [Saul and his men] who seek to destroy David. They lie in ambush on a foggy day [when visibility is poor] in order to take David by surprise *(Rashi).*

Ibn Ezra, however, identifies these men as the informers [of Ziph] who revealed David's secret hideaway to Saul.

יָבֹאוּ בְּתַחְתִּיּוֹת הָאָרֶץ — *They shall enter the lowest depths of the earth.*

David prays: 'These lowly men attempted to condemn me and to drag me to *Gehinnom.* Let them sink to the lowest depths instead' *(Radak).*

11. יַגִּירֻהוּ עַל יְדֵי חָרֶב — *He shall drag him by the sword.*

Radak explains that the root הַגָּרָה, *to flow,* refers primarily to liquids [see *Lamentations* 3:49]. In this verse it means *the sword will cause* blood *to flow.* Since the word denotes the movement of objects from place to place, it

מְנָת שֻׁעָלִים יִהְיוּ: יב וְהַמֶּלֶךְ יִשְׂמַח סג
בֵּאלֹהִים יִתְהַלֵּל כָּל־הַנִּשְׁבָּע בּוֹ כִּי יִסָּכֵר יב
פִּי דוֹבְרֵי־שָׁקֶר:

also indicates that the corpse of the enemy will be dragged about ignominiously. The singular form is utilized because David is addressing his foremost enemy, Saul. [Saul, in fact, was finally killed by the sword and his corpse was disgraced.]

מְנָת שֻׁעָלִים יִהְיוּ — *A portion of foxes shall they be.*

Radak explains that David reverts to the plural יִהְיוּ, *they shall be*, because he is now addressing Saul's many followers. He asks that their corpses be abandoned to the wild beasts of prey.

According to *Rashi*, 'Let their homes and settlements become desolate, inhabited only by wild foxes.'

12. וְהַמֶּלֶךְ יִשְׂמַח בֵּאלֹהִים — *But the king shall be glad with God.*

Rashi contends that David here refers to himself as king, for although Saul still reigned, Samuel had already anointed David as his immediate successor.

My adversaries taunt me, predicting that I shall never ascend to the throne. Destroy them, I pray, and invest me with monarchy so that I may rejoice in God's choice *(Radak)*.

Sforno maintains that David is praying on King Saul's behalf. 'Although he pursues me relentlessly, I refuse to curse him [for he is still the anointed of God]. Rather I pray that his troubled, melancholy spirit should find joy in fulfilling God's command to vanquish our gentile foes, so that he will no longer have to seek joy in pursuing me.' [According to *Sforno*, the curse of the

63
12

a portion of foxes shall they be.
12 But the king shall be glad with God,
glorified will be everyone who swears by Him;
For the mouth of falsifiers
will be stopped.

preceding verse was not directed at Saul, as *Radak* explains.]

יִתְהַלֵּל כָּל הַנִּשְׁבָּע בּוֹ — *Glorified will be everyone who swears by Him.*

When the world sees that You have saved me, all righteous men who cleave to You will be recognized as praiseworthy *(Rashi).*

These God-fearing men are those totally honest people who have the exclusive right to swear by Your Name *(Radak).*

As the prophet (*Jeremiah* 9:22-23) says, אַל יִתְהַלֵּל חָכָם בְּחָכְמָתוֹ, *Let not the wise man glory in his wisdom, neither let the mighty man glory in his might; let not the rich man glory in his riches; but let he who glories glory only in this: that he understands and knows Me (Rashbam).*

כִּי יִסָּכֵר פִּי דוֹבְרֵי שָׁקֶר — *For the mouth of falsifiers will be stopped.*

This refers to those who swear falsely in the Name of God *(Radak).*

David said, 'I do not suffer most from Saul himself, but from liars who slander me to him and invite his wrath with false tales about me. When these villains are silenced, my men and I will rejoice' *(Metzudas David).*

[Then we will no longer be trapped in the wilderness of Judah; we will be able to *behold You in the Sanctuary, to see Your might and Your glory* (*v.*3).]

מזמור סד

64

The preceding Psalm described David in exile. Although physically isolated from God, spiritually David remained completely absorbed in the service of the Almighty. This total concentration rendered David oblivious to all sinister threats.

Centuries later, in the exile of Babylon, Daniel, a descendant of the royal line of David, duplicated the selfless dedication of his illustrious ancestor. Midrash Shocher Tov *and* Rashi *explain that this psalm is based on the events narrated in the sixth chapter of the Book of* Daniel.

Immediately upon his ascension to the Babylonian throne, Darius the Mede appointed 120 satraps to govern the vast empire. The satraps were responsible to three ministers, of whom Daniel was the most capable and distinguished. Jealous of Daniel's prominence, the satraps and viziers plotted his downfall.

They convinced Darius to issue a decree prohibiting his subjects from addressing petitions to God or man for the first thirty days of the new king's reign. All requests would be addressed exclusively to Darius during this period, in order to enhance his authority and prestige at the very outset of his rule. The satraps decreed that anyone disobeying their edict would be cast into the lion's pit.

All obeyed the decree save Daniel, who continued to pray to God three times daily. No threat, not even the spector of the lion's pit, could divert Daniel from the service of God. Like David, Daniel thirsted only for God. Daniel's well deserved reward and his miraculous salvation will be described in the commentary to this psalm.

סד
א־ה

א־ב לַמְנַצֵּחַ מִזְמוֹר לְדָוִד: שְׁמַע־אֱלֹהִים קוֹלִי
ג בְשִׂיחִי מִפַּחַד אוֹיֵב תִּצֹּר חַיָּי: תַּסְתִּירֵנִי
ד מִסּוֹד מְרֵעִים מֵרִגְשַׁת פֹּעֲלֵי אָוֶן: אֲשֶׁר
שָׁנְנוּ כַחֶרֶב לְשׁוֹנָם דָּרְכוּ חִצָּם דָּבָר מָר:
ה לִירוֹת בַּמִּסְתָּרִים תָּם פִּתְאֹם יֹרֻהוּ וְלֹא

2. שְׁמַע אֱלֹהִים קוֹלִי — *Hear, O God, my voice expressing my woes.*

Radak and *Metzudas David* render שִׂיחִי as *my tale of woes* [cf. *Psalms* 55:3].

However, שִׂיחַ is often interpreted as a reference to fervent prayer [cf. *Berachos* 26b]. *Midrash Shocher Tov* explains that this alludes to Daniel, who ignored the decree of Darius by maintaining his regime of prayer. Daniel would pray daily in his upper chamber, open the windows facing Jerusalem, and kneel in supplication to God (*Daniel* 6:11).[1]

Many commentaries wonder why Daniel endangered his life in order to pray. This was not a case where יֵהָרֵג וְאַל יַעֲבֹר, *one must let oneself be killed rather than transgress.* This rule applies at all times only to three cardinal sins: idolatry, immorality, and murder. However, where coercion is aimed at conversion one must sacrifice his life for קִידּוּשׁ הַשֵּׁם, *Sanctification of God's Name,* even for a Jewish custom. Since the king's intent here was for his own glory, without intent to convert Jews, Daniel was not obligated or even permitted to jeopardize his life.

Alshich (comm. to *Daniel*) explains that for this reason Daniel prayed in the secrecy of his upper chamber and not in the synagogue where he had no doubt prayed previously. In order not to anger the king and endanger his own life, he chose to ostensibly abide by the king's decree, while furtively upholding his obligation to God.

Malbim (comm. to *Daniel*) interprets Daniel's defiance of the king's decree not as a conscious act of martyrdom, but as a miscalculation as to the danger of his actions. The king's decree prohibited *whoever shall make a request (Daniel* 6:8) to address himself to anyone but Darius. Daniel made no petition or request; he merely offered praise, blessing, and thanksgiving to God as was his daily custom.

However, because the satraps were determined to find Daniel guilty of transgressing the king's decree, they interpreted his prayer as a specific petition. [See *comm. Daniel* 6:11, ArtScroll ed. for lengthy discussion of Daniel's martyrdom.]

מִפַּחַד אוֹיֵב תִּצֹּר חַיָּי — *From dread of the foe preserve my life.*

According to *Midrash Shocher Tov,* this refers to the verse: *These men* [his enemies] *assembled and found Daniel praying and supplicating before his God (Daniel* 6:12).

R' Saadiah Gaon (Daniel 6:12) comments that they stealthily surrounded Daniel's home and asked Daniel's maidservant what he was doing. When she answered, 'He is kneeling and praying to his God,' they immediately entered and personally witnessed this 'crime,' which they swiftly reported to the king.

3. תַּסְתִּירֵנִי מִסּוֹד מְרֵעִים — *Hide me from the counsel* [lit. *the secret*] *of the wicked.*

[On the outside the satraps and

1. It is interesting to note that the house where Daniel prayed became a landmark and a holy site in Babylon. Many centuries after Daniel's death, the Sages of the *Talmud* would travel to pray at Daniel's home (see *Eruvin* 21a and *Rashi, ibid).*

64
1-5

F*or the Conductor,*
a song of David.
2 *Hear, O God, my voice expressing my woes;*
from dread of the foe preserve my life.
3 *Hide me from the counsel of the wicked,*
from the assembly of evildoers,
4 *Who have sharpened their tongue*
like the sword,
And aimed their arrow —
a bitter word —
5 *To shoot in secrecy at the innocent;*
suddenly they shot, and they are unafraid.

viziers claimed to be deeply concerned with consolidating the power and prestige of the king; secretly, however, their sole desire was to destroy Daniel.]

מֵרְגְשַׁת פֹּעֲלֵי אָוֶן — *From the assembly of evildoers.* [Cf. 2:1 לָמָּה רָגְשׁוּ גוֹיִם.]

Even after receiving the accusation against Daniel, King Darius wanted to forgive his beloved and highly respected prime minister; but all of the satraps הַרְגִּשׁוּ עַל מַלְכָּא, *assembled around the king* (*Daniel* 6:16), insisting that the law of the land must be strictly enforced and that Daniel must be punished (*Rashi*).

4. אֲשֶׁר שָׁנְנוּ כַחֶרֶב לְשׁוֹנָם — *Who have sharpened their tongue like the sword.*

The satraps spread לָשׁוֹן הָרַע, *slanderous tales,* about Daniel to deprive him of the king's favor (*Rashi*).

דָּרְכוּ חִצָּם דָּבָר מָר — *And aimed their arrow — a bitter word.*

Literally, דָּרְכוּ means to *step on* the bow in order to string it and prepare it for shooting (*Ibn Ezra*).

The arrows were smeared with poison to make them doubly lethal (*Targum*).

When the wicked slander their victims at close range, the impact of the slander resembles the thrust of the sword. When they slander from a distance their barbed words resemble poisoned arrows shot from a bow (*Norah Tehillos*).

5. לִירוֹת בַּמִּסְתָּרִים תָּם — *To shoot in secrecy at the innocent.*

The wicked slander their victims surreptitiously, in order to deprive them of an opportunity for self-defense (*Radak*).

[Much to his dismay, King Darius was finally forced to accede to the demands of the satraps and ministers: Daniel was thrown into the lion's den. In *Daniel* 6:18 we read: *And a stone was brought and was placed over the opening of the pit, and the king sealed it with his signet ring and with the signet rings of his nobles, so that his will regarding Daniel not be changed.* The commentators explain that the king placed a stone barrier at the entrance of the den to circumvent the cunning of his nobles, for he feared that they would secretly throw stones or shoot arrows at Daniel and later falsely attribute his death to the lions (*R' Saadiah Gaon*).][1]

1. *Rashi* (*Daniel* 6:18) explains that in all of Babylon there are no stones; fences and buildings were made of clay bricks produced from mud (see *Genesis* 11:3). However, God summoned

ו יִירָאוּ: יְחַזְּקוּ־לָמוֹ | דָּבָר רָע יְסַפְּרוּ
לִטְמוֹן מוֹקְשִׁים אָמְרוּ מִי יִרְאֶה־לָּמוֹ:
ז יַחְפְּשׂוּ־עוֹלֹת תַּמְנוּ חֵפֶשׂ מְחֻפָּשׂ וְקֶרֶב
ח אִישׁ וְלֵב עָמֹק: וַיֹּרֵם אֱלֹהִים חֵץ פִּתְאוֹם
ט הָיוּ מַכּוֹתָם: וַיַּכְשִׁילֻהוּ עָלֵימוֹ לְשׁוֹנָם

6. יְחַזְּקוּ לָמוֹ דָּבָר רָע — *They urge an evil matter upon him.*

Feigning concern for the king's authority, the satraps deviously encouraged Darius to issue an evil decree *(Rashi).*

Otzar Nechmad renders יְחַזְּקוּ, *they intensify,* to suggest that whenever the wicked notice the slightest flaw in the behavior of the righteous, they purposely exaggerate its significance, to make it appear a very *evil matter.* [Thus, when the satraps sought to find fault with Daniel (*Daniel* 6:5-6), they could accuse him only of praying to God, for his general behavior was beyond reproach.]

יְסַפְּרוּ לִטְמוֹן מוֹקְשִׁים — *They speak of concealing snares.*

Ostensibly, the satraps were motivated purely by loyalty to the king; actually their sole intention was to set a trap for Daniel *(Rashi).*

אָמְרוּ מִי יִרְאֶה לָּמוֹ — *They say, 'Who will see them?'*

Foolishly, they ask, 'Who shall see us?', forgetting that God knows every thought and sees every deed *(Radak).*

7. יַחְפְּשׂוּ עוֹלֹת — *They search out pretexts.*

They seek libelous accusations to use against Daniel, as Scripture says (*Daniel* 6:5): *Then the viziers and the satraps tried to find a libel against Daniel with regard to the kingdom; but they could find neither fault nor corruption because he was faithful; and there was found neither error nor corruption in him (Rashi).*

תַּמְנוּ חֵפֶשׂ מְחֻפָּשׂ — *They complete a diligent search.*

[The crafty nobles were undaunted by their inability to uncover a misdeed with which to accuse Daniel.] They strained their ingenuity to fabricate a complaint against their hated enemy, and finally *they accomplished* [i.e., *completed*] their goal *(Radak; Metzudas David).*

Our text reads תַּמְנוּ, *they complete,* but *Rashi's* version has טָמְנוּ, *they conceal.* This suggests that when the satraps finally devised their wily plot against Daniel, *they concealed* their true intentions deep within their hearts, to avoid arousing the king's suspicion (see *Minchas Shai).*

וְקֶרֶב אִישׁ וְלֵב עָמֹק — *Within man and deep in heart.*

[Although the nobles delved into the depths of their hearts to find fault with Daniel, their effort was futile, for Daniel had also searched the inner recesses of his soul as he prayed to God. The merit derived from this sincere self-scrutiny protected Daniel from the satraps' plot.

[*Midrash Shocher Tov* teaches that when Darius came to inquire about

angels to bring a huge stone from the Land of Israel to cover the mouth of the lion's den. According to some commentators, an angel in the form of a lion sat at the edge of the pit to frighten away intruders *(Midrash Shocher Tov).*

R' Saadiah Gaon (*Daniel* 6:23) adds that the prophet Habakuk and his Judean field workers miraculously appeared in the pit. They prepared a lavish banquet for Daniel, and together they sang songs praising God's wondrous mercy.

[6] *They urge an evil matter upon him,*
they speak of concealing snares;
they say, 'Who will see them?'
[7] *They search out pretexts,*
they complete a diligent search;
within man and deep in heart.
[8] *Then God shot an arrow at them suddenly;*
suddenly their wounds appeared.
[9] *They were caused to stumble*
by their very own tongue;

Daniel's welfare the next morning, Daniel did not respond immediately to the king's questions because he was in the midst of reciting the *Shema*. Daniel's devotion to God was so complete that no one, not even the king himself, could distract the prophet during his prayers (even though *halachah* permits one to interrupt *Shema* to greet one who might otherwise kill him. See *Berachos* 13a).]

8. וַיֹּרֵם אֱלֹהִים חֵץ פִּתְאוֹם – *Then God shot an arrow at them suddenly.*

This form of punishment was especially appropriate, for Daniel's wicked enemies had shot at him without warning (*v.* 5) *(Ibn Ezra).*

Daniel remained in the lion's den overnight; in the morning, he emerged unscathed. His enemies sought to deny the miraculous nature of his salvation by claiming that the lions did not molest Daniel because their appetites had been satiated by a previous meal.

The king, outraged by this allegation, announced that Daniel's enemies must spend the night in the lions' den in order to test the validity of their defamatory claim.

Darius took the nobles (120 satraps and 2 viziers), their wives (122 women), and one child of each (122 children; a total of 366 people) and swiftly shot them like arrows into the den. The ferocious, hungry lions, who outnumbered the people four to one, devoured them instantly. The lions shattered their bones before they even touched the floor of the lion's den *(Rashi; Midrash Shocher Tov).*

הָיוּ מַכּוֹתָם – [*Suddenly*] *their wounds appeared* [lit. *came to be*].

Radak explains that the word פִּתְאוֹם, *suddenly*, modifies both the clause which precedes it and the clause which follows it.

9. וַיַּכְשִׁילֻהוּ עָלֵימוֹ לְשׁוֹנָם – *They were caused to stumble by their very own tongue.*

The tongues which they had used to condemn Daniel ultimately turned against them *(Rashi).*

[Darius cast them into the lion's den only to test their own claim that the lions' appetites had already been satisfied. Had the satraps remained silent, Darius would not have subjected them to this trial.]

The punishment, too, was tailored to the satraps' plots against Daniel (*v.* 4), for they had *sharpened their tongue like the sword (Ibn Ezra).*

י יִתְנוֹדְדוּ כָּל־רֹאֵה בָם׃ וַיִּירְאוּ כָּל־אָדָם
וַיַּגִּידוּ פֹּעַל אֱלֹהִים וּמַעֲשֵׂהוּ הִשְׂכִּילוּ׃
יא יִשְׂמַח צַדִּיק בַּיהוה וְחָסָה בוֹ וְיִתְהַלְלוּ
כָּל־יִשְׁרֵי־לֵב׃

יִתְנוֹדְדוּ כָּל רֹאֵה בָם — *All who see them shake their head.*

Observers shake their heads in scorn and derision *(Rashi).*

10. וַיִּירְאוּ כָּל אָדָם וַיַּגִּידוּ פֹּעַל אֱלֹהִים — *Then all men came to fear, and declared the work of God.*

[Upon witnessing the miraculous rescue of Daniel and the terrible revenge visited upon his foes, King Darius wrote: *To all the peoples, nations, and languages that live in all the earth, your peace should multiply! I hereby issue a decree that: throughout the extent of my kingdom let them tremble before, and fear, the God of Daniel — Who is the living God and everlasting; His kingdom is that which will not be destroyed, and His rule is till eternity. He saves and rescues, and performs signs and wonders in heaven and on earth — Who has saved Daniel from lions (Daniel* 6:26-28).

וּמַעֲשֵׂהוּ הִשְׂכִּילוּ — *And His deed they comprehended.*

They realized that all of God's punishments requite a person for his actions 'measure for measure', i.e., Divine punishment always 'fits the crime' *(Chozeh David).*

[God is Master of the universe in general and Sovereign of the animal kingdom in particular. Animals instinctively obey their master. Therefore, when man successfully preserves the Divine image in which he was created, then he too commands the obedience of the animals (see 49:13).

[The *Zohar* emphasizes that the lions were totally subdued in the presence of Daniel because the prophet embodied the image of their Divine Master.

[Everyone who observed Daniel glimpsed in him a reflection of God Himself; in this way, they indirectly gained an improved understanding of God's deeds.]

11. יִשְׂמַח צַדִּיק בַּה׳ — *Let the righteous one be glad in HASHEM.*

[Even after Daniel's miraculous salvation, God continued to give Daniel additional reasons for rejoicing, as Scripture attests (*Daniel* 6:29): *And this Daniel was successful throughout the reign of Darius and in the* [subsequent] *reign of Cyrus the Persian.*]

All who see them shake their head.
10 *Then all men came to fear,*
and declared the work of God;
and His deed they comprehended.
11 *Let the righteous one be glad in HASHEM,*
and take refuge in Him;
And let all the upright in heart find glory.

Migdal David notes that the final verse of this psalm resembles the last verse of Psalm 32: שִׂמְחוּ בַה׳ וְגִילוּ צַדִּיקִים וְהַרְנִינוּ כָּל יִשְׁרֵי לֵב, *Be glad in HASHEM and rejoice, O righteous. Cry out in joy, all upright of heart.*

The difference between the two verses is that the former is a command which exhorts the righteous to find joy in their faith, whereas the latter is a Divine promise that God will help those who seek this joy to find it.

וְחָסָה בוֹ – *And take refuge in Him.*

When the righteous witness that the faith they placed in God was justified, they resolve to trust in God with even greater devotion in the future *(Radak).*

וְיִתְהַלְלוּ כָּל יִשְׁרֵי לֵב – *And let all the upright in heart find glory.*

They may glory in the fact that because of their integrity, they have merited Divine salvation *(Rashi).*

[The *Talmud (Sanhedrin* 93b) observes that Daniel was glorified in an extraordinary manner: an entire book of Scripture received his name. This fulfilled the prophecy of *Isaiah* (56:5): שֵׁם עוֹלָם אֶתֵּן לוֹ, *I will grant him an everlasting name,* for *Chida* notes that the numerical value of the word שֵׁם, *name* – 340 – is equal to that of סֵפֶר, *book.*]

Finally, *Bris Avraham* notes the difference between the צַדִּיק and the יָשָׁר (cf. comm. of *Malbim* to *Psalms* 33:1). The *righteous* (צַדִּיק) adheres to the commands of God in all of his actions, but in his mind he is still troubled by questions and doubts. Because of his intellectual uncertainty, he needs Divine aid to overcome the temptations posed by the Evil Inclination. Thus, *the righteous are glad in HASHEM,* i.e., in His assistance.

In contrast, the *upright* (יָשָׁר) recognizes God's truth so clearly that he needs no Divine assistance to overcome temptation. Since the upright themselves deserve credit for their accomplishments, *they find glory* 'independently,' without reference to God.

מזמור סה 65

This psalm is a prayer which David composed at a time of terrible national disaster. In II Samuel 21, *we read:* And there was a famine in the days of David for three years, year after year, and David sought out the presence of Hashem. *In this psalm, David entreats God to send abundant rains and rich harvests* (Malbim; Norah Tehillos).

Ibn Ezra (v. *10) adds that at the moment the drought struck, the nation was also invaded by a foreign army. Since this psalm was composed at a time when the nation was threatened both from within and from without, the psalmist voices his longing for the advent of the Messiah. Although the Messiah's arrival is eagerly awaited at all times, anticipation of his coming is heightened at times of national emergency, for the Messiah will solve all of Israel's problems, both internal and external, economic and political* (Yaavetz HaDoresh).

In conclusion, the psalmist expresses his wish for an agricultural renaissance in which the Holy Land would flourish once more, freeing the children of Israel to concentrate on their true mission, the service of God.

סה א־ב לַמְנַצֵּחַ מִזְמוֹר לְדָוִד שִׁיר: לְךָ דֻמִיָּה
א־ד תְהִלָּה אֱלֹהִים בְּצִיּוֹן וּלְךָ יְשֻׁלַּם־נֶדֶר:
ג־ד שֹׁמֵעַ תְּפִלָּה עָדֶיךָ כָּל־בָּשָׂר יָבֹאוּ: דִּבְרֵי

1. מִזְמוֹר לְדָוִד שִׁיר — *With musical accompaniment, by David, a song.*

[See *comm.* to *Psalms* 30:1, where מִזְמוֹר is identified as the accompaniment of כְּלֵי זֶמֶר, *musical instruments,* and שִׁיר is described as the lyrics of the *song.*

Although plagued by starvation, David never ceased to praise God, anticipating his future salvation.

Hirsch notes that שִׁיר, the masculine form, refers to the final redemption of the future, while שִׁירָה, the feminine form, alludes to those acts by which the Almighty lays the groundwork for the ultimate salvation. [Cf. *comm.* to *Psalms* 33:3. Thus this psalm, which refers to the famine of David's times, also contains a deeper theme: the ultimate Messianic redemption.]

2. לְךָ דֻמִיָּה תְהִלָּה — *Silence is Your praise.*

This translation follows *Rashi,* who explains that any effort to recount all of God's virtues is utterly futile, since His wondrous attributes are infinite. Indeed, every attempt to completely enumerate His praises only detracts from His glory, for it implies that His praises are finite and within human understanding.

[Conversely, when man stands before his Creator in silent recognition of his own inadequacy, this constitutes the most eloquent testimony to God's magnificence, which defies human comprehension.]

The Sages of the *Talmud (Megillah* 18a) expressed this idea in the adage, מִלָּה בְּסֶלַע מַשְׁתּוּקָא בִּתְרֵין, *If a word is worth a silver coin, then silence is surely worth two,* and סַמָּא דְכוּלָּה מַשְׁתּוּקָא, *silence is the most potent of all formulas.*

Lachmei Todah renders לְךָ דֻמִיָּה תְהִלָּה: *Your silence is Your praise,* alluding to God's patience, which restrains Him from punishing sinners immediately after they commit an offense.

Ibn Ezra, Radak, and *Sforno* render דֻמִיָּה as *waiting, hoping,* for the Holy Ark which was in Zion. The masses assembled there to pay homage. The words of praise which they prepared *waited* on their lips, hoping for an opportunity to be uttered in Your presence. Ever since the destruction of the Temple, the children of Israel have eagerly awaited the moment when they will be redeemed from exile to worship in Zion.

Indeed, this wholehearted yearning for God constitutes an unparalleled tribute to the Almighty, as the psalmist pledges (71:14), *And I shall await* [You] *continually and* [thus] *add to all of Your praises (Sefer HaIkkarim).*

אֱלֹהִים בְּצִיּוֹן — *O God in Zion.*

This phrase refers to *God who dwells in Zion,* because it was there that the gentiles devastated the sacred Temple. Although this atrocity deserves to be avenged with unbridled Divine might and fury, God restrains Himself with amazing patience. This *silence is God's praise (Rashi;* see *Lachmei Todeh,* above).

Only in Zion is God's omnipotence revealed, as the psalmist declares (99:2), *HASHEM is great in Zion and He is exalted above all the nations.* It is in Zion, therefore, that Israel is awed into *silence,* recognizing that any attempt to enumerate God's praises is futile *(Beer Avraham).*

Even in Zion, where legions of Levites were available to chant hymns of praise, דֻמִיָּה, *silence,* surpassed all words *(Meir Tehillos).*

Yaavetz HaDoresh suggests that when drought and famine struck the

65
1-3

For the Conductor, with musical accompaniment, by David, a song.
2 *Silence is Your praise, O God in Zion,*
and for Your sake the vow is fulfilled.
3 *O heeder of prayer,*
unto You does all flesh come.

land of Israel, the entire nation assembled in Zion to fast and pray for salvation.

וּלְךָ יְשֻׁלַּם נֶדֶר — *And for Your sake the vow is fulfilled.*

For centuries, the Jewish nation awaited the opportunity to serve You selflessly in the Temple, in order to fulfill the oath which they had taken at Sinai (*Exodus* 24:7): נַעֲשֶׂה וְנִשְׁמָע, *We shall do* [this refers to the performance of the Torah's precepts] and *we shall listen* [this refers to the understanding of the commandments] *(Sforno).*

Even when they are dispersed into exile, they vow to serve You once again in Zion *(Radak).*

[When the starving nation of Israel gathered to pray for rain and bountiful harvests, they made many solemn vows to God, which they hoped to fulfill shortly.]

3. שֹׁמֵעַ תְּפִלָּה — *O Heeder of prayer.*

God hears the prayers of all mankind in the Holy Temple, which is situated in Zion; the prophet (*Isaiah* 56:7) described the *Beis HaMikdash* as a בֵּית תְּפִלָּה, *House of Prayer (Ibn Ezra).*

No mortal can hear prayers as God does. A human king cannot even hear the words of two men who speak at the same time; certainly he cannot understand the pleas of the multitudes who cry out simultaneously. However, the Holy One, Blessed be He, hears the individual prayers of all mankind, even though they are uttered coinstantaneously *(Midrash Shocher Tov).*

This defies the normal laws of nature, for ordinarily the sound of a single voice can be understood by ten ears, but the sound of ten voices cannot be understood by only one ear (*Pesikta Rabbasi* 21:6).

The *Midrash (Shemos Rabbah* 21:4) notes that the vast variety of prayers are described here in the singular form, as תְּפִלָּה, because a special angel gathers the prayers offered in all of the synagogues and fashions them into one perfect entreaty, which crowns God like an עֲדִי, *jeweled tiara.* [According to *Yefeh Toar*, this word is related to עָדֶיךָ.]

עָדֶיךָ כָּל בָּשָׂר יָבֹאוּ — *Unto You does all flesh come.*

The *Beis HaMikdash* is a universal *House of Prayer*, dedicated לְכָל הָעַמִּים, *to all the nations (Isaiah* 56:7; *Ibn Ezra).*

In this sacred shrine, יָבוֹא כָל בָּשָׂר לְהִשְׁתַּחֲוֹת לְפָנַי אָמַר ה׳, *'All flesh shall come to bow before me,' says HASHEM (Isaiah* 66:23; *Radak).*

God is not like a human king, who discriminates between rich and poor, powerful and weak. The Holy One, Blessed be He, treats *all flesh* as equals. He listens attentively to the prayers of every individual (*Shemos Rabbah* 21:4).

Shevet M'Yisrael observes that the reference to בָּשָׂר, *flesh,* alludes to the Talmudic dictum (*Sotah* 5a): A man's plea is not heard unless he humbles himself by making his heart become soft flesh [rather than tough, insensitive muscle].

Furthermore, there are heretics who perpetuate the false claim that God hears only the prayers which request perfection of the soul and spirit, but not those which concern the body. The psalmist refutes this notion, declaring that our Father in heaven eagerly awaits every prayer, even those dedicated to

עֲוֺנֹת גָּבְרוּ מֶנִּי פְּשָׁעֵינוּ אַתָּה תְכַפְּרֵם:
ה אַשְׁרֵי | תִּבְחַר וּתְקָרֵב יִשְׁכֹּן חֲצֵרֶיךָ
נִשְׂבְּעָה בְּטוּב בֵּיתֶךָ קְדֹשׁ הֵיכָלֶךָ:
ו נוֹרָאוֹת | בְּצֶדֶק תַּעֲנֵנוּ אֱלֹהֵי יִשְׁעֵנוּ

mundane, material concerns of the *flesh (Mabit).*

[Therefore, the children of Israel can expect God to listen to their prayers in time of famine even though these petitions relate to the sustenance of the *flesh.*]

4. דִּבְרֵי עֲוֺנֹת גָּבְרוּ מֶנִּי — *Talk of sins overwhelms me.*

We fully recognize that this famine is not a chance happening, but a Divinely ordained punishment for our many iniquities *(Ibn Ezra).*

It is futile to attempt to catalog our countless errors and flaws. Therefore, we do not itemize our failings, but simply pray that You will pardon all of our transgressions *(Rashi).*

Alshich observes that David personally accepts the blame for this calamity, since he is the nation's leader. Because David occupies such a prominent position, even his minute flaws are noticed by the masses and thereby cause desecration of God's Name. David laments, *Even minor iniquities* (דִּבְרֵי עֲוֺנֹת) are magnified and *become overwhelming* (גָּבְרוּ מֶנִּי) *because they were performed by me* and thus assume grave importance.

פְּשָׁעֵינוּ אַתָּה תְכַפְּרֵם — *Our transgressions — You will pardon them.*

[The commentaries note that the verse begins in the singular, but ends in the plural.]

Radak explains that this inconsistency was intended to emphasize that the psalm speaks for the multitudes of Jews who have languished in exile throughout the generations.

Sforno perceives this as David's confession: 'Since I realize that my own iniquities are overwhelming, my merits are not sufficient to overcome them and bring forgiveness on behalf of the entire congregation. Therefore, I must beseech You, O God, to mercifully pardon our transgressions.'

In conclusion, *Sfas Emes* comments that the righteous leader is the heart of the nation. His private sin causes the public to transgress, for his offense triggers a decline in the spiritual level of the entire people [see *Overview, Tehillim* Vol. I, Section IV]. David pleads, 'Since my personal iniquities overwhelmed me, I caused our national transgressions. Since I am responsible, I beg You to *pardon them.'*

5. אַשְׁרֵי תִּבְחַר וּתְקָרֵב — *Praises to the one You choose and draw near.*

According to *Radak,* this alludes to the generation of exiles which God will *choose* for redemption. He will *draw* them *near* by causing their return to *Eretz Yisrael* and Jerusalem.

Bamidbar Rabbah (83:2) interprets this as a reference to God's devoted followers, the great men of Jewish history. Some were merely chosen, i.e., singled out for distinguished service, but some were also drawn near, thus being shown special Divine favor.

David was chosen as Scripture says (78:70), *He chose David His servant.* After David sinned, he was rejected; Absalom forced David to leave Jerusalem, God's city. However, under the influence and guidance of his revered teacher, Eira HaYari [who taught him to repent], David was drawn near once again.

יִשְׁכֹּן חֲצֵרֶיךָ — *To dwell in Your courts.*

[4] *Talk of sins overwhelms me,*
our transgressions — You will pardon them.
[5] *Praises to the one You choose and draw near*
to dwell in Your courts,
To be sated with the goodness of Your house,
the holiness of Your Sanctuary.
[6] *With awesome works of righteousness*
You answer us,
O God of our salvation,

This alludes to the prohibition which forbids all men (except for David and his descendants) to sit and dwell in the Temple courtyard (*Sotah* 40b). This distinction indicates David's special favor in the eyes of God *(Alshich).*

נִשְׂבְּעָה בְּטוּב בֵּיתֶךָ — *To be sated with the goodness of Your house.*

Sforno interprets this as a prayer: O Lord, grant us an abundant flow of the sanctity which streams from Your Temple. Please overlook the fact that we are unworthy of such generosity.

Alshich adds that the Temple was the source of all spiritual satisfaction. The *Midrash* calls the *Beis HaMikdash* בֵּית הַשּׁוֹאֵבָה, *the house of elevation,* because it was from this consecrated spot that Israel became spiritually elevated by the Holy Spirit [cf. *Succah* 50b and *Tosafos, s.v.* חד תני ibid.].

According to *Vidal HaTzorfati* and *Shaloh HaKodosh,* the psalmist here offers advice to the devoted man who seeks to *draw near* to God. David advises that this closeness can only be accomplished by spurning all material pleasures and by finding satisfaction solely in the *goodness* of God.

קְדֹשׁ הֵיכָלֶךָ — *The holiness of Your Sanctuary.*

It is customary to recite this verse during the circumcision *(Bris Milah)* ceremony. The *Zohar (Lech Lecha)* states that the ten words in this verse correspond to the ten Divine canopies which are granted to those who fulfill the *mitzvah* of circumcision.

Through the covenant of circumcision, the people of Israel were *chosen* and *drawn near* to God *(Iyun Tefillah).* The children of Israel ascend higher and higher, until they reach the *holiness* of the celestial *sanctuary,* where their souls cleave to God *(Sharbit HaZohar, Siddur Otzar Tefillos).*

6. נוֹרָאוֹת בְּצֶדֶק תַּעֲנֵנוּ — *With awesome works of righteousness You answer us.*

Your *righteousness* is evident because You defend us from the hostile pagans and drive them off with *awesome* blows *(Rashi).*

From this we learn that we need not fear, so long as we remain worthy of God's mercy. Just as You stave off the external threat of the enemy, You will protect us from the internal danger of famine and drought *(Ibn Ezra).*[1]

1. The *Talmud (Yoma* 69b) says that when the pagan hordes openly desecrated the sacred Temple, it seemed as if God were no longer נוֹרָא, *awesome.* Afterwards, however, when Israel managed to survive being scattered in exile among multitudes of murderous enemies, people wondered, 'How can one helpless sheep endure, surrounded by seventy hungry wolves?' This proves that the nations realize that we have remained the chosen people of God, despite our suffering. They don't destroy us, for they fear God's נוֹרָאוֹת, *awesome works.*

ז מִבְטָח כָּל־קַצְוֵי־אֶרֶץ וְיָם רְחֹקִים: מֵכִין
ח הָרִים בְּכֹחוֹ נֶאְזָר בִּגְבוּרָה: מַשְׁבִּיחַ |
שְׁאוֹן יַמִּים שְׁאוֹן גַּלֵּיהֶם וַהֲמוֹן לְאֻמִּים:
ט וַיִּירְאוּ יֹשְׁבֵי קְצָוֹת מֵאוֹתֹתֶיךָ מוֹצָאֵי־
י בֹקֶר וָעֶרֶב תַּרְנִין: פָּקַדְתָּ הָאָרֶץ |

מִבְטָח כָּל קַצְוֵי אֶרֶץ וְיָם רְחֹקִים – *O Trust of earth's far ends and distant seas.*

All men, even those who inhabit the most remote locations, turn to You when in need, for Your kingdom stretches to the very ends of the earth *(Rashi).*

The exiles of Israel are scattered not only to קַצְוֵי אֶרֶץ, *the earth's far ends,* but also to קַצְוֵי יָם, *the distant seas.* This refers to the far-flung, isolated islands. They yearn to be gathered once again into the center of the world, Jerusalem *(Radak; Sforno).*

Midrash Shocher Tov interprets this homiletically: The celestial Gates of Prayer are not always open, but the Gates of Repentance are open forever.

Just as the sea is always accessible to everyone who wants to bathe there, we *trust* that the 'sea' of repentance is constantly open to the person who seeks to immerse himself in it.

Radak explains that a lesson may be derived from this natural phenomenon.

Our exiled nation may appear to be moribund or lifeless; the gentiles taunt us mercilessly, saying that the Jewish people will never experience a national renaissance. Nevertheless, the exile is actually a long, lonely incubation period, during which time God prepares the proper conditions for our future rebirth, which will inaugurate an era of unparalleled national growth and success.

7. מֵכִין הָרִים בְּכֹחוֹ – *Who readies mountains with His strength.*

Rashi observes that although the rocky surface of the mountainside does not appear to be arable, God prepares the ground with special weather conditions and rains; as a result even this poor soil produces vegetation. (According to *Targum,* these plants sustain the mountain goats.) Elsewhere, the psalmist refers to God as the One *Who prepares rain for the earth, Who makes the mountains grow grass* (147:8).

נֶאְזָר בִּגְבוּרָה – *Who is girded with might.*

God can display His *might* whenever it becomes necessary, for the Almighty is constantly prepared and *girded* with His own unfailing strength *(Radak).*

Rashi explains that the psalmist refers here to God's גְּבוּרָה, *might,* because he is marveling at the rainfall [which cures drought and famine and brings abundant crops]. The *Talmud (Taanis* 2a) describes the Divine system of watering the earth as גְּבוּרוֹת גְּשָׁמִים, *the powers of the rain.*

8. מַשְׁבִּיחַ שְׁאוֹן יַמִּים – *Who calms the roar of the seas.*

All of the commentaries are in agreement as to this translation of מַשְׁבִּיחַ, *calms.* Similarly, we read (89:10) אַתָּה מוֹשֵׁל בְּגֵאוּת הַיָּם בְּשׂוֹא גַלָּיו אַתָּה תְשַׁבְּחֵם, *You rule the proud swelling of the sea; when its waves arise, You calm them (Rashi; Ibn Ezra).*

[Ordinarily, מַשְׁבִּיחַ is translated *improves.* It is possible to find a relationship between that rendition and the translation here, for whoever aspires to better himself feels unfulfilled and unsettled. Once he achieves the desired improvement, his uneasiness is stilled.]

שְׁאוֹן גַּלֵּיהֶם – *The roar of their waves.*

Just as You control the mighty forces of the sea, so do You control the mighty nations. The nations roar and threaten Israel, yet You restrain them and redeem Israel from their midst *(Radak).*

O Trust of earth's far ends and distant seas,
7 *Who readies mountains with His strength,*
Who is girded with might,
8 *Who calms the roar of the seas,*
the roar of their waves
and the multitude of nations.
9 *Inhabitants of the furthest ends*
are frightened by Your signs,
with the appearance of morning and evening
You cause joy.
10 *You paid heed to the earth*

The roar of the seas refers to the gentile masses; *the roar of the waves* refers to their haughty rulers, who arrogantly place themselves above the common people *(Sforno).*

וַהֲמוֹן לְאֻמִּים — *And the multitude of nations.*

The translation follows *Targum* and *Ibn Ezra.*

However, *Metzudas David* and *Hirsch* render הֲמוֹן as *tumult, roar,* derived from הָמָה.

This denotes the loud sound of agitated motion created by a noisy multitude. *Ibn Ezra* observes that God is Master over both the forces of nature and the forces of mankind. Therefore, He will save Israel from famine and from foes.

Radak (v. 9) perceives this as an allusion to the exodus from Egypt: He who stilled *the roar of the seas* when He split the waters before the Children of Israel is destined to still the multitude of nations and rescue Israel from their midst.

9. וַיִּירְאוּ יֹשְׁבֵי קְצָוֹת מֵאוֹתֹתֶיךָ — *Inhabitants of the furthest ends are frightened by Your signs.*

Every day, God impresses His sovereignty upon all of mankind by displaying celestial signs which demonstrate His awesome mastery over the forces of nature. At times God employs the supernatural in order to draw man's attention to His mighty rule. After He split the sea, God caused all of mankind to recognize the miracle, as Scripture says (*Exodus* 15:14): *The nations heard and were afraid; trembling took hold of the inhabitants of Philistia.* Similarly, all men shall fear Him in the future, when He gathers in the exiles of Israel *(Radak).*

According to *Metzudas David,* אוֹתֹתֶיךָ refers to the *signs* of rumbling thunder and flashing lightning, which strike fear in all hearts [cf. *Berachos* 59a].

מוֹצָאֵי בֹקֶר וָעֶרֶב תַּרְנִין — *With the appearance of morning and evening You cause joy.*

Mankind is awed by the precise routine of the celestial luminaries: the sun rises punctually every morning *(Radak).* The undeviating schedule of daily appearances fosters a sense of security in man *(Metzudas David).* Even the luminaries themselves seem to rejoice in their routine, as Scripture says (*Job* 38:7): בְּרָן יַחַד כּוֹכְבֵי בֹקֶר, *When the morning stars together sing for joy (Radak).*

Mankind pays homage to God for creating this flawless solar system. In their morning prayer, Jews recite the benediction בָּרוּךְ ... יוֹצֵר הַמְּאוֹרוֹת, *Blessed are You... Who fashions the*

וַתְּשֹׁקְקֶהָ רַבַּת תַּעְשְׁרֶנָּה פֶּלֶג אֱלֹהִים
מָלֵא מָיִם תָּכִין דְּגָנָם כִּי־כֵן תְּכִינֶהָ:
יא תְּלָמֶיהָ רַוֵּה נַחֵת גְּדוּדֶהָ בִּרְבִיבִים
יב תְּמֹגְגֶנָּה צִמְחָהּ תְּבָרֵךְ: עִטַּרְתָּ שְׁנַת

luminaries. At night, Jews say, ...בָּרוּךְ הַמַּעֲרִיב עֲרָבִים, *Blessed are You... Who causes nightfall to descend (Rashi).*

Sforno perceives in this verse a prayer for restoration of the earth's antediluvian perfection: May it be Your will that the sun return to its original axis (which was perfectly aligned with the rotation of our planet), so that the earth will again enjoy perpetual spring.

10. פָּקַדְתָּ הָאָרֶץ וַתְּשֹׁקְקֶהָ — *You paid heed to the earth and watered her.*

Some commentaries relate וַתְּשֹׁקְקֶהָ to תַּשְׁקֶה, *You water,* explaining: Whenever You desire to benefit mankind, You water the earth with extra rains *(Rashi).*

Indeed, immediately prior to the formation of Adam (and before he sinned), You improved the soil for his sake, as Scripture states (*Genesis* 2:6), *A mist ascended from the earth and watered the whole surface of the soil (Sforno).*

Ibn Ezra explains that during David's lifetime, Israel was simultaneously endangered by two threats: The foe laid siege to their land, but God *remembered the land* and rescued the people, drought and famine plagued Israel, but God *watered her* with rain.

Others relate תְּשֹׁקְקֶהָ to תְּשׁוּקָה, *craving (Ibn Ezra).* The *Midrash (Shir HaShirim Rabbah* 7:11) comments that a woman craves only her husband, Israel craves only its Father in Heaven, and rain desires only to descend to earth.

Radak renders וַתְּשֹׁקְקֶהָ, *You cause* [the earth] *to crave,* suggesting: When You punish the nations which defy You, You hold back the rains until the parched earth craves moisture. Only then do You mercifully water the land. Similarly, Israel languishes in exile and longs to be revived by the fresh dew of redemption.

רַבַּת תַּעְשְׁרֶנָּה — *You enriched her abundantly.*

The root of this word is עָשִׁיר, *rich,* which suggests that God sends abundant rain so that the world will prosper *(Radak);* at the dawn of Creation, God cultivated the earth without any help from man, as Scripture states (*Genesis* 2:9), *And HASHEM, God, caused to grow from the ground every tree that was pleasing to the sight and good for food (Sforno).*

In explicating the significance of the word עָשִׁיר, *Shir HaShirim Rabbah* (7:11) teaches that if man is worthy, the Creator will make the land עָשִׁיר, *rich,* but if he is unworthy, the earth will produce only עֲשִׂירִי, *one tenth,* of its capacity.

פֶּלֶג אֱלֹהִים מָלֵא מָיִם — *[From] the tent of God filled with water.*

The *Talmud (Taanis* 8b) describes פֶּלֶג as a קוּבָּה, *tent,* or *compartment,* in the heavens, where אֱלֹהִים, *God,* stores the rain which eventually descends to the earth [see *Targum*].

Radak, however, identifies פֶּלֶג as the *large pool of water* formed after it rains. The word אֱלֹהִים is utilized to emphasize the extraordinary size of this body of water, which was created in such a brief time. These pools provide water for man and beast and also moisten the dry soil.

תָּכִין דְּגָנָם — *You prepare their grain.*

Even after You water the earth, You continue to assure the success of the crop by channeling favorable winds to the fields and by protecting the tender

and watered her,
You enriched her abundantly,
from the tent of God filled with water.
You prepare their grain,
for thus do You prepare it.
11 *Her ridges You water generously,*
settling in her furrows.
With showers You soften her,
her growth You bless.
12 *You crown the year of Your goodness*

shoots from pestilence and blight *(Radak).*

כִּי כֵן תְּכִינֶהָ – *For thus do You prepare it.*

According to *Radak,* this refers to the protection of the grain, as described above. Obviously, generous rains are of no value if the crop is later devastated by blight or by storms.

Sforno maintains that this statement delineates God's original master plan for mankind: You fashioned the world in a way that would release man from all mundane pursuits, because the earth was intended to produce the staples of life (grains and fruits) without the need for human exertion. This utopian existence would *prepare* mankind to concentrate exclusively on the service of God.

[Here lies the solution to the threat of famine, for when climatic and agricultural conditions prove unfavorable to human survival, this indicates that mankind had forsaken its mission (i.e., Divine service). At these times, God ceases to *prepare* the earth for humanity. When men return to the pursuit of their ordained purpose and destiny, the earth will return to its normal pattern of productivity.]

11. תְּלָמֶיהָ רַוֵּה – *Her ridges You water generously.*

The psalmist continues to recount the blessings of the water cycle.

The תְּלָמִים, *ridges,* are the mounds of dirt which are formed by plowing. God causes these rows to be watered generously by the rains *(Radak).*

נַחֵת גְּדוּדֶהָ – *Settling in her furrows.*

Radak defines גְּדוּדִים, lit. *scratches,* as *the deep furrows* between the *ridges* created by plowing. [The rainwater *settles* in the *furrows* and nourishes the seeds planted there.]

Metzudas David translates גְּדוּדֶהָ as *her bands of men,* referring to the hungry people who wander around the earth in search of food. They derive נַחַת, *satisfaction,* from the rains, which banish drought and famine from the land.

בִּרְבִיבִים תְּמֹגְגֶנָּה – *With showers You soften her.*

The heavy rains come and soften the soil, which was formerly hard and untillable *(Radak).*

צִמְחָהּ תְּבָרֵךְ – *Her growth You bless.*

After the rains of Heavenly blessing, the crops flourish, growing to heights far surpassing those that would ordinarily be expected *(Sforno).*

12. עִטַּרְתָּ שְׁנַת טוֹבָתֶךָ – *You crown the year of Your goodness.*

When You decide to prosper a year,

יג טוֹבָתֶךָ וּמַעְגָּלֶיךָ יִרְעֲפוּן דָּשֶׁן: יִרְעֲפוּ
יד נְאוֹת מִדְבָּר וְגִיל גְּבָעוֹת תַּחְגֹּרְנָה: לָבְשׁוּ
כָרִים | הַצֹּאן וַעֲמָקִים יַעַטְפוּ־בָר
יִתְרוֹעֲעוּ אַף־יָשִׁירוּ:

You send the rains, which crown it with goodness *(Rashi).*

This decision takes place on the first day of the year, *Rosh HaShanah,* when Israel crowns God as their sovereign *(Panim Yafos).*

Meiri suggests that the wealth and prosperity described in these verses is no more than an allegory, alluding to genuine success, i.e., spiritual and intellectual development. Just as the finest earth lies fallow and dormant if not blessed with Heavenly rain, the powers of the mind and soul are locked up until Divine inspiration stimulates and releases them.

וּמַעְגָּלֶיךָ יִרְעֲפוּן דָּשֶׁן — *And Your paths drip with abundance.*

When You open the channels of rain, You graciously release all of the sources of Heavenly abundance, and they flow down the *path* to earth *(Alshich).*

Radak identifies God's מַעְגָּל, *path,* as the clouds which *drip* down the rain which creates abundance on earth.

Ibn Ezra, however, maintains that מַעְגָּל refers to the countless new rivulets formed after heavy rainfall, for they testify to abundance.

It is significant, notes the *Panim Yafos,* that the letters of דָּשֶׁן are numerically equivalent to 354. The lunar year, on which the Jewish calendar is based, is composed of 355 days. On the first day *Rosh HaShanah,* God decides the degree to which He will bless the other 354 days with דָּשֶׁן, *abundance.*

13. יִרְעֲפוּ נְאוֹת מִדְבָּר — *They drip onto pastures of wilderness.*

Just as *Your paths drip abundance* onto inhabited areas for the sake of mankind, so do *they drip onto the wilderness,* to benefit the wild animals which pasture there *(Radak).*

וְגִיל גְּבָעוֹת תַּחְגֹּרְנָה — *And the hills gird themselves.*

This is symbolic: when the rains cease and drought strikes the countryside, the scorched hills seem to be shrouded in sackcloth and mourning; but when the rains revive the soil and cover it with rich produce, the hills appear to be girded with happiness *(Radak).*

14. לָבְשׁוּ כָרִים הַצֹּאן — *The meadows don sheep.*

and Your paths drip with abundance.
13 *They drip onto pastures of wilderness*
and the hills gird themselves with joy.
14 *The meadows don sheep*
and the valleys cloak themselves with fodder.
They shout for joy,
they even sing!

The translation of כָּרִים, *meadows,* follows *Rashi, Radak,* and *Ibn Ezra.* [Only in one other place in Scriptures is כַּר rendered thus; in *Isaiah* 30:23, we read יִרְעֶה מִקְנֶיךָ ... כַּר נִרְחָב, *He will graze Your cattle ... in the broad meadow.*]

The lush vegetation which grows as a result of the rains attracts countless sheep to the meadows. They graze together so densely that they cover the earth like a swathe of thick cloth.

[Throughout Scripture, כָּרִים usually means *sheep.* See 37:20, *Deuteronomy* 32:14.]

Targum [based on *Rosh HaShanah* 8a] renders: The כָּרִים, *rams, clothe* [a euphemism for impregnate] *the* צֹאן, *ewes.* The mating season takes place sometime in early spring, when the *valleys cloak themselves with fodder.*

וַעֲמָקִים יַעַטְפוּ בָר — *And the valleys cloak themselves with fodder.*

Every inch of the surface will be productive, without any empty, fallow space *(Metzudas David).*

It seems superfluous to say that the valleys will be well watered, for we have already learned that even the high hills and mountains will receive adequate rainfall. With this apparently unnecessary clause, the psalmist indicates that the valleys will not be flooded by an overabundance of rain *(Radak).*

יִתְרוֹעֲעוּ אַף יָשִׁירוּ — *They shout for joy, they even sing.*

When a dry spell snaps, famine ends and prosperity returns. Therefore, men shout and sing for joy *(Rashi; Metzudas David).*

Ibn Ezra interprets this as a continuation of the preceding symbolism: When the hillsides burst forth with vigorous new growth, they seem to *shout for joy.*

According to *Radak,* this describes the fresh winds which blow gently through the full-grown stalks of grain, producing a soft, pleasant hum which sounds like a hymn of joy.

[Similarly, when Israel returns from exile they will be rejuvenated and invigorated to sing out of sheer ecstasy.]

מזמור סו 66

David composed this psalm in the twilight of his career, when God released him from the threat of the many hostile nations which surrounded him. Relieved of his concerns about the present, David was free to dream of the Messianic future (Ibn Yachya).

The psalmist first turns to Israel's glorious past, replete with wonders and miracles. The salvation of days gone by inspires the faith that such events are destined to be repeated on an even grander scale in the future, when God grants Israel its ultimate redemption (Meiri).

Meiri *also suggests that the original version of this psalm was composed at the time of the exodus from Egypt. It foretells the splendor of the Temple, which was destined to be built by Solomon. Later, David adapted this work to the circumstances of his and future generations.*

Indeed, Sforno *observes that this psalm provides an eternal lesson in the art of supplication. David teaches the exiles to exert themselves in prayer to God and to emulate the example of their forefathers, who were granted redemption because of their unparalleled devotion in prayer.*

In light of this, we can understand why the Vilna Gaon (Maaseh Rav *194) designates this as the 'Song of the day' for the sixth day of Passover: these verses serve as a most appropriate introduction to the climactic redemption at the sea, which occurred on the seventh of Passover.*

סו
א־ד

א לַמְנַצֵּחַ שִׁיר מִזְמוֹר הָרִיעוּ לֵאלֹהִים כָּל־
ב הָאָרֶץ: זַמְּרוּ כְבוֹד־שְׁמוֹ שִׂימוּ כָבוֹד
ג תְּהִלָּתוֹ: אִמְרוּ לֵאלֹהִים מַה־נּוֹרָא
ד מַעֲשֶׂיךָ בְּרֹב עֻזְּךָ יְכַחֲשׁוּ־לְךָ אֹיְבֶיךָ: כָּל־
הָאָרֶץ | יִשְׁתַּחֲווּ לְךָ וִיזַמְּרוּ־לָךְ יְזַמְּרוּ

1. לַמְנַצֵּחַ שִׁיר מִזְמוֹר — *For the Conductor, a song with musical accompaniment.*

The psalmist begins with three musical instructions, thereby alluding to Israel's redemption from three countries: Babylon, Media, and Greece. Each of these joyous events merits its own musical composition *(Alshich).*

In addition, these three terms refer to the three Temples [where songs of praise were offered and will again be offered to God] *(Eretz HaChaim).*

הָרִיעוּ לֵאלֹהִים כָּל הָאָרֶץ — *Exult to God all the earth.*

The psalmist addresses himself to Israel: 'Conduct yourselves in a manner which will inspire love and respect in the eyes of the world. Then the nations will admire you and will shout for joy when God redeems you' *(Sforno).*

2. זַמְּרוּ כְבוֹד שְׁמוֹ — *Sing to the glory of His Name.*

When Israel is in exile, God's Name is disgraced and derided by the nations; they taunt us, 'Where is your God? Why does He not come to your aid?' Therefore, when you are redeemed make sure to proclaim God's true glory to the world! *(Radak).*

Earn the respect of the nations, for this will lead mankind to praise God for having chosen so glorious a nation as Israel *(Sforno).*

Tehillos Hashem notes that זַמְּרוּ is related to זְמוֹרָה, *branch.* It signifies, 'disperse and disseminate God's glory,' just as a tree's branches spread out far from its trunk.

שִׂימוּ כָבוֹד תְּהִלָּתוֹ — *Make that glory His fitting praise.*

Sefer HaIkkarim observes that a human king depends upon the honor and acclaim of his subjects. If he were to reject it, the mortal king would be stripped of his power and majesty.

Only the Divine King of kings embodies true glory, which is eternal and does not depend on human bondage. Therefore, שִׂימוּ, *make* God's exclusive possession of genuine כָבוֹד, *glory,* תְּהִלָּתוֹ, *His praise (Shevet M'Yisrael).*

3. אִמְרוּ לֵאלֹהִים מַה נּוֹרָא מַעֲשֶׂיךָ — *Say unto God, 'How awesome are Your works!'*

Rashi explains that since מַעֲשֶׂיךָ, *Your works,* is plural, the plural adjective נוֹרָאוֹת would normally have been employed.

The use of the singular form נוֹרָא suggests the following interpretation: The vast number of *Your works* does not detract from the significance of each individual deed, for every act You perform is נוֹרָא, *awesome,* in its own right.

According to a different interpretation, the verse can be rendered: No mortal can perceive Your Divine essence directly. Only by studying *Your works* can man hope to gain insight into Your being, which is נוֹרָא, *awesome.*[1]

1. By limiting God's praise through the diminutive singular form נוֹרָא, the psalmist teaches us a significant lesson: only part of a person's praiseworthy attributes and accomplishments should be mentioned in his presence. Here God is addressed directly (*Say unto God*); thus, אוֹמְרִים מִקְצָת שִׁבְחוֹ בְּפָנָיו, *We recite only part of His praise in His Presence.* When He is not addressed directly, this restriction does not apply, as we see in 136:1; there God is not spoken to

For the Conductor,
a song with musical accompaniment:
Exult to God all the earth!
2 *Sing to the glory of His Name,*
make that glory His fitting praise.
3 *Say unto God,*
'How awesome are Your works!'
Because of Your abundant power,
Your enemies acknowledge their lies to You.
4 *All the earth will bow to You*
and they will sing to You,
they will sing to Your Name, Selah.

בְּרֹב עֻזְּךָ יְכַחֲשׁוּ לְךָ אֹיְבֶיךָ — *Because of Your abundant power, Your enemies acknowledge their lies to You.*

When You demonstrate Your powerful control over the events of this world by causing cataclysms such as plagues of pestilence, famine, thunderstorms, and war, the wicked cringe with fear and confess the כַּחַשׁ, *lies,* and sins of which they are guilty' *(Radak).*

However, even this confession is an insincere כַּחַשׁ, *deception,* a homage motivated solely by fear. In their hearts, the wicked remain unfaithful to the Almighty *(Sforno; Rashbam).*

Their insincerity and opportunism were possible only because their humble confessions were not accompanied by the intellectual recognition of God and His sovereignty. Rather, כחשו, the wicked became gaunt and emaciated by starvation and suffering, which compelled their feigned 'confessions' *(Rashbam; Tanchuma).*

Radak renders יְכַחֲשׁוּ literally as *they deny,* to indicate that when they ultimately realize Your ability to destroy them, the nations will *deny* that they ever persecuted Israel.

According to *Shemos Rabbah* (20:10), the gentile monarchs who originally denied Hashem's sovereignty were forced to retract and *deny* their blasphemy. Pharaoh, Nebuchadnezzar, and Sennacherib mocked God before they eventually admitted to His majesty and might.

4. כָּל הָאָרֶץ יִשְׁתַּחֲווּ לְךָ וִיזַמְּרוּ לָךְ — *All the earth will bow to You and they will sing to You.*

As the prophet *Zephaniah* (3:9) foretells, *Then I will transform the nations to a pure language, that they may all call upon the Name of HASHEM to serve Him with one consent (Radak).*

This transformation will take place in two stages. First, the nations will be totally crushed by their new-found awareness of their instrinsic degradation (יִשְׁתַּחֲווּ לְךָ). Later, their bowed spirits will be lifted in song (וִיזַמְּרוּ לָךְ) when they recognize God's exalted majesty *(Norah Tehillos).*

directly and He is praised more: הוֹדוּ לַה׳ כִּי טוֹב כִּי לְעוֹלָם חַסְדּוֹ, *O give thanks to HASHEM, for He is [completely] good, for His loving-kindness endures forever (Bereishis Rabbah 32:3).*

[This is one of the common cases in Scripture where God is used as an example to teach rules of propriety that apply not to Him, but to human beings. In our case, there is no essential difference between speaking *to* God or *of* Him, since He is Omnipresent.]

ה שִׁמְךָ סֶלָה: לְכוּ וּרְאוּ מִפְעֲלוֹת אֱלֹהִים
ו נוֹרָא עֲלִילָה עַל־בְּנֵי אָדָם: הָפַךְ יָם |
לְיַבָּשָׁה בַּנָּהָר יַעַבְרוּ בְרָגֶל שָׁם נִשְׂמְחָה־
ז בּוֹ: מֹשֵׁל בִּגְבוּרָתוֹ | עוֹלָם עֵינָיו בַּגּוֹיִם
°יָרוּמוּ תִּצְפֶּינָה הַסּוֹרְרִים | אַל °ירימו לָמוֹ

יְזַמְּרוּ שִׁמְךָ סֶלָה — *They will sing to Your Name, Selah.*

The songs which previous redemptions inspired were short-lived, interrupted by destruction and exile; but the tunes composed in honor of the ultimate redemption will continue סֶלָה, *forever* [see *comm.* 3:3] *(Tehillos Hashem).*

5. לְכוּ וּרְאוּ מִפְעֲלוֹת אֱלֹהִים — *Go and see the works of God.*

[Cf. *comm.* to 46:9 לְכוּ חֲזוּ מִפְעֲלוֹת ה׳.]

These words are what all men on earth are destined to say to one another *(Radak).*

Ibn Ezra renders לְכוּ as *come to me,* as in *Isaiah* 1:18, to indicate that every man will invite his neighbor to join in the discovery of God's ways.

נוֹרָא עֲלִילָה עַל בְּנֵי אָדָם — *Awesome in deed toward mankind.*

God may do as He pleases with mankind, for His actions have no external constraints. Therefore, all men stand in awe before Him *(Radak).*

Men are also terrified by God's omniscience. Since their every action is known to Him, they tremble lest He find fault with them *(Rashi).*

Rabbeinu Bachaya relates עֲלִילָה to עִלָּה, *cause* for God Himself is the Prime Cause of all events.

Hirsch elaborates that even before the dawn of Creation, the Sovereign of the universe envisaged an ultimate goal for all worldly affairs. To realize this goal, God set into motion an awesomely complex series of interwoven causes and effects.

Throughout history, the Almighty guided and manipulated the development of events in order to reach the goals which He had originally set.

Midrash Tanchuma (Vayeshev 4) notes that the chronicle of Joseph's elevation to royal power has become a classical illustration of Divine orchestration of human affairs.

Countless, apparently unrelated incidents meshed in order to draw the entire House of Israel to Egypt, for God's original plan had ordained that the foundation of Jewish history would be set there, in the form of a cruel bondage and a miraculous redemption. Once the Divine wheels of history are set in motion, no earthly power can stand in their path.

6. הָפַךְ יָם לְיַבָּשָׁה — *He changed the sea into dry land.*

The psalmist now enumerates some of God's awesome accomplishments *(Radak).* [The splitting of the Sea of Reeds was an extraordinary miracle because it totally transformed nature.]

In addition, the entire makeup of the Egyptian nation was drastically changed at that time. Not only did the Egyptians perish on earth, but even their שַׂר לְמַעְלָה, *sovereign angel in heaven,* was slain [i.e, the nation was stripped of its spiritual essence and its unique role in the Divine scheme of universal history was altered] *(Alshich).*

בַּנָּהָר יַעַבְרוּ בְרָגֶל — *Through the river they passed on foot.*

This refers to Israel's miraculous crossing of the Jordan River *(Joshua* Chapter 3) as the Jews entered the Land of Canaan *(Targum; Radak).*

[Unlike the Sea of Reeds, the Jordan did not split open. Rather, as its waters

5 *Go and see the works of God,*
awesome in deed toward mankind.
6 *He changed the sea into dry land,*
through the river they passed on foot;
there we rejoiced in Him.
7 *He rules the world with His might,*
His eyes oversee the nations.
Let not the rebellious exalt themselves, Selah.

raced downstream they halted abruptly, their course dammed by a huge, invisible barrier, which caused the waters to pile up in a towering wall (*Joshua* 3:16) that reached a height of many miles (*Sotah* 34a). Further downstream, beneath the pillar, Israel crossed the completely dry river bed on foot.]

[Also בְרָגֶל, lit. *by foot*, alludes to the fact that the waters of the Jordan only halted after the priests, who were carrying the Ark, dipped their feet into the edge of the river (*Joshua* 3:15).]

שָׁם נִשְׂמְחָה בּוֹ — *There we rejoiced* [lit. *we will rejoice*] *in Him.*

We rejoiced when we crossed over the Jordan *(Ibn Ezra).*

Rashi, however, interprets this as a reference to the Sea of Reeds, which rejoiced at the opportunity to fulfill God's wishes by splitting.

The Children of Israel were also gladdened at the sea, for God's Name was sanctified throughout the entire world in a manner which was unmatched by the damming of the Jordan River. At the sea, Israel expressed their joy with Song (*Exodus* 15:1), whereas at the Jordan they remained silent *(Chozah David).*

Radak renders נִשְׂמְחָה literally as *we will rejoice,* to indicate that our rejoicing will occur in Messianic times, when God *with His scorching wind will shake His hand over the river and will smite it into seven streams and cause men to cross over dry-shod. And there shall be a highway for the remnant of His people that shall remain from Assyria, just as there was for Israel in the day that they came up out of the land of Egypt (Isaiah* 11:15-16).

7. מֹשֵׁל בִּגְבוּרָתוֹ עוֹלָם — *He rules the world with His might.*

The translation of עוֹלָם as *world* follows *Targum* and *Metzudas David. Sforno* adds that God alone rules the world, not the ministering angels.

However, *Ibn Ezra* and *Radak* render עוֹלָם: *forever,* to indicate that after the final redemption of Israel, God's undisputed sovereignty over the world will endure *forever.*

Tehillas Hashem interprets גְבוּרָתוֹ as a reference to God's *mighty* anger, which is aroused by Israel's transgressions: *He rules over* (or controls) *His anger forever.*

עֵינָיו בַּגּוֹיִם תִּצְפֶּינָה — *His eyes oversee the nations.*

God has always been lenient with the nations and overlooked their offenses. In the future, however, He will watch them closely and punish them strictly, in accordance with the letter of the law *(Radak; Sforno).*

When God is angered by the shortcomings of Israel, He need only turn His watchful gaze towards the gentiles. When compared with their depravity, Israel's offenses become insignificant, providing God ample justification to control His mighty anger *(Noam Megodim).*

הַסּוֹרְרִים אַל יָרוּמוּ לָמוֹ סֶלָה — *Let not the rebellious exalt themselves, Selah.*

Since God originally treated the wicked leniently, they misinterpreted

ח סֶלָה: בָּרְכוּ עַמִּים | אֱלֹהֵינוּ וְהַשְׁמִיעוּ
ט קוֹל תְּהִלָּתוֹ: הַשָּׂם נַפְשֵׁנוּ בַּחַיִּים וְלֹא־
י נָתַן לַמּוֹט רַגְלֵנוּ: כִּי־בְחַנְתָּנוּ אֱלֹהִים
יא צְרַפְתָּנוּ כִּצְרָף־כָּסֶף: הֲבֵאתָנוּ בַמְּצוּדָה
יב שַׂמְתָּ מוּעָקָה בְמָתְנֵינוּ: הִרְכַּבְתָּ אֱנוֹשׁ
לְרֹאשֵׁנוּ בָּאנוּ־בָאֵשׁ וּבַמַּיִם וַתּוֹצִיאֵנוּ

this as a sign of Divine weakness. They took advantage of His mercy and flouted the law with impunity. These rebels are destined to be vanquished *(Radak; Sforno).*

8. בָּרְכוּ עַמִּים אֱלֹהֵינוּ — *Bless our God, O Nations.*

Ibn Ezra suggests that *Nations* may refer to the Jebusites, who were under Israelite dominion and were thus obligated to obey such an exhortation, or it may refer to Israel itself [the chosen of all peoples].

Rashi and *Radak* explain this as an address to all non-Jews. When mankind realizes that the incessant persecution of the exile has failed to annihilate our nation, they should bless God for the miracles He wrought to assure our survival [i.e., they should thank God for aborting their schemes to exterminate His chosen people, for such a heinous crime would have aroused His unbridled wrath (cf. *comm.* to 117:1).]

Dorash Moshe interprets this exhortation in light of the Talmudic dictum that no proselytes will be accepted in Messianic times, for fear that the convert's professed love for God and Torah is insincere and that his true motive is the wish to share in Israel's glory (*Yevamos* 24b). According to this view, the psalmist teaches that if the nations wish to *bless our God* by joining His rank, they must do so now, while He is still אֱלֹהֵינוּ, *the Dispenser of Strict Justice,* who shows no special favor to Israel. Once He redeems Israel, conversion will no longer be possible.

9. הַשָּׂם נַפְשֵׁנוּ בַּחַיִּים — *He who set our soul in life.*

God preserved us throughout the travails of exile *(Radak)* in a manner which defies the laws of nature and of history *(Sforno).*

He *set our soul* on the righteous path which leads to eternal *life* in the hereafter *(Targum; Ibn Yachya).*

וְלֹא נָתַן לַמּוֹט רַגְלֵנוּ — *And did not allow our foot to falter.*

He reinforced our steadfast resolve to recognize no deity other than Him. He did not let us fall prey to the lure of strange gods and alien religions *(Sforno).*

10. כִּי בְחַנְתָּנוּ אֱלֹהִים — *For You examined us, O God.*

[Exile is the ultimate test of our loyalty to God. The pressure of this precarious, abnormal existence on alien, hostile soil has tested every fiber of our faith.]

We have passed this Divine examination, and our loyalty is clearly above reproach *(Sforno).*

צְרַפְתָּנוּ כִּצְרָף כָּסֶף — *You refined us as if refining silver.*

Our exile has functioned as a crucible, enabling You to eliminate the undesirable dross from our midst. Many heretic, apostate, and defiant sinners have perished and disappeared from our ranks *(Sforno).*

Those who remain have been refined by the process of repentance [which was spurred by the dangers of the exile] *(Rashi).*

[8] *Bless our God, O Nations,*
let the sound of His praise be heard.
[9] *He who set our soul in life*
and did not allow our foot to falter.
[10] *For You examined us, O God,*
You refined us as if refining silver.
[11] *You installed us in the cage,*
You placed constraint upon our loins,
[12] *You mounted a mortal over our heads;*
we entered fire and water

11. הֲבֵאתָנוּ בַמְּצוּדָה — *You installed us in the cage.*

You trapped us in a cramped prison *(Rashi)* so well fortified that only a miracle could permit us to escape from its confines *(Radak; Ibn Yachya).*

[The impregnable nature of th's prison explains why the term מְצוּדָה, which really means *fortress* (see 18:3), is used to describe it.]

Hirsch observes that the existence which the exiled Jew has endured in his ghetto resembles that of a man enclosed in a cage in two respects:

First, the Jew has been barred from normal contact and relations with the outside world; second, the Jew has been a defenseless target, vulnerable to attacks from all sides. This unique test has revealed Israel's inherent moral nobility, from which there have been remarkably few defections throughout the millenia of our persecution. The salient fact of Israel's history is not the number of its defectors, but the inspiring steadfastness with which it has remained loyal to its mission.

שַׂמְתָּ מוּעָקָה בְמָתְנֵינוּ — *You placed constraint upon our loins.*

The root עָקָה means *painful oppression* (see 55:4) which restrains free movement *(Rashi; Ibn Ezra).*

The gentiles arbitrarily exercise their unlimited authority to restrict our privileges. We are constrained from actions which are permitted to all other citizens *(Hirsch).*

12. הִרְכַּבְתָּ אֱנוֹשׁ לְרֹאשֵׁנוּ — *You mounted a mortal over our heads.*

Prior to our exile, no frail mortal ruled us and we looked to You alone as our Sovereign *(Radak);* but in exile we are subject to the whim of the lowest of men, the scum of the earth *(Sforno).* Thus the prophet *Isaiah* (26:13) laments, *Other lords besides You have sovereignty over us.*

בָּאנוּ בָאֵשׁ וּבַמַּיִם — *We entered fire and water.*

Our suffering may be compared to fire, which consumes an object, and water, which drowns it. The tragedies of the exile should have overwhelmed us and obliterated our name; yet, with Your aid, we have survived *(Radak).*

R' Avraham Azulai notes that the psalmist likens adversity to fire and water, which are both vehicles of ritual purification [see *Numbers* 31:23], for *golus* has had the same cleansing effect on the spirit of the Jewish people.

The *Talmud (Megillah* 11a) teaches that the Babylonian Exile under the dominion of Nebuchadnezzar is signified by *fire* [because this tyrant intimidated Israel with the threat of death in a furnace]. The Egyptian exile under

יג לָרְוָיָה: אָבוֹא בֵיתְךָ בְעוֹלוֹת אֲשַׁלֵּם לְךָ
יד נְדָרָי: אֲשֶׁר־פָּצוּ שְׂפָתָי וְדִבֶּר־פִּי בַּצַּר־
טו לִי: עֹלוֹת מֵחִים אַעֲלֶה־לָּךְ עִם־קְטֹרֶת
אֵילִים אֶעֱשֶׂה בָקָר עִם־עַתּוּדִים סֶלָה:
טז לְכוּ־שִׁמְעוּ וַאֲסַפְּרָה כָּל־יִרְאֵי אֱלֹהִים

the rule of Pharoah is connoted by *water* [since Pharoah attempted to drown all male infants in the Nile].[1]

וַתּוֹצִיאֵנוּ לָרְוָיָה — *And You withdrew us to abundance.*

[See *comm.* to 23:5, כּוֹסִי רְוָיָה, *my cup overflows.*] When God provides salvation, He does not merely bestow a meager measure of sustenance upon His beneficiaries. Rather, He generously provides them with more than they need or deserve.

13. אָבוֹא בֵיתְךָ בְעוֹלוֹת — *I shall enter Your house with burnt offerings.*

The psalmist now speaks in the singular, as the collective voice of the exiles who pledge to fulfill the vows they took in *golus.* This will be accomplished when God rebuilds His house, the Temple *(Radak).*

These future sacrifices will represent thanksgiving. Rather than complain about our exile, we will express our appreciation for the purifying effect which *golus* has had on our souls *(Norah Tehillos).*

אֲשַׁלֵּם לְךָ נְדָרָי — *I shall pay You my vows.*

The *Talmud (Chagigah* 7a) observes that in *Proverbs* (25:17), King Solomon discourages frequent visits to the *Beis HaMikdash,* saying, *Let your foot be seldom in your neighbor's house, lest he be sated with you and hate you,* whereas here David seems eager to bring offerings constantly.

The *Talmud* explains that Solomon was referring to sin and guilt offerings. It is certainly preferable that no offenses be committed, making such sacrifices rare. However, David was eager to dedicate voluntary burnt offerings and peace offerings, which are a desirable display of intense love for God.

14. אֲשֶׁר פָּצוּ שְׂפָתָי — *Which my lips uttered* [lit. *opened (Targum)*].

This refers to extraordinary pledges prompted by situations of great distress, as exemplified by Yiftach, who said (*Judges* 11:35) of the vow he took when entering battle, וְאָנֹכִי פָּצִיתִי פִי, *for I have opened my mouth (Ibn Ezra; Hirsch).*

The duress of exile prompts Israel to utter vows of equal gravity [for *golus,* too, is a continuous battle] *(Radak).*

15. עֹלוֹת מֵחִים אַעֲלֶה לָּךְ — *Burnt offerings of fat animals I shall offer up to You.*

Rashi and Radak indentify מֵחִים as a cognate of מוֹחַ, *bone marrow,* the vital substance which symbolizes robust health and corpulence.

Vayikra Rabbah relates מֵחִים to מָחָה, *wipe out,* teaching that this verse may

1. The *Talmud* teaches that if misfortune drives a desperate man to lower himself before another person when requesting charity, this humiliation is considered as painful as death by *fire and water* together (*Berachos* 6b).

Furthermore, the Sages (*Bava Metziah* 75a) perceived that even the man who is forced to swallow his pride by soliciting a loan is extremely sensitive because of the damage done to his self-respect. Therefore, if the creditor knows that the debtor does not yet possess the means to repay the loan, he may not even pass in front of him, lest the debtor interpret this as a hint that payment of the debt is due, for this will cause the debtor anguish which equals the suffering inflicted by *fire and water.*

and You withdrew us to abundance.
13 *I shall enter Your house with burnt offerings,*
I shall pay You my vows,
14 *Which my lips uttered,*
and my mouth spoke in my distress.
15 *Burnt offerings of fat animals*
I shall offer up to You,
With the burning of rams,
I will prepare bullocks with goats, Selah.
16 *Go and hearken, all you who fear God,*
and I will relate what He did for my soul.

be illustrated by the example of the king who was served a sumptuous repast. The monarch was so delighted by the very first course that he 'wiped his plate clean.' [Similarly, the supplicant prays that the intense devotion which accompanies his עוֹלָה should render it exceedingly desirable to God. If the holy fires of the altar quickly consume every fragment of the animal's flesh, this will indicate Divine pleasure and acceptance of the supplicant's offering.]

עִם קְטֹרֶת אֵילִים – *With the burning of rams.*

The translation follows *Radak* and *Metzudas David*, who interpret this as a reference to the הַקְטָרַת הַחֲלָבִים, *the burning of the fat*, of the ram offering.

However, *Targum* understands these words to denote two separate offerings: קְטֹרֶת, *burnt incense*, and אֵלִים, *rams*.

Tanchuma (Tetzavah 15) states that David yearned to emulate the deeds of the נְשִׂיאִים, *princes*, of the twelve tribes, who offered incense as the first part of their special sacrifice at the dedication of the Tabernacle (*Numbers* Chap. 7).

אֶעֱשֶׂה בָקָר עִם עַתּוּדִים סֶלָה – *I will prepare* [lit. *make*] *bullocks with goats, Selah.*

This phrase supports the opinion (see *Tanchuma* above) that David was patterning his offering after the offering of the נְשִׂיאִים, *princes*, of the twelve tribes; for these were the only individuals who brought such a vast variety of offerings, including bullocks, goats, rams [and incense] (*Vayikra Rabbah* 88:3).

16. לְכוּ שִׁמְעוּ ... כָּל יִרְאֵי אֱלֹהִים – *Go and hearken, all you who fear God.*

Each and every God-fearing man will exhort his comrade with this advice (*Radak*).

Rashi identifies the יִרְאֵי אֱלֹהִים as the sincere proselytes who converted to the Jewish faith. [See *Rashi* to 115:13.]

[In verse 5, the psalmist declared לְכוּ וּרְאוּ מִפְעֲלוֹת אֱלֹהִים, *Go and see the works of God*. That declaration served as an introduction for an overview of Jewish history (*vs.* 6-12) as it is visible to the mortal eye of בְּנֵי אָדָם, *the sons of man*.

Now, however, the psalmist delves even deeper and calls upon the truly God-fearing to *hearken*, i.e., to understand *(Sforno)* what effect the Almighty's guidance of history has had on the development of the Jewish soul (לְנַפְשִׁי).]

וַאֲסַפְּרָה ... אֲשֶׁר עָשָׂה לְנַפְשִׁי – *And I will relate what He did for my soul.*

The order of this verse is interrupted. According to *Sforno*, this interruption indicates that this deeply significant

יז אֲשֶׁר עָשָׂה לְנַפְשִׁי: אֵלָיו פִּי־קָרָאתִי
יח וְרוֹמַם תַּחַת לְשׁוֹנִי: אָוֶן אִם־רָאִיתִי
יט בְלִבִּי לֹא יִשְׁמַע | אֲדֹנָי: אָכֵן שָׁמַע אֱלֹהִים
כ הִקְשִׁיב בְּקוֹל תְּפִלָּתִי: בָּרוּךְ אֱלֹהִים
אֲשֶׁר לֹא־הֵסִיר תְּפִלָּתִי וְחַסְדּוֹ מֵאִתִּי:

message must be repeated: First *I will relate* to all of Israel and then I will emphasize to *all who fear God* exactly *what He has done* to develop the boundless spiritual resources of *my soul.*

17. אֵלָיו פִּי קָרָאתִי – *Unto Him (with) my mouth I called.*

Ibn Ezra notes that the grammatically proper reading would have been בְּפִי, *with my mouth.*

Binah L'ittim explains that David loved God with such intensity and selfless devotion that he feared lest he use his most precious organ, his mouth, improperly. Therefore, he dedicated his entire power of speech to the Almighty and begged Him to choose the proper words of prayer and praise. Thus, this clause should be understood as follows: אֵלָיו פִּי, *Unto Him* [is consecrated] *my mouth,* [therefore, the prayers which God composed] קָרָאתִי, *I called out.*

וְרוֹמַם תַּחַת לְשׁוֹנִי – *And He was extolled by* [lit. *beneath*] *my tongue.*

Throughout the duration of the exile, we never ceased to call out to God in supplication, and we extolled His majesty [without pause] *(Rashi).*

Our translation renders רוֹמַם as a verb: *I extolled Him,* thus He was מְרוֹמָם, *extolled,* תַּחַת לְשׁוֹנִי, *by my tongue (Rashi; Radak).*

Literally, תַּחַת לְשׁוֹנִי means *beneath* my tongue, alluding to the heart, which fashions words and provides the intellectual support *beneath* verbal statements *(Radak).* In addition, hidden deep *beneath my heart* are splendid ideas for extolling God, but these sublime insights cannot be articulated *(Ibn Ezra).*

Noam Elimelech stresses David's selflessness. Even when *unto Him I called,* requesting my personal needs, the underlying motive *beneath my tongue* was to have the opportunity וְרוֹמַם, *to extol* God for my success. No matter how desperate my situation, I always addressed God in a low, calm voice, whispering and suppressing the words *beneath my tongue,* for I firmly believe that God is Omnipresent and draws near to the prayers of every supplicant. The Sages (*Berachos* 24b) said that someone who raises his voice in prayer resembles the false prophets [who screamed and ranted to their deaf idols] *(Beis Elokim).*

18. אָוֶן אִם רָאִיתִי בְלִבִּי – *If I perceived iniquity in my heart.*

[I know that it is impossible for thoughts of iniquity to be harbored in my heart, for it is filled only with love for the Almighty; its bursts with extolment which defies expression (*v.* 17).]

לֹא יִשְׁמַע אֲדֹנָי – *My Lord would not have listened.*

Even if a sinful thought stole into my heart, God graciously overlooked it and ignored it *(Rashi; Radak).*

From this the Sages of the *Talmud* (*Kiddushin* 40a) derived the important principle that מַחֲשָׁבָה רָעָה אֵין הקב״ה מְצַרְפָהּ לְמַעֲשֶׂה, *The Holy One, Blessed be He, does not consider an evil thought to be an evil deed.* He pardons the iniquitous thought as long as it does not result in an evil deed. However, when it does lead to sin, then the offender is punished for both his forbidden action and his sinful thought.

The *Shaloh Hakodosh* maintains that

17 *Unto Him with my mouth I called*
and He was extolled by my tongue.
18 *If I perceived iniquity in my heart,*
my Lord would not have listened.
19 *In truth, God has heard,*
He has hearkened to the sound of my prayer.
20 *Blessed be God, Who has not withdrawn*
my prayer or His loving-kindness from me.

this amnesty applies only to adventitious thoughts of sin; but if a person deliberately concentrates his mental capabilites upon iniquitous machinations, then his sinful scheming cannot be condoned by God. The Rabbis (*Yoma* 29a) condemned this serious offense in the dictum: הִרְהוּרֵי עֲבֵירָה קָשִׁים מֵעֲבֵירָה, *The thought of sin is more pernicious than sin itself.*

[This is because thought affects the intellect, which is the enduring essence of man, whereas a physical deed may affect only the body, which is merely man's temporary shell. When sin is etched into the mind, eternal damage may result.][1]

19. אָכֵן שָׁמַע אֱלֹהִים – *In truth* [*Targum* בְּקוּשְׁטָא; see *Exodus* 2:14] *God has heard.*

His favorable response to my petition attests to the *truth* and sincerity of my plea. For, although God would pardon *the iniquity in my heart (v.* 18), such improper thoughts would taint the purity of my supplication and render it unacceptable *(Ibn Ezra).*

As the psalmist declares (145:18), קָרוֹב ה׳ לְכָל קֹרְאָיו לְכֹל אֲשֶׁר יִקְרָאֻהוּ בֶאֱמֶת, *HASHEM is close to all who call upon Him, to all who call upon Him sincerely (Rashbam).*

הִקְשִׁיב בְּקוֹל תְּפִלָּתִי – *He has hearkened to the sound of my prayer.*

My anguish and the desperation of my plight were not sufficient cause to enlist the aid of God. What aroused Him was the ring of truth – the sincere קוֹל, *sound,* of my prayers. Thus, even judging me strictly in His role as אֱלֹהִים, *the Dispenser of Strict Justice,* He deemed me truly worthy of His salvation *(Norah Tehillos).*

20. בָּרוּךְ אֱלֹהִים – *Blessed be God.*

[He is blessed not only when merciful, but even when He acts as אֱלֹהִים, *the Dispenser of Strict Justice.*]

אֲשֶׁר לֹא הֵסִיר תְּפִלָּתִי וְחַסְדּוֹ מֵאִתִּי – *Who has not withdrawn my prayer or His kindness from me.*

Even while אֱלֹהִים afflicted me and my heart grew faint from agony, He continued to lift my spirits and inspired *my prayer (Kli Chemdah).*

This inspiration was the unique *loving-kindness* which God displayed to me *(Ibn Ezra).*

The *Talmud (Berachos* 5a) teaches that sometimes God ordains that pious men of extraordinary devotion undergo suffering and tribulations known as יִסּוּרִים שֶׁל אַהֲבָה, *afflictions of* [Divine] *love.* This suffering is not sent as a

1. The *Talmud* qualifies this rule, which grants pardon for casual thoughts of iniquity: (1) It only applies to a God-fearing Jew whose soul is basically good. Thus, if he even considers doing a *mitzvah,* he is rewarded as if he actually accomplished that good deed. Evil, however, is completely alien to the Jewish soul; therefore, adventitious sinful thoughts can be disregarded.

On the other hand, the evil thoughts of an idolater, whose soul is corrupted, *are punished;*

punishment or as atonement for past sins (for its recipients are righteous men), but as an opportunity to increase future reward. When the devout accept their afflictions with joy and praise of the Divine Will which ordained them, their merits increase in direct proportion to the severity with which their faith in God has been tested.

These *afflictions of* [Divine] *love* can be distinguished from the afflictions of Divine punishment in that the former do not interfere with the afflicted man's pursuit of Torah study or with his prayer, for this verse says, *Blessed be ELOHIM* [for His strict judgment] *Who has not allowed my prayer* [which tells of] *His loving-kindness to depart from me.*

The psalmist concludes on a hopeful note: When all of Israel witnesses the many acts of kindness which God performed for me, they will gain confidence in God's determination to redeem them from the long exile *(Metzudas David).*

since these evil thoughts reflect the idolater's true nature, they cannot be overlooked by God. However, the idolater's occasional noble impulses and good intentions are not rewarded until they result in meritorious conduct, and the thought is authenticated by concrete action.
(2) If a Jew becomes so perverted that he starts to think of serving idols, then these thoughts cannot be dismissed casually and are accorded the status of an actual deed.
(3) If a Jew sins once and then repeats the sin once again, הוּתְּרָה לוֹ, it becomes permissible to him, in the sense that his conscience no longer recoils from this offense, but begins to tolerate it. Lacking restraint, even a casual impulse to sin will lead to actual transgression; therefore, the thought itself is deemed a sin.

Panim Yafos observes that the psalmist alludes to this by adopting the singular form, אָוֶן, *iniquity,* saying, *Had I perceived iniquity in my heart,* for if a person sins only once, then iniquity is not detected in his heart, but after the sin is repeated, iniquity does become apparent.

מזמור סז 67

The Holy One, Blessed be He, revealed this extraordinary psalm to Moses and later to David. Both men were granted a holy vision, in which this psalm was engraved on a sheet of the purest gold, which was fashioned in the shape of a seven-branched candelabrum (menorah).

David duplicated this psalm in its menorah *design and etched it onto his shield, so that he could study its teachings before entering into battle; this meritorious conduct assured David's victory (*Chida, Midbar Kedeimos מערכת ד׳ אות כ״א. Chida *notes that he copied this statement from the original manuscript of* Rabbi Shlomo Luria, *the* Maharshal). *A diagram of the psalm in its traditional* menorah *form appears in an appendix at the end of this volume.*

Avodas HaKodesh *says that whoever concentrates daily on this* menorah *and its message is considered as if he actually kindled the* menorah *in the* Beis HaMikdash; *such a person is surely destined to inherit the World to Come. Whoever recites it while concentrating on its* menorah *design will surely be safeguarded from all evil and enjoy great success.*

It is customary to recite this psalm before Sefiras HaOmer *on the forty-nine days between Passover and Shavuos (*Alshich; Akeidas Yitzchak; Kesef Mezukak*).*

In addition, many congregations chant this psalm with a special tune immediately preceding the evening prayer at the conclusion of the Sabbath.

סז א־ב **לַמְנַצֵּחַ בִּנְגִינֹת מִזְמוֹר שִׁיר: אֱלֹהִים**
א־ד **יְחָנֵּנוּ וִיבָרְכֵנוּ יָאֵר פָּנָיו אִתָּנוּ סֶלָה:**
ג **לָדַעַת בָּאָרֶץ דַּרְכֶּךָ בְּכָל־גּוֹיִם יְשׁוּעָתֶךָ:**
ד **יוֹדוּךָ עַמִּים | אֱלֹהִים יוֹדוּךָ עַמִּים כֻּלָּם:**

1. לַמְנַצֵּחַ בִּנְגִינֹת מִזְמוֹר שִׁיר — *For the Conductor, upon* Neginos, *a song with musical accompaniment.*

Alshich emphasizes that this psalm has a universal message. The four musical instructions of this introductory verse correspond to the four realms (mineral, vegetable, animal and human) which make up the world; all four kingdoms were in a state of imperfection until the Torah was given at Sinai.

The following seven verses, which make up the body of this psalm, contain forty-nine words, corresponding to the seven weeks (49 days) which precede the giving of the Torah on Shavuos. On each of these days, Israel entered another one of 'the forty-nine gates of wisdom' *(Yosef Tehillos).*

The seven verses also allude to the seven branches of the menorah, which are the source of intellectual illumination for Israel.

This psalm describes the bounteous blessings and the redemption which await the children of Israel if they dedicate themselves to cultivating the rich spiritual and intellectual heritage contained in the Torah.

2. אֱלֹהִים יְחָנֵּנוּ וִיבָרְכֵנוּ — *May God favor us and bless us.*

Radak interprets this as a special request made by the Jews in exile: [Since our fortunes steadily decline] may God increase His blessings for us every day!

Sforno adds: *Favor us* although we are undeserving; bless us with fertility, for the terrible persecutions of *galus* have decimated our ranks.

Hirsch explains that חָנַן refers to the granting of intellectual abilities, as in the first request in the daily silent prayer, the *Shemoneh Esrei,* which begins אַתָּה חוֹנֵן לְאָדָם דַּעַת, *It is You Who favor man with wisdom.* [Even during the harsh exile, when so many basic needs are unmet, intellectual advancement always remains the prime concern of the Jewish people.]

Rashbam observes that this request reflects the style of the priestly blessing: יְבָרֶכְךָ ה׳, *May HASHEM bless you;* וִיחֻנֶּךָּ, *And show you favor (Numbers* 6:24, 25).

יָאֵר פָּנָיו אִתָּנוּ סֶלָה — *May He display His luminous countenance with us, Selah.*

May He grant us success in all of our endeavors *(Radak).*

May He illuminate our minds so that we may perceive the wondrous lessons of the Torah *(Sforno).*

May we forever be a reflection of the Divine intellect, and thus display the צֶלֶם אֱלֹהִים, *the image of God,* which makes man capable of knowing God's will and endowing his physical existence with Divine holiness *(Tehillos Hashem).*

Rashbam observes that this wish alludes to the priestly benediction *(Numbers* 6:25) יָאֵר ה׳ פָּנָיו אֵלֶיךָ, *May HASHEM shine His face towards you.*

3. לָדַעַת בָּאָרֶץ דַּרְכֶּךָ — *To make known Your way on earth.*

We ask for intellectual enlightenment so that we may be equipped to spread Your teachings throughout the world. We yearn to guide mankind toward an appreciation of *Your way,* which refers to Your beneficence *(Rashi; Sforno).*

Mankind is baffled by the seemingly chaotic development of human affairs. If You will shine Your countenance upon Israel, this will demonstrate to all men that You do in fact guide world events upon a well defined path towards a clear-cut goal. Then mankind

For the Conductor, upon Neginos
a song with musical accompaniment.
2 May God favor us
and bless us,
May He display His luminous countenance
with us, Selah.
3 To make known Your way on earth,
among all the peoples Your salvation.
4 Then nations will acknowledge You,
O God,
The nations will acknowledge You —
all of them.

will come to recognize דַּרְכֶּךָ, *Your way,* in all affairs בָּאָרֶץ, *on earth (Hirsch).*

Hirsch notes that God's *way* is a dual concept, for it includes both the manner in which God guides world events and the pattern of conduct which God has directed man to follow. By shining His countenance upon the Jewish nation, God will make known both facets of His *way:* Mankind will recognize that human history is guided along Divinely designed paths towards the fulfillment of Divinely ordained goals; the blessings with which God favors the Jewish people will also lead mankind to adhere to the pattern of human conduct prescribed by God's Law and exemplified by the Jews.

This will fulfill the prophecy (*Isaiah* 11:9): *The earth shall be full of the knowledge of HASHEM, as the waters cover the sea (Radak).*

בְּכָל גּוֹיִם יְשׁוּעָתֶךָ — *Among all the peoples Your salvation.*

God's interest is not confined to Israel; He is also concerned with the welfare and salvation of the other peoples. One purpose of Israel's exile and dispersion was to expose all of the nations to the Torah's teachings, so that they might have an opportunity to accept the truth and be saved. The Sages (*Pesachim* 87b) taught that the Holy One, Blessed be He, exiled Israel among the nations in order to add proselytes to the Jewish people *(Shaarei Chaim).*

4. יוֹדוּךָ עַמִּים אֱלֹהִים — [*The*] *nations will acknowledge You, O God.*

Gradually, Israel's benign influence will spread the Divine teachings amongst the nations, until every nation will acknowledge God and pay Him homage *(Hirsch).*[1]

1. *Rav Yosef Engel (Droshos Otzros Yosef* 8) demonstrates that the purpose of the *mitzvah* of סְפִירַת הָעוֹמֶר, *counting the Omer,* is to foster a heightened appreciation of God and of one's fellow man. The climax of this awareness is on the thirty-third day, *Lag B'Omer.*

The *Omer* period is designated as a time of mourning for the twenty-four thousand disciples of R' Akiva who died at this time; they suffered this punishment because they neither respected nor appreciated each other properly *(Yevamoos* 62b).

The plague which struck them ceased on the thirty-third day because it was then that they finally absorbed the lesson of the *Omer* and increased their appreciation for God and man.

The psalmist alludes to this here, because אֱלֹהִים is the thirty-third word in this composition of forty-nine words. It marks the climax: יוֹדוּךָ עַמִּים אֱלֹהִים, *The nations will acknowledge You, O God.*

סז ה־ח

ה יִשְׂמְחוּ וִירַנְּנוּ לְאֻמִּים כִּי־תִשְׁפֹּט עַמִּים
מִישֹׁר וּלְאֻמִּים | בָּאָרֶץ תַּנְחֵם סֶלָה:
ו יוֹדוּךָ עַמִּים | אֱלֹהִים יוֹדוּךָ עַמִּים כֻּלָּם:
ז אֶרֶץ נָתְנָה יְבוּלָהּ יְבָרְכֵנוּ אֱלֹהִים
ח אֱלֹהֵינוּ: יְבָרְכֵנוּ אֱלֹהִים וְיִירְאוּ אוֹתוֹ
כָּל־אַפְסֵי־אָרֶץ:

יוֹדוּךָ עַמִּים כֻּלָּם — *The nations acknowledge You—all of them.*

Ultimately, the message of God will penetrate every corner of the land and all nations will worship Him *(Hirsch).*

5. יִשְׂמְחוּ וִירַנְּנוּ לְאֻמִּים — *Nations will be glad and sing for joy.*

עַם and לְאוֹם both mean *nation.* לְאוֹם refers to the *state* which governs a people and represents to the outside world the particular striving of that people. So long as nations are selfish and acquisitive, their outside stance, their nationalistic posture, will reflect selfishness; but ultimately, all national governments will discard their present policy of selfish isolation and recognize that the welfare of all men depends on the establishment of a harmonious community of nonaggressive nations joyously united in the worship of God.

עַם is *a unified national community,* separate from all other nations. International dissension and animosity are inevitable, so long as each nation seeks only its own welfare *(Hirsch).*

Kli Chemdah comments that the tolerant לְאֻמִּים, *states,* respected the exiles of Israel as their equals; they regarded them as representatives of a worthy fellow nation, rather than as despised foreigners. Since these states with their enlightened goals of world unity and mutual respect are compatible with Israel's Messianic aspirations, they will rejoice upon the advent of the Redeemer.

כִּי תִשְׁפֹּט עַמִּים מִישֹׁר — *Because You will judge the nations with fairness.*

[Each individual עַם, *national community,* considers itself superior and refuses to treat Israel as its equal. They are destined to undergo Divine judgment for their failure to ensure מִישֹׁר, *fairness, equity.*]

וּלְאֻמִּים בָּאָרֶץ תַּנְחֵם סֶלָה — *And the nations on earth You will guide, Selah.*

[In this world, the לְאֻמִּים, *states,* strive to achieve מִישֹׁר, *equity* and *fairness,* as a means toward the creation of a stable world balance of power. They seek to create an international order whose benefits would exceed the advantages experienced by the self-seeking, uncooperative עַמִּים, *national communities.* Although their motives are to further their own ends rather than to serve God, they nevertheless move in the direction of establishing a moral, ethical order; for that they deserve to be rewarded. The *states* will receive their reward when God openly guides human affairs to the establishment of an eternal human brotherhood which recognizes no borders or nationalities.]

6. יוֹדוּךָ עַמִּים אֱלֹהִים — *[Then] nations will acknowledge You, O God.*

This is a repetition of verse 4. According to *Sforno* and *Rashbam,* verse 4 introduces verse 5, signifying that the nations will given thanks when You judge them with fairness [and restore the harmony of the social order]. Verse 6 introduces verse 7, indicating *the nations will acknowledge* [i.e., give thanks] — when *the earth has yielded its produce* [and the earth's original agricultural abundance is restored].

According to *Hirsch,* the use of the word *Selah* to conclude verses 2, 5, and

5 *Nations will be glad*
and sing for joy
Because You will judge the nations
with fairness,
And the nations on earth
You will guide, Selah.
6 *Then nations will acknowledge You,*
O God,
The nations will acknowledge You —
all of them.
7 *The earth has yielded its produce,*
may God, our own God, bless us.
8 *May God bless us*
and may all the ends of the earth fear Him.

8 indicates that the psalm is divided into three parts. They correspond to the three distinct phases in which mankind will fulfill its ultimate Divinely ordained mission. First (*vs.* 1-2), only the Jewish people will come to recognize and to obey God's will. Second (*vs.* 3-5), the leaders of all the nations will submit to God's authority and worship Him. Third and finally (verses 6-8), all people will learn to worship God directly; at this point, their national leaders will become superfluous and give up their positions of privilege and power.

As *Hirsch* explains the repetition of this verse, the general populace will be initially incapable of recognizing God's majesty and His Law on their own. Only under the guidance and influence of their intelligent leaders will they develop sufficient insight to offer thanks to God and to serve Him.

Later, when the recognition of God's sovereignty spreads worldwide, all men will submit to God and render homage to Him without any intermediary. Then the newly enlightened *nations* (i.e., the general populace) *will acknowledge* God of their own accord, without requiring their leaders' example and instructions.

7. אֶרֶץ נָתְנָה יְבוּלָהּ — *The earth has yielded its produce.*

[The political renaissance of the future will be accompanied by an agricultural rebirth, for the world's spiritual development will pervade the earth and affect the soil. The *Talmud* (*Sanhedrin* 98a) notes that the advent of Redemption will be heralded by agricultural changes: *You mountains of Israel shall sprout forth your branches and yield your fruit to my people Israel, for they are at hand to arrive (Ezekiel* 36:8).]

Radak explains that prior to the Redemption, sin will pollute the atmosphere and disturb the balance of the water cycle. God warned Israel not to stray after false gods, for the result would be וְעָצַר אֶת הַשָּׁמַיִם וְלֹא יִהְיֶה מָטָר וְהָאֲדָמָה לֹא תִתֵּן אֶת יְבוּלָהּ, *He will hold back the heavens and there will be no rain, and the earth will not give forth its produce (Deuteronomy* 11:17).

In the future, however, the earth will yield its bounty effortlessly without any human cultivation or labor. Moreover, it will produce a finished product, not merely the raw, unprocessed crop. The Sages say (*Kesubos* 111b) that the trees are destined to grow baked loaves of the finest flour *(Tehillos Hashem).*

יְבָרְכֵנוּ אֱלֹהִים אֱלֹהֵינוּ — *May God, our own God, bless us.*

It is in the power of Israel to transform אֱלֹהִים, the Divine Name which denotes God's sovereignty over all the nations, into their personal deity, אֱלֹהֵינוּ, *our God,* who attends to their needs with special concern. Israel turns to God with unreserved devotion. He reciprocates by vouchsafing His uniquely paternal Providence to the Jewish people *(Kedushas Levi).*

8. **יְבָרְכֵנוּ אֱלֹהִים** — *May God bless us.*

After the Redemption, the nation of Israel will spread throughout the earth, as God had promised the Patriarch Jacob (*Genesis* 28:14): וְהָיָה זַרְעֲךָ כַּעֲפַר הָאָרֶץ וּפָרַצְתָּ יָמָּה וָקֵדְמָה וְצָפֹנָה וָנֶגְבָּה, *And your seed shall be like the dust of the earth and shall spread abroad to the west and to the east and to the north and to the south (Sforno).*

וְיִירְאוּ אוֹתוֹ כָּל אַפְסֵי אָרֶץ — *And may all the ends of the earth fear Him.*

Even the most remote civilizations, isolated at the ends of the earth, are destined to recognize God's glory *(Ibn Ezra).*

When the nations witness the splendid fortunes of Israel after the Redemption, they will be imbued with awe before the Almighty for they will reason that God favored the Jewish people only because of their God-fearing behavior. The nations will conclude that they should follow Israel's example; thus, they will join Israel in rendering homage to God *(Rashi).*

מזמור סח 68

The theme of this composition is the Revelation at Sinai, which the psalmist describes with unsurpassed eloquence and ecstasy. This Revelation at Sinai affected the whole world; it was a cataclysmic event, an upheaval second only to the Creation in its colossal proportions.

From this traumatic transformation, Israel emerged as the Chosen People, a nation rising heavenward in obedience to the Divine summons; and as this one nation ascended, the seventy alien societies fell, eternally estranged, for they had rejected God's invitation to join His ranks.

As God drew closer to Israel, the nations recoiled further from the Jewish people; each fresh outpouring of Divine love for the sacred nation was met with a new wave of bitter hatred from the gentiles. The Talmud *explains* (Shabbos *89b) that Mount Sinai (סִינַי) received this name because it is the source of the nations' hatred (שִׂנְאָה) for the Jews. It also was called Chorev (חוֹרֵב), the* Talmud *continues, because from this mountain, devastation (חוּרְבָּן), descended upon the nations. Therefore, the opening verses of this psalm describe the gentiles' many attempts to surround and destroy Israel.*

The Gaon *of* Vilna (Maaseh Rav *196) designates this as the Song of the Day for the second day of Shavuos, which is the festival commemorating the Sinaitic Revelation.*

סח א־ב לַמְנַצֵּחַ לְדָוִד מִזְמוֹר שִׁיר: יָקוּם אֱלֹהִים
א־ג יָפוּצוּ אוֹיְבָיו וְיָנוּסוּ מְשַׂנְאָיו מִפָּנָיו:
ג כְּהִנְדֹּף עָשָׁן תִּנְדֹּף כְּהִמֵּס דּוֹנַג מִפְּנֵי־אֵשׁ

1. לַמְנַצֵּחַ — *For the Conductor.*

Literally, this word may also be rendered: *To Him who causes victory* [see *comm.* 4:1]. The opening verses of this psalm are a plea for victory over the nations who assault and threaten Israel [see *Prefatory Remarks*].

Dorash Moshe points out that the first two letters of this word, ל, *lamed* and מ, *mem*, together have a numerical value of 70, indicating that the psalmist prays to be נָצֵח, *victorious* over the seventy gentile nations of the world.

Rashi identifies Amalek as the specific foe here. [Amalek, a vicious, godless enemy, was the first nation to attack Israel as the Jews were journeying towards Sinai to accept the Torah.]

Ibn Yachya and *Malbim* contend that these introductory verses refer instead to Ammon, Moab, Edom, and Aram, which beleaguered Israel in the reign of David [see II *Samuel*, Chapter 8; see also *Ibn Ezra, Psalms* 68:1].

Radak maintains that this prayer alludes to Sennacherib of Assyria, who laid siege to Jerusalem, the citadel of King Chizkiyahu.

Meiri suggests that the psalmist here foretells the encircling of the Holy City which will occur during the Messianic battle of Gog and Magog.

2. יָקוּם אֱלֹהִים — *Let God arise.*

[This verse is based on *Numbers* 10:35, וַיְהִי בִּנְסֹעַ הָאָרֹן וַיֹּאמֶר מֹשֶׁה קוּמָה ה׳ וְיָפֻצוּ אֹיְבֶיךָ וְיָנֻסוּ מְשַׂנְאֶיךָ מִפָּנֶיךָ, *And it came to pass when the Ark journeyed forward that Moses said: 'Arise, HASHEM, and let Your foes be scattered and let those who hate You flee before You.'*

Since the Torah given at Sinai was the source of the gentiles' undying hatred of Israel (see *Prefatory Remarks*), it is fitting that the very same Torah, deposited in the Holy Ark, should lead Israel into battle against its adversaries.]

Whereas Moses addressed God directly, in the second person, and described Him as the *Dispenser of Mercy:* קוּמָה ה׳, *Arise HASHEM*, David speaks indirectly, in the third person, and pleads with the *Dispenser of Strict Justice:* יָקוּם אֱלֹהִים, *Let God arise (Chazah Zion; Toras Chesed).*

Eretz HaChaim explains that Moses was primarily concerned with the merciful salvation of Israel and was content to have the militant gentile nations scattered. David, however, perceived that the nations of every generation posed a mortal danger to Israel, a threat which demanded a severe, final response. Therefore, he invoked God's strict justice to utterly destroy the enemies, saying *(v.* 3), *'Let the wicked perish in the face of God.'*

יָפוּצוּ אוֹיְבָיו — *Let His enemies be scattered.*

Rashi (Numbers 10:35) describes these enemies as massed in tight assault formation. [Thus David prays, 'Let their strong ranks be broken and their staunch fighters dispersed.']

According to *Malbim*, the אוֹיֵב is far more dangerous than the שׂוֹנֵא. The former actually demonstrates his hatred with malicious actions, whereas the latter merely harbors animosity in his heart [see *comm.* of *Malbim* to 18:18].

Since the אוֹיֵב actually engages in battle, he will be beaten and *scattered*. The שׂוֹנֵא, however, stands back in the rear, concentrating on battle strategy. When Israel triumphs, he *flees*.

וְיָנוּסוּ מְשַׂנְאָיו מִפָּנָיו — *And let His foes* [lit., *those who hate Him*] *flee before Him.*

Rashi (Numbers 10:35) comments that these are the pursuers [who chase

68
1-3

For the Conductor, by David,
a song with musical accompaniment.
2 Let God arise,
let His enemies be scattered;
And let His foes
flee before Him.
3 As smoke is dispersed,
so disperse them;
As wax melts before the fire,

after Israel. David prays, 'Let them now take to their heels and flee before the might of Israel.']

Rashi goes on to explain that מְשַׂנְאָיו, *those who hate Him* (i.e., God), refers to whoever despises and attacks Israel. Similarly, we read (83:3-4): וּמְשַׂנְאֶיךָ נָשְׂאוּ רֹאשׁ, *And those who hate You have lifted* [*their*] *head*. How is their hatred demonstrated? עַל עַמְּךָ יַעֲרִימוּ סוֹד, *They take deceptive counsel against Your nation.* [1]

3. כְּהִנְדֹּף עָשָׁן תִּנְדֹּף — *As smoke is dispersed, so disperse* [*them*].

The success of the wicked is an illusion resembling the thick smoke billowing through a chimney. This seemingly solid mass will soon dissipate into a wisp, as the wind drives the smoke away. This echoes the verse (37:20) וְאֹיְבֵי ה׳ ... כָּלוּ בֶעָשָׁן כָּלוּ, *The foes of HASHEM ... they vanish, in smoke they vanish (Midrash Shocher Tov).*

Smoke and vapor, which always rise, symbolize the haughty man whose pride stirs him with aspirations to climb even higher on the ladder of power and success *(Sforno).*

Like a dark and ominous column of smoke rising heavenward, the wicked momentarily seem to represent real danger. Yet smoke's nature dictates that it must gradually fade away, a process hastened by the wind. Similarly, evil cannot long endure; it will fade away of its own accord, and its disintegration will be accelerated by God's hidden guidance of the events of human history. All evildoers will perish, because the very nature of evil is ephemeral and lacks enduring reality *(Hirsch).*

כְּהִמֵּס דּוֹנַג מִפְּנֵי אֵשׁ — *As wax melts before the fire.*

The psalmist does not use the simile of wax completely consumed בָּאֵשׁ, *in the fire,* but speaks only of the wax melted מִפְּנֵי אֵשׁ, *before the fire (Tehillas Hashem).*

Shaarei Chaim explains that in the previous verse, two categories of adversaries were described. The אוֹיֵב, *foe,* poses an actual physical threat. He must be completely destroyed, like smoke, which vanishes in the wind.

However, the שׂוֹנֵא, *enemy,* merely contemplates evil in his heart. If he changes his attitude, he can be saved.

1. [The root of anti-Semitism is *not* the instinctive loathing and revulsion which people feel for an alien. Rather, this perverse enmity manifests a deep strait of bitter antagonism against all that is truly sacred and representative of God's universal dominion. The enemy of Israel despises the burdensome authority of God.

This truth is illustrated by Hitler, who explained that he was motivated to obliterate the Jewish people 'because they cursed civilization with a conscience.'

Although the anti-Semite may espouse other religions with fanatic zeal, this is merely *deceptive counsel* (83:4), i.e., an attempt to cunningly disguise his godlessness.]

סח ד־ה

ד יֹאבְדוּ רְשָׁעִים מִפְּנֵי אֱלֹהִים: וְצַדִּיקִים
יִשְׂמְחוּ יַעַלְצוּ לִפְנֵי אֱלֹהִים וְיָשִׂישׂוּ
ה בְשִׂמְחָה: שִׁירוּ | לֵאלֹהִים זַמְּרוּ שְׁמוֹ סֹלּוּ
לָרֹכֵב בָּעֲרָבוֹת בְּיָהּ שְׁמוֹ וְעִלְזוּ לְפָנָיו:

Thus, he resembles melted wax which retains its substance, although its outer shape is transformed.

Malbim observes that this verse parallels the preceding verse, which repeated Moses' proclamation as the camp of Israel journeyed in the wilderness. By day, the camp was led by the עַמּוּד עָנָן, *Pillar of Cloud*, which cleared a path before them. Now the psalmist requests a similar salvation: *Disperse all obstacles and enemies in their path as smoke is dispersed.*

By night, the עַמּוּד אֵשׁ, *Pillar of Fire* went before them. Therefore, the psalmist makes a parallel request, that the present enemy melt *before the fire.*

יֹאבְדוּ רְשָׁעִים מִפְּנֵי אֱלֹהִים — *So let the wicked perish in the face of God.*

Rashi observes that in the days of Moses, God's wrath was kindled against the opponents of Israel. Moses addressed the Holy Ark as it returned from battle, וּבְנֻחֹה יֹאמַר שׁוּבָה ה׳ רִבְבוֹת אַלְפֵי יִשְׂרָאֵל, *And when it came to rest, he said: 'Rest, HASHEM, upon the myriads and thousands of Israel'* (*Numbers* 10:36).

[This implies, 'Let the enemy armies perish but allow the armies of Israel to return home unscathed, with their full regiments of myriads and thousands' (*Daas Zekeinim, Numbers* 10:36).]

4. וְצַדִּיקִים יִשְׂמְחוּ יַעַלְצוּ לִפְנֵי אֱלֹהִים — *But as for the righteous — let them be glad, let them exult before God.*

Eretz HaChaim comments that the Holy Ark scattered the enemies of the Almighty, but the devout unite and rejoice in the Ark's presence, as Scripture states, *And David danced before* [the Ark of] *HASHEM with all his might* (II *Samuel* 6:14). In addition, the Ark was a source of joy for all in its vicinity; when the Ark was housed in the home of Oved Edom of Gat for three months, his family was greatly blessed by its presence (II *Samuel* 6:11).

[In *comm.* to 9:3, it was explained that עָלַץ is related to חָלַץ, *to release from bonds;* it is an expression of joyous release from depression and confinement.

The wicked feel cramped and very uneasy in the presence of God. The sight of the Temple or the Holy Ark inhibits their instinctive pursuit of the profane and restricts their promiscuous abandon.

The righteous, however, are inspired by the holy precincts. All of their dormant talents and energies are suddenly released, as they strive to serve their Creator. This sudden self-realization gives rise to an indescribable sense of exultation.]

Alshich and *Sforno* perceive here a reference to that fire which simultaneously melts the wicked like wax (*v.* 3), and strengthens the righteous. The *Talmud* (*Nedarim* 8b) teaches that in the future, God will remove the blazing sun from its protective sheath. Then, its fierce heat will consume the wicked, while it heals the righteous.

וְיָשִׂישׂוּ בְשִׂמְחָה — *Let them rejoice with gladness.*

The short-lived *gladness* derived from material pleasures eventually leaves a vacuum in the heart, but the spiritual *gladness* derived from God's service causes the devout to *rejoice* perpetually (*Binah L'ittim*).

Radak maintains that this psalm refers to the downfall of Sennacherib [see *v.* 1], which took place on the first night of Passover. He explains that *so let the wicked perish in the face of God.*

4 *But as for the righteous —*
let them be glad,
Let them exalt before God;
let them rejoice with gladness.

5 *Sing to God,*
make music for His Name,
Extol Him
Who rides in Aravos, With YAH His Name
and exult before Him.

when King Chizkiyahu and his nation were saved from the Assyrian host they *rejoiced* over the Jews' redemption from Egypt [which is commemorated by the Festival of Passover] *with* [additional] *gladness* because of their deliverance from Sennacherib.

5. שִׁירוּ לֵאלֹהִים זַמְּרוּ שְׁמוֹ — *Sing to God, make music [for] His Name.*

[See *comm.* to 30:1.]

When the children of Israel *rejoice with gladness (v. 4)*, every celebrant will encourage his comrade to exult and sing hymns of praise *(Ibn Ezra).*

They will say זַמְּרוּ [cognate with זוֹמֵר, *to prune*] שְׁמוֹ, implying, 'If you remove the distractions which distort clear perception of His Name and deeds, then you will be inspired to sing' *(Chasam Sofer).*

סֹלּוּ — *Extol (Rashi; Radak; Ibn Ezra; Rashbam).*

[Cf. *Proverbs* 4:8 סַלְסְלֶהָ וּתְרוֹמְמֶךָּ, *Extol her and she will elevate you.*]

Rabbi Moshe (quoted in *Ibn Ezra*), *Radak*, and *Hirsch* relate סֹלּוּ to סָלַל, *to raise up*, from which are derived מְסִלָּה, *highway*, and סוּלָּם, *ladder*. [Cf. *Isaiah* 62:10, סֹלּוּ סֹלּוּ הַמְסִלָּה, *Build up, build up, the road.* See *comm.* to 3:3.]

Chasam Sofer paraphrases this exhortation: 'Construct a mental highway upon which your spirits can rise towards God!'

לָרֹכֵב — *(To) Him Who rides.*

רֹכֵב denotes the total mastery of the horseman over his steed. The metaphor is used to describe the firm guidance with which God directs the events of the world *(Radak; Hirsch).* We find similar references later in this psalm, where we read of רֶכֶב אֱלֹהִים, *the chariot of God (v.* 18), which appeared at Sinai, and רֹכֵב בִּשְׁמֵי שְׁמֵי קֶדֶם, *The Rider upon the loftiest of primeval heavens (v.* 34) *(Ibn Ezra).*

[God manifests His mastery only to the extent that people recognize it. As man's comprehension increases, God's guidance expands, as Scripture states, רֹכֵב שָׁמַיִם בְּעֶזְרֶךָ, *He rides the heavens with your* [Israel's] *help (Deuteronomy* 33:26).]

בָּעֲרָבוֹת — *In Aravos.*

This is the highest heaven, where God sits upon [i.e., *rides*] His great throne *(Targum).*

This heaven controls the motions and orbits of all the lower spheres *(Radak).*

The *Talmud (Chagiga* 12a) describes the loftiest of the seven celestial heavens as עֲרָבוֹת, *Aravos,* where 'God stores righteousness, justice, and charity.' There rest the treasuries of life, peace, and blessing. The highest of the heavenly spheres also holds the souls of the *tzaddikim,* the souls which have not yet come to life, and the dew by means of which God will resuscitate the dead.

ו אֲבִי יְתוֹמִים וְדַיַּן אַלְמָנוֹת אֱלֹהִים בִּמְעוֹן
ז קָדְשׁוֹ: אֱלֹהִים | מוֹשִׁיב יְחִידִים | בַּיְתָה

God called it עֲרָבוֹת because the righteous deeds of the *tzaddikim* were עֲרֵבִים, *sweet and desirable*, to Him. He planted their accomplishments in this heaven, where they bear the fruit of providing the universe with spiritual enrichment (*Midrash Shocher Tov*, 114).

[This means that by virtue of the deeds and understanding of the righteous, God attains a higher degree of spiritual mastery. It was His will that His Presence be obscure on earth, but that it become revealed as a result of the spiritual achievements of virtuous people.]

בְּיָהּ שְׁמוֹ — *With YAH His Name.*

This signifies, *extol Him* with this unique designation (*Radak*). This Divine Name denotes God's awesomeness, as the prophet (*Isaiah* 26:4) says, כִּי בְּיָהּ ה׳ צוּר עוֹלָמִים which *Targum* renders: *Through the awesome might of HASHEM you will find Salvation.* This is similar to a previous exhortation of the psalmist (2:11), *Serve HASHEM in awe and rejoice with trembling (Rashi).*

The *Talmud* (*Menachos* 29b) interprets *Isaiah* 26:4 thus: With the letters of יָהּ, *YAH*, HASHEM fashioned (צוּר) the worlds. First, He created the World to Come with the smallest letter, י, *yud*, because that world is reserved for the humble people who minimize their worth. Their number is very small.

Then He made This World with the letter ה, *he*, which is open on the bottom, to symbolize that life offers many temptations to succumb to sin, and thus to descend to damnation. The small opening at the top of the left leg of the ה implies that only a fraction of mankind will rise to heaven (*Maseches Heicholos*, Chapter 7).

וְעִלְזוּ לְפָנָיו — *And exult before Him.*

The verse begins with the Name אֱלֹהִים, which denotes God as the *Dispenser of Strict Justice*, but concludes with a reference to יָהּ, which is only half of the Name יהו״ה, which denotes God as the *Dispenser of Mercy. Sforno's* commentary implies that God does not exercise His full mercy as long as He must dispense severe but just punishments. Nevertheless, even when the Divine mercy must be tempered, *exult before Him*, for He utilizes all His attributes only to benefit man.

6. [In the preceding verse, the people were encouraged to compose a hymn to praise and extol God. They responded with the following composition, which continues until the end of this psalm (*Rashi*).]

אֲבִי יְתוֹמִים וְדַיַּן אַלְמָנוֹת — *Father of orphans and Judge of widows.*

Radak comments that although God soars in the loftiest heights of *Aravos*, He remains intimately involved in the affairs of the weakest and least prominent people. He is a father to the orphan, who desperately needs a parent.[1] Since she is often beleaguered by those who encroach upon her estate and possessions, the אַלְמָנָה, *widow*, resembles an אִלֵּם, *mute*, unable to plead on her own behalf (*Hirsch*). Therefore God protects the widow by defending her before the court.

The *Talmud* (*Megillah* 31b) notes that this juxtaposition of verses 5 and 6 illustrates the rule: כָּל מָקוֹם שֶׁאַתָּה מוֹצֵא גְבוּרָתוֹ שֶׁל הַקב״ה שָׁם אַתָּה מוֹצֵא

1. When *Rambam* (*Hilchos Nachalos* 11:12) codifies the laws governing the אַפּוֹטְרוֹפּוֹס, *trustee*, whom the court appoints as guardian over the estate of the orphans, he concludes, 'Although the trustee is not required to render an exact accounting of his transactions, he should personally keep a scrupulously precise account for himself, bearing in mind that the protector of the orphans is none other than God Himself, *Who rides in Aravos* and Who is *Father of orphans.*

6 *Father of orphans and Judge of widows*
is God in the habitation of His holiness.
7 *God gathers the lonely into a family,*

עַנְוְתָנוּתוֹ, *whenever Scripture refers to God's might, it immediately mentions His humbleness.*

Rashi interprets this verse as a metaphorical reference to Israel, a people abandoned by the world like a homeless orphan. Only God is our Father. At the time of the destruction, the tragedy was compounded because יְתוֹמִים הָיִינוּ וְאֵין אָב, *we have become orphans and fatherless (Lamentations* 5:3), implying that even our Father in Heaven rejected us.

At that time, Jerusalem was desolate: הָיְתָה כְּאַלְמָנָה, *it became like a widow (Lamentations* 1:1). In that bitter moment, God became *Judge of widows* (i.e., of Jerusalem).

Even in exile, however, we are not completely lost; we are not like orphans or widows whose protection is dead. Rather, God is only temporarily estranged from His people. He resembles the father and husband who journeyed to a distant land but will eventually return *(Midrash Shocher Tov,* 2).

אֱלֹהִים בִּמְעוֹן קָדְשׁוֹ — *Is God in the habitation of His holiness.*

Although God's glory soars to the celestial heights, He still cares for the lowest creatures on earth and guides their ways *(Ibn Ezra).*

7. אֱלֹהִים מוֹשִׁיב יְחִידִים בַּיְתָה — *God gathers* [lit. *settles*] *the lonely into a family* [lit. *house*].

[The word בַּיְתָה, *house,* does not refer to an architectural structure but to the family as a social unit.] When the children of Israel were isolated and scattered throughout the land of Egypt, God gathered them together to create a unified nation *(Rashi).*

Meiri adds that in contrast to the Egyptian masses, the Jews were not nameless serfs. Each one was a יָחִיד, *individual,* outstanding, distinguished, and of unique merit. When the sons of Jacob descended to Egypt, they were a small band of extraordinary individuals; the Jews maintained their personal identity until they later departed in multitudes as עַם סְגוּלָּה, *a treasured nation.*

Similarly, at the time of the future Messianic redemption, the Jews will be isolated and dispersed to the very ends of the earth. Yet, God will gather them בַּיְתָה, *to their ancient homeland,* the Land of Israel.

The Rabbis *(Sotah* 2a) interpret this passage homiletically as a reference to the Divine art of matchmaking, for it is a superhuman task to take יְחִידִים, *lonely individuals,* who may be strangers and emotional opposites with conflicting personal priorities and preferences, and to fuse them into one unit. God alone can *gather* [*them*] *into a family,* because at the moment of conception, a בַּת קוֹל, *heavenly voice,* proclaims the Divine decree that the body and soul of the future mates should develop in such a manner that they later become a single harmonious whole. Because the partners were intended and fashioned for one another, the marriage ceremony which takes place later is tantamount to the reunion of two temporarily separated parts of an organism which are being returned to their original unity.[1]

1. A Roman noblewoman once asked Rabbi Yose ben Chalafta how long it took God to create the world. 'Six days,' he replied.

'And what has He been doing since then?', she inquired.

'He sits and makes matches,' said Rabbi Yose.

'What!' cried the matron incredulously. 'This is the Divine craft? Why, even I can make

מוֹצִיא אֲסִירִים בַּכּוֹשָׁרוֹת אַךְ סוֹרְרִים
ח שָׁכְנוּ צְחִיחָה: אֱלֹהִים בְּצֵאתְךָ לִפְנֵי עַמֶּךָ
ט בְּצַעְדְּךָ בִישִׁימוֹן סֶלָה: אֶרֶץ רָעָשָׁה | אַף־

מוֹצִיא אֲסִירִים בַּכּוֹשָׁרוֹת — *He releases the prisoners at suitable moments.*

God redeemed Israel from Egypt in the most *suitable* (כָּשֵׁר) season of the year — springtime — for then the weather is optimal for traveling on the road; it is neither too hot nor too cold *(Rashi).*

Ibn Ezra, Radak, and *Meiri* translate כּוֹשָׁרוֹת as *bonds* (cognate with קוֹשָׁרוֹת with the כ, *kaf,* in place of the ק, *kuf*): *God releases the prisoners from their bonds.*

However, *Hirsch* notes that בַּכּוֹשָׁרוֹת literally means *with their bonds.* [This teaches that even though the Jews had been physically liberated from Egypt, spiritually, they remained in bondage, for they were enslaved by ignorance, doubts, and their personal desires. The Children of Israel achieved spiritual independence only after God enlightened their minds by the revelation of the Torah at Sinai.]

The Sages render בַּכּוֹשָׁרוֹת as a contraction of the words בֶּכִי, *weeping,* and שִׁירוֹת, *songs.* When Israel was released from bondage, it was a time of *weeping* for the Egyptians and of *song* for the Jews, who were redeemed in the merit of their worthy forefathers *(Tanchuma, Boh* 1).

According to the *Midrash,* this phrase also relates to the formation of the family unit (mentioned at the beginning of this verse). When God matches a couple, their union is undoubtedly suitable and has the potential for happiness. Ultimately, however, only the efforts of husband and wife determine whether or not the match will succeed. If they appreciate the wisdom of God's choice, the resulting happiness will cause them to sing שִׁירוֹת, *songs,* of joy and gratitude; but if they refuse to accept their Divinely designated mates, they will be engulfed in unhappy בֶּכִי, *weeping (Bereishis Rabbah* 68:4).

Furthermore, if the couple is God-fearing, they will מוֹצִיא אֲסִירִים בַּכּוֹשָׁרוֹת, *bring forth* scholarly sons who are able to decide what is halachically אָסוּר, *prohibited,* or כָּשֵׁר, *permitted;* but if the couple is not meritorious, their son will be an ignoramus whose parched mind is barren of Torah knowledge.

אַךְ סוֹרְרִים שָׁכְנוּ צְחִיחָה — *Only the rebellious dwell in the thirsty land.*

When the Jews were redeemed from Egypt, they left behind a parched and barren land which had been ravaged by plagues. The erstwhile Jewish אֲסִירִים, *prisoners,* had been redeemed בַּכּוֹשָׁרוֹת, *at the suitable moment* — springtime, the most pleasant season of the year *(Rashi).*

[The verse implies that the Egyptians deserved this punishment because they were סוֹרְרִים, *rebellious,* against God.]

According to *Radak,* this entire verse refers to the downfall of Sennacherib, who beseiged Jerusalem with his hordes. The Jews, trapped in the city, were a handful of יְחִידִים, *lonely individuals,* but God *released these*

matches!' [*Radal* explains that she denied that Divine Providence was a factor in the successful matching of men and women.]

'Perhaps it is easy for you to accomplish this,' declared Rabbi Yose, 'but in God's eyes, making matches is as difficult as splitting the sea.'

The noblewoman took one thousand manservants and one thousand maidservants and lined them up in two rows facing one another. She walked between the rows and arbitrarily decided, 'This one will marry this one; this one will marry this one.' She then sent the new couples home for the night.

[In line with the above-noted comment of *Radal,* she arrogantly attempted to demonstrate

68 *He releases the prisoners*
8 *at suitable moments,*
Only the rebellious
dwell in the thirsty land.
8 *O God when You went forth*
before Your nation,
When You marched through the wilderness, Selah.

prisoners from their bonds, with all the captives who had been kept in the camp of the Assyrians. An angel smote the Assyrian soldiers, burning their souls but leaving their bodies intact. Since these *rebellious* upstarts who challenged the sovereignty of God died without any bodily wounds, it appeared as if they died of thirst *in the thirsty land.*

8. אֱלֹהִים בְּצֵאתְךָ לִפְנֵי עַמֶּךָ – *O God, when You went forth before Your nation.*

In the wilderness, God's Pillar of Cloud went before them by day and His Pillar of Fire, by night *(Targum; Sforno).*

God's Holy Ark went out to battle before them to assure their victory *(Radak).*

According to *Pirkei d'Rabbi Eliezer* (Chapter 41), this alludes to the Jews' deep sleep on the night prior to the receiving of the Torah at Sinai. The night was very short, and the people overslept until two hours after daybreak. *God went forth* from heaven and arrived at Sinai *before the nation.* Moses hastily went through the camp to arouse the people, saying, 'Arise, for the Groom has already arrived, and He is waiting to escort His bride to the wedding canopy! God is waiting to enter into a Torah covenant with Israel.'

[Ever since, it has been customary for Jews to stay awake the entire night of Shavuos, in order to atone for that first Shavuos night, when they overslept (*Mogen Avrhohom; Orach Chaim* 494).]

בְּצַעְדְּךָ – *When You marched.*

Hirsch defines צַעַד as a *slow, measured stride.* God did not hurry through the wilderness; He caused Israel to journey slowly and deliberately, so that the Jews would sense God's nearness and His guidance with their every step.

בִישִׁימוֹן – *Through* [lit. *in*] *the wilderness.*

God directed His gracious providence towards Israel throughout their forty-year sojourn in the שְׁמָמָה, *desolation (Targum);* this Divine providence was especially evident when the Jews arrived at Sinai, which is also known as חוֹרֵב, *desolation (Sforno).*

[God gave the Torah in an uninhabited wilderness in order to emphasize that the authority of the Torah is not limited to one specific society or civilization. Torah life can flourish even in a forsaken wasteland.]

that such human relationships were random and unregulatd by God's wisdom. This being the case, God withdrew the guidance He normally extends to people engaged in matchmaking.]

The following morning, all the servants converged upon her. One had a head wound, another had an injured eye, a third had a broken leg. Each shouted that he could not tolerate his new mate.

Thereupon, the noblewoman summoned Rabbi Yose and admitted, 'There is no god like your God, and no truth comparable to your Torah. Your statement [that God alone makes fitting matches] is proper and just' *(Bereishis Rabbah* 68:4).

סח
י־יא

שָׁמַיִם נָטְפוּ מִפְּנֵי אֱלֹהִים זֶה סִינַי מִפְּנֵי
אֱלֹהִים אֱלֹהֵי יִשְׂרָאֵל: גֶּשֶׁם נְדָבוֹת תָּנִיף
אֱלֹהִים נַחֲלָתְךָ וְנִלְאָה אַתָּה כוֹנַנְתָּהּ:
יא חַיָּתְךָ יָשְׁבוּ־בָהּ תָּכִין בְּטוֹבָתְךָ לֶעָנִי

סֶלָה — *Selah* [lit. *forever;* see *comm.* 3:3].

In the wilderness, God demonstrated that He provides a deliverance from distress *forever,* i.e., at all times *(Rashi).*

9. אֶרֶץ רָעָשָׁה — *The earth roared.*

When the Torah was given, Mount Sinai quaked in the presence of God, as Scripture states (*Exodus* 19:18), *And the entire mountain trembled greatly.* The mighty nations of the earth also shuddered in awe as God's might was revealed at Sinai *(Radak).*

אַף שָׁמַיִם נָטְפוּ — *Even the heavens dripped.*

The skies over Sinai became dark and forbidding, as if they were about to *drip* with rain. Similar language is used in 18:12: *He made darkness His concealment ... dark waters and thick clouds (Radak).*

מִפְּנֵי אֱלֹהִים — *Before the Presence of* [lit. *because of*] *God.*

The earth and the heavens quaked in fear because of אֱלֹהִים, *the Dispenser of Strict Justice,* for He created the world on the condition [*Avodah Zarah* 5a] that the universe will endure only if Israel accepts the Torah. If the Torah is rejected, then the world has no purpose, and the entire universe will return to nothingness *(Tehillos Hashem).*

זֶה סִינַי — *This is Sinai.*

Clouds of smoke billowed from Sinai as from a fiery oven *(Targum).* [This signified God's awesome presence.]

מִפְּנֵי אֱלֹהִים אֱלֹהֵי יִשְׂרָאֵל — *Before the Presence of God, the God of Israel.*

Dorash Moshe points out that the numerical value of סִינַי, *Sinai,* (130) is equal to that of סֻלָּם, *ladder,* because Sinai is the *'ladder'* upon which the souls of Israel ascend in order to stand *before the Presence of God.*

10. גֶּשֶׁם נְדָבוֹת תָּנִיף אֱלֹהִים — *A generous rain did You lavish* [lit. *pour*], *O God.*

Even as *the heavens dripped* afflictions and suffering upon the gentiles who rejected the Torah (*v.* 9), the skies lavished bountiful, blessed rains upon the Jews, who accepted the Torah *(Radak).*

The Children of Israel were overawed when they heard the voice of the Almighty at Sinai. Their souls soared heavenward, leaving their bodies limp and lifeless. God then showered them with the same life-giving dew with which He will revive the dead at תְּחִיַּת הַמֵּתִים, *the Resurrection of the Dead,* and they came back to life *(Targum; Shabbos* 88a).

[God caused the Children of Israel to undergo this experience so that He could imbue them with a firm belief in the Resurrection of the Dead, for this is a cardinal principle of Jewish faith. At the very moment when He gave the Children of Israel the Torah, God implanted within them the faith that they could judge and anticipate the greatest reward not in This World, but following the Resurrection.]

נַחֲלָתְךָ וְנִלְאָה — [*When*] *Your heritage was weary.*

When *Your heritage* (the Holy Land and the Chosen People) — *was weary for rain, You lavished it* [rain] *generously (Targum; Rashi).*

אַתָּה כוֹנַנְתָּהּ — *You established it firmly.*

After the juggernaut of the Assyrian army swept through Judea, the

9 *The earth roared — even the heavens dripped*
before the Presence of God.
This is Sinai — before the Presence of God,
the God of Israel.
10 *A generous rain did You lavish,*
O God,
When Your heritage was weary
You established it firmly.
11 *Your flock settled there.*
You prepare for the poor
with Your goodness, O God.

defenders of Jerusalem were *weary*. Yet, as always, You miraculously protected *Your heritage* and *You established it firmly (Radak)*, as Scripture states (*Exodus* 15:17), מִקְּדָשׁ אֲדֹנָי כּוֹנְנוּ יָדֶיךָ, *The Temple, my Lord, Your hands established (Sforno).*

11. חַיָּתְךָ יָשְׁבוּ בָהּ — *Your flock* [lit. *living creature*] *settled there* [lit. *in it*].

The translation of חַיָּתְךָ follows *Rashi, Ibn Ezra,*, and *Radak*. It is based on *II Samuel* 23:11. The psalmist compares the faithful of Israel to sheep who flock to their master.

They all assemble בָהּ, *therein*, i.e, in the Land of Israel *(Ibn Ezra)* and in Jerusalem *(Radak).*

Alshich observes that these words explain what the Jews gained when their souls soared from their bodies at Sinai. God invested their spirits with new חִיּוּת, *vitality*, for their strength had been sapped by the Egyptian bondage. Afterwards, יָשְׁבוּ בָהּ, the reinvigorated souls *settled* back into their original bodies.

תָּכִין בְּטוֹבָתְךָ לֶעָנִי אֱלֹהִים — *You prepare for the poor with Your goodness, O God.*

God actually benefited the Jews by requiring them to wander in the wilderness for forty years, for when the Canaanites first heard that Israel was coming to *Eretz Yisrael* [after the Revelation at Sinai], they devastated their land to render it worthless to the Jewish people. However, when the Jews failed to arrive as expected, the Canaanites engineered a complete reconstruction. In this manner, God *prepare[d]* [the land] *with goodness for the poor* and homeless Jewish people *(Rashi).*

In later years, *You prepare[d]* a victory *for the poor* remnants of Judea, who were miraculously saved from Sennacherib's army *(Radak).*

The *Talmud (Eruvin* 54a) interprets this verse as an allusion to the Torah scholar who renounces the pleasures of this world to concentrate on his holy studies. The devout, dedicated scholar treats himself like a חַיָּה, *an animal,* which is not concerned with the manner in which its food is prepared, but swiftly devours whatever it needs in order to survive. If he lives with such perfect sincerity, then God assures him not only of success in his studies, but also in his material needs. Of him it is said, *You prepare for the poor with Your goodness, O God.*

יב אֱלֹהִים: אֲדֹנָי יִתֶּן־אֹמֶר הַמְבַשְּׂרוֹת צָבָא
יג רָב: מַלְכֵי צְבָאוֹת יִדֹּדוּן יִדֹּדוּן וּנְוַת־בַּיִת
יד תְּחַלֵּק שָׁלָל: אִם תִּשְׁכְּבוּן בֵּין שְׁפַתָּיִם
כַּנְפֵי יוֹנָה נֶחְפָּה בַכֶּסֶף וְאֶבְרוֹתֶיהָ

12. אֲדֹנָי יִתֶּן אֹמֶר – *My Lord gave His* [lit. *the*] *word.*

He revealed the words of Torah to His nation, Israel *(Targum)*, and simultaneously He *gave* [*them*] *His word* [i.e., His promise], as recorded in verse 14 *(Rashi)*. [See 12:7 אִמֲרוֹת ה׳ אֲמָרוֹת טְהֹרוֹת.]

הַמְבַשְּׂרוֹת צָבָא רָב – *Announcing to the great legion.*

[The commentaries note the peculiarity of the word הַמְבַשְּׂרוֹת, which is plural and in the feminine gender.]

Here the psalmist alludes to an ancient practice whereby women would announce the latest local news in their songs; similarly, God announced His word to the great legions *(Ibn Ezra; Radak; Sforno)*.

God appointed two great מְבַשְּׂרוֹת, *announcers*, Moses and Aaron, to teach Torah to the legions of Israel *(Targum)*.

Each word which God uttered at Sinai split [מְשַׁבְּרוֹת] into seventy מְבַשְּׂרוֹת, *announcements*, i.e., seventy languages, so that the *great legions* of the gentile nations could hear the Divine teachings (*Shabbos* 88b).[1]

Similarly, it was *announced* that *the great legion* of the Assyrian army besieging Jerusalem would be destroyed at the word of God *(Radak)*.

At the time of the future Messianic redemption, too, God's word will herald the defeat of all who oppose His design *(Meiri)*.

13. מַלְכֵי צְבָאוֹת יִדֹּדוּן יִדֹּדוּן – *Kings of legions flee, they flee.*

[The root of יִדֹּדוּן is נָדַד, *to wander* or *to move.* The repitition of the word signifies that at Sinai there were two directions of movement.]

Each word which God uttered at Sinai was so awe-inspiring that it caused the legions of Israel to *flee* [i.e., retreat] twelve *mil* [about 6 miles] from the mountain. Later the ministering angels helped them to *flee* [i.e., return] to their original position at Sinai (*Shabbos* 88a).

When Israel conquered Canaan, the kings of the gentile legions were forced to flee repeatedly *(Radak)*.

וּנְוַת בַּיִת תְּחַלֵּק שָׁלָל – *And the dweller within apportions booty.*

[נְוַת is derived from נָוֶה, *dwelling.* The feminine form alludes to the wife, who is the homemaker and *dwells* in the privacy of the house.]

Radak notes that women are singled out in appreciation for their unique contribution to the war effort. It is they who soothe the battle-weary warriors and comfort the wounded with tender words.

This also refers to the Torah scholar's wife who tends to the needs of the household while her husband engages

1. The root of all languages in the world is Hebrew, the Holy Tongue. Hebrew was spoken exclusively, until God confused the tongues of mankind at the Tower of Babel. He then distorted the Holy Tongue in seventy different ways, and seventy derivatives of Hebrew emerged. These languages were so corrupt that it was impossible to recognize their holy source *(Shaloh Hakodosh)*.

At Sinai, God desired to draw the seventy nations back to His sanctity. He sought to demonstrate to them that the essence of their language is also holy. Therefore, He split every Hebrew word He uttered into seventy languages to display the spark of holiness which is at the core of every foreign tongue *(Sfas Emes)*.

[12] *My Lord gave His word,*
announcing to the great legion.
[13] *Kings of legions flee, they flee,*
and the dweller within apportions booty.
[14] *Were You to nestle between boundaries —*
dove's feathers plated with silver,

in the intellectual "battles" of Torah study. She is destined to share equally in her spouse's spiritual rewards; as Rabbi Akiva said to his disciples concerning his devoted wife, Rachel, 'Mine and yours [all of our Torah studies] are hers' *(Kesubos* 63a; *Chomas Anoch).*

A similar system is practiced in every Jewish war: the spoils are apportioned equally between those who go out to battle and those who are assigned to stay behind to guard the homefront *(see Numbers* 31:27; *Ibn Ezra).*

The Israelite conquerors of Canaan *apportioned* the spoils of their victories in this manner *(Rashi).*

When Israel received the Torah, the nations envied and admired Israel's selfless dedication to God. They *apportioned* honor to the Torah, which is called (119:162) precious שָׁלָל, *booty (Mechilta Yisro* 20:9).

14. אִם תִּשְׁכְּבוּן בֵּין שְׁפַתָּיִם — *Were you to nestle* [lit. *lie down*] *between boundaries.*

This alludes to the Torah scholar who sacrifices all physical comforts in his whole-hearted dedication to his studies. Issachar excelled in this virtue; Jacob praised him, saying (*Genesis* 49:14): *He resembles the beast of burden* [traveling continuously, day and night, with no permanent place of rest]. *He lies down (only) between boundaries* [of the cities]. This suggests that Issachar limits his sleep to brief naps at irregular intervals. (The words מִשְׁפְּתָיִם and שְׁפַתָּיִם are derived from שָׂפָה, *lip* or *riverbank,* signifying a border or limitation.)

The Lord gave His word and pledged to *the legion*[s] of Israel (*v.* 12) that if they would dedicate themselves to Torah with similar self-sacrifice, bountiful joy and success would be theirs. See *Rashi* and *Bereishis Rabbah* 99:10.

Radak defines שְׁפַתָּיִם as the sooty oven into which a cooking pot is lowered. According to his rendition, the verse teaches that if the Children of Israel humble themselves, shunning social status and lofty positions in favor of their Divine service, then despite the dirt and soot which may cover them in the course of their duties, they will surely emerge as clean and white as *a dove plated with* [spotless] *silver.*

Targum renders שְׁפַתָּיִם as קִלְקְלָתָא *dung heap* [related to אַשְׁפָּה]; thus the verse would mean: *The wicked kings sink into filth because they defy God, while Israel soars to the heavens like a dove.*

כַּנְפֵי יוֹנָה — *Dove's feathers.*

Rashi translates כַּנְפֵי as *plumes,* i.e., the outer feathers, which are primarily for ornament.

The *Talmud (Shabbos* 49a) explains that Israel is likened to a *dove;* just as the feathers of the dove protect the bird, so do the *mitzvos* protect Israel from danger.

נֶחְפָּה בַכֶּסֶף — *Plated with silver.*

Reading the word שְׁפַתָּיִם as the word שְׂפַת יָם, *seashore, Rashbam* and *Targum* refer this verse to the abundance of silver and gold, lost by the drowning Egyptians, with which Israel was covered, at the shore of the Sea of Red.

According to *Radak,* this refers to the silver and gold which Israel plundered from the abandoned Assyrian camp.

טו בְּיַרַקְרַק חָרוּץ: בְּפָרֵשׂ שַׁדַּי מְלָכִים בָּהּ
טז תַּשְׁלֵג בְּצַלְמוֹן: הַר־אֱלֹהִים הַר־בָּשָׁן הַר
יז גַּבְנֻנִּים הַר־בָּשָׁן: לָמָּה | תְּרַצְּדוּן הָרִים

וְאֶבְרוֹתֶיהָ – *And her pinions.*

This is the actual אֵבֶר, *limb,* of the wing, which keeps the dove airborne, not merely the ornamental feathers *(Rashi).*

בִּירַקְרַק – *With brilliant gold.*

Rashi explains that although יָרֹק means *green,* the doubling of the final two letters to form יְרַקְרַק indicates a lack of greenness. The pure gold which comes from the lands of *Chavilah* and *Kush (Genesis* 2:11,12) does *not* have a reddish or *greenish* tint, as is often found in gold of lesser purity. [*Tosafos, Sukkah* 31b *s.v.* יָרוֹק כְּכַּרְתִי, describes יָרֹק (especially as used in this verse) as *yellow.*]

חָרוּץ – *Brilliant* [cf. *Proverbs* 8:19].

This word literally means *sharp.* In connection with intellectual capacity, it denotes initiative or diligence. It is also used to describe the worth of precious metals *(Hirsch).*

15. בְּפָרֵשׂ שַׁדַּי מְלָכִים – *When Shaddai prostrates kings.*

Literally, פָּרֵשׂ means *to spread out.* God vanquishes the kings and spreads them out flat on the ground, in a pose of total submission. Specifically, Scripture recounts such an occurrence after God smote the Assyrian camp (*II Kings* 19:35): *Behold, they were all dead corpses* [spread out on the face of the earth] *(Radak).*

Rashi perceives this as an allusion to the Torah scholars [the true *kings* of the world; see *Proverbs* 8:15] who unravel the knottiest halachic problems and *spread them out* [i.e., resolve them] like a smoothly pressed garment (see *Deuteronomy* 22:17).

שַׁדַּי – *Shaddai.*

The psalmist uses this particular Divine name because it designates God as the Master who triumphs over all adversaries *(Ibn Ezra).*

Since the king of Assyria spoke with brazen arrogance against Shaddai, he therefore deserved to be crushed with the full force connoted by this mighty name *(Radak).*

The root of the Name שַׁדַּי is דַּי, *enough, desist.* Therefore, its use in the verse suggests, 'May the Almighty, Who called a halt to the process of Creation by shouting, 'דַּי, *Enough!'* (*Chagigah* 12a). bring an end to our suffering at the hans of the gentile kings *(Zerah Yaakav).*

בָּהּ תַּשְׁלֵג בְּצַלְמוֹן – *Those in shadowy darkness shall be whitened.*

When God sends salvation, the Jewish people, who were shrouded in a צֵל, *dark shadow,* of gloom, will become illuminated with bright joy *(Radak).*

Ibn Ezra identifies צַלְמוֹן as a mountain whose peak is always capped with snow. It is located on the eastern bank of the Jordan River. [Possibly, since the snow never melts there it seems as if the mountain peak is perpetually under a cool צֵל, *shadow.*]

Targum renders צַלְמוֹן as צַלְמָוֶת, *the shadow of death,* i.e., *Gehinnom, Hell,* which is the destination of the wicked kings.

16. הַר אֱלֹהִים הַר בָּשָׁן – *The mountain of God, the mountain of Bashan.*

[The psalmist now demonstrates the superiority of Mount Sinai over all other peaks and explains why Sinai was the most suitable location for the Revelation.]

The word *Bashan* is used to praise any desirable geographic location because there was a specific place in *Eretz Yisrael* called *Bashan,* where the pasture land was exceptionally lush and abundant. Animals who grazed there were noted for their size and strength. [See *comm.* to 22:13 אַבִּירֵי בָשָׁן].

And her pinions with brilliant gold.
15 *When Shaddai prostrates kings,
those in shadowy darkness shall be whitened.*
16 *The mountain of God,
the mountain of Bashan;
the mountain of Gavnunim,
the mountain of Bashan.*
17 *Why do you prance,
you mountains of Gavnunim,*

Although Mount Sinai was in a barren, parched wilderness, it was considered a הַר בָּשָׁן, *an exceptional mountain,* because the Holy Spirit came to rest upon it and it was designated as הַר אֱלֹהִים, *the Mountain of God (Radak).*

[God chose Sinai precisely because it was the lowest and most insignificant mountain, to teach that Torah knowledge can only be acquired by the humble scholar who seeks no recognition for his accomplishments.]

הַר גַּבְנֻנִּים הַר בָּשָׁן – *The mountain of Gavnunim, the mountain of Bashan.*

[Unlike Sinai, which is *exceptional* because of its spiritual excellence, the other great mountains are called בָּשָׁן, *exceptional,* because of their unusual physical dimensions.]

The word גַּבְנֻנִּים is derived from גָּבוֹהַּ, *tall.* The plural usage indicates exceptional height. Furthermore, the highest peak of this lofty mountain is surrounded on all sides by many lesser ridges called גַּבְנֻנִּים *(Radak; Meiri).*

[The word גַּב also means *back,* signifying that these lower ridges serve as a 'backdrop' setting off the lofty pinnacle, whose height is even more evident when compared to the lower surrounding mountains.

Indeed, because of the tall mountain's height, it was unacceptable as the place for receiving the Torah; for height symbolizes arrogance, the repugnant character flaw which disqualifies the student from achieving Torah excellence.][1]

17. לָמָּה תְּרַצְּדוּן הָרִים גַּבְנֻנִּים – *Why do you prance, you mountains of Gavnunim.*

Radak and *Menachem* (cited by *Rashi)* translate תְּרַצְּדוּן as תְּרַקְּדוּן, *dance* or *cavort.* The tall mountains are like proud creatures who *prance* about to display their beauty and height. Their efforts, however, do not avail, for God already designated Sinai as His chosen mountain.

The *Talmud (Megillah* 29b) perceives תְּרַצְּדוּן as a contraction of תִּרְצוּ דִין, *you desire judgment,* for God judged between all of the mountains and Sinai to decide which was most suitable for the giving of the Torah. Mount Tabor

1. The *Talmud (Megillah* 29b) notes that גַּבְנֻנִּים alludes to גִּבֵּן, *elongated eyebrows,* a blemish which disqualifies a priest from serving in the Temple (*Leviticus* 21:20). [These eyebrows are so long that they droop down and cover the eyes (*Rashi, Leviticus* 21:20). Just as exceptional length renders the eyebrows unfit for the priestly services, so does exceptional height render the mountains unfit for receiving the Torah.]

The *Talmud (Megillah* 29b) concludes that this teaches us that a man whose soul is blemished by arrogance is as much of a cripple as a man whose body is maimed with a physical wound.

גַּבְנֻנִּים הָהָר חָמַד אֱלֹהִים לְשִׁבְתּוֹ אַף־
יח יהוה יִשְׁכֹּן לָנֶצַח: רֶכֶב אֱלֹהִים רִבֹּתַיִם
יט אַלְפֵי שִׁנְאָן אֲדֹנָי בָם סִינַי בַּקֹּדֶשׁ: עָלִיתָ
לַמָּרוֹם | שָׁבִיתָ שֶּׁבִי לָקַחְתָּ מַתָּנוֹת בָּאָדָם

and Mount Carmel both came to demand judgment; but God dismissed their claims, saying, 'Your peaks are defiled by the idols erected there. Only Sinai has preserved its purity' *(Bereishis Rabbah* 99:1).

According to *Rashi, Radak* and *Sforno,* this verse does not refer to Mount Sinai but to Mount Moriah, the location of the Holy Temple. *Rashi* translates תְּרַצְּדוּן as *attack from ambush,* indicating that the other mountains [i.e., the mighty gentile nations] assault the Temple Mount and seek to destroy it.

הָהָר חָמַד אֱלֹהִים לְשִׁבְתּוֹ — *[Towards] the mountain which God has desired for His abode?*

God chose Mount Sinai because of its low elevation, which symbolizes the desirable trait of humility *(Targum).*

Ramban (Exodus 25:1) explains that the main purpose of the מִשְׁכָּן, *Tabernacle,* and מִקְדָּשׁ, *Temple,* was to provide a suitable repository for the Torah given at Sinai. The stone tablets which were given on that mountain were safeguarded in the Holy Ark, which was enshrined in the Holy of Holies. Therefore the extraordinary love which God had for Sinai was later transferred to the Mount Moriah, which became His permanent abode.

אַף ה׳ יִשְׁכֹּן לָנֶצַח — *Even HASHEM will dwell there forever.*

Once God's holy spirit settled on Mount Moriah, it never departed. See *Rambam, Hilchos Beis HaBechirah* 6:16.

[The psalmist no longer designates God as אֱלֹהִים, *the Dispenser of Strict Justice,* but as ה׳, *the Dispenser of Mercy,* thereby suggesting that although it was necessary for God to exercise His strict justice by destroying the Temple Mount, we look forward to the day when the Almighty *will dwell there* as HASHEM of Mercy *forever.*]

18. רֶכֶב אֱלֹהִים רִבֹּתַיִם — *The chariot of God is twice ten thousand.*

When God revealed Himself to Israel at Sinai, He was escorted by *twice ten thousand, thousands of Shin'an,* which are angels. His use of this elaborate retinue displayed His great affection for His chosen people *(Rashi).*

A mortal king goes out to war with a great army, but sends much smaller delegations on peace missions. In contrast, the Holy One, Blessed be He, goes out to war alone, as Scripture states, ה׳ אִישׁ מִלְחָמָה, *HASHEM is a Man* [all alone] *of war (Exodus* 15:3); however, when He went to give Israel the Torah [the source of all contentment and peace], He was accompanied by many myriads of angels *(Sifri, BeHaaloscha* 12:5).

אַלְפֵי שִׁנְאָן — *Thousands of* Shin'an.

Rashi views שִׁנְאָן as cognate with שְׁנוּנִים, *sharp, prompt,* signifying thousands of efficient angels who speedily discharge their Divine mission.

Ibn Ezra renders שִׁנְאָן as שְׁנַיִם. Thus אַלְפֵי שִׁנְאָן should be rendered *two thousand,* which in combination with the plural רִבֹּתַיִם, *myriads,* gives a total of 22,000. *Ibn Ezra* comments that this may allude to the number of Levites in the wilderness.

God foresaw that all the tribes, with the exception of Levi, would eventually forsake the Torah; therefore, it was only in Levi's merit that God descended upon Sinai *(Tanchuma, Tzav* 10).

According to *Targum,* this means two thousand angels who were instructed

Towards the mountain
which God has desired for His abode?
Even HASHEM will dwell there forever.
18 *The chariot of God is twice ten thousand,*
thousands of Shin'an
My Lord is among them,
at Sinai in holiness.
19 *You ascended on high,*
having taken captives.
You took gifts for man,

[שׁוֹנָה] by God directly, and *twice ten thousand* aflame with a celestial fire.

The *Midrash* (*Shemos Rabbah* 29:2) defines שִׁנְאָן as שֶׁנָּאִים, *that are beautiful,* referring to the ministering angels.

Sforno explains that these are angels שֶׁנָּאִים, *which move and change,* because they take on different forms when engaged in different missions. Each time they come in a prophetic vision, they take on a new appearance.

אֲדֹנָי בָם סִינַי בַּקֹּדֶשׁ – *My Lord is among them, at Sinai in holiness.*

According to Rabbi Yochanan, God descended at Sinai with six hundred thousand ministering angels who placed crowns on the head of each man of Israel as a reward for the holy zeal with which the Israelites accepted the Torah (*Tanchuma, Tetzaveh* 11).

19. עָלִיתָ לַמָּרוֹם – *You ascended on high.*

Rashi and *Targum* (based on *Shabbos* 89a) maintain that this refers to Moses, whose ascent on Mount Sinai was considered as an entry into the heavens.

When the ministering angels complained to the Holy One, Blessed be He, that a mortal did not belong among them, God replied, 'He ascended to take the Torah.'

The angels argued, 'This precious treasure, which was hidden away for the equivalent of 974 generations before the world was created, should not be given to mortal man.'

God then summoned Moses to counter the arguments of the angels. Moses reasoned with them, 'Angels do not need the Torah. You have no parents to honor, no possibility of conforming to the requirements of *kashrus,* and no Egyptian bondage to remember.'

The holy angels admitted the truth of Moses' words and consented to allow the Torah out of the heavenly domain, since its precepts apply only to man and to his world.

According to *Radak, Meiri* and *Sforno,* this verse refers to the conquest of *Eretz Yisrael* by the gentile armies who sent the Jews into exile. At that time it appeared as if God had completely forsaken the earth to the wicked *and* [*had*] *ascended on high.*

שָׁבִיתָ שֶּׁבִי – *Having taken* [lit. *You captured*] *captives.*

The angels sought to keep the Torah captive' in the heavens, until Moses captured it for mankind by his convincing arguments.

The length of the לֻחֹת, *tablets,* was six handbreaths. During the original struggle, the top two handbreadths were in the hands of God, the bottom two were grasped by the hands of Moses and two unclaimed handbreadths remained in the middle (*Shemos Rabbah* 28:1; *Yerushalmi Taanis* 4:5).

כ וְאַף סוֹרְרִים לִשְׁכֹּן | יָהּ אֱלֹהִים: בָּרוּךְ
אֲדֹנָי יוֹם | יוֹם יַעֲמָס־לָנוּ הָאֵל יְשׁוּעָתֵנוּ
כא סֶלָה: הָאֵל | לָנוּ אֵל לְמוֹשָׁעוֹת וְלֵיהוִֹה
כב אֲדֹנָי לַמָּוֶת תּוֹצָאוֹת: אַךְ־אֱלֹהִים יִמְחַץ

[Finally Moses *captured* all of the Torah for Israel].

Following the interpretation of *Radak, Meiri,* and *Sforno,* this means that the marauding gentile army overran the Holy Land and *took many captives.*

לָקַחְתָּ מַתָּנוֹת בָּאָדָם – *You took gifts for man.*

Moses brought the Torah down from heaven as a gift for mankind *(Targum; Rashi).*

In addition, when the angels accepted the truth of Moses' arguments, they displayed their friendship by giving him spiritual gifts. Even the Angel of Death was generous to Moses and revealed to him the secret of stopping a plague by burning incense (*Shabbos* 89b).

[According to the preceding interpretation, the word לָאָדָם, *for man* would have been more appropriate. Literally, בָּאָדָם means *in man,* indicating that the Torah was presented to humanity because its precepts find their fulfillment only *in man* rather than in angels (see *Tanchuma Ki Sisa* 17).]

The degenerate nations, whose barbarity resembles that of the beasts, did not deserve the Torah. Only the Jews, who are the epitome of morality and civilization, merited it; they alone are called אָדָם, *man,* par excellence (*Ezekiel* 34:31). Thus Moses *took the gifts* בָּאָדָם, *by virtue of man,* i.e., Israel (*Pesikta Rabbasi* 48:4).

Radak interprets these words: You took *away* from man (i.e., Israel) the presents which You once bestowed upon him. After man sinned, Your holy spirit departed from him and You no longer protected him.

וְאַף סוֹרְרִים לִשְׁכֹּן יָהּ אֱלֹהִים – *That even rebels may dwell with YAH God.*

Since the Torah was given, God's Holy Spirit clings to Israel under all circumstances, even when they rebel and anger Him *(Rashi).*

Radak renders: When You were angered by Israel, even the rebellious gentiles such as the brazen king of Assyria sought to conquer and dwell with YAH God in the holy city of Jerusalem.

20. בָּרוּךְ אֲדֹנָי – *Blessed be my Lord.*

Rashi explains that the following is the song mentioned above (*v.* 5), *Sing to God, make music for His Name.* [Sing to God because of the gift He gave us at Sinai.]

Sing to God because of the victory He gave Israel over the Assyrian host *(Radak).*

יוֹם יוֹם – *Day by day.*

Bless Him for His past kindness and anticipate His future kindness with additional blessings *(Malbim).*

יַעֲמָס לָנוּ – *He burdens us.*

In addition to the basic precepts which are incumbent upon the Children of Israel, God daily adds new commands, trials, and challenges, thus increasing our *burden (Targum).*

He does this in order to reward us with maximum goodness every day; He seeks to *burden* us with all the kindness we can possibly bear *(Rashi).*

God's ultimate goal is not to *burden us;* rather, He desires that we be a burden [i.e., dependent] on Him, as Scripture states, (*Isaiah* 46:3) בֵּית יִשְׂרָאֵל הָעֲמֻסִים מִנִּי בֶטֶן, *the House of Israel who are borne by me from birth (Shemos Rabbah* 25:9).

הָאֵל יְשׁוּעָתֵנוּ סֶלָה – *The God of our salvation, Selah.*

This is how God acts toward us *day*

that even rebels may dwell with YAH God.
20 *Blessed be my Lord,*
day by day
He burdens us,
the God of our salvation, Selah.
21 *The God is for us*
a God of salvations.
Though HASHEM/ELOHIM, my Lord,
has many avenues toward death—
22 *God will cleave only the head of His foes,*

by day: for every threat and *burden,* He provides us with a *salvation (Rashi).*

[God saved Israel from Sennacherib, King of Assyria, because the nation assumed the full *burden* of Torah study. The *Talmud (Sanhedrin* 94b) explains that in the merit of this intense עוֹל, *burden,* of Torah study, God protected His nation against the conquest attempted by Sennacherib.]

21. הָאֵל לָנוּ אֵל לְמוֹשָׁעוֹת – *[The] God is for us a God of salvations.*

Even when God acts strictly with us, it is for the purpose of saving us from an even harsher punishment. The man who suffers from poverty must realize that this is the Lord's way of providing him an *avenue* of escape from *death.* Since the pauper is considered a dead man (*Nedarim* 64b), this bitter punishment can take the place of real death and provide salvation from it *(Kiflayim L'tushiya).*

וְלֵיהוִה אֲדֹנָי – *Though HASHEM / ELOHIM, my Lord.*

Alshich points out that although the Divine Name used here is HASHEM, the vowel dots appended to it are those of אֱלֹהִים, *Elohim.*

[This teaches that it is in His role of HASHEM, *the Dispenser of Mercy,* that He tempers His love with the seemingly harsh lessons associated with the Name אֱלֹהִים, *Elohim, the Dispenser of Strict Justice.* Minor afflictions are intended to save a man from major tragedies by facilitating his recognition that he has displeased His Creator and by spurring him to repentance before he commits even graver offenses against God.]

לַמָּוֶת תּוֹצָאוֹת – *Has many avenues toward death.*

Rashi translates תּוֹצָאוֹת as *paths or exits* [leading from life] to death. God saves Israel, but He opens before their enemies many avenues of death.

God has a vast arsenal of lethal weapons at His disposal for annihilating our foes. He smote the Egyptians with ten different plagues and then drowned them in the sea. He hurled deadly hailstones upon the Canaanites (*Joshua* 10:11) and incited such bedlam amidst the Philistine ranks that the soldiers slew each other (I *Samuel* 14:20). This variety of deaths is endless *(Radak).*

The *Talmud (Berachos* 8a) teaches that God created 903 different forms of death, corresponding to the numerical value of תּוֹצָאוֹת.

22. אַךְ אֱלֹהִים יִמְחַץ רֹאשׁ אֹיְבָיו – *God will cleave only the head of his foes.*

God will slay them unaided and alone, without spear or sword, as He did when His angel slew one hundred and eighty thousand Assyrians in one instant *(Radak).*

רֹאשׁ אֹיְבָיו קָדְקֹד שֵׂעָר מִתְהַלֵּךְ
כג בַּאֲשָׁמָיו: אָמַר אֲדֹנָי מִבָּשָׁן אָשִׁיב אָשִׁיב
כד מִמְּצֻלוֹת יָם: לְמַעַן | תִּמְחַץ רַגְלְךָ בְּדָם
כה לְשׁוֹן כְּלָבֶיךָ מֵאֹיְבִים מִנֵּהוּ: רָאוּ
הֲלִיכוֹתֶיךָ אֱלֹהִים הֲלִיכוֹת אֵלִי מַלְכִּי

The destruction will be direct and complete; it will be aimed at *the head,* which is the most important part of the body *(Meiri).*

Yaavetz HaDoresh translates רֹאשׁ אֹיְבָיו as *the first of His foes,* i.e., Esau's grandson Amalek, the first enemy to attack the Jews as they left Egypt. Of Amalek, Scripture says, רֵאשִׁית גּוֹיִם עֲמָלֵק, *the first of nations is Amalek (Numbers* 24:20).

קָדְקֹד שֵׂעָר — *The hairy skull.*

This refers to the skull of Esau, who is described as אִישׁ שָׂעִר, *a hairy man (Genesis* 27:11; *Rashi).*

Esau seeks to conceal his wickedness beneath a facade of false piety. He resembles the swine which tries to prove that it is Kosher by displaying its split hooves *(Sforno).* [Therefore, Esau's skull will be split measure for measure.]

Meiri explains that the קָדְקֹד is the very center of the skull, where the hairline usually parts the hair into two separate sections. [Hence, this word is composed of two equal parts, קד and קד.]

Since the קָדְקֹד is the topmost point of the head, whenever Heavenly decrees descend upon a person, they are described as falling upon this spot [see 7:17 and *Deuteronomy* 33:16-17].

מִתְהַלֵּךְ בַּאֲשָׁמָיו — *Of him who saunters with his guilt.*

The wicked man calmly follows his daily routine and is untroubled by his burden of *guilt;* he refuses to repent *(Radak).*

He continues to follow his evil ways and adds new offenses to his record of *guilt (Sforno).*

23. אָמַר אֲדֹנָי מִבָּשָׁן אָשִׁיב — *My Lord promised, 'I will bring back from Bashan.'*

Rashi renders: I will rescue them from exile among *the mighty ones of Bashan* [cf. 22:13].

According to *Radak,* this is a Divine pledge to *turn back* or thwart the Assyrian invasion of Israel. Since the enemy first infiltrated Jewish territory on the eastern side of the Jordan River, in the land once known as *Bashan,* the entire campaign was named *Bashan.*

אָשִׁיב מִמְּצֻלוֹת יָם — *I will bring back from the depths of the sea.*

I shall gather in the exiles of Israel from all over the land and even from the islands of the sea *(Rashi; Sforno).*[1]

1. When the Second Temple was destroyed, four hundred Jewish boys and girls were seized and transported by ship to Rome for immoral purposes. When the youths realized the foul fate which awaited them, they asked the oldest and wisest of their group, 'If we drown ourselves in the sea, will we still merit a portion in the World to Come?'

The wise youth cited this verse, *'My Lord promised 'I will bring back from Bashan* [i.e., those threatened by בּוּשָׁה, *immoral disgrace*], *I will bring back from the depths of the sea'* [i.e., those who drown themselves to preserve their purity and to sanctify God's Name]. Upon hearing this, the maidens all leaped into the sea without hesitation. The youths immediately followed their example. Concerning these young martyrs, the psalmist laments, כִּי עָלֶיךָ הֹרַגְנוּ כָל הַיּוֹם, *For Your sake we are killed all the time* (44:23).

the hairy skull of him who saunters with his guilt.

23 *My Lord promised,*
'I will bring back from Bashan,
I will bring back from the depths of the sea;
24 *That your foot may wade*
through blood;
That the tongue of your dogs
may have its portion from the enemies.'
25 *They saw Your ways, O God,*
the ways of my God, my King, in holiness.

24. לְמַעַן תִּמְחַץ רַגְלְךָ בְּדָם — *(So) that your foot may wade through blood.*

Literally, מָחַץ means *to split* [see *Judges* 5:26]. Here it describes the parting of a liquid by wading through it: 'When the heads of our bitter foes are split, we shall wade in their blood' *(Rashi; Hirsch).*

Radak understands תִּמְחַץ as *to redden* [see *Isaiah* 63:1] the feet with the enemies' blood and *to redden* the tongues of the dogs who lick the blood.

לְשׁוֹן כְּלָבֶיךָ מֵאוֹיְבִים מִנֵּהוּ — [*That*] *the tongue of your dogs* [*may have*] *its portion from the enemies.*

Rashi (based on *Daniel* 1:10) translates מִנֵּהוּ as *its portion* of daily sustenance (from מָנָה, *a portion).* The Israelites' dogs shall find themselves amply provided with meat, bones, and blood from the remains of the enemy.

Midrash Shocher Tov comments that this refers to the drowned bodies of the Egyptians which were washed up on the shore of the Sea of Reeds. The Jews' dogs devoured the hands and limbs of the slave drivers who tortured the Israelites in Egypt.

25. רָאוּ הֲלִיכוֹתֶיךָ אֱלֹהִים — *They saw Your ways, O God.*

[At the sea, Israel *saw Your way* of dealing justly with mankind, according to their deserts. They witnessed their dogs devouring the cruel hands which once beat the Jews. When they noticed that some Egyptians drowned swiftly and painlessly while others suffered slow, excruciating deaths, they realized that each man was punished in accordance with the extent of his wickedness.]

God revealed His ways so clearly at the Sea, the *Mechilta (Parshas Beshalach)* says, that the humblest maidservant at the sea witnessed more than Ezekiel ben Buzi saw in all his prophecies *(Ibn Yachya).*

Furthermore, they saw Your concern for their welfare. When You split the sea, You fashioned not one, but twelve separate הֲלִיכוֹת, *ways,* a specially designed path for each tribe *(Alshich).*

Years later, when Israel witnessed the death of the Assyrian camp, they fully recognized *Your ways* in guiding the fate of mankind *(Radak).*

הֲלִיכוֹת אֵלִי מַלְכִּי בַקֹּדֶשׁ — *The ways of my God, my King, in holiness.*

[The eyes of Israel scrutinized the annals of history wisely. In every event they searched out the hand of God. The Divine Hand is evident to those who desire to discover His holiness in order to emulate God's sacred ways.]

כו בַקֹּדֶשׁ: קִדְּמוּ שָׁרִים אַחַר נֹגְנִים בְּתוֹךְ
כז עֲלָמוֹת תּוֹפֵפוֹת: בְּמַקְהֵלוֹת בָּרְכוּ
כח אֱלֹהִים אֲדֹנָי מִמְּקוֹר יִשְׂרָאֵל: שָׁם בִּנְיָמִן |
צָעִיר רֹדֵם שָׂרֵי יְהוּדָה רִגְמָתָם שָׂרֵי
כט זְבֻלוּן שָׂרֵי נַפְתָּלִי: צִוָּה אֱלֹהֶיךָ עֻזֶּךָ עוּזָּה

26. קִדְּמוּ שָׁרִים אַחַר נֹגְנִים — *First went singers, then musicians.*

At the sea, they first sang words of praise; only later were they joined by instrumental accompaniment *(Rashi).*

This demonstrates the intensity of their joy. Ordinarily, the orchestra begins the music in order to enliven the singers, who then join in. At the sea, the miracles which Israel witnessed sent their spirits soaring. The Jews broke into song before the musicians even had a chance to begin playing *(Yaavetz HaDoresh).*

Rashi, drawing upon the *Midrash (Shemos Rabbah* 23:7), identifies the שָׁרִים as the Children of Israel, who were given precedence over the angels. Although the angels were most eager to chant hymns of praise to the Almighty, He forced them to wait, explaining, 'It is not that I wish to make you appear inferior; rather, I must let the mortals sing first, lest those among them who are destined to die very soon lose their unprecedented opportunity to sing to Me. Since you angels are eternal, you are not threatened by sudden death.'

בְּתוֹךְ עֲלָמוֹת תּוֹפֵפוֹת — *In the midst of timbrel-playing maidens.*

The male singers were in the midst [of the camp], surrounded by the women, led by Miriam [who sang outside] *(Rashi; Radak).*

[*Exodus* 15:20 states, *And Miriam the prophetess, the sister of Aaron, took the timbrel in her hand, and all the women went out after her with timbrels and dancing.* The women left the camp because it is immodest to dance in the presence of men and it is forbidden for men to hear them singing (*Berachos* 24a). As an additional precaution, they drowned out their voices in the din of the crashing timbrels.

The tempo of the timbrel has a singularly irresistible effect, particularly on women. The *Talmud (Moed Kattan* 9b) says, 'A lady of sixty is rejuvenated into a little girl of six when she hears the sound of the timbrel; she runs (to dance). Therefore, all the women of Israel (including Miriam, who was eighty-six years old) are described here as nimble and graceful עֲלָמוֹת, *maidens.* (See *Pardeis Yosef, Shemos* 15:20).]

27. בְּמַקְהֵלוֹת בָּרְכוּ אֱלֹהִים אֲדֹנָי — *In congregations bless God, my Lord.*

[Israel did not cross the sea as a single קָהָל, *congregation,* but as twelve separate tribes or מַקְהֵלוֹת, *congregations.* Nevertheless, when it came time to sing God's praises, they all joined together as one.]

אֲדֹנָי מִמְּקוֹר יִשְׂרָאֵל — *From the source of Israel.*

Even the toddler on his father's knee and the infant at his mother's breast witnessed the glory of God at the sea and burst forth in song. Even the fetus in his mother's womb sang a hymn of praise, as it says, *In congregations bless God, my Lord — from the* מְקוֹר, *womb* [i.e., the *source* of human life] *of Israel (Berachos* 50b; *Yerushalmi Sotah* 5:4).

This alludes to the virtuous Jewish wives who fiercely protected their chastity, despite the fact that the Jews were at the mercy of the lewd Egyptians for hundreds of years. They kept the pedigree of Israel as pure as a fresh fountain by guarding the *source,* i.e.,

[26] *First went singers, then musicians;*
In the midst of timbrel-playing maidens.
[27] *In congregations bless God,*
my Lord — from the source of Israel.
[28] *There Benjamin, the youngest, rules them,*
the princes of Judah stoned them,
the princes of Zebulun,
the princes of Naphtali.
[29] *Your God decreed your might,*

the womb, from defilement. Since God's assistance enabled them to retain their purity, it is the subject of this song of praise *(Alshich).*

28. שָׁם בִּנְיָמִן צָעִיר רֹדֵם — *There Benjamin, the youngest, rules them.*

When Israel stood poised at the edge of the sea before it split, the tribes began to quarrel. Each argued that it deserved to be the first to plunge into the water. [Actually, the shore of the sea was long enough for everyone to have jumped into the water together, but each tribe wanted the honor of carrying the coffin of Joseph, for Israel had been assured that the sea would part in Joseph's merit *(Mahari Pinto).*] Suddenly, the tribe of Benjamin leaped into the sea [without Joseph's coffin], as the verse states, *Benjamin* רֹדֵם, i.e., רַד יָם, *went down into the Sea! (Sotah* 36b).

Because the tribe of Benjamin courageously assumed the role of leadership at the Sea, one of its members, King Saul, later became the first Jewish monarch. This is also alluded to in the word רֹדֵם, which is cognate with רֹדֶה, *to rule (Targum; Rashi).*

שָׂרֵי יְהוּדָה רִגְמָתָם — *The princes of Judah stoned them.*

Since Judah was the tribe Divinely ordained for the monarchy, Judah reacted forcefully to Benjamin's apparent usurpation of its royal power. Judah stoned Benjamin, forcing the tribe to return to shore. Then, led by their prince, Nachshon ben Aminodov, the true tribe of monarchy jumped into the sea *(Sotah* 36b; *Alshich).*

Although the monarchy was later transferred from the House of Saul the Benjaminite to the House of David the Judean, the Temple was constructed predominantly on the territory of Benjamin and only partially on the estate of Judah. Since Benjamin descended to the sea first, the Holy Spirit descended upon his territory first (*Mechilta Beshalach,* 14).

שָׂרֵי זְבֻלוּן שָׂרֵי נַפְתָּלִי — *The princes of Zebulun, the princes of Naphtali.*

[They assisted Judah in stoning Benjamin.]

According to *Radak,* the verse alludes to the Assyrian attack on the Jewish nation. The Ten Tribes of Israel were already in exile; all that remained were a few scattered individuals, primarily from the tribes of Zebulun and Naftali. The noble men of these remnants came to Jerusalem to assist the tribes of Judah and Benjamin רִגְמָתָם, *gathered,* there. At that time, Benjamin courageously רֹדֵם, *overwhelmed,* the enemy in battle. When victory was achieved, all the different tribes, i.e., מַקְהֵלוֹת, *congregations,* united to bless God.

29. צִוָּה אֱלֹהֶיךָ עֻזֶּךָ — *Your God decreed* [lit. *has commanded*] *Your might.*

[At the moment of Israel's miraculous

ל אֱלֹהִים זוּ פָּעַלְתָּ לָּנוּ: מֵהֵיכָלֶךָ עַל־
לא יְרוּשָׁלָםִ לְךָ יוֹבִילוּ מְלָכִים שָׁי: גְּעַר חַיַּת
קָנֶה עֲדַת אַבִּירִים | בְּעֶגְלֵי עַמִּים מִתְרַפֵּס
בְּרַצֵּי־כָסֶף בִּזַּר עַמִּים קְרָבוֹת יֶחְפָּצוּ:

triumph, all recognized that God had decreed that Israel be invincible.]

Some attribute these words to the tribe of Judah, who declared that its might and royal power were from God (*Dorash Moshe*).

According to other commentators, these are the words of King David (*Ibn Ezra*) or King Chizkiyahu (*Radak*).

עוּזָּה אֱלֹהִים זוּ פָּעַלְתָּ לָּנוּ — *This might, O God, You have wrought for us.*

The translation follows *Radak*. *Rashi*, however, interprets this as Israel's grateful blessing to God: 'Be mighty, for You have wrought all this good for our sake!'

30. מֵהֵיכָלֶךָ עַל יְרוּשָׁלָםִ — *Out of Your Temple on to Jerusalem.*

Your majesty overflows out of Your Sanctuary in the *Beis HaMikdash* and spreads over the entire city of Jerusalem. This was particularly evident at the time of the downfall of Assyria, which had conquered the world. Only Jerusalem remained impregnable, for it was fortified by the sanctity emanating from the *Beis HaMikdash* (*Radak*).

לְךָ יוֹבִילוּ מְלָכִים שָׁי — *To You the kings shall deliver tribute.*

Hirsch points out that the word שָׁי is only found here, in 76:12, and in *Isaiah* 18:7. In each case, the word signifies a special gift which the nations will someday offer as tribute to God.

Just as God's glory is spread over Jerusalem, it shall eventually cover the entire earth. Then all the nations will pay tribute to Him and to the Messiah (*Esther Rabbosi* 1:4).

31. גְּעַר — *Destroy.*

When followed by a noun prefixed with a ב, *beis*, this verb means *to rebuke harshly* [see *Targum*]. Here, however, it is translated *destroy* (*Radak* and *Ibn Ezra, Psalms* 9:6).

חַיַּת קָנֶה — *The beast of reed*[s].

This describes the greedy and overbearing nation which tramples the peoples of the world just as a wild boar crashes through flimsy reeds. Many Talmudic and Midrashic sources identify this conqueror as the Roman Empire [see 80:14]. However, *Rashi* maintains that this verse refers to Ishmael, i.e., to the Arabs.

According to the *Zohar (Parshas Pinchos)*, this alludes to the humble origin of the mighty Roman Empire. When Solomon sinned with his wives, God began to transfer the sovereignty, of Israel to Rome. To symbolize this, the Almighty sent the angel Gabriel to thrust a lone קָנֶה, *reed* into the Mediterranean Sea; eventually, debris collected around this reed and formed the Italian Peninsula (*Shabbos* 56b). [This signifies that Rome was essentially weak; its strength lay in its diplomatic skill in fashioning powerful alliances. Basically these nations were like debris or waste which clings together and solidifies into a strong position.]

This enemy attacks with long spears resembling *reeds (Radak; Meiri).*

Everything which Rome does is recorded with the very same 'reed pen' (*Pesachim* 118a). [Rome laid claim to being the epitome of culture and civilization. However, her 'pen' created not only Western law, literature, and art, but also the most inhuman decrees of torture and death against Israel and other nations (*Midrash Shocher Tov, Psalm* 2). At the core, the Romans were

this might, O God, You have wrought for us.
30 *Out of Your Temple on to Jerusalem —*
to You the kings shall deliver tribute.
31 *Destroy the beast of reeds,*
the assembly of bulls
among the calves of nations,
who ingratiates himself for pieces of silver;
Who scatters nations and desires battles.

ruthless, militaristic barbarians, no better than the wild *beast of the reeds.*]

עֲדַת אַבִּירִים בְּעֶגְלֵי עַמִּים — *The assembly of bulls* [lit. *mighty ones*] *among the calves of nations.*

Meiri cites 22:13, where the mightiest of nations are compared to *bulls.* They intimidate the weaker nations, who resemble tender calves.

מִתְרַפֵּס — *Who ingratiates himself.*

This corrupt nation would stoop to the lowest depths and grovel for love of money *(Meiri; Radak; Rashi).*

Hirsch notes that the root of this word is רֶפֶס or רֶפֶשׁ, *mud, mire,* indicating that the sophistication and culture of Rome are a crude facade. They would sell their pride and wallow in filth and *mud* for the sake of money.

Midrash Shocher Tov (*Psalms* 2) understands מִתְרַפֵּס as a contraction of מַתִּיר פַּס, *they open the palm* of their hand to accept bribes.

בְּרַצֵּי כָסֶף — *For pieces of silver (Radak).*

Hirsch comments that רַצֵּי is related to רָצַץ, *to break into pieces.* [Since this nation lacks the slightest trace of self-respect, they would sell their souls for a mere scrap of silver.]

Rashi translates רַצֵּי as רִצּוּי, *appeasement,* i.e., they are pleased only by money.

בִּזַּר עַמִּים — *Who scatters nations.*

The ב should be read as a פ, changing the word to פִּזַּר, *scatters (Rashi; Radak).*

קְרָבוֹת יֶחְפָּצוּ — [*Who*] *desires battles.*

This militaristic nation lives by the sword and constantly seeks an excuse to enter into hostilities with other nations *(Rashi).*[1]

1. The word קְרָבוֹת may also be identified with קָרוֹב, *close relative.* Based on this verse the Sages of the *Talmud (Pesachim* 118b) discovered the formula for comprehending Israel's erratic fortunes in exile.

Israel will prosper in exile only as long as the Jews safeguard their unique identity as God's chosen nation, a people set apart. When Israel seeks to assimilate into its gentile environment, however, it is violently rejected by its host nation. Just as the human body cannot tolerate the intromission of foreign matter and rejects it violently, so does the body of nations forcibly expel Israel when the Jewish nation attempts to enter its midst.

Thus, בִּזַּר עַמִּים, God *scatters* Israel *among* the far-flung *nations.* He drives them out of the country where they have wrongly come to feel 'at home' because their sense of equality has caused them to forget that they are alien. They are rejected because קְרָבוֹת יֶחְפָּצוּ, *they desire closeness* [from קָרוֹב, *relative*] with the gentiles.

This lesson was vividly illustrated by Israel's first exile in Egypt. As long as the Jews voluntarily segregated themselves from the Egyptians and cloistered themselves in Goshen, they were held in esteem; but once they spread throughout the land and attempted to assimilate into Egyptian society, they were oppressed and threatened with annihilation *(Beis HaLeivi, Parshas Shemos).*

לב יָאֱתָיוּ חַשְׁמַנִּים מִנִּי מִצְרָיִם כּוּשׁ תָּרִיץ
לג יָדָיו לֵאלֹהִים: מַמְלְכוֹת הָאָרֶץ שִׁירוּ
לד לֵאלֹהִים זַמְּרוּ אֲדֹנָי סֶלָה: לָרֹכֵב בִּשְׁמֵי
לה שְׁמֵי־קֶדֶם הֵן יִתֵּן בְּקוֹלוֹ קוֹל עֹז: תְּנוּ עֹז
לֵאלֹהִים עַל־יִשְׂרָאֵל גַּאֲוָתוֹ וְעֻזּוֹ
לו בַּשְּׁחָקִים: נוֹרָא אֱלֹהִים | מִמִּקְדָּשֶׁיךָ אֵל
יִשְׂרָאֵל הוּא נֹתֵן | עֹז וְתַעֲצֻמוֹת לָעָם
בָּרוּךְ אֱלֹהִים:

32. יָאֱתָיוּ חַשְׁמַנִּים מִנִּי מִצְרָיִם – *Nobles shall come from Egypt.*

Menachem explains that חַשְׁמַנִּים are the inhabitants of the land of חַשְׁמוֹנָה. However, *Radak* and *Ibn Ezra* identify them as the *nobles* of all the nations. Similarly, we find that the aristocratic family of Matisyahu, the high priest, was called חַשְׁמוֹנָאִי.

The *Talmud (Pesachim* 118b) says that in the future, the degrading exile will end. Israel will no longer strive to come close to the nations [see footnote *v.* 31]; rather, the nations will attempt to ally themselves with Israel. Even our archenemy, Egypt, will offer tribute (see *v.* 30).

Although the Messiah's first reaction will be to reject the gifts proffered by the nation which once oppressed us so cruelly, God will insist that the tribute be accepted, since Egypt had provided the family of the Patriarch Jacob hospitality in time of famine.

According to *Midrash Shocher Tov,* the name חַשְׁמַנִּים is a contraction of חָשׁוּ, *they hastened,* to bring מָנִים, *costly gifts.* Also they are מְמוּנִים, *completely prepared* to join our nation as proselytes.

כּוּשׁ תָּרִיץ יָדָיו לֵאלֹהִים – *Kush shall hasten its hands to God.*

Kush [commonly identified with Ethiopia] will eagerly follow the example set by Egypt and immediately bring tribute to the Messiah (*Pesachim* 118b).

According to *Radak,* before Sennacherib besieged Jerusalem, he conquered the empires of Egypt and Kush; he then held their noblemen captive in his camp while he encircled the Holy City. When these princes witnessed the wondrous destruction of the Assyrian host, they recognized the greatness of our God. They survived the plague, threw themselves into the hands of God's chosen people, and converted to Judaism.

33. מַמְלְכוֹת הָאָרֶץ שִׁירוּ לֵאלֹהִים – *O Kingdoms of the earth, sing to God.*

In this world, the gentile kingdoms fail to appreciate the greatness of the Almighty, who allows His chosen people to suffer so much at their hands. In the future, however, the kingdoms will realize that God only afflicted the Jews in His role as אֱלֹהִים, *the Dispenser of Strict Justice,* i.e., for their own benefit. At that time, the gentiles will sing God's praises *(Alshich).*

34. לָרֹכֵב בִּשְׁמֵי שְׁמֵי קֶדֶם – *To the Rider upon the loftiest of primeval heavens* [lit. *the heavens of heavens of old*].

This refers to the highest of the seven heavens, *Aravos,* as mentioned earlier in *v.* 5, *Extol Him who rides in Aravos.* Unlike this temporary world and its mortal inhabitants, the highest heavens and the angels who dwell there have existed from antiquity and will continue to exist forever *(Radak).*

32 *Nobles shall come from Egypt*
Kush shall hasten its hands to God.
33 *O Kingdoms of the earth,*
sing to God,
make music to my Lord, Selah!
34 *To the Rider upon*
the loftiest of primeval heavens
Behold He bestows with His voice,
a mighty voice.
35 *Attribute might to God,*
Whose majesty hovers over Israel
And Whose might is in the clouds.
36 *You are awesome, O God,*
from Your sanctuaries, O God of Israel —
It is He Who grants might and power
to the nation, blessed be God.

Previously, the kingdoms of earth attributed their sovereignty and success to the celestial signs, the heavenly bodies which they thought controlled man's fate and fortune; but when Israel ascends above all of the nations, they will recognize that God alone rules the heavens, just as the rider determines the path of his horse *(Sforno).*

הֵן יִתֵּן בְּקוֹלוֹ קוֹל עֹז — *Behold He bestows with His voice, a mighty voice.*

In the future, God will proclaim His complete sovereignty over all the earth. He will sweep away the lesser celestial forces which had previously been His agents and His intermediaries *(Sforno).*

35. תְּנוּ עֹז לֵאלֹהִים — *Attribute might to God.*

The *mighty voice* which will go forth *(v.* 34) will proclaim *(Ibn Ezra)* that the power which the nations previously exercised over Israel was not their own but was a Divine endowment *(Alshich).* The strength of the Messiah will also be ascribed to the Almighty *(Sforno).*

In a sense, the source of all God's might is Israel: When the children of Israel follow the wishes of the Omnipresent, they reinforce the strength of the One above (see *Mechilta Beshalach* 15:6). The Divine wisdom had ordained that God's actions be a reflection of Israel's deeds; the strength of Israel's commitment *give*[s] *might to God (Rashbam; Binah L'ittim).*

עַל יִשְׂרָאֵל גַּאֲוָתוֹ — *Whose majesty* [lit., *pride*] *hovers over Israel.*

God can only be proud, so to speak, when Israel is faithful and obedient to His word *(ARIzal).* Then, He displays the extent of His majesty and pride by acting generously to His precious people *(Ibn Ezra),* and by making them triumphant over their foes *(Rashbam).* Similarly, the prophet (*Isaiah* 49:3) spoke of *Israel, in whom I will be glorified (Sforno).*

וְעֻזּוֹ בַּשְּׁחָקִים — *And Whose might is in the clouds.*

[When God's sovereignty is recognized on earth, He is empowered, so to speak, to exercise His might over the celestial forces above.]

36. נוֹרָא אֱלֹהִים מִמִּקְדָּשֶׁיךָ — *You are awesome, O God, from Your sanctuaries.*

Radak and *Ibn Ezra* perceive the plural form *Your sanctuaries* as an allusion to the dual existence of the *Beis Hamikdosh:* there is a spiritual Temple in the heavens which corresponds to the Temple on earth [the one below cannot be destroyed until its heavenly counterpart is obliterated].

In addition, *Radak* suggests that the plural form alludes to the various sections and chambers of the *Beis Hamikdosh.* The *Sanctuary* was divided into different levels of holiness.

The entire world was awestruck when God destroyed His most sacred and cherished place. This impressed upon all men the exacting demands of God's strict justice.

The *Talmud (Zevachim* 115b) says that the word may also be read מִמְּקוּדָּשֶׁיךָ, *from Your holy people,* meaning that God is especially demanding of His most pious and devout nation. When they are punished for even the slightest deviation from scrupulous adherence to the law, the world is filled with fear and awe.

אֵל יִשְׂרָאֵל הוּא נֹתֵן עֹז וְתַעֲצֻמוֹת לָעָם — *O God of Israel — it is He Who grants might and power to the nation.*

God will grant royal *might* to the Messiah and extraordinary *power* to the entire nation, as the prophet (*Micah* 5:7) foretells: *And the remnant of Jacob shall be among the nations in the midst of many peoples like a young lion among the flocks of sheep (Sforno).*

בָּרוּךְ אֱלֹהִים — *Blessed be God.*

This psalm begins with the prayer (*v.* 2) יָקוּם אֱלֹהִים, *Let God arise,* and it concludes with a response to this impassioned plea. In the future, God will demonstrate that the Divine justice which He had dispensed with such apparent harshness was actually disguised beneficence.

At that time, the entire world will enthusiastically bless אֱלֹהִים, *God, Dispenser of Strict Justice,* for everything He has done *(Yaavetz HaDoresh).*

מזמור סט 69

The great irony of Jewish history is that our exiled nation has spent more time on foreign soil than in its own homeland. Uprooted violently from their natural setting, the Jewish people have wandered for almost twenty centuries. Our people have not merely survived without a country to call their own — they have even flourished during the exile.

The fact of Jewish survival grows even more amazing when one considers the hostile environments into which our people have been thrust. Israel resembles a delicate and vulnerable rose. Just as the rose is protected by its thorns, the Jewish people are protected by the Torah, which fortifies us so that we may endure the hardships and dangers of our exile (Hirsch). *This concept of exile provides the theme of this psalm.*

Hirsch *observes that the psalmist, David, has a prophetic vision of generations of brave Jews surviving the dark centuries of exile, sustained by the thoughts contained in this psalm. First, the downtrodden outcasts recount the tragic tale of their wanderings and woes* (v. 2-30). *Finally however, they draw on the deep reserves of faith which permeate the Jewish heart, and they shout out a triumphant hymn of everlasting devotion to God* (v. 31-37). *Thus, from the crucible of suffering emerges a mold of ironclad faith which has withstood the tests of the ages.*

Another major theme, David's ancestry, is discussed at length in Overview to Megillas Ruth, *ArtScroll edition, and in* The Book of Our Heritage (Vol. 3), *'Sivan,' by Eliyahu Kitov.*

סט א־ה

א־ב לַמְנַצֵּחַ עַל־שׁוֹשַׁנִּים לְדָוִד: הוֹשִׁיעֵנִי
ג אֱלֹהִים כִּי בָאוּ מַיִם עַד־נָפֶשׁ: טָבַעְתִּי |
בִּיוֵן מְצוּלָה וְאֵין מָעֳמָד בָּאתִי בְמַעֲמַקֵּי־
ד מַיִם וְשִׁבֹּלֶת שְׁטָפָתְנִי: יָגַעְתִּי בְקָרְאִי
ה נִחַר גְּרוֹנִי כָּלוּ עֵינַי מְיַחֵל לֵאלֹהָי: רַבּוּ |
מִשַּׂעֲרוֹת רֹאשִׁי שֹׂנְאַי חִנָּם עָצְמוּ

1. עַל שׁוֹשַׁנִּים — *Upon Shoshanim.*

[See 45:1; 60:1.]

Here David sings of the exile of Israel, which began with the exile of the members of Sanhedrin, who are likened to שׁוֹשַׁנִּים, *roses (Targum).*

In exile, the seventy nations attack Israel, just as the thorns which surround the *rose* prick its delicate petals *(Rashi).*

The chief characteristics of the *rose* are its bright red color and its remarkable fragrance. These symbolize the main features of exile: Israel's wanderings have been stained by the blood of martyrdom, but the soul of our people has become permeated with the sublime fragrance of purity *(Alshich).*

2. הוֹשִׁיעֵנִי אֱלֹהִים — *Save me, O God.*

[Although Israel is accustomed to harsh treatment in the exile (for God manifests Himself to His people as אֱלֹהִים, *Dispenser of Strict Justice),* nevertheless, Divine salvation is to be expected when the very existence of the Jewish nation is endangered by the enemy.]

כִּי בָאוּ מַיִם עַד נָפֶשׁ — *For the waters have reached until the soul!*

The nations are likened to water, as the psalmist says (18:17), *He drew me out of deep waters (Ibn Ezra).* Israel, up to its neck in troubles, is on the verge of death *(Radak).*

[Israel can endure the physical suffering of exile; but the nation cannot tolerate the erosion of its unique spiritual values by the heresy and immorality which pervade the exile.]

3. טָבַעְתִּי בִּיוֵן מְצוּלָה — *I am sunk in deep mire* [lit. *quicksand of the shadowy deep; cf. Psalms* 40:3 טִיט הַיָּוֵן].

Israel laments: The exiled nation has a double problem; not only is it drowning in the waters of the מְצוּלָה, [lit. *shadowy deep*], but also it cannot extricate itself, because it is mired in יָוֵן [lit. *quicksand*] *(Radak).*

Contact with the gentile world introduced me to enticing new lusts. I am drawn into their grip, like a man sucked into quicksand *(Migdal David).*

Sforno says that מְצוּלָה refers to the Babylonian exile. This land was so low and muddy that the prophet (*Isaiah* 44:27) calls it צוּלָה, *shadowy deep.*

[*Sforno* analyzes every word in this psalm, demonstrating how each phrase refers to a different incident in Israel's long exile. However, we have omitted most of his comments because they would require excessive explanation and background material.]

וְאֵין מָעֳמָד — *(And) there is no foothold.*

[Assimilation threatens from all sides. There appears to be no way to maintain a separate, independent identity on an equal footing with other nations. Israel seems to be doomed.]

בָּאתִי בְמַעֲמַקֵּי מַיִם — *I have entered deepest waters.*

[Another double threat is mentioned here: Not only is Israel drowning in *deep waters,* but also a *swift current* is sweeping the nation, preventing its escape.]

וְשִׁבֹּלֶת שְׁטָפָתְנִי — *(And) a rushing current sweeps me away.*

69
1-5

For the Conductor, upon Shoshanim,
by David.
[2] Save me, O God,
for the waters have reached until the soul!
[3] I am sunk in deep mire,
there is no foothold.
I have entered deepest waters;
a rushing current sweeps me away.
[4] I am wearied by my crying,
my throat is parched,
My eyes failed
as I waited for my God.
[5] More abundant than the hairs of my head
are those who hate me groundlessly.
Mighty are those who would cut me off,

[שִׁבֹּלֶת is related to שְׁבִיל, *path.* The gentile lifestyle runs counter to the Jewish way of life. It makes a strong impression upon the Jew who is struggling to survive in a hostile environment, and it threatens to 'sweep him away' from his Jewish tradition.]

4. יָגַעְתִּי בְקָרְאִי — *I am wearied by my crying* [lit. *calling*].

Like a drowning man screaming desperately for help, I called out until my throat became dry [and my cries were of no avail] *(Radak).*

נִחַר גְּרוֹנִי — *My throat is parched.*

Esau's prowess lies in his sword, but the power of Jacob rests in his throat. When Jacob raises his voice in prayer, he usually is answered. Yet, in the gloom of exile, God did not respond to the Jews' supplications; therefore, their voices grew hoarse from incessant prayer *(Chozeh David).*

כָּלוּ עֵינַי מְיַחֵל לֵאלֹהָי — *My eyes failed as I waited for my God.*

[Although I waited continuously for the dawn of redemption, and strained my eyes until they grew weak, God did not even show me a glimmer of hope or communicate the slightest response to my plea.]

5. רַבּוּ מִשַּׂעֲרוֹת רֹאשִׁי שֹׂנְאַי חִנָּם — *More abundant than the hairs of my head are those who hate me groundlessly.*

Countless enemies have eagerly searched for an opportunity to attack Israel without any provocation, because they see that history bears out the Talmudic prognosis (*Gittin* 56a): Whoever afflicts Israel attains a position of world leadership *(Tehillos Hashem).*

עָצְמוּ מַצְמִיתַי — *Mighty are those who would cut me off.*

If the enemies merely multiplied like hairs, then their threat would not be overwhelming, for each hair is but a flimsy wisp which is easily bent back. However, my peril is truly great, because the strength of each individual enemy has increased, so that each has become a mighty and formidable adversary which threatens to raze me *(Beer Avraham).*

מַצְמִיתַי אֹיְבַי שֶׁקֶר אֲשֶׁר לֹא־גָזַלְתִּי אָז
ו אָשִׁיב: אֱלֹהִים אַתָּה יָדַעְתָּ לְאִוַּלְתִּי
ז וְאַשְׁמוֹתַי מִמְּךָ לֹא־נִכְחָדוּ: אַל־יֵבֹשׁוּ בִי |
קֹוֶיךָ אֲדֹנָי יֱהֹוִה צְבָאוֹת אַל־יִכָּלְמוּ בִי
ח מְבַקְשֶׁיךָ אֱלֹהֵי יִשְׂרָאֵל: כִּי־עָלֶיךָ
ט נָשָׂאתִי חֶרְפָּה כִּסְּתָה כְלִמָּה פָנָי: מוּזָר
י הָיִיתִי לְאֶחָי וְנָכְרִי לִבְנֵי אִמִּי: כִּי־קִנְאַת

אֹיְבַי שֶׁקֶר — *My falsehood-seeking foes.*

I dedicate my life to truth and refuse to join my foes in their pursuit of lies and false ideals. For this they cannot forgive me *(Rashi).*

שֹׂנְאַי חִנָּם, *those who hate me groundlessly,* pose much less of a threat. Since their hatred is groundless, they fabricate no slanderous tales to besmirch my reputation; but אֹיְבַי שֶׁקֶר, *my falsehood-seeking foes,* justify their bitter enmity by spreading false, malicious accusations against me *(Beer Avraham;* see *Targum).*

אֲשֶׁר לֹא גָזַלְתִּי אָז אָשִׁיב — *What I never stole I will then return.*

When the gentile mobs gather to do me harm, I have no choice but to appease them with bribes. Thus, I am compelled to *return that which I never stole,* i.e., I give them money which I do not owe them *(Rashi).*

According to *Radak:* The gentiles accuse me of thefts which I never committed and force me to repay money which I never stole.

6. אֱלֹהִים אַתָּה יָדַעְתָּ לְאִוַּלְתִּי — *O God, You know my folly.*

In the previous verse, Israel vigorously denied the false charges hurled by the gentiles. Israel now hastens to admit that she has indeed been guilty of sins — but not of those invented by the malicious enemy. God alone is aware of the full extent of these wrongdoings, but He also knows that these sins were caused by ignorance and foolishness *(Hirsch).*

The אִוֶּלֶת is the sin committed for no reason. [The Sages teach: A man does not sin unless he is seized by a spirit of madness (*Sotah* 5a).] Therefore, a senseless offense is punished by the senseless attack of שֹׂנְאַי חִנָּם, *those who hate me without cause (Beer Avraham).*

וְאַשְׁמוֹתַי מִמְּךָ לֹא נִכְחָדוּ — *And my guilty acts from You are not hidden.*

God recognizes that the hidden root of my *acts of guilt* is the lust for pleasure and gratification; but now, I realize that I was enticed by false fantasies, for the pleasures I so eagerly anticipated were truly harmful and evil. Since I lied to myself, I was plagued by (*v.* 5) אֹיְבַי שֶׁקֶר, *my enemies who lie (Beer Avraham).*

7. אַל יֵבֹשׁוּ בִי קֹוֶיךָ — *Let them not be shamed through me, those who wait for You* [cf. 25:3].

Israel has long awaited Divine redemption; if their hopes are ultimately dashed, then all other men awaiting Divine salvation will also be disappointed *(Radak; Rashi).*

According to *Malbim,* בּוּשָׁה is the inner *shame* one feels for himself whereas כְּלִימָה is public *disgrace* suffered at the hands of others [see *comm.* to 35:3]. When those who wait for God see that their hopes go unfulfilled, they are personally 'shamed' by the realization that they have been unworthy of Divine assistance.

אֲדֹנָי ה׳ צְבָאוֹת — *My Lord HASHEM/ELOHIM of Legions.*

my falsehood-seeking foes.
What I never stole
I will then return.
6 *O God You know my folly,*
and my guilty acts from You are not hidden.
7 *Let them not be shamed through me,*
those who wait for You;
My Lord HASHEM/ELOHIM of Legions,
let them not be disgraced through me,
those who seek You,
O God of Israel.
8 *Because for Your sake humiliation*
I have borne,
Disgrace covered my face.
9 *I became a stranger to my brothers,*
and an alien to my mother's sons.

[When the ineffable four-letter Name of God follows אֲדֹנָי, it is vowelized and read as אֱלֹהִים, *Elohim.*]

You are the Master of the celestial legions above, and Lord of the legions of Israel below. Since You can manipulate all creation at will, we beg You to redeem Israel *(Radak).*

אַל יִכָּלְמוּ בִי מְבַקְשֶׁיךָ – *Let them not be disgraced through me, those who seek You.*

Malbim continues: If those who seek You publicly are not answered they will suffer public כְּלִמָּה, *disgrace,* by being embarrassed before others.

אֱלֹהֵי יִשְׂרָאֵל – *O God of Israel.*

Israel beseeches God to remember His promise that he would accompany them into exile: *When they are in the land of their enemies I will not reject them, neither will I abhor them, to destroy them utterly and to break my covenant with them, for I am HASHEM their God (Leviticus 26:44; Hirsch).*

8. כִּי עָלֶיךָ נָשָׂאתִי חֶרְפָּה – *Because for Your sake humiliation I have borne.*

Humiliation is the most intense form of insult and degradation suffered at the hands of others [see *comm.* to *Psalms* 35:4].

This *humiliation* would have ended in a moment had I only accepted the religion of my tormentors; but *for Your sake* I have gladly borne the burden of the Jewish faith *(Radak).*

כִּסְּתָה כְלִמָּה פָנָי – *Disgrace covered my face.*

All the nations know that if Israel were to repent her sins she would immediately be redeemed. The continuation of the exile is therefore a public *disgrace,* because it reveals Israel's stubborn refusal to mend her ways *(Beer Avraham).*

9. מוּזָר הָיִיתִי לְאֶחָי – *I became a stranger to my brothers.*

Beer Avraham differentiates between the נָכְרִי, *alien,* and the זָר, *stranger;* the former is a citizen of a foreign nation. The latter is someone from one's own nation who had been close but has become estranged.

בֵּיתְךָ אֲכָלָתְנִי וְחֶרְפּוֹת חוֹרְפֶיךָ נָפְלוּ
יא עָלָי: וָאֶבְכֶּה בַצּוֹם נַפְשִׁי וַתְּהִי לַחֲרָפוֹת
יב לִי: וָאֶתְּנָה לְבוּשִׁי שָׂק וָאֱהִי לָהֶם לְמָשָׁל:
יג יָשִׂיחוּ בִי יֹשְׁבֵי שָׁעַר וּנְגִינוֹת שׁוֹתֵי שֵׁכָר:

Rashi explains that Esau was a very close relative of Israel, a full brother sharing the same father and mother. In exile, Israel *became a stranger* to Esau, for he refused to recognize their family bond.

Radak, however, contends that *stranger* refers to Ishmael, who was only a half-brother to the Jews, through the Patriarch Abraham. [See *comm.* to verse 22 for a description of how the Ishmaelites betrayed the exiled Jews.]

וְנָכְרִי לִבְנֵי אִמִּי — *And an alien to my mother's sons.*

According to *Radak* this describes Esau, who, unlike Ishmael, is a full brother to Israel. [Despite their close blood relationship, Esau was completely alienated from his Jewish brethren. The *Talmud (Kiddushin* 18a) describes Esau as an apostate Jew.]

10. כִּי קִנְאַת בֵּיתְךָ אֲכָלָתְנִי — *Because envy of Your House devoured me.*

The gentiles saw the great love which You displayed for us while Your House, the *Beis HaMikdash* stood [see *Yoma* 54a]. It was this love that aroused their envy *(Rashi).*

Olellos Ephraim perceives in these words an allusion to the moral decay which undermined the social and spiritual fabric of the Jewish nation and caused the Temple to be destroyed. *Envy* and senseless hatred caused the House of God to be *devoured* [*Yoma* 9b], and the Temple will only be rebuilt when mutual consideration and brotherly love prevail.

According to the *Talmud (Zevachim* 54b), this is a reference to David's personal life. On the night that David first fled from Saul, Samuel designated David as Saul's successor. The prophet then gave David a scroll containing secret instructions concerning the construction of the Temple. (At that time, the nation was still using the temporary, portable Tabernacle.) The privilege of receiving these secrets kindled the jealousy of David's archenemy, Doeg the Edomite, which is referred to here [see footnote to 52:2].

וְחֶרְפּוֹת חוֹרְפֶיךָ נָפְלוּ עָלָי — *And the humiliations of those who scorn You have befallen me.*

O God, You proclaimed that You will surely redeem Israel. The gentiles mock us, however, for we continue to writhe in their clutches, with no salvation in sight. They deny Your ability to redeem us. This insult to You is reflected in the humiliation they heap upon us. They also place their faith in false idols, which is another form of insult to You *(Radak).*

11. וָאֶבְכֶּה בַצּוֹם נַפְשִׁי — *And I wept while my soul was fasting.*

My soul is constantly shrouded in gloom and mourning *(Radak).* This is especially so on the fast days which commemorate our national tragedy *(Hirsch).* Other conquered nations bemoan only their physical suffering, but Israel laments her spiritual losses *(Alshich).*

וַתְּהִי לַחֲרָפוֹת לִי — *And it was humiliating* [lit. *humiliations*] *for me.*

I was embarassed by my weeping, for it produced no results. You ignored my tears and left me in exile *(Metzudas David).*

You Yourself, O God, became a source of humiliation to me, when the gentiles reviled me in an attempt to shatter my faith in You and to draw me to their false beliefs *(Radak).*

10 *Because envy of Your House devoured me,*
and the humiliations of those who
scorn You have befallen me
11 *And I wept while my soul was fasting*
and it was humiliating for me.
12 *I made sackcloth my garment,*
I became for them a byword.
13 *They gossip about me, those who sit*
by the gate;
The drinking songs of drunkards.

12. וָאֶתְּנָה לְבוּשִׁי שָׂק — *I made sackcloth my garment.*

The donning of sackcloth made of coarse animal hair is a sign of humiliation and repentance. The wearer symbolically chastises himself for having behaved as an impulsive, uncontrolled animal. In general, this display of contrition is too extreme for the common man; it is practiced only by men of extraordinary piety. The *Midrash* teaches that Jacob introduced the practice of wearing sackcloth. This tradition has been maintained by Jews throughout the generations. Scripture (*I Chronicles* 21:16) indicates that this practice is reserved only for great men: *And David and the Sages, all robed in sackcloth, fell down on their faces (Shnei Luchos HaBris, Maseches Rosh HaShanah,* first gloss).

וָאֱהִי לָהֶם לְמָשָׁל — *I became for them a byword.*

[See 44:15: תְּשִׂימֵנוּ מָשָׁל בַּגּוֹיִם, *You made us a byword among the peoples.*]

Among the gentiles, the word 'Jew' became a byword used to describe anything base and despicable *(Radak; Hirsch).*

13. יָשִׂיחוּ בִי יֹשְׁבֵי שָׁעַר — *They gossip about me, those who sit by the gate.*

[Any mass gathering is termed 'sitting by the gate,' for the gate was the public area of the city.] When the heathens assemble in their theaters and circuses, the Jews are the butt of their vile jokes (*Pesicha, Eichah Rabbasi* 17).

[Furthermore, שַׁעַר also means *the price* of commodities sold at *the gate* of the marketplace. Anti-Semites attribute inflation to the Jews, whom they falaciously accuse of exploiting the consumer and driving up the prices. The Jew-haters spread absurd rumors to support their libels.] They allege: 'The Jews squander all their weekly earnings on their Sabbath. They have no firewood for cooking, so they smash their beds and burn the boards. This forces them to sleep on the floor. Since the hard ground makes them ache they massage their sores with large quantities of oil, which is why oil has become so expensive!' (*Eichah Rabbasi* 17 and 3:5).

וּנְגִינוֹת שׁוֹתֵי שֵׁכָר — *The drinking song of drunkards* [lit. *And the songs of beer drinkers*].

Not only do the dignitaries who sit prominently *by the gate* of the city ridicule the Jews, but even the lowest drunkards dare to deride us *(Midrash Chachomim).*

They celebrate their holidays by emphasizing our sorrows. Gleefully they sing, 'The Jews wait forever for Messiah, but he never comes!' *(Maharam Markado).*

יד וַאֲנִי תְפִלָּתִֽי־לְךָ | יהוה עֵת רָצוֹן אֱלֹהִים
טו בְּרָב־חַסְדֶּךָ עֲנֵנִי בֶּאֱמֶת יִשְׁעֶךָ: הַצִּילֵנִי
מִטִּיט וְאַל־אֶטְבָּעָה אִנָּצְלָה מִשֹּׂנְאַי
טז וּמִמַּעֲמַקֵּי־מָיִם: אַל־תִּשְׁטְפֵנִי | שִׁבֹּלֶת
מַיִם וְאַל־תִּבְלָעֵנִי מְצוּלָה וְאַל־תֶּאְטַר־
יז עָלַי בְּאֵר פִּיהָ: עֲנֵנִי יהוה כִּי־טוֹב חַסְדֶּךָ

14. וַאֲנִי תְפִלָּתִי לְךָ ה׳ — *But as for me, my prayer is to You, HASHEM.*

David declared to the Holy One, Blessed be He, 'Master of the Universe, when the gentiles celebrate their festivals they eat, drink, and sing at their feasts all day long, without once mentioning Your Name. We are different. On the Jewish Sabbath, we do not forget You. We interrupt our eating, drinking, and relaxation to gather in the sacred House of God for the Afternoon Prayer, in which we praise you for all that you have provided' *(Midrash).* [1]

Furthermore, whenever the gentiles ridicule and threaten me, my only defense against them is *my prayer unto You,* pleading for *kindness* and *salvation (Radak; Meiri).*

עֵת רָצוֹן — *At an opportune time* [lit. *a time of favor*].

Part of my prayer is the wish that the timing of such prayer be favorable to You (*Rashi; Yerushalmi, Makkos* 2:6).

If he engages in incessant prayer, the supplicant can be certain that he will eventually arrive at a propitious moment *(Radak).*

One should take care to pray with the congregation, for whenever they gather to pray is *a favorable time* before God (*Berachos* 7b).

Israel's most fervent prayer is that God hasten the advent of Messiah and bring about the redemption at the most *favorable time (Meiri).*

Siddur Otzar Hatefillos (Sabbath Afternoon) explains that the era of chaos preceding the final redemption will span nine months, similar to the duration of pregnancy and birth. The agony will come to its climax on the late afternoon of the last Sabbath. Then we will find favor in the eyes of God, and He will begin to turn our suffering into joy.

אֱלֹהִים בְּרָב חַסְדֶּךָ עֲנֵנִי בֶּאֱמֶת יִשְׁעֶךָ — *O God, in the abundance of Your kindness, answer me with the truth of Your salvation.*

The redemption and the reconstruction of the *Beis HaMikdash* are extraordinary gifts which cannot become a reality through ordinary Divine *kindness.* They require רָב חַסְדֶּךָ, *an abundance of Your kindness,* as in (5:8): וַאֲנִי בְּרֹב חַסְדְּךָ אָבוֹא בֵיתֶךָ, *As for me, through Your abundant kindness, I will enter Your House (Tefilloh L'Moshe).*

15. The following verses comprise the text of David's prayer to HASHEM *at a favorable time (Radak).*

1. Because we interrupt our festivities with the Torah reading during the *Minchah* service of the Sabbath afternoon it is customary to recite this verse at that time (*Tur, Orach Chaim* 292). However, it is not recited on the afternoon of a יוֹם טוֹב, *festival,* because the Torah is not read then. This verse is reserved for an עֵת רָצוֹן, *a favorable time,* when Israel pleases God by reading His holy Scriptures (*Beis Yosef, Orach Chaim* 292).

Since the gentiles ridicule Jewish Sabbath observance, it is particularly appropriate that this verse is read on the Sabbath as a retort to them (see *Perisha, Orach Chaim* 292).

[14] *But as for me, my prayer is to You, HASHEM,*
at an opportune time,
O God, in the abundance of Your kindness,
answer me with the truth of Your salvation.
[15] *Rescue me from the mire*
so that I sink not;
let me be rescued from my enemies
and from the deep waters.
[16] *Let no swift current sweep me away,*
nor let the shadowy depths swallow me,
and do not let the pit close its mouth over me.
[17] *Answer me, HASHEM,*
for Your kindness is good;

הַצִּילֵנִי מִטִּיט וְאַל אֶטְבָּעָה — *Rescue me from the mire so that I sink not.*

Radak observes that this verse and the following one, which describe Israel as being on the brink of tragedy, seem to contradict verse 3, which pictures Israel as a doomed nation, already engulfed in woe: *I am sunk in deep mire ... I have entered deepest waters; a rushing current sweeps me away. Radak* explains that the earlier verse depicts the immediate emergency, in which Israel is indeed sunk in the mire of exile and inundated with countless miseries. This verse, however, represents Israel's concern for the future. Israel entreats that she not be damned to an eternal exile from which there is no escape.

16. אַל תִּשְׁטְפֵנִי שִׁבֹּלֶת מַיִם — *Let no swift current sweep me away.*

Let no mighty king drag me away into foreign exile *(Targum).*

וְאַל תִּבְלָעֵנִי מְצוּלָה — *Nor let the shadowy depths swallow me.*

[In verse 3, מְצוּלָה is merely translated as *deep*, but a more accurate rendition takes note of the word's relation to צֵל, *shadow.* At this depth, the sun's rays do not penetrate, and the area is shrouded in a dark shadow. This symbolizes a desperate situation of bleak exile, without even a ray of hope for redemption.]

וְאַל תֶּאְטַר עָלַי בְּאֵר פִּיהָ — *And do not let the pit close its mouth over me.*

תֶּאְטַר is related to אִטֵּר יַד, *the left-handed man,* who cannot use his right hand because it is אִטֵּר, *closed off,* from normal functions *(Rashi; Radak; Ibn Ezra).*

[Similarly, the exile seals Israel off from normal existence; the nation resembles a prisoner incarcerated in a deep well.]

Targum identifies the בְּאֵר, *well,* as *Gehinnom* (Purgatory). [Cf. *Eruvin* 19a and *comm.* to 16:11.]

17. עֲנֵנִי ה׳ כִּי טוֹב חַסְדֶּךָ — *Answer me, HASHEM, for Your kindness is good.*

Divine kindness is not merely a temporary benefaction, but an eternal *good* which has no injurious aftermath. You kindly designated us as Your Chosen People, but if we will be doomed in exile forever, then Your original kindness was short-lived and not truly *good (Yaavetz HaDoresh).*

יח כְּרֹב רַחֲמֶיךָ פְּנֵה אֵלָי: וְאַל-תַּסְתֵּר פָּנֶיךָ
יט מֵעַבְדֶּךָ כִּי-צַר-לִי מַהֵר עֲנֵנִי: קָרְבָה אֶל-
כ נַפְשִׁי גְאָלָהּ לְמַעַן אֹיְבַי פְּדֵנִי: אַתָּה
יָדַעְתָּ חֶרְפָּתִי וּבָשְׁתִּי וּכְלִמָּתִי נֶגְדְּךָ כָּל-
כא צוֹרְרָי: חֶרְפָּה | שָׁבְרָה לִבִּי וָאָנוּשָׁה
וָאֲקַוֶּה לָנוּד וָאַיִן וְלַמְנַחֲמִים וְלֹא

כְּרֹב רַחֲמֶיךָ פְּנֵה אֵלָי — *According to the abundance of Your mercy turn towards me.*

Do not determine my fate on the basis of my merits, for they are lacking; rather relate to me with Your boundless mercy, which knows no limitations *(Radak).*

18. וְאַל תַּסְתֵּר פָּנֶיךָ מֵעַבְדֶּךָ — *(And) hide not Your face from Your servant.*

[Exile must be understood as a new condition of Israel's eternal mission, rather than purely as a punishment. When Israel is banished from its own land, it assumes the challenge of serving as an example to its neighbors of how to live in accordance with God's will despite adverse circumstances. When it does so, it reflects its role as a people fashioned in God's image.

Therefore, the banished people asks, 'O God, if You conceal Your countenance from Your servant, Israel — thus making it difficult for us to fathom Your will — how can we be a reflection of Your sacred image?']

כִּי צַר לִי מַהֵר עֲנֵנִי — *Because I am distressed — answer me quickly.*

Since my situation is desperate, Your immediate response is imperative if I am to survive *(Radak).*

19. קָרְבָה אֶל נַפְשִׁי גְאָלָהּ — *Draw near to my soul — redeem it.*

Israel declares, 'My body will remain imprisoned in foreign hands as long as My soul is captivated by the allure of alien ideologies. Therefore, I pray, *redeem* my soul, for only this spiritual liberation will assure the פִּדְיוֹן, *ransom* of my body' *(Beis Elokim).*

The Torah states *(Leviticus* 25:25): *If your brother becomes poor and sells some of his estate then his near kinsman shall come to redeem it.* This teaches that the closer the relative, the greater his obligation to redeem his kin. No one is more closely related to the human soul than God, for the soul of man is חֵלֶק אֱלוֹהַ מִמַּעַל, *part of the Divine Being.* Thus, God, so to speak, is obligated to redeem His 'close relative,' Israel *(Malbim).*

לְמַעַן אֹיְבַי פְּדֵנִי — *Because of my foes, ransom me.*

Radak paraphrases: Release me from exile, for if You fail to do so, my foes will deny Your omnipotence and question Your ability to direct the affairs of the world.

Malbim differentiates between *redemption* and *ransom* as follows: a person is *redeemed* by relatives because of his close ties with them; someone is *ransomed* because of his intrinsic worth.

Unlike the human soul, which is considered akin to God, the body is not a close 'relative' of the Divine Spirit. Nevertheless, the body does deserve to be 'ransomed' on its own merits, lest it be wantonly destroyed by the threatening foe.

20. אַתָּה יָדַעְתָּ חֶרְפָּתִי וּבָשְׁתִּי וּכְלִמָּתִי — *You know my humiliation, my shame, and my disgrace.*

You know that I have suffered every

according to the abundance of Your mercy
turn towards me.
18 *Hide not Your face from Your servant,*
because I am distressed —
answer me quickly.
19 *Draw near to my soul — redeem it;*
because of my foes, ransom me.
20 *You know of my humiliation,*
my shame, and my disgrace;
before You are all my tormentors.
21 *Humiliation has broken my heart*
and I am deathly sick.
I longed for comfort,
but there was none,
and for consolers,
but I found none.

type of degradation during my exile (*Radak*).

נֶגְדְּךָ כָּל צוֹרְרָי — *Before You are all my tormentors.*

Often my tormentors cunningly sought to conceal their plots, not realizing that everything is revealed נֶגְדְּךָ, *before You* (*Radak*).

נֶגְדְּךָ can also be translated *against You*, to suggest: You know that the disgrace and humiliation which I suffer is on Your account, because I am Your representative. *All of my tormentors are actually against You* (*Vidal HaTzorfati*).

21. חֶרְפָּה שָׁבְרָה לִבִּי וָאָנוּשָׁה — *Humiliation has broken my heart and I am deathly sick.*

אָנוּשָׁה has been translated as *I am deathly sick* (*Rashi*); *I am pained* (*Radak*), or *I have given up hope* [derived from יֵאוּשׁ, *despair*] (*Rav Shlomo Atiah*).

Beer Avraham explains that the degradation and abuse heaped upon Israel robbed the people of their basic sense of human dignity. Thus, אָנוּשָׁה means *I have sunk to the level of* אֱנוֹשׁ, *frail, flimsy mortal.*

וָאֲקַוֶּה לָנוּד וָאַיִן — *I longed for comfort, but there was none.*

Literally, לָנוּד means *to shake* [see *Job* 2:11], for the person who comes to offer consolation usually shakes his head as a sign of compassion for the mourner (*Metzudas David*). [Israel bitterly recollects that throughout the exile, no gentile nation ever felt sympathy for her sorrow.]

וְלַמְנַחֲמִים וְלֹא מָצָאתִי — *And for consolers, but I found none.*

[Even if no nation truly felt our pain, at least the gentiles could have offered words of sympathy and solace in order to lighten our misery. Yet even this minimal display of human kindness was not forthcoming from our callous neighbors.]

כב מָצָאתִי: וַיִּתְּנוּ בְּבָרוּתִי רֹאשׁ וְלִצְמָאִי
כג יַשְׁקוּנִי חֹמֶץ: יְהִי־שֻׁלְחָנָם לִפְנֵיהֶם לְפָח
כד וְלִשְׁלוֹמִים לְמוֹקֵשׁ: תֶּחְשַׁכְנָה עֵינֵיהֶם
כה מֵרְאוֹת וּמָתְנֵיהֶם תָּמִיד הַמְעַד: שְׁפָךְ־
כו עֲלֵיהֶם זַעְמֶךָ וַחֲרוֹן אַפְּךָ יַשִּׂיגֵם: תְּהִי־
טִירָתָם נְשַׁמָּה בְּאָהֳלֵיהֶם אַל־יְהִי יֹשֵׁב:
כז כִּי־אַתָּה אֲשֶׁר־הִכִּיתָ רָדָפוּ וְאֶל־מַכְאוֹב

22. וַיִּתְּנוּ בְּבָרוּתִי רֹאשׁ – *They put poison in my meal.*

[בָּרוּתִי, *my meal,* is cognate with בִּרְיָה, described in II *Samuel* 13:7 as the special meal prepared to nurse a sick person back to health (בְּרִיאוּת). It also is the first meal prepared for mourners returning from the burial of a relative (סְעוּדַת הַבְרָאָה).

Not only did the gentiles fail to console the Jews, but even when Israel sought to comfort herself by nursing her own wounds and soothing her own suffering, the gentiles disturbed the Jews and poisoned their spirits with fresh insults and attacks (see *Radak).*]

וְלִצְמָאִי יַשְׁקוּנִי חֹמֶץ – *And for my thirst they gave me vinegar.*

Instead of quenching my thirst, they sought to intensify my agony by making me even thirstier.

This alludes to an incident of treachery documented by the *Midrash (Eichah Rabbah 2:2):* When the Jewish captives were led through their land, the Ishmaelites greeted the Jews with apparent friendliness and sympathy. First, the Ishmaelites gave them well salted food. Then they handed them leather bags which seemed to be full of water, to slake their burning thirst. However, when the unsuspecting Jews raised the bags to their lips, nothing but hot, dry air entered their weakened bodies and they fell dead. [See footnote to *Eichah* 1:19, ArtScroll edition.]

23. יְהִי שֻׁלְחָנָם לִפְנֵיהֶם לְפָח – *Let their table become a snare before them.*

Let them fall victim to their own attempt on my life! They put poison into the meal set on my table, but let them be so involved in their wicked scheming that they mix up their own meal with mine and eat the poison they prepared for me *(Beer Avraham).*

וְלִשְׁלוֹמִים לְמוֹקֵשׁ – *Let their very peace become a trap.*

May the very conditions which they long for as their goal of selfish peace become the source of their misfortune *(Rashi; Radak).*

[They seek to deny me tranquility while retaining their own composure and serenity. Deny them their wish; instead, trouble them and trap them in a web of anxiety and frustration.]

24. תֶּחְשַׁכְנָה עֵינֵיהֶם מֵרְאוֹת – *Let their eyes be too darkened to see* [lit. *from seeing*].

The vision of the wicked is distorted and dim. It leads them to failure and ruination; but the vision of the righteous is straight and true, guiding them in their spiritual ascent (*Midrash Esther Rabbah* 7:9).

וּמָתְנֵיהֶם תָּמִיד הַמְעַד – *And as for their loins, let them falter continually.*

Since the wicked do not see properly, they will stumble and falter. They will lose their high positions of power and prestige. The psalmist refers to the loins, because they support the body's upright posture *(Radak).*

25. שְׁפָךְ עֲלֵיהֶם זַעְמֶךָ – *Pour Your wrath upon them.*

22 *They put poison in my meal,*
and for my thirst they gave me vinegar.
23 *Let their table become a snare before them;*
let their very peace become a trap;
24 *Let their eyes be too darkened to see;*
and as for their loins,
let them falter continually.
25 *Pour Your wrath upon them,*
and let the fierceness of Your anger
overtake them.
26 *Let their palace be desolate,*
in their tents let there be no dweller.
27 *For the nation You smote,*
they pursued,

Even when God chastises the righteous, He does so with love and concern. He does not drown them in one huge wave of agony, but metes out their suffering in small doses [see footnote to 6:2]. However, since He seeks to obliterate the wicked, He pours out His wrath over them in a single overwhelming torrent *(Yaavetz HaDoresh).*

God mercifully diverted His anger from the Jews themselves. He poured out his wrath upon the sticks and stones of the Temple rather than upon the Jewish nation. [See ArtScroll *Eichah, comm.* to 2:5,6; and 4:11.] The cruel gentiles, though, do not deserve the Divine compassion. Therefore, unleash the full measure of Your fury upon them! *(Shaarei Chaim).*

וַחֲרוֹן אַפְּךָ יַשִּׂיגֵם — *And let the fierceness of Your anger overtake them.*

If they should attempt to flee before Your wrath, do not let them escape. *Overtake them* with Your anger *(Radak).*

26. תְּהִי טִירָתָם נְשַׁמָּה — *Let their palace be desolate.*

They laid waste to Your palace, the *Beis HaMikdash;* therefore, let their splendid castles be desolate *(Norah Tehillos).*

בְּאָהֳלֵיהֶם אַל יְהִי יֹשֵׁב — *In their tents let there be no dweller.*

Throughout the centuries of exile, the gentiles never let us dwell peacefully in our tents; therefore, let them also be driven from their homes *(Norah Tehillos).*

27. כִּי אַתָּה אֲשֶׁר הִכִּיתָ רָדָפוּ — *For [the nation] You smote they pursued.*

God wanted to discipline His errant children of Israel through the gentiles, but they overstepped their authority. The Divine plan permitted the gentiles to smite Israel with restraint, in order to prod the Jews to mend their ways; but the cruel nations were filled with malicious zeal for their mission. Their unbridled, vicious persecution of the Jews was totally unauthorized *(Rashi; Radak).*

Therefore, God's fury is now aroused against these gentiles, as the prophet (*Zechariah* 1:15) warns: *I am greatly enraged by the nations who are at ease, for I was but a little displeased* [with Israel] *but they* [the nations] *helped to increase the evil (Yaavetz HaDoresh).*

כח חֲלָלֶיךָ יְסַפֵּרוּ: תְּנָה־עָוֺן עַל־עֲוֺנָם וְאַל־
כט יָבֹאוּ בְּצִדְקָתֶךָ: יִמָּחוּ מִסֵּפֶר חַיִּים וְעִם
ל צַדִּיקִים אַל־יִכָּתֵבוּ: וַאֲנִי עָנִי וְכוֹאֵב
לא יְשׁוּעָתְךָ אֱלֹהִים תְּשַׂגְּבֵנִי: אֲהַלְלָה שֵׁם־
לב אֱלֹהִים בְּשִׁיר וַאֲגַדְּלֶנּוּ בְתוֹדָה: וְתִיטַב

It was for this reason that Pharaoh and his people were punished for oppressing the Jews in Egypt, for God had only permitted him to enslave the Jews, but not to torture and kill them *(Otzar Nechmad).*

וְאֶל מַכְאוֹב חֲלָלֶיךָ יְסַפֵּרוּ — *And they relate the pain of Your mortally wounded.*

[In their cruel glee, they proudly tell of the suffering they inflicted on those whom You have permitted them to punish.]

Radak explains that although חָלָל usually means a *corpse,* that cannot be the correct translation here, because dead men feel no pain [see *Shabbos* 13b]. Here חָלָל means *mortally wounded,* on the brink of death.

If not for the Divine decree, the gentiles could not harm Israel in the least. If they were to realize that they are no more than human agents fulfilling a Divine command, all would go well; but they deny the Divine source of their power and boast of *the pain* which they think they have inflicted on the Jews whom, in truth, You, O God, have wounded — not they *(Tehillos Hashem).*

28. תְּנָה עָוֺן עַל עֲוֺנָם — *Add iniquity to their iniquity.*

Radak understands the word עָוֺן as an alternate for עוֹנֶשׁ, *punishment.* Thus, cause them to suffer new punishment, in addition to that which they already deserve.

Not only should they be condemned for the iniquity of pursuing Israel (*v.* 27), but also they must be judged guilty for bragging about the pain they added to Israel's wounds *(Ibn Ezra).*

Since their boasting proves that everything they did to Israel was motivated exclusively by cruelty, rather than by disinterested obedience to the Divine command, even pain which they *were* authorized to inflict on us is considered an *iniquity* which is added to their major sin [persecuting Israel excessively] *(Ibn Yachya).*[1]

וְאַל יָבֹאוּ בְּצִדְקָתֶךָ — *And let them not be privy* [lit. *enter*] *to Your righteousness.*

'You are destined to deal righteously with Israel in the future, allotting them abundant good. Do not allow the undeserving gentiles to have access to that goodness, which should be reserved exclusively for the righteous *(Radak).*

29. יִמָּחוּ מִסֵּפֶר חַיִּים — *Let them be wiped away from the Book of Life.*

Rashbam illustrates this verse poetically: All of the earth is the Book of God and all its inhabitants are

1. The *Ramban* in *Genesis* 15:4 (cited in footnote to the ArtScroll edition of *Yonah* 1:14), discusses the philosophical implicaton of the murder of someone whose death had been predetermined on *Rosh HaShanah.* Because a murderer acted out of his own motives, unaware of the Divine decree, he cannot plead that he was carrying out God's will. Since he commits the crime out of personal vindictiveness or hopes of gain, he is guilty, despite the fact that he fulfills God's plan. Pharaoh deserved punishment because he enslaved the Jews solely out of personal vindictiveness. The same applies to Sennacherib (see *Isaiah* 10:5-6) and to Nebuchadnezzar (see *Isaiah* 14:23, 14 and 47:6, 8).

and they relate the pain
of Your mortally wounded.
28 *Add iniquity to their iniquity*
and let them not be privy to Your righteousness.
29 *Let them be wiped away from the Book of Life,*
and with the righteous let them not be inscribed.
30 *But I am afflicted and pain-racked,*
Your salvation, O God, shall raise me high
31 *I shall praise the Name of God with song,*
and I shall magnify it with thanksgiving;

inscriptions. At death, all are erased from the Divine rolls.

Radak maintains that the psalmist is referring to the 'Book of Eternal Life' in the World to Come. In that sacred volume, the wicked have no place.

וְעִם צַדִּיקִים אַל יִכָּתֵבוּ – *And with the righteous let them not be inscribed.*

The *Talmud (Rosh HaShanah* 16b) states that the fate of each person is recorded in one of three special books which are opened on Rosh HaShanah. The perfectly righteous men are immediately inscribed and sealed in the Book of Life. The completely wicked men are immediately inscribed and sealed is the Book of Death. The fate of the others hangs in the balance from Rosh HaShanah until Yom Kippur. If they prove to be worthy, they merit inscription in the Book of Life. If they prove to be unworthy, they are inscribed in the Book of Death.

30. וַאֲנִי עָנִי וְכוֹאֵב – *But I am afflicted and pain-racked.*

Take note of the intense pain caused by the suffering of the exile, and quickly send Your salvation *(Radak).*

Not only is he עָנִי, *afflicted,* by physical pain, he is also the victim of poverty. The chaotic times at the end of the centuries of exile will precipitate a world-wide economic crisis; therefore, the Sages (*Sanhedrin* 97a) say that the advent of Messiah will not come until the last penny vanishes from the purse *(Chazah Zion).*

יְשׁוּעָתְךָ אֱלֹהִים תְּשַׂגְּבֵנִי – *Your salvation, O God, shall raise me high.*

Only Your assistance can lift me from my dismal situation *(Radak).*

31. אֲהַלְלָה שֵׁם אֱלֹהִים בְּשִׁיר – *I shall praise the Name of God with song.*

[The psalmist now enters the final phase of his composition. After recounting the many pains visited upon Israel in exile by אֱלֹהִים, *God, the Dispenser of Strict Justice,* the nation comes to realize that these very blows reinforced the Jewish character and made it impregnable, protected against the incessant onslaughts of the hostile environment.

This God-given strength sends a wave of spiritual exaltation through the loyal and obedient nation of God and fills its soul with song.]

וַאֲגַדְּלֶנּוּ בְתוֹדָה – *And I shall magnify it with thanksgiving.*

When God delivers me from the exile [and returns me to the Holy Land], I shall dedicate a קָרְבָּן תּוֹדָה, *thanksgiving offering,* in recognition of His kindness *(Radak).*

לג לַיהוה מִשּׁוֹר פָּר מַקְרִן מַפְרִיס: רָאוּ
עֲנָוִים יִשְׂמָחוּ דֹּרְשֵׁי אֱלֹהִים וִיחִי
לד לְבַבְכֶם: כִּי־שֹׁמֵעַ אֶל־אֶבְיוֹנִים יהוה
לה וְאֶת־אֲסִירָיו לֹא בָזָה: יְהַלְלוּהוּ שָׁמַיִם

32. וְתִיטַב לַה׳ מִשּׁוֹר פָּר — *And it shall please HASHEM more than a full-grown bullock.*

The *Talmud (Chullin* 60a) states that during the creation of the world, all animals first appeared on earth at the peak of maturity. At that time, Adam sacrificed a newborn שׁוֹר, *bullock,* which was already as mature as a פָּר, *bull.* Our verse alludes to Adam's offering. The *Talmud* infers from *Leviticus* 22:27 that for the purpose of Temple offerings even on the day of birth, the newborn calf is called a שׁוֹר, *bullock*, but it is not called a פָּר, *bull,* until it is three years old *(Rashi).*

The songs of praise and thanksgiving which Israel will sing to God upon its redemption will surpass the exquisite offering which Adam dedicated to HASHEM *(Radak).*

מַקְרִן מַפְרִיס — *Possessed of horns and hoofs.*

The *Talmud (Avodah Zarah* 8a) relates that Adam sinned on the very day on which he had been created. When the sun began to sink beneath the horizon, Adam lamented, 'Woe unto me! Because of my sin, the world is doomed to drown in darkness and to return to chaos. This must be the death penalty which Heaven has ordained for me!'

Adam and Eve both wept bitterly throughout the night.

When the first rays of daylight appeared, Adam realized that the darkness of night was not a punishment but part of the earth's daily cycle. In relief and gratitude, Adam sacrificed a full-grown ox. The ox had been created fully grown on the sixth day of Creation. Like all animals, it emerged from the earth. Our phrase, *horns and hoofs,* indicates that the ox came into being in that order: first the horns emerged, followed by the rest of its body, ending with the hoofs *(Rashi).*

R' Yehuda said in the name of Shmuel: 'The ox which Adam sacrificed possessed but one horn growing out of the center of its forehead.' Adam sinned because his lower animal nature overcame his Divinely granted intellect and spirit. Thus, he distorted his priorities by giving precedence to the flesh before the soul. This was a revolt against the spiritual mastery of God, the Oneness of His Name.

The ox which Adam later sacrificed in repentance symbolized that he had put his values and priorities back into order.

The word קֶרֶן, *horn,* also means *principal,* denoting 'the main thing.' The one horn sprouting from the center of the ox's head signified that henceforth uppermmost in Adam's mind, at the center of his thoughts, Adam had but one concern — to recognize that God is the one and only authority. Only His will should be obeyed. Secondary are the physical needs of man, symbolized by the *hoofs,* which support the animal's entire body. The *hoofs* are פָּרוּס, *split,* a sign that the desires of the flesh are many and diverse *(Maharsha; Avodah Zarah* 5a, *Nefesh HaChaim* 1:20).

Alshich interprets the symbolism of the *ox* differently. Throughout Rabbinical literature, the קֶרֶן, *horn,* is always associated with goring and damage. In the case of Adam, the *horn,* i.e., the damage caused by the sin, came

32 *And it shall please HASHEM more than*
a full-grown bullock
possessed of horns and hoofs.
33 *The humble shall see it*
— they shall be glad,
you who seek God,
let your hearts revive.
34 *For HASHEM hearkens to the destitute,*
and His prisoners He does not despise.
35 *Heaven and earth shall praise Him;*

first. Only afterwards did Adam offer the kosher animal (identified by its split *hoofs)* to appease God. The offering of Messianic times will surpass this. At that time, Israel will offer a sacrifice of thanksgiving only for the sake of expressing its love for God, without needing atonement for any prior sin.

33. רָאוּ עֲנָוִים יִשְׂמָחוּ — *The humble shall see it — they shall be glad.*

Only the humble will be gladdened by the future salvation, for they alone will witness it. The arrogant will be destroyed *(Radak).*

דֹּרְשֵׁי אֱלֹהִים וִיחִי לְבַבְכֶם — *You who seek God let your hearts revive.*

The heart enveloped in gloom is considered dead, whereas the joyous heart abounds with energy and life. Redemption will lift the faithful ones of Israel from the shrouds of misery and will revive their hearts with gladness *(Radak).*

[For centuries, God's presence was hidden in the shadows; His influence over human affairs remained unseen. Only the devout who searched for Him caught a glimpse of His veiled hand in the events of history. However, when human history draws to an end, God will reveal His ways for all to see. Those who persistently sought to discover God will truly rejoice, for their dream of comprehending His ways will be realized. See *Hirsch.*]

34. כִּי שֹׁמֵעַ אֶל אֶבְיוֹנִים ה׳ — *For HASHEM hearkens to the destitute.*

Although the poor man is helpless or fettered by pain, this does not mean that God has forsaken him. On the contrary, his very affliction attests to God's respect for him. The Almighty desires to hear his fervent prayers for salvation and to purify his spirit by means of his afflictions *(Hirsch).*

וְאֶת אֲסִירָיו לֹא בָזָה — *And His prisoners He does not despise.*

The nations hold Israel in utter contempt because they arrogantly regard the Jews as their prisoners. In truth, the Jews are only the prisoners of God, the proof being that the Almighty can release them at any moment He desires. Unlike the haughty gentiles, God *does not despise His prisoners.* He will graciously hearken to their plea for redemption *(Radak).*

35. יְהַלְלוּהוּ שָׁמַיִם וָאָרֶץ — *Heaven and earth shall praise Him.*

[In the darkness of exile, God's praises were hidden, but when Israel is redeemed, the world will recognize His greatness. Israel will faithfully publicize His goodness until it is known throughout the earth and is even echoed by the heavens.]

Elsewhere, David offers a similar paean to God (I *Chronicles* 16:31) יִשְׂמְחוּ הַשָּׁמַיִם וְתָגֵל הָאָרֶץ וְיֹאמְרוּ בַגּוֹיִם ה׳ מָלָךְ, *The heavens shall be glad, and the*

לו וְאָרֶץ יַמִּים וְכָל־רֹמֵשׂ בָּם: כִּי אֱלֹהִים |
יוֹשִׁיעַ צִיּוֹן וְיִבְנֶה עָרֵי יְהוּדָה וְיָשְׁבוּ שָׁם
לז וִירֵשׁוּהָ: וְזֶרַע עֲבָדָיו יִנְחָלוּהָ וְאֹהֲבֵי
שְׁמוֹ יִשְׁכְּנוּ־בָהּ:

earth shall rejoice and they shall proclaim to the peoples, 'HASHEM reigns!' (Radak).

יַמִּים וְכָל רֹמֵשׂ בָּם — *The seas and all that moves therein.*

This too echoes the prophecy of the psalmist concerning the day when all of the univese shall acclaim God (96:11): יִרְעַם הַיָּם וּמְלֹאוֹ, *The sea and its fullness shall shout for joy (Radak).*

36. כִּי אֱלֹהִים יוֹשִׁיעַ צִיּוֹן וְיִבְנֶה עָרֵי יְהוּדָה — *For God shall save Zion and build the cities of Judah.*

The psalmist mentions Zion and Judah because they are the most prominent locations in the Holy Land. Also, Judea is the territory of the royal tribe. While these Holy places were under gentile rule, they were themselves considered exiles *(Radak).*

וְיָשְׁבוּ שָׁם וִירֵשׁוּהָ — *And they shall settle there and possess it.*

When Israel first conquered the land, it was only granted to the Jews temporarily, as evidenced by their later exile. In the future, however, *Eretz Yisrael* will become their eternal possession and estate *(Zerah Yaakov).*

the seas and all that moves therein;
36 *For God shall save Zion*
and build the cities of Judah.
And they shall settle there
and possess it.
37 *The offspring of His servants shall inherit it,*
and lovers of His Name shall dwell there.

37. וְזֶרַע עֲבָדָיו יִנְחָלוּהָ — *The offspring of His servants shall inherit it.*

This refers to the descendants of the Patriarchs Abraham, Isaac, and Jacob *(Metzudas David).*

This promise will be fulfilled in the days of Messiah *(Ibn Ezra).*

וְאֹהֲבֵי שְׁמוֹ יִשְׁכְּנוּ בָהּ — *And lovers of His Name shall dwell there.*

This alludes to the Talmudic dictum that no proselytes will be accepted into Judaism in Messianic times (*Yevamos* 24b). Only those who join Israel in the misery of exile are considered sincere converts, stirred by a genuine love for God and His word. Those who request conversion in Messianic times are suspected of ulterior motives, such as the desire to share in the glory and reward of Israel.

Therefore, the psalmist concludes, in the future era of triumph and redemption only the veterans of the tortuous exile will dwell in the Holy Land, for only they have proven that they are *those who love His Name (Yaavetz HaDoresh).*

מזמור ע 70

In the preceding psalm, David begged God to redeem the entire Jewish nation from exile. Here he makes a personal plea for his own return. Midrash Shocher Tov *illustrates David's wish with a parable:*

David may be likened to the shepherd who grazed the flocks of the king. The king became vexed by the shepherd and so he chased away the flock, tore down the animal shed, and dismissed the shepherd. After a time, the king gathered in the sheep and rebuilt the shed, but he did not restore the shepherd to his position. The shepherd lamented, 'Behold the sheep are gathered in, the shed is rebuilt, but I am not remembered!'

In the preceding psalm, (v. 36) *David said,* God shall save Zion and build the cities of Judah, *as if to say, 'Behold the shed is rebuilt';* and they shall settle there and take possession of it, *as if to say, 'Behold the sheep are gathered in.' In this psalm, David, the shepherd, asks, 'Shall I not be remembered?' Therefore this composition is dedicated* לְדָוִד לְהַזְכִּיר, unto David, For Remembrance.

David gazed prophetically into the future and rejoiced over the rebirth of the nation. However, he feared that God would hold the leaders solely responsible for the sins of the people. Thus, as king and founder of the royal line, he and his descendants would be eternally doomed to exile and oblivion. Fully acknowledging his responsibility for the errors of his subjects, David nevertheless asks God to remember to credit him also for the merits of the people, by virtue of which they are redeemed. If the sheep are worthy to return home, this certainly reflects credit on the faithful shepherd who guided the flock.

א־ב לַמְנַצֵּחַ לְדָוִד לְהַזְכִּיר: אֱלֹהִים לְהַצִּילֵנִי
ג יהוה לְעֶזְרָתִי חוּשָׁה: יֵבֹשׁוּ וְיַחְפְּרוּ
מְבַקְשֵׁי נַפְשִׁי יִסֹּגוּ אָחוֹר וְיִכָּלְמוּ חֲפֵצֵי

1. לַמְנַצֵּחַ לְדָוִד לְהַזְכִּיר — *For the Conductor, unto David, For Remembrance.*

[This superscription appears only at the beginning of one other composition, psalm 38:1, which commences מִזְמוֹר לְדָוִד לְהַזְכִּיר. See *comm.* there.]

Radak and *Meiri* comment that David may have composed this work when he fled from Saul or when he escaped from Absalom. A desperate fugitive, David felt forsaken by God. Therefore he pleaded *for Remembrance.*

[At that time, David foresaw that the entire nation of Israel was destined to experience a sense of abandonment in exile. Therefore, he also bore their future problems in mind when he composed this work. Specifically, David addressed the anguish of the Jewish leaders (see *Prefatory Remarks).*]

Midrash Shocher Tov records God's promise: 'If Israel remembers Me, I shall remember them, as the prophet says, *Ephraim is a darling son to Me, indeed a child of delight, for as often as I speak of him, I do remember him even more; therefore, My heart yearns for him, I will surely have mercy on him, says* HASHEM *(Jeremiah* 31:19).'

2. אֱלֹהִים לְהַצִּילֵנִי — *O God — to rescue me.*

Verses 2-6 of this psalm are almost identical to verses 14-18 of psalm 40.

Malbim determines that David composed psalm 40 while he was escaping from Saul. He composed psalm 70 at the age of sixty-five, when he was fleeing from Absalom [see *II Samuel* 15:7; *Radak; Mahari Kara*].

This chronology is supported by the fact that psalm 71, which is a continuation of this psalm, refers to David's old age in verses 9 and 19 [see *Radak* to 71:1].

According to *Malbim,* this background explains the superscription לְהַזְכִּיר, *for Remembrance:* David pleads with the Almighty, 'Remember the miraculous rescue from Saul which You provided when I was young and repeat it now, in my old age, as I flee from Absalom!'

[The differences between psalm 40 and psalm 70 can also be understood in the light of this chronology. In 40:14, David invoked the Divine Attribute of Mercy, crying out, 'רְצֵה ה׳ לְהַצִּילֵנִי, *Will it, HASHEM, rescue me!'* Since David knew that he was innocent in all his dealings with Saul, he felt entitled to HASHEM's mercy. However, when David fled from the army of Absalom, he realized that he was being justly punished for his sin concerning Bath Sheba, for the Prophet Nathan had forewarned him: *I will raise up evil against you from out of your own house (II Samuel* 12:11).

Therefore, David used the Divine Name אֱלֹהִים, which refers to God as *the Dispenser of Divine Justice,* pleading 'Despite my sins, take note of my sincere penitence and contrition. Please hasten לְהַצִּילֵנִי, *to my rescue!'*

ה׳ לְעֶזְרָתִי חוּשָׁה — *O HASHEM, to my assistance, hasten!*

After You, אֱלֹהִים, *the Dispenser of Divine Justice,* have consented to rescue me, do not delay the day of my salvation. Arouse the Name of HASHEM the Dispenser of Divine Mercy to have compassion and to hasten to my assistance *(Otzar Nechmad).*

3. יֵבֹשׁוּ וְיַחְפְּרוּ מְבַקְשֵׁי נַפְשִׁי — *Shamed and disgraced be those who seek my life.*

[In 40:15, the words יֵבֹשׁוּ וְיַחְפְּרוּ are followed by the word יַחַד, *together,*

For the Conductor, unto David,
For Remembrance.
2 *O God — to rescue me,*
O HASHEM, to my assistance, hasten!
3 *Shamed and disgraced*
be those who seek my life,
repulsed and humiliated
be those who wish me evil.

implying that all the men who joined in Saul's pursuit of David were united *(together)* by one intention: *to seek my* (David's) life in order to protect Saul's kingdom. In our psalm, however, the word יַחַד, *together,* is omitted, because no such unity existed in the camp of Absalom. His followers were enmeshed in conflicting conspiracies which splintered them into several groups. David refers to this internal strife in 55:16: *I saw violence and strife in the city* of Jerusalem, Absalom's headquarters.

Absalom tried to fool the people and the Sanhedrin (see 35:11,12, *comm.* and footnote). However, Achitophel, Absalom's most intimate counselor, secretly plotted to overthrow the young prince and to seize the throne (see *Prefatory Remarks,* Psalm 3). Another advisor, Chushai HaArki, was an undercover agent representing David's interests; therefore he purposely misled Absalom. The masses became disillusioned with Absalom and secretly prayed for his downfall (*Yerushalmi Sotah* 1:8; see *comm.* to 55:19).

Also, in 40:15, מְבַקְשֵׁי נַפְשִׁי, *those who seek my life,* is followed by the word לִסְפּוֹתָהּ, *to put an end to,* which is excluded here. Again the reason is that *all* of Saul's men sought *to put an end to* David's life, out of loyalty to Saul. However, the motives of Absalom's followers were varied].

יִסֹּגוּ אָחוֹר וְיִכָּלְמוּ חֲפֵצֵי רָעָתִי — *Repulsed* [lit. *retreat*] *and humiliated be those who wish me evil.*

Shevet M'Yisrael explains that this is a reference to Shimi ben Gera, who cursed David as he fled from Absalom, saying: *'Hashem has given the monarchy to Absalom your son,* וְהִנְּךָ בְּרָעָתֶךָ, *and behold you are caught in your own evil' (II Samuel* 16:8).[1]

David's request, *let them be repulsed,* was ultimately fulfilled, for after Absalom was slain, Shimi was repulsed and forced to retract his previous hostility to David. Scripture recounts: *And Shimi ben Gera hurried... and came down with the men of Judah to meet King David... And Shimi ben Gera fell down before the king... And he said to the king, 'Let my lord neither reckon my iniquity against me, nor remember that which your servant did perversely on the day that my lord king went out of Jerusalem... For your servant knows that I have sinned. Therefore, behold I am the first one of all the House of Joseph to come down today to greet my lord, the king' (II Samuel* 19:17-21).

1. The curse hurled by Shimi ben Gera provides us with an essential key to understanding much of David's suffering at the hands of his foes.

Yalkut Shimoni (II Samuel 151) says that Shimi was referring to the carriage of Bath Sheba, which enjoyed a prominent position in the royal entourage. Shimi viewed this as the height of audacity, since he considered Bath Sheba the root of all David's difficulties. How dare David

ד רָעָתִי: יָשׁוּבוּ עַל־עֵקֶב בָּשְׁתָּם הָאֹמְרִים
ה הֶאָח | הֶאָח: יָשִׂישׂוּ וְיִשְׂמְחוּ | בְּךָ כָּל־
מְבַקְשֶׁיךָ וְיֹאמְרוּ תָמִיד יִגְדַּל אֱלֹהִים
ו אֹהֲבֵי יְשׁוּעָתֶךָ: וַאֲנִי | עָנִי וְאֶבְיוֹן אֱלֹהִים
חוּשָׁה לִּי עֶזְרִי וּמְפַלְטִי אַתָּה יהוה אַל־
תְּאַחַר:

4. יָשׁוּבוּ עַל עֵקֶב בָּשְׁתָּם — *Let them be turned back by their deserved shame.*

The word עֵקֶב refers to deserved recompense, whether it is reward for good or punishment for evil. Thus, may their punishment fit their crime. Since these enemies intended to put me to shame, let them come to shame, *(Radak).*

[In 40:16, the verse reads יָשֹׁמּוּ, *Let them be astounded (Rashi) by their deserved shame.* Because David recognized Saul as God's anointed king, he had no desire to ascend to the throne during Saul's lifetime. David did seek to foil Saul's vigorous attempts to kill him; he wanted to *astound* Saul, demonstrating that he was invulnerable to the king's attempts on his life.

Absalom, on the other hand, had treacherously usurped David's throne. Therefore, David requested that Absalom be *turned back* (יָשׁוּבוּ), i.e., deposed from the throne which he had unlawfully assumed.]

עַל־עֵקֶב בָּשְׁתָּם — *By their deserved shame.*

[See commentary to 40:16 for discussion of עֵקֶב. *Targum* here renders *because they lay in ambush for me.* The עֵקֶב, *heel,* is the lowest part of the body, hidden from view; thus, it is synonymous with an ambuscade (see *Joshua* 8:13). This alludes to the treachery of Absalom and his party. They feigned loyalty to David while secretly plotting against the aging king.]

הָאֹמְרִים הֶאָח הֶאָח — *Those who say, 'Aha! Aha!'*

As I fled, they cheered with glee, 'Aha! Aha! Rejoice! Rejoice!' *(Radak).*

[Similarly, 35:21 states: *They broadly opened their mouths against me. They say, 'Aha! Aha! Our own eyes have seen!'*]

Likewise, the nations of the world rejoiced over the destruction of Jerusalem and the exile of the Jews, as Scripture (*Ezekiel* 26:2) says, *Tyre spoke of Jerusalem saying, 'Aha!' (S'forno).*

[In 40:16, we read הָאֹמְרִים לִי הֶאָח הֶאָח, *those who say to me, 'Aha! Aha!'.* As explained in detail in *comm.* to *v.* 3, all of Saul's men were united by one purpose only — the desire to capture David. Therefore, their taunts were directed only לִי, *to me,* i.e., to David.

persist in keeping this very woman as his esteemed queen? 'Since you do not chase her out,' Shimi argued, *'Behold you are caught in your own evil!'*

Meshech Chochma (Parshas Nitzovim) explains the *Talmud's (Yoma* 86b) teaching that complete repentance for a particular sin requires that a person overcome temptation the next time he has a similar opportunity to commit the same sin. The greater the similarity of circumstances in the two instances of temptation, the greater the evidence that the sinner has repented when he avoids repeating his sin. David had 'sinned' with Bath Sheba when she was Uriah's wife, according to this prescription for repentance, David would have had to divorce Bath Sheba and have her remarry, in order to prove that he had conquered his passion for her. Since her remarriage would duplicate her original status as another man's wife, David's temptation would be similar to his original test.

However, the *Talmud (Sanhedrin* 18a) forbids a queen to remarry after her relationship with

4 *Let them be turned back by their deserved shame*
those who say 'Aha! Aha!'
5 *Let them rejoice and be glad in You,*
all who seek You,
And let them always say, 'God
be magnified' — the lovers of Your salvation.
6 *As for me, I am poor and destitute.*
O God, hasten to me!
You are my assistance and He Who causes my escape,
HASHEM, do not delay!

Absalom's camp, however, was splintered into a number of factions which did not share common goals. They rejoiced and they gloated over the prospects of victory, but not all of them directed their taunts toward David.]

5. יָשִׂישׂוּ וְיִשְׂמְחוּ בְּךָ כָּל מְבַקְשֶׁיךָ — *Let them rejoice and be glad in You, all who seek You.*

[Despite their protestations of righteousness, Absalom and his clique were selfish men who sought fortune and power. David's followers, in contrast, were motivated neither by personal ambition nor by hatred for Absalom. They were devout men dedicated to the sanctification of God's Name. They realized that by supporting the monarch, whose mission is to symbolize God's authority and majesty, they glorify God.

However, Absalom's group rejoiced only at David's downfall, as the psalmist laments, *But when I limped they rejoiced and gathered* (35:15).]

וְיֹאמְרוּ תָמִיד יִגְדַּל אֱלֹהִים — *And let them always say, 'God be magnified.'*

[The reading in 40:17 is יֹאמְרוּ תָמִיד. The ו, *vav*, is added here to denote additional praises which will be inspired by the victory over Absalom.

In 40:17, the exclamation is יִגְדַּל ה׳, *HASHEM be magnified!* (see *comm.*). As explained in *comm.* to *v.* 2 (אֱלֹהִים לְהַצִּילֵנִי), David here uses the Name אֱלֹהִים, *the Dispenser of Strict Justice*, because the rebellion of Absalom was a Divine punishment for David's sin.]

With time, one's love for a finite object will wane and disappear. Love for the eternal God, whose majesty is infinite, however, will steadily increase. Those who seek Him discover new attributes תָּמִיד, *always.* As their awareness of God's glory increases, so does their love for Him, and they exclaim, *'God be magnified!'* This implies the request that their awareness of His splendor grow ever greater *(Sefer HaIkkarim).*

the king is terminated. Thus, Bath Sheba's divorce would accomplish nothing; she would merely become a forsaken woman, prohibited to all other men, while David would be permitted to remarry her.

The tragedy of David's life, therefore, was beyond repair. Although he dedicated himself to repentance, he could never fully eradicate his sin. Consequently a trace of sin always remained, providing his enemies with ammunition to use in their attacks on him.

Actually, all those who hated David, hated God; they despised David because he represented God. By sinning, however, David provided these foes with an excuse to blaspheme God, who had chosen David as His anointed. Therefore, when the prophet chastised David, he stressed (II *Samuel* 12:14): אֶפֶס כִּי נִאֵץ נִאַצְתָּ אֶת אֹיְבֵי ה׳ בַּדָּבָר הַזֶּה, *behold, by this deed you have provided the foes of Hashem with an excuse to blaspheme Him.* It is this taint which can never be completely erased.

אֹהֲבֵי יְשׁוּעָתֶךָ — *The lovers of Your salvation.*

[In 40:11 we read אֹהֲבֵי תְּשׁוּעָתֶךָ. See *comm.* to 71:15 for an explanation of the difference according to *Hirsch.*]

6. וַאֲנִי עָנִי וְאֶבְיוֹן — *As for me, I am poor and destitute.*

Chased from his palace, toppled from his throne, despised by his own son, David was indeed as wretched and as impoverished as a desperate pauper *(Radak).*

[With these words, David reminds God of one of his greatest merits: his arduous preparations for the construction of the Holy Temple. David, the successful ruler of a prosperous people, the conqueror of rich nations, became *poor and destitute* because he dedicated his enormous treasures to the purchase of materials for the *Beis HaMikdash.*

David pleads that God reward his devotion by speedily returning him to his throne, so that he might continue his efforts for the glorfication of God's name.][1]

Chazah Zion says that these words allude to the future suffering of Israel. After the destruction of the First Temple, the Jews were like an עָנִי, *poor man,* who is only nominally impoverished; but after the devastation of the Second Temple, Israel was stripped of every asset. Then the nation resembled the אֶביון who is תָּאֵב לְכָּל, *in need of everything,* possessing not even the basic necessities for survival.

אֱלֹהִים חוּשָׁה לִּי — *O God hasten to me!*

[In 40:18 we read אֲדֹנָי יַחֲשָׁב לִי, *My Lord, think of me.*

Radak (ibid.) identifies יַחֲשָׁב with חָשׁוּב, *worthy, important,* i.e., 'May I be considered worthy in the eyes of my Lord.' That request could only be made when David fled from Saul because David knew that he was completely innocent in all his dealings with his tormentor. However, when Absalom pursued David, David knew that he was being justly punished for his sins and so he could not ask God to consider him חָשׁוּב, *worthy,* of assistance on his own merit.]

עֶזְרִי וּמְפַלְטִי אַתָּה — *You are my assistance and He Who causes my escape.*

Our verse refers to God's assistance in the masculine form: עֶזְרִי. This is in contrast to 40:18 where we read עֶזְרָתִי, in the feminine form. *Minchas Shai* cites the *Midrash (Kohelles Rabbah* 7:27) which proves from this that the Holy Spirit which envelops the prophets form sometimes speaks in the masculine form and sometimes in the feminine form.

ה׳ אַל תְּאַחַר — *HASHEM, do not delay!*

[In Psalm 40, David addresses himself to the Dispenser of Strict Justice and says אֱלֹהַי אַל תְּאַחַר, *My God, do not delay!* Throughout *this* composition David recognized his guilt and therefore referred to God as the strict and just אֱלֹהִים. However, in conclusion he now pleads for the mercy of ה׳, *the Dispenser of Kindness.*

In *Psalm* 40 David considered himself innocent of Saul's terrible accusations and thought himself worthy of HASHEM's kindness; but he concludes with a plea that even if he is guilty and fit to be punished by אֱלֹהִים, *God,* nevertheless God should not delay His salvation.]

1. *Chida* in *Devash L'pi* (מַעֲרֶכֶת טו) explains that Adam was responsible for introducing poverty into the world; as a result of his sin, all men were cursed with the responsibility to support themselves,as Scripture states, *'By the sweat of your brow shall you get bread to eat' (Genesis* 3:19).

David's seventy years of life, a gift from Adam, were dedicated to rectifying Adam's sin [see *Overview Tehillim,* Vol. I, part I]. David could have been the world's most affluent man, but he gladly impoverished himself for the benefit of the rest of mankind suffering from Adam's curse. Since the greatest blessing which he could bestow on mankind was the construction of the Temple, David gave all his money for that cause.

מזמור עא 71

This composition is a continuation of the previous psalm; therefore, it does not require a superscription. These verses provide further insight into David's agitated feelings as he fled from his son, Absalom.

When he had fled from Saul as a youth, David had been sustained by the hope that a long life still lay before him, during which time he would ascend to the throne. Now, in his old age, as the specter of death loomed before him, David truly feared that he might not live to regain his royal crown. David therefore pleaded with God to rejuvenate him, to draw even closer to him, and to endow his final years with unprecedented splendor.

David's passionate words express the feelings of all those who have reached advanced age. This psalm is their special prayer — a fervent request that their venerable years be blessed with dignity and grace, a prayer that meaningful accomplishments will crown a lifetime of achievement. It is a plea that God banish the emptiness and boredom which atrophy the body and frustrate the soul.

In addition, says Meiri, *David identified the afflictions of his own old age with the anguish of the entire Jewish nation, which was destined to grow worn and weary during the protracted exile. Here David prays not only for his own rejuvenation, but also for the spiritual revival of the entire Jewish people.*

עא
א־ה

א בְּךָ־יהוה חָסִיתִי אַל־אֵבוֹשָׁה לְעוֹלָם:
ב בְּצִדְקָתְךָ תַּצִּילֵנִי וּתְפַלְּטֵנִי הַטֵּה־אֵלַי
ג אָזְנְךָ וְהוֹשִׁיעֵנִי: הֱיֵה לִי | לְצוּר מָעוֹן
לָבוֹא תָּמִיד צִוִּיתָ לְהוֹשִׁיעֵנִי כִּי־סַלְעִי
ד וּמְצוּדָתִי אָתָּה: אֱלֹהַי פַּלְּטֵנִי מִיַּד רָשָׁע
ה מִכַּף מְעַוֵּל וְחוֹמֵץ: כִּי־אַתָּה תִקְוָתִי אֲדֹנָי

1. בְּךָ ה׳ חָסִיתִי — *In You, HASHEM, I took refuge.*

[The first three verses of this psalm are very similar to 31:2-4, which refers to David's flight from Saul (see *comm.* there). These lines were composed thirty-five years later, as David fled from Absalom.

At that time, the vast majority of the people and most of the Sanhedrin abandoned David. Therefore, the forsaken king could turn to God alone for refuge. Similarly, Israel in exile has no one to turn to but God.]

אַל אֵבוֹשָׁה לְעוֹלָם — *Let me not be shamed, ever.*

Midrash Shocher Tov observes that even though the gentiles disgrace the exiled Jews in this world, the Jews are assured that they will not be shamed in the World to Come, as the prophet says, *Israel is saved by HASHEM, a salvation for all times; they will not be shamed or disgraced forever and ever (Isaiah* 45:17).

[David accepted humiliation at the hands of Absalom, for he viewed it as a Divine punishment for his sin. He was prepared to endure his exile until he repented sufficiently to find favor in God's eyes. He pleads only that his rejection not be לְעוֹלָם, *forever.*]

2. בְּצִדְקָתְךָ תַּצִּילֵנִי וּתְפַלְּטֵנִי — *In Your righteousness rescue me and give me escape.*

David does not claim to deserve Divine salvation from Absalom because of his own *righteousness;* rather, he invokes God's righteousness. David recognizes that this tragic episode represents Divine retribution for his sin with Bath Sheba, for the prophet Nathan had warned him (II *Samuel* 12:11), *'Behold, I will raise up evil against you from out of your own house' (Radak).*

הַטֵּה אֵלַי אָזְנְךָ וְהוֹשִׁיעֵנִי — *Incline Your ear to me and save me.*

David realizes that his sins have formed a barrier which prevents his prayers from ascending heavenward to God. Therefore, David begs God to show him special favor by 'bending His ear' to David's mouth, so that his prayers can reach God directly, without any obstacle *(Yaavetz HaDoresh).*

3. הֱיֵה לִי לְצוּר מָעוֹן — *Be for me a sheltering rock* [lit. *a rock of a palace*].

[In 31:3, we read הֱיֵה לִי לְצוּר מָעוֹז, *become for me a mighty rock,* because when David fled from Saul, he wanted only a *mighty rock* for protection. Here, though, David's gravest concern was not for his personal safety, but for the preservation of his kingship and of his unique role as God's anointed leader of Israel. He requests that his מָעוֹן, *palace,* in Jerusalem, which symbolizes his monarchy, be returned to him *(Radak).*]

לָבוֹא תָּמִיד — *To enter for all times.*

[Weary from a lifetime of incessant challenges and flight, David now seeks peace and security for all times.]

צִוִּיתָ לְהוֹשִׁיעֵנִי — *You ordered my salvation.*

Continue to protect me as in the past, by sending Your guardian angels to escort me, as Scripture says (91:11),

71
1-5

In You HASHEM I took refuge,
let me not be shamed, ever.
2 *In Your righteousness rescue me*
and give me escape,
Incline Your ear to me
and save me.
3 *Be for me a sheltering rock*
to enter for all times —
You ordered my salvation,
for my Rock and my Fortress are You.
4 *My God! Give me escape*
from the wicked one's dominion,
From the hand of the scheming
and the violent.
5 *For You are my hope,*
My Lord HASHEM/ELOHIM —

כִּי מַלְאָכָיו יְצַוֶּה לָּךְ לִשְׁמָרְךָ בְּכָל דְּרָכֶיךָ, *He commands His angels for you, to guard you on all your ways (Radak).*

This may also refer to the Divine command which prohibits the males of Moab from entering the congregation of Israel, but permits the females to enter (see *Deuteronomy* 23:4). Because of this law, David's great-grandmother, Ruth the Moabite, was allowed to marry Boaz. Here David offers thanksgiving for that Divine command which enabled him לָבוֹא תָּמִיד, *to enter* [the Jewish nation] *for all times (Yaavetz HaDoresh).* [See also Overview V to *Ruth,* ArtScroll ed.]

כִּי סַלְעִי וּמְצוּדָתִי אָתָּה — *For my Rock and my Fortress are You.*

[In 18:3, David uses the same words to thank God for delivering him from Saul.]

4. אֱלֹהַי פַּלְּטֵנִי מִיַּד רָשָׁע — *My God, give me escape from the wicked one's dominion* [lit. *hand*].

The wicked one refers to Absalom *(Radak).* [It was Absalom who threatened his father's life and publicly violated David's ten concubines. (See *II Samuel* 16:20-17:2.)]

מִכַּף מְעַוֵּל וְחוֹמֵץ — *From the hand* [lit. *palm*] *of the scheming and the violent.*

The *Targum* renders מְעַוֵּל as מָרֵי עֵילָא, *the master of schemes,* a title which perfectly fits Achitophel, Absalom's treacherous advisor (see *Radak*). [It was he who incited Absalom to acts of חָמָס, *violence.*]

חוֹמֵץ is cognate with חוֹמֵס, *the violent robber,* because the letters ץ and ס are often interchanged in Hebrew usage *(Rashi; Radak).*

[The word כַּף, *palm,* denotes a stronger grip than יַד, *hand* (see *comm.* to 18:1). Since Achitophel posed a greater threat to David than did Absalom, David asks to be freed from his clutches.]

5. כִּי אַתָּה תִקְוָתִי — *For You are my hope.*

I fully recognize Your omnipotence; therefore, I place my trust and hope in no power other than You *(Radak).*

ו יְהוִה מִבְטַחִי מִנְּעוּרָי: עָלֶיךָ | נִסְמַכְתִּי
מִבֶּטֶן מִמְּעֵי אִמִּי אַתָּה גוֹזִי בְּךָ תְהִלָּתִי
ז תָמִיד: כְּמוֹפֵת הָיִיתִי לְרַבִּים וְאַתָּה
ח מַחֲסִי־עֹז: יִמָּלֵא פִי תְּהִלָּתֶךָ כָּל־הַיּוֹם
ט תִּפְאַרְתֶּךָ: אַל־תַּשְׁלִיכֵנִי לְעֵת זִקְנָה

מִבְטַחִי מִנְּעוּרָי — *My security since my youth.*

Yaavetz Hadoresh explains that in order to appreciate the significance of these words, we must understand the tragic circumstances of David's youth. [See *The Book of Our Heritage, Vol.* 3, 'Sivan,' by Eliyahu Kitov for a full discussion of this topic.] David was misunderstood and despised even by his own father and brothers. This was all part of the Divine design by which David learned to find his security exclusively in God, rather than in men.

6. עָלֶיךָ נִסְמַכְתִּי מִבֶּטֶן — *On You have I relied from birth* [lit., *the belly*].

From the moment of birth, You watched over me and provided me with ample sustenance. Even before I emerged from the בֶּטֶן, *belly,* You prepared food for me מִמְּעֵי אִמִּי, *from the innards of my mother* [this refers to the milk produced within her breasts] *(Radak).*

מִמְּעֵי אִמִּי אַתָּה גוֹזִי — *From the innards of my mother You drew me.*

The translation of גוֹזִי follows *Rashi, Radak,* and *Metzudas David.*

Malbim however, relates גוֹזִי to גוֹזֵז, *shear or cut,* because one of the miracles of procreation is God's ability to fashion one body within another, while sustaining both as separate entities. As the embryo takes shape in the mother's womb, it is separated so that it can develop independently within the placenta. Thus, *from the innards of my mother you cut me off.*

According to the *Talmud (Niddah* 30b-31a), גוֹזִי is a term for taking an oath; while the child is still within the mother's womb, the angels make him swear to lead a righteous life [see footnote to 24:4].

[This demonstrates that the enormity of God's compassion and concern extends to the very roots of human existence. The Divine spark is implanted even in the fetus, for as *Maharshah (Niddah* 30b-31a) points out, גוֹזִי, *my oath,* has the numerical value of 26, which is equal to the numerical value of HASHEM's name.]

בְּךָ תְהִלָּתִי תָמִיד — *Of You is my praise always.*

I feel myself to be blessed and praiseworthy at all times because of the goodness You bestow upon me *(Radak).*

7. כְּמוֹפֵת הָיִיתִי לְרַבִּים — *I became an example for the multitude.*

Many witnessed my tragic downfall and were chastened by my example. They began to mend their ways lest they too be condemned to share the ignominious fate which was my punishment for my sins *(Rashi; Radak).*

David's entire existence was meant to set the standard of piety and devotion for his people. Even his shortcomings were part of a Divine design to enlighten all of Israel, as the *Talmud (Avodah Zarah* 4b) says: David did not truly deserve to commit his sin concerning Bath Sheba, but God caused the sin so that David should set an example of penitence for the masses. If any man becomes discouraged and doubts his ability to atone for his sins, we reassure him, saying, 'Learn a lesson from David, who erred and spent the rest of his life in intensive, sincere repentance!' *(Tehillos Hashem).*[1]

71
6-9

My security since my youth.
6 *On You have I relied from birth;*
from the innards of my mother You drew me,
Of You is my praise always.
7 *I became an example for the multitude,*
for You were my mighty refuge.
8 *Let my mouth be filled with Your praise,*
all day long with Your glory,
9 *Do not cast me off in time of old age,*

וְאַתָּה מַחֲסִי עֹז — *For You [were] my mighty refuge.*

I set a positive example for the people as I fled from Absalom because they saw that I counted on You alone and that You responded by giving me full support *(Ibn Ezra).*

Despite my sins, [You accepted my repentance and] You returned me to my throne *(Radak).*

8. יִמָּלֵא פִי תְּהִלָּתֶךָ — *Let my mouth be filled with Your praise.*

[No man can fill his mouth with joyous praise when he is overwhelmed with the anguish of exile. Such *praise* can only be uttered upon experiencing the triumph of final salvation. As the *Talmud (Berachos* 31a) says: One cannot fill his mouth with mirth in this world, for Scripture states, אָז יִמָּלֵא שְׂחוֹק פִּינוּ, (Only) *then* (at the final redemption), *shall laughter fill our mouths* (126:2).]

From the words of this verse, the *Talmud (Berachos* 50b) derives the law that blessings should not be recited while a person has food in his mouth. Rather, his *mouth* should literally *be filled with Your praise.*

כָּל הַיּוֹם תִּפְאַרְתֶּךָ — *All day long with Your glory.*

I find glory in naught but the fact that You deemed me worthy of Your salvation *(Radak).*

9. אַל תַּשְׁלִיכֵנִי לְעֵת זִקְנָה — *Do not cast me off in time of old age.*

[*Avos* 5:21 teaches that זִקְנָה, *old age,* begins at sixty. David was sixty-five when Absalom rebelled.]

Just as You were with me in my youth, please accompany me now, in my old age *(Ibn Ezra).*

Even if I have grown old, i.e., accustomed to my sinful ways, please do not reject me *(Rashi).*

David said to the Holy One, Blessed be He, 'When I was young and strong, I put my life in danger to lead Your sons, the children of Israel, into battle. But now that I have grown old, [they no longer appreciate me and] they say *"when will* [the old man] *die and his name perish?"* ' (41:6).

The Holy One, Blessed be He, responded in the words of the prophet *(Isaiah* 46:4), *'Even to old age I am the same, and even to white hairs I shall carry you, I have made and I shall carry*

1. Indeed, when David fled from Absalom his main concern was that he might set a bad example for the people. The *Talmud (Sanhedrin* 107a) teaches that David was so distraught that he even decided to make it appear as if he were worshiping idols.

When David's wise counselor and confidant, Chushai HaArki, observed this, he asked in amazement, 'Shall it then be said that a devout king like you worshiped idols?'

David replied, 'It would be even worse for people to say, "A pious king like David was killed by his own sons" ' [for if such a calamity befalls a righteous king, people will question the value of righteous living. This doubt will greatly undermine the faith of the masses

י כִּכְלוֹת כֹּחִי אַל־תַּעַזְבֵנִי: כִּי־אָמְרוּ אוֹיְבַי
יא לִי וְשֹׁמְרֵי נַפְשִׁי נוֹעֲצוּ יַחְדָּו: לֵאמֹר
אֱלֹהִים עֲזָבוֹ רִדְפוּ וְתִפְשׂוּהוּ כִּי־אֵין
יב מַצִּיל: אֱלֹהִים אַל־תִּרְחַק מִמֶּנִּי אֱלֹהַי
יג °חוּשָׁה לְעֶזְרָתִי °חישה: יֵבֹשׁוּ יִכְלוּ שֹׂטְנֵי נַפְשִׁי

the burden, indeed I shall bear and rescue (Aggadas Bereishis 35).

כִּכְלוֹת כֹּחִי אַל תַּעַזְבֵנִי — *When my strength fails forsake me not.*

The *Baal Shem Tov* would say that even a young man can find himself 'cast into old age' for if he loses his enthusiasm for life, and slows down in his energetic pursuit of God's service, then he is virtually an old man. Therefore, even the youth should pray that his strength not fail him, so that God's vibrant spirit will not forsake him, leaving him feeble and decrepit.

Shaar bas Rabbim explains these words in light of the *Talmudic* dictum *(Avodah Zarah* 19a): Praiseworthy is the man who repents when he is still in the prime of manhood. If the sinner conquers his turbulent passions during his youth, this is a sign of true contrition; but if the sinner delays repentance until he has become frail and impotent, devoid of temptation, what does his repentance prove?

The tragedy which David experienced with Absalom in his old age caused him to repent the sins of his earlier years; but he feared that his sincere remorse might be deemed insignificant, since he was already elderly and feeble. Therefore he prays, *'Do not cast away my repentance in the time of old age; when my strength gives out, do not forsake me.'*

10. כִּי אָמְרוּ אוֹיְבַי לִי — *For my foes say of me.*

My foes take counsel together and say of me, *'God has forsaken him' (v.* 11). 'We can deal with David as we please, for God has abandoned him as a result of his sins' *(Rashi).*

וְשֹׁמְרֵי נַפְשִׁי נוֹעֲצוּ יַחְדָּו — *And those who watch for my life* [lit. *soul*] *consult together.*

This refers to the stalwart nobles who were once David's comrades, and vigilantly guarded his welfare. Now they have turned against him, and plot his doom *(Rashi; Radak).*

In an alternative interpretation, *Radak* suggests that the description *those who watch out for my soul* fits David's veteran enemies, who spied on him, alert for the most opportune moment to attack the helpless fugitive.

11. לֵאמֹר אֱלֹהִים עֲזָבוֹ — *Saying, 'God has forsaken him.'*

David laments: My enemies celebrate because my own flesh and blood has challenged my rule. They claim that this proves that I have been utterly abandoned by both God and man *(Radak).*

The *Talmud (Sotah* 21a) notes that

(Rashi).] David said, 'It is preferable that I worship idols [and be disgraced personally] than that the name of God be publicly desecrated. [David reasoned, 'If my son kills me after my feigned idolatry, God's name will be sanctified, because people will say that I was justly punished, for my idol worship.']

Chushai assured David that this drastic step was unnecessary. He explained that it was well known to the people that David was condemned to suffer at the hands of his upstart son because he sinned.

Chushai explained that the Holy Torah purposely juxtaposes the portion dealing with the בֵּן סוֹרֵר וּמוֹרֶה, *the rebellious, insolent son,* and the portion discussing the יְפַת תֹּאַר, *the woman*

71
10-13

when my strength fails — forsake me not.
10 *For my foes say of me, and those who watch*
for my life consult together,
11 *Saying: 'God has forsaken him,*
pursue and catch him,
For there is no rescuer.'
12 *O God, be not far from me,*
O My God, hasten to my assistance.
13 *Let them be shamed and consumed —*
the adversaries of my soul.

David's enemies lost sight of David's stature as a Torah giant. They forgot that although sin can counterbalance the merit gained by performing a precept, it cannot cancel out the merit acquired by engaging in Torah study. The *Talmud* concludes that had David's foes only realized the tremendous protection which David enjoyed by virtue of his Torah study, they would not have dared to antagonize him. God never forsakes the dedicated Torah student, for the student refuses to abandon his quest for God's teachings.

רִדְפוּ וְתִפְשׂוּהוּ כִּי אֵין מַצִּיל — *Pursue and catch him for there is no rescuer.*

With these words, each of David's adversaries and pursuers encouraged his comrades to intensify their efforts to kill the king. They declared, 'David's legendary military prowess is a thing of the past. God has spurned him; his might has vanished' *(Radak).*

12. אֱלֹהִים אַל תִּרְחַק מִמֶּנִּי — *O God, be not far from me.*

[Remember that despite my sins, I still represent You in the world. If I am defeated, Your Name will be besmirched together with mine.]

Hirsch paraphrases: Prove to my enemies that You are never far from those who diligently study the Torah. Even if Torah scholars sin, their study enables them to repent, as the Sages comment: 'If only they had continued studying My Torah when they abandoned Me!' for immersion in this holy pursuit would eventually have brought the sinners back to God *(Yalkut Shimoni* to *Jeremiah* 16:11).

אֱלֹהַי לְעֶזְרָתִי חוּשָׁה — *O my God, hasten to my assistance.*

[See *comm.* to 22:20.]

13. יֵבֹשׁוּ יִכְלוּ שֹׂטְנֵי נַפְשִׁי — *Let them be shamed and consumed — the adversaries of my soul.*

At first, defeat will merely shame them, but as they experience repeated disaster, they will ultimately be devastated and consumed *(Alshich).*

of beautiful appearance, the attractive gentile girl captured in battle and taken in marriage by the Jewish soldier. The Torah teaches that the man who follows his lusts and takes such a wife is doomed to reap bitter fruits from the union. He will sire a barbarian who seethes with unbridled passions and revolts against all authority.

David had taken the captured Princess Ma'achah, the daughter of Talmai, King of Geshur, as a war bride. Thus, it was clear to all that a seditious son such as Absalom was destined to bedevil David some day. Indeed, David was inadvertently setting a מוֹפֵת, *example,* which benefited the people, for they now witnessed the full extent of God's justice, which punishes even a person as righteous as David, if he fails to heed the Torah's warnings.

יד יֶעֱטוּ חֶרְפָּה וּכְלִמָּה מְבַקְשֵׁי רָעָתִי: וַאֲנִי
תָּמִיד אֲיַחֵל וְהוֹסַפְתִּי עַל־כָּל־תְּהִלָּתֶךָ:
טו פִּי | יְסַפֵּר צִדְקָתֶךָ כָּל־הַיּוֹם תְּשׁוּעָתֶךָ כִּי
טז לֹא יָדַעְתִּי סְפֹרוֹת: אָבוֹא בִּגְבֻרוֹת אֲדֹנָי
יז יֱהוִֹה אַזְכִּיר צִדְקָתְךָ לְבַדֶּךָ: אֱלֹהִים

יֶעֱטוּ חֶרְפָּה וּכְלִמָּה מְבַקְשֵׁי רָעָתִי — *Let them be enwrapped in humiliation and disgrace — those who seek my harm.*

[My enemies sought to undermine the authority of the Torah and underestimated its efficacy in restoring the sinner to God. As a result, they considered my spiritual *hurt* incurable. Disgrace them by proving their analysis to be completely wrong.]

14. וַאֲנִי תָּמִיד אֲיַחֵל — *As for me, I shall always hope.*

Even when tragedy and despair threaten to engulf me, my confidence in You will not be shaken. I eagerly await an opportunity *to add to all of Your praises (Rashi; Radak).*

According to *Kli Yakar*, these words reflect Israel's incessant yearning for redemption. אֲיַחֵל is an acrostic of the twelfth of *Maimonides'* Thirteen Principles of Faith (Principle 12): אִם יִתְמַהְמֵהַּ חַכֵּה לוֹ, [Even though] *he* [Messiah] *may tarry, wait for him.*

וְהוֹסַפְתִּי עַל כָּל תְּהִלָּתֶךָ — *That I will add to all Your praises.*

I await Your salvation because it will provide me with the opportunity to add to Your many praises *(Radak).*

Sefer HaIkkarim comments that the most eloquent praise which man can offer to God is to *continually hope* with silent, uncomplaining faith for His salvation.]

Tehillah L'David notes that although David composed or edited one hundred and fifty תְּהִילוֹת for the *Book of Psalms*, He yearned to compose still more praises; however, his lifelong suffering and persecution prevented the realization of this dream. Therefore David and all of Israel *continually hope* for the Messianic era, in which countless new psalms will be composed. The numerical value of עַל כָּל, lit. *beyond all*, is 150, suggesting that in the future, the number of psalms will be far *beyond all* of the original 150.

15. פִּי יְסַפֵּר צִדְקָתֶךָ — *My mouth shall tell of Your righteousness.*

My entire being is suffused with feelings of love and gratitude to You, to the extent that praises flow effortlessly from my mouth *(Alshich).*

David now begins a paean of praise in gratitude for the clemency which God granted him. In truth, he deserved to die following his sin with Bath Sheba. However, when David acknowledged his transgression, and confessed חָטָאתִי, *I have sinned* [*II Samuel* 12:13], his sentence was commuted to יִסּוּרִים, *suffering*, which purified his soul and atoned for his misdeed [see *Psalms* 51].

David describes this Divine mercy as צְדָקָה, *righteousness*, and views the pain inflicted upon him by Absalom as part of the compassionate Divine plan which leads transgressors back to God *(Hirsch).*

כָּל הַיּוֹם תְּשׁוּעָתֶךָ — *All day long of Your salvation.*

Hirsch points out the subtle difference between תְּשׁוּעָה and יְשׁוּעָה: the word יְשׁוּעָה, related to the word יֵשׁ, denotes a triumph over dangers which imperil one's very יֵשׁ, *being*. The word תְּשׁוּעָה, however (derived from שׁוֹעַ, *wealthy*, as in *Isaiah* 32:5), indicates deliverance from threats to one's property, influence, or power.

[Although Absalom did not destroy

Let them be enwrapped in humiliation
and disgrace—those who seek my harm.
14 *As for me, I shall always hope*
that I will add to all Your praises.
15 *My mouth shall tell of Your righteousness,*
all day long of Your salvation
for I do not know their numbers.
16 *I shall come with the mighty deeds*
of my Lord, HASHEM/ELOHIM,
I will mention Your righteousness,
Yours alone.

David's life, i.e., his יֵשׁ, *being,* he did temporarily succeed in usurping David's royal power and influence. Hence, David's final victory from Absalom is appropriately termed a תְּשׁוּעָה.]

כִּי לֹא יָדַעְתִּי סְפֹרוֹת — *For I do not know their numbers.*

I am forced to sing Your praises incessantly, and to *relate Your righteousness all day long,* because Your wonders are infinite and, therefore, impossible to count *(Radak).*

16. אָבוֹא בִּגְבֻרוֹת... — *I shall come with the mighty deeds of my Lord, HASHEM/ELOHIM.*

I shall come to offer hymns of praise inspired by HASHEM's mighty acts *(Rashi).*

When I go out to battle my enemies, I place my faith in God's *might,* rather than in human power *(Radak).*

Thus, when I emerge victoriously, I claim no glory for myself, but only *make mention of Your righteousness, Yours alone (Meiri).*

[David composed this psalm at the age of sixty-five (see *Prefatory Remarks* and *comm.* to *v.* 9). He looked forward to old age, as he says in 90:10, יְמֵי שְׁנוֹתֵינוּ בָהֶם שִׁבְעִים שָׁנָה וְאִם בִּגְבוּרֹת שְׁמוֹנִים שָׁנָה, *The days of our years are seventy, or if with might, eighty years* (see *Avos* 5:24).]

[Repentance endowed the aged David with tremendous new reservoirs of moral vigor, to which he never had access in his youth. Consequently, he also sought renewed physical vigor so that he might reach previously unattainable heights in the service of God.]

אַזְכִּיר צִדְקָתְךָ לְבַדֶּךָ — *I will mention Your righteousness, Yours alone.*

Since Adam had presented seventy years of his life to David as a gift [see *Overview, Tehillim* vol. I, part I], David expressed appreciation to Adam. 'However,' reasoned David, 'If God will let me live until I reach גְבֻרוֹת, *might,* i.e., eighty years, then for those ten additional years I am indebted to God *alone,* and I will make mention of His righteousness exclusively' *(Chazah Zion).*[1]

1. [In 39:5 we read David's plea, *Let me know, O HASHEM, my end and the measure of my days, what is it?* In the *footnote* to that verse, we learn that God refused to tell David when he would die.

My son, Eliyahu Meir, נ״י, observes that since David knew that he had received exactly seventy years of life as a gift from Adam, (as explained in the *Overview* to *Tehillim* vol. 1, part I), he should have known precisely when his death would occur.

This verse, however, teaches that David *did* harbor hopes of living longer than seventy

עא לְמַּדְתַּנִי מִנְּעוּרָ֑י וְעַד־הֵ֝נָּה אַגִּיד
יח נִפְלְאוֹתֶֽיךָ׃ יח וְגַם עַד־זִקְנָ֨ה ׀ וְשֵׂיבָה
אֱלֹהִ֣ים אַל־תַּעַזְבֵ֑נִי עַד־אַגִּ֣יד זְרוֹעֲךָ֣

17. אֱלֹהִים לִמַּדְתַּנִי מִנְּעוּרָי — *O God, You have taught me from my youth.*

From my earliest youth, You taught me to accept You as אֱלֹהִים, *the Strict Dispenser of Divine Justice.* It was You Who raised me as a lonely shepherd in a harsh and hostile environment, for no tender parents ever sheltered me. As the Patriarch Jacob described the rugged lot of the shepherd, *'By day drought consumed me, and the frost by night, and my sleep departed from my eyes'* (*Genesis* 31:40).

Ferocious combat was my youthful pastime, rather than innocent child's play: *Your servant slew both the lion and the bear (I Samuel* 17:36). This conditioned me to fear no mortal danger. Scripture records that David said, 'HASHEM, *Who delivered me from the paw of the lion and the paw of the bear, He will deliver me from the hand of the Philistine (I Samuel* 17:37).

My tender mind was molded with trust in God; as I grew older this youthful faith became even firmer, imbuing me with unshakeable confidence to face the vicissitudes of life *(Chazah Zion).*

In addition, O God, You have endowed me from youth with the ability to discern Your generosity and Providence in all phases of life *(Radak).*

וְעַד הֵנָּה אַגִּיד נִפְלְאוֹתֶיךָ — *And until this moment I declare Your wonders.*

[The Sage Elisha ben Avuyah taught that lessons mastered in childhood can be compared to ink written on fresh paper *(Avos 4:25).*

The vivid lessons of David's youth left an indelible imprint on his soul. His early psalms were like unfinished symphonies; throughout David's life, he added new verses in praise of God.

Although the aged David's bones grew brittle and his skin turned dry, his spirit remained youthful and undaunted. He continued to extol each new Divine revelation with his original youthful sense of awe (see *Radak; Alshich).*]

18. וְגַם עַד זִקְנָה וְשֵׂיבָה אֱלֹהִים אַל תַּעַזְבֵנִי — *And even until old age and hoariness, O God, forsake me not.*

[*Avos* 5:24 states: The man of sixty has attained זִקְנָה, *old age. Rashi* comments that at sixty, a man's hair begins to turn white. *Meiri* notes that when one reaches this age, he tends to lose his interest in worldly matters. This being so, the *Mishnah* advises him to take advantage of this natural phenomenon and concentrate his remaining years on the worship of the Holy One, taking heed of his approaching death.

Sixty is the age of complete mental maturity, for the Sages (*Kiddushin* 32b) teach that the word זָקֵן *(zaken), old,* is a loose abbreviation of the words *zeh-kanah-chochma,* one who has acquired wisdom.

David hoped that God would remain near him in his old age and grant him that wisdom which is attainable only at the peak of maturity.]

עַד...שֵׂיבָה — *Until... hoariness.*

[The *Mishnah* in *Avos* 5:24 continues: The man of seventy has attained שֵׂיבָה, *hoary old age.* The Torah commands, *You shall stand up before the man of* שֵׂיבָה *(Leviticus* 19:32). Since Heaven has seen fit to grant him advanced age, he deserves honor *(Magen Avos).*

years, on his *own* merit. It is also possible that he feared that his life might be shortened to less than seventy years, because of his sins. For these reasons he sought to know the exact *measure of his days.*]

17 *O God, You have taught me from my youth,*
and until this moment
I declare Your wonders.
18 *And even until old age and hoariness*
O God, forsake me not
Until I proclaim
Your strength to the generation,

Seventy is considered the natural end to a full life (see 90:10), and David himself died at seventy, as Scripture states, וַיָּמָת בְּשֵׂיבָה טוֹבָה שְׂבַע יָמִים, *and he died in full, hoary old age, full of days (I Chronicles* 29:28).

Meiri (Avos 5:24) comments: The old man of seventy is no longer capable of any worldly pursuits. Therefore, he should dedicate his time and energy for God's sake.

Magen Avos quotes *Rabbeinu Yonah*: As a man approaches his end, let him stir himself to repentance, in the realization that his life will not continue indefinitely.

When a wise philosopher first noticed the white strands in his hair, he remarked, 'These are the messengers of death.' If a person ignores this opportunity for repentance, the prophet criticizes him: *Hoariness has cast* [*its mark on him*], *and he knows it not (Hosea* 7:9). David asks that God be with him in this critical period of his life, as he approaches his final destiny.]

According to *Yalkut Shimoni* 804, the word שֵׂיבָה is cognate with יְשִׁיבָה, *sitting*. This would suggest: when I was young and powerful, I could stand on my own two feet — yet You came to my assistance and performed wonders to save me. Now that I am feeble and compelled to sit, please do not forsake me.[1]

עַד אַגִּיד זְרוֹעֲךָ — *Until I proclaim Your strength.*

When I was young, it was possible for people to be misled by my physical strength and to attribute my amazing victories to my personal prowess. Now, although I am old and weak, I still continue to be triumphant. This proves that it is *Your strength* alone which supports me *(Radak; Malbim).*

Malbim adds that זְרוֹעַ literally means *the upper arm*, which is the source of the lower hand's strength (see *comm.* to 44:4). God is the זְרוֹעַ, i.e., the ultimate source of all human strength manifested in the lower world.

לְדוֹר — *To the generation.*

Radak identifies this as the present generation, i.e., David's contemporar-

1. The *Midrash (Bereishis Rabbah* 59:3) quotes Abraham, who asked, 'Dear God, now that You have granted me זִקְנָה, *old age*, please also grant me שֵׂיבָה, *hoariness.*' Abraham's request can be explained by drawing upon the introduction of *R' Shimon Shkop* to *Shaarei Yosher:*

The *Talmud (Bava Metziah* 87a) states that until Abraham, no man showed the signs of old age. Fathers and sons looked exactly alike; thus, when someone wanted to speak to Abraham, he sometimes mistakenly spoke to Isaac, and vice versa. Therefore, Abraham requested that he be given the appearance of old age, as Scripture states *(Genesis* 24:1), וְאַבְרָהָם זָקֵן בָּא בַּיָּמִים, *And Abraham was old, advanced in age.*

Abraham wanted to look his age in order to arouse his student's respect for his teachings concerning the one true God. He was a זָקֵן, *elder scholar*, and he began the Torah tradition among the Jewish people by establishing and heading a Yeshiva *(Yoma* 28b). Abraham deemed it essential that he be endowed with the glorious dignity of old age in order to arouse his students' respect and thereby facilitate their acceptance of the revolutionary belief in one God, which he sought to instill in their hearts.

עא יט לְדוֹר לְכָל־יָבוֹא גְּבוּרָתֶךָ: וְצִדְקָתְךָ
יט־כא אֱלֹהִים עַד־מָרוֹם אֲשֶׁר־עָשִׂיתָ גְדֹלוֹת
°הִרְאִיתַנִי כ אֱלֹהִים מִי כָמוֹךָ: אֲשֶׁר °הראיתנו |
°תְּחַיֵּנִי צָרוֹת רַבּוֹת וְרָעוֹת תָּשׁוּב °תחיינו
°תַּעֲלֵנִי כא וּמִתְּהוֹמוֹת הָאָרֶץ תָּשׁוּב °תעלנו: תֶּרֶב |

ies. *Targum* renders this as לְדָר דָּרֵי, *for generation after generation*. [David hopes that these lessons taught to his generation will be so powerful that they will leave an impression for generations to come.]

לְכָל יָבוֹא גְּבוּרָתֶךָ — *To all who will yet come — Your might.*

May the venerable remnants of the present generation recount Your greatness to the next generation. I shall perpetuate Your Name by recording *Your might* in the Book of *Psalms* for future generations to read *(Radak)*.

[Inspired by these tales of *Your might*, future generations will have the fortitude to endure their exile.]

19. וְצִדְקָתְךָ אֱלֹהִים עַד מָרוֹם — *And Your righteousness, O God, is unto the high heavens.*

Here David continues to reveal the details of the promise he began in the preceding verse: *I will proclaim ... Your righteousness* which is *unto the high heavens (Rashi)*. Your righteousness surpasses that of any human *tzaddik*. It defies description because it is far beyond human comprehension *(Ibn Ezra)*.

According to *Pesikta Rabbosi (47:1)*, God's compassion and concern extend not only to the lowly denizens of this earth but also to the lofty heavenly bodies. Since the moon had no light of its own, it appeared to be doomed to shrouded oblivion. God mercifully positioned it in the heavens in such a way that it would reflect the sun's brilliance and thus assume a position of prominence in the skies.

Hirsch reminds us that David (who is here fleeing from Absalom) speaks as a penitent lauding God for the extraordinary charity and righteousness which He demonstrates to the remorseful sinner.

Indeed, repentance rises to the high heavens, as the Sages note (*Yoma* 86b), *Teshuvah* (repentance) is of unsurpassed greatness for its effects rise to God's heavenly throne. God has provided the sincere penitent with the opportunity to eradicate the very roots of his transgression and to make a fresh start.

אֲשֶׁר עָשִׂיתָ גְדֹלוֹת — *You, [Who] have done great things.*

Your accomplishments are so great that they defy description *(Alshich)*.

אֱלֹהִים מִי כָמוֹךָ — *O God, who is like You?*

Your greatness inspires all who witness it to extol Your virtues, as did Moses and all of Israel when they joyously proclaimed (*Exodus* 15:11), 'מִי כָמֹכָה בָּאֵלִם ה, *Who is like You among the mighty HASHEM?' (Radak)*.

20. אֲשֶׁר הִרְאִיתַנִי צָרוֹת רַבּוֹת וְרָעוֹת — *You [Who] have shown me many and grievous troubles.*

Although the word is written הִרְאִיתַנוּ with a ו, *vav* (denoting the plural form), it is pronounced with a י, *yud*, (which) indicates the singular form). This discrepancy implies that David has applied his personal experience to the history of the entire nation. David traces his own transition from hunted fugitive to honored monarch and prophesies that the Jewish people will undergo a similar metamorphosis from exile to redemption. David foresees that just as he was

To all who will yet come —
Your might.
19 *And Your righteousness,*
O God, is unto the high heavens,
You, Who have done great things,
O God, Who is like You?
20 *You, Who have shown me*
many and grievous troubles, revive me again.
And from the depths of the earth
raise me again.

chased from Jerusalem by his son before returning in triumph to the Holy City, so will Israel eventually return from the Diaspora to their cherished homeland (*Radak; Hirsch;* see *Pesikta Rabbosi* 34:6).

[Ironically, the Jews were exiled from Jerusalem because of the treachery of the 'sons' of Israel, who betrayed their fatherland and brought destruction upon their own people; similarly, David was chased from Jerusalem by the treachery of his son Absalom.]

תָּשׁוּב תְּחַיֵּינִי — *Revive me again.*

[The exile of a nation normally signifies its demise as a unified entity. Thus the redemption of an exiled people is comparable to the resurrection of the dead.

Death also haunted David's family. The infant born from his initial union with Bath Sheba died soon after birth. David's son Amnon was treacherously murdered by Absalom, and Absalom himself was eventually slain.]

וּמִתְּהוֹמוֹת הָאָרֶץ תָּשׁוּב תַּעֲלֵנוּ — *And from the depths of the earth raise me again.*

David compares his woes to a deep abyss *(Ibn Ezra).* The word תַּעֲלֵנוּ, *bring us up* (referring to the entire nation) is written in the plural but the pronunciation is in the singular, תַּעֲלֵנִי, *bring me up* (referring to David himself) *(Radak).*

[This alludes to the fact that after death, Absalom sank to the lowest depths of hell. When David learned of his son's demise, *the king was sorely distressed and went up to the chamber over the gate and wept, and as he went, he said: 'My son Absalom, my son, my son Absalom! I would have died for you, O Absalom, my son, my son!' (II Samuel* 19:1).

The *Talmud (Sotah* 10b) asks why it was necessary for David to cry out eight times on behalf of his deceased son, referring to him both as *Absalom* and *my son.* The *Talmud* explains that David's first seven cries raised Absalom from the seven levels of *Gehinnom.* With David's eighth cry, some Sages maintain, Absalom's severed head was rejoined to his body. Others say that this final prayer elevated Absalom's soul so that it became worthy to enter the World to Come.

Maharsha (*Sotah* 10b) explains that ordinarily, even a father's great merits cannot save his sinful child from punishment (see *Tosafos, Sotah* 10b). In this case, however, Absalom was suffering in part for the sins of David. The prophet had warned David that his sin concerning Bath Sheba would have bad influence on his family: *'I will raise up evil against you from out of your own house' (II Samuel* 12:11).

Therefore, Absalom was in *Gehinnom* partly because of his father. David recognized this when he screamed, *'I would have died for you, O Absalom,*

כב גְּדֻלָּתִי וְתִסֹּב תְּנַחֲמֵנִי: גַּם־אֲנִי | אוֹדְךָ
בִכְלִי־נֶבֶל אֲמִתְּךָ אֱלֹהָי אֲזַמְּרָה לְךָ
כג בְכִנּוֹר קְדוֹשׁ יִשְׂרָאֵל: תְּרַנֵּנָּה שְׂפָתַי כִּי
כד אֲזַמְּרָה־לָּךְ וְנַפְשִׁי אֲשֶׁר פָּדִיתָ: גַּם־
לְשׁוֹנִי כָּל־הַיּוֹם תֶּהְגֶּה צִדְקָתֶךָ כִּי־בֹשׁוּ
כִּי־חָפְרוּ מְבַקְשֵׁי רָעָתִי:

my son, my son!' Therefore, David's prayers succeeded, because by praying for Absalom he was, in reality, praying for himself.

This perhaps is the meaning of the double usage: *From the depths of the earth* תַּעֲלֵנִי *bring me* (David) *up*, and thereby תַּעֲלֵנוּ *bring us*, i.e., both David and Absalom, *up*].

21. תֶּרֶב גְּדֻלָּתִי — *Increase my greatness.*

Increase my greatness to a level which even surpasses the glory I enjoyed before my decline. In reference to the Jewish nation, this means that when the Messiah redeems Israel, the Jews will enjoy tremendous prestige which will exceed any temporary pre-eminence which they had ever enjoyed in former times *(Radak).*

[After David recovered his throne from Absalom, he enjoyed greater power and recognition than ever before.]

וְתִסֹּב תְּנַחֲמֵנִי — *And turn to comfort me.*

[David asks that he be granted consolation for the death of his son and that Israel be comforted for the suffering it endures in exile.]

22. גַּם אֲנִי אוֹדְךָ בִכְלִי נֶבֶל ... אֲזַמְּרָה לְךָ בְכִנּוֹר — *I too shall thank You on the* Neivel *instrument ... I shall sing to You on the* Kinor.

[See *comm.* to 33:22 for a complete description of these musical instruments.]

Exile stifles all sounds of music and joy, but when You *increase my greatness* at the time of the Messianic redemption, I will respond by increasing my songs of thanks to you *(Radak).*

אֲמִתְּךָ אֱלֹהָי — *For Your faithfulness, my God.*

You promised to return us from exile, and we shall rejoice when You faithfully fulfill Your word *(Radak).*

קְדוֹשׁ יִשְׂרָאֵל — *O Holy One of Israel.*

[When the individual or the nation of Israel as a whole becomes defiled by sin, it is You Who inspires them to return to the heights of holiness, so that they become worthy of redemption.]

23. תְּרַנֵּנָּה שְׂפָתַי כִּי אֲזַמְּרָה לָּךְ — *My lips shall rejoice when I sing to You.*

When my lips sing to the accompaniment of the *Neivel* and *Kinor (Rashi),* the ecstatic phrases of song will echo the joy bursting from my heart, and every utterance will be completely sincere.

Similarly the psalmist declared (84:3), לִבִּי וּבְשָׂרִי יְרַנְּנוּ אֶל אֵל חָי, *Both my heart and my flesh will rejoice towards the living God (Radak).*

David implies, 'The fact that I enjoy the privilege of singing to You is ample cause to rejoice. Indeed, song is the very

71
21-24

[21] *Increase my greatness,*
and turn to comfort me.
[22] *I, too, shall thank You, on the* Neivel *instrument,*
for Your faithfulness, my God,
I shall sing to You on the Kinor,
O Holy One of Israel.
[23] *My lips shall rejoice when I sing to You,*
and my soul which You have redeemed.
[24] *My tongue, too, all day long*
shall utter Your righteousness.
For they are shamed,
for they are humiliated —
those who seek my harm.

purpose of my entire existence, for Adam endowed me with seventy years of his life only so that my songs should rectify the damage inflicted by his sins' *(Alshich).*

וְנַפְשִׁי אֲשֶׁר פָּדִיתָ — *And my soul which You have redeemed.*

David continues, 'My soul, which is a fragment of the soul of Adam, finds serenity and redemption from sin only through inspired song' *(Alshich).*

[Furthermore, I was redeemed from the threat of Absalom only by virtue of my sacred compositions praising God.]

24. גַּם לְשׁוֹנִי כָּל הַיּוֹם תֶּהְגֶּה צִדְקָתֶךָ — *My tongue, too, all day long shall utter Your righteousness.*

Today I sing to the accompaniment of musical instruments, but even when such instruments are absent, my tongue will continue to sing of Your righteousness *(Ibn Ezra).*

[In his commentary to 12:4, *Malbim* states that שְׂפָתַיִם, *lips,* always denote external communication, the spoken work which relates the desires of the flesh; but לָשׁוֹן, *tongue,* refers to internal speech, the intimate thoughts of man's heart which are expressed only to his Creator. David says, 'My (external) lips shall rejoice (*v.* 23) and my (internal, spiritual) tongue too shall speak of Your righteousness.']

כִּי בשׁוּ כִּי חָפְרוּ מְבַקְשֵׁי רָעָתִי — *For they are shamed, for they are humiliated — those who seek my harm.*

My spirit soars as I sing, while they are covered with disgrace *(Radak).*

Absalom and his followers suffered every type of ignominy and disgrace; they met with total defeat and their revolt was crushed *(Alshich).*

מזמור עב 72

*T*his psalm concludes the second Book of *Tehillim. It is also the final psalm dedicated to specific events in David's lifetime (see comm. to v. 20).*

Radak states that David was near death when he composed this hymn. It was the most triumphant day of his career — the day on which he crowned his beloved son, Solomon, as his successor to the royal throne. This magnificent event represented the realization of David's primary goal, the culmination of all his prayers.

That glorious day brought unprecedented celebration. David's loyal followers blessed him, 'As HASHEM has been with my master, the king, so shall He be with Solomon, and may He make his throne even greater than the throne of my master the king, David' ... And they blew the shofar, and all the people said, 'Long live King Solomon!' ... And the people played the flutes and rejoiced with great joy, so that the very earth was shattered by their voices ... And also, thus said the king, 'Blessed be HASHEM, the God of Israel, Who has today provided a successor to sit on my throne, and my own eyes see it' I Kings *1:37, 39-40, 48).*

David entertained great hopes for his son. As his death approached, David reviewed the events of his life and realized that many of his cherished plans for creating a perfect society based on the laws of the Torah remained unfulfilled. With his last breath, David charged his temporal and spiritual heir, Solomon, with the task of creating a utopian world order predicated on Divine righteousness and justice.

Solomon came very close to realizing his father's great ambition, and to the extent to which he succeeded, his rule resembled the future reign of Messiah. Thus, Sforno *and* Radak *note, the verses of this psalm apply both to Solomon and to his descendant, the long-awaited Messiah.*

א לִשְׁלֹמֹה | אֱלֹהִים מִשְׁפָּטֶיךָ לְמֶלֶךְ תֵּן
ב וְצִדְקָתְךָ לְבֶן־מֶלֶךְ: יָדִין עַמְּךָ בְצֶדֶק
ג וַעֲנִיֶּיךָ בְמִשְׁפָּט: יִשְׂאוּ הָרִים שָׁלוֹם לָעָם

1. לִשְׁלֹמֹה — *For Solomon.*

Why was the great gift of wisdom and justice granted to Solomon? Scripture relates (I *Kings* 3:5-12): *In Givon HASHEM appeared to Solomon in a dream of the night, and God said, 'Ask of me what I shall give you.'*

And Solomon said, ' You have done great kindness to my father, David, because he walked before You with truth and righteousness and with uprightness of heart, and You kept for him this great kindness and gave him a son to sit on his throne, as it is this day. And now, HASHEM, my God, You have made Your servant king in the place of David, my father, and I am but a little child; I know not how to go out or come in. [Solomon was only twelve years old when he became king. (*Seder Olam Rabbah* 14).] *Give therefore to Your servant an understanding heart to judge Your nation, that he may discern between good and evil, for who is able to judge this, Your very numerous nation?'*

And it pleased HASHEM that Solomon had asked this thing. And God said to him, 'Since you have requested this and you have not requested for yourself long life and you did not request for yourself riches and you did not ask for the life of your enemies, but You did request for yourself discernment, to understand judgment, behold, I have acted in accordance with your words, and I have given you a wise and understanding heart, so that there has been none who compares to you before you, and after you none shall arise like you'.

Rashi explains that David composed this psalm when he foresaw that such extraordinary wisdom would be granted to his son.

Targum renders לִשְׁלֹמֹה, *by Solomon,* maintaining that this psalm is a prophetic hymn composed by Solomon, dedicated to the future Messiah.

Radak notes that the Messiah is referred to as שְׁלֹמֹה, which is a contraction of שֶׁהַשָּׁלוֹם שֶׁלוֹ, *peace is his,* as in (*Songs* 8:12) הָאֶלֶף לְךָ שְׁלֹמֹה, *the thousand is for you, Solomon.*

אֱלֹהִים מִשְׁפָּטֶיךָ לְמֶלֶךְ תֵּן — *O God, Your judgments to the king—do give.*

David prays, 'O God, please endow my son (and the future Messiah) with the wisdom to follow the laws of the Torah without error and to render equitable decisions, based exclusively on Torah dictates' *(Rashi; Radak).*

Perfect, total justice cannot be performed by a finite, mortal judge, unless he is guided by the wisdom of God, Who is the sole source of universal justice *(Malbim).*

According to *Midrash Shocher Tov,* David refers here to a specific request: 'O God, You can distinguish between innocence and guilt without the aid of witnesses or warnings; please grant Solomon this ability.'

David's request was fulfilled when two women came before Solomon, each claiming to be the mother of a certain infant. Solomon brilliantly proved the identity of the real mother, without the aid of witnesses (I *Kings* 3:16-28).

At that moment, a Divine proclamation corroborated Solomon's judgment. Thus all of Israel knew with certainty that God had granted wise judgment to this king (see *Maccos* 23b).

וְצִדְקָתְךָ לְבֶן מֶלֶךְ — *And Your righteousness to the prince!* [lit. *son of the king*].

This also refers to Solomon *(Rashi)* and to the Messiah *(Radak).*

It is insufficient for a king to base his ruling solely on a rigid code of law. The responsible magistrate should temper justice with mercy and should help the

72
1-3

For Solomon. O God,
Your judgments to the king — do give,
and Your righteousness to the prince!
2 *May he judge Your nation with righteousness,*
and Your poor with justice.
3 *May the mountains bring the nation peace,*

litigants to fulfill the requirements of the law *(Rashi; Zerah Yaakov).*

[When a new king is establishing his rule and building his dynasty, he often cannot afford to be lenient, lest he undermine his royal authority. Thus, *God, Your* (authority for strict) *judgment to the (first) king — do give;* but that king's son, who has inherited a stable, secure throne, can often afford to show clemency and compassion. Thus, grant *Your righteousness* (and a spirit of mercy) *to the son of the king.*]

According to *Rashi,* David asks that any harsh Divine *judgment* to be meted out to his family be inflicted directly upon him, the *king.* Thus David's son Solomon, *the son of the king,* would enjoy *righteousness* and serene peace and would not be condemned to suffer for his father's sins.

2. יָדִין עַמְּךָ בְצֶדֶק — *May he judge Your nation with righteousness.*

Mishnas Rabbi Eliezer 4 says that Solomon's uncanny judgment frightened everyone, including hardened criminals, into acting *with righteousness.* When the people heard of the famous case of the two mothers (in which Solomon saw the truth unaided by any tangible evidence or witnesses), they said, 'We had better not steal or break the law, lest Solomon discover our crimes.'

The *Zohar* (II 78a) says that since the Holy Spirit rested upon Solomon's wondrous throne, all who approached it were frightened and awed. A threatening figure perched on the throne would shake violently when anyone lied. Thus Solomon could detect a deceiver without the aid of witnesses.

[See *Targum Sheni* to *Megillas Esther* Chapter 1.]

וַעֲנִיֶּיךָ בְמִשְׁפָּט — *And Your poor with justice.*

May Solomon treat the downtrodden and the poor in accordance with the law and show no favoritism to the powerful and the rich *(Radak).*

Hirsch explains that the paupers are called *Your poor* because God Himself has decreed that they be impoverished. The Divine order of the world, *Hirsch* notes, is predicated on the unequal distribution of wealth [see *commentary* and footnote to 61:8]. If all men were economically equal and self-sufficient, then there would be no opportunity for צֶדֶק, *righteousness,* and charity in this world.

3. יִשְׂאוּ הָרִים שָׁלוֹם לָעָם — *May the mountains bring the nation peace.*

Rashi interprets this literally: When the mountains are filled with abundant grain and crops, the people are satisfied. Prosperity creates contentment, which fosters feelings of friendship and brotherhood. Thus, peace will flourish in the land.

Radak understands this allegorically: *The mountains* refers to the mighty monarchs of the gentile nations. Awed by Solomon's wisdom and might, they will seek to make peace with him throughout his reign. This also will occur in the Messianic era, which will be devoid of hostility.

According to *Sforno, the mountains* alludes to the high government officials appointed by the king. These smug bureaucrats tend to become petty tyrants who exploit the people under

ד וּגְבָעוֹת בִּצְדָקָה: יִשְׁפֹּט | עֲנִיֵּי־עָם יוֹשִׁיעַ
ה לִבְנֵי אֶבְיוֹן וִידַכֵּא עוֹשֵׁק: יִירָאוּךָ עִם־
ו שָׁמֶשׁ וְלִפְנֵי יָרֵחַ דּוֹר דּוֹרִים: יֵרֵד כְּמָטָר
ז עַל־גֵּז כִּרְבִיבִים זַרְזִיף אָרֶץ: יִפְרַח־בְּיָמָיו

their rule. Solomon, however, will choose his ministers and officials wisely; therefore, they will *bring peace* and good will to the populace, rather than dissension and animosity.

וּגְבָעוֹת – *And the hills.*

The low hills also *bring peace to the nation* by charitably providing their rich fruits and produce *(Rashi).*

According to *Sforno, the hills* refers to the lower echelons of governmental authority, including petty officials and the wives of the ministers. They too will be compassionate and charitable.

4. יִשְׁפֹּט עֲנִיֵּי עָם – *May He judge the nation's poor.*

In *v.* 2, the psalmist speaks of עֲנִיֶּיךָ, *Your* [i.e., God's] *poor,* whose lot was determined by the Divine design which ordained unequal distribution of wealth to provide an opportunity for kindness and charity.

However, *the nation's poor* mentioned in this verse refers to those whose poverty can be traced to unjust social conditions caused by national disregard for human rights and for man's responsibility to his fellow man. These underprivileged citizens are the victims of a national indifference to kindness and charity *(Hirsch).*

יוֹשִׁיעַ לִבְנֵי אֶבְיוֹן – *And save the children of the destitute.*

Sforno explains that this refers to the children of rich parents who have suddenly lost their wealth. Since the plight of such youngsters who had been accustomed to affluence and ease is particularly distressing, the king will provide them with a generous allowance.

וִידַכֵּא עוֹשֵׁק – *And crush the oppressor.*

This refers to a cowardly charlatan who secretly deceives his victims and thus exploits them. These despicable men will cower before Solomon's extraordinary ability to unearth hidden lies *(Ibn Ezra).*

5. יִירָאוּךָ עִם שָׁמֶשׁ – *So that they will fear You at sunrise* [lit. *with the sun*].

This translation follows *Targum* and *Metzudas David.*

The *Talmud* (*Berachos* 9b) teaches that the devout men called *Vasikin,* who sought to fulfill the Torah's precepts perfectly, would recite the *Shema* immediately before sunrise and recite the *Shemoneh Esrei* service as the sun came over the horizon, in order to fulfill this verse.

Midrash HaNeelam explains that God created the brilliant sun so that man could view the awesome wonders of creation and come to fear God, the Creator.

However, *Rashi, Radak,* and *Ibn Ezra* render: Let them learn from Solomon to fear You and let this fear endure forever, i.e., as long as the sun and the moon continue to shine.

Malbim adds: May their fear of God be consistent — just as the sun and moon remain stable in their orbits.

[David's greatest wish was to restore mankind to the utopian status it enjoyed before Adam sinned. *Ramban (Genesis* 2:9) teaches that Adam originally resembled the heavenly host, which the *Talmud (Sanhedrin* 42a) describes as creatures of truth, whose achievement is truth, and who do not deviate from their appointed mission. (See *Overview, Tehillim* Vol. I part 1).]

וְלִפְנֵי יָרֵחַ – *And before the moon's appearance.*

Again the translation follows *Targum* and *Metzudas David.* The *Talmud*

and the hills — through charity.
4 *May he judge the nation's poor,*
and save the children of the destitute;
and crush the oppressor.
5 *So that they will fear You at sunrise*
and before the moon's appearance,
generation after generation.
6 *May he descend like rain upon mown grass,*
like showers watering the earth.

(*Berachos* 29b) cites the view that it is commendable to recite the afternoon prayers (the *Minchah* service) immediately prior to sunset, just as the moon begins to appear. However, this practice is not generally followed, for fear that the proper moment may be missed. (The afternoon prayers should be completed before sunset.)

דּוֹר דּוֹרִים — *Generation after generation.*

Solomon's lesson will be transmitted from father to son; thus the tradition will continue unbroken (*Metzudas David*).

The teachings of Messiah will endure to an even greater degree. When he teaches the nation to fear God, the people's faith will never lapse (*Radak*).

6. יֵרֵד כְּמָטָר עַל גֵּז — *May he descend like rain upon mown grass.*

This verse teaches that the ideal king should *descend* to the level of the common people and concern himself with their lives. As a result, his words will penetrate deep into their hearts, like the rain which saturates the earth; but if the king serves only the elite members of society, then his influence on the nation as a whole will be minimal (*Rashi; Hirsch*).

The rain which falls after the grass is mown is especially beneficial (see *Amos* 7:1), for then the moisture can irrigate not only the roots, but also the fresh tips of the grass.

In an allegorical sense, the cut grass connotes people who have been admonished for their shortcomings. Since people are normally averse to receiving chastisement and rebuke, reproof must be given in a roundabout, tactful way; but if the king displays genuine concern for his subjects, then they will accept even blunt criticism from him, realizing that his remarks are motivated by his sincere concern for their welfare (*Malbim*).

[Even if the monarch's criticism is sharp and cutting, the people will drink up his words thirstily, like freshly mown grass which soaks up water.]

כִּרְבִיבִים זַרְזִיף אָרֶץ — *Like showers watering the earth.*

[רְבִיבִים, derived from רַב, *great*, and רְבָבָה, *a myriad*, denotes a great downpour of rain.]

Rashi states that זַרְזִיף means *raindrops* (see *Yoma* 87a). The words of the benevolent king will quench the spiritual thirst of the nation, just as a shower of raindrops provides lifegiving moisture for the parched earth and inspires tremendous joy (*Radak; Sforno*).

Radak says that Solomon's reign fulfilled David's great expectations of utopian bliss: *And Judah and Israel dwelt securely, each man under his vine and under his fig tree, from Dan to Beer Sheva, all the days of Solomon* (*I Kings* 5:5).

The Messiah's reign will not only be a paradise of material wealth, but also one

ח צַדִּיק וְרֹב שָׁלוֹם עַד־בְּלִי יָרֵחַ: וְיֵרְדְּ מִיָּם
ט עַד־יָם וּמִנָּהָר עַד־אַפְסֵי־אָרֶץ: לְפָנָיו
י יִכְרְעוּ צִיִּים וְאֹיְבָיו עָפָר יְלַחֵכוּ: מַלְכֵי

of spiritual truth. The term זַרְזִיף is a contraction of two words which describe the Messiah's times: (זִיף) זִיוּף *falsehood; deceit*, will become זָר, *alien; unknown*, because Messiah will banish deception from the world *(Sforno)*.

7. יִפְרַח בְּיָמָיו צַדִּיק — *In his days may the righteous man flourish.*

The righteous man refers to the entire nation of Israel. In Solomon's days, as long as the Jews remained righteous, they flourished, as Scripture states, (I Kings 4:20) *Judah and Israel are many, like the sand on the sea — a multitude, they eat and drink and are happy (Rashi).*

At that time the nation developed spiritually, blossoming both in brilliant Torah study and scrupulous *mitzvah* observance. This can only occur when the Jews are settled securely in their own land *(Sforno)*. [Similar spiritual growth will take place in the time of the Messiah.]

וְרֹב שָׁלוֹם — *With abundant peace.*

And he had peace on all sides round about him. And Judah and Israel dwelt in safety ... [and Solomon said] *'Now HASHEM, my God, has granted me rest on every side, there is neither adversary nor evil attack'* (I Kings 5:4-5, 18).

All of David's prayers on Solomon's behalf were completely fulfilled, except for this. David requested eternal peace, but God ordained that the reign of the House of David would endure only as long as David's descendants remained faithful to His word. When they betrayed God, he withdrew His protection from them *(Rashi)*.

עַד בְּלִי יָרֵחַ — *Till there is no moon.*

[These words describe the ultimate degree of serenity, stability, and success. The commentaries offer numerous interpretations for this enigmatic description.]

Peace will last until the end of time, until even the moon (an indicator of time) is no more *(Rashi; Radak)*.

The prophet *Isaiah* (60:19,20) describes the Messianic redemption thus: *The sun will no longer serve you with light by day, and for brightness, the moon will no longer give you light; HASHEM will be your eternal light, and your God will be your splendor. Your sun will not set again, nor will your moon be gathered in, for HASHEM will be an everlasting light for you and your days of mourning will be completed.*

At that time, God's glory will outshine the sun and the moon; therefore, they will no longer be needed *(Hirsch)*.

Even the idolaters, the worshipers of the moon, will be no more *(Targum)*.

People will feel so secure that even if the moon does not shine and the night is pitch black, they will walk the streets without any fear *(Vidal HaTzorfati)*.

In exile, the gentiles shine (with success) like the sun, while Israel resembles the moon, which has no light of its own. Peace and autonomy will bring the 'waning moon' status of Israel to an end *(Eretz Hachaim)*.[1]

8. וְיֵרְדְּ מִיָּם עַד יָם — *May he dominate from sea to sea.*

Solomon (and Messiah) will have sovereignty over all of the territory of

1. The *Midrash (Shemos Rabbah* 15:26) derives from the verse הַחֹדֶשׁ הַזֶּה לָכֶם, *This month* [lit. *this new moon*] *shall be for you (Exodus* 12:2) that the royal dynasty of Israel will resemble the cycle of the moon: It will endure for thirty generations, just as the month lasts thirty days. The light of Jewish sovereignty began to rise in the time of the Patriarch Abraham, who was universally recognized as *the prince of God (Genesis* 23:6) followed by

[7] *In his days may the righteous man flourish*
with abundant peace till there is no moon.
[8] *May he dominate from sea to sea,*
and from river to the ends of the earth.
[9] *May nobles kneel before him,*
and may his foes lick the dust.

Eretz Yisrael, from יַם סוּף, *Sea of Reeds* (in the south), to the יַם פְּלִשְׁתִּים *Sea of Philistines* (the Mediterranean, in the north and west. See *Exodus* 23:31) *(Rashi; Radak)*.

Sforno explains that the dominion implied by the word וְיֵרְדְּ is not an impersonal government by proxy; rather it means that the king personally leads the people. [The word is related to רֵד, *go down*, meaning that the monarch descends to the level of the people and is intimately involved in their affairs.]

וּמִנָּהָר עַד אַפְסֵי אָרֶץ — *And from river to the ends of the earth.*

The boundaries of *Eretz Yisrael* also extend from נְהַר פְּרָת, *the Euphrates River*, on the northeast and the נְהַר מִצְרַיִם, *the River of Egypt*, in the southwest (see *Genesis* 15:18). This encompasses all of the territory which was promised to the Patriarchs *(Alshich)*.

Solomon ruled over all this land, and beyond, as Scripture attests, (*I Kings* 5:4) *He* [Solomon] *had dominion over all the land beyond the river, from Tifsach to Azah, and over all the kings who were beyond the river (Rashi; Radak).*

9. לְפָנָיו יִכְרְעוּ צִיִּים — *May nobles kneel before him.*

This translation of צִיִּים follows *Rashi*, who bases his view on the *Targum* to *Numbers* 24:24 [Similarly, *Targum* on this verse renders צִיִּים as אִיפַּרְכַיָא, *governors.*]

Others say that צִיִּים are the inhabitants of אֶרֶץ צִיָּה, *the parched desert*, suggesting: Even these isolated tribes will hear of Solomon's majesty and come to pay homage to him *(Radak)*.

Ibn Ezra, however, relates צִיִּים to צִי, *the navy* (see *Isaiah* 33:21). Thus, ships from far and near will sail to Israel to serve Solomon.

וְאֹיְבָיו עָפָר יְלַחֵכוּ — *And may his foes lick the dust.*

Any attempt to challenge Solomon's authority will meet with failure and frustration. *His foes* will be forced to *lick the dust* in his presence, in fear of his power *(Radak)*.

Isaac, Jacob, Judah, Peretz, Chetzron, Rom, Aminodov, Nachshon, Salmon, Boaz, Oved, and Jesse. Then came David (whose name, דָּוִד, has the numerical value of 14). He lived in the fourteenth generation (counting from Abraham) and resembled the moon, which is almost full on the fourteenth day of the month. Solomon was the fifteenth generation; in his days, the glory of David's line reached full perfection, comparable to that of the full moon on the fifteenth day of the month.

Then the decline began: The situation deteriorated from generation to generation. [See *Yechezkel*, ArtScroll ed. Appendix II.] The waning light of the Davidic line disappeared entirely in the thirtieth generation, with King Tzidkiyahu. Nebuchadnezzar blinded King Tzidkiyahu and sent him into exile, symbolizing the total eclipse of the monarchy. This is the meaning of this verse: [Because of Jewish sovereignty] *there will be an abundance of peace, until* [the thirtieth generation, when] *the moon is no more.* (see *Overview Tehillim* Vol. I, Part VIII).

תַּרְשִׁישׁ וְאִיִּים מִנְחָה יָשִׁיבוּ מַלְכֵי שְׁבָא
יא וּסְבָא אֶשְׁכָּר יַקְרִיבוּ: וְיִשְׁתַּחֲווּ־לוֹ כָל־
יב מְלָכִים כָּל־גּוֹיִם יַעַבְדוּהוּ: כִּי־יַצִּיל אֶבְיוֹן
יג מְשַׁוֵּעַ וְעָנִי וְאֵין־עֹזֵר לוֹ: יָחֹס עַל־דַּל
יד וְאֶבְיוֹן וְנַפְשׁוֹת אֶבְיוֹנִים יוֹשִׁיעַ: מִתּוֹךְ

10. מַלְכֵי תַרְשִׁישׁ וְאִיִּים מִנְחָה יָשִׁיבוּ — *The kings of Tarshish and the isles shall return with tribute.*

In I *Kings* 10:21-23 we read the fulfillment of David's prayer: *And all King Solomon's drinking vessels were of gold, and all the vessels of the house of the forest of Lebanon were of pure gold, none were of silver, because it was not considered of any worth in the days of Solomon. For the king had at sea the navy of Tarshish with the navy of Hiram; once every three years the navy of Tarshish arrived bringing gold and silver, ivory and apes and peacocks. So King Solomon surpassed all the kings of the earth in riches and in wisdom.*

[Throughout Scriptures, *Tarshish* is described as a major seaport which dispatched great merchant fleets to the ends of the earth. See *comm.* to 48:8, *Genesis* 10:4, and *Jonah* 1:3.]

יָשִׁיבוּ — [*They*] *shall return.*

This usage is unexpected; *they shall bring* would seem to be more appropriate here. *Radak* and *Ibn Ezra* explain that this verse means that the nations will return to offer tribute to Solomon every year.

According to the *Midrash (Bereishis Rabbah* 78:12), this refers to the Messiah. All the gifts which Jacob gave to Esau, all the bribes which Jews have used to still the animosity of their oppressors through the ages, [and all the property which the gentiles have forcibly plundered from us] will be returned to the Messiah when the nations subject themselves to his sovereignty *(Tehillos Hashem).*

מַלְכֵי שְׁבָא וּסְבָא אֶשְׁכָּר יַקְרִיבוּ — *The kings of Sheba and Seba shall offer gifts.*

The fulfillment of this verse is described in *I Kings* (10:1, 2, 10): *And when the Queen of Sheba heard of the fame of Solomon, for the sake of* HASHEM, *she came to test him with riddles. And she came to Jerusalem with a great retinue, with camels that bore spices and very much gold and precious stones ... And she gave the king one hundred and twenty talents of gold, and very many spices and precious stones; never again did such an abundance of spices arrive to compare with that which the Queen of Sheba gave to Solomon.*

[Perhaps אֶשְׁכָּר, translated by *Targum* as *gifts,* is related to שְׂכַר, *reward,* which would imply that the Queen of Sheba bestowed her *gifts* on Solomon as a reward for the knowledge he had shared with her so generously: *And King Solomon gave to the Queen of Sheba all her desire, whatever she asked, (I Kings* 10:13).][1]

11. וְיִשְׁתַּחֲווּ לוֹ כָל מְלָכִים — *All the kings shall prostrate themselves before him.*

David's prayer for his son was answered when *all the earth sought the presence of Solomon, to hear his wisdom which God had put in his heart. And every man brought his tribute, ves-*

1. The *Talmud (Bava Basra* 15b) maintains that מַלְכַּת שְׁבָא does not mean *the Queen of Sheba,* rather it means מַלְכוּת שְׁבָא, *the royalty of Sheba. Maharsha (ibid.)* explains that the Queen of Sheba was not merely the wife of the king, rather she herself was the ruling monarch and this was a rare phenomenon in history.

10 *The kings of Tarshish and the isles*
shall return with tribute,
The kings of Sheba and Seba
shall offer gifts.
11 *All the kings*
shall prostrate themselves before him,
All the peoples
shall serve him.
12 *For he will deliver the crying destitute one*
and the poor one with none to help him.
13 *He will pity the impoverished and destitute;*
the souls of destitute ones he will save.

sels of silver and vessels of gold, and raiment and armor, and spices, horses and mules, each year according to its due (I Kings 10:24-35).

כָּל גּוֹיִם יַעַבְדוּהוּ – *All the peoples shall serve him.*

They will not serve him out of fear, but out of love and admiration *(Sforno).*[1]

All the homage and adulation paid to Solomon will be paid to the Messiah as well *(Radak).*

12. כִּי יַצִּיל אֶבְיוֹן מְשַׁוֵּעַ – *For he will deliver the crying destitute one.*

Solomon was to earn the love and admiration of the entire world because of his towering moral stature. His court was universally recognized as the international tribunal of justice; the needy regarded him as their defender; he was the friend of the weak and persecuted.

Princes turned to him to arbitrate national disputes; weak nations called upon him for salvation from their powerful neighbors. Even paupers, feeble and powerless individuals, felt that Solomon cared for their personal problems; they too appeared before him *(Radak; Ibn Ezra; Hirsch).*

וְעָנִי וְאֵין עֹזֵר לוֹ – *And the poor one with none to help him* [lit. *without a helper for him*].

[Although others spurn the cries of the ragged paupers who seek justice against tyranny, Solomon courageously championed their unpopular, but just cause.]

13. יָחֹס עַל דַּל וְאֶבְיוֹן – *He will pity the impoverished and destitute.*

Solomon did not use the huge amount of tribute brought to him by all the nations for his own pleasure. He distributed all excess wealth to alleviate the plight of the deprived *(Alshich).*

[The Torah prohibits the king from amassing a fortune of silver and gold in excess of his annual expenses for supporting his army and retinue (*Deuteronomy* 17:17), lest too much wealth fill his heart with pride. Similarly he is constrained from having too many horses or too many wives (*Deuteronomy* 17:16,17).

1. The universal homage paid to Solomon was not restricted to human beings. *Targum Sheini* (1:1) to *Megillas Esther* states that the fish of the sea and the birds of the sky, domestic animals and wild beasts came to Solomon's palace and presented themselves for slaughter, so that they might merit to be part of Solomon's meal.

וּמֵחָמָס יִגְאַל נַפְשָׁם וְיֵיקַר דָּמָם בְּעֵינָיו:
טו וִיחִי וְיִתֶּן־לוֹ מִזְּהַב שְׁבָא וְיִתְפַּלֵּל בַּעֲדוֹ
טז תָּמִיד כָּל־הַיּוֹם יְבָרֲכֶנְהוּ: יְהִי פִסַּת־בַּר |
בָּאָרֶץ בְּרֹאשׁ הָרִים יִרְעַשׁ כַּלְּבָנוֹן פִּרְיוֹ

The *Talmud (Sanhedrin* 21b) states that Solomon transgressed both the prohibition against too many wives and the law of limiting the size of the royal stables; but despite Scriptural reports of Solomon's enormous wealth, the *Talmud* does *not* accuse him of possessing an overabundance of riches. The reason, as *Alshich* explains, is that Solomon used all his extra funds either for the Temple or to benefit the underprivileged.]

Sforno comments that Solomon was particularly sensitive to the plight of those who became impoverished because of inflation. When the rich plundered the poor by inflating the prices of such staples as grain, Solomon combatted this practice.

וְנַפְשׁוֹת אֶבְיוֹנִים יוֹשִׁיעַ — *The souls of destitute ones He will save.*

The rich employer exploits his poor laborer and works him to death. Solomon saved these wretched slaves from their desperate plight *(Sforno).*

14. מִתּוֹךְ וּמֵחָמָס יִגְאַל נַפְשָׁם — *From fraud and from violence he will redeem their soul.*

Literally תּוֹךְ means *inside,* suggesting that the deceitful man tries to conceal the injury and damage which he inflicts on his victim. In contrast, חָמָס describes acts of open *violence (Rashi; Ibn Ezra; Radak;* see *comm.* to *Psalms* 55:12).

Specifically, says *Sforno,* Solomon used his might and prestige to prevent kings from tyrannizing their helpless subjects.

וְיֵיקַר דָּמָם בְּעֵינָיו — *And their blood will be precious in his eyes.*

[Solomon's acute sense of justice was stirred by his great esteem for human life and by his sensitivity to human suffering. It was anathema for him to advance the cause of his monarchy at the expense of human misery.]

15. וִיחִי וְיִתֶּן לוֹ מִזְּהַב שְׁבָא — *So he will live! And He will grant him of the gold of Sheba.*

This translation follows *Rashi:* Solomon will live on, and God will provide him with the wealth he needs to pursue his universal philanthropy.

According to *Ibn Ezra, Radak,* and *Metzudas David,* the verse signifies that Solomon's charity will infuse the poor with new life. Not only will the poor live, they will be prosperous, for Solomon will generously bestow upon them the tribute of gold he received from Sheba.

וְיִתְפַּלֵּל בַּעֲדוֹ תָמִיד — *And He will pray for him continually.*

God's blessings will pour down upon Solomon incessantly *(Rashi).*

The poor, the beneficiaries of Solomon's magnanimity, will shower an endless flow of prayers and blessings upon him *(Radak; Ibn Ezra; Metzudas David).*

16. יְהִי פִסַּת בַּר בָּאָרֶץ — *May an abundance of grain* [lit. *a loaf of bread*] *be in the land.*

Rashi determines that פִּסַּת is cognate with פִּסְיוֹן, *enlargement; increase* [see *Leviticus* 13:7]. This *abundance* will create unprecedented contentment, which, in turn, will foster the פִּיוּס, *reconciliation,* of those who became estranged from God.

Radak adds that, at that time, when a man plants a mere פַּס, *fistful,* of seeds, a

72
14-16

[14] *From fraud and from violence*
he will redeem their soul,
And their blood will be precious
in his eyes.
[15] *So he will live!*
And He will grant him of the gold of Sheba,
And He will pray for him continually
and bless him every day.
[16] *May an abundance of grain be*
in the land on the mountain tops,
May its fruit rustle
like the Lebanon;

vast field of grain will sprout from it.[1]

Sforno interprets this as an allegory: the wise and just king will concentrate his full pedagogic skills on a פִּסַּת, *handful* of devoted disciples, who will then disseminate his universal message of equity and decency.

בְּרֹאשׁ הָרִים — *On the mountain tops.*

[Not only will the rich soil bear fruit, even the barren and inaccessible mountain tops will become verdant and amazingly productive.]

The *Talmud (Kesubos* 111b) foretells that in the future, a stalk of wheat [planted in the valley *(Maharshah)*] will grow to incredible heights, until it towers above the mountaintops.

יִרְעַשׁ כַּלְּבָנוֹן פִּרְיוֹ — *May its fruit rustle like the Lebanon.*

Each kernel of wheat will be as large as the huge fruits growing in the lush forest of Lebanon. They will equal the size of the large kidneys of a cow *(Rashi).*

In order to harvest these giant kernels from the tremendously high stalks, HASHEM will send a wind to shake the finest flour from the kernels. When this floats gently to earth, people will gather fistfuls, which will sustain them generously (*Kesubos* 111b).

The *Talmud (Yoma* 39b) also relates that when Solomon built the Holy Temple, he planted a variety of golden fruit trees which miraculously produced golden fruits. The wind would rustle through the trees and shake the precious fruit making it fall to the earth, providing a generous income for the priests who worked in the Temple.

When the gentiles entered the Temple courtyard to destroy it, these wondrous trees shriveled and died. In the future, however, they will be restored to their former splendor.

1. The *Talmud (Shabbos* 30b) records Rabban Gamliel's teaching that in the days of the Messiah, the land of Israel will produce loaves of baked bread [every day], in fulfillment of this verse.

One incredulous student mocked this statement, retorting, 'Does Scripture not teach, *there is nothing new under the sun?' (Koheles* 1:9).

Rabban Gamliel replied, 'I will show you something very similar which is already in existence.' He showed the student mushrooms, which sprout to full maturity overnight.

[Actually the sceptic's question was unfounded, because before Adam's sin, the earth did produce perfect, finished loaves of bread, which stopped coming after the sin.]

יז וְיָצִיצוּ מֵעִיר כְּעֵשֶׂב הָאָרֶץ: יְהִי שְׁמוֹ |
°יִנּוֹן לְעוֹלָם לִפְנֵי־שֶׁמֶשׁ °ינין שְׁמוֹ וְיִתְבָּרְכוּ
יח בוֹ כָּל־גּוֹיִם יְאַשְּׁרוּהוּ: בָּרוּךְ | יהוה
אֱלֹהִים אֱלֹהֵי יִשְׂרָאֵל עֹשֵׂה נִפְלָאוֹת

וְיָצִיצוּ מֵעִיר כְּעֵשֶׂב הָאָרֶץ – *May they blossom forth from the city like the grass of the earth.*

In the same way that agricultural marvels will bloom in the fields, demographic miracles will abound in the cities: an unprecedented population explosion will fill the urban areas with teeming masses *(Radak).*

Jerusalem, in particular, will witness spectacular growth of her Jewish population (*Rashi*, based on *Kesubos* 111b).

Hirsch observes that David envisioned his son's rule as providing the guidance needed for the city to function properly as the basis of society, and he wished to see his people thrive in the city, just as grass blooms in the fields. In our culture, the harmony and beauty of creation are more apparent in unpopulated areas than they are in cities. However, when our national life is conducted with integrity and purity, and based on the service of God, then the city will radiate more breathtaking beauty and spiritual splendor than any 'natural wonder' of the physical world. The masses who are dedicated to the fulfillment of the Divine mission are truly God's greatest wonder.

17. יְהִי שְׁמוֹ לְעוֹלָם – *May his name survive forever.*

May Solomon be recognized forever as a paragon of wisdom and wealth *(Rashi).* May his name be equaled only by the great name of the Messiah *(Ibn Ezra).*

With the mere mention of the Messiah's name, the resultant yearning for his appearance hastens his arrival *(Beis Elokim).*

לִפְנֵי שֶׁמֶשׁ יִנּוֹן שְׁמוֹ – *May his dynasty endure as long as the sun.*

Radak explains that יִנּוֹן is cognate with נִין, *descendant,* to indicate that just as descendants perpetuate the memory of their ancestors, so should the fame of the king endure for as long as the sun shines, until the end of time. *Rashi* adds that this term for descendants is usually reserved for the heirs of the royal line.

According to *Pirkei D'Rabbi Eliezer* (ch. 32), יִנּוֹן alludes to *youth,* intimating that the Messiah is destined to bring about the resurrection of the dead.[1]

The *Talmud (Sanhedrin* 98b) marshals a number of opinions concerning the name of the Messiah. Some interpret these words literally, maintaining that יִנּוֹן שְׁמוֹ, *Yenon will be his* [actual] *name.* Other suggested names are מְנַחֵם, *Menachem,* שִׁילֹה, *Shiloh,* and חֲנִינָה, *Chaninah.* [Some commentaries have observed that the initial letters of all four suggested names spell מָשִׁיחַ, *Messiah!*]

וְיִתְבָּרְכוּ בוֹ – *And may men bless themselves by him.*

A father will bless his son, 'May you

1. *Kovetz Shiurim* Vol. II:29 quotes the responsa of *Radvaz* (II: 644), who explains there will be *two* resurrections. The general resurrection for all men will take place after the Messianic era. However, at the advent of the Messianic era a limited revival of the dead will occur, bringing back to life the outstanding individuals, the great scholars and men of piety, of each generation. This is also the opinion of the *Ritva,* who explains that it is only right that these dedicated persons should enjoy the bliss and rewards of the Messianic times. [See *Ikrei Hadat, Yoreh Deah Hilchos Aveilus* appendix 66.]

The *Talmud (Yoma* 5b) indicates that in the Messianic era Moses and Aaron will be alive once again and they will be available to make halachic decisions. [See *Pesachim* 114b, *Tosafos*

May they blossom forth from the city
like the grass of the earth.
17 *May his name survive forever,*
may his dynasty endure as long as the sun,
And may men bless themselves by him;
may all peoples praise him.
18 *Blessed be HASHEM, God, the God of Israel,*
Who alone does wondrous things.

be as wise and wealthy as Solomon' *(Rashi).*

כָּל גּוֹיִם יְאַשְּׁרֻהוּ – *May all peoples praise him.*

[The sterling qualities of Solomon and the Messiah will be universally admired.]

18. בָּרוּךְ ה׳ אֱלֹהִים אֱלֹהֵי יִשְׂרָאֵל – *Blessed be HASHEM, God, the God of Israel.*

In the final three verses of this composition, the author offers praise and thanks to God, not only for the inspiration to complete this psalm, but also for the privilege of completing the second Book of *Tehillim (Radak).*

Blessed be ה׳, *the Dispenser of Kindness* and blessed be אֱלֹהִים, *the Dispenser of Strict Justice (Sforno).*

Blessed be the Almighty, Who, despite His exalted position as *HASHEM* and God of the entire universe, still supervises us personally as *the God of Israel (Ibn Yachya).*

עֹשֵׂה נִפְלָאוֹת לְבַדּוֹ – *Who alone does wondrous things.*

God intervenes personally, rather than through an intermediary *(Malbim).* He performs miracles for Israel exclusively (i.e., *alone*), thus demonstrating that He alone, *the God of Israel,* is the true Lord. All pagan deities are false *(Radak).*

Radak contends that David here refers to a specific miracle: He asks that God send a heavenly flame to burn on the altar of Solomon's Temple, in order to demonstrate to the world that Solomon was worthy of *wondrous things alone,* i.e., in his own merit.

The *Talmud (Niddah* 31a) illustrates these words with a parable: As two merchants were about to board a ship, a sharp thorn pierced one man's foot, forcing him to miss the ship. Disappointed, the merchant cursed his luck. Soon however, word arrived that the ship had sunk. All aboard were lost. Now the wounded merchant burst forth in song, thanking God for his good fortune.

This is the meaning of the verse, *He does wondrous things alone:* often God acts *alone* in such hidden ways that even the beneficiary of His miracles doesn't immediately recognize his own good fortune!

s.v. אֶחָד זָכָר לְפֶּסַח and *Sanhedrin* 51b, *Rashi s.v.* הֲלָכָה לָמָּה לִי.] *Rav Saadiah Gaon* states that Moses will be revived together with all other prophets of Jewish history, who will assist him.

The *Yalkut Shimoni* to *Job,* Chapter 38, 924 tells us of Rav Yoshiya's final wish: 'Dress me in white shrouds. Put shoes on my feet and a staff in my hand and put me on my side [in the grave] so I will be ready when Messiah comes and calls me to life.'

The *Talmud (Sanhedrin* 92a) says that the righteous ones who will be resurrected [in the Messianic era, *Rashi*] will never be returned to their graves.

Finally the Sages (*Sotah* 48b) speak of the future and place the revival of the dead *before* the advent of Messiah, the scion of David. In light of the above sources, this must refer to the outstanding leaders, not to the masses.

יט לְבַדּוֹ: וּבָרוּךְ | שֵׁם כְּבוֹדוֹ לְעוֹלָם וְיִמָּלֵא
כ כְבוֹדוֹ אֶת־כָּל־הָאָרֶץ אָמֵן | וְאָמֵן: כָּלּוּ
תְפִלּוֹת דָּוִד בֶּן־יִשָׁי:

19. וּבָרוּךְ שֵׁם כְּבוֹדוֹ לְעוֹלָם — *Blessed be His glorious Name forever.*

God has but one real name, which is ה׳, *HASHEM*. All other references to Him are merely descriptions of his countless powers and abilities *(Ibn Ezra).*

[When men are only aware of God's actions, they may err and attribute these deeds to false deities.] The climax of the Messianic mission is to bring mankind to an awareness of God's true identity as the one and only Divine power. The prophet (*Zechariah* 14:9) foretells: *On that day HASHEM will be One and His Name will be One (Radak).*

וְיִמָּלֵא כְבוֹדוֹ אֶת כָּל הָאָרֶץ — *And may all the earth be filled with His glory.*

This verse will be fulfilled only when men are imbued with a keen awareness of God's majesty, as the prophet (*Isaiah* 11:9) foretells, *for the earth shall be filled with the knowledge of HASHEM, as the waters cover the sea (Radak).*

אָמֵן וְאָמֵן — *Amen and Amen.*

The word בָּרוּךְ, *blessed be,* is found in the previous verse and repeated here. Since God is blessed twice, a double *Amen* is needed to verify both benedictions *(Midrash Chachomim).*

The repetition of *Amen* expresses the hope that God be glorified both in This World and in the World to Come *(Zera Yaakov).*

20. כָּלּוּ תְפִלּוֹת דָּוִד בֶּן יִשָׁי — *The prayers of David, the son of Jesse, are ended.*

As was explained in the *Prefatory Remarks,* this psalm was composed by David on his deathbed. It commemorates the last significant act of David's lifetime, the coronation of Solomon.

The Book of *Tehillim* ends with this psalm only in the sense that it is the last of the psalms that were inspired by specific events in David's lifetime. The

19 *Blessed be His glorious Name forever*
And may all the earth be filled with His glory.
Amen and Amen

20 *The prayers of David,*
the son of Jesse, are ended.

following three books are predominantly songs of general praise for God.

The psalmist purposely laid out his book in this fashion, so that this inspired work would end with a tremendous outpouring of Divine praise (*Radak, Psalms* 72:1).

Rabbi Meir, quoted in the *Talmud* (*Pesachim* 117b), explains that the entire Book of *Tehillim* was composed by David. He teaches that כָּלּוּ should not be read *are ended,* but should be interpreted as a contraction of the two words כָּל אֵלּוּ, *all of these,* are the prayers of David.

[Although a number of psalms are ascribed to ten other righteous men (see *Rashi,* to 1:1), in truth they composed their songs merely as a personal recollection. It was David who rewrote all of the psalms so that they would relate to the souls of all men at all times. See *Overview Tehillim,* Vol. I, part IV, 'The sweet singer of Israel'.]

R' Yosef Kimchi, quoted by his son, *Radak,* points out that it does not say that David's זְמִירוֹת, *psalms,* or הוֹדָאוֹת, *songs of thanksgiving,* are ended; rather the verse mentions David's תְּפִלּוֹת, *prayers.*

David's praises of God will never end, but his *prayers* were inspired by his sins, his failures and his tragedies. In his *prayers,* David begs for atonement for himself and for his entire people.

With the advent of the perfect king, the Messiah, Israel will finally rid itself of all folly and failure. A nation redeemed and restored to grandeur, Israel will then live in a utopia, with no need for anguished pleas. Therefore, although תְּפִלּוֹת, *prayers,* will come to an end, songs of praise and thanksgiving will resound joyously forever.

מזמור עג 73

The *third book of* Tehillim *begins with this psalm. Whereas the first two books of* Psalms *are dedicated primarily to specific, personal events in the lives of individuals, the last two books concern general, universal themes which demonstrate God's goodness. The introductory verse of this psalm is a resounding declaration of faith which eloquently sets the tone for the ensuing compositions:* Truly God is [*naught but*] good to Israel!

The psalmist surveyed Jewish history — past, present, and future — and beheld only misery and travail for the Jews, while evil men flourished. Countless other observers have had their faith weakened by the same gnawing question: מַדּוּעַ דֶּרֶךְ רְשָׁעִים צָלֵחָה, Why does they way of the wicked prosper (Jeremiah *12:1*).

Assaf addresses those plagued by indecision and doubt. 'Do not be troubled by seeming inconsistencies,' he counsels, 'for everything God does to Israel is good. He causes you to suffer now, so that the fruits of your good deeds may be preserved for the future world of reward' (Radak; Rashi). *Remember this and no complaints will ever escape your lips; instead, your heart will overflow with endless hymns of gratitude.*

עג
א־ה

א מִזְמוֹר לְאָסָף אַךְ טוֹב לְיִשְׂרָאֵל אֱלֹהִים
ב ◦נָטָיו לְבָרֵי לֵבָב: וַאֲנִי כִּמְעַט ◦נטוי רַגְלָי כְּאַיִן
ג ◦שֻׁפְּכוּ ◦שפכה אֲשֻׁרָי: כִּי־קִנֵּאתִי בַּהוֹלְלִים
ד שְׁלוֹם רְשָׁעִים אֶרְאֶה: כִּי אֵין חַרְצֻבּוֹת
ה לְמוֹתָם וּבָרִיא אוּלָם: בַּעֲמַל אֱנוֹשׁ אֵינֵמוֹ

1. מִזְמוֹר לְאָסָף — *A song of Assaf.*

[A short biographical sketch of Assaf is provided in the *commentary* to 50:1. Psalm 73 begins a series of eleven compositions by Assaf. Assaf authored twelve psalms in all; thus he was the most prolific psalmist after David himself.]

אַךְ — *Truly* [lit. *only*].

This word signifies without any doubt or reservation that only this fact is true *(Sforno).*

No matter what happens to me, this conviction will remain firm, even when all other beliefs are shattered *(Radak).*

אַךְ טוֹב לְיִשְׂרָאֵל אֱלֹהִים — *Truly God is good to Israel.*

Even when God sits in judgment as אֱלֹהִים, *the Dispenser of Divine justice (Pesikta Zutrasa, Eikev),* He is nevertheless *truly good;* the seemingly harsh punishments He administers are goodness in disguise *(Midrash Shocher Tov).*

לְבָרֵי לֵבָב — *To the pure of heart.*

This refers to those who have, through concentrated effort, eliminated (בּוֹרֵר) all impurities and deficiencies from their hearts. Their faith is perfectly flawless *(Hirsch).* Their hearts are בָּרִיא, *healthy* and *robust,* in their genuine conviction that God is good *(Midrash Shocher Tov).*

[Only such a person can overcome the crisis of faith, as we read previously: *Who may ascend the mountain of HASHEM, and who may stand in the place of His sanctity?* נְקִי כַפַּיִם וּבַר לֵבָב, *One with clean hands and a pure heart* (24:3, 4).]

2. וַאֲנִי כִּמְעַט נָטָיו רַגְלָי — *But as for me, my feet were nearly turned astray.*

Before I set my mind to research and contemplate the ways of God, I was no better than any other sceptic *(Sforno).* I was overcome by doubts, and I almost turned my path of life towards the direction of heresy and disbelief *(Radak).*

According to the opinion that Assaf was one of the sons of Korach (see *commentary* to 50:1), this means that Assaf was swallowed by the earth, together with his rebellious father, Korach. His *feet* [i.e., his destiny] *were nearly turned astray* towards the brink of *Gehinnom,* but at the last moment Assaf repented and was saved *(Vayikrah Rabbah 17:1).*

כְּאַיִן — *Like nothing.*

Without faith, I was walking on thin air with *nothing* to support me *(Radak).*

In an instant, in almost no time — I was swallowed up *(Metzudas David).*

שֻׁפְּכוּ אֲשֻׁרָי — *My steps would have been washed aside* [lit. *poured out*].

Hirsch explains that אָשׁוּר denotes a powerful, purposeful stride; שָׁפַךְ, *to be spilled like water,* signifies the opposite of firm steps directed towards a goal. Since water has no shape of its own, its path is not self-determined, but depends upon the surrounding terrain.

Similarly, the Godless man does not determine his path in life according to any strong inner convictions or purpose; rather he lets himself be affected by superficial, external considerations.

3. כִּי קִנֵּאתִי בַּהוֹלְלִים — *For I envied the madmen.*

Rashi derives הוֹלְלִים from מָהוּל, *mixed up* [i.e., confounded or confused]. Because of their mad

73
1-5

A *Song of Assaf*
truly God is good to Israel,
to the pure of heart.
2 *But as for me,*
my feet were nearly turned astray,
Like nothing —
my steps would have been washed aside;
3 *For I envied the madmen*
when I saw the peace of the wicked.
4 *Because there are no fetters to their death*
and their vitality is sound.
5 *In the toil of frail humans*
they are nowhere,

obsession with futile worldly pleasures, these *madmen* have perverted their order of priorities. Their own personal gratification has taken precedence over all other considerations; therefore, they think nothing of stealing or committing any other crime in order to satisfy their desires *(Radak).*

According to *Tanchuma HaKadum, Metzorah* 11, the הוֹלְלִים will even commit cold-blooded murder. (חֲלָלִים means *corpses;* the letters ה, *heh,* and ח, *ches,* are often interchanged.

The *Midrash (Vayikrah Rabbah* 17:1) notes that the wicked הוֹלְלִים bring יְלָלָה, *cries of anguish,* to their victims.

שְׁלוֹם רְשָׁעִים אֶרְאֶה — *When I saw the peace of the wicked (Targum).*

When I witnessed crime which escaped punishment and violence which was rewarded with tranquility, my faith in a just God began to waver *(Radak).*

I began to suspect that the whole world was a topsy-turvy den of הוֹלְלוֹת, *mad confusion,* for the wicked prosper while the righteous suffer. I started to envy the *madman,* who is insensitive to all intellectual anguish. Why was I cursed with a conscience which made me revolt against sin, while the wicked blithely disregard the Law of God, with apparent impunity? *(Eitz Hadaas).*

4. כִּי אֵין חַרְצֻבּוֹת לְמוֹתָם — *Because there are no fetters to their death.*

חַרְצֻבּוֹת means *bonds* or *shackles,* as in *Isaiah* 58:6. Not only do the wicked live their lives wantonly, unencumbered by limitations or restraints, but they even die unmolested. They remain healthy and comfortable until the moment of death.

The righteous, in contrast, die slowly and painfully, after enduring long illness. As excruciating pain racks their frail bodies, it would seem more merciful for God to release them from their tormented existence, but invisible *fetters* seem to shackle them to their suffering *(Rashi; Radak).*

Rashi also cites the Sages *(Shabbos* 31b) who say that חַרְצֻבּוֹת is a contraction of two words; the wicked are not חַרֵדִין, *afraid,* or עֲצֵבִין, *distressed,* by the specter of the day of death and the final reckoning.

וּבָרִיא אוּלָם — *And their vitality is sound.*

Some say that אוּלָם is related to אֵל, אַיִל, or אֵלִים, all of which mean *strength* and *vitality* [see 22:20] *(Radak; Sforno; Ibn Yachya).*

According to the *Midrash (Vayikra Rabbah* 17:1), this refers to the אוּלָם, *vestibule,* which was the entrance hall

ו וְעִם־אָדָם לֹא יְנֻגָּעוּ: לָכֵן עֲנָקַתְמוֹ גַאֲוָה
ז יַעֲטָף־שִׁית חָמָס לָמוֹ: יָצָא מֵחֵלֶב עֵינֵמוֹ
ח עָבְרוּ מַשְׂכִּיּוֹת לֵבָב: יָמִיקוּ | וִידַבְּרוּ בְרָע
ט עֹשֶׁק מִמָּרוֹם יְדַבֵּרוּ: שַׁתּוּ בַשָּׁמַיִם פִּיהֶם

in the *Beis HaMikdosh.* Since it was a very large room, forty cubits tall and twenty cubits wide *(Middos* 3:7), supported by massive columns and sturdy stones, it became a symbol of solid strength. Similarly, the powerful evildoers seem to be firmly and permanently entrenched.

5. בַּעֲמַל אֱנוֹשׁ אֵינֵמוֹ — *In the toil of frail humans they are nowhere* [i.e., not involved].

The wicked prosper greatly, without any effort or exertion *(Radak; Ibn Ezra).*

Specifically, עָמָל refers to fruitless toil, hard labor which produces no beneficial results. Frail, fallible humans often engage in such frustrating, futile efforts. Every action performed by these wicked men, however, meets with instant, unfailing success *(Hirsch).*

Targum renders: These men are not involved in the toil of those who exert themselves to study Torah.

וְעִם אָדָם לֹא יְנֻגָּעוּ — *And with mankind they are not plagued.*

During an epidemic, even the righteous are plagued, yet these wicked men remain unscathed. Catastrophes which destroy other men leave them untouched *(Ibn Ezra; Radak).*

Even the most common ailments (such as toothache, headache, or eyestrain) do not affect them *(Midrash Shocher Tov).*

6. לָכֵן עֲנָקַתְמוֹ גַאֲוָה — *Therefore their necklace is pride.*

Since they have been released from all human drudgery and pain, they grow arrogant *(Rashi).* They flaunt their arrogance as if it were a precious jeweled necklace *(Radak).*

Their apparent immunity to common human maladies leads them to imagine that they are a special breed, set apart from common folk. Therefore, they wear a special badge around their necks to identify themselves as a superior race *(Alshich).*

Ibn Yachya observes that their very posture betrays their conceit, for they stretch out their necks and lift their heads high as they strut about haughtily (cf. *Isaiah* 3:16).

יַעֲטָף שִׁית חָמָס לָמוֹ — *Enwrapping their body in their own violence.*

Specifically, *Rashi* identifies שִׁית, *form,* as the שֵׁתוֹת, *buttocks* (see *II Samuel* 10:4; *Isaiah* 20:4), which are associated with shameful nakedness. The violent crimes of the wicked bring them tremendous profits. They grow exceedingly fat and their corpulence envelops every part of their body.

Radak translates שִׁית as a *garment* [see *Proverbs* 7:10], i.e., the wicked cloak themselves with a garment of crime and violence.

Sforno explains that they use their ill-gotten gains to purchase respectability so that their 'nakedness,' i.e., their shameful reputation, will be concealed *(Sforno).*

Others translate שִׁית as *the foundation* (see *Isaiah* 19:10), to signify that the lives of the wicked are predicated on violence *(Meiri).*

7. יָצָא מֵחֵלֶב עֵינֵמוֹ — *Bulging from corpulence are their eyes.*

Hunger, poverty, or many tears cause the eyes to sink deep into their sockets, but thick cushions form around the eyes of the fat man and they seem to make his eyes bulge out *(Rashi; Midrash Shocher Tov).*

According to *Radak* and *Rabbi*

And with mankind
they are not plagued.
6 *Therefore their necklace is pride*
enwrapping their body
in their own violence.
7 *Bulging from corpulence*
are their eyes,
They went beyond
the fantasies of the heart.
8 *They consume,*
and speak of foul oppression,
Out of haughtiness
they speak.
9 *They direct their mouth against Heaven,*

Moshe (in *Ibn Ezra*), the fatty folds cover their eyes, making it appear as if their eyes 'came out,' blinded by abundant wealth.

עָבְרוּ מַשְׂכִּיּוֹת לֵבָב — *They went beyond the fantasies of the heart.*

The heart is called שֶׂכְוִי because it is שׁוֹכֶה, *observant,* in that it possesses the faculty of imagination. Any luxury which the heart of the wicked imagined was granted to them; they received pleasures even beyond their greatest expectations *(Rashi; Radak).*

Midrash Shocher Tov refers this to God's generous fulfillment of a person's most heartfelt wishes: 'If someone desired a vineyard, I made him duke over an entire province [replete with vineyards]. If a soldier wanted to be an officer, I made him commander-in-chief' *(Midrash Shocher Tov).*

8. יָמִיקוּ — *They consume.*

Literally this means that they 'melt,' 'dissolve,' or 'waste away' (see *Zechariah* 14:12). The wicked mercilessly deride their enemies. Their foul words of scorn and derision destroy all who stand in their path *(Rashi; Radak).*

וִידַבְּרוּ בְרָע עֹשֶׁק — *And [they] speak of foul oppression.*

They are impudent. They make no effort to conceal their crimes, but instead boast of their evil deeds *(Ibn Ezra; Radak).*

מִמָּרוֹם יְדַבֵּרוּ — *Out of haughtiness they speak.*

They speak without inhibition, as if there were no heavenly authority to restrain them *(Ibn Ezra; Radak).*

Indeed, they audaciously claim that their speech is Divinely inspired מִמָּרוֹם, *from above.* They claim that their unbridled success is tantamount to Heavenly approval of their deeds *(Tehillos Hashem).*

9. שַׁתּוּ בַשָּׁמַיִם פִּיהֶם — *They direct their mouth against Heaven.*

They hurl blasphemous abuse heavenward and deny the power of God. Scripture records that Pharaoh defiantly asked, 'מִי ה' אֲשֶׁר אֶשְׁמַע בְּקֹלוֹ, *Who is HASHEM that I should obey His voice?' (Exodus* 5:2). Sennacherib and Nebuchadnezzar issued similar challenges to God's authority *(Rashi; Midrash Shocher Tov).*

°יָשׁוּב י וּלְשׁוֹנָם תִּהֲלַךְ בָּאָרֶץ: לָכֵן | °יָשִׁיב עַמּוֹ
יא הֲלֹם וּמֵי מָלֵא יִמָּצוּ לָמוֹ: וְאָמְרוּ אֵיכָה
יב יָדַע־אֵל וְיֵשׁ דֵּעָה בְעֶלְיוֹן: הִנֵּה־אֵלֶּה
יג רְשָׁעִים וְשַׁלְוֵי עוֹלָם הִשְׂגּוּ־חָיִל: אַךְ־רִיק
יד זִכִּיתִי לְבָבִי וָאֶרְחַץ בְּנִקָּיוֹן כַּפָּי: וָאֱהִי
טו נָגוּעַ כָּל־הַיּוֹם וְתוֹכַחְתִּי לַבְּקָרִים: אִם־

וּלְשׁוֹנָם תִּהֲלַךְ בָּאָרֶץ — *And their tongue struts on earth.*

According to the *Talmud (Arachin* 15b), this verse describes those who spread לָשׁוֹן הָרַע, *evil tales: Their tongue struts through the earth,* dragging along hopeless victims. The crimes perpetrated by their mouths grow and grow until their enormity reaches the highest heavens.

In general, slanderers first deny only the decency of their fellow men, but eventually deny God. This is illustrated by 12:5, which condemns *those who have said: 'With our tongues we shall prevail, our lips are with us, who is master over us?' (Yerushalmi Peah* 1:1).

The vicious, unrestrained slanderers first heap scorn and derision upon the holy men on earth; even the righteous prophets do not escape their ridicule. They brazenly trample them in the dust. Naturally, they even set their mouths against HASHEM *(Radak; Ibn Ezra; Rambam Hilchos Tumas Tzoraas* 16:10).

The Sages say that the evil talebearer is comparable to the barking dog and suffers the fate of that lowly creature. Just as the dog is forced to lick filth and dirt with its tongue in its search for food, so will these wicked men eventually be reduced to searching through the earth for food. Thus, *their* [starving] *tongue walks through the earth* [in search of food] *(Rav Yitzchak Chayes).*

10. לָכֵן יָשׁוּב עַמּוֹ הֲלֹם — *Therefore He turns His people here.*

God has bestowed remarkable success upon the wicked. Thus God Himself causes (so to speak) His faithful followers to neglect His ways and to *turn* towards the lifestyle of the wicked *(Rashi).*

[The כְּתִיב, *spelling,* of the word is יָשִׁיב, *return,* but the קְרִי, *pronunciation,* is יָשׁוּב, *repeat.*] According to *Radak,* this word describes God's conduct toward the evildoers. God does not merely show favor to the wicked occasionally or haphazardly, rather, He 'repeatedly' favors them with a set pattern of special privileges.

הֲלֹם — *Here.*

This translation follows *Rashi* and *Radak,* based on *Exodus* 3:5 and *Judges* 18:3.

Rashbam renders הֲלֹם as *a blow to the head* (see *Judges* 5:26), which indicates that the minds of the righteous are dazed and confused by the success of the wicked.

וּמֵי מָלֵא יִמָּצוּ לָמוֹ — *And abundant waters seem drained by them.*

The teachings of the Torah are likened to a full reservoir of fresh, flowing water; but the success of the wicked — who flaunt their contempt for these sacred teachings — undermines the prestige of the Torah to such an extent that even the Torah's adherents may come to see the Torah as a diminishing trickle rather than a powerful reservoir *(Rashi).*

Radak renders: The triumph of evil over good causes the devout to drink the full cup (מֵי מָלֵא) of bitter disappointment, draining (יִמָּצוּ) it to the bitter dregs.

11. וְאָמְרוּ אֵיכָה יָדַע אֵל — *And they say, 'How does God know?'*

and their tongue struts on earth.
10 *Therefore He turns*
His people here,
And abundant waters seem
drained by them.
11 *And they say, 'How does God know?*
Is there knowledge in the Most High?'
12 *Behold these are the wicked —*
always at ease, they accumulate wealth.
13 *Surely in vain*
have I kept my heart pure,
And washed my hands
in cleanliness.
14 *For I was plagued all day long,*
and chastised every morning.

[Former believers, now bitterly disillusioned, challenge the very foundations of our faith.] They ask, 'How can we be assured of the existence of an omniscient God?' *(Rashi).*

וְיֵשׁ דֵּעָה בְעֶלְיוֹן — *(And) 'Is there knowledge in the Most High?'*

He dwells above, but we dwell below; He is pure spirit, but we are coarse flesh. How then, can He involve Himself with our mundane affairs? *(Alshich).*

He is the Most High Judge, the Supreme Arbiter; how can He allow iniquity to go unpunished, while the righteous receive no reward? *(Radak).*

12. הִנֵּה אֵלֶּה רְשָׁעִים — *Behold these are the wicked.*

See how they flaunt the Torah with insolence! *(Rashi).*

וְשַׁלְוֵי עוֹלָם — *Always at ease* [lit. *tranquil forever*].

[שַׁלְוָה describes inner emotional *serenity,* as opposed to שָׁלוֹם, *peace,* from external threats (see commentary of *Malbim* to 122:7).

Not only are the wicked free from external threats, but they even enjoy peace of mind, completely untroubled by pangs of conscience.

Their wealth seems to increase in direct proportion to the atrocities they commit.]

13. אַךְ רִיק זִכִּיתִי לְבָבִי — *Surely in vain have I kept my heart pure.*

The disillusioned observer falls deeper and deeper into despair. He wonders, 'Why should I struggle to purify my thoughts and actions if I will nevertheless be plagued like a sinner?' *(Rashi; Radak).*

וָאֶרְחַץ בְּנִקָּיוֹן כַּפָּי — *And (I) washed my hands in cleanliness.*

Since my hands are involved in the fulfillment of many of the Torah's precepts, I have always scrupulously guarded them from any unseemly act *(Ibn Ezra).*

14. וָאֱהִי נָגוּעַ כָּל הַיּוֹם — *For I was plagued all day long.*

Although I tried to be good, I found myself plagued incessantly by the evildoers! *(Radak).*

וְתוֹכַחְתִּי לַבְּקָרִים — *And chastised* [lit. *my chastisement*] *every morning.*

No matter how hard I struggled to

אָמַרְתִּי אֲסַפְּרָה כְמוֹ הִנֵּה דוֹר בָּנֶיךָ
טז °הוא בָגָדְתִּי: וָאֲחַשְּׁבָה לָדַעַת זֹאת עָמָל °היא
יז בְעֵינָי: עַד־אָבוֹא אֶל־מִקְדְּשֵׁי־אֵל אָבִינָה
יח לְאַחֲרִיתָם: אַךְ בַּחֲלָקוֹת תָּשִׁית לָמוֹ
יט הִפַּלְתָּם לְמַשּׁוּאוֹת: אֵיךְ הָיוּ לְשַׁמָּה

remain unsullied, I experienced new misfortune daily. This Divine chastisement indicated that I was not pursuing the proper path *(Hirsch)*.

According to *Midrash Shocher Tov*, this describes the בּוֹקֶר, *dawn*, of the Messianic era, when God will institute a completely new form of wondrous chastisement. Now, when a man plucks a fig on the Sabbath, the fig tree remains silent. In the future, however, when a sinner approaches the fig tree, the tree will shout, 'Today is the Sabbath!'

Now a man can sin undisturbed in the privacy of his home, but in the future, the very stones in the walls of his house will be aroused, and they will scream out chastisement and warning.

15. אִם אָמַרְתִּי אֲסַפְּרָה כְמוֹ – *Had I said, 'I will tell how it is.'*

These are the words of the psalmist Assaf *(Rashi; Ibn Ezra)*, or of all the devout leaders of Jewry through the generations of exile *(Radak)*: I cannot bear to accept for myself or to reveal to others the full extent of the crisis of faith confronting the righteous men who suffer.

הִנֵּה דוֹר בָּנֶיךָ בָגָדְתִּי – *Behold, the generation of Your children I would have betrayed.*

I would have made the masses who would heed my arguments into traitors *(Rashi; Malbim)*. So powerful are the questions which I pose against Divine justice, that anyone who ponders them will be moved to betray his former religious convictions. This is even true of *Your sons*, i.e., men who had previously felt extremely close to You *(Metzudas David)*.

16. וָאֲחַשְּׁבָה לָדַעַת זֹאת – *And when I reflected to understand this.*

Although I dared not tell others how perplexing the dilemma really was, I nevertheless allowed myself to ponder this matter in the privacy of my own mind *(Radak)*. I tried to understand and justify God's apparently unjust actions *(Rashi)*.

עָמָל הוּא בְעֵינָי – *It was iniquity in my [own] eyes.*

I contemplated this problem in my mind's eye *(Radak)*.

After lengthy contemplation, God's ways still seemed tainted with עָמָל, *iniquity (Rashi)*.

Hirsch translates עָמָל as *useless toil*, which suggests the rendering: all of my mental efforts were futile.

17. עַד אָבוֹא אֶל מִקְדְּשֵׁי אֵל – *Until I entered into the sanctuaries of God.*

The apparent unfairness of life continued to puzzle me as long as my vision remained profane, for I measured success according to material attainment and physical comfort.

Then I shifted my gaze to loftier things, and began to concentrate on the enrichment of the soul. I recognized that although suffering was tearing down my body, it was building my soul into a magnificent sanctuary of eternal bliss.

At that moment, I realized that the wicked are bankrupt, for they squandered all their merits in This World, and are condemned to eternal damnation in the Hereafter *(Rashbam; Radak)*.

I learned to change my attitude and to lift up my sights in *the Sanctuary of God*, the Holy Temple. There the

15 Had I said,
'I will tell how it is,'
Behold, the generation of Your children
I would have betrayed.
16 And when I reflected to understand this,
it was iniquity in my eyes,
17 Until I entered into the sanctuaries of God;
then I understod their end.
18 Only on slippery places
do You set them,
You throw them down
to darkness.

devoted priests and the greatest scholars of Israel revealed to me the secret of true success *(Ibn Ezra).*

Inspired by the Holy Spirit, I gazed into the future and saw the fate of those who dared to attack *the Sanctuaries* [such as Sennacherib, Nebuchadnezzar, and Titus]. From these archvillains I learned that success is an illusion by which God ensnares the wicked, enabling them to arrive at their ultimate doom *(Rashi).*

Hirsch notes that the psalmist refers to מִקְדְּשֵׁי, *the Sanctuaries (plural),* because the Temple was divided into a few sections, each of which played an essential role in reflecting God's presence and glory.

אָבִינָה לְאַחֲרִיתָם – *Then I understood their end.*

The holy priests taught me that man was not created to enjoy the present, but to improve his final lot in the World of Souls. This *end* is the only thing that really counts *(Ibn Ezra).*

I learned an important lesson from the end of Jewish history. A third Holy Temple is destined to be built, and its splendor will outshine that of both previous Temples together [because it will be built upon a foundation of destruction and suffering.] Then the secrets of existence will be revealed with unprecedented clarity and we will truly understand the value of the righteous man's affliction *(Beer Avraham).*

18. אַךְ בַּחֲלָקוֹת תָּשִׁית לָמוֹ – *Only on slippery places do You set them.*

The clever hunter first prepares a deadly trap and afterwards clears a path through the forest to his snare. The hunter's unsuspecting prey then bounds effortlessly over the smooth path, unaware that the hunter prepared the way in order to lure him to his death.

Similarly, the unhindered success of the wicked is part of God's scheme to lead them quickly into oblivion *(Malbim).*

[See *comm.* to 35:6 יְהִי דַרְכָּם חֹשֶׁךְ וַחֲלַקְלַקּוֹת, *May their way be dark and exceedingly slippery.*

חֲלָקוֹת also means *broken pieces.* In this context, the wicked do not realize that their prosperity in This World is only a חֵלֶק, *fragment,* of the reward which awaits the righteous in the Hereafter.]

הִפַּלְתָּם לְמַשּׁוּאוֹת – *You throw them down to darkness.*

The translation follows *Ibn Ezra,* who sees מַשּׁוּאוֹת as cognate with שׁוֹאָה, *darkness* or *desolation* [see *commentary* to 35:8].

כ כְּרָגַע סָפוּ תַמּוּ מִן־בַּלָּהוֹת: כַּחֲלוֹם
כא מֵהָקִיץ אֲדֹנָי בָּעִיר | צַלְמָם תִּבְזֶה: כִּי
כב יִתְחַמֵּץ לְבָבִי וְכִלְיוֹתַי אֶשְׁתּוֹנָן: וַאֲנִי־
כג בַעַר וְלֹא אֵדָע בְּהֵמוֹת הָיִיתִי עִמָּךְ: וַאֲנִי

Ibn Ezra also suggests that the root of מַשּׁוּאוֹת is נשא, as in הַנָּחָשׁ הִשִּׁיאַנִי, *the serpent deceived me (Genesis* 3:13). Thus, the wicked lull themselves with fantasies and deceptions, and fail to face up to the somber fact that their dreamlike prosperity will soon turn into a nightmare.

According to *Sforno*, the downfall of the wicked will be so devastating that all who hear of it will be מִשְׁתָּאֶה, *amazed, dumbfounded.*

19. אֵיךְ הָיוּ לְשַׁמָּה כְרָגַע — *How have they turned desolate in an instant!*

[The powerful lesson I learned *in the sanctuaries (v.* 17) instantly transformed my way of thinking. I realized that the prosperity of the wicked is only a fleeting fantasy.]

סָפוּ תַמּוּ — *They came to an end, they are consumed* [lit. *finished*].

[For the righteous, This World is only a beginning, a corridor leading into the main hall — the Hereafter; but for the wicked everything will *end* here. They will be *consumed* by their own passions and pleasures.]

מִן בַּלָּהוֹת — *Through terrors.*

[בַּלָּהוֹת is related to בֶּהָלָה, *confusion, hysteria.*]

Hirsch notes that this word is related to בָּלָה, *to wear out, to erode.* Thus, the acquisitions of the wicked are impermanent, subject to the ravages of time. Their fleeting prosperity swiftly comes to an *end* and is *consumed* because of steady erosion and decay.

20. כַּחֲלוֹם מֵהָקִיץ — *Like a dream with no awakening.*

According to *Rashi*, the following verses describe the sudden downfall of the Assyrian host of Sennacherib, which was destroyed while besieging Jerusalem. The psalmist's prophetic vision of this annihilation serves to reinforce his new-found conviction that the success of the wicked serves only to pave their path to doom.

Thus, the awesome host of Assyria was lulled to sleep by dreams of total victory; but the dream proved to have no קֵץ, *conclusion* or *fulfillment;* God's angel smote the sleeping army.

Radak renders *like a dream from which one awakens* — to find that the bliss he witnessed was imaginary. Thus will the wicked be rudely aroused to a shocking awareness of their doom.

אֲדֹנָי בָּעִיר צַלְמָם תִּבְזֶה — *So, my Lord, in the city You will render their appearance odious.*

In Jerusalem, *the city* the Assyrians sought to conquer, the bodies of the enemy soldiers *became odious* and deformed, because they were all burned *(Rashi).*

R' Yosef Kimchi (quoted by his son, *Radak*) maintains that this refers to תְּחִיַּת הַמֵּתִים, *the resurrection of the dead.* בָּעִיר (related to עֵר, *awake*) means that the slumbering dead bodies will be *aroused.* The righteous will ascend to perfection and eternity, while the *appearance* of the wicked will be disgraced and distorted.

Meiri concludes that ultimately people will recognize that the prosperity of the wicked was a sham. It was all צֶלֶם, *form,* mere external glitter without any inner substance.

21. כִּי יִתְחַמֵּץ לְבָבִי — *For my heart was in ferment.*

Before I beheld this downfall of Assyria, I was deeply agitated by the success of the wicked *(Rashi).*

Just as fermentation causes substances to rise and swell, so was my heart bursting with pain *(Sforno).*

19 *How have they turned*
desolate in an instant!
They came to an end,
they are consumed through terrors.
20 *Like a dream with no awakening,*
so, my Lord, in the city
You will render
their appearance odious.
21 *For my heart was in ferment,*
and my mind was on edge.
22 *And I am senseless and know nothing,*
like a beast was I with You.

The ferment in my heart was not a healthy one. Rather, it resembled the wine which fermented improperly and turned into sour vinegar. Similarly, I was so embittered that nothing in my life tasted sweet anymore *(Radak).*

וְכִלְיוֹתַי אֶשְׁתּוֹנָן – *And my mind* [lit. *my kidneys*, cf. 7:10, 16:7] *was on edge.*

The word אֶשְׁתּוֹנָן is derived from שָׁנוּן, *sharp*, like the well honed blade of a sword or the sharp edge of an arrowhead. The commentaries understand this comparison in a number of ways.

Rashi seems to interpret it as a sign of advanced anxiety: My nerves were on edge. [Indeed, *Targum* relates אֶשְׁתּוֹנָן to אֵשׁ, *fire*, rendering: My mind was aflame with rage and frustration.]

Radak interprets: When I debated this matter with others, I became sarcastic and cynical. Caustic opinions and sharp comments shot from my mouth.

According to *Rabbeinu Yonah*: I mulled over this matter and allowed it to sit and ferment in my mind, until my wits were sharpened like a sword and I finally began to observe events with greater clarity and precision. I then realized that without contemplation, *I am senseless and know nothing (v. 22).*

22. וַאֲנִי בַעַר וְלֹא אֵדָע – *And I am senseless and know nothing.*[1]

[See *commentary* to 49:11, יַחַד כְּסִיל וָבַעַר יֹאבֵדוּ, *together the foolish and senseless perish.*]

Hirsch (here and in *Genesis* 45:17) explains that the בַּעַר lacks basic intelligence and resembles the בְּעִיר, *animal.*

The true root of the word is בער, *burning*, which describes the animal who is 'ablaze' with Divinely implanted instinctual desires which cannot be bridled. Similarly, the man described as בַּעַר heeds only the sensual fires of his flesh and totally disregards his mind, which becomes blank and devoid of sensibility.

Thus, says the psalmist, 'Before I understood the secret of existence, I was no better than a senseless animal' *(Radak; Ibn Ezra).*

בְּהֵמוֹת הָיִיתִי עִמָּךְ – *Like a beast* [lit. *animals*] *was I with You.*

In self-defense, I must mention that

1. The *Midrash (Koheles Rabbah* 1:12) states that these words were worthy to be the opening lines of this entire Book of *Psalms.* As *R' David Luria (Radal)* explains, these words display the humility of the prophet who acknowledges his own inadequacy, recognizing that it was the word of God which illuminated his mind and liberated it from animal lust. The enlightment of the confused mind is, in fact, one aim of the Book of *Psalms.*

כד תָּמִיד עִמָּךְ אָחַזְתָּ בְּיַד־יְמִינִי: בַּעֲצָתְךָ
כה תַנְחֵנִי וְאַחַר כָּבוֹד תִּקָּחֵנִי: מִי־לִי
כו בַשָּׁמָיִם וְעִמְּךָ לֹא־חָפַצְתִּי בָאָרֶץ: כָּלָה
שְׁאֵרִי וּלְבָבִי צוּר־לְבָבִי וְחֶלְקִי אֱלֹהִים
כז לְעוֹלָם: כִּי־הִנֵּה רְחֵקֶיךָ יֹאבֵדוּ הִצְמַתָּה

despite my tremendous mental upheaval and confusion, my body always remained faithful to You. When it came to the actual performance of precepts, I ignored my doubts and questions and exercised simple faith, strictly adhering to Your commands, just as a beast obeys its master without hesitation *(Rashi)*. [See *footnote* to 36:7, אָדָם וּבְהֵמָה תוֹשִׁיעַ ה׳, *man and beast You save, HASHEM.*]

Later, when contemplation sharpened my thinking, I realized that the apparent bliss of the wicked is nothing to envy at all. Only their body — the beastlike part of man — has benefited from prosperity, while their Godlike aspect has withered from neglect *(Malbim)*.

23. וַאֲנִי תָמִיד עִמָּךְ — *But I am always with You.*

The idea is similar to 16:8: שִׁוִּיתִי ה׳ לְנֶגְדִּי תָמִיד, *I have set HASHEM before me always,* which signifies: I am aware of His Presence at all times, and I do not take my mind off Him for a moment *(Sforno)*. [I exert myself to appreciate His goodness under all circumstances.]

אָחַזְתָּ בְּיַד יְמִינִי — *You grasped my right hand.*

The verse (16:8) concludes, כִּי מִימִינִי בַּל אֶמּוֹט, *because He is at my right hand I shall not falter (Sforno).*

Because I exerted my intellectual powers to concentrate on God, and because I struggled to banish all doubts from my mind, I merited Divine inspiration, which resolved all of my questions and reinforced my faith *(Radak)*. [Thus was I directed toward the *right hand*, i.e., the proper path.]

24. בַּעֲצָתְךָ תַנְחֵנִי — *With Your counsel You will guide me.*

Since *You grasped my right hand* to prevent me from slipping into doubt and despair, I beseech You to continue to support and *guide me* in the future. Teach me new lessons about Your Essence, as long as I live *(Radak)*.

וְאַחַר — *And then* [lit. *afterwards*].

This means after my death, which will come at the end of a long life dedicated to discovering You *(Radak)*.

Rashi, Radak and *Hirsch* point out that in most editions, the word וְאַחַר has the separating accent sign רְבִיעַ מוּגְרָשׁ, which sets it apart from the word which follows.

כָּבוֹד תִּקָּחֵנִי — *With glory You will receive me.*

My soul is my כָּבוֹד, *glory* [see 30:13]. After an entire life of pursuing the Divine, my soul will be fit to be received in the most glorious part of paradise *(Radak)*.

Radak emphasizes that his interpretation is based on the accentuation of these words, which separates אַחַר from כָּבוֹד. *Sforno,* however, reads these words together as אַחַר כָּבוֹד, *after glory,* to imply: After my soul is glorified in this world, You will receive me in the next world.

Based on this reading, *Rashi* explains that after Sennacherib achieved the full measure of glory in this world, תִּקָּחֵנִי, God took it all away from him with one swift stroke of death.

25. מִי לִי בַשָּׁמָיִם — *Whom have I* [lit. *who is for me*] *in heaven?*

The wicked have chosen various

73
23-27

23 *But I am always with You,*
You grasped my right hand.
24 *With Your counsel*
You will guide me,
And then, with glory
You will receive me.
25 *Whom have I in heaven?*
And beside You
I wish for nothing on earth.
26 *My flesh and my heart yearn —*
Rock of my heart
And my portion is God forever.
27 *For behold, those far from You*
shall perish,

celestial bodies (sun, moon, or stars) as their gods. Others worship the ministering angels in heaven. I shun all these and rely on no one in heaven, except for You *(Rashi; Radak).*

וְעִמְּךָ לֹא חָפַצְתִּי בָאָרֶץ — *And beside You I wish for nothing on earth.*

Others worship the terrestrial forces, namely, the four elements: water, fire, earth, and wind. I have no interest in these either. I turn to You alone for my salvation *(Radak; Sforno).*

26. כָּלָה שְׁאֵרִי וּלְבָבִי — *My flesh and my heart yearn* [lit. *go out*].

Flesh refers to the bones, muscles, and skin, comprising the entire organic system of which all living creatures are composed. *Heart* refers to the basic spark of life which endows these organisms with the power to exist and function. In this respect, both man and animal are alike. This flesh is destined to *go out,* i.e., it will disintegrate after death *(Radak).*

Even during my lifetime, my *flesh and heart* pine for God's closeness and *go out* [in frenzied search of it] *(Rashi).*

[Thus, I have no interest in the prosperity of the wicked for I concentrate my desire on loftier matters.]

צוּר לְבָבִי — *Rock of my heart.*

This refers to the unique human intellect. It is the *rock* of man's heart, the immortal spark of life which never grows dim *(Radak).*

וְחֶלְקִי אֱלֹהִים לְעוֹלָם — *And my portion is God forever.*

The intellect is the Divine part of man — a fragment of God's own essence, so to speak — which is enveloped by a garment of flesh *(Radak).*

[Thus: my soul, sculptured by suffering, polished by pain, will endure long after the beastlike flesh of the wicked decays.]

27. כִּי הִנֵּה רְחֵקֶיךָ יֹאבֵדוּ — *For behold, those far from You shall perish.*

[The goal and ambition of the devout Jew is to emulate God and to cling to His ways.] These evil men purposely estrange themselves from God and divorce their thoughts and deeds from all that is Divine. Their wish will be fulfilled when they are utterly banished from God's presence in the Hereafter *(Sforno).*

עג כח כָּל־זוֹנֶה מִמֶּךָּ׃ וַאֲנִי | קִרְבַת אֱלֹהִים לִי
כח טוֹב שַׁתִּי | בַּאדֹנָי יֱהוִֹה מַחְסִי לְסַפֵּר כָּל־
מַלְאֲכוֹתֶיךָ׃

Therefore, I will not admire their success, for each pleasure they enjoy makes them even further *removed from You (Alshich).*

הִצְמַתָּה כָּל זוֹנֶה מִמֶּךָּ – *You cut down all who stray from You.*

[While my body suffered, my soul flourished and grew. As I learned to appreciate Your chastisement, I advanced and developed; but those who turned their backs to You (because of their success), remained emotionally and intellectually immature. Their growth was interrupted and stunted.]

28. וַאֲנִי קִרְבַת אֱלֹהִים לִי טוֹב – *But as for me, God's closeness is my goodness.*

They find pleasure in their alienation, but I find joy only in the proximity of God, both in this world and in the next *(Radak).*

שַׁתִּי בַּאדֹנָי אֱלֹהִים מַחְסִי – *I have put my refuge in my Lord, HASHEM/ELOHIM.*

I feel secure because He watches over me with הַשְׁגָּחָה פְּרָטִית, intense personal providence and supervision *(Malbim).*

לְסַפֵּר כָּל מַלְאֲכוֹתֶיךָ – *So that I may relate all of Your mission.*

You cut down all who
stray from You.
28 *But as for me,*
God's closeness is my goodness,
I have put my refuge
in my Lord, HASHEM/ELOHIM,
So that I may relate
all of Your mission.

This translation follows *Targum* and *Rashi.* Literally, a מַלְאָךְ, *angel,* is a *messenger* charged with transmitting God's wishes. Similarly the psalmist perceives in his heart a flash of Divine inspiration which contains a message for mankind. He communicates this faithfully to his audience. The psalmist has no greater desire than to continue to discharge this duty.

Radak renders מַלְאֲכוֹתֶיךָ as *Your works* (cognate with מְלָאכָה). According to this view, the righteous man understands that the future reward is the enrichment of the Divine intellect. This is a long process beginning with an appreciation of God's terrestrial *works* of physical nature. From an appreciation of the mundane, the mind advances to comprehend the works of God in heaven.

[Each of the *works of God* contains a special message which the devout man yearns to decipher, so that he may enjoy a deeper awareness of God's wishes. This is truly the mission of life. In discharging it, man can elevate himself to the rank of an angel.]

מזמור עד 74

The preceding psalm addressed the question of why the righteous suffer. Here the psalmist studies the most painful example of this apparent injustice, the pitiful plight of the Jew in exile.

Pesikta Rabbosi *32:2 states that four prophets protested against the strictness of God's judgment and questioned its equity. One of the protestors was Assaf, who demanded,* Why O God, have You abandoned us for eternity?

The Holy One, Blessed be He, was quick to respond, 'O, Assaf, am I truly guilty of abandoning the Jews? Actually, it is they who have forsaken Me, as Scripture states, Israel has abandoned that which is good (Hosea *8:2). The prophet refers to God, for there is no good greater than He!*

Israel counters that it is not only the Jews who are endangered by the exile, but even God's own stature in the world is imperiled by the fact that He has not redeemed His Chosen People. Since the continuation of the exile encourages Israel's enemies to blaspheme against God, He must combat this heresy vigorously. The psalm therefore concludes, Arise, O God, champion Your cause! Remember Your insults from the degenerate all day long. Forget not the voice of Your tormentors, the tumult of Your opponents arising always.

עד
א־ד

א מַשְׂכִּיל לְאָסָף לָמָה אֱלֹהִים זָנַחְתָּ לָנֶצַח
ב יֶעְשַׁן אַפְּךָ בְּצֹאן מַרְעִיתֶךָ: זְכֹר עֲדָתְךָ |
קָנִיתָ קֶּדֶם גָּאַלְתָּ שֵׁבֶט נַחֲלָתֶךָ הַר־צִיּוֹן
ג זֶה | שָׁכַנְתָּ בּוֹ: הָרִימָה פְעָמֶיךָ לְמַשֻּׁאוֹת
ד נֶצַח כָּל־הֵרַע אוֹיֵב בַּקֹּדֶשׁ: שָׁאֲגוּ צֹרְרֶיךָ

1. מַשְׂכִּיל לְאָסָף – *A Maskil by Assaf.*

[See *comm.* to 32:1. מַשְׂכִּיל is derived from שֵׂכֶל, *wisdom, enlightenment.* Assaf was a brilliant thinker who utilized his wisdom to instruct people.

Rabbi Moshe Isserles (Rama) in *Toras HaOlah* (I,11) writes that the great Greek scholar and philosopher Socrates acquired the basic principles of his wisdom from the teachings of Assaf and Achitophel. As a result, Socrates recognized the falsehood of the Greek myths and idols, and vigorously challenged them.]

לָמָה אֱלֹהִים זָנַחְתָּ לָנֶצַח – *Why, O God, have You abandoned* [*us*] *for eternity?*

The first (Babylonian) Exile was limited to seventy years; but this second (Roman) Exile still continues, with no end in sight *(Sforno).* We are not merely *lost;* rather You intentionally cast us away from You *(Radak).*

יֶעְשַׁן אַפְּךָ – [*Will*] *Your wrath smolder.*

The word אַף [lit. *nose*] is used to denote *wrath* because the angry man grows hot and smoke seems to issue from his nostrils *(Rashi; Radak).*

[Not only is the exile interminably long, but it is also filled with violence and hostility. Even when the roaring fires of persecution subside, the gentile's hatred for the Jews still smolders in his heart, awaiting the moment when it can flare up again.]

בְּצֹאן מַרְעִיתֶךָ – *Against the sheep of Your pasture.*

The events of the exile seem incompatible with Your role as Shepherd of Israel, for the shepherd's job is to protect his flocks, while You seem to have abandoned us to all forms of danger and destruction *(Maharam Markado).*

Even when a shepherd is forced to strike his straying sheep to force them back on the proper path, he does not remain angry with them. Why then, does Your wrath continue to burn against us even after You have punished us *(Hirsch)?*

2. זְכֹר עֲדָתְךָ קָנִיתָ קֶּדֶם – *Remember Your congregation, which You acquired of old.*

In this verse, the psalmist calls upon God to recall three major historical facts which demonstrate that Israel is God's Chosen Nation and deserves Divine redemption *(Malbim).*

First, Israel cannot be allowed to disappear in the dark exile, for the Jewish nation is the very purpose of all creation. Even before the actual Creation, *ex nihilo,* God determined to create Israel, the celestial throne, the Torah, the Patriarchs, the Holy Temple, and the Messiah. Israel was the very first 'thought' which God conceived, for the Jewish people is the foundation of the world (*Rashi; Bereishis Rabbah* 81:4).

This primeval preference for Israel was demonstrated when God chose the Patriarchs and the Twelve Tribes of Israel to represent Him in this world *(Malbim).*

גָּאַלְתָּ שֵׁבֶט נַחֲלָתֶךָ – *You redeemed the tribe of Your heritage.*

The second event to remember is the Divine redemption granted to the Jews in Egypt. By this redemption, You

74
1-4

A Maskil *by Assaf:*
Why, O God,
have You abandoned us for eternity;
Will Your wrath smolder against
the sheep of Your pasture?
2 *Remember Your congregation*
which You acquired of old,
You redeemed the tribe of Your heritage,
this Mount of Zion where You dwelled.
3 *Lift Your footsteps to wreak eternal ruin*
for the foe's evildoing in the Sanctuary.
4 *Your tormentors roared amidst Your meeting place,*

acquired Israel as Your estate. Please liberate us from this exile, just as You saved us in the past *(Targum; Radak).*

The psalmist refers to all Twelve Tribes as one שֵׁבֶט, *tribe,* because the Jews left Egypt in complete unity and solidarity; they were united by their complete trust in God *(Maharam Markado).* Also, they were not yet divided into separate מַחֲנוֹת, *camps,* under distinctive דְגָלִים, *banners (Norah Tehillos).*

[Here Assaf alludes to Israel's deep desire to regain this national solidarity in the future.]

הַר צִיּוֹן זֶה שָׁכַנְתָּ בּוֹ – *This Mount of Zion, where You dwelled.*

Third, O God, look down upon Zion, the site of Your Temple, formerly splendid and now in ruins. Remember how Your Holy Spirit dwelled there before the destruction, and return once more to this sacred abode *(Radak; Malbim).*

3. הָרִימָה פְעָמֶיךָ לְמַשֻּׁאוֹת נֶצַח – *Lift Your footsteps to wreak eternal ruin.*

This translation of פְּעָמֶיךָ follows *Targum, Radak, and Sforno,* who render: *Lift Your feet* to hasten towards the gentile foe *(Tehillos Hashem). Lift Your feet* high in order to crush Your enemies underfoot with even greater force *(Sforno).* [*Rashbam* renders פַּעַם as *a blow* which falls with great force because it is delivered from a height.]

Rashi suggests that פַּעַם is related to פְּעִימָה, *terror* [see *Genesis* 41:8, וַתִּפָּעֶם רוּחוֹ, *and his spirit was alarmed*]. The psalmist calls upon God to implant and to intensify fears and anxieties in the enemy so that they will be driven to complete שׁוֹאָה, *destruction.*

כָּל הֵרַע אוֹיֵב בַּקֹּדֶשׁ – *For the foe's evildoing in the Sanctuary.*

The execution of the hated enemy must be exceptionally brutal because this foe was determined to destroy not merely the masonry of the Temple, but also its unique sanctity. Titus, for example, defiled the Holy of Holies by laying with a prostitute upon an open Torah scroll.

Indeed, most decrees promulgated by the Roman oppressors were aimed at tearing Israel from the source of קֹדֶשׁ, *sanctity,* by prohibiting the study of Torah and the performance of the precepts *(Sforno).*

4. שָׁאֲגוּ צוֹרְרֶיךָ בְּקֶרֶב מוֹעֲדֶךָ – *Your tormentors roared amidst Your meeting place.*

Rashi notes that the Temple is the place where God and Israel convene, as

ה בְּקֶרֶב מוֹעֲדֶךָ שָׂמוּ אוֹתֹתָם אֹתוֹת: יִוָּדַע
ו כְּמֵבִיא לְמָעְלָה בִּסְבָךְ־עֵץ קַרְדֻּמּוֹת: וְעַתָּ
פִּתּוּחֶיהָ יָּחַד בְּכַשִּׁיל וְכֵילַפֹּת יַהֲלֹמוּן:
ז שִׁלְחוּ בָאֵשׁ מִקְדָּשֶׁךָ לָאָרֶץ חִלְּלוּ

Scripture states וְנוֹעַדְתִּי לְךָ שָׁם, *And I will meet you there (Exodus* 25:22).

[It was this unique bond which the gentiles sought to sever when they defiled the *meeting place.* They roared with glee as they ravaged the Temple. Titus unsheathed his sword and stabbed the holy פָּרוֹכֶת, *curtain (Gittin* 56b), for he imagined that he could thereby cut God away from Israel.]

שָׂמוּ אוֹתֹתָם אֹתוֹת — *They made their signs for signs.*

Blood started to flow from the curtain when Titus stabbed it. He interpreted this as an אוֹת, *sign,* that he had slain God Himself (*Gittin* 56b). The blood was actually a Divine sign to Israel that God was 'suffering' over their tragic plight.

Thus, *they* [the Romans] made אוֹתֹתָם, *their signs* [the ones intended for encouraging Israel], for אֹתוֹת, *signs* [for themselves and in their own favor] *(Sforno).*

According to *Midrash Shocher Tov* quoted by *Rashi* and *Radak,* these words refer to the destruction of the first *Beis HaMikdash* at the hands of Nebuchadnezzar. He received heavenly signs which were meant to encourage his assault on Jerusalem and he was wise enought to pay heed to those messages. Thus, *they* [the attackers] *made their* [Heaven-sent] *signs for* [meaningful] *signs.*

Nebuchadnezzar had not been sure whether to attack Israel or Ammon, so he had consulted seers, who foretold victory over Israel. He then shot arrows into the air, aimed in all directions. He observed that all of the arrows flew towards the south, in the direction of the Holy Land (Babylon is in the north). Thus assured, he confidently marched to Jerusalem.

5. יִוָּדַע כְּמֵבִיא לְמָעְלָה — *They are considered like one bringing on high.*

When the Temple was built, many people took up their *hatchets* and went into the *thicket* to chop *trees* to supply wood for the Temple's construction. They performed this *mitzvah* with such joy and devotion that God appreciated and considered their contributions as a sacrifice brought *on high,* before the celestial throne *(Radak).*

Similarly, the enemy sought to destroy the Temple, only in order to destroy the sanctity of God *on high.* The attack on the wood and stones was considered as an assault on God *(Rashi).*

Midrash Tanchuma (Pikudei 4) illustrates this with a parable: The king's enemy attempted to assassinate the monarch but found the well guarded king inaccessible. Undaunted, the sinister enemy decided to vent his hatred on the king's statue by toppling it over at its base.

Similarly, the gentiles would like to assault the Almighty, whom they hate. Finding this impossible, they attack God's resemblance — Israel. Since our nation is the foundation upon which God's sanctity rests in this world, if Israel is toppled, God's majestic presence falls, too.

בִּסְבָךְ עֵץ קַרְדֻּמּוֹת — *In the thicket of trees — the hatchets.*

When the Temple was built, the dedicated people took to the woods with hatchets to chop lumber for construction *(Radak).*

When Nebuchadnezzar destroyed the Temple, he sent a shipment of arms to his commander-in-chief, Nevuzaradon. It consisted of three hundred donkey loads of hatchets made of the strongest steel, which could cut through steel. Nevuzaradon hurled them at the gates

they made their signs for signs.
5 *They are considered like one bringing on high,*
in the thicket of trees — the hatchets.
6 *And now its entranceways —*
altogether —
With hatchets and axes
they break them down.
7 *They sent Your Sanctuary up in flames;*

of Jerusalem, but to no avail, for they shattered against the stout portals of the Holy City. With so many smashed hatchet handles strewn about, the area resembled a *thicket of trees*. This unprecedented failure proved to the enemy that by attacking Israel, he was attacking God. *They* [the foe] *are considered like one bringing* [the battle] *on high* [to wage war against heaven] (*Rashi* based on *Sanhedrin* 96a).

[Also, just as a tangled thicket 'swallows' and enmeshes all that enter it, so did the wooden gates 'swallow' and destroy the hatchets. See *Rashi*.]

6. וְעַתָּה פִּתּוּחֶיהָ יָּחַד — *And now its entranceways—altogether.*

According to *Rashi*, פִּתּוּחֶיהָ is cognate with פֶּתַח, *entranceway*. Although the enemy realized that God was miraculously protecting the city, this did not deter him from continuing his vigorous attempt to smash the city's *entranceways* and *gates*.

Targum, *Radak*, and *Metzudas David* render this as *its engravings* or *its carvings*, related to פִּתּוּחֵי חֹתָם, *the engravings of the signet* (*Exodus* 28:11). According to this view, the enemy was bent on wiping out the beauty and ornament of the Holy City.

Hirsch adds that even after the structure of the Temple lay in ruins, the enemy searched through the debris for any remaining engraved fragments bearing the holy design of the Temple. Israel's enemies sought to destroy God's glory and to eradicate every vestige of Judaism.

בְּכַשִּׁיל וְכֵילַפּוֹת יַהֲלֹמוּן — *With hatchets and axes they break them down.*

[At first, God frustrated the enemy's attempts to breach the city's walls. God did so to demonstrate that He still loved Israel and was reluctant to punish them.

This was also a test for the enemy. By disregarding God's initial displeasure, they proved that they were bent on devastating Jerusalem for their own purposes, whether or not this conformed to God's will.]

Finally, Nevuzaradon, his supply of hatchets exhausted, gave up his futile attack and shouted in despair, 'I must flee from here, lest the Almighty smite me as He smote the entire host of Sennacherib, the Assyrian king!'

At that moment, a Heavenly Voice encouraged him, 'Nevuzaradon, the time has come for the Temple to be razed and for the Sanctuary to be burned!'

Nevuzaradon had but one hatchet left in his arsenal. He hurled it at the gates and smashed them (*Sanhedrin* 96b).

Radak explains that כַּשִּׁיל and כֵּילַפּוֹת are synonymous with קַרְדוֹם, *hatchet*. *Rashi* describes them as the tools of the carpenter. *Hirsch* says that כַּשִּׁיל is derived from כשל, *to fall*. Thus כַּשִּׁיל is a *hammer* which causes chips to fall from wood. כֵּילַפּוֹת is related to קלף, *to peel*, and refers to a chisel or plane.

7. שִׁלְּחוּ בָאֵשׁ מִקְדָּשֶׁךָ — *They sent Your Sanctuary up in flames* (*Radak*).

The *Talmud* (*Sanhedrin* 96b) continues that Nevuzaradon's forces stormed through the breached gates and

ח מְשְׁכַּן־שְׁמֶךָ: אָמְרוּ בְלִבָּם נִינָם יָחַד
ט שָׂרְפוּ כָל־מוֹעֲדֵי־אֵל בָּאָרֶץ: אוֹתֹתֵינוּ
לֹא־רָאִינוּ אֵין־עוֹד נָבִיא וְלֹא־אִתָּנוּ יוֹדֵעַ

slew all who stood in their way, until they arrived at the *Beis HaMikdash,* which they set afire.

Nevuzaradon was filled with pride over his unprecedented accomplishment, for no one else had ever succeeded in damaging the House of God.

At that moment, a Heavenly Voice proclaimed, 'You yourself have not accomplished anything! A slain nation is what you have slain, You burned a burned Sanctuary, and You ground up flour which was already ground.'

[Israel survives on earth only because it is sustained by its collective national soul in heaven. When sin saps the vitality of that heavenly soul, it withers and dies. Then the Jewish nation becomes vulnerable and weak.

Similarly, there is a *Beis HaMikdash* in heaven which corresponds to the Temple on earth. This celestial sanctuary fills the earthly Temple with God's holy Presence; but when the flames of iniquity consume the heavenly abode, nothing remains on earth but an empty shell, which crumbles under its own weight (see *Maharsha, Sanhedrin* 96b).]

לָאָרֶץ חִלְּלוּ מִשְׁכַּן שְׁמֶךָ — *To the very earth they desecrated the abode of Your Name.*

When the flames first licked at the base of the Temple, the entire edifice began to rise heavenward to return to the source of its sanctity; but God was determined to demonstrate His extreme displeasure with the Jewish people. Therefore, a heavenly force pushed the *abode of God's Name* back down *to the earth,* so that the enemy could desecrate it. This destruction vividly demonstrated to the Jews that they had brought about a profanation of His Name *(Sanhedrin 96a; Mahrasha, ibid.).*

8. אָמְרוּ בְלִבָּם נִינָם יָחַד — *They said in their hearts their — their monarchs all together.*

Rashi explains that נִינָם is a term describing *monarchy,* as in *Psalms* 72:17, יִנּוֹן שְׁמוֹ, which refers to the King Messiah. The kings who attacked Israel all initiated hostilities with an assault on God and His abode: The Philistines destroyed the Tabernacle at Shiloh, Nebuchadnezzar laid waste the First Temple, and Titus razed the Second Temple.

According to *Radak* and *Ibn Ezra,* נִינָם is related to אַל תּוֹנוּ, *You shall not damage (Leviticus* 25:14), and refers to the fact that the enemy sought to 'damage' and destroy Israel יָחַד, *all together.*

Targum and *Sforno* render נִינָם as cognate with נִין, *descendant.* The enemy realized that Israel can only be eradicated through spiritual genocide and assimilation. The נִינָם, *future generations,* of Israel must be weaned from their heritage and joined יָחַד, *together,* with the gentile masses. Therefore, the enemy *burnt all of the meeting places of God on earth.* They destroyed the synagogues and the houses of Torah study, in an attempt to strip our descendants of their Jewish identity forever.

שָׂרְפוּ כָל מוֹעֲדֵי אֵל בָּאָרֶץ — *They burned all of God's meeting places on earth.*

In the Temple, all Jews met to join in Divine service, in order to sanctify God's Name on earth and to publicly accept His sovereignty *(Midrash Shocher Tov).*

The Great Sanhedrin met in the לִשְׁכַּת הַגָּזִית, *the Chamber of Hewn Stone,* which was adjacent to the Temple, to compose the annual calendar and to determine the dates of מוֹעֲדֵי אֵל, *the holidays and festivals of God (Midrash Hagadol, Vayikra).*

to the very earth they desecrated the abode of Your Name.

8 *They said in their hearts —*
their monarchs all together —
They burned all of God's meeting places on earth.

9 *Our signs we have not seen;*
there is no longer a prophet,
And none among us
knows how long —

9. אֹתוֹתֵינוּ לֹא רָאִינוּ — *Our signs we have not seen.*

Assaf now foresees the final stages of the bleak Exile, and laments, 'Through the words of Your prophets, You promised us that at this advanced stage of Exile, we would begin to see clear signs of imminent redemption, but we have not yet witnessed any such signs (*Rashi*).

In the past, even after You abandoned us to the hands of the enemy, You swiftly returned to show us signs of favor. For example, after the Philistines devastated Shiloh and captured the Holy Ark, You toppled their idols and plagued their populace in a wondrous manner which clearly displayed Your displeasure (see *I Samuel*, chapter 5); but when Titus profaned the Holy of Holies, he escaped unscathed and You demonstrated no sign of displeasure (*Sforno*).

אֵין עוֹד נָבִיא — *There is no longer a prophet.*

After the death of the last prophets — Haggai, Zachariah, and Malachi — no man was granted the knowledge of when the redemption would take place .[1]

We eagerly await the advent of Elijah, the prophet of Redemption, who will appear before the Messiah; but even he tarries (*Radak*).

וְלֹא אִתָּנוּ יוֹדֵעַ עַד מָה — *And none among us knows how long.*

Although prophecy is now extinct, we do possess the works of the early prophets who foretold the time of the Redemption. However, God purposely concealed the exact date of our deliverance even from the early prophets, as Scripture states (*Daniel* 12:4): *But you, Daniel, conceal the words and seal the book until the end of*

1. See *Sanhedrin* 11a and *Rashi* to *Yoma* 21b. *Sefer HaDoros* sets the date of the prophets' demise in the year 3442 after Creation, the thirty-fourth year of the Second *Beis HaMikdash.*

Seder Olam Rabbah, chapt. 30 comments: Until now, the prophets spoke with the Holy Spirit, but henceforth, *Bend your ear and give heed to the words of the Sages* (*Proverbs* 22:1).

Meiri (to *Sanhedrin* 11a) explains that the Holy Spirit only descends on a happy, serene man (see *Shabbos* 31a). Throughout the era of the Second Temple and afterwards, the Jews were constantly persecuted by gentile oppressors. As a result, even the holy Sages lacked the peace of mind which is a prerequisite of prophecy.

The *Gaon of Vilna* (comm. to *Proverbs* 16:4) observes that when the prophets were still alive, any man could approach them for intimate guidance. The prophet could plumb the innermost depths of a person's soul and discover his purpose in life. Since prophecy has vanished, however, man can no longer interpret these signs of personal identity through prophecy. Therefore, they remain concealed.

י עַד־מָה: עַד־מָתַי אֱלֹהִים יְחָרֶף צָר יְנָאֵץ
יא אוֹיֵב שִׁמְךָ לָנֶצַח: לָמָּה תָשִׁיב יָדְךָ
°חֵיקְךָ יב וִימִינֶךָ מִקֶּרֶב °חוקך כַלֵּה: וֵאלֹהִים
מַלְכִּי מִקֶּדֶם פֹּעֵל יְשׁוּעוֹת בְּקֶרֶב הָאָרֶץ:
יג אַתָּה פוֹרַרְתָּ בְעָזְּךָ יָם שִׁבַּרְתָּ רָאשֵׁי
יד תַנִּינִים עַל־הַמָּיִם: אַתָּה רִצַּצְתָּ רָאשֵׁי

time, when many shall travel about and knowledge shall be increased (Midrash Shocher Tov).

Even after prophecy disappeared, God still communicated with the people through the בַּת קוֹל, *Heavenly Voice (Sanhedrin* 11a), but now even that voice has ceased, so we have no way of knowing the future *(Dodi L'Tzvi).*

The *Talmud (Sanhedrin* 97a) lists numerous signs which herald the imminent arrival of Messiah; among these are cataclysms, crises, wars, and plagues. However, concludes the *Talmud*, there is really *none in our midst who knows until when* the Exile will endure, for all these signs have appeared, yet Messiah tarries (כָּלוּ כָּל הַקִּיצִין*). Rav* teaches that only a mass movement of תְּשׁוּבָה, *repentance*, among the Jewish people can hasten our salvation *(Zerah Yaakov).*

10. עַד מָתַי אֱלֹהִים יְחָרֶף צָר — *How long, O God, will the tormentor revile?*

After razing the *Beis HaMikdash*, the *tormentor* Titus traveled over the sea to make a triumphant entry into Rome. A storm arose and great waves threatened to sink Titus' ship. He *reviled* God and said, 'It appears that this God of the Jews is truly helpless. His power only extends over the sea, for He drowned Pharaoh and Sisro in the sea, but on land He can do nothing!' *(Gittin* 56b).

How long, O God, must we be forced to hear such insults from the arrogant tormentors? *(Sforno).*

יְנָאֵץ אוֹיֵב שִׁמְךָ לָנֶצַח — *Shall the foe blaspheme Your Name forever?*

The foe accuses our God of impotence and claims that He is incapable of delivering us from exile *(Radak).*

Malbim differentiates between the צָר, *tormentor*, who *reviles* God out loud and in public, and the אוֹיֵב, *foe*, who *blasphemes* in the privacy of his heart [by denying God's power and ability]. Both must be rebuked.

11. לָמָּה תָשִׁיב יָדְךָ וִימִינֶךָ — *Why do You withdraw Your hand, even Your right hand?*

יָדְךָ, *Your hand*, refers to the left hand *(Menachos* 36a; *Radak; Ibn Ezra)*, which symbolizes גְּבוּרָה, *strong judgment.* The psalmist wonders why God withdrew His strong *hand* and did not administer harsh judgments to the marauding gentiles.

יְמִינְךָ, *Your right hand*, signifies חֶסֶד, *merciful kindness.* Even this Divine attribute was withdrawn, and God showed no compassion for the downtrodden Jews *(Alshich).*

The prophet laments (*Eichah* 2:3): הֵשִׁיב אָחוֹר יְמִינוֹ מִפְּנֵי אוֹיֵב, *He withdrew His right hand in the presence of the enemy (Radak).* [See *comm.*, ArtScroll edition of *Eichah* 2:3.]

מִקֶּרֶב חֵיקְךָ כַלֵּה — *From within Your bosom—remove it!*

Remove Your right hand from your bosom *(Rashi).*

This hand symbolizes initiative and action. The lazy man tucks his hand comfortably into his bosom and avoids work. Here God is exhorted to campaign vigorously against the foe until complete revenge has been accomplished *(Radak).*

10 *How long, O God,*
will the tormentor revile?
Shall the foe blaspheme
Your Name forever?
11 *Why do You withdraw Your hand,*
even Your right hand?
From within Your bosom —
remove it!
12 *For God is my King from yore,*
working salvations in the midst of the earth.
13 *You shattered the sea*
with Your might,
You smashed sea serpent's heads
upon the water.

Radak also suggests that this can mean 'Remove the enemies from Your bosom, for as long as You protect them no harm can befall them.'

[The word is read חֵיקְךָ, *Your bosom* but is written חוּקְךָ, *Your decree* or *alloted portion.* The written form suggests that the enemy seems to have merited a special, undeserved allotment of Divine favor and security. The psalmist hopes that this unwarranted blessing will be removed.]

12. וֵאלֹהִים מַלְכִּי מִקֶּדֶם — *For God is my King from yore.*

Although God is Master of the entire universe, He takes special interest in us, the Children of Israel. Therefore, He is *my King,* in particular *(Ibn Yachya).*

That was true in days *of old,* before we were driven into exile. Now, as we suffer without respite, it seems as if He is no longer *my King (Radak).*

פֹּעֵל יְשׁוּעוֹת בְּקֶרֶב הָאָרֶץ — *Working salvations in the midst of the earth.*

O God, although Your exalted throne is in the highest heavens, remember how in days *of old* You would descend to *the midst of the earth,* the land of Israel's enemies, to champion the cause of Your Chosen People *(Radak).*

Then, for our sake, You miraculously changed the course of nature and interfered with the normal cycles *in the midst of the earth* in order to save Israel *(Malbim).*

13. אַתָּה פוֹרַרְתָּ בְעָזְּךָ יָם — *You shattered the sea with Your might.*

You worked salvtion in the midst of the earth by splitting *the Sea of Reeds (Malbim).*

The sea was not merely split in half; rather it was *shattered* into twelve separate paths, one for each tribe *(Mechilta, Beshalach* 14:15, *Alshich, v.* 18).

שִׁבַּרְתָּ רָאשֵׁי תַנִּינִים עַל הַמָּיִם — *You smashed the sea serpents' heads upon the water.*

Radak observes that Pharaoh, the King and self-proclaimed 'deity' of Egypt, is described as הַתַּנִּים הַגָּדוֹל הָרֹבֵץ בְּתוֹךְ יְאֹרָיו, *the great sea serpent who crouches in his rivers (Ezekiel* 29:3).

The water, especially the Nile River, was Pharaoh's special element. His power was based on it because its annual overflow provided the basis of Egypt's agricultural prosperity. Therefore, Pharaoh met his downfall on the water to demonstrate that his

טו לִוְיָתָן תִּתְּנֶנּוּ מַאֲכָל לְעַם לְצִיִּים: אַתָּה
בָקַעְתָּ מַעְיָן וָנָחַל אַתָּה הוֹבַשְׁתָּ נַהֲרוֹת
טז אֵיתָן: לְךָ יוֹם אַף־לְךָ לָיְלָה אַתָּה הֲכִינוֹתָ
יז מָאוֹר וָשָׁמֶשׁ: אַתָּה הִצַּבְתָּ כָּל־גְּבוּלוֹת
יח אָרֶץ קַיִץ וָחֹרֶף אַתָּה יְצַרְתָּם: זְכָר־זֹאת

reliance on this element was futile *(Hirsch)*.

14. אַתָּה רִצַּצְתָּ רָאשֵׁי לִוְיָתָן — *You crushed the heads of Leviathan.*

This is another description of Pharaoh, as Scripture states (*Isaiah* 27:1): *On that day HASHEM shall punish with His harsh sword, His great and strong one, the Leviathan, the fleeing serpent, and Leviathan the crooked serpent, and He will kill the sea serpent that is in the sea (Rashi).*[1]

The heads refer to Pharaoh's minions, the captains and generals who headed his armies *(Radak)*.

תִּתְּנֶנּוּ מַאֲכָל לְעַם לְצִיִּים — *You served him as food to the nation of legions.*

This translation of צִיִּים, *legions,* follows *Rashi* based on *Numbers* 24:24. As the *legions* of Israel fled from Egypt, You gave Israel Pharaoh's treasures as spoils.

Radak renders צִיִּים as *parched wilderness* [see *comm.* to *Psalms* 72:9]. When Israel escaped from Egypt into the parched desert, they were supplied by the booty from Egypt.

15. אַתָּה בָקַעְתָּ מַעְיָן וָנָחַל — *You split open fountain and stream.*

You caused fresh water to flow in the parched wasteland, as Scripture states (*Psalms* 18:15): יְבַקַּע צֻרִים בַּמִּדְבָּר, *He splits open rocks in the wilderness (Radak; Ibn Ezra).*

אַתָּה הוֹבַשְׁתָּ נַהֲרוֹת אֵיתָן — *You dried the mighty rivers.*

This refers to the might torrent of the Jordan River; [in early spring] its bank can hardly contain its waters, because it is fed by the flow of many small tributaries [i.e., mighty rivers]. You stopped the flow of the Jordan and dried the riverbed so that Israel could cross over to Canaan in the time of Joshua *(Rashi; Radak)*.

16. לְךָ יוֹם אַף לְךָ לָיְלָה — *Yours is the day, Yours [also] is the night.*

In the preceding verse, the psalmist stressed that our one God is the Master over all forces in the universe. This implies an essential harmony and interaction of forces even though some of the ongoing processes in nature appear to contradict and oppose one another. For example, the same God who causes water to spring forth from rock also dried up the watery deep.

God daily demonstrates His mastery over all natural forces and processes. In his beneficence, He causes the dawn to break so that men should be aroused to action, and He causes darkness to fall so that men should be forced to rest and gather strength, while the wild beasts are afforded an opportunity to hunt undisturbed, under cover of darkness *(Radak)*.[1]

Furthermore, God performed great miracles for Israel both by day and by

1. The heathens of old could not comprehend God's omnipotence. They said, 'He who controls good cannot possibly control evil.' They fabricated the myth that the upper half of man, the lofty intellectual sphere, is ruled by the good god Ormazd, while the lower half of man, the seat of dark passions, is controlled by Ahriman (*Sanhedrin* 39a).

Similarly, they claimed, 'He who created day did not create night.' To refute this, Jews mention God's role as Creator of day in our night prayers. בּוֹרֵא יוֹם וָלָיְלָה...וּמַעֲבִיר יוֹם וּמֵבִיא

14 *You crushed the heads of Leviathan,*
You served him as food
to the nation of legions.
15 *You split open fountain and stream,*
You dried the mighty rivers.
16 *Yours is the day, Yours is the night,*
You prepared the luminary and the sun.
17 *You established all the boundaries of earth,*
summer and winter — You fashioned them.
18 *Remember this —*

night. Our grateful nation showed its appreciation by dedicating hymns of praise to the Almighty both by day and by night (*Bereishis Rabbah* 86:2).

Allegorically, *the day* signifies the bright moment of Israel's redemption. Just as God will surely be with us then, we must be firm in our faith that He is with us even now, in the dark night of our bitter exile *(Rashi)*.

אַתָּה הֲכִינוֹתָ מָאוֹר וָשָׁמֶשׁ — *You prepared the luminary and the sun.*

מָאוֹר, *luminary,* refers to the moon *(Targum),* which reflects the light of *the sun.* It also refers to the stars *(Rashbam).*

Radak explains that God *prepared* these celestial bodies for the benefit of the earth. The illumination and heat provided by *the sun* are essential for all life. The moon controls the tides and causes certain plants to grow (see *Deuteronomy* 33:14). It also provides invaluable illumination in the gloom of night.

The stars provide an indispensable navigational guide for sailors or for men lost in the uncharted desert. Also, the stars represent spiritual forces which exert tremendous power over both the vegetable and mineral kingdoms. The *Talmud (Chullim* 7b) teaches that the growth of every blade of grass on earth is controlled by a heavenly force (מַזָּל).

According to *Rashi,* this verse should be understood allegorically: Even in the dark night of exile, You illuminated our lives with the bright light of Torah.

17. אַתָּה הִצַּבְתָּ כָּל גְּבוּלוֹת אָרֶץ — *You established all the boundaries of earth.*

You created seven distinctly different climate zones *(Ibn Ezra)*; each contributes a unique meterological benefit to the entire earth *(Radak).*

You established geographic divisions on earth and designed separate continents inhabited by diverse peoples *(Ibn Yachya).*

Finally, You fostered the growth of seventy nations, as Scripture states (*Deuteronomy* 32:8): *He established the boundaries of the nations according to the number of the Children of Israel (Chazah Zion).*

קַיִץ וָחֹרֶף אַתָּה יְצַרְתָּם — *Summer and winter — You fashioned them.*

Here, too, the psalmist emphasizes that God is the sole Creator, for what could be more different than the intense heat of *summer* and the snow of *winter (Radak).*

לַיְלָה, *He creates day and night...He causes the day to pass and He brings on the night,* and we mention the night in our daytime prayers. יוֹצֵר אוֹר וּבוֹרֵא חֹשֶׁךְ, *He fashions light and creates darkness (Rabbeinu Yonah* on *Berachos* 11b).

אויֵב חֵרֵף | יהוה וְעַם־נָבָל נִאֲצוּ שְׁמֶךָ׃
יט אַל־תִּתֵּן לְחַיַּת נֶפֶשׁ תּוֹרֶךָ חַיַּת עֲנִיֶּיךָ
כ אַל־תִּשְׁכַּח לָנֶצַח׃ הַבֵּט לַבְּרִית כִּי־מָלְאוּ
כא מַחֲשַׁכֵּי־אֶרֶץ נְאוֹת חָמָס׃ אַל־יָשֹׁב דַּךְ
כב נִכְלָם עָנִי וְאֶבְיוֹן יְהַלְלוּ שְׁמֶךָ׃ קוּמָה
אֱלֹהִים רִיבָה רִיבֶךָ זְכֹר חֶרְפָּתְךָ מִנִּי־
כג נָבָל כָּל־הַיּוֹם׃ אַל־תִּשְׁכַּח קוֹל צֹרְרֶיךָ
שְׁאוֹן קָמֶיךָ עֹלֶה תָמִיד׃

18. זְכָר זֹאת אוֹיֵב חֵרֵף ה׳ — *Remember this — how the foe reviled HASHEM.*

Remember, O God, that although You performed all these wonders (enumerated in the preceding verses), the foe persisted in insulting You by questioning Your ability and might *(Radak).*

Titus, for example, claimed that Your power extends only over the sea *(Sforno;* see *comm.* to *v.* 10).

According to *Ibn Ezra,* the psalmist is calling upon the foe himself to *remember* his own ugly calumniation of God.

וְעַם נָבָל נִאֲצוּ שְׁמֶךָ — *And the degenerate nation blasphemed Your Name.*

Sforno identifies this *nation* as the uncouth Persian kingdom [which ruled over Israel during the first thirty-four years of the Second *Beis HaMikdash.* See *Avodah Zarah* 9a].

19. אַל תִּתֵּן לְחַיַּת נֶפֶשׁ תּוֹרֶךָ — *Deliver not to the wild beast the soul of Your turtledove.*

Rome, the mighty empire given to barbaric cruelty, is called *(Psalms* 68:30) חַיַּת קָנֶה, *the wild beast of the reeds (Chazah Zion),* whereas Israel, the weak and defenseless nation, is likened to the gentle *dove,* as we read *(Songs* 2:14): יוֹנָתִי בְּחַגְוֵי הַסֶּלַע, *O my dove,* [trapped] *in the crannies of the rock! (Radak;* see *comm.* to ArtScroll *Shir HaShirim* 1:15 for a lengthy comparison of Israel to the dove).

Rashi observes that the dove is a classic symbol of fidelity, for once a male dove becomes intimate with a female, he will never take a different mate (see *Eruvin* 100b). Although God abandoned Israel and left her bereft, like a lonely widow, Israel never exchanged Him for a different god [see *Targuma D'HaTargum*].

Targum interprets תּוֹרֶךָ as 'those who study Your תּוֹרָה, *Torah.'* This refers to the scholars, who moan like a *turtledove* over the tragedy of the Exile [turtledoves are noted for their plaintive cooing] *(Sforno).*

חַיַּת עֲנִיֶּיךָ אַל תִּשְׁכַּח לָנֶצַח — *The life of Your poor forget not forever.*

[Here חַיַּת means *life, soul* — referring to the spirit of the Jewish people. Let this impoverished folk not fall prey forever to the wild nations in their interminable Exile.]

Specifically this describes the simple masses who only pursue the basic staples of *life (Sforno).*

20. הַבֵּט לַבְּרִית — *Gaze upon the covenant.*

This refers to *the covenant* which You forged with our forefathers *(Rashi; Radak; Sforno).*

Even when Israel has no merit in their favor, except for the merit of the covenant of circumcision, God still redeems them *(Agadas Bereishis* 17).

כִּי מָלְאוּ מַחֲשַׁכֵּי אֶרֶץ נְאוֹת חָמָס — *For the dark places of the earth are full, the habitations of violence.*

how the foe reviled HASHEM,
And the degenerate nation
blasphemed Your Name.
19 Deliver not to the wild beast
the soul of Your turtledove,
The life of Your poor
forget not forever.
20 Gaze upon the covenant,
for the dark places of the earth are full,
the habitations of violence.
21 Let not the oppressed turn back in shame,
let the poor and destitute praise Your Name.
22 Arise, O God,
champion Your cause!
Remember Your insults
from the degenerate all day long.
23 Forget not the voice of Your tormentors,
the tumult of Your opponents rising always.

Israel is exiled to remote *places* which are *dark*, gloomy, and forbidding. In those dangerous *habitations*, the Jews fall prey to the *violence* of their enemies *(Radak).*

21. אַל יָשֹׁב דַּךְ נִכְלָם — *Let not the oppressed turn back in shame.*

When the man crushed by the oppressor approaches You in sincere prayer, answer him and do not let him return empty-handed *(Rashi).*

Heed the pleas of Israel, the nation oppressed in exile *(Radak).*

עָנִי וְאֶבְיוֹן יְהַלְלוּ שְׁמֶךָ — *Let the poor and destitute praise Your Name.*

When those who suffer in exile realize that their travail is not in vain [for it hastened the Redemption], they will praise Your Name *(Alshich).*

22. קוּמָה אֱלֹהִים רִיבָה רִיבֶךָ — *Arise, O God, champion Your cause!*

The campaign against the enemy is indeed *Your cause* for our oppressors have reviled and blasphemed Your Name *(Radak; Ibn Ezra).*

זְכֹר חֶרְפָּתְךָ מִנִּי נָבָל כָּל הַיּוֹם — *Remember Your insults from the degenerate all day long.*

Targum renders נָבָל as מַלְכָּא טִפְשָׁא, *the foolish king* [for all who dare to challenge HASHEM are either fools or madmen].

23. אַל תִּשְׁכַּח קוֹל צֹרְרֶיךָ — *Forget not the voice of Your tormentors.*

Your tormentors roared amidst Your meeting place (*v.* 4). Do not forget that brutal, barbaric sound of devastation *(Ibn Ezra).*

שְׁאוֹן קָמֶיךָ עֹלֶה תָמִיד — *The tumult of Your opponents rising always.*

[The *Talmud (Yoma* 20b) says that *the tumult* which rises from the vast metropolis of Rome is so loud that the din travels from one end of the world to the other, obliterating other noises.

This is an allegory which illustrates the universal dominion of Rome, whose influence is so great that it overwhelms all other cultures and ideologies. Thus, Rome threatens to eradicate God's Presence from the earth.

Therefore, the psalmist concludes with a plea that the tumultuous challenge of Rome be wiped away, so that God may rule over the earth undisturbed.]

מזמור עה 75

The preceding psalm concludes with the ominous words, the tumult of Your opponents rising always. *This terrible din is amplified by the screams of Israel in exile, as they suffer at the hands of their tormentors, they shout a plea:* Al Tashcheis, Do not destroy! (Chozeh David).

Israel's anguish will intensify as the end of the exile draws near. At that time, calamities will befall Israel in rapid succession. The world will be engulfed in the colossal conflict of Gog and Magog, which will scar the face of the earth. Trampled and terrified, Israel will turn to God with the fervent prayer, Al Tashcheis, Do not destroy! (Meiri; Ibn Yachya).

God will respond with the assurance that salvation is imminent. He is only waiting for the most propitious moment to bring complete ruin upon His foes. Then, All the pride of the wicked I shall cut down; exalted shall be the pride of the righteous (v. *11).*

עה
א־ד

א לַמְנַצֵּחַ אַל־תַּשְׁחֵת מִזְמוֹר לְאָסָף שִׁיר:
ב הוֹדִינוּ לְּךָ | אֱלֹהִים הוֹדִינוּ וְקָרוֹב שְׁמֶךָ
ג סִפְּרוּ נִפְלְאוֹתֶיךָ: כִּי אֶקַּח מוֹעֵד אֲנִי
ד מֵישָׁרִים אֶשְׁפֹּט: נְמוֹגִים אֶרֶץ וְכָל־
יֹשְׁבֶיהָ אָנֹכִי תִכַּנְתִּי עַמּוּדֶיהָ סֶּלָה:

1. לַמְנַצֵּחַ אַל תַּשְׁחֵת — *For the Conductor,* Al Tashcheis [lit. *do not destroy*].

[See *comm.* to 57:1 for a discussion of this superscription.]

This psalm is dedicated to the final era of the exile, the period of the קִיבּוּץ גָלֻיוֹת, *the ingathering of the exiles (Radak).*

[Then Israel will need special merits and Divine mercy because, as the *Talmud* relates in *Sanhedrin* (97a; and *Sotah* (49b), the final period of the exile will be especially difficult.]

מִזְמוֹר לְאָסָף שִׁיר — *A song by Assaf, with musical accompaniment.*

[See *comm.* to *Psalm* to 30:1 שִׁיר מִזְמוֹר.]

By virtue of the genuine appreciation which Israel has for God and in the merit of the songs of praise and the joyous music which they compose in His honor, they will certainly deserve to be saved from destruction *(Alshich).*

2. הוֹדִינוּ לְּךָ אֱלֹהִים הוֹדִינוּ — *We thanked You, O God, we gave thanks.*

These are the words Israel will utter when the exiles are gathered. The repetition emphasizes the sincerity of Israel's thanks *(Radak),* and stresses that Israel thanks God for *all* of His actions, even when their beneficent purpose is not discerned by man *(Rashi).*

Midrash Shocher Tov renders: Haven't we thanked You in the past for Your wondrous deeds? Repeat Your wonders and we will surely repeat our words of thanks.

וְקָרוֹב שְׁמֶךָ — *And Your Name is near.*

[God's real Name is ה׳, *HASHEM, the Dispenser of Kindness*]. Throughout the perils of exile, You have been nearby, swift to respond to our cries with Your Name of compassion, as *Psalms* 145:18 states, קָרוֹב ה׳ לְכָל קֹרְאָיו, *HASHEM is near to all those who call upon Him (Radak; Sforno).*

סִפְּרוּ נִפְלְאוֹתֶיךָ — *Your wonders they declared.*

In the past, our ancestors never missed an opportunity to relate Your wondrous deeds *(Rashi).* This refers especially to the holy prophets of old who constantly spoke to Israel about the splendor of *Your Name (Ibn Ezra).*

In the future, when You gather in the exiles, both Israel (who will personally experience the Redemption) and the gentiles (who will witness it) will relate *Your wonders* and thank You for fulfilling the promises made by the prophets of old *(Radak).*

3. כִּי אֶקַּח מוֹעֵד — *When I will choose the appointed time.*

[Now God replies to Israel's query as to why He delays their redemption. It is postponed because Israel's redemption is not an isolated event in history, but the introduction of a new world order which will revolutionize the course of human affairs.

At that time, the entire earth will be run according to comprehensive laws of unerring uprightness and justice; even the most minute and insignificant matters will be affected by this transformation. God is biding His time, waiting for the right moment to introduce this new system, for incomplete justice is no justice at all. See *Radak; Metzudas David.*]

According to *Rashi,* these are the

75
1-4

For the Conductor,
Al Tashcheis.
A song by Assaf,
with musical accompaniment.
2 *We thanked You, O God,*
we gave thanks
And Your Name is near;
Your wonders they declared.
3 *When I will choose the appointed time,*
I shall judge with fairness.
4 *Melted are the earth*
and all of its inhabitants;
I firmly established its pillars, Selah.

words of Israel, a continuation of their pledge (begun in *v.* 2) to thank God and declare His wonders. כִּי אֶקַּח מוֹעֵד *is rendered: When I take a holiday.* It implies: During holidays, I will not emulate the customs of the gentiles who while away their holidays with lewd talk and foolish levity. Rather, I shall train all of my thoughts on God's deeds and *I shall judge* those Divine acts *with fairness* in order to fully appreciate them. [Thus, each holiday will be a holy day.]

Shaloh Hakadosh translates כִּי אֶקַּח מוֹעֵד, *when I take my time,* and study world events slowly and painstakingly, then I always arrive at the conclusion that Your judgments are fair and upright; but if I am rash and form my opinions hastily, they are usually unfair and crooked.

אֲנִי מֵישָׁרִים אֶשְׁפֹּט — *I shall judge with fairness.*

God promises that He will eventually judge the enemies with complete fairness and give them their just punishment *(Radak).* Israel will praise God on each holiday according to its special theme, and will show appreciation for God's justice *(Rashi).*

4. נְמוֹגִים אֶרֶץ וְכָל יֹשְׁבֶיהָ — *Melted are the earth and all of its inhabitants.*

At the appointed time of Divine retribution, all the inhabitants of the earth will witness how God will take revenge on the adversaries of Israel. Realizing their own crimes, all who see this will cringe in fear and their hearts will melt *(Radak).*

Rashi explains that this refers to the past, when the Torah was transmitted at Sinai. At that fateful moment, the future of the entire universe was in serious doubt, for at Creation God had stipulated that if Israel refused to accept the Torah, the existence of the world would be meaningless and that He would then 'melt' the World back into Chaos and Void [see *Avodah Zarah* 5a].

According to *Mechilta (Beshalach* 15:15), when the Canaanites heard that Israel was commanded to destroy them, their hearts dissolved in fear, as Scripture states: נָמֹגוּ כֹּל יֹשְׁבֵי כְנָעַן, *All the inhabitants of Canaan melted away (Exodus* 15:15).

אָנֹכִי תִכַּנְתִּי עַמּוּדֶיהָ סֶּלָה — *I firmly established its pillars, Selah.*

When the gentiles who witness my revenge realize that I am the Almighty who can melt the world at will, they will also recognize that I am the Lord who is able to firmly establish and perpetuate the earth *(Radak).*

ה אָמַרְתִּי לַהוֹלְלִים אַל־תָּהֹלּוּ וְלָרְשָׁעִים
ו אַל־תָּרִימוּ קָרֶן: אַל־תָּרִימוּ לַמָּרוֹם
ז קַרְנְכֶם תְּדַבְּרוּ בְצַוָּאר עָתָק: כִּי לֹא
ח מִמּוֹצָא וּמִמַּעֲרָב וְלֹא מִמִּדְבַּר הָרִים: כִּי־
ט אֱלֹהִים שֹׁפֵט זֶה יַשְׁפִּיל וְזֶה יָרִים: כִּי כוֹס

[The final era of exile will be a tumultuous, confusing time. The existing social order will melt and disappear. All this will transpire in order to make people understand that the sole basis of existence is firm belief in God.]

When, at Sinai, the world was threatened with extinction, it was אָנֹכִי, *I*, Israel, who saved it and *firmly established* it by accepting the Torah, with the proclamation of faith (*Exodus* 24:7): נַעֲשֶׂה וְנִשְׁמָע, *We shall do and we shall obey (Rashi).*

Furthermore, I [Israel] accepted God's command, (*Exodus* 20:2): אָנֹכִי ה׳ אֱלֹהֶיךָ, *I am HASHEM, Your God (Shir HaShirim Rabbah* 12:1).

5. אָמַרְתִּי לַהוֹלְלִים אַל תָּהֹלּוּ — *I said to the madmen, 'Be not insane.'* [See *comm.* to 5:6.]

[In the final era of exile, הוֹלְלוּת, *madness*, will replace reason and logic. The never-ending torrent of crises will leave the world stunned and dazed.

Through these cataclysmic events, God will reeducate the world, which is gripped by a *mad* appetite for more and more material wealth (see *Radak; Sforno*). In their selfish pursuit of pleasure, they sought to forget God; but He will force them to remember that His word is the only island of sanity which survives in the sea of madness.

The nations will also come to realize that it is madness to blame Israel for all of the world's problems and to use this as an excuse to persecute the Jews (see *Rashi).*

וְלָרְשָׁעִים אַל תָּרִימוּ קָרֶן — *And to the wicked, 'Raise not your pride'* [lit. *horn*].

[The exile was meant to subdue the קֶרֶן, *pride (Targum),* of the wicked, but they perverted this opportunity for character development by increasing their arrogance, instead of diminishing it. When they prospered in exile, they boasted (*Deuteronomy* 8:17): *My power and the might of my hand have gotten me this wealth* (see *Radak* and *Sforno).*]

6. אַל תָּרִימוּ לַמָּרוֹם קַרְנְכֶם — *Raise not to the heights Your pride.*

[The mad pursuit of luxury and wealth in the final days of the exile will be spurred by a false sense of *pride* and accomplishment. Men will imagine that they have reached *the heights* of technology, culture, and civilization; they will therefore believe that they have earned the right to spoil themselves (see *Alshich*).]

תְּדַבְּרוּ בְצַוָּאר עָתָק — *You who speak with insolence and insult (Targum).*

[The צַוָּאר, *neck*, is an allegory for stubborn, unyielding *insolence.* The haughty men strut about with outstretched necks. Material wealth has caused them to feel that they are masters of their own destinies; as a result, they have no respect for God.]

7. כִּי לֹא מִמּוֹצָא וּמִמַּעֲרָב — *For neither from sunrise* [lit. *the exit*] *nor from sunset* [lit. *the west*].

[In the final epoch, men will desperately comb the face of the earth in a relentless effort to exploit its riches, but such enterprises are futile if not Divinely sanctioned.]

Wealth does not result from the merchandise which a man exports from the east *(sunrise)* to the ends of the earth, i.e., the west *(sunset).* Even if a

5 *I said to the madmen, 'Be not insane';*
and to the wicked, 'Raise not your pride.'
6 *Raise not to the heights your pride,*
You who speak with insolence and insult.
7 *For neither from sunrise nor from sunset,*
nor from the wilderness comes glorification.
8 *For God is the Judge,*
He lowers one and raises another.
9 *For a cup is in HASHEM's hand*

trader would send a mighty merchant fleet to every port or dispatch prospectors to [mineral-laden] deserts and mountains, he would not necessarily prosper, because the will of God is the only factor which determines financial success (*Rashi*, based on *Bamidbar Rabbah* 22).

וְלֹא מִמִּדְבָּר הָרִים — *Nor from the wilderness comes glorification.*

The word הָרִים is related to הַרָמָה, *elevation, success.* No manner of exertion, even the most lucrative trading expedition to a remote desert, can guarantee *success (Rashi; Radak; Midrash Shocher Tov).*

Targum, however, renders הָרִים simply as *mountains*, suggesting that the mountains of the *wilderness* are not a guaranteed source of riches.

8. כִּי אֱלֹהִים שֹׁפֵט — *For God is the Judge.*

He alone has the final word as to who will prosper and who will fail. Therefore let no man *raise his pride to the heights (v.* 6), for he deserves no credit for his wisdom, strength, or riches *(Ibn Ezra).* No human effort can alter the decree which God issues on these matters *(Alshich).*

[The *Talmud (Beitzah* 16a) states that everyone's annual income is determined on the days of judgment between Rosh HaShanah and Yom Kippur. *Rashi* explains that a person must therefore exercise great care not to spend too much, lest he exceed this annual allocation.]

זֶה יַשְׁפִּיל וְזֶה יָרִים — *He lowers one and raises another.*

This world may be likened to a water wheel which irrigates a field. It scoops water from the stream below and lifts the water to the elevated field. Then it descends again, empty. Men's fortunes tend to rise and fall in a similar manner (*Shemos Rabbah* 31:14).

A noblewoman once asked Rabbi Shimon ben Chalafta, 'What has God been doing since He completed the world in the first six days of Creation?' The Sage replied, 'Since that time until this very day, God has been making ladders upon which He lowers one man while He raises another.' God impoverishes one man, in order to give his wealth to another, more deserving man (*Bamidbar Rabbah* 22:8).[1]

9. כִּי כוֹס בְּיַד ה׳ — *For a cup is in HASHEM's hand.*

The prophet Isaiah (51:17) cries out, *'Awake, Awake, stand up O Jerusalem, You who have drunk from the hand of*

1. Property is called נְכָסִים because possessions נִכְסִים, *vanish*, from the hands of one owner and reappear in the hands of another. Coins are called זוּזִים because they are constantly זָזִים, *moving away*, from one man to another. Funds are called מָמוֹן, because we ask their possessor, 'Why do you bother to מוֹנֶה, *count*, the money? It will soon be gone!' Pieces of currency are called מָעוֹת because we wonder מַה לְעֵת, 'What is the value of something which lasts only a short time?' (*Bamidbar Rabbah* 22:7).

עה
י־יא

בְּיַד־יהוה וְיַיִן חָמַר | מָלֵא מֶסֶךְ וַיַּגֵּר מִזֶּה
אַךְ־שְׁמָרֶיהָ יִמְצוּ יִשְׁתּוּ כֹּל רִשְׁעֵי־אָרֶץ:
י וַאֲנִי אַגִּיד לְעֹלָם אֲזַמְּרָה לֵאלֹהֵי יַעֲקֹב:
יא וְכָל־קַרְנֵי רְשָׁעִים אֲגַדֵּעַ תְּרוֹמַמְנָה
קַרְנוֹת צַדִּיק:

HASHEM the cup of His fury, the dregs of the benumbing cup you have drunk and You have drained.'

In exile, the Jews drank their full of this bitter brew, but when the exiles are gathered in, the enemy will have his turn to drink from the cup of misery *(Radak; Rashi).*

Then, all will clearly see that *God is the Judge, He lowers one* [the enemy] *as He lifts up another* [Israel] *(Maharam Arma'ah).*

וְיַיִן חָמַר — [*With*] *strong wine (Rashi).*

[חָמַר is cognate with חָמוּר, *strong, relentless.* Here it means *undiluted wine* which is full-bodied and high in potency. This is an allegory alluding to the full force of Divine retribution, unrestrained by any mercy or compassion.]

Radak adds that חָמַר refers to red wine, for this color characterizes superb wines of the finest vintage (see *Proverbs* 23:31).

מָלֵא מֶסֶךְ — *The pouring is full.*

That bitter cup will be *full* in order to give each of our tormentors the *full* share of misery they deserve *(Rashi).*

וַיַּגֵּר מִזֶּה — *And overflows from it.*

The *cup* of sorrow is so *full* that its contents spill over its rim *(Radak).*

אַךְ שְׁמָרֶיהָ יִמְצוּ יִשְׁתּוּ כֹּל רִשְׁעֵי אָרֶץ — *Only its dregs they shall drain and drink — all the wicked of the earth.*

The wine at the top of the cup is bitter, but *the dregs* which sink to the bottom are the bitterest of all. Those whose crimes were relatively mild will drink from the top of the cup, but the infamous *wicked of the earth* will be forced to swallow the worst of punishments *(Ibn Ezra).*

with strong wine the pouring is full,
and overflows from it.
Only its dregs
they shall drain and drink —
all the wicked of the earth.
10 *But as for me, I shall tell it forever;*
I shall sing to the God of Jacob!
11 *And all the pride of the wicked*
I shall cut down;
Exalted shall be the pride of the righteous!

10. וַאֲנִי אַגִּיד לְעֹלָם — *But as for me, I shall tell it forever.*

I do not enjoy the downfall of the wicked, *per se*; rather, I take pleasure in the opportunity it affords me to relate the power of God's vengeance *(Rashi; Radak)*. I publicize this so that people may learn from these examples to mend their ways *(Ibn Ezra)*.

אֲזַמְּרָה לֵאלֹהֵי יַעֲקֹב — *I shall sing to the God of Jacob!*

I will laud God's faithfulness, for even when He sent the seed of Jacob into exile, He remained their God and protector *(Radak)*.

11. וְכָל קַרְנֵי רְשָׁעִים אֲגַדֵּעַ — *And all the pride of the wicked I shall cut down.*

When *the pride of the righteous will be exalted* at the ingathering of exiles and Israel will emerge victorious from the war of Gog and Magog, then the prestige of the wicked will be diminished *(Radak)*.

תְּרוֹמַמְנָה קַרְנוֹת צַדִּיק — *Exalted shall be the pride of the righteous!*

This refers to Israel, the only one of the world's nations which represents righteousness *(Radak)*, for they are the people of the God of righteousness *(Rashi)*.

[The קֶרֶן is literally a *horn*, the symbol of self-defense and might, which gives a person prestige.] In the future, the trappings of Jewish sovereignty will be returned, as I *Samuel* 2:10 states, *And He shall give might to His king and exalt the horn of* מְשִׁיחוֹ*, His anointed*, and as *Psalms* 132:17 states, *There I will make the horn of David flourish; I have set up a lamp for* מְשִׁיחִי*, My anointed one (Midrash Shocher Tov).*

מזמור עו

76

The preceding psalm spoke of the final days of Jewish exile; this psalm, continuing that theme, describes the war of Gog and Magog, which will be waged at the end of the exile (Radak v. *13). This final battle has a historical precedent in the siege of Jerusalem by Sennacherib, who amassed an army composed of all the nations he had conquered.*

At an earlier date, the armies of Assyria had led the Ten Tribes of Israel into exile. Only the small Kingdom of Judah remained; it was led by King Chizkiyahu, who ruled over the two tribes of Judah and Benjamin. This illustrious monarch's very name testifies to the source of his authority, for Chizkiyahu literally means My strength is HASHEM (Sanhedrin *94a).*

HASHEM did not fail those who trusted in Him, for Assyria was annihilated and God's fame spread far and wide: God is recognized in Judah, in Israel His Name is great (v. *2).*

Similarly, God's majesty is now concealed in the shrouds of exile. The future triumph over Gog and Magog will signal the return of Divine prestige. God's glory will gradually spread, until it is recognized throughout the world.

All the nations will be stricken, but Divine protection will envelop Jerusalem like a tabernacle, as the psalm says, When His Tabernacle was in Salem [*Jerusalem*] and His dwelling in Zion (v. *3).*

Rav Hai Gaon *transmitted a Rabbinical tradition that the war of Gog and Magog is destined to take place in the month of Tishrei [in conjunction with* Sukkos, *the Feast of Tabernacles*] (Tur; Orach Chaim *490).*

Therefore, the Gaon of Vilna (Maaseh Rav *234) designates this psalm as the* שִׁיר שֶׁל יוֹם, the Song of the Day, *for the first day of* Sukkos.

עו א־ב לַמְנַצֵּחַ בִּנְגִינֹת מִזְמוֹר לְאָסָף שִׁיר: נוֹדָע
א־ד בִּיהוּדָה אֱלֹהִים בְּיִשְׂרָאֵל גָּדוֹל שְׁמוֹ:
ג־ד וַיְהִי בְשָׁלֵם סוּכּוֹ וּמְעוֹנָתוֹ בְצִיּוֹן: שָׁמָּה

1. לַמְנַצֵּחַ בִּנְגִינֹת – *For the Conductor, with instrumental music.*

As explained in the *Prefatory Remarks*, this psalm discusses King Chizkiyahu's response to Sennacherib's assault on the city of Jerusalem. The Sages explain that Chizkiyahu failed to react properly to the wondrous salvation he received from the hand of God *(Sanhedrin* 94a). The Holy One, Blessed be He, intended to make Chizkiyahu the Messiah, and to make the siege of Sennacherib the war of Gog and Magog. However, the Divine Attribute of Strict Justice protested, arguing, 'Sovereign of the Universe, King David recited many songs and praises in Your honor, yet You did not designate him as Your Messiah. Since Chizkiyahu — for whom You have performed so many miracles — failed to sing even one song in Your praise, how can he deserve to be Your Messiah?' This convinced God to abandon His plan.

With this psalm, Assaf sought to compensate for Chizkiyahu's failure by composing an especially ecstatic song of praise, embellished by a vast variety of נְגִינֹת, *instrumental music (Midrash Chachamim).*[1]

מִזְמוֹר לְאָסָף שִׁיר – *A song of Assaf, with musical accompaniment.*

Gog and Magog will hurl insults against God, as *Psalms* 89:52 states: *For Your foes revile You, HASHEM, they revile the footsteps of Your Messiah.* Sennacherib and his minions also blasphemed God with impunity. The best weapon to combat these vicious insults are songs in praise of God. Indeed, the *Talmud (Sanhedrin* 95b) teaches that as Sennacherib's army slumbered, God enabled them to hear the songs of the חַיּוֹת, *the celestial angels,* and their souls expired *(Be'er Moshe, II Kings* 19:35).

2. נוֹדָע בִּיהוּדָה אֱלֹהִים – *God is recognized* [lit. *known*] *in Judah.*

[Only Judah withstood Sennacherib's onslaught because Chizkiyahu placed no trust in military might. Instead he sought protection in intensive study of the Torah, which is the medium through which the will of God is recognized.

Chizkiyahu decreed that anyone who failed to study Torah would be condemned to die as a traitor and a deserter.

No Jew was exempted from this universal conscription. As a result, every man, woman, boy and girl was well versed even in the most intricate laws of the Torah *(Sanhedrin* 94b). In the most literal sense, *God is recognized in Judah.*]

In the future, God [and His Messiah] will first be recognized in Judah, where Gog and Magog will fall. From there His fame will spread *throughout Israel* and the entire world *(Radak).*

1. The *Midrash (Shir HaShirim Rabbah* 4:19) explains that Chizkiyahu did not feel that it was necessary for him to sing praises to God. He reasoned, 'For the ordinary, secular man Divine miracles are indeed unexpected and must be acknowledged. But since my life is dedicated exclusively to the study of Torah, extraordinary Divine intervention on my behalf is to be expected. My Torah study can be considered equivalent to the songs which others compose.'

Chizkiyahu's conduct was judged improper for he placed too much confidence in his own merits and personal righteousness [see *Berachos* 10b]. Had he been more humble, he would have appreciated God's mercy enough to compose at least one song of praise in His honor *(comm. of Eitz Yoseif* to *Shir HaShirim Rabbah* 4:19).

76
1-3

For the Conductor,
with instrumental music,
A song of Assaf
with musical accompaniment.
2 God is recognized in Judah;
in Israel His Name is great.
3 When His tabernacle was in Salem,
and His dwelling in Zion.

בְּיִשְׂרָאֵל גָּדוֹל שְׁמוֹ — *In Israel His Name is great.*

[The Ten Tribes of Israel were lost in exile because they estranged themselves from God and served idols; but when Sennacherib's colossal host fell before God's might, His holy Name became *great* even throughout the ranks of the alienated, distant tribes of *Israel.*

This spark of recognition of God will be kept alive in the hearts of the lost tribes for thousands of years, until the advent of Messiah which spurs their complete return to the fold.]

This also refers to the reign of Chizkiyahu's ancestor, David, for he was first recognized only by his own tribe of Judah. David ruled in the city of Hebron for two and a half years. Afterwards, he was acclaimed by all and his name became *great throughout Israel (Chomas Anoch).*

3. וַיְהִי בְשָׁלֵם סֻכּוֹ — *When His tabernacle was in Salem.*

When the world was created God designated Jerusalem as a haven of holiness, a sacred tabernacle where He could protect His sons on earth and pray for their welfare.

Jerusalem was originally called שָׁלֵם, *Salem,* 'the city of perfection and peace.' Its ruler was Shem, Noah's pious son, who called himself Malchi-zedek [lit. *My King is righteousness*]. Shem was כֹהֵן לְאֵל עֶלְיוֹן, *the priest dedicated to God, Most High (Genesis* 14:18).

Later, *Abraham called the name of that place* ה' יִרְאֶה, *HASHEM sees (Genesis* 22:14), for when God views that place, He remembers the merits of the Patriarchs.

God pondered, 'Which name shall I prefer? If I use Shem's designation שָׁלֵם, *Salem,* Abraham will be neglected. If I call it by Abraham's name יִרְאֶה, *Yireh,* then Shem will be hurt. Therefore, I will combine both names and call if יְרוּשָׁלַיִם, *Jerusalem* [cf. *Tosafos, Taanis* 16a s.v. הַר].

The physical embodiment of that heavenly tabernacle (סֻכּוֹ) was the *Beis HaMikdash,* but Israel's sins profaned it and caused its ruin. However, it will eventually be rebuilt, as the prophet foretells *(Amos* 9:11): בַּיּוֹם הַהוּא אָקִים אֶת סֻכַּת דָּוִיד הַנֹּפֶלֶת, *On that day, I shall raise up the tabernacle of David that is fallen (Midrash Shocher Tov; Bereishis Rabbah* 56:10).

Sforno renders סֻכּוֹ as a *concealment, ambuscade,* where a lion secretly lies in wait for his prey. This signifies that the enemy (Sennacherib or Gog and Magog) fails to recognize that tremendous forces hidden within the sacred environs of Jerusalem will someday spring forth and destroy him.

וּמְעוֹנָתוֹ בְצִיּוֹן — *And His dwelling in Zion.*

[It was from this holy spot that salvation arose. *Midrash Shocher Tov* (22:2) relates that as Sennacherib encircled Jerusalem, King Chizkiyahu and the prophet Isaiah sat [praying] in

שִׁבַּר רִשְׁפֵי־קָשֶׁת מָגֵן וְחֶרֶב וּמִלְחָמָה
ה סֶלָה: נָאוֹר אַתָּה אַדִּיר מֵהַרְרֵי־טָרֶף:
ו אֶשְׁתּוֹלְלוּ | אַבִּירֵי לֵב נָמוּ שְׁנָתָם וְלֹא־
ז מָצְאוּ כָל־אַנְשֵׁי־חַיִל יְדֵיהֶם: מִגַּעֲרָתְךָ
ח אֱלֹהֵי יַעֲקֹב נִרְדָּם וְרֶכֶב וָסוּס: אַתָּה |

the Holy Temple. A flame burst from their midst and consumed the entire Assyrian host. This triumph firmly established God's dwelling in Jerusalem and enhanced Chizkiyahu's majesty, as well.

Amidst the rich spoils of Sennacherib's camp, the Jews found King Solomon's wondrous throne. They returned the throne to the palace (which had once been Solomon's dwelling place) and set Chizkiyahu up on it *(Yalkut HaMakiri, Isaiah* 14:12).]

4. שָׁמָּה שִׁבַּר רִשְׁפֵי קָשֶׁת — *There He broke the flying bows.*

This refers to the swift arrows which fly from the bowstring *(Rashi; Radak).*

[This signifies the Assyrian juggernaut which sped across the world unchallenged, until its momentum was finally broken at the gates of Jerusalem.

The *Midrash (Koheles Rabbah* 9:27) states that Chizkiyahu armed his men with lethal weapons, which remained concealed under their plain white robes (which betokened peace and reconciliation). Chizkiyahu was prepared to stop the foe with three things: prayer, tribute, and, if all else failed, war. Prayer and Torah study proved to be sufficient to halt the enemy's advance.]

מָגֵן וְחֶרֶב וּמִלְחָמָה סֶלָה — *Shield, sword, and battle, Selah.*

The defeat of Gog and Magog will display the utter futility of weapons and armed might. All the tools of war will be broken as *Isaiah* (2:4) foretells: *They shall beat their swords into plowshares and their spears into pruning hooks, nation shall not lift up sword against nation, neither shall they learn war anymore (Sforno).*

5. נָאוֹר אַתָּה — *Enlightened are You.*

Most commentators recognize the root of נָאוֹר as אוֹר, *light*. When, *in Judah, God is recognized,* the illumination of truth will spread throughout the world, revealing the infinite magnitude of God's might, which vanquishes vast armies with a single blow *(Radak).* This splendid light will be reflected on the shining face of Messiah *(Sforno).*

Rashi identifies נָאוֹר with נאר, *to sweep out,* which suggests that as a result of the foes' defeat, God's world will be 'swept' clean of all adversaries.

אַדִּיר מֵהַרְרֵי טָרֶף — *More powerful than the mountains of prey.*

The forbidding peaks where predators such as lions dwell are called *the mountains of prey.* The enemies of Israel are as powerful and ferocious as these wild beasts, but You, O God are far more powerful than they *(Radak).*

6. אֶשְׁתּוֹלְלוּ אַבִּירֵי לֵב — *Bereft of reason were the stout-hearted.*

Rashi notes that *Job* 12:17 reads, מוֹלִיךְ יוֹעֲצִים שׁוֹלָל, *He leads counselors away bereft of reason.* [The root of the word is שָׁלָל, *loot, booty,* to indicate that the wise are 'plundered' of their most precious possession: their intelligence and sense of judgment.]

If the *stout-hearted* attackers of Jerusalem had exercised their intellects properly, they would have repented and curbed their stubborn, rebellious nature *(Zerah Yaakov).*

According to *Radak,* this means that when the attackers of Jerusalem fall,

4 *There He broke the flying bows,*
shield, sword, and battle, Selah.
5 *Enlightened are You,*
more powerful than the mountains of prey.
6 *Bereft of reason were the stout-hearted,*
they slept their sleep,
And all the men of war
did not find their ability.
7 *At Your rebuke,*
O God of Jacob,
He will be stunned
along with chariot and horse.
8 *O You,*

their riches will be plundered by the inhabitants of the beleaguered city.

נָמוּ שְׁנָתָם — *They slept their sleep.*

The word נָמוּ is related to תְּנוּמָה, *slumber.* The vigorous warriors who threatened the city were suddenly paralyzed, robbed of their strength. They fell into the deep sleep of death and never awoke.

וְלֹא מָצְאוּ כָל אַנְשֵׁי חַיִל יְדֵיהֶם — *And all the men of war did not find their ability* [lit. *their hands*].

They lost their ability to handle their weapons properly *(Targum).*[1]

7. מִגַּעֲרָתְךָ אֱלֹהֵי יַעֲקֹב — *At Your rebuke, O God of Jacob.*

[*Jacob* designates the Children of Israel when they are downtrodden and weak. You rebuke their enemies for them when they cannot defend themselves.]

נִרְדָּם וְרֶכֶב וָסוּס — *He will be stunned along with chariot and horse.*

Not only the foot soldiers, but even the mighty king of Gog and Magog himself will fall into the slumber of death *(Radak).*

A horse is normally alert, for it never sleeps deeply (*Sukkah* 26b). [Nevertheless, the cavalry horses of the marauding army will fall into deep slumber, even though they are attached to cumbersome chariots *(Kiflayim L'Tushiya).*]

1. [This also alludes to the events related in the Midrash (*Shir Hashirim Rabbah* 4:19). Among the legions which besieged Jerusalem were the armies of Egypt, led by Pharaoh, and the forces of Ethiopia, led by King Tarheka. They secretly planned to help Chizkiyahu. When Sennacherib learned of their betrayal, he tied the kings up, hand and foot.

When the angel of doom smote the Assyrians at midnight, the lives of Israel's two allies were spared.

In the morning, Chizkiyahu discovered these two survivors imprisoned in the camp. Recognizing their loyalty, he undid their bonds, and they returned home to relate the wonders of God's might to their subjects.

Thus, while all the men of war [who attacked Israel] *did not find their hands* [when they were smitten], these faithful allies regained their freedom and the use of their hands, which had been tied.]

נוֹרָא אַתָּה וּמִי־יַעֲמֹד לְפָנֶיךָ מֵאָז אַפֶּךָ:
ט מִשָּׁמַיִם הִשְׁמַעְתָּ דִּין אֶרֶץ יָרְאָה
י וְשָׁקָטָה: בְּקוּם־לַמִּשְׁפָּט אֱלֹהִים לְהוֹשִׁיעַ
יא כָּל־עַנְוֵי־אֶרֶץ סֶלָה: כִּי־חֲמַת אָדָם תּוֹדֶךָּ
יב שְׁאֵרִית חֵמֹת תַּחְגֹּר: נִדְרוּ וְשַׁלְּמוּ
לַיהוה אֱלֹהֵיכֶם כָּל־סְבִיבָיו יֹבִילוּ שַׁי
יג לַמּוֹרָא: יִבְצֹר רוּחַ נְגִידִים נוֹרָא לְמַלְכֵי־
אָרֶץ:

8. אַתָּה נוֹרָא אַתָּה — *O You, awesome are You!*

When You triumph over the foe, Your awesome might manifests itself in full measure. Then all will see that it is *You*, and *You* alone, Who rules the earth *(Sforno)*.

וּמִי יַעֲמוֹד לְפָנֶיךָ מֵאָז אַפֶּךָ — *And who can stand before You when You are wrathful?*

Indeed, throughout history no nation has survived God's wrath, save Israel; for God's displeasure with Israel stems solely from His eternal love for His Chosen People. His wrath is calculated to spur Israel to repentance, so that the Jewish nation will deserve future Divine providence *(Shevet M'Yisrael)*.

9. מִשָּׁמַיִם הִשְׁמַעְתָּ דִּין — *From heaven You made judgment heard.*

You dispatched Your prophet Isaiah to announce to the world the sentence of doom which Your tribunal passed against Sennacherib *(Rashi)*. You are destined to inform the world of the imminent downfall of Gog and Magog *(Ibn Yachya)*.

[This alludes to *Yalkut Shimoni (II Kings* 236), which describes the celestial signs foretelling Chizkiyahu's victory. For three days, Chizkiyahu was ill and bed-ridden. On the third day, God stopped the cycle of the sun in Chizkiyahu's honor, and caused it to go ten degrees backwards in order to lengthen the day. That night, Sennacherib was destroyed (see *II Kings* 20:8-11).]

אֶרֶץ יָרְאָה וְשָׁקָטָה — *The earth feared, then grew calm.*

At first, the Holy land was convulsed with fear, anxiously awaiting Sennacherib's invasion. Upon his defeat, tranquility and calm were restored *(Rashi)*.

The downfall of so awesome an adversary thrust a shaft of fear into the hearts of all of our potential adversaries throughout the earth. Their eager aspirations for the conquest of the Holy Land were stilled and *grew calm (Radak)*.

Allegorically,this verse alludes to the giving of the דִּין, *Law*, at Mount Sinai. From the very beginning of the earth's existence, God stated that the sole purpose of Creation was that Israel should accept the Torah. If they refused, the continuation of the world would be meaningless, and God would return it to primeval chaos. Thus the *earth feared* and trembled lest Israel refuse the Torah; but when Israel enthusiastically accepted it, and thereby guaranteed the perpetuation of the earth's existence, *the earth grew calm (Shabbos* 88a; *Avodah Zarah* 3a).

[This provides an important insight into the subsequent events of history. Whenever we see the world convulsed in turmoil and violence, we may interpret this as a sign that the

awesome are You!
And who can stand before You
when You are wrathful.
9 *From heaven You made judgment heard,*
the earth feared, then grew calm.
10 *When God arises to pass judgment,*
to save all the earth's humble, Selah.
11 *For the rage of man causes You homage;*
and as for the remnant, You restrain anger.
12 *Make vows and fulfill them to HASHEM,*
your God,
All you who surround Him
they will present gifts to the Awesome One.
13 *He will cut down the spirit of the nobles,*
He is awesome to the monarchs of the earth.

foundation of society, the Torah, is being rejected by mankind.]

10. בְּקוּם לַמִּשְׁפָּט אֱלֹהִים — *When God arises to pass judgment.*

The agitation and unrest of the earth will finally be calmed when God judges the wicked *(Radak)* and saves the righteous, such as Chizkiyahu and his followers *(Rashi).*

לְהוֹשִׁיעַ כָּל עַנְוֵי אֶרֶץ סֶלָה — *To save all the earth's humble, Selah.*

[King Chizkiyahu was the epitome of humility. He gladly denied himself the honors and pompous trappings of royalty. The Sages testify (*Pesikta D'Rav Kahana* 6:59) that his daily diet consisted of no more than two bunches of greens and some meat. Although Israel mocked his humble dining habits, he was content. The king's conduct taught his subjects to be satisified with a frugal subsistence, as *Talmud (Shabbos* 113b) teaches that the verse *(Ruth* 2:14): *And she was satisfied* [*with little*] describes Israel in the days of Chizkiyahu.]

11. כִּי חֲמַת אָדָם תּוֹדֶךָּ — *For the rage of man causes You homage.*

When catastrophic setbacks fill the wicked with frustration and rage, the innocent and the righteous do *homage* to Your ability to dispense justice. Indeed, the wicked themselves are led to praise God; for example, Nebuchadnezzar lauded the Almighty for saving Chananyah, Mishael, and Azaryah from the flaming inferno *(Rashi).* Thus, *the rage of* [wicked] *man* is turned to *homage (Radak).*

Furthermore, when God is filled with rage against a certain man, His purpose is to test this man's ability to appreciate Divine rebuke to the extent of *rendering homage* to God for His chastisement *(Toras Chesed).*

שְׁאֵרִית חֵמֹת תַּחְגֹּר — *And as for the remnant, You restrain anger.*

When the worst of the wicked are intimidated by the display of Your great might, the שְׁאֵרִית, *remainder,* signifying the men of lesser evil, will learn to *restrain* their venomous anger against You and to keep still *(Rashi).*

Rashi also suggests that this refers to God, rendering תַּחְגֹּר as *You gird,* to suggest: You are destined to gird all of Your zealous *anger* to the very last *remnant,* in an all-out campaign against the wicked.

Sforno comments that this will be the final war; after it there will be no future חֵמֹת, *hostilities (Sforno).*

12. נִדְרוּ וְשַׁלְּמוּ לַה׳ אֱלֹהֵיכֶם כָּל סְבִיבָיו – *Make vows and fulfill them to HASHEM, your God, all you who surround Him.*

The downfall of the wicked will bring about a return to the proper world order, which has God as its focal point. His spirit will dwell in the Temple and Israel will settle around that sacred spot *(Targum).* All the nations will gather around the land of Israel in order to be close to God (see *Radak).* They will recognize His sovereignty; everyone will make vows in God's honor, and the pledges will be fulfilled.

[*Zekan Aharon* describes *Eretz Yisrael* as the 'navel of the earth.' This alludes to its central position in creation and to its function as the conduit of God's sustenance, just as the umbilical cord brings nourishment to the unborn infant.]

יֹבִילוּ שַׁי לַמּוֹרָא – *They will present gifts to the Awesome One.*

Then all the nations will recognize that God is the One to be feared *(Radak),* and they will present offerings to Him in the *Beis HaMikdash (Targum).*

However, the gentiles will pay tribute only out of fear, whereas Israel *will make vows* [out of love] *and fulfill them* [with devotion] *(Sforno).*

Nevertheless, everyone will dedicate more than mere animal sacrifices. They will devote all their intellectual and emotional resources to the service of HASHEM *(Nefutzos Yehudah).*

13. יִבְצֹר רוּחַ נְגִידִים – *He will cut down the spirit of the nobles.*

The term for the harvest of the vine is בְּצִירָה (see *Deuteronomy* 24:21); here, the word signifies that the arrogant gentile princes will be 'cut' from life as easily as grapes are plucked from the vine *(Radak).*

נוֹרָא לְמַלְכֵי אָרֶץ – *He is awesome to the monarchs of the earth.*

The wrath of God *(Ibn Ezra)* and the King Messiah *(Sforno)* will melt the courage of the enemy monarchs, as *Psalms* 2:5 predicts: *Then, He will speak to them in His anger, and His fury will terrify them.* Only then will the universal triumph of God be complete.

מזמור עז

77

This psalm explains the purpose of Israel's long and arduous sojourn in exile.

While settled peacefully on its native soil, the contented nation lapsed into a spiritual slumber and neglected its Divine mission. The latent moral and spiritual energy of the Chosen People remained dormant deep within the Jewish heart.

The awesome challenges of exile activated these powerful resources. The searing pain of incessant persecution aroused the Jewish soul. The heart of Israel soared heavenward and the voice of the anguished people cried out fervently to the Almighty (see Hirsch*).*

The psalmist searches through the chronicles of ancient Jewish history to demonstrate that God saved Israel even in their bleakest moments. Since the Almighty wrought miracles of salvation in the past, why does He not perform miracles in the present exile? Certainly, He remains omnipotent.

However, it is God's wish to wring every last tear from our eyes, to squeeze every last cry of repentance from our hearts, so that we might be thoroughly worthy of the final, total redemption. May it come speedily in our times!

עז
א־ה

א־ב לַמְנַצֵּחַ עַל־°ידיתון לְאָסָף מִזְמוֹר: קוֹלִי
°ידותון אֶל־אֱלֹהִים וְאֶצְעָקָה קוֹלִי אֶל־אֱלֹהִים
ג וְהַאֲזִין אֵלָי: בְּיוֹם צָרָתִי אֲדֹנָי דָּרָשְׁתִּי
יָדִי | לַיְלָה נִגְּרָה וְלֹא תָפוּג מֵאֲנָה הִנָּחֵם
ד נַפְשִׁי: אֶזְכְּרָה אֱלֹהִים וְאֶהֱמָיָה אָשִׂיחָה |
ה וְתִתְעַטֵּף רוּחִי סֶלָה: אָחַזְתָּ שְׁמֻרוֹת עֵינָי

1. לַמְנַצֵּחַ עַל יְדוּתוּן — *For the Conductor, on Yedusun.*

Rashi (based on *Shir HaShirim Rabbah* 4:3) derives יְדוּתוּן from the word דָּת, *decree.* Every psalm introduced with this word refers to the evil decrees and oppressive edicts which the enemy imposes on Israel [see *Prefatory Remarks* to Psalm 39].

לְאָסָף מִזְמוֹר — *By Assaf, a song.*

[Assaf's unique talent was the ability to find something to sing about even in the bleakest gloom. See *commentary* to *Psalms* 79:1.]

2. קוֹלִי אֶל אֱלֹהִים וְאֶצְעָקָה — *My voice is raised to God and I cry aloud.*

Indeed when Israel stands helpless and alone in exile, its only weapon is its voice, as the *Midrash (Bereishis Rabbah* 65:16) states: *The voice is the voice of Jacob (Genesis* 27:22) signifies that when the voice of Jacob is lifted in prayer in the houses of worship, then the bloody hands of Esau cannot harm the Jewish people.

Furthermore, the *Talmud (Gittin* 57b) teaches that no human prayer ever brings results unless some offspring of Jacob participate in the prayer service.

קוֹלִי אֶל אֱלֹהִים וְהַאֲזִין אֵלָי — *My voice is raised to God and He gives ear to me.*

The psalmist repeats this phrase to emphasize that Israel cries out to God, and to God alone. Therefore, Jews deserve God's attention and His compassionate response *(Radak).*

Sforno adds that the repetition underlines the dual aspect of Israel's prayers; Jews beseech God to save them from the direct persecution of the enemy and to alleviate the indirect suffering of the exile, caused by economic and social problems.

3. בְּיוֹם צָרָתִי אֲדֹנָי דָּרָשְׁתִּי — *On the day of my distress, my Lord I sought.*

This distress of exile accomplished its purpose, which was to elevate me. Even at the height of my agony I never sought mere relief from pain; I asked for spiritual renewal and Divine guidance *(Targum).*

[I accepted each pang of suffering as a forceful invitation to *seek out my Lord.*]

יָדִי — *My wound* [lit. *my hand*].

Rashi and *Radak* render יָדִי as *my wound,* based on *Exodus* 9:3, where the plague with which God smites the Egyptians is called יַד. Here the psalmist refers to Israel's heart, which was deeply wounded by the suffering in the dark לַיְלָה, *night,* of exile.

Targum reads the words together: — דָּרַשְׁתִּי יָדִי, *I sought my hand,* meaning, 'I sought that God's hand should rest upon me and guide me with prophetic vision [see *Ezekiel* 1:3, 3:22] in order that I might navigate through the gloom of exile.'

יָדִי לַיְלָה נִגְּרָה וְלֹא תָפוּג — *My wound oozes* [lit. *flows*] *through the night, and does not cease.*

Just as blood pours from an open wound incessantly, so do the Jews constantly cry and moan in exile *(Radak).*

There is no bandage which can help heal this nasty wound *(Tehillos Hashem).*

77
1-5

For the Conductor,
on Yedusun by Assaf, a song.
2 My voice is raised to God
and I cry aloud,
My voice is raised to God
and He gives ear to me.
3 On the day of my distress,
my Lord I sought.
My wound oozes through the night,
and does not cease;
my soul refuses comfort.
4 I remember God and I moan,
I speak and my spirit swoons, Selah.
5 You grasped my eyelids

מֵאֲנָה הִנָּחֵם נַפְשִׁי — *My soul refuses comfort.*

I attempt to console myself with the knowledge that God promised to redeem us someday. However, the distress of the exile is so intense that my soul refuses to be calmed *(Radak).*

Although my body suffers physical pain, it can find consolation in the fact that pain purges the body of its inclination towards lust and sin. However, *my soul refuses comfort* from this consideration, because the Jewish spirit can only find peace in the pursuit of prayer and Torah, yet both of these occupations have been interrupted by the travails of exile *(Toras Chacham).*

4. אֶזְכְּרָה אֱלֹהִים וְאֶהֱמָיָה — *I remember God and I moan.*

I remember how God favored me when I was in His good graces *(Rashi),* and how He championed my cause against my adversaries *(Sforno).*

אָשִׂיחָה — *I speak.*

I constantly tell others of the kindness which I once enjoyed from God *(Rashi);* I contrast that blissful period with my present woes and dismay (see *Radak).*

King Solomon said in his wisdom (*Proverbs* 12:25): *If there is worry in a man's heart, let him speak it out* [to others]. I tried to ease my anxiety with this form of therapy; but it was to no avail, because my pain was so intense *(Tehillos Hashem).*

וְתִתְעַטֵּף רוּחִי סֶלָה — *And my spirit swoons, Selah.*

Literally, וְתִתְעַטֵּף means *to be enveloped,* because the person who swoons in pain doubles over and seems to be rolled up or 'enveloped' within himself, as in *Eichah* 2:20: הָעֲטוּפִים בְּרָעָב, *who swoon from hunger (Radak).*

5. אָחַזְתָּ שְׁמֻרוֹת עֵינָי — *You grasped my eyelids.*

The man who remains awake deep into the night is called the שׁוֹמֵר, *watcher,* of the night [cf. *Isaiah* 21:8], and the אַשְׁמוּרֶת, *watch,* is the time when watchmen awaken for the next shift in the night *(Rashi; Radak).*

Furthermore, the eyelids are called שְׁמֻרוֹת, *watches,* for they protect the eye *(Ibn Ezra; Sforno; Rabbi Moshe* quoted in *Radak).*

The psalmist laments: Throughout the long night of exile so many

ו נִפְעַמְתִּי וְלֹא אֲדַבֵּר: חִשַּׁבְתִּי יָמִים
ז מִקֶּדֶם שְׁנוֹת עוֹלָמִים: אֶזְכְּרָה נְגִינָתִי
בַּלָּיְלָה עִם־לְבָבִי אָשִׂיחָה וַיְחַפֵּשׂ רוּחִי:
ח הַלְעוֹלָמִים יִזְנַח | אֲדֹנָי וְלֹא־יֹסִיף לִרְצוֹת
ט עוֹד: הֶאָפֵס לָנֶצַח חַסְדּוֹ גָּמַר אֹמֶר לְדֹר
י וָדֹר: הֲשָׁכַח חַנּוֹת אֵל אִם־קָפַץ בְּאַף
יא רַחֲמָיו סֶלָה: וָאֹמַר חַלּוֹתִי הִיא שְׁנוֹת

problems plagued me that I could not close my eyes to sleep peacefully. Agony kept my eyes open and on the alert (like those of a night watchman on guard duty), but I became dizzy and groggy from exhaustion.

נִפְעַמְתִּי וְלֹא אֲדַבֵּר — *I was alarmed and could not speak.*

At night my worries keep me awake, and during the day, I am so bewildered and lost that I cannot speak *(Radak).*

Moreover, I see that the future holds even greater woes for my persecuted people. Although I am alarmed by the specter of doom, I dare not alert them, lest they be gripped by uncontrollable panic *(Sforno).*

6. חִשַּׁבְתִּי יָמִים מִקֶּדֶם — *I have pondered olden days.*

[Unable to bear the harsh realities of the present exile and unwilling to face the future (which threatens to be even worse), Israel looks back to the glorious days of the past.]

I contemplate the countless acts of kindness which You performed for our ancestors in the past *(Rashi).* In particular, You extracted our people from previous periods of exile and turned their mourning to joy *(Radak).*

The *Midrash (Shemos Rabbah* 45:2) translates חִשַּׁבְתִּי as *I calculated* to suggest, 'I figured out how long we were in Egypt, how long we spent in Babylon, and how long we suffered under the rule of the Greeks.

It is clear that this exile has endured far longer than all previous ones. Therefore, it must be our sins which delay the final redemption *(Shevet M'Yisroel).*

שְׁנוֹת עוֹלָמִים — *Ancient years.*

[The good days of the past seem ages away as if they took place in a totally different world. How I wish those wonderful times would return!]

7. אֶזְכְּרָה נְגִינָתִי בַּלָּיְלָה — *I recall my music in the night.*

As I languish in the dark *night* of exile, I recall the joyous music which I offered in the *Beis HaMikdash* in days of old *(Rashi).*

עִם לְבָבִי אָשִׂיחָה — *With my heart I meditate (Targum; Rashi).*

Despite my anguish, I keep my feelings private lest my difficult experiences shock others or weaken their faith and their resolve to serve God *(Alshich).*

וַיְחַפֵּשׂ רוּחִי — *And my spirit searches.*

I search desperately for Divine guidance because prophecy has vanished and I have no way of predicting the duration of this long exile *(Shevet M'Yisroel).*

8. הַלְעוֹלָמִים יִזְנַח אֲדֹנָי — *Is it for eternity that my Lord rejects me?*

Has God abandoned me to perpetual exile? *(Rashi).*

וְלֹא יֹסִיף לִרְצוֹת עוֹד — *Nevermore to be appeased?*

This is not the first time He was angry with Israel, but in former times, He was eventually appeased. Now, however, it seems that His wrath will never be appeased *(Rashi).*

77
6-11

I was alarmed and could not speak.
6 I have pondered olden days,
ancient years.
7 I recall my music in the night,
with my heart I meditate,
ad my spirit searches.
8 Is it for eternity that my Lord rejects me,
nevermore to be appeased?
9 Is His kindness forever ended,
His last word said for all generations?
10 Has God forgotten graciousness,
and sealed in anger His mercy?
11 And I said, 'It is to intimidate me,

9. הֶאָפֵס לָנֶצַח חַסְדּוֹ — *Is His kindness forever ended?*

[Since God's kindness is infinite, how can it be that it has now come to *an end?*].

גָּמַר אֹמֶר לְדֹר וָדֹר — *His last word said for all generations?*

Has God issued a *final decree* which prohibits Him forever from lessening His wrath? *(Rashi).*

Have all the *words* (אֹמֶר) of consolation and hope expressed by the prophets come to *an end* (גָּמַר), so that there is no hope for future generations? *(Radak).*

10. הֲשָׁכַח חַנּוֹת אֵל — *Has God forgotten graciousness?*

Rashi offers two translations for חַנּוֹת. According to the first translation, the verse would mean: Has God forgotten His tendency to be חוֹנֵן, *gracious?* According to the second translation, it would mean: Has He forgotten the many חֲנִינוֹת, *supplications,* which we addressed to Him, as we begged for Divine mercy?

Alshich adds: Has the merciful God not promised (*Exodus* 33:19): וְחַנֹּתִי אֶת אֲשֶׁר אָחֹן, *I shall be gracious to whom I shall be gracious,* which indicates that even upon the undeserving, He will bestow חִנָּם, *free,* grace?

אִם קָפַץ בְּאַף רַחֲמָיו סֶלָה — [*And*] *(has He) sealed in anger His mercy?*

The word קָפַץ literally means *to clench one's fist* in a hoarding gesture, as in *Deuteronomy* 15:7: *Is God permanently hoarding His abundant supply of mercy because of His anger? (Rashi; Radak).*

11. וָאֹמַר חַלּוֹתִי הִיא — *And I said, 'It is to intimidate me'* [lit. *it is my terror*].

[In the preceding verses, the psalmist posed the question, 'Why does *this* exile continue without end?' Now he attempts to answer that query.]

I sense that God is trying to intimidate me in order to beat my rebellious heart into submission. Therefore, He pursues me with the חִיל, *terror,* of *galus (Rashi).*

Radak identifies the root of חַלּוֹתִי as חָלָל, *corpse,* implying: When I was discouraged, I declared that I would not emerge alive from this interminable exile.

Sforno and *Rashbam* translate חַלּוֹתִי as *my prayer* [see *Exodus* 32:11 וַיְחַל מֹשֶׁה]. According to this view, Israel says, 'In my terrible predicament, the

°אֶזְכּוֹר

יב יְמִין עֶלְיוֹן: °אזכיר מַעַלְלֵי־יָהּ כִּי־
יג אֶזְכְּרָה מִקֶּדֶם פִּלְאֶךָ: וְהָגִיתִי בְכָל־פָּעֳלֶךָ
יד וּבַעֲלִילוֹתֶיךָ אָשִׂיחָה: אֱלֹהִים בַּקֹּדֶשׁ
טו דַּרְכֶּךָ מִי־אֵל גָּדוֹל כֵּאלֹהִים: אַתָּה הָאֵל
טז עֹשֵׂה פֶלֶא הוֹדַעְתָּ בָעַמִּים עֻזֶּךָ: גָּאַלְתָּ

only solution can be *my prayer,* for only prayer will *transform the right hand of the Most High.'*

According to *Pesikta D'Rav Kahana* 17, חַלּוֹתִי is cognate with חִלּוּל, *desecration.* In this context, it would suggest: *HASHEM swore* [to protect us] *with His right hand (Isaiah* 62:8). Why has that oath been nullified and God's right hand transformed? Because of 'my desecration' of the Divine covenant. Israel is at fault — not God.

שְׁנוֹת יְמִין עֶלְיוֹן — *This change of the Most High One's right hand.*

Scripture states that in the exile הֵשִׁיב אָחוֹר יְמִינוֹ מִפְּנֵי אוֹיֵב, *God withdrew His right hand in the presence of the enemy (Eichah* 2:3). Since this very hand used to embrace Israel, God's שְׁנוֹת, *changed* or *transformed behavior* must be designed to intimidate the Jewish nation *(Rashi),* or to stir them to fervent prayer *(Sforno; Rashbam).*

Radak translates שְׁנוֹת as the plural of שָׁנָה, *years.* Israel says: 'I remember the glorious former *years* when God's *right hand* was *Most High* and He redeemed us from Egypt and Babylon. I am confident that He will deliver His people again.'

12. אֶזְכּוֹר מַעַלְלֵי יָהּ — *I recall the works of YAH.*

My heart meditates and my spirit searches (v. 7) the ancient days of Jewish history for a solution to the problem of exile. I find comfort in the study of God's past wonders *(Alshich).*

The word is קְרִי, *read,* אֶזְכּוֹר: *I recall the works of God* and find consolation in the manifestations of His Omnipotence. The spelling is אַזְכִּיר, *I remind* [*others*], of God's works, as well *(Radak).*

כִּי אֶזְכְּרָה מִקֶּדֶם פִּלְאֶךָ — *When I remember Your ancient wonders.*

In Egypt, too, the Jews were discouraged and gave up hope. So long was the exile, so relentless was the bondage, that no man dared to hope for Divine intervention. Yet, You performed miracles and liberated us. When I consider this ancient lesson, my heart is filled with new hope for redemption from this bleak, endless *galus (Radak).*

13. וְהָגִיתִי בְכָל פָּעֳלֶךָ — *I shall meditate upon all Your deeds.*

The translation of וְהָגִיתִי follows *Metzudas David* [see *commentary* to *Psalms* 1:2].

Alshich and *Chazah Zion* explain that there are certain topics which may be pondered in the privacy of the mind, but never expressed by the tongue. Solomon said in his wisdom (*Proverbs* 25:2): כְּבֹד אֱלֹהִים הַסְתֵּר דָּבָר, *The glory of God is to conceal a matter.* This refers to the secrets of the six days of Creation. These profound mysteries may not be transmitted verbally (*Bereishis Rabbah* 9; *Chagigah* 11b).

Therefore *When I remember Your wonders of old (v.* 12), I recall the dawn of Creation and meditate on that deep subject, without speaking of it.

Radak however, renders וְהָגִיתִי as *I will relate,* implying: In order to console my downtrodden brethren, I will recount Your miraculous works in Egypt and at the splitting of the sea.

וּבַעֲלִילוֹתֶיךָ אָשִׂיחָה — *And speak about Your works.*

this change of the Most High One's right hand.'
12 *I recall the works of YAH,*
when I remember Your ancient wonders.
13 *I shall meditate upon all Your deeds*
and speak about Your works.
14 *O God, in sanctity is Your way,*
what power is as great as God?
15 *You are the God Who works wonders,*
You manifested Your might among the nations.

The secrets of how the world was created must remain concealed, but the manifest wonders of nature *should* be discussed, for these amazing phenomena proclaim the sovereignty of God and His mastery over all realms of existence. Of these works, Solomon said (*Proverbs* 25:2): וּכְבֹד מְלָכִים חֲקֹר דָּבָר, *But the glory of Kings is to investigate a matter.*

Therefore, Israel declares: 'Of (these) works I shall openly speak!' *(Alshich; Chazah Zion).*

14. אֱלֹהִים בַּקֹּדֶשׁ דַּרְכֶּךָ – *O God, in sanctity is Your way.*

[Many observers of Jewish history have scrutinized the events of our long and turbulent past and have become confused by the inconsistency of events. Success and failure, sovereignty and servitude, joy and tragedy have alternated with no apparent pattern; but the psalmist discerns the Divine Hand in the vicissitudes of our history, and he recognizes that all these changes of fortune ultimately lead to the sanctification of God's Name (see *Rashi).*]

Radak suggests that the climax of this sanctification was achieved when God's Holy Spirit descended on Mount Sinai and the Holy Torah was granted to Israel, as *Psalms* 68:18 states: אֲדֹנָי בָם סִינַי בַּקֹּדֶשׁ, *My Lord is in their midst at Sinai, at the sanctity.*

מִי אֵל גָּדוֹל כֵּאלֹהִים – *What power is as great as our God?*

There are many celestial forces which control the earth. These powers are called אֵלִים or אֱלֹהִים, which literally mean *powerful ones, angels (commentary* to *Psalms* 8:6 and to *Genesis* 6:2). One must never forget that these are merely Divine agents to carry out the will of the one and only God, Who controls all forces. There is none as great as He *(Radak).*

15. אַתָּה הָאֵל עֹשֵׂה פֶלֶא – *You are the God who works wonders.*

You demonstrated Your miracles at the revelation at Mount Sinai *(Radak).*

הוֹדַעְתָּ בָעַמִּים עֻזֶּךָ – *You manifested Your might among the nations.*

Initially, God gave several nations an opportunity to accept the Torah. When they refused it, He offered the Torah to the children of Israel, who eagerly accepted.

In His Omniscience, God certainly knew that the gentiles would reject the Torah, but He offered it to them, nonetheless,. to demonstrate His evenhandedness.

In this way, God made known *to the nations* that He was justified in punishing them for their sins, because He had given them a chance to discover and to fulfill His will, as revealed in the Torah *(Tanchuma, V'Zos HaBerachah* 4).

יז בִּזְרוֹעַ עַמֶּךָ בְּנֵי־יַעֲקֹב וְיוֹסֵף סֶלָה: רָאוּךָ
מַּיִם | אֱלֹהִים רָאוּךָ מַּיִם יָחִילוּ אַף יִרְגְּזוּ
יח תְהֹמוֹת: זֹרְמוּ מַיִם | עָבוֹת קוֹל נָתְנוּ
יט שְׁחָקִים אַף־חֲצָצֶיךָ יִתְהַלָּכוּ: קוֹל רַעַמְךָ |

16. גָּאַלְתָּ בִּזְרוֹעַ עַמֶּךָ — *With Your powerful arm You redeemed Your nation.*

Literally, זְרוֹעַ means *arm* as in *Exodus* 6:6, which states that God redeemed Israel בִּזְרוֹעַ נְטוּיָה, *with an outstretched arm.* This expression indicates that God had to apply immense pressure on the Egyptians, who refused to liberate Israel *(Radak).*

Indeed it was most difficult for God to justify Israel's miraculous redemption from Egypt, for the Jews had allowed themselves to be influenced by the corrupt and lewd Egyptian culture to the extent that they even adopted their master's ways. For example, the Jews were uncircumcized, had long hair, and wore garments containing both wool and linen. [This combination of fibers, known as *shatnez,* is prohibited by the Torah *(Deuteronomy* 22:11).]

However, God redeemed the Jews despite their degradation because of His oath to the Patriarchs that He would redeem their descendants. The term זְרוֹעַ, *arm,* is an allusion to an oath because one who swears raises his arm *(Shir HaShirim Rabbah* 2:2).

[See *commentary* to *Psalms* 44:4, where *Malbim* explains that the term זְרוֹעַ is used whenever HASHEM saves Israel although they are unworthy of Divine aid.]

בְּנֵי יַעֲקֹב וְיוֹסֵף סֶלָה — *The sons of Jacob and Joseph, Selah.*

Joseph is mentioned since he was the cause of Jacob's descent to Egypt. It was he who provided for all of his brethren during their sojourn in that land *(Radak; Targum).*

God later used זְרוֹעַ, *force,* to split the sea in the merit of Joseph's coffin, which the Jews were carrying from Egypt *(Shevet M'Yisroel).*

[See *comm.* to the following verse for an explanation of other factors involved in the splitting of the sea.]

17. רָאוּךָ מַּיִם אֱלֹהִים — *The waters saw You, O God.*

Moses stretched his hand over the sea at God's command, but the sea refused to split. Even when Moses displayed the covenant of circumcision, the coffin of Joseph and the holy staff on which the ineffable Name of God was engraved, the sea refused to part [claiming that it was a servant of God and had no right to deviate from its Divinely ordained course].

Finally, God revealed His glory to the sea; then the waters split in trepidation and awe *(Pirkei D'Rabbi Eliezer* 42).

רָאוּךָ מַּיִם יָחִילוּ — *The waters saw You and were terrified.*

At the sea, Israel was terribly afraid of the Egyptian host. When they cried out to You in frantic prayer *(Exodus* 14:10), You responded by threatening the waters, so that they would split *(Sforno).*

אַף יִרְגְּזוּ תְהֹמוֹת — *Even the depths trembled.*

At that moment, all of the waters in the entire world parted, including the water in springs, wells, pits, bowls and barrels. Even the celestial reservoir of water and the waters in the *depths* of the earth parted *(Mechilta, Beshalach* 14:21; *Shemos Rabbah* 21:6).

Alshich (v. 20) explains that God made this miracle a universal one for two reasons: first, He wanted to publicize His Omnipotence throughout

[16] *With Your powerful arm*
You redeemed Your nation,
the sons of Jacob and Joseph, Selah.
[17] *The waters saw You, O God,*
the waters saw You and were terrified,
even the depths trembled.
[18] *Clouds streamed water, heavens sounded forth,*
even Your arrows went abroad.
[19] *The rumble of Your thunder*
rolled like a wheel,

the entire world; second, God wanted to disprove the arguments of those who attributed the miracle to natural phenomena. Since a westerly wind blew over the sea the night before it parted (*Exodus* 14:21), many denied God's might by attributing the splitting of the sea to the wind; but when *all* the waters in the world split, this reasoning was shown to be false.

18. זֹרְמוּ מַיִם עָבוֹת — *Clouds streamed water.*

God marshaled many forces of nature to throw the Egyptian host into frenzy and turmoil, as (*Exodus* 24:24) states: *And HASHEM looked out over the Egyptian camp through the pillar of fire and the cloud, and He brought confusion to the Egyptian camp.* The clouds poured torrents of rain on the enemy, which added to the tumult *(Radak).*

קוֹל נָתְנוּ שְׁחָקִים — *Heavens sounded forth.*

This refers to the thunder [mentioned in the next verse] *(Radak).*

אַף חֲצָצֶיךָ יִתְהַלָּכוּ — *Even Your arrows went abroad.*

חֲצָצֶיךָ is related to חִצֶּיךָ, *Your arrows (Rashi),* and refers to the hailstones which poured down upon the Egyptians at the sea *(Radak).*

Some say that this refers to the seventh of the ten plagues: בָּרָד, *hail (Maharam Markado).*

It may also signify the hailstones which struck the Canaanite kings when Israel fought to conquer the Holy Land *(Radak).*

19. קוֹל רַעַמְךָ בַּגַּלְגַּל — *The rumble of Your thunder rolled like a wheel.*

Ibn Ezra observes that thunder is caused by atmospheric turbulence which causes the clouds to 'roll' and collide [creating a terrifying crash].

You caused this awesome sound to 'roll' across the waters like a spinning גַּלְגַּל, *wheel,* causing panic and confusion in the Egyptian camp *(Rashi).*[1]

Radak suggests that גַּלְגַּל refers to the circular orbit' of the celestial bodies which control the rain and thunder. Also גַּלְגַּל refers to the wheels of Pharaoh's chariots. God caused them to fall off and the chariots were dragged tortuously (*Exodus* 14:25).

1. In fact, the intimidation of the wicked is the true purpose of thunder. The *Talmud (Berachos* 59a) teaches that thunder was created in order to humble the arrogant sinner by exposing his own frailty and insignificance (*Maharsha, Berachos* 59a). Therefore, upon hearing thunder, we utter the benediction: *Blessed be He Whose power and might fill the world.*

כ־כא °וּשְׁבִילְךָ כ

בְּגַלְגַּל הֵאִירוּ בְרָקִים תֵּבֵל רָגְזָה וַתִּרְעַשׁ
הָאָרֶץ: בַּיָּם דַּרְכֶּךָ °ושביליך בְּמַיִם
כא רַבִּים וְעִקְּבוֹתֶיךָ לֹא נֹדָעוּ: נָחִיתָ כַצֹּאן
עַמֶּךָ בְּיַד־מֹשֶׁה וְאַהֲרֹן:

Actually, the horses shied away from the sea, but miraculously, the chariots became self-propelled and dragged the horses and their riders to their watery doom *(Mechilta Beshalach* 14:25).

הֵאִירוּ בְרָקִים תֵּבֵל — *Lightning bolts lit the world.*

This refers to *Exodus* 14:20: *And it lit up the night (Radak).* [The lightning enabled Israel to see the foe.]

רָגְזָה וַתִּרְעַשׁ הָאָרֶץ — *The earth trembled and roared.*

The frenzied Egyptians trembled in terror and awe *(Radak).*

20. בַּיָּם דַּרְכֶּךָ — *In the sea was Your way.*

You paved the route to redemption in the sea so that Israel might follow Your lead (*Ibn Ezra; Radak; Sforno).* The Egyptians met their doom traveling on that very same road *(Shemos Rabbah* 25:6).

וּשְׁבִילְךָ בְּמַיִם רַבִּים — *And Your path went through the mighty waters.*

Actually, שְׁבִילְךָ is plural, *Your paths,* because God divided the sea into twelve separate avenues, one for each tribe (see *Psalms* 136:13; *Radak).*

A wall of water separated each path, but God furnished the walls with windows [so that each tribe could see how the others were escaping and thus be encouraged to continue] *(Pirkei D'Rabbi Eliezer* 42).

וְעִקְּבוֹתֶיךָ לֹא נוֹדָעוּ — *But Your footsteps remained unknown.*

After the Jews made their escape, the watery walls collapsed and the sea surface returned to its original place, thus drowning the Egyptians *(Radak).*

Despite the tremendous changes which had been miraculously wrought in the sea, nature reverted to normalcy immediately after the miracle ended. No trace of the preceding upheaval remained *(Hirsch).*

21. נָחִיתָ כַצֹּאן עַמֶּךָ — *You led Your nation like a flock.*

Your concern for Israel did not end when they escaped from the dangers of the sea. You continued to lead them through the wilderness for forty years *(Radak).*

With complete confidence and faith, Israel followed You into the barren desert, completely disregarding the desolation and the absence of food and water.

77
20-21

Lightning bolts lit the world,
the earth trembled and roared.
20 *In the sea was Your way,*
and Your path went through the mighty waters,
But Your footsteps
remained unknown.
21 *You led Your nation like a flock,*
by the hand of Moses and Aaron.

Just as sheep are not generally taken into a barn or shelter, Israel lacked permanent shelter during these forty years.

Just as sheep are never led to a fodder trough, but forage for their own food, Israel lacked provisions in the wilderness and lived from day to day.

Finally, just as sheep obediently follow the lead of their shepherd, Israel followed the lead of Moses and Aaron *(Bamidbar Rabbah* 23:2).

בְּיַד מֹשֶׁה וְאַהֲרֹן – *By the hand of Moses and Aaron.*

God chose the most dedicated and reliable leaders, Moses and Aaron, for His people. These devoted shepherds stand out in sharp contrast to the corrupt and selfish leaders of later generations. Of the latter, the prophet (*Ezekiel* 34:2, 3) says: *Thus says my Lord, HASHEM, 'Woe to the shepherds of Israel who have fed themselves; should not the shepherds graze the flocks? You eat the fat and clothe yourselves with the wool, you slaughter the healthy lambs, but you do not feed the sheep (Ben Beisi).*

The *Midrash (Shemos Rabbah* 2:3) sets down the rule that the Holy One, Blessed be He, does not elevate any man to a great position of leadership until He tests him first in small matters. Moses and David, for example, were humble shepherds prior to their rise to greatness. In their integrity, they grazed their sheep in the wilderness in order to keep them from eating and stealing the grass in pastures belonging to others.

God said to them, 'You have been found trustworthy in pasturing the sheep of other men; now come lead my flock, Israel!' [see *footnote, Psalms* 23:1].

In these final verses, the psalmist presents proofs from Jewish history that God can create a wondrous redemption of universal proportions. Therefore, if God has not delivered us it can only be a result of our shortcomings. Obviously, we have not improved ourselves sufficiently and therefore must endure further afflictions until our purification has been completed and we have become all that God desires us to be *(Metzudas David)*.

מזמור עח 78

In this composition, the psalmist surveys the history of Israel from the bondage in Egypt until the reign of King David. The events of this period, spanning more than 400 years, do not seem to follow any apparent order. However, the discerning student of Jewish history quickly discovers that the varied events of these four centuries all stem from a single source: God's desire that His holy Torah should be the supreme authority over Israel. God humbled the Jews as slaves in Egypt so that they would be prepared to accept the exclusive sovereignty of the Torah at Sinai. God then settled them as an independent nation in the Holy Land, so that He might appoint a monarch who would rule the Jewish people in the name of the Torah. The monarch whom God chose was David. David's son Solomon built the Beis Hamikdosh, the sacred Temple in which God's Torah was enshrined and venerated as the Supreme Law.

But the authority of David did not go unchallenged. From the earliest times, the powerful tribe of Ephraim, the heir of the royal line of Joseph, demanded dominion. They were proud that Joshua ben Nun, the conqueror of the land, was from the tribe of Ephraim and that the Tabernacle had been situated in Shiloh, in the territory of Ephraim, for 369 years (see Ibn Ezra v. *9).*

Even when the spiritual and political capital of Israel was transferred to Jerusalem, Ephraim did not forget its former glory. Yeravam ben Nevat of Ephraim arose to challenge Solomon. He eventually caused the Ten Tribes to secede from Judean rule; these tribes were known collectively as Ephraim.

Malbim *and* Hirsch *explain that this psalm is a firm proclamation that God recognizes none but David and his seed as the true Torah rulers of all Israel:* He despised the tent of Joseph the tribe of Ephraim He did not choose; but chose the tribe of Judah, Mount Zion which He loves (v. *67, 68).*

עח
א־ה

א מַשְׂכִּיל לְאָסָף הַאֲזִינָה עַמִּי תּוֹרָתִי הַטּוּ
ב אָזְנְכֶם לְאִמְרֵי־פִי: אֶפְתְּחָה בְמָשָׁל פִּי
ג אַבִּיעָה חִידוֹת מִנִּי קֶדֶם: אֲשֶׁר שָׁמַעְנוּ
ד וַנֵּדָעֵם וַאֲבוֹתֵינוּ סִפְּרוּ־לָנוּ: לֹא נְכַחֵד |
מִבְּנֵיהֶם לְדוֹר אַחֲרוֹן מְסַפְּרִים תְּהִלּוֹת
ה יְהוָה וֶעֱזוּזוֹ וְנִפְלְאֹתָיו אֲשֶׁר עָשָׂה: וַיָּקֶם

1. מַשְׂכִּיל לְאָסָף — *A Maskil by Assaf.*

[See *comm.* to *Psalms* 32:1. מַשְׂכִּיל, is derived from שֵׂכֶל, *wisdom, enlightment.* The message of this psalm is so essential that Assaf took pains to assure that it would be accurately transmitted to the entire nation. The *Talmud (Pesachim* 117a) states that any psalm introduced with the word *Maskil* was publicized and explained to the entire congregation by a skilled interpreter and orator.]

הַאֲזִינָה עַמִּי תּוֹרָתִי — *Give ear, my nation, to my Torah.*

[These brief words capture the theme of this entire lengthy psalm: Obey the Torah!] Accept it as a Divine gift מִן הַשָּׁמַיִם, *from heaven (Sefer Halkkarim). (Sefer Halkkarim).*

Recognize David the Judean as the only king authorized by the Torah, as Scripture states (*Genesis* 49:10), לֹא יָסוּר שֵׁבֶט מִיהוּדָה, *The ruler's staff shall not depart from Judah (Ibn Yachya).*

Study Jewish history as recorded in the Torah and observe the punishment of those who disregarded the Torah *(Alshich).* At the same time, appreciate God's kindness towards those whom He seeks to improve through Torah *(Sforno).*

[Many commentators identify תּוֹרָתִי, *my Torah,* as the Written Law and אִמְרֵי פִי, *the words of my mouth,* as the Oral Law.]

הַטּוּ אָזְנְכֶם לְאִמְרֵי פִי — *Bend Your ear to the words of my mouth.*

The Jewish scholar approaches the study of history as a sacred pursuit, for he realizes that beneath the surface the concealed hand of God guides all events. The study of the miraculous and benevolent providence of God is tantamount to actual Torah study.

The Almighty says, *'Bend Your ear to* carefully hear *the words of My mouth,'* i.e., the simple stories of Jewish history recorded in the Scriptures, because if you delve beneath the surface, you will find yourself listening to תּוֹרָתִי, *My Torah,* and you will gain sacred inspiration from the lessons of history *(Malbim).*

2. אֶפְתְּחָה בְמָשָׁל פִּי — *I will open my mouth with a parable.*

Parable refers to the actual words of the Torah itself *(Rashi).* [The Torah resembles a parable because it couches eternal, ineffable truths in stories which illustrate abstract concepts in simple human terms. See *comm.* to 49:5: אַטֶּה לְמָשָׁל אָזְנִי, *I will bend my ear to the parable.*]

The word אֶפְתְּחָה, *I will open,* is used in conjunction with a מָשָׁל, *parable,* because a *parable* is a simple tale which helps to unlock complex and hidden truths which would otherwise be too difficult to comprehend *(Norah Tehillos).*

אַבִּיעָה חִידוֹת מִנִּי קֶדֶם — *I will utter* [lit. *pour forth*] *riddles from ancient times.*

[To the untrained eye historical events appear to be perplexing, incomprehensible riddles. Only the profound Torah scholar can penetrate the inner core of history's many riddles. When they are thoroughly understood, the inner meaning of history *pours forth,* enabling people to comprehend the seemingly incomprehensible.]

78
1-4

A Maskil *by Assaf,*
Give ear, my nation, to my Torah;
Bend your ear
to the words of my mouth.
2 *I will open my mouth with a parable,*
I will utter riddles from ancient times.
3 *What we heard and know*
and our fathers told us,
4 *We shall not withhold from their sons —*
to the final generation —
Relating the praises of HASHEM,
His might and His wonders that He has wrought.

3. אֲשֶׁר שָׁמַעְנוּ וַנֵּדָעֵם — *What we heard and know.*

We have heard Torah traditions and narratives from many sources; since righteous, devout men have transmitted these truths to us, we have accepted them without question. We know them to be absolutely true *(Ibn Ezra).*

[There is no inconsistency in our historical sources, for there is only *one* authentic version, in which every detail of the story corroborates another detail. Among secular historical chronicles, there is no such unity; instead, contradictory versions of history abound, and each 'historian' espouses 'his story'.]

וַאֲבוֹתֵינוּ סִפְּרוּ לָנוּ — *And our fathers told us.*

The main reason for our unshakable confidence in our tradition is that *our fathers* transmitted it to us. No one loves us more than our parents do; thus they certainly would not want to deceive or mislead us *(Radak; Ibn Ezra).*

4. לֹא נְכַחֵד מִבְּנֵיהֶם — *We shall not withhold from their sons.*

We are grateful to our fathers and ancestors for transmitting their Torah tradition to us. We will display our appreciation by sharing this tradition with all of their sons and descendants *(Rashi; Ibn Ezra)* who were not fortunate enough to receive a proper Torah education *(Radak).*

[We realize that we are but a link in the long chain of tradition. However, if even the smallest link is missing, the entire chain is broken. Therefore, we are determined to forge a link to the future, so that the next generation will be connected to our venerable past.]

לְדוֹר אַחֲרוֹן מְסַפְּרִים תְּהִלּוֹת ה׳ — *To the final generation — relating the praises of* HASHEM.

The scholars and bearers of our tradition are obligated to teach our uneducated brethren until they become sufficiently inspired and well informed to transmit the Torah to their own children. These children will relay it to their children, until the very last generation *(Radak).*

[In order to generate that degree of intense enthusiasm which can survive from one generation to the next, it is not enough to teach dry, lifeless facts. The scholar must vigorously and constantly relate the *praises of* HASHEM.]

וֶעֱזוּזוֹ וְנִפְלְאֹתָיו אֲשֶׁר עָשָׂה — *His might and His wonders that He has wrought.*

His might refers to God's sovereignty over the entire universe, the heavens above and the earth below; *His wonders*

עֵדוּת | בְּיַעֲקֹב וְתוֹרָה שָׂם בְּיִשְׂרָאֵל אֲשֶׁר
צִוָּה אֶת־אֲבוֹתֵינוּ לְהוֹדִיעָם לִבְנֵיהֶם:
ו לְמַעַן יֵדְעוּ | דּוֹר אַחֲרוֹן בָּנִים יִוָּלֵדוּ יָקֻמוּ
ז וִיסַפְּרוּ לִבְנֵיהֶם: וְיָשִׂימוּ בֵאלֹהִים כִּסְלָם
וְלֹא יִשְׁכְּחוּ מַעַלְלֵי־אֵל וּמִצְוֹתָיו יִנְצֹרוּ:
ח וְלֹא יִהְיוּ | כַּאֲבוֹתָם דּוֹר סוֹרֵר וּמֹרֶה דּוֹר
לֹא־הֵכִין לִבּוֹ וְלֹא־נֶאֶמְנָה אֶת־אֵל רוּחוֹ:
ט בְּנֵי אֶפְרַיִם נוֹשְׁקֵי רוֹמֵי־קֶשֶׁת הָפְכוּ

refers to the miracles which demonstrated *His might (Sforno).*

5. וַיָּקֶם עֵדוּת בְּיַעֲקֹב — *He established a testimony in Jacob.*

Ibn Ezra explains that עֵדוּת refers to the laws which are firmly *established* and which are accepted without question, because logic and common sense bear *testimony* to the significance of these precepts.

Malbim adds that עֵדוּת describes simple 'Bible stories,' the historical and biographical narratives of Scripture. These appeal even to the common folk, the masses, who are referred to as יַעֲקֹב [see *comm.* to *Psalms* 14:7].

Tehillos Hashem points out that our tradition dates back to the Patriarchs, who fulfilled the Torah's precepts even before the Law was formally given at Sinai. This was especially true of Jacob, who symbolizes Torah and truth. It was he who gathered his sons around his deathbed in order to hand the *testimony* over to them *(Chazah Zion).*

וְתוֹרָה שָׂם בְּיִשְׂרָאֵל אֲשֶׁר צִוָּה אֶת אֲבוֹתֵינוּ — *And emplaced a Torah in Israel which He commanded our fathers.*

Ibn Ezra contines that תּוֹרָה refers to *mitzvos* whose value is not apparent and which do not appeal to the human logic of the masses. These are not accepted voluntarily and must be צִוָּה, *commanded,* from Sinai.

Malbim notes that תּוֹרָה means the understanding of the deep moral lessons and complex historical value of each narrative of the Torah. The ignorant commonfolk of *Jacob* cannot appreciate this; only יִשְׂרָאֵל, *Israel,* the intellectual elite, grasp the true import of these lessons.

6. לְמַעַן יֵדְעוּ דּוֹר אַחֲרוֹן — *So that the last generation may know.*

The chain of tradition must be continued until the end of time *(Radak).*

בָּנִים יִוָּלֵדוּ יָקֻמוּ וִיסַפְּרוּ לִבְנֵיהֶם — *Sons yet to be born — they will arise and tell their own sons.*

The fathers teach their young sons, and when the sons *arise* to maturity, they, in turn, will transmit the tradition to their offspring *(Radak).*

7. וְיָשִׂימוּ בֵאלֹהִים כִּסְלָם — *So that they may place their hope in God.*

The stories of the wonders which God performed in days of old inspire hope in the hearts of the present generation *(Radak).*

וְלֹא יִשְׁכְּחוּ מַעַלְלֵי אֵל — *And not forget the works of God.*

Constant repetition of these wondrous stories of God are an assurance that God will not be forgotten by Israel *(Radak).*

וּמִצְוֹתָיו יִנְצֹרוּ — *But safeguard His commandments.*

When our faith in God is reinforced by hearing His words, we shall be inspired to be more scrupulous in *safeguard*[ing] *His commandments (Radak).*

5 *He established a testimony in Jacob*
and emplaced a Torah in Israel,
Which He commanded our fathers,
to make them known to their sons.
6 *So that the last generation may know —*
sons yet to be born —
They will arise
and tell their own sons;
7 *So that they may place their hope in God,*
and not forget the works of God,
but safeguard His commandments;
8 *That they not become like their fathers,*
a wayward and rebellious generation,
A generation that did not dedicate its heart aright
and whose spirit was not faithful with God.
9 *The sons of Ephraim, armed bowsmen,*

8. וְלֹא יִהְיוּ כַּאֲבוֹתָם דּוֹר סוֹרֵר וּמֹרֶה — *That they not become like their fathers, a wayward and rebellious generation.*

This refers to the generation which was first in Egypt and later in the wilderness *(Rashi).* [Although they witnessed countless miracles, their stubborn and rebellious spirit was not subdued and humbled before God.]

דּוֹר לֹא הֵכִין לִבּוֹ — *A generation that did not dedicate its heart aright.*

[This generation enjoyed the unprecedented privilege of receiving the Torah, yet, since they did not dedicate their hearts to complete faith in God, they remained rebellious.]

וְלֹא נֶאֶמְנָה אֶת אֵל רוּחוֹ — *And whose spirit was not faithful with* [lit. *toward*] *God.*

[Although they possessed a faith which far surpassed that of later generations, they were inconsistent and unreliable. Upon slight provocation, they often became insolent toward HASHEM.]

9. בְּנֵי אֶפְרַיִם — *The sons of Ephraim.*

[The main theme of the psalm commences here. Although the generation of the wilderness was unreliable and rebellious, Torah study and observance gradually tamed their hearts; submission and obedience eventually replaced insolence.

But one tribe retained its original arrogance and ignored the tradition of our fathers.]

There was a time-honored tradition that the sojourn of the Jews in Egypt would endure no longer than four hundred years, commencing from the moment of Isaac's birth. Only Ephraim paid no heed to this calculation, insisting that the four hundred years had started thirty years earlier, at the time of the בְּרִית בֵּין הַבְּתָרִים, *the covenant of the parts,* which occurred when Abraham was 70. [See *Chiddushei Griz HaLevi, Parshas Bo.*]

Yagnon, a grandson of Ephraim, arose as a false prophet, claiming that God had commanded him to lead the

י בְּיוֹם קְרָב׃ לֹא שָׁמְרוּ בְּרִית אֱלֹהִים
יא וּבְתוֹרָתוֹ מֵאֲנוּ לָלֶכֶת׃ וַיִּשְׁכְּחוּ
יב עֲלִילוֹתָיו וְנִפְלְאוֹתָיו אֲשֶׁר הֶרְאָם׃ נֶגֶד
אֲבוֹתָם עָשָׂה פֶלֶא בְּאֶרֶץ מִצְרַיִם שְׂדֵה־

people out of Egypt. None responded to this claim except for the tribe of Ephraim; they were of the royal line of Joseph and were also men of prowess and might. Gathering their wives and children, they left Egypt. According to one tradition, their Egyptian overlords pursued and overtook them, killing tens of thousands of warriors (*Pirkei D'Rabbi Eliezer* 48).[1]

[Only part of the tribe of Ephraim participated in this tragic episode of rash, premature flight. However, even those who stayed behind were exceptionally proud and stubborn. In the following verses, the psalmist shows that all the wonders which God performed in Egypt and in the wilderness failed to humble their hearts. See *Ibn Ezra; Radak.*]

נוֹשְׁקֵי רוֹמֵי קָשֶׁת — *Armed bowsmen* [i.e., archers].

They dared to ignore the Divine warning not to leave Egypt prematurely, because their strength and their skill with weapons caused them to grow proud *(Rashi; Ibn Ezra).*

Rashi explains that נוֹשְׁקֵי is derived from נֶשֶׁק, *arms,* and רוֹמֵי means *to shoot* (or fling) high in the air (cf. *Exodus* 15:1).

הָפְכוּ בְּיוֹם קְרָב — *They retreated on the day of battle.*

[The aristocrats of Ephraim mocked their brethren who languished in the Egyptian bondage. They accused them of cowardice, of being paralyzed by fear and by a 'slave mentality';] but despite Ephraim's bold words, on the day of battle their courage failed them. They fled in terror before the enemy who then completely annihilated them *(Targum; Rashi).*

10. לֹא שָׁמְרוּ בְּרִית אֱלֹהִים — *They did not safeguard the covenant of God.*

[God had struck a covenant with Israel, promising that He would redeem them at the appointed time; they were not to leave Egypt earlier. Ephraim disregarded this holy pact.

Now the psalmist launches into a lengthy description of the rebelliousness of the entire Israelite nation throughout their sojourn in the wilderness. Although the criticism is leveled at the nation as a whole, it seems that the remainder of the tribe of Ephraim was particularly guilty of insubordination. Thus the following verses are a continuation of the theme introduced in the preceding verse.]

Ibn Ezra and *Radak* explain that the Israelites abandoned the Divine covenant of Torah which they had entered at Sinai.

Shaarei Chaim says that this refers to the fact that during the forty years in the desert, all the tribes (with the exception of Levi) failed to circumcize their sons, neglecting God's covenant

1. Another source *(Shemos Rabbah* 20:11) says that Ephraim marched toward *Eretz Yisrael* across the lands of the Philistines, who attacked and destroyed them (see *I Chronicles* 7:21). Their bodies were left unburied; thirty years later, when the other tribes made their exodus from Egypt, great heaps of their sun-bleached bones littered the roads of Philistia.

As a result, God did not lead Israel to freedom via Philistia (*Exodus* 13:17), because He knew that if the Jewish people witnessed this gruesome testimony of defeat, their spirit would be utterly crushed. They would regret their flight from Egypt and return timidly to their former masters.

they retreated on the day of battle.
10 *They did not safeguard the covenant of God,*
and after His teaching they refused to go.
11 *They forgot His works,*
and His wonders that He had shown them.
12 *In the presence of their fathers He did marvels,*
in the land of Egypt, in the field of Zoan.

with the seed of Abraham.

וּבְתוֹרָתוֹ מֵאֲנוּ לָלֶכֶת — *And after His teaching they refused to go.*

Whenever they traveled in the wilderness, the Holy Ark containing the Torah traveled before them and led the way; but often the stubborn nation *refused to follow,* saying *(Numbers* 14:4), 'נִתְּנָה רֹאשׁ וְנָשׁוּבָה מִצְרָיְמָה, *Let us appoint a* [*new*] *leader and return to Egypt' (Norah Tehillos).*

11. וַיִּשְׁכְּחוּ עֲלִילוֹתָיו — *They forgot His works.*

[God worked miracles and manipulated all of nature in Egypt so that Israel might learn an unforgettable lesson about His universal mastery, yet the people chose to forget these teachings.]

וְנִפְלְאוֹתָיו אֲשֶׁר הֶרְאָם — *And His wonders that He had shown them.*

God's *wonders* are usually concealed from the eyes of man *(Ibn Ezra).* [In Egypt, however, He displayed them clearly, so that they might learn to fear Him.]

12. נֶגֶד אֲבוֹתָם עָשָׂה פֶלֶא — *In the presence of their fathers He did marvels.*

Rashi (based on *Bereishis Rabbah* 92:2) explains that when God divided the waters of the sea, He caused the Patriarchs Abraham, Isaac, and Jacob to descend from heaven so that they could witness the redemption of their children. [Thus they saw the fulfillment of God's promise that their offspring would be redeemed and their oppressors punished *(Genesis* 15:13-14).]

Sforno, however, contends that this refers to the fathers who were enslaved in Egypt. They witnessed a true miracle in that *the more they* [the Egyptians] *afflicted them, the more they multiplied and grew (Exodus* 1:12). [The Jews were exceptionally prolific in Egypt; Jewish women who were subjected to oppression gave birth to sextuplets.]

בְּאֶרֶץ מִצְרַיִם שְׂדֵה צֹעַן — *In the land of Egypt, in the field of Zoan.*

Radak comments that *Zoan* is synonymous with *Egypt* because it is Egypt's capital city, and the center of its affairs [see *Numbers* 13:22; *Isaiah* 30:4].

Alshich notes that the words אֶרֶץ, *land,* and שָׂדֶה, *field,* allude to a specific miracle which took place in these locations. The *Talmud (Sotah* 11b) says that the Jewish mothers in Egypt gave birth in the *fields* under the cover of apple trees so that their oppressors would not discover their newborn sons and kill them. God fashioned a protective trench beneath each infant; there the babies were miraculously nursed on milk and honey. When they grew older, these children began to emerge from their hiding places and gathered in flocks. Their fathers went out to greet them; miraculously every child recognized his own father, despite the fact that he had never seen him before. Thus, *before their fathers he did marvels.*

יג צֹעַן: בָּקַע יָם וַיַּעֲבִירֵם וַיַּצֶּב־מַיִם כְּמוֹ־
יד נֵד: וַיַּנְחֵם בֶּעָנָן יוֹמָם וְכָל־הַלַּיְלָה בְּאוֹר
טו אֵשׁ: יְבַקַּע צֻרִים בַּמִּדְבָּר וַיַּשְׁקְ כִּתְהֹמוֹת
טז רַבָּה: וַיּוֹצִא נוֹזְלִים מִסָּלַע וַיּוֹרֶד כַּנְּהָרוֹת
יז מָיִם: וַיּוֹסִיפוּ עוֹד לַחֲטֹא־לוֹ לַמְרוֹת
יח עֶלְיוֹן בַּצִּיָּה: וַיְנַסּוּ־אֵל בִּלְבָבָם לִשְׁאָל־

13. בָּקַע יָם וַיַּעֲבִירֵם — *He split the sea and brought them across.*

[Not only did God divide the waters of the sea, but He also made a completely dry corridor, well stocked with food, fruit, and other luxuries, so that they could cross in comfort.]

וַיַּצֶּב מַיִם כְּמוֹ נֵד — *And He stood the water like a wall.*

God did not merely carve a pathway through the water; He also piled the water into a towering wall which soared high into the sky, in order that the miracle would be noticed by far-off peoples *(Alshich).*

14. וַיַּנְחֵם בֶּעָנָן יוֹמָם — *He led them with a cloud by day.*

God's kindness did not end at the sea. He carefully guided them through the uncharted wilderness, leading them with His pillar of *cloud (Radak).*

This *cloud* covering also protected them from the scorching desert sun *(Ibn Ezra).*

וְכָל הַלַּיְלָה בְּאוֹר אֵשׁ — *And all night long with a fiery light.*

This lit up the way and illuminated the entire camp, so they had no need for candles or torches *(Ibn Ezra; Radak).*

Alshich explains the seeming redundancy of the words בְּאוֹר אֵשׁ, *by the light of a fire.* The blazing heat of the desert is relieved by a nighttime cooling. But if the column of fire leading the nation were to give off heat, there would never be a cool respite from the fiery inferno. Thus, the verse stresses *by the 'light' of a fire*, indicating that this fire emitted light but not heat.

15. יְבַקַּע צֻרִים בַּמִּדְבָּר — *He sundered rocks in the wilderness.*

At the very outset of their sojourn in the wilderness, an adequate water supply became a vital concern. When they entered the wilderness of Sin and camped at Rephidim, there was no water to drink. The thirsty masses clamored for water, and threatened Moses. God therefore commanded him to smite the rock with his staff; then water streamed forth in abundance *(Rashi,* based on *Exodus* 17:1-7).

Although Moses struck only one צוּר, *rock,* the psalmist speaks of many צֻרִים, *rocks,* because at the moment this huge boulder was split, many other rocks thoughout the wilderness also burst open and gushed with water *(Yalkut Shimoni* 819).

[Thus an entire network of lush oases was prepared to supply all of Israel's future needs in the desert. Why, then, does Scripture state again and again that Israel lacked for water? Since this miraculous supply of water existed solely by virtue of Israel's ability to believe in the Almighty's miracles, whenever the spiritual level of the nation declined and they began to doubt God's wondrous powers, their water supply was cut off. See *Alshich.*]

Radak notes that although the psalmist is enumerating the miracles which occurred in the desert, he is not adhering to their precise chronological order; for example, here the wonder of the water at Rephidim is listed first, but in the Torah, two earlier miracles are recorded: that of the מָן, *manna,* and that of the שְׂלָיו, *quail.*

וַיַּשְׁקְ כִּתְהֹמוֹת רַבָּה — *And provided drinks like the abundant depths.*

[The water which sprang from the

13 *He split the sea and brought them across,*
and He stood the water like a wall.
14 *He led them with a cloud by day,*
and all night long with a fiery light.
15 *He sundered rocks in the wilderness,*
and provided drinks like the abundant depths.
16 *He brought forth flowing waters from the rock*
and caused waters to descend like rivers.
17 *But they continued further to sin against Him,*
to defy the Most High One in the thirsty desert.
18 *They tested God in their hearts,*

rock was not merely an accumulation of surface moisture; rather, Moses succeeded in tapping the very source of water in the depths of the earth.]

Rashi says this refers to the crossing of the sea. Although the waters of the sea were saline, springs of fresh water sprang from the depths so that the people could refresh themselves while they crossed the sea floor.

16. וַיּוֹצִא נוֹזְלִים מִסָּלַע – *He brought forth flowing waters from the rock.*

[In the merit of Miriam the prophetess, Moses' pious sister, a unique well accompanied the Israelite camp in the wilderness. The well was a round rock, perforated with holes like a sieve (*cf. Shabbos* 35a; *Rashi, ibid.*). It rolled along in the desert as the Jews traveled; when they stopped, the rock came to rest in the middle of the camp and water flowed from its holes.]

וַיּוֹרֶד כַּנְּהָרוֹת מָיִם – *And caused waters to descend like rivers.*

Using his scepter of authority, the נָשִׂיא, *prince*, of each tribe would trace a shallow channel in the sand from the בְּאֵר שֶׁל מִרְיָם, *the well of Miriam*, to the campsite of his tribe. The water would begin to נוֹזֵל, *flow*, from the well along this channel until it grew into a mighty torrent resembling a running river (*Rashi*).

The well also formed one large river which encircled the camp of each tribe. If a person wanted to visit a friend from a different tribe, he would have to travel there in a small boat (*Tosefta, Succah* 3:3).

17. וַיּוֹסִיפוּ עוֹד לַחֲטֹא לוֹ – *But they continued further to sin against Him.*

[It was with water that God demonstrated His greatest benevolence towards Israel. Yet the more generosity He displayed, the more Israel complained about the lack of water and increased their sinful behavior against God (see *Radak*).]

לַמְרוֹת עֶלְיוֹן בַּצִּיָּה – *To defy the Most High One in the thirsty* [*parched*] *desert.*

In the parched desert, these wandering fugitives required God's assistance more than ever; nevertheless, they rejected Him there and refused to obey Him (*Ibn Ezra*).

They claimed that since God is *Most High*, He could have no interest in so insignificant and lowly a place as the barren desert (*Eretz HaChaim*). [Thus, they denied the Omnipresence of Divine Providence and despaired of receiving Divine aid.]

18. וַיְנַסּוּ אֵל בִּלְבָבָם – *They tested God in their hearts.*

This refers to their demand for meat. Scripture states: *And the mixed*

יט אֹכֶל לְנַפְשָׁם: וַיְדַבְּרוּ בֵּאלֹהִים אָמְרוּ
כ הֲיוּכַל אֵל לַעֲרֹךְ שֻׁלְחָן בַּמִּדְבָּר: הֵן
הִכָּה־צוּר | וַיָּזוּבוּ מַיִם וּנְחָלִים יִשְׁטֹפוּ

multitude that was in their midst fell into lust, and the children of Israel also wept again and said, 'Who shall feed us meat?' (Numbers 11:4).

They really had no need for meat, for the manna had a superb taste and supplied all of their nutritional needs. They demanded meat in order to test God's ability [to supply their needs in the desert] *(Radak).*

The *Midrash (Tanchuma, Yisro* 3) cites a difference of opinion as to the precise nature of Israel's testing of God. R' Yehudah taught that the people argued: 'God claims to be in our midst, yet whenever a king leaves his palace to visit his subjects in the provinces, he wines and dines his people lavishly. If God treats us in this manner, we will know that He is truly King and we will serve Him; but if He does not, we will rebel.'

The Rabbis claim that the Jews applied a different test. *Scripture (Exodus* 16:7) states: עַל רִיב בְּנֵי יִשְׂרָאֵל וְעַל נַסֹּתָם אֶת ה׳ לֵאמֹר הֲיֵשׁ ה׳ בְּקִרְבֵּנוּ אִם אָיִן, *because of the strife of the Children of Israel and because they tested HASHEM saying, 'Is HASHEM in our midst or not?'* [i.e., they sought God's constant Presence]. This refers to an ultimatum which the Jews presented: If God can fathom our inner thoughts and desires, thus proving that He is *in our midst,* we shall serve Him; but if He does not know these desires, then He is not in our midst and we will refuse to serve Him.[1]

[This *Midrash Tanchuma* provides us with an example of how terribly one may err by studying Scripture without the benefit of the תּוֹרָה שֶׁבְּעַל פֶּה, *Oral Law.*

A superficial reading of the Biblical narrative would leave one with the false impression that the Israelites in the desert were a motley band of refugees who, having experienced oppression and deprivation, now tried desperately to make up lost time with endless *materialistic* demands.

Yet the *Midrash* teaches that these Jews were noble men of unparalleled devotion. All of their demands were actually spiritual: they sought God's closeness so that their souls would be suffused with His sanctity. Their sin was that they made firm demands rather than humble *requests,* and that they challenged God to meet these demands.

How ludicrous, then, is the arrogance of those who look down upon the generation of the wilderness and label them as Jews of little faith! Our ancestors were giants of the spirit; in comparison to them, we are less than dwarfs, for our souls are all but smothered by physical desires.]

לִשְׁאָל אֹכֶל לְנַפְשָׁם — *By requesting food they could crave.*

[The word נֶפֶשׁ, *soul,* also means *desire* or *craving* (see *Genesis* 23:8).

The children of Israel drew so close to God in the wilderness that they resembled celestial beings. Even their food, the manna, was unique, as verse 25 states, לֶחֶם אַבִּירִים אָכַל אִישׁ, *man ate the bread of angels.*

Despite its superb taste, however, the

1. *Shemos Rabbah* (21:10) describes God's boundless generosity: זֶה אַרְבָּעִים שָׁנָה ה׳ אֱלֹהֶיךָ עִמָּךְ לֹא חָסַרְתָּ דָּבָר, *These forty years HASHEM your God has been with you; you have lacked nothing.* All that they *did* require was דָּבָר which can be translated *a thing,* but which literally means *a word.* This suggests that they had only to express their wish, and it was fulfilled immediately. R' Shimon maintains that speech was unnecessary; in his view, they merely had to think of their desire, and God fulfilled it.

by requesting food they could crave.
19 *And they spoke against God! They said,*
'Can God prepare a table in the wilderness?
20 *Behold, he struck a rock and water flowed*
and streams flooded forth —

manna was not a physical food and therefore, the human body could not develop a craving for it. Manna was purely functional. The Jews ate this ethereal, heavenly food because their rational mind dictated that since man requires energy to live and serve God, he should eat the manna, which was the most efficient nutrient possible.

The masses could not live up to the spiritual demands of the manna. Although they were only a little lower then the angels, the people were still affected by a (natural) human desire for food which they could crave.

They complained, 'וְעַתָּה נַפְשֵׁנוּ יְבֵשָׁה אֵין כֹּל בִּלְתִּי אֶל הַמָּן עֵינֵינוּ, *But now our soul* [i.e., our craving] *is shriveled; there is nothing at all besides the manna before our eyes'* (*Numbers* 11:6).

Therefore, the people הִתְאַוּוּ תַּאֲוָה, *lusted for a lust* (*Numbers* 11:4), which means literally that they yearned for something for which they could feel a lustful craving.

However, the manna did create in man the craving to study Torah and to know the ways of God. Had they been virtuous, the people would have found contentment in this spiritual pursuit. (See *Alshich. Numbers* 11:4, and *Introduction* to *Shav Shmaitza*, חַזוּת).]

19. וַיְדַבְּרוּ בֵּאלֹהִים — *And they spoke against God!*

The psalmist now records the mutinous thoughts which they harbored in their hearts (*Radak*).

אָמְרוּ הֲיוּכַל אֵל לַעֲרֹךְ שֻׁלְחָן בַּמִּדְבָּר — *They said, 'Can God prepare a table in the wilderness?'*

They said: 'We know that even in the desert God is capable of supplying individual sources of food, such as water or manna, but can He *prepare a* [*full*] *table* of all types of nourishment? Can He even supply meat?'

They reasoned, moreover, 'The manna is not such an extraordinary thing, because solid nutrients also descend from the sky in the form of snow or hailstones; nor is water from a rock so remarkable, for moisture often condenses and collects under a cool boulder; but meat has never come down from the desert skies!' (*Radak*).

According to the *Midrash* (*Shemos Rabbah* 25:7), the nations of the world doubted that God could supply any provisions at all for the Jews in the desert. God therefore opened the gates of heaven and rained down so much manna that it piled up to towering heights which were visible from great distances. The psalmist referred to this in the verse *You prepare a table before me, in full view of my tormentors* (23:5). The verse continues, *You anointed my head with oil* — which alludes to the fatty meat of the שְׂלָיו, *quail*. It concludes *my cup overflows* — which alludes to the waters of Miriam's well.

20. הֵן הִכָּה צוּר וַיָּזוּבוּ מַיִם — *'Behold, he struck a rock and waters flowed.'*

According to *Radak*, this refers to the *rock* which Moses *smote* at Rephidim (Exodus 17:6) at the beginning of the forty year journey in the wilderness.

The *Midrash* (*Bamidbar Rabbah* 19:9) teaches that this verse alludes to the incident of מֵי מְרִיבָה, *Waters of Strife*, which took place at the end of the forty years in the wilderness (*Numbers* 20:7-14).

God told Moses to speak to the rock,

הֲגַם־לֶחֶם יוּכַל תֵּת אִם־יָכִין שְׁאֵר לְעַמּוֹ׃
כא לָכֵן | שָׁמַע יהוה וַיִּתְעַבָּר וְאֵשׁ נִשְּׂקָה
כב בְיַעֲקֹב וְגַם־אַף עָלָה בְיִשְׂרָאֵל׃ כִּי לֹא
הֶאֱמִינוּ בֵּאלֹהִים וְלֹא בָטְחוּ בִּישׁוּעָתוֹ׃
כג וַיְצַו שְׁחָקִים מִמָּעַל וְדַלְתֵי שָׁמַיִם פָּתָח׃

but instead, he hit it twice. The first blow brought forth only a few drops, for Scripture states, *he smote a rock and waters* יָזוּבוּ, *trickled forth.* Some Jews mocked Moses, asking scornfully,'Son of Amram, are these meager waters meant only for nursing infants or for weaned babes?'

וּנְחָלִים יִשְׁטֹפוּ – *'And streams flooded forth.'*

Moses took offense at this jest, and smote the rock a second time, releasing a torrent which drowned those who had mocked him, as Scripture implies in the words *and streams overflowed (Bamidbar Rabbah* 19:9).

הֲגַם לֶחֶם יוּכַל תֵּת – *'Can He give even bread?'*

Ibn Ezra and *Radak* translate לֶחֶם as *meat,* as in קָרְבָּנִי לַחְמִי, *My sacrifice* [of flesh] *My bread (Numbers* 28:2). This refers to the improper request for meat at קִבְרוֹת הַתַּאֲוָה, *Graves of Desire (Numbers* 11:4-6).

אִם יָכִין שְׁאֵר לְעַמּוֹ – *'Can He supply meat* [lit. *flesh*] *for His nation?*

This refers to the similar query which was expressed in *Numbers* 11:13 *(Ibn Ezra).* [See *comm.* to *v.* 27 concerning the implications of the word שְׁאֵר, *flesh.*]

21. לָכֵן שָׁמַע ה׳ וַיִּתְעַבָּר – *Therefore HASHEM heard and was enraged.*

Although they never expressed aloud their doubts about God's ability, God *heard* their unspoken thoughts and was angered *(Radak).*

וְאֵשׁ נִשְּׂקָה בְיַעֲקֹב – *And a fire was kindled against Jacob.*

Rashi observes that נִשְּׂקָה is related to הֵיסֵק, *to ignite.*

Radak explains that the eleventh chapter of *Numbers* relates two tragic episodes which occurred in the very same place. The people were מִתְאֹנְנִים, *complaining,* against God. They did not believe that God could take them into the land of Canaan and miraculously destroy their enemies. The people had no faith in God and were determined to fight for themselves. They demanded that spies be sent to scout the land, so that they could prepare for conventional battle [see *Deuteronomy* 1:21-22].

Because of their brazen lack of faith, *a fire was kindled against Jacob,* as *Numbers* 11:1, 3 states: *And HASHEM heard, and His wrath flared, and the fire of HASHEM burnt in their midst, and it consumed those in the outermost part of the camp ... And he* [Moses] *called the name of that place* תַּבְעֵרָה, *Conflagration, because the fire of HASHEM burnt in their midst.*

וְגַם אַף עָלָה בְיִשְׂרָאֵל – *And wrath also flared against Israel.*

After the fires of תַּבְעֵרָה died, a new cry of protest was heard from the camp, and they stirred up a craving for meat. Then, וַיִּחַר אַף ה׳ מְאֹד, *the wrath of HASHEM burned greatly (Numbers* 11:10). Those who fomented this protest were slain by the hand of God and were buried on the spot in קִבְרוֹת הַתַּאֲוָה, *Graves of Desire,* synonymous with תַּבְעֵרָה *(Radak).*

Malbim (Numbers 11:10) explains that although only a small group of sinners actually protested, *God's wrath flared against* [all of] *Israel.* However,

Can He give even bread?
Can He supply meat for His nation?'
21 *Therefore HASHEM heard and was enraged*
and a fire was kindled against Jacob,
and wrath also flared against Israel.
22 *For they had no faith in God,*
and trusted not in His salvation.
23 *Though He instructed the clouds above,*
and the doors of heaven He opened,

the heavenly fire burned only יַעֲקֹב, *Jacob*, which signfies the lowest stratum of the nation, i.e., the actual sinners. [When the Patriarch Jacob reached his highest spiritual level, God gave him the additional name Israel *(Genesis* 32:29). Therefore, the greatest Jews are symbolically referred to as Israel; while the masses are called Jacob.]

22. כִּי לֹא הֶאֱמִינוּ בֵּאלֹהִים – *For they had no faith in God.*

They tested God because they had no faith in His ability to supply them with meat in the desert *(Radak).*

וְלֹא בָטְחוּ בִּישׁוּעָתוֹ – *And trusted not in His salvation.*

Neither did they believe that God could destroy their enemies, and enable them so to enter Canaan unopposed *(Radak).*

23. וַיְצַו שְׁחָקִים מִמָּעַל – *Though He instructed the clouds above.*

The Israelites had been granted unparalleled miracles — such as the manna, which fell from the clouds above. Such miracles should have reinforced their belief; as a result their faithlessness to God was particularly condemnable *(Ibn Ezra; Radak).*

The *Talmud (Chagigah* 12b) states that there are seven levels of רָקִיעַ, *firmament.* The lowest is וילון [*vilon*], *curtain.* The second lowest level is שְׁחָקִים, *clouds,* which literally means *grinders,* for in this firmament stands a 'mill' which grinds up manna to be eaten by the righteous in the Hereafter. [The 'mill' refers to the transitionary process which enables a purely spiritual food to become capable of ingestion by physical beings.]

וְדַלְתֵי שָׁמַיִם פָּתָח – *And the doors of heaven He opened.*

Alshich offers a profound insight: Every physical substance on earth originated as a spiritual force emanating from the highest firmament, the lofty realm of the Divine. This spiritual force descended through each layer of heaven and eventually assumed its material form on earth. The descent was gradual and, at each level, the spiritual form was 'cloaked' with another 'loaf' of physical being.

The manna, however, was unique. It did not pass through the many layers of firmament, nor did it descend through the וילון, *curtain,* which serves as the final 'cloak' of the material world. God merely *opened the doors of heaven,* and the manna fell straight down, with its purity unadulterated. Therefore, the manna was a pure nutrient, containing no residue or waste matter.

כד וַיַּמְטֵר עֲלֵיהֶם מָן לֶאֱכֹל וּדְגַן־שָׁמַיִם נָתַן
כה לָמוֹ: לֶחֶם אַבִּירִים אָכַל אִישׁ צֵידָה שָׁלַח
כו לָהֶם לָשֹׂבַע: יַסַּע קָדִים בַּשָּׁמָיִם וַיְנַהֵג

24. וַיַּמְטֵר עֲלֵיהֶם מָן לֶאֱכֹל — *And rained upon them manna to eat.*

[When the manna fell it was ready to eat, so that the Jews could be free to spend their time on loftier pursuits. This is the intent of the *Mechilta (Beshalach* 17:16), which teaches that the privilege of expounding upon the Torah was given only to those who (divorced themselves from material pursuits and) ate manna.

In addition, the man who ate manna became suffused with intense faith in God. When the people first saw the manna, they asked, 'מָן הוּא, *what is it?'* (*Exodus* 16:15). It is significant that the letters of מָן הוּא also form the word אֱמוּנָה, *faith.*]

וּדְגַן שָׁמַיִם נָתַן לָמוֹ — *And the grain of heaven He gave them.*

Although the manna fell ready to eat — like bread — it could also be ground and used — like unprocessed grain — to make a variety of delicacies *(Kiflayim L'tushia).*

[The benediction recited over bread is הַמּוֹצִיא לֶחֶם מִן הָאָרֶץ, *Blessed be He Who brings forth bread from the earth.* Torah scholars have disagreed concerning which blessing was recited over the manna (see *Bnai Yissochor, Sabbath Maamar* 3:1).

Sefer Chassidim (1640) contends that the proper benediction was הַמּוֹצִיא לֶחֶם מִן הַשָּׁמַיִם, *Blessed be He Who brings forth bread from heaven,* but other rabbis maintain that no blessing was necessary. The *Talmud (Berachos* 35a) states: It is forbidden to derive pleasure from עוֹלָם הַזֶּה, *This World,* without reciting a benediction. However, since the manna had its source in heaven, rather than in This World, the rabbis held that it did not require any benediction *(Pardes Yosef, Beshalach* 16:4).]

25. לֶחֶם אַבִּירִים אָכַל אִישׁ — *The bread of angels* [lit. *of the powerful*] *mankind ate.*

The *Talmud (Yoma* 75b) cites R' Akiva's statement that manna was the food of אַבִּירִים, *angels.* R' Yishmael asks rhetorically, 'Do angels really eat?' [R' Akiva evidently understands the words *bread* and *eat* figuratively. Although angels do not need food, they do require a constant flow of Divine will and Divine illumination to sustain them. Since the manna contained sparks of Divine light, it not only strengthened the body, but also fortified the soul.

Shevet M'Yisrael cites the dictum of the Sages *(Bava Metzia* 86b) that the Children of Israel received the manna because of the merit of Abraham, who provided bread and meat for the three angels who visited him. Since Abraham offered human food to angels, God rewarded him by offering angel food to his descendants — the seed of Abraham.]

R' Yishmael, however, renders אַבִּירִים as אֵבָרִים, *limbs.* In his view, the *bread* supplied energy which was completely absorbed by all the limbs of the body; no waste was produced to be eliminated from the body.[1]

אָכַל אִישׁ — *Mankind ate.*

According to *Midrash Shocher Tov,* the psalmist here refers to all of Israel collectively as אִישׁ, *one man.*

The *Talmud (Yoma* 75b) states that אִישׁ refers to Joshua. The measure of

1. *Ramban (comm.* to *Genesis* 2:17) cites the opinion of natural scientists who claim that death was man's preordained lot from the beginning of Creation. Adam was sustained by the earth's products which are subject to decay. Therefore it was inevitable that Adam had to eventually die and decompose.

[24] *And rained upon them manna to eat,
and the grain of heaven He gave them.*
[25] *The bread of angels mankind ate,
provision He sent them for satisfaction.*
[26] *He made the east wind blow
in heaven*

manna granted him equaled the portions of the entire congregation of Israel put together. In this interpretation, the word אַבִּירִים would be rendered *powerful ones*, and it refers to the entire nation. Thus, Joshua, the *man*, was given a portion equal to the sum total of theirs.

This statement seems to contradict the Torah's teaching that every person received an equal measure of manna. *Scripture (Exodus* 16:18) states that even if one man gathered more manna and another man gathered less, when they came home they discovered that their baskets each contained precisely one *omer* measure.

In his commentary to *Numbers* 1:4, *Malbim* explains that manna had a dual identity: it was לֶחֶם, *bread*, in its external appearance, but אַבִּירִים, *angel food*, in its inner essence. Since the ignorant people completely ignored the Divine nature of the manna, it became for them nothing but bread to satisfy their physical hunger; it was *not* absorbed in their limbs and it did not turn into a wondrous variety of tastes.

The wise, however, recognized the true blessing of the manna and appreciated their unique opportunity for spiritual growth. Thus every soul was illuminated to the extent that it sought the spiritual nourishment contained in the manna. Because no one's desire for wisdom equaled that of the diligent student Joshua, he extracted from the manna a spiritual portion which equaled that of all Israel combined.

צֵידָה שָׁלַח לָהֶם לָשֹׂבַע – *Provision He sent them for satisfaction.*

[Not only was the manna nutritious and satisfying, but it was also sent in a sanitary package of fresh dew which fell conveniently wherever they camped. Thus, there was no need to carry cumbersome packs of provisions through the desert (see *Radak).*

The *Talmud (Berachos* 48a) says that Moses composed the *Bircas HaMazon* [Grace after Meals] for Israel when they started to eat the manna and became content (see *Gilyonei HaShas, Berachos* 48b).]

26. יַסַּע קָדִים בַּשָּׁמָיִם – *He made the east wind blow in heaven.*

[In verse 21, the psalmist began to recount God's wrath over Israel's demand for meat. He departed from that theme to describe the miraculous gift of the manna, which truly made meat unnecessary. It is interesting to note that the Torah (*Numbers* 11:4-9) also provides a lengthy description of the manna immediately after relating the Jews' protest over meat. Now the psalmist returns to the original theme and describes how God supplied birds for meat.]

Scripture relates: *And a wind blew from Hashem and brought quails from the sea (Numbers* 11:31). This was a southeasterly wind *(Radak).*

Ramban disagrees with the scientists and observes that primeval man was immortal. The food which Adam ate before he sinned resembled ethereal manna which absorbed into the limbs and did not decompose. Only after the sin was Adam's diet changed to regular, degradable food, which rendered Adam susceptible to death and decomposition.

כז בְּעֻזּוֹ תֵימָן: וַיַּמְטֵר עֲלֵיהֶם כֶּעָפָר שְׁאֵר
כח וּכְחוֹל יַמִּים עוֹף כָּנָף: וַיַּפֵּל בְּקֶרֶב מַחֲנֵהוּ
כט סָבִיב לְמִשְׁכְּנֹתָיו: וַיֹּאכְלוּ וַיִּשְׂבְּעוּ מְאֹד
ל וְתַאֲוָתָם יָבִא לָהֶם: לֹא־זָרוּ מִתַּאֲוָתָם
לא עוֹד אָכְלָם בְּפִיהֶם: וְאַף אֱלֹהִים | עָלָה
בָהֶם וַיַּהֲרֹג בְּמִשְׁמַנֵּיהֶם וּבַחוּרֵי יִשְׂרָאֵל

וַיְנַהֵג בְּעֻזּוֹ תֵימָן — *And with His strength He steered the south wind.*

Hirsch explains that the sea was to the east of their camp and the quail were actually situated to the southeast. Thus an east wind was needed to steer the quail across the sea, and a southerly wind was necessary to blow the quail towards the Israelite camp.

27. וַיַּמְטֵר עֲלֵיהֶם כֶּעָפָר שְׁאֵר — *He rained upon them meat like dust.*

The first wonder was that the quail fell in abundance, like teeming rain *(Alshich; Radak).*

[Ordinarily, the word שְׁאֵר, *meat, flesh,* is used figuratively in reference to a close relative [see *Leviticus* 18:6].

The *Midrash (Bamidbar Rabbah* 15:24) explains that with this uncommon usage, the psalmist alludes to the fact that although the children of Israel expressed a desire for animal flesh, they actually were motivated by carnal desire for forbidden flesh. This craving was a result of the restrictions which the Torah had recently imposed upon them, in forbidding unions with close שְׁאֵר, *flesh,* meaning *relatives.*

Therefore, when the Jews seemed to be mourning their lack of meat, the Torah reveals (*Numbers* 11:10), *And Moses heard the people weeping* לְמִשְׁפְּחֹתָיו, *over their families,* which signifies 'over the restrictions placed over their family life.']

וּכְחוֹל יַמִּים עוֹף כָּנָף — *And winged birds like the sand of the seas.*

The second wonder was that the quail fell to the ground, despite the fact that birds in flight normally remain securely airborne. When the quail dropped to the ground like dead weight, they resembled sand settled on the shore of the sea *(Alshich).*

28. וַיַּפֵּל בְּקֶרֶב מַחֲנֵהוּ — *And He dropped it amidst His camp.*

The third wonder was that God guided the flight pattern of the quail so that they landed precisely in the middle of the camp *(Alshich),* as *Numbers* 11:3 states: וַיִּטֹּשׁ עַל הַמַּחֲנֶה — *And they fell upon the camp (Radak).*

סָבִיב לְמִשְׁכְּנוֹתָיו — *Around His dwellings.*

Scripture continues: *About a day's journey on this side [of the camp] and about a day's journey on the other side round about the camp, and about two cubits high on the face of the earth (Numbers* 11:31).

Although these birds usually flee from areas inhabited by man, in this case they crowded around the camp *(Alshich).*

29. וַיֹּאכְלוּ וַיִּשְׂבְּעוּ מְאֹד — *Then they ate and were very sated.*

They ate far too much of this fowl. In *Numbers* 11:20, God warned: *You shall eat ...* עַד אֲשֶׁר יֵצֵא מֵאַפְּכֶם, *until it comes out of your nostrils (Radak).*

וְתַאֲוָתָם יָבִא לָהֶם — *For He brought them their craving.*

The translation follows *Ibn Ezra.* However, *Alshich* renders: *And their craving was that He should bring [more] to them;* i.e., they continued to crave more and more meat.

Alshich adds that this alludes to the

And with His strength
He steered the south wind.
27 *He rained upon them meat like dust*
and winged birds like the sand of the seas,
28 *And He dropped it amidst His camp,*
around His dwellings.
29 *Then they ate and were very sated,*
for He brought them their craving.
30 *They had not yet loathed their craving,*
their food was still in their mouth,
31 *When the wrath of God rose against them*
and slew their most corpulent;
The chosen of Israel
He bent over.

opinion of the Sages that the repetitive phrase הִתְאַוּוּ תַּאֲוָה, *they craved a craving* (*Numbers* 11:4) means that they really desired both animal flesh and carnal pleasure. Therefore, even after they had their fill of meat, they still wanted God to bring them something more (see *comm.* to *Psalms* 78:20).

30. לֹא זָרוּ מִתַּאֲוָתָם — *They had not yet loathed their craving.*

God warned, *You shall eat so much,* וְהָיָה לָכֶם לְזָרָא, *it will be loathsome to you* (*Numbers* 11:20).

עוֹד אָכְלָם בְּפִיהֶם — *Their food was still in their mouth.*

But they never reached that point of loathing, for, *while the meat was yet between their teeth, before it was chewed, the wrath of HASHEM was inflamed against the people and HASHEM smote the people with a very great plague* [*Numbers* 11:33] (*Rashi; Radak; Ibn Ezra*).

31. וְאַף אֱלֹהִים עָלָה בָהֶם — *When the wrath of God rose against them.*

The sin of the Golden Calf had preceded this transgression. Since they were guilty of two offenses, God's anger against them was of great intensity (*Zerah Yaakov*).

וַיַּהֲרֹג בְּמִשְׁמַנֵּיהֶם — *And slew their most corpulent.*

According to *Radak*, this refers to the strong, healthy Jews. *Ibn Ezra* maintains that this signifies the rich pleasure seekers.

The *Midrash* (*Bamidbar Rabbah* 15:24) identifies מִשְׁמַנֵּיהֶם as the cream of Israelite society, the elite members of Sanhedrin. [Although they had been guilty of other sins prior to this event, this enormous sin provided God with an opportunity to punish them for all their misdeeds.]

וּבַחוּרֵי יִשְׂרָאֵל הִכְרִיעַ — *The chosen of Israel He bent over.*

The term בָּחוּר is usually applied to young men, youth. Literally, בָּחוּר means *chosen one*. Here it refers to the foremost sages of Israel, who were also smitten in this plague (*Rashi; Bamidbar Rabbah* 15:24).

Hirsch points out that the term כָּרַע is also found in *Judges* 5:27; it signifies the *bending* or *crumpling* of the body which occurs at death.

לב הִכְרִיעַ: בְּכָל־זֹאת חָטְאוּ־עוֹד וְלֹא
לג הֶאֱמִינוּ בְּנִפְלְאוֹתָיו: וַיְכַל־בַּהֶבֶל יְמֵיהֶם
לד וּשְׁנוֹתָם בַּבֶּהָלָה: אִם־הֲרָגָם וּדְרָשׁוּהוּ
לה וְשָׁבוּ וְשִׁחֲרוּ־אֵל: וַיִּזְכְּרוּ כִּי־אֱלֹהִים
לו צוּרָם וְאֵל עֶלְיוֹן גֹּאֲלָם: וַיְפַתּוּהוּ בְּפִיהֶם

32. בְּכָל זֹאת חָטְאוּ עוֹד — *Nevertheless, they transgressed further.*

The incident of the quail was only one of their ten נִסְיוֹנוֹת, *challenges,* against God *(Ibn Ezra).*[1]

They continued to defy God's will by sending מְרַגְּלִים, *spies,* by joining Korach's rebellion against Moses, and by demanding water at מֵי מְרִיבָה, *the Waters of Strife (Radak).*

וְלֹא הֶאֱמִינוּ בְּנִפְלְאֹתָיו — *And had no faith in His wonders.*

They doubted God's ability to bring them safely into the Holy Land. They should have said, 'The God who performed wonders for us in Egypt can certainly repeat these miracles in Canaan' *(Alshich).*

33. וַיְכַל בַּהֶבֶל יְמֵיהֶם — *So He ended their days in vanity.*

All of the hardships which they endured in order to escape from the Egyptian bondage were in vain, because nothing came of the redemption. They left Egypt in order to enter the Holy Land; instead their corpses fell in the desolate wilderness *(Ibn Ezra).*

All those who had been twenty or over at the time of the sin of the spies were condemned to die during the forty year sojourn in the desert. The men died at the age of sixty *(Radak).*

[The sin of the spies took place on the Ninth of Av of the Jews' second year in the wilderness. Consequently, their punishment for the sin of believing the false report of the spies was also meted out on *Tishah b'Av* during their years in the wilderness; each year, the men who had reached the age of sixty died on that day.]

וּשְׁנוֹתָם בַּבֶּהָלָה — *And their years in terror.*

The *Midrash* relates that throughout their years in the wilderness, on the eve of the Ninth of Av, a herald would announce, 'Everyone go out and dig a

1. The *Mishnah (Avos* 5:6) states, 'With ten trials did our forefathers try the Holy One, Blessed be He, in the wilderness, as it is stated, *They have put me to the test ten times now, and have not hearkened to my voice (Numbers* 14:22).

The *Talmud (Arachin* 15a-b) recounts these ten trials. First, before crossing the Sea of Reeds, the Jews said to Moses, *Is it because there are no graves in Egypt that you took us to die in the wilderness? (Exodus* 14:11). Second, when they emerged from the Sea, they became contentious and said, 'Just as we are coming out safe on this side, so are the Egyptians emerging from the other side.' In order to calm them, God caused the Sea to spew forth the corpses of the drowned Egyptians (*Exodus* 14:30). Third, at *Marah,* they refused to drink the bitter water and murmured against Moses (*Exodus* 15:23-24). Fourth, at *Rephidim* there was no water and the people quarreled with Moses (*Exodus* 17:1-2). Fifth, although God warned the people that they were not to go out to search for Manna on the Sabbath, some people defied the warning and went out to gather some; they found none (*Exodus* 25-27). Sixth, earlier, Moses had commanded them to leave no manna from one morning to the next; yet some did save some manna, and it bred worms (*Exodus* 19-20). Seventh, the nation later complained about a lack of food and mourned for the 'luxuries' and 'fleshpots' which they had left behind in Egypt (*Exodus* 16:2-3). Eighth, they complained again about the Manna and demanded meat (*Numbers* 11:4-6). Ninth, they made the golden calf (*Exodus* 32). Tenth, in the wilderness of Paran, they dispatched spies, in defiance of the promises of God (*Numbers* 13-14).

[32] *Nevertheless, they transgressed further
and had no faith in His wonders.*
[33] *So He ended their days in vanity
and their years in terror.*
[34] *When He slew them —
then they would seek Him,
They would repent
and pray to God.*
[35] *They would remember that God was their rock,
and the Most High God their redeemer.*
[36] *They seduced Him with their mouths,*

grave. Every Israelite dug himself a grave and slept in it that night. The next morning, the herald would cry out, 'Let the living separate themselves from the dead!' The survivors left their graves in peace, while the dead [those who had reached sixty years of age] were buried in the graves where they slept.

Worms crawled from their navels up to their mouths and they died in the same ignominious fashion as did the spies [see *Taanis* 30b, *Tosafos* s.v. יוֹם שֶׁבּוֹ].

Although God, in His mercy, took the lives only of the sixty year olds, there was no guarantee that such would be the case every year. Thus, everyone felt fear that he might remain in his grave on the coming *Tishah b'Av* and this year might be his last on earth (*Alshich*).

34. אִם הֲרָגָם וּדְרָשׁוּהוּ — *When He slew them — then they would seek Him.*

Radak suggests that this may be understood in two ways. First, after the victims of God's wrath were slain for their transgressions, the survivors were aroused to seek out God. Second, following the sin of the מְרַגְּלִים, *spies*, when God condemned the entire congregation to death in the wilderness, they sought to appease Him by displaying new-found enthusiasm for entering Eretz Yisrael.

וְשָׁבוּ וְשִׁחֲרוּ אֵל — *They would repent and pray to God.*

The word שִׁחֲרוּ comes from שַׁחַר, *dawn*, because the earnest supplicant arises early to commune with his Maker before engaging in any other pursuit (*Ibn Ezra*).

Radak explains that it was at dawn that the Children of Israel frantically attempted to display their contrition for doubting God's ability to take them into the land: *And they rose up early in the morning and went to the top of the mountain saying, 'We are here and we shall go up to the place which HASHEM has promised, for we have sinned* (*Numbers* 14:40).

35. וַיִּזְכְּרוּ כִּי אֱלֹהִים צוּרָם — *They would remember that God was their rock.*

They came to understand that even when God appears as אֱלֹהִים, *the Dispenser of Strict Justice*, He is truly concerned with their welfare and desires to support them (*Zerah Yaakov*).

וְאֵל עֶלְיוֹן גֹּאֲלָם — *And the Most High God their Redeemer.*

They realized that the very God who redeemed them from Egypt was the Supreme Being who could take them into the land of Canaan (*Ibn Ezra*).

36. וַיְפַתּוּהוּ בְּפִיהֶם — *They seduced Him with their mouths.*

Although they went through the

לז וּבִלְשׁוֹנָם יְכַזְּבוּ־לוֹ: וְלִבָּם לֹא־נָכוֹן עִמּוֹ
לח וְלֹא נֶאֶמְנוּ בִּבְרִיתוֹ: וְהוּא רַחוּם | יְכַפֵּר
עָוֺן וְלֹא־יַשְׁחִית וְהִרְבָּה לְהָשִׁיב אַפּוֹ
לט וְלֹא־יָעִיר כָּל־חֲמָתוֹ: וַיִּזְכֹּר כִּי־בָשָׂר
מ הֵמָּה רוּחַ הוֹלֵךְ וְלֹא יָשׁוּב: כַּמָּה יַמְרוּהוּ

motions of sincere penitence (*v.* 34), God knew that their *beguiling* words were not sincere *(Radak).*

The *Tosefta (Bava Kama* 7:3) goes even further, claiming that Israel was *never* sincere towards God. Even when they proclaimed (*Exodus* 24:7) *'All that HASHEM has said* נַעֲשֶׂה וְנִשְׁמָע, *We will do and we will obey,'* they did not truly mean it, but they attempted to deceive God!

[However, in that instance God did not criticize them; instead, He praised their devotion and rewarded their loyalty by bestowing crowns of Divine glory upon them (*Shabbos* 88a).

Rabbi Boruch Sorotzkin Zt"l points out that in a moment of inspiration, a man's heart soars far beyond its ordinary bounds and he makes verbal commitments which exceed his normal abilities. Such enthusiasm is desirable, for it spurs man to challenges which would otherwise have been beyond his scope.

At Sinai, the Jews were swept away by a spiritual fervor. Thus, for that brief moment, they meant what they said — even though they were not really prepared to live up to it; but here, after they sinned, they deceitfully professed true repentance.

וּבִלְשׁוֹנָם יְכַזְּבוּ לוֹ — *And with their tongues they deceived Him.*

[The *comm.* on *v.* 18 cites the opinion that Israel was constantly testing God to determine whether He truly knew the thoughts of their hearts. According to this view, whenever the Jews sinned, it was because they imagined that God was unaware of their true intentions; therefore, they dared to *deceive Him with their tongues.*]

37. וְלִבָּם לֹא נָכוֹן עִמּוֹ — *But their heart was not constant with Him.*

Although they professed repentance, they had not sincerely resolved never to repeat their sins *(Sforno).*

וְלֹא נֶאֶמְנוּ בִּבְרִיתוֹ — *Nor were they faithful with His covenant.*

[At Sinai, they entered a solemn covenant to be loyal to God and to His commands, but later they betrayed this agreement.]

38. וְהוּא רַחוּם יְכַפֵּר עָוֺן — *But He, the Merciful One, is forgiving of iniquity.*

God knew that the 'penitence' of Israel was a worthless pretense. By definition, *teshuvah* (repentance) requires a change of heart. Nevertheless, other people might witness this display of apparent regret and imagine it to be genuine. If God were to ignore Israel's show of repentance, people might question His desire to forgive repentant transgressors.

Thus, in order to preserve His reputation as *the Merciful One,* and to encourage sincere pentitents, God even forgave tthe *iniquity* of the undeserving *(Radak).*[1]

1. This verse is recited at the beginning of the evening *(Maariv)* prayer service (*Rambam, Hilchos Tefillah* 9:9). The *Tur (Orach Chaim* 237) explains that the morning *(Shacharis)* prayer and the afternoon *(Minchah)* prayer correspond to the daily *Tamid* sacrifice in the Temple, which brought atonement for Israel. Since the *Tamid* was not brought at night, we seek atonement by praying, *He, the Merciful One, is forgiving of iniquity* — i.e., His forgiveness is granted even though we do not offer an evening sacrifice. [Therefore, this verse

and with their tongues they deceived Him.
37 *But their heart was not constant with Him,*
nor were they faithful with His covenant.
38 *But He, the Merciful One,*
is forgiving of iniquity, and does not destroy.
Frequently He withdraws His anger,
not arousing His entire rage.
39 *For He remembered that they were but flesh,*
a fleeting breath, not returning.
40 *How often they defied Him in the wilderness*

וְלֹא יַשְׁחִית — *And does not destroy.*

[The *Talmud (Bava Kama* 60b) states that when God gives the מַשְׁחִית, 'destroyer' (i.e., the Angel of Death) permission to wreak havoc, the destroyer smites both the guilty and the innocent. However, God gives the Angel of Death this power only on rare occasions, such as during the plague of the firstborn in Egypt. Ordinarily, the compassionate God holds the forces of violence in check (see *Alshich).*]

וְהִרְבָּה לְהָשִׁיב אַפּוֹ וְלֹא יָעִיר כָּל חֲמָתוֹ — *Frequently He withdraws His anger, not arousing His entire rage.*

Malbim differentiates between אַף, *anger*, which is openly displayed, and חֵמָה, *rage*, which is concealed in the heart (see *comm.* to *Psalms* 6:2).

As a result of Israel's sins, God's אַף, *anger* flared; and they were burnt by fire and stricken by plague. In His compassion, God agreed to *withdraw His anger* as much as possible, to minimize the damage inflicted on Israel.

However, He contained His חֵמָה, *rage* completely, because when *inner anger* and *outer rage* join, they create a destructive force of enormous power.

39. וַיִּזְכֹּר כִּי בָשָׂר הֵמָּה — *For He remembered that they were but flesh.*

This is the main reason for God's compassion for humanity. Who recognizes the frailty of man as well as his Maker? God Himself offered the following rationale for man's sins: How can man quash his desire for flesh if his physical body is no more than weak flesh? It is only natural for man to be attracted to a food which is similar to his own body *(Ibn Ezra; Radak).*

רוּחַ הוֹלֵךְ וְלֹא יָשׁוּב — *A fleeting breath, not returning.*

God sought to justify their conduct with an additional excuse: since his life is so short, how can man be blamed for wanting to grab a little pleasure from this world? *(Ibn Ezra).*

Moreover, God must be quick to forgive man while he still lives, for life lasts no longer than *a fleeting breath.*

Radak points out that this verse does not contradict our belief in תְּחִיַּת הַמֵּתִים, *the resurrection of the dead,* for that is an extraordinary miracle, outside the realm of nature.

40. כַּמָּה יַמְרוּהוּ בַמִּדְבָּר — *How often they defied Him in the wilderness.*

Israel put God to the test many times. Sometimes they were motivated by a perverse spirit of rebelliousness and stubbornness; rebelliousness spurred

should be recited even before *Maariv* on the eve of the Sabbath *(Eitz Yoseif, Otzar Hatefillos).*]

Tur continues that it was the custom to administer the punishment of מַלְקוֹת, *stripes*, just before nightfall, after the sins of the day were over. Since the stripes bring atonement and

מא בַּמִּדְבָּר יַעֲצִיבוּהוּ בִּישִׁימוֹן: וַיָּשׁוּבוּ
מב וַיְנַסּוּ אֵל וּקְדוֹשׁ יִשְׂרָאֵל הִתְווּ: לֹא־זָכְרוּ
מג אֶת־יָדוֹ יוֹם אֲשֶׁר־פָּדָם מִנִּי־צָר: אֲשֶׁר־
שָׂם בְּמִצְרַיִם אֹתוֹתָיו וּמוֹפְתָיו בִּשְׂדֵה־

the sins of the Golden Calf, Korach's revolt, and the incident at Beis Peor *(Malbim).*

יַעֲצִיבוּהוּ בִּישִׁימוֹן — *And caused Him grief in the desolation.*

At other times, they tested God because they were discouraged and frustrated by the endless desolation of the barren wasteland. Their dejection and grief led them to complain about the 'dull' manna and the lack of water *(Malbim).*

41. וַיָּשׁוּבוּ וַיְנַסּוּ אֵל — *Over and over they tested God.*

Even after they tested God with the *meat* and saw that their faithless behavior aroused His intense wrath, they stubbornly continued to test the Almighty, at מֵי מְרִיבָה, *the Waters of Strife,* and on many other occasions which are not enumerated in the Torah.

The psalmist refers to God as אֵל, which literally means *All Powerful* [*comm.* to 50:1 and footnote to 22:2], because their tests were prompted by their doubts concerning God's Omnipotence *(Radak).*

וּקְדוֹשׁ יִשְׂרָאֵל הִתְווּ — *And of the Holy One of Israel [they] demanded signs.*

תָּו is a *sign;* הִתְוָה means *to make a sign (Ezekiel* 9:4). Here the Israelites asked God for conclusive *signs* to answer their query (*Exodus* 17:7), *'Is HASHEM in our midst or not?'(Rashi).*

Radak renders הִתְווּ, *they drew boundaries,* to indicate that they made *signs* to denote God's imagined limitations.

As *the Holy One of Israel,* God had already demonstrated to the world His unlimited ability to perform miracles, yet Israel still questioned God's infinite power.

Hirsch explains that the generation of the wilderness believed that God's might and His providence did not extend to every area of life.

The purpose of the wandering in the wilderness was to instill complete faith that every aspect of existence, even the most mundane, is in the hands of God. To the extent that Israel lacked total trust in God, they reverted to the sort of spiritual degeneration which resulted in the destruction of the Tribe of Ephraim in the generation preceding the psalmist Assaf. (See *Pref. Remarks).*

42. לֹא זָכְרוּ אֶת יָדוֹ — *They remembered not His hand.*

[Now the psalmist launches into a description of the miraculous plagues with which God punished Egypt. If the Jews had only remembered how intimately God's hand was involved in manipulating the course of nature in Egypt, then they would never have questioned His desire or His ability to control all of the forces in the wilderness.]

יוֹם אֲשֶׁר פָּדָם מִנִּי צָר — *[Nor] the day He redeemed them from the tormentor.*

Divine forgiveness, they would recite this verse three times during the procedure. The verse contains thirteen words [corresponding to God's thirteen attributes of Mercy] and three times thirteen equals thirty-nine, which is the standard number of stripes. [The custom to delete this verse before *Maariv* on the eve of the Sabbath and of Yom Tov is based on this, because stripes were not administered at such times *(Avudraham; Eitz Yoseif; Otzar Hatefillos).*]

The *Zohar Chadash* explains that as the darkness of night descends, the flames of *Gehinnom* [hell] blaze with greater fury. Therefore, we recite this verse then to remind God of His mercy. On Sabbath eve this is unnecessary, because the flames of hell die down on the day of rest.

and caused Him grief in the desolation!
41 Over and over they tested God
and of the Holy One of Israel
they demanded signs.
42 They remembered not His hand,
nor the day He redeemed them
from the tormentor.
43 How He set His signs in Egypt,
and His wonders in the field of Zoan,

Egypt was the most formidable society of that age, the most developed power, the world's mightiest overlord. Yet Israel watched as this awesome adversary was rendered powerless by God, while they — a weak and broken band of exhausted slaves — were suddenly catapulted to greatness. What could provide more conclusive evidence of God's Omnipotence *(Hirsch)?*

43. אֲשֶׁר שָׂם בְּמִצְרַיִם אֹתוֹתָיו — [*Nor*] *How He set His signs in Egypt.*

According to *Malbim*, אותות refers to *signs*, i.e., plagues preceded by advance warning, and מוֹפְתִים refers to *wonders*, punitive plagues which struck without prior warning. When God warned the Egyptians of the impending plague and clearly revealed the nature of the disaster which they were to expect, that was an אות, *sign*. The Egyptians were forewarned of the plague of דָּם, *blood*, צְפַרְדֵּעַ, *frogs*, עָרוֹב, *wild beasts*, דֶּבֶר, *pestilence*, בָּרָד, *hailstones*, אַרְבֶּה, *locusts*, and מַכַּת בְּכוֹרוֹת, *the smiting of the firstborn.*

These signs attested to God's ability to control all elements of nature.

The other plagues were מוֹפְתִים, *wonders*, which punished Egypt for its recalcitrance in responding to God's will.

Rabbi Shimon bar Yochai says that in each instance, Moses and Aaron warned Pharoah for seven days before the plague began; and the plague itself lasted twenty-three days (a total of one month). A seven day interval elapsed between one plague and the next (*Midrash Shocher Tov;* see *Shemos Rabbah* 9:14 and *Yefei Toar* ad. loc.).

Midrash Shocher Tov offers a different translation of these words: *He placed His signs on the Egyptians.* This suggests that the names and symptoms of all the plagues were actually imprinted on the skin of the guilty victims.

וּמוֹפְתָיו בִּשְׂדֵה צֹעַן — *And His wonders in the field of Zoan.*

Malbim explains that three plagues beset the Egyptians without any prior warning: כִּנִּים, *lice*, שְׁחִין, *boils*, and חֹשֶׁךְ, *darkness.* After each set of two *sign* plagues, the warnings of which the Egyptians had ignored, they were afflicted with a third *wonder* plague in order to punish them for their arrogance in disregarding God's word [see *Ramban* on *Exodus* 8:15 and *Hirsch*].

The אותות, *signs*, were calculated to cause the Egyptians to recognize and to obey God's will. The מוֹפְתִים, *wonders* occurred in the field of Zoan because their target was the abundance and prosperity of the land and its people.

Maharam Markado explains that only seven signs are described here, because only in regard to these seven did Moses make a statement such as, *And you shall know that I am HASHEM.* [See *Exodus* 7:17 (blood), 8:6 (frogs), 8:18 (wild beasts), 9:3 (pestilence), 9:14 (hail), 10:2 (locusts), and 11:4 (smiting of the Firstborn).]

In this psalm, God chastises Israel

מד צֹעַן: וַיַּהֲפֹךְ לְדָם יְאֹרֵיהֶם וְנֹזְלֵיהֶם בַּל־
מה יִשְׁתָּיוּן: יְשַׁלַּח בָּהֶם עָרֹב וַיֹּאכְלֵם
מו וּצְפַרְדֵּעַ וַתַּשְׁחִיתֵם: וַיִּתֵּן לֶחָסִיל יְבוּלָם

because in the wilderness they quickly forgot all of the *signs* which He had displayed in Egypt. Therefore, the psalmist emphasizes precisely those plagues which were specifically designated as vehicles for recognizing and resembling God's power. After witnessing these plagues, the Jews should never have doubted God's Omnipotence.

Chazoh Zion adds that a human king always tries to catch his enemy unaware, for surprise is an important element in a successful attack. The King of kings, however, issued explicit warnings with details of the plagues with which He would punish Pharoah and Egypt.

44. וַיַּהֲפֹךְ לְדָם יְאֹרֵיהֶם – *And changed their rivers into blood.*

The Egyptians worshipped the Nile River, its tributaries and its irrigation canals. Whenever God punishes a nation, He strikes first at their gods; therefore, the very first plague transformed the river into putrid blood.

In addition, the Egyptians tried to prevent Jewish wives from immersing themselves in a מִקְוָה, *ritual bath*, following menstruation. Therefore, God punished them by changing the river where *they* bathed into blood *(Kesef Mezukak)*.

The *Midrash* also stresses that each plague represented punishment for a particular wrong that the Egyptians did to the Jews. Since they forced Jews to labor as lowly drawers of water, their waters were turned to blood.[1]

וְנוֹזְלֵיהֶם בַּל יִשְׁתָּיוּן – *And their flowing waters He made undrinkable.*

Hirsch explains that יְאֹרֵיהֶם refers to channels diverted from the Nile to irrigate the soil; נוֹזְלֵיהֶם refers to their drinking water.

An Israelite and an Egyptian went to fill their jugs at the fountain. The Jew drew out water while the gentile found his pail filled with blood. The clever Egyptian made a proposal to the Israelite, 'Come, let us fill up one jug together.' When they put their lips to the jug to drink at the same time, the Jew sipped fresh water while the gentile quaffed a mouthful of blood.

The only way the Egyptian could drink was if he purchased water from the Jew. The arrangement reaped handsome profits for Israel and made them wealthy (*Midrash Shocher Tov; Shemos Rabbah* 9:10).

45. יְשַׁלַּח בָּהֶם עָרֹב וַיֹּאכְלֵם – *He sent against them a mixture of beasts which devoured them.*

This too was appropriate punishment, because the Egyptians degraded the Jewish men by assigning them the job of babysitting for Egyptian children. Therefore, God sent wild beasts to devour the children *(Midrash; Tehillos Hashem)*.

According to *Midrash Shocher Tov,*

1. *Midrash Tanchumah* points out that the sequence of the plagues corresponds to the strategy of a general laying siege to a rebellious city. Thus, the plague of blood corresponds to poisoning the city's water supply; the frogs, to trumpeters whose terrifying noise sows fear amongst the inhabitants; the lice, to arrows shot into the city; the wild animals, to barbaric mercenaries sent as shock troops to make the initial assault on the fortifications; the pestilence, to a deadly disease with which the enemy infects the city; the boils, to chemicals used to burn the people's skin; the hailstones, to heavy missiles with which the enemy smashes the city's walls; the locusts, to vast enemy legions which swarm over the city and overwhelm it; the darkness, to imprisonment of the enemy in dark dungeons; the slaying of the firstborn, to execution of the ringleaders responsible for the insurrection. [See *ArtScroll Haggadah* p. 128.]

[44] *And changed their rivers into blood
and their flowing waters He made undrinkable.*
[45] *He sent against them a mixture of beasts
which devoured them,
And frogs
that brought them ruin.*
[46] *And He gave the* chasil *their crop,*

they were first attacked by swooping ferocious birds sweeping down from above and then they were mangled by lions, tigers, and bears from below.

Normally a beast is fearless only when it is in its accustomed hunting ground; when it is uprooted to alien surroundings, it becomes intimidated. Therefore, when God transported the beasts to Egypt, He miraculously transported with them their natural habitats *(Peh Kadosh, Exodus* 8:17).

Ibn Ezra explains that although the frogs actually were sent before the beasts, the plague of wild beasts is mentioned first because it was so much more severe.

Malbim points out that of the seven plagues which came with prior warning, six came in double form (the plague of blood was the exception). For instance, when God brought the עָרוֹב, *beasts,* upon Egypt, all the creatures in the world swarmed over the land, including frogs. If so, why was it necessary for God to send a special plague of *frogs*? The frogs were not sent primarily as a punishment, but as an extra opportunity to display God's power. Accordingly, the frogs are mentioned here after the beasts, to indicate their secondary role (see *Alshich).*

וּצְפַרְדֵּעַ וַתַּשְׁחִיתֵם — *And frogs that brought them ruin.*

The swarms and multitudes of frogs are described in the singular because one frog emerged from the river first and bred myriads of others *(Shemos Rabbah* 10).

The Egyptians thought that their solid marble palaces would keep out the frogs, but the creatures declared, 'We are messengers sent by Almighty God!' Then the massive stone blocks shattered before them *(Midrash Shocher Tov).*

The frogs mutilated the bodies of the Egyptians; וַתַּשְׁחִיתֵם, *they castrated them,* and *ruined* their ability to procreate *(Rashi).*

[This punishment was inflicted because the Egyptians had tried to curtail the prolific fertility of the Jews *(Exodus* 1:12).]

46. **וַיִּתֵּן לֶחָסִיל יְבוּלָם** — *And He gave the* chasil *their crop.*

Since the Egyptians had forced the Israelites to tend their farms and vineyards, locusts were sent to consume all that grew there *(Midrash Tanchuma).*[1]

1. The prophet *Joel* (1:4) speaks of four species of locusts: *gozzom, arbeh, yellek,* and *chasil.* These attacked the land of Israel in his times and *the likes of these never existed in past times, nor will ever exist afterwards (Joel* 2:2).

The Torah describes the plague of locusts in Moses' time in similar terms: *Before them there were no such locusts as they, nor will there ever be afterwards (Exodus* 10:14). *Rashi* notes there that this apparently contradicts the account in Joel.

Rashi explains that although the total number of locusts in Joel's time was never equalled, that multitude was composed of four different species of locusts as listed above. The plague in Moses' time was composed of fewer locusts, but they were all of a single species, *arbeh.* Never in history did such a mass of a single species of locusts converge on a country.

Ramban (Exodus 10:14) challenges *Rashi's* theory, citing this verse as proof that not only

מז וְיגִיעָם לָאַרְבֶּה: יַהֲרֹג בַּבָּרָד גַּפְנָם
מח וְשִׁקְמוֹתָם בַּחֲנָמַל: וַיַּסְגֵּר לַבָּרָד בְּעִירָם
מט וּמִקְנֵיהֶם לָרְשָׁפִים: יְשַׁלַּח־בָּם | חֲרוֹן אַפּוֹ
עֶבְרָה וָזַעַם וְצָרָה מִשְׁלַחַת מַלְאֲכֵי
נ רָעִים: יְפַלֵּס נָתִיב לְאַפּוֹ לֹא־חָשַׂךְ מִמָּוֶת

וִיגִיעָם לָאַרְבֶּה – *And their wearying labor to the locust.*

[Not only is אַרְבֶּה the name of an individual species of these insects, but it is also their generic name because these creatures always come in tremendous hordes, and the root of אַרְבֶּה is רַב, *many.*]

47. יַהֲרֹג בַּבָּרָד גַּפְנָם – *He killed their vines with hail.*

Since the Egyptians forced the Jews to be stonecutters, hailstones were rained upon them *(Midrash Tanchumah).*

The *hail* is another example of an apparently unnecessary plague, since the locusts would afterwards devour all the vegetation. Although the main punishment was the omminous locusts, the hailstones were sent to display God's awesome might. For this reason, the psalmist here records locusts *before* hailstones, reversing their actual chronological order *(Malbim).*

וְשִׁקְמוֹתָם בַּחֲנָמַל – *And their* shikmah *trees with* chanamal.

Radak and *Metzudas Zion* describe the *shikmah* as a type of fig tree (see *Amos* 7:14) [others translate it as *sycamore*]. Although the plagues devastated all forms of flora, the psalmist singled out the vines and the *shikmah* because they comprise the majority of the vegetation of Egypt.

Rashi identifies חֲנָמַל, *chanamal,* as a species of locust, quoting *Midrash Shocher Tov* which renders בַּחֲנָמַל as a contraction of the words בָּא חָן וּמָל, *it came, encamped,* and *cut down.*

Radak cites *Rav Saadiah Gaon,* who translates חֲנָמַל as *hailstones* which were so large that they broke down trees as they fell (see *Ibn Ezra).*

48. וַיַּסְגֵּר לַבָּרָד בְּעִירָם – *He delivered their cattle to the hail.*

The translation follows *Targum* and *Metzudas Zion.*

Rashi renders וַיַּסְגֵּר as *He barred the way,* for when the Egyptian herdsmen saw the hailstones beginning to fall, they quickly attempted to lead their livestock to shelter. However, the hailstones formed a massive wall which barred their passage.

וּמִקְנֵיהֶם לָרְשָׁפִים – *And their flocks to fiery bolts.*

Targum, Radak and *Ibn Ezra* propose this translation of רְשָׁפִים based on the fact that the hailstones defied the established laws of nature, for fire *flared up amidst the hail (Exodus* 9:24).

Rashi, however, renders רְשָׁפִים as *soaring birds* (based on *Job* 5:7). When the Egyptian herdsmen saw that the mounds of hailstones prevented them from saving their flocks, they quickly slaughtered some animals and attempted to carry the carcasses home on their shoulders. Suddenly swift birds swooped from the sky and snatched the carcasses away.

the *arbeh* species but also the *chasil* species of locusts attacked Egypt. *Ramban* explains that the plague of *locusts* in Egypt was unique because locusts normally descend only upon an arid land. Thus the appearance of locust hordes in the most humid Nile River basin was truly an unsurpassed wonder.

and their wearying labor to the locust.
47 *He killed their vines with hail,*
and their shikmah *trees with* chanamal.
48 *He delivered their cattle to the hail*
and their flocks to fiery bolts.
49 *He dispatches against them*
His fierceful anger,
Wrath, rage, and distress,
a delegation of evil messengers.
50 *He leveled a path for His anger,*
He spared not their soul from death,

49. יְשַׁלַּח בָּם חֲרוֹן אַפּוֹ — *He dispatches against them His fierceful anger.*

Ibn Ezra maintains that this refers to the plague of hail, which was so terrifying and intimidating that Pharoah afterwards confessed, *'I have sinned this time; HASHEM is righteous and I and my nation are wicked'* (Exodus 9:27).

R' Eliezer interprets *fierceful anger* as a description of the Ten Plagues each of which was fourfold in nature: *Wrath, rage, distress, and a delegation of evil messengers.* These four parts of the plague parallel the four elements: Air, water, fire, and earth. R' Akiba understands that each plague contained five parts — their composite being, identified here as *fierceful anger*, representing the fifth *(Akeidas Yitzchak; see Haggadah,* ArtScroll ed.).

עֶבְרָה וָזַעַם וְצָרָה — *Wrath, rage, and distress.*

According to *Radak*, this entire verse is a general reference to all of the ten plagues which manifested the full intensity of God's awesome wrath.

Hirsch identifies the root of עֶבְרָה as לעבר, *to overstep*, certain boundaries, alluding to an anger which is so overwhelming as to defy containment. According to *Hirsch*, זַעַם implies Divine wrath which strikes its target visibly and directly. It is apparently related to לזהם, *to loathe.*

מִשְׁלַחַת מַלְאֲכֵי רָעִים — *A delegation of evil messengers* [lit. *angels*].

Every plague was a message dispatched by God to convey a lesson to the Egyptians *(Radak).*

The psalmist chooses his words carefully. He does not say מַלְאָכִים רָעִים, *evil angels*, rather מַלְאֲכֵי רָעִים, *the angels of the evil ones*, i.e., the evil forces of the wicked which come back to punish them *(Chazah Zion).*

50. יְפַלֵּס נָתִיב לְאַפּוֹ — *He leveled a path for His anger.*

God's anger went forth on a *level path* without hindrance or obstacle *(Radak).*

Although His wrath was great, He kept it within bounds. The messengers of evil who enforced the plagues confined their damage to the guilty Egyptians. For instance, God leveled a path for the avenging angel to strike at the homes of the Egyptian firstborn, but kept the angel away from the Israelite dwellings *(Rashi).*

לֹא חָשַׂךְ מִמָּוֶת נַפְשָׁם — *He spared not their soul from death.*

He did not give them an extra minute to live. He decreed that they die at the earliest possible opportunity *(Radak).*

נא נַפְשָׁם וְחַיָּתָם לַדֶּבֶר הִסְגִּיר: וַיַּךְ כָּל־
בְּכוֹר בְּמִצְרָיִם רֵאשִׁית אוֹנִים בְּאָהֳלֵי־
נב חָם: וַיַּסַּע כַּצֹּאן עַמּוֹ וַיְנַהֲגֵם כָּעֵדֶר
נג בַּמִּדְבָּר: וַיַּנְחֵם לָבֶטַח וְלֹא פָחָדוּ וְאֶת־
נד אוֹיְבֵיהֶם כִּסָּה הַיָּם: וַיְבִיאֵם אֶל־גְּבוּל
נה קָדְשׁוֹ הַר־זֶה קָנְתָה יְמִינוֹ: וַיְגָרֶשׁ
מִפְּנֵיהֶם | גּוֹיִם וַיַּפִּילֵם בְּחֶבֶל נַחֲלָה
נו וַיַּשְׁכֵּן בְּאָהֳלֵיהֶם שִׁבְטֵי יִשְׂרָאֵל: וַיְנַסּוּ

וְחַיָּתָם לַדֶּבֶר הִסְגִּיר — *And their bodies* [lit. *their vitality*] *He delivered to pestilence.*

חַיָּתָם may be translated *their bodies (Rashi), their souls (Radak),* or *their livestock (Targum; Radak; Metzudas Zion).*

Midrash Shocher Tov explains that an assault of דֶּבֶר, *pestilence,* accompanied each of the other nine plagues as they were visited upon the Egyptians.

51. וַיַּךְ כָּל בְּכוֹר בְּמִצְרָיִם — *He struck down every first-born in Egypt.*

The Passover *Haggadah* emphasizes that it was God Himself who slew the first-born: אֲנִי וְלֹא מַלְאָךְ...אֲנִי וְלֹא שָׂרָף...אֲנִי הוּא וְלֹא אַחֵר, *I and no angel... I and no seraph... it is I and no other.* If so, who is the מַשְׁחִית, *destroyer,* of whom it is written *(Exodus* 12:23): *God will not let the destroyer come into your houses to strike* on Pesach night?

The *Vilna Gaon* maintains that this destroyer is the Angel of Death. On a normal night, he would have claimed a number of victims among the large Jewish population. If any Jew had died on the night of Passover, however, the Egyptians would have believed that the Jews too were affected by the slaying of the firstborn. Therefore the Angel of Death was forbidden to smite even those Jews who would have died a natural death. [See Artscroll *Haggadah* p. 121.]

Malbim comments that בְּכוֹר, *the first-born,* refers to the oldest member of each family — the one who happened to be born before all other present members of the household. In the land mass of Egypt proper, all of these first-born were slain. The plague even affected foreigners who were living on Egyptian soil at the time.

רֵאשִׁית אוֹנִים בְּאָהֳלֵי חָם — *The primary strength in the tents of Cham.*

Malbim continues that another type of *firstborn* is the first child conceived of *first-born* is the first child conceived of each father, who is called the prime 21:17). This first-born is not as readily apparent as the first-born of each mother, and only those who were first-born of their fathers who were actually of Egyptian blood [the descendants of Ham who was the father of מִצְרַיִם (see *Genesis* 1:6)] were slain during this plague; foreigners living in Egypt were not killed if they were the first-born of their fathers but not of their mothers. Those first-born of Hamitic blood were slain not only in the actual territory of Egypt but wherever they were on Passover night [i.e., in any *tent of Ham*].

52. וַיַּסַּע כַּצֹּאן עַמּוֹ — *Then He caused His nation to journey like sheep.*

God guided Israel out of Egypt with consideration, according to their own pace *(Radak).*

וַיְנַהֲגֵם כָּעֵדֶר בַּמִּדְבָּר — *And guided them like a flock in the wilderness.*

He resembled a shepherd who is conscientious about providing for his sheep, yet lenient in overlooking their disobedience.

And their bodies He delivered
to pestilence.
51 *He struck down every first-born in Egypt,*
the primary strength in the tents of Cham.
52 *Then he caused His nation to journey like sheep,*
and guided them like a flock in the wilderness.
53 *He led them with confidence so they had no fear,*
for their foes the sea had covered.
54 *And He brought them to His sacred boundary,*
to this mountain which His right hand acquired.
55 *Then He drove away peoples before them*
and apportioned them a measured estate,
And settled the tribes of Israel
in their tents.

Israel responded by running after Moses and Aaron into the wilderness, just as a flock follows its devoted keeper *(Midrash Shocher Tov).*

53. וַיַּנְחֵם לָבֶטַח וְלֹא פָחָדוּ — *He led them with confidence so they had no fear.*

Ordinarily, sheep feel vulnerable and afraid in a desolate wilderness. Yet, Israel found a sense of security in the desert *(Malbim).*

וְאֶת אוֹיְבֵיהֶם כִּסָּה הַיָּם — *For their foes the sea had covered.*

When the Egyptian chariots pursued them and chased them to the sea, the Jews panicked momentarily: *and they were very much afraid and the children of Israel cried out to HASHEM (Exodus* 14:10). However, God immediately allayed their fears by showing them that the waters were swallowing their foes *(Radak).*

54. וַיְבִיאֵם אֶל גְּבוּל קָדְשׁוֹ — *And He brought them to His sacred boundary.*

This refers to the Holy Land *(Radak),* to Jerusalem *(Ibn Ezra),* and to the Temple Mount *(Targum).*

הַר זֶה קָנְתָה יְמִינוֹ — *To this mountain which His right hand acquired.*

Malbim explains that God thereby fulfilled His promise to Israel: תְּבִאֵמוֹ וְתִטָּעֵמוֹ בְּהַר נַחֲלָתְךָ, *You shall bring them and You shall plant them in the mountain of Your inheritance (Exodus* 15:17); [this was the ultimate purpose of their redemption from Egypt].

55. וַיְגָרֶשׁ מִפְּנֵיהֶם גּוֹיִם — *Then He drove away peoples before them.*

God drove out the seven great nations of Canaan *(Rashi; Ibn Ezra).*

וַיַּפִּילֵם בְּחֶבֶל נַחֲלָה — *And apportioned them a measured estate.*

Literally, וַיַּפִּילֵם means *He cast.* God commanded Israel to cast lots in order to apportion the land of Israel among the tribes *(Metzudas David).*

Some read וַיַּפִּילֵם together with the preceding stich: *He drove out the peoples before them and He cast them* [the nations] *down (Radak).*

וַיַּשְׁכֵּן בְּאָהֳלֵיהֶם שִׁבְטֵי יִשְׂרָאֵל — *And settled the tribes of Israel in their tents.*

The Jews took over the homes of the seven nations who were driven out *(Rashi).*

וַיַּמְרוּ אֶת־אֱלֹהִים עֶלְיוֹן וְעֵדוֹתָיו לֹא
נז שָׁמָרוּ: וַיִּסֹּגוּ וַיִּבְגְּדוּ כַּאֲבוֹתָם נֶהְפְּכוּ
נח כְּקֶשֶׁת רְמִיָּה: וַיַּכְעִיסוּהוּ בְּבָמוֹתָם
נט וּבִפְסִילֵיהֶם יַקְנִיאוּהוּ: שָׁמַע אֱלֹהִים
ס וַיִּתְעַבָּר וַיִּמְאַס מְאֹד בְּיִשְׂרָאֵל: וַיִּטֹּשׁ
סא מִשְׁכַּן שִׁלוֹ אֹהֶל שִׁכֵּן בָּאָדָם: וַיִּתֵּן לַשְּׁבִי

56. וַיְנַסּוּ וַיַּמְרוּ אֶת אֱלֹהִים עֶלְיוֹן – *Yet they tested and rebelled against the Most High God.*

[First, the psalmist related that Israel rebelled in the wilderness, despite God's kindness to them there and in Egypt.] Now the narrative switches to the era of the שׁוֹפְטִים, *Judges,* who led Israel after the death of Joshua and the elders. Then, too, the people tested God *(Rashi; Radak).*

Alshich explains that their descent into sin was gradual. First they merely *tested* God; only later did they openly *rebel* against Him. They claimed that God is עֶלְיוֹן, *Most High,* in heaven above, but that He is too great to concern Himself with the ways of man below. Nevertheless, at that stage they still did follow Him and they kept His commandments.

וְעֵדוֹתָיו לֹא שָׁמָרוּ – *And did not observe His testimonies.*

Alshich notes that the Jewish people cannot long exist without belief in הַשְׁגָּחָה פְּרָטִית, *personal Divine Providence, and surveillance,* for the precepts were meant to be *testimonies* to God's intimate involvement with man. Since they denied Divine Providence, Israel ultimately abandoned these *testimonies.*

57. וַיִּסֹּגוּ וַיִּבְגְּדוּ כַּאֲבוֹתָם – *They drew back and betrayed as their fathers had.*

[The nation's spiritual progress under the guidance of Moses and Joshua later came to naught, for *in those days* (of the Judges) *there was no king in Israel; every man did that which was right in his own eyes (Judges* 21:25). Lacking proper discipline and guidance, the nation regressed to the rebellious state of their forefathers.]

נֶהְפְּכוּ כְּקֶשֶׁת רְמִיָּה – *They became warped* [lit. *they changed*] *like a treacherous bow.*

The warped bow is unreliable in that it does not shoot in the direction towards which the archer aims *(Rashi).*

Indeed the faulty weapon endangers the archer, because it backfires against him. Similarly, the children of Israel were intended to be the 'weapon' of God, shooting forth arrows of faith to destroy the pagan beliefs of a Godless world; but then the Children of Israel grew warped and, like a crooked bow, they turned their projectiles *against* God and attacked His faith instead of defending it *(Malbim).*

Radak renders קֶשֶׁת רְמִיָּה as *a deceitful archer* who pretends to take aim away from his intended target in order to catch his victim off guard.

There were times when the influence of a Judge did turn Israel in the proper direction. However, that influence was so weak that it dissipated the moment the Judge died; then the Jews suddenly turned to the opposite direction — to idols.

58. וַיַּכְעִיסוּהוּ בְּבָמוֹתָם – *They angered Him with their high altars.*

In the days of Eli the High Priest and Samuel the Prophet there were idolaters among the Jews. [They built בָּמוֹת, *high altars,* dedicated to heathen gods.] Samuel inspired the people to return to the path of righteousness when the Holy Ark of the Tabernacle was

56 *Yet they tested and rebelled*
against the Most High God,
And did not observe
His testimonies.
57 *They drew back and betrayed*
as their fathers had,
They became warped
like a treacherous bow.
58 *They angered Him*
with their high altars,
And with their idols,
they aroused His jealousy.
59 *God heard and His anger overflowed*
and He greatly despised Israel.
60 *He abandoned the Tabernacle of Shiloh,*
the tent where He dwelled among men.

miraculously returned from Philistine captivity *(Radak).*

וּבִפְסִילֵיהֶם יַקְנִיאוּהוּ – *And with their idols, they aroused His jealousy.*

[*Radak (comm.* to *II Kings* 17:28) explains that it was jealousy which inspired the Jews to stray after heathen idols, for Israel envied the prosperity of the pagan nations around them. They imagined that if they were to serve these idols, they would experience similar success. All they accomplished, however, was to arouse God's jealousy.]

59. שָׁמַע אֱלֹהִים וַיִּתְעַבָּר – *God heard and His anger overflowed.*

[As explained in the commentary to *v.* 49, עֶבְרָה is derived from לעבר, *to overstep, to go over.* It alludes to an overwhelming wrath which cannot be contained. When Israel serves idols, it steps out of the perimeter of faith and passes into the sphere of disobedience and denial of the Divine.]

וַיִּמְאַס מְאֹד בְּיִשְׂרָאֵל – *And He greatly despised Israel.*

[Denial of God led to moral corruption and perversion which made Israel completely abhorrent to God.]

For this reason, God caused the Holy Ark — the earthly home for the Divine spirit — to be taken from Israel by the Philistine army *(Radak).*

60. וַיִּטֹּשׁ מִשְׁכַּן שִׁלוֹ – *He abandoned the Tabernacle of Shiloh.*

[The *Tabernacle* stood in Shiloh 369 years (*Zevachim* 118b). The Holy Ark rested there throughout that period, until God abandoned Shiloh and caused the Ark to be taken by the Philistines.]

אֹהֶל – *The tent.*

This Tabernacle was not a conventional building. Although its walls were built of solid stone, its roof resembled a *tent,* for it was made of curtains spread out from wall to wall (*Zevachim* 118a).

אֹהֶל שִׁכֵּן בָּאָדָם – *The tent where He dwelled among men.*

Alshich explains that God has no desire to set His spirit upon inanimate beams and stones. The Tabernacle is merely a means to channel God's spirit into the midst of human life, as Scrip-

סב עֻזּוֹ וְתִפְאַרְתּוֹ בְיַד־צָר: וַיַּסְגֵּר לַחֶרֶב עַמּוֹ
סג וּבְנַחֲלָתוֹ הִתְעַבָּר: בַּחוּרָיו אָכְלָה־אֵשׁ
סד וּבְתוּלֹתָיו לֹא הוּלָּלוּ: כֹּהֲנָיו בַּחֶרֶב נָפָלוּ
סה וְאַלְמְנֹתָיו לֹא תִבְכֶּינָה: וַיִּקַץ כְּיָשֵׁן | אֲדֹנָי
סו כְּגִבּוֹר מִתְרוֹנֵן מִיָּיִן: וַיַּךְ־צָרָיו אָחוֹר
סז חֶרְפַּת עוֹלָם נָתַן לָמוֹ: וַיִּמְאַס בְּאֹהֶל

ture states: וְעָשׂוּ לִי מִקְדָּשׁ וְשָׁכַנְתִּי בְּתוֹכָם, *And they shall make me a Temple so that I may dwell in their midst (Exodus* 25:28).

61. וַיִּתֵּן לַשְּׁבִי עֻזּוֹ — *He placed His might into captivity.*

This refers to God's Torah *(Targum)* in the form of the Ark and the Tablets of the Law *(Rashi).*

Ordinarily, the *might* of these holy objects fortified Israel in battle, but this *might* deserted them as they faced the Philistine host because the Jews no longer merited such miraculous intervention *(Malbim).*

וְתִפְאַרְתּוֹ בְּיַד צָר — *And His glory into the tormentor's hand.*

Previously, glorious miracles had been performed for Israel by means of the Ark. Now this sacred symbol fell ingloriously into the hands of the Philistines *(Malbim).*

62. וַיַּסְגֵּר לַחֶרֶב עַמּוֹ — *He delivered His nation to the sword.*

I Samuel 4:10 records, *And there was a very great slaughter and there fell from Israel thirty thousand foot soldiers.*

וּבְנַחֲלָתוֹ הִתְעַבָּר — *And against His estate His anger overflowed.*

His wrath was not confined to His guilty people. God's anger even engulfed *His estate,* which refers to His chosen place, the Tabernacle *(Malbim).*

63. בַּחוּרָיו אָכְלָה אֵשׁ — *His young men* [lit. *chosen ones*] *the fire consumed.*

Ordinarily, recently married *young men* are exempt from military duties which would separate them from their new brides (*Deuteronomy* 24:5). But when the war is an obligatory one for the defense of the homeland, then even these newlyweds are summoned to battle (*Sotah* 44b). Thus it transpired that even young Jewish soldiers were devoured by Philistine fire *(Malbim).*

וּבְתוּלֹתָיו לֹא הוּלָּלוּ — *And His maidens* [lit. *virgins*] *had no marriage song* [lit. *were not praised.*]

In addition to the tragic loss of young newlyweds, many brides awaiting marriage were bereaved.

The hall of the wedding feast is called בֵּית הִלּוּלָה, *the place of praise,* because it is meritorious to enhance the joy of bride and groom by lauding their virtues. Many weddings never took place because of the tragic battlefield deaths of potential grooms *(Rashi; Radak; Malbim).*

64. כֹּהֲנָיו בַּחֶרֶב נָפָלוּ — *His priests fell by the sword.*

... *And the Ark of God was captured and the two sons of Eli* [the High Priest] *Chofni and Pinchas, were slain (I Samuel* 4:11) with other priests who accompanied the Ark into battle *(Radak).*

וְאַלְמְנֹתָיו לֹא תִבְכֶּינָה — *And His widows did not weep.*

At that time, Pinchas' wife was pregnant. When she heard the tragic news, she went into premature labor, which led to an extremely difficult birth and to her death (*I Samuel* 4:19). Therefore, she had no opportunity to mourn her husband's death *(Rashi).*

Moreover in her dying words (*I Samuel* 4:21-22), her lament centered on the capture of the Holy Ark, which she

61 *He placed His might into captivity*
and His glory into the tormentor's hand.
62 *He delivered His nation to the sword*
and against His estate His anger overflowed.
63 *His young men, the fire consumed*
and His maidens had no marriage song.
64 *His priests fell by the sword*
and His widows did not weep.
65 *Then the Lord awoke like one sleeping,*
like a warrior rousing himself with song
from wine.
66 *He struck His enemies into retreat,*
eternal disgrace He bestowed on them.
67 *He despised the tent of Joseph,*

recognized as a far greater tragedy than the death of her own husband *(Metzudas David).*

65. וַיִּקַץ כְּיָשֵׁן אֲדֹנָי – *Then the Lord awoke like one sleeping.*

This figurative language suggests that, for a time, God seemed to ignore the sins of Israel; thus He was likened to a sleeping man oblivious to surrounding events *(Radak).*

כְּגִבּוֹר מִתְרוֹנֵן מִיָּיִן – *Like a warrior rousing himself with song from wine.*

The intoxicated *warrior* lacks no strength, but he is momentarily rendered helpless because of his drunken stupor. He therefore attempts to rouse himself by shouting or singing (רִינָּה).

Similarly, the All-Merciful God attempts to cast a blind eye on Israel's sins, but when the time comes to react, He lashes out against them, to show that His attention is focused on them again *(Radak).*

66. וַיַּךְ צָרָיו אָחוֹר – *He struck His enemies into retreat.*

Radak comments that as a result of their sins, Israel was routed in battle: *And the Philistines fought, and Israel was beaten, and they fled every man to his tent (I Samuel* 4:10).

Targum, Rashi, and *Malbim* interpret this verse differently. Despite God's justifiable anger against Israel, He was nevertheless aroused to defend the honor of His Holy Ark, which had been disgraced and defiled at the hands of the heathens.

God therefore punished the Philistines by disgracing them in a most ignominous manner: He smote them from their אָחוֹר, *rear,* with a plague of hemorrhoids *(I Samuel* 6:1).

חֶרְפַּת עוֹלָם נָתַן לָמוֹ – *Eternal disgrace He bestowed on them.*

The capture of the Holy Ark by the Philistines was a source of everlasting disgrace to Israel *(Radak).*

The plague of diarrhea which afflicted Philistia caused them eternal shame *(Rashi; Malbim).*

67. וַיִּמְאַס בְּאֹהֶל יוֹסֵף – *He despised the tent of Joseph.*

Although the Philistines returned the Holy Ark, it was never again deposited in Shiloh; nor was the Tabernacle ever

סח יוֹסֵף וּבְשֵׁבֶט אֶפְרַיִם לֹא בָחָר: וַיִּבְחַר
אֶת־שֵׁבֶט יְהוּדָה אֶת־הַר צִיּוֹן אֲשֶׁר
סט אָהֵב: וַיִּבֶן כְּמוֹ־רָמִים מִקְדָּשׁוֹ כְּאֶרֶץ
ע יְסָדָהּ לְעוֹלָם: וַיִּבְחַר בְּדָוִד עַבְדּוֹ וַיִּקָּחֵהוּ
עא מִמִּכְלְאֹת צֹאן: מֵאַחַר עָלוֹת הֱבִיאוֹ
לִרְעוֹת בְּיַעֲקֹב עַמּוֹ וּבְיִשְׂרָאֵל נַחֲלָתוֹ:
עב וַיִּרְעֵם כְּתֹם לְבָבוֹ וּבִתְבוּנוֹת כַּפָּיו יַנְחֵם:

reconstructed on any part of the territory of Joseph *(Radak; Malbim).*

וּבְשֵׁבֶט אֶפְרַיִם לֹא בָחָר — *The tribe of Ephraim He did not choose.*

In addition, the tribe of Ephraim was eternally disqualified for the monarchy *(Malbim).*

68. וַיִּבְחַר אֶת שֵׁבֶט יְהוּדָה — *But He chose the tribe of Judah.*

[The psalm now reaches its climax: the choice of the royal house of David, the descendant of Judah.]

אֶת הַר צִיּוֹן אֲשֶׁר אָהֵב — *Mount Zion which He loves.*

[Not only did God elevate the men of Judah to royalty; He also assigned supreme prominence to the territory of Judah.]

69. וַיִּבֶן כְּמוֹ רָמִים מִקְדָּשׁוֹ — *And He built His Temple like the high heavens.*

Just as He created the heavens with 'two hands,' so did He fashion the *Beis HaMikdash*, Holy Temple, with 'two hands' *(Rashi).*

[This figure of speech connotes God's total involvement and concern in the construction of the Temple.]

The significance of the Temple derives from the fact that its function was to connect *the high heavens* with the earth below and to transmit the celestial sanctity to earth *(Malbim).*

כְּאֶרֶץ יְסָדָהּ לְעוֹלָם — *Like the earth He established it forever.*

Just as *the earth* is permanent, so is the Temple's location in Zion immutable. [See *Rambam, Hilchos Beis HaBechirah* 6:16]. Unlike the Tabernacle, which was removed from Shiloh, the Temple will never be moved to a different site *(Radak).*

70. וַיִּבְחַר בְּדָוִד עַבְדּוֹ — *He chose David, His servant.*

Just as God's choice of Zion is everlasting, His choice of David and his descendants will never be abrogated *(Radak).*

[God promised this because David was עַבְדּוֹ, *His servant,* whose dedication to God was unsurpassed.]

וַיִּקָּחֵהוּ מִמִּכְלְאוֹת צֹאן — *And took him from the sheep corrals.*

The root of מִכְלְאֹת is כֶּלֶא, *prison,* a reference to the pens where the sheep are held securely *(Metzudas Zion).*

[Ordinarily, when a shepherd locks his sheep in their pens, he forgets about them because he feels confident that they are safe. David, however, stayed with his sheep even after they were locked in their pens, because he was genuinely concerned for their welfare. He ensured that they were comfortable and had sufficient food and water.

Such intimate concern is the sign of a true leader, who sees his role as one of increased responsibility, rather than increased privilege. This attitude contrasts sharply with that of the leaders of Ephraim, who were mainly concerned with the special perquisites and privileges of the monarchy and who neglected their duties.]

71. מֵאַחַר עָלוֹת — *From behind the nursing ewes.*

the tribe of Ephraim He did not choose.

68 But He chose the tribe of Judah,
Mount Zion which He loves.
69 And He built His Temple like the high heavens,
like the earth He established it forever.
70 He chose David, His servant,
and took him from the sheep corrals.
71 From behind the nursing ewes,
He brought him to tend
to Jacob, His nation,
and Israel, His estate.
72 He tended them
according to the wholesomeness of his heart,
And by the skill of his hands
he led them.

The mother sheep are called עָלוֹת because they nurse their young *(Radak; Ibn Ezra)*. The young lambs are called עוֹלְלִים, *sucklings (Metzudas Zion)*.

[The sucklings are tender and must be handled very gently. Also the mothers' milk supply decreases readily if they are exhausted or distressed (see *Genesis* 33:13). Therefore, only a devoted shepherd can give these creatures the care they need.]

הֱבִיאוֹ לִרְעוֹת בְּיַעֲקֹב עַמּוֹ — *He brought him to tend to* [lit. *within*] *Jacob, His nation.*

Malbim explains that the Jewish nation is both a political and a religious community. The political aspect is called *Jacob*, and the religious aspect is called *Israel*. When David assumed sovereignty, it became his duty to tend to *Jacob* — the political entity — *His nation.*

[The psalmist takes pains to add that David's role was לִרְעוֹת בְּיַעֲקֹב, *to tend within Jacob;* this indicates that he did not hold himself aloof from the masses, but he joined their ranks and influenced them from *within.*]

וּבְיִשְׂרָאֵל נַחֲלָתוֹ — *And* [lit. *within*] *Israel His estate.*

Malbim continues that the title *Israel* denotes the religious nature of Jewish society, which is bound together by faithful piety more than by politics. David, the devoted servant of God, also provided strong spiritual leadership.

72. וַיִּרְעֵם כְּתֹם לְבָבוֹ — *He tended them according to the wholesomeness of his heart.*

This describes David's faithful service as the spiritual leader of the nation of Israel *(Malbim)*.

וּבִתְבוּנוֹת כַּפָּיו יַנְחֵם — *And by the skill* [lit. *understanding*] *of his hands* [lit. *palms*] *he led them.*

The seat of תְּבוּנָה, *understanding,* is the mind; the mind relays its messages to the hands, which then act with skill *(Radak; Metzudas David)*.

This refers to David's role as the political and temporal leader of Jacob *(Malbim)*. [His success in this area is attributed to his ability to translate his spiritual Torah, תְּבוּנָה, *understanding,* from abstract theory into actual accomplishments.]

Hirsch notes that this verse does not use the usual word for *His hands* — יָדָיו — because that term implies the wielding of power over one's subjects. David did not regard the people as his temporal fiefs or subjects, but as God's sacred charges who had been placed in כַּפָּיו, *his palms*, so that he might care for them and lead them on the Divine path of righteousness. This attitude is the reason why the monarchy of Judah succeeded where all others failed.

מזמור עט 79

A*ssaf composed many psalms, whose relationship to his personal life is not readily apparent. In this case however,* Midrash Shocher Tov *explains that Assaf's approach to this subject can be understood by means of a parable:*

> *A beggar's daughter once went to fill her earthenware jug at a well. Much to her dismay, the rope snapped and her jug fell deep into the well. The poor girl was crushed by the loss of her only vessel, for she knew that no one would make an effort to retrieve such an inexpensive utensil. Suddenly, however, the king's daughter arrived to draw some well water in her golden pitcher. Accidently, this precious pitcher also tumbled into the well. Upon observing this, the beggar's daughter burst into a joyous dance, saying 'The person who descends into the pit to retrieve the princess' precious pitcher will be able to retrieve my jug as well!'*

Midrash Shocher Tov *explains that Assaf had been distressed when his father, Korach, was swallowed into the bowels of the earth (see* Numbers *16:31-33). He lost all hope for his father's return, until he received a prophetic vision that the gates of the Temple would also be swallowed by the earth, while the rest of the Sanctuary was destroyed. The vision concluded with these very same gates being raised it to their former glory.*

Then Assaf became ecstatic. He composed this psalm, saying, 'He who shall descend to the bowels of the earth to retrieve the Temple's gates will also raise my father, Korach.'

א מִזְמוֹר לְאָסָף אֱלֹהִים בָּאוּ גוֹיִם | בְּנַחֲלָתֶךָ
טִמְּאוּ אֶת־הֵיכַל קָדְשֶׁךָ שָׂמוּ אֶת־
ב יְרוּשָׁלַםִ לְעִיִּים: נָתְנוּ אֶת־נִבְלַת עֲבָדֶיךָ
מַאֲכָל לְעוֹף הַשָּׁמָיִם בְּשַׂר חֲסִידֶיךָ
ג לְחַיְתוֹ־אָרֶץ: שָׁפְכוּ דָמָם | כַּמַּיִם סְבִיבוֹת

1. מִזְמוֹר לְאָסָף — *A song of Assaf.*

Since this woeful composition describes the Temple's destruction, it would seem that a more appropriate title for the psalm would be 'A dirge of Assaf.'

The *Talmud* employs a parable which elucidates the true meaning of the title *A song of Assaf.* A king once erected a beautiful bridal canopy for the nuptials of his son. The son, however, was so stubborn and rude that he infuriated his father. The King stormed into the wedding hall and vented his rage on the gorgeous canopy, ripping it to shreds.

So too did the stubbornness of Israel exceedingly anger God. However, the Lord was merciful and directed His anger at the stones and beams of the Holy Temple rather than at the Jews themselves. Although the people of Israel were severely punished, they were saved from total destruction.

Assaf had the wisdom to perceive and interpret the חוּרְבָּן, *destruction,* in this light. Therefore, he dedicated a song of praise to God's mercy (*Kiddushin* 31b).

אֱלֹהִים — *O God.*

The psalmist begins with a cry of deep anguish which beseeches God for an answer *(Radak).*

בָּאוּ גוֹיִם בְּנַחֲלָתֶךָ — *The nations have entered into Your estate.*

The psalmist asks how God could have allowed this trespass since the Torah states: *The stranger who draws near shall die (Numbers* 1:52). This warning does not only apply to non-Jews, but even the two sons of Aaron, the High Priest died when they entered the Sanctuary without permission (*Leviticus* 10:1-2). When King Uziah offered incense to You in the Sanctuary, he was stricken with leprosy and the earth shook and roared in protest of his sin. How did these gentiles enter the Holy of Holies and emerge unscathed?

God replies that the Jews were punished because they had entered the Sanctuary without permission. The marauding gentiles, however, broke into the Temple upon God's invitation, as *Jeremiah* 1:15 states: *'Behold, I will call upon all the families of the kingdoms of the north,' says HASHEM, and they shall come and each one shall set up his throne at the entrance of the gates of Jerusalem (Midrash Shocher Tov).*

טִמְּאוּ אֶת הֵיכַל קָדְשֶׁךָ — *They defiled the Sanctuary of Your holiness.*

Even if we were to ignore the damage which the gentiles inflicted upon the Temple, we could not be oblivious to the fact that their mere entry defiled its sanctity *(Rav Avraham Azulai).*

שָׂמוּ אֶת יְרוּשָׁלַיִם לְעִיִּים — *They turned Jerusalem into heaps of rubble (Radak).*

[This connotes that the neat and orderly city of Jerusalem, the architectural marvel of the entire world, was transformed into heaps of rubble.]

Chozeh David teaches that even this destruction can be viewed as a cause for מִזְמוֹר, *song.* Rabbi Akiva rejoiced when he saw the foxes emerge from the ruins of the Holy of Holies (*Maccos* 23b), for he firmly believed that just as God had fulfilled His promise to devastate Jerusalem, so would He ultimately keep His pledge to

79
1-3

A song of Assaf, O God!
The nations have entered into Your estate,
They defiled the Sanctuary of Your holiness,
they turned Jerusalem into heaps of rubble.
2 *They have placed the corpse of Your servants*
as food for the birds of the sky,
the flesh of Your devout ones
to the beasts of the earth.
3 *They shed their blood like water*

reconstruct the city until it even surpasses its former grandeur![1]

2. נָתְנוּ אֶת נִבְלַת עֲבָדֶיךָ מַאֲכָל לְעוֹף הַשָּׁמָיִם – *They have placed the corpse of Your servants as food for the birds of the sky.*

It would seem that the Jews who lived at the time of the destruction were sinners who were unworthy of the title, *Your servants.*

The *Talmud (Sanhedrin* 47a) explains that חֲסִידֶיךָ, *Your devoted ones,* (in the latter part of this verse) refers to those who were always pious. However, עֲבָדֶיךָ, *Your servants,* describes those who were wicked before death. Nevertheless, since these men were mercilessly executed by the gentile murderers, their terrible suffering provided atonement for their sins. Therefore they merited the glorious title עֲבָדֶיךָ, *Your servants.*

Radak adds that there were a handful of good men hiding in Jerusalem at the time of the destruction; these men truly merited the title *Your servants.* [Nevertheless, their influence was limited, and they did not inspire the masses to repentance.]

בְּשַׂר חֲסִידֶיךָ לְחַיְתוֹ אָרֶץ – *The flesh of Your devout ones to the beasts of the earth.*

First the נְבֵלוֹת, *corpses,* of the Jews were abandoned to scavenging birds. Then the gentiles came and threw the בָּשָׂר, *flesh,* of the corpses to their domestic animals [i.e., their dogs and cats] for food *(Malbim).*

This illustrates the severity of Divine justice. If a man demands that his friend repay a debt, and the debtor proves that he is penniless, then the creditor has no way to compel repayment.

God, however, may demand that an evil man pay with his life. After the sinner's death, God may even inflict punishment on his rotting flesh. In addition, after the flesh is gone, the dry bones may be dragged from their grave

1. [A parable: A royal palace was found in total disarray. Its gorgeous curtains had been stripped away, the furniture was turned upside down, and the exquisite marble floors were covered with filthy water.

The casual observer would consider the palace an abandoned ruin, but the perceptive viewer would discern a definite pattern in this turmoil. He would realize that not one object has been left untouched and conclude that a thorough spring cleaning is in progress. To facilitate this cleaning, the magnificent edifice had been taken apart.

Similarly, Rabbi Akiva noticed that the destruction of the Temple was a systematic overturning of every stone, beam, and vessel. He recognized that the devastation was not random; it conformed faithfully to a Divine 'master plan.' Foxes even roamed through the ruins with impunity, exactly as the prophet had predicted.

This provided conclusive proof that the destruction was actually a preparation for the future Temple, which would be pure and untainted. Therefore, Rabbi Akiva rejoiced.]

ד יְרוּשָׁלָםִ וְאֵין קוֹבֵר: הָיִינוּ חֶרְפָּה
ה לִשְׁכֵנֵינוּ לַעַג וָקֶלֶס לִסְבִיבוֹתֵינוּ: עַד־מָה
יהוה תֶּאֱנַף לָנֶצַח תִּבְעַר כְּמוֹ־אֵשׁ
ו קִנְאָתֶךָ: שְׁפֹךְ חֲמָתְךָ | אֶל־הַגּוֹיִם אֲשֶׁר
לֹא־יְדָעוּךָ וְעַל מַמְלָכוֹת אֲשֶׁר בְּשִׁמְךָ לֹא
ז קָרָאוּ: כִּי אָכַל אֶת־יַעֲקֹב וְאֶת נָוֵהוּ

and exposed to disgrace *(Midrash Shocher Tov).*

3. שָׁפְכוּ דָמָם כַּמַּיִם סְבִיבוֹת יְרוּשָׁלָיִם — *They shed their blood like water round about Jerusalem.*

Their blood was deemed as cheap as water, which is spilled indiscriminately *(Ibn Ezra).*

The tragedy of this bloodshed was even greater in that it did not take place in a forsaken wilderness, but in the heart of the Jews' own homeland, *around Jerusalem (Malbim).*

וְאֵין קוֹבֵר — *And there was no burier.*

Indeed, God showed more concern for the blood of common creatures than He did for the blood of Israel. Israel's blood was left uncovered and uncared for, yet the Torah commands (*Leviticus* 17:13): *He who hunts the beast or the bird that may be eaten, he shall pour out its blood and cover it with dust (Midrash Shocher Tov).*

Metzudas David explains that although a few Jews survived, they were too terrified to emerge from their hiding places to bury their slain brethren.

4. הָיִינוּ חֶרְפָּה לִשְׁכֵנֵינוּ — *We were a disgrace to our neighbors.*

Even the handful of Jews who did survive were not completely spared, for they were a disgrace in the eyes of their gentile neighbors *(Ibn Ezra).*

[Compare this verse with *Psalms* 44:14: תְּשִׂימֵנוּ חֶרְפָּה לִשְׁכֵנֵינוּ לַעַג וָקֶלֶס לִסְבִיבוֹתֵינוּ.]

לַעַג וָקֶלֶס לִסְבִיבוֹתֵינוּ — *The mockery and scorn of those around us.*

Hirsch suggests that the word קֶלֶס which means *praise* when used in the prayerbook, refers here to the 'self-glorification' and conceit of the non-Jews. They scorned us and used our disgrace as a means to exalt themselves.

5. עַד מָה ה' תֶּאֱנַף לָנֶצַח — *Until when HASHEM, Will you be angry forever?*

Radak maintains that this psalm is dedicated to the destruction of the First Temple. Although the ensuing exile endured for only seventy years, for those who languished on foreign soil it seemed to last לָנֶצַח, *forever.*

Sforno observes that this refers to the gentile conquerors who certainly intended to uproot the Torah and destroy Israel *forever.*

תִּבְעַר כְּמוֹ אֵשׁ קִנְאָתֶךָ — *Will Your jealousy burn like fire?*

A fire will rage as long as combustible material is available. Does that mean, O God, that Your anger will continue to blaze until every last Jew is devoured? *(Maharam Arma'ah).*

6. שְׁפֹךְ חֲמָתְךָ אֶל הַגּוֹיִם אֲשֶׁר לֹא יְדָעוּךָ — *Pour forth Your wrath at the nations that know You not.*

The wording is אֶל הַגּוֹיִם, *at the nations,* rather than עַל הַגּוֹיִם *upon the nations (Hirsch).* [This refers to nations totally lacking knowledge of God. God's wrath is directed *toward* them as a threat and as a warning.][1]

1. During the Passover *Seder,* a fourth cup of wine is poured before the recital of *Hallel.* At that time, an extra cup is filled for Elijah the Prophet, the messenger of redemption and the forerunner of the Messiah.

Since the destruction of the first Temple, the Jewish people have been subjected to the

round about Jerusalem,
and there was no burier.
4 *We were a disgrace to our neighbors,*
the mockery and scorn of those around us.
5 *Until when, HASHEM, will You be angry forever?*
Will Your jealousy burn like fire?
6 *Pour forth Your wrath*
at the nations that know You not,
And upon the kingdoms that do not
call upon Your Name.
7 *For they have devoured Jacob,*
and desolated His habitation.

וְעַל מַמְלָכוֹת אֲשֶׁר בְּשִׁמְךָ לֹא קָרָאוּ – *And upon the kingdoms that do not call upon Your Name.*

This refers to the more advanced *kingdoms* which *do* recognize God's greatness but which fail to obey God's will *(Malbim).* [As a result of their awareness of God and His dictates, their crimes are inexcusable. Therefore, Divine wrath pours out עַל, *upon,* them and not merely אֶל, *at,* them as a warning.]

These nations do not follow the example of our forefather Abraham, of whom Scripture states (*Genesis* 21:33): *And there He called upon the Name of HASHEM, the eternal God (Sforno).*

[Indeed, they constantly try to blot out all evidence of God's influence and presence.]

7. כִּי אָכַל אֶת יַעֲקֹב – *For they have devoured Jacob.*

The heathens destroyed the one nation which does *recognize You* and invoke Your Name: Jacob. They were motivated by sheer brutality and selfishness, not by a desire to fulfill Your desire to punish the Jews. This is evident beyond any doubt, because, as mentioned in the previous verse, they never claimed to know You , and never before attempted to *call upon Your Name (Chozek David).*

וְאֶת נָוֵהוּ הֵשַׁמּוּ – *And desolated His habitation.*

The ultimate proof of the gentiles' impure intentions is their wanton, malicious devastation of Your Temple. If they had the slightest concern for spreading the recognition of Your Name, why didn't they spare at least a vestige of this unique *habitation* where Your spirit dwelled in clearly-revealed grandeur *(Chozeh David).*

Radak points out that the prophet *Zechariah* (1:4, 15) also hurls this accusation against the nations: *So said HASHEM of Legions, I am jealous for*

tyranny of four great empires: Babylon, Persia, Greece, and Rome. (Rome represents the present exile.) The fourth cup evokes our prayer that the fourth exile come to an end and that our oppressors and tormentors perish.

The doors of the home are then thrown open, to signify that we need not fear our foes. The assembled family and guests recite verses 6 and 7 of this psalm, beginning with the fervent plea, *pour forth Your wrath at the nations that know You not.* Thus we welcome to our homes the Prophet Elijah, who will announce the fulfillment of our dream: the return of all Jews to Zion and Jerusalem.

ח הֵשַׁמּוּ: אַל־תִּזְכָּר־לָנוּ עֲוֺנֹת רִאשֹׁנִים
מַהֵר יְקַדְּמוּנוּ רַחֲמֶיךָ כִּי דַלּוֹנוּ מְאֹד:
ט עָזְרֵנוּ | אֱלֹהֵי יִשְׁעֵנוּ עַל־דְּבַר כְּבוֹד־שְׁמֶךָ
וְהַצִּילֵנוּ וְכַפֵּר עַל־חַטֹּאתֵינוּ לְמַעַן שְׁמֶךָ:
י לָמָּה | יֹאמְרוּ הַגּוֹיִם אַיֵּה אֱלֹהֵיהֶם יִוָּדַע
°בַּגּוֹיִם °בגיים לְעֵינֵינוּ נִקְמַת דַּם־עֲבָדֶיךָ
יא הַשָּׁפוּךְ: תָּבוֹא לְפָנֶיךָ אֶנְקַת אָסִיר כְּגֹדֶל
יב זְרוֹעֲךָ הוֹתֵר בְּנֵי תְמוּתָה: וְהָשֵׁב

Jerusalem and for Zion with a great zeal. And I am very angered at the nations that are at ease, for I was only a little angry [with Israel] but they helped to escalate the evil decree.

8. אַל תִּזְכָּר לָנוּ עֲוֹנוֹת רִאשֹׁנִים — *Recall not against us the iniquities of the ancients.*

The translation follows *Ibn Ezra* and *Radak,* who emphasize that עֲוֹנֹת רִאשֹׁנִים, should not be rendered, 'our former iniquities,' which would imply 'the sins of our youth.'

Ordinarily, if a son continues in the footsteps of his sinful father, his punishment is doubly severe, as Scripture states: *Bringing punishment for the iniquities of the fathers upon the sons (Exodus 34:7).* Here the psalmist cries out, 'The terrible burden of our own sin is crushing enough. Please do not also reckon against us the sins of our ancestors and predecessors!'

מַהֵר יְקַדְּמוּנוּ רַחֲמֶיךָ — *Speedily — let Your mercy come to meet us.*

Before we sink to the point where we become liable both for our own sins and the legacy of sin which we inherited from our fathers, please have mercy on us and send us an opportunity to earn the merit of complying with Your will. By virtue of this, we will certainly be saved from harsh punishment *(Sforno).*

כִּי דַלּוֹנוּ מְאֹד — *For we have fallen very low.*

We no longer have the strength to withstand the rigors of the long exile *(Radak).*

Alshich translates: 'For we have become exceedingly דַּל, *impoverished.*' He interprets the entire verse in this vein. In the time of the First Temple, our predecessors were guilty of the three cardinal sins: idolatry, adultery, and bloodshed. Do not remember these sins against us now, for in the time of the Second Temple, we were no longer guilty of those iniquities.

Our main sin at this time is שִׂנְאַת חִנָּם, *causeless hatred,* and jealousy of our fellow man (*Yoma* 9b). The result of this evil is that we have become exceedingly impoverished, for poverty breeds envy and animosity. [The *Yerushalmi, Yoma* 1:9, observes: Because they loved money they came to hate one another.] Therefore, please cure our malady at its source and speedily let Your mercy come to meet us with a generous solution to our financial woes.

9. עָזְרֵנוּ אֱלֹהֵי יִשְׁעֵנוּ עַל דְּבַר כְּבוֹד שְׁמֶךָ — *Assist us, O God of our salvation, for the sake of Your Name's glory.*

We were doomed because we desecrated Your Name. Help us to rectify this by providing an opportunity to sanctify Your Name. And if that requires us to die a martyr's death, then fortify our will to suffer for the sake of Your glory *(Alshich).*

8 *Recall not against us*
the iniquities of the ancients.
Speedily — let Your mercy come to meet us
for we have fallen very low.
9 *Assist us, O God of our salvation,*
for the sake of Your Name's glory.
Rescue us and atone for our sins
for Your Name's sake.
10 *Why should the nations say,*
'Where is their God?'
Let Him be acknowledged among the nations
before our eyes as revenge
For the spilt blood of Your servants.
11 *Let the groan of the prisoner come before You,*
as befits the greatness of Your power.
Spare those condemned to die.

וְהַצִּילֵנוּ וְכַפֵּר עַל חַטֹּאתֵינוּ לְמַעַן שְׁמֶךָ — *Rescue us and atone for our sins for Your Name's sake.*

Alshich continues: Although we are prepared to die for Your Name, we prefer that You deliver us from death, so that we may dedicate the actions of our lives to enhancing Your glory. We pray that such deeds will render us worthy of forgiveness.

10. לָמָּה יֹאמְרוּ הַגּוֹיִם אַיֵּה אֱלֹהֵיהֶם — *Why should the nations say, 'Where is their God?'*

Why do You forsake us in exile so long that the nations become incredulous and ask, what sort of god is this hidden deity of the Jews? If He is truly a god, why does He not champion the cause of His people? *(Metzudas David).*

יִוָּדַע בַּגּוֹיִם לְעֵינֵינוּ נִקְמַת דַּם עֲבָדֶיךָ הַשָּׁפוּךְ — *Let Him be acknowledged among the nations before our eyes as revenge for the spilt blood of Your servants.*

[When they see that every drop of Jewish blood is properly avenged, they will recognize that God is indeed our champion. In addition, let His revenge take place *before our eyes,* so that it will be clear that it is being done for our sake.]

11. תָּבוֹא לְפָנֶיךָ אֶנְקַת אָסִיר — *Let the groan of the prisoner come before You.*

Israel in exile is like a prisoner in jail *(Ibn Ezra).* [No matter how much freedom and equality the Jews enjoy, as long as economic or political circumstances keep them from their homeland, they are like shackled prisoners.]

כְּגֹדֶל זְרוֹעֲךָ הוֹתֵר בְּנֵי תְמוּתָה — *As befits the greatness of Your power. Spare those condemned to die.*

The word הוֹתֵר, *release,* is derived from הַתֵּר, *to open,* the shackles of exile *(Targum; Radak).* It may also be related to יַתֵּר, *to leave a remainder.* This would refer to the survivors who live through the exile *(Ibn Ezra; Radak),* even though they were condemned to die.

יג
לִשְׁכֵנֵינוּ שִׁבְעָתַיִם אֶל־חֵיקָם חֶרְפָּתָם
יג אֲשֶׁר חֵרְפוּךָ אֲדֹנָי: וַאֲנַחְנוּ עַמְּךָ | וְצֹאן
מַרְעִיתֶךָ נוֹדֶה לְּךָ לְעוֹלָם לְדוֹר וָדֹר
נְסַפֵּר תְּהִלָּתֶךָ:

12. וְהָשֵׁב לִשְׁכֵנֵינוּ שִׁבְעָתַיִם אֶל חֵיקָם — *Repay our neighbors sevenfold — into their bosom.*

These heathen neighbors betrayed the Torah, which is מְזֻקָּק שִׁבְעָתָיִם, *clarified sevenfold (Pslams* 12:7), and destroyed the Temple, which is at the *bosom* (i.e., the center) of the world (*Ezekiel* 43:13). Correspondingly, their punishment is directed at their *bosom (Eichah Rabbah* 3), for this represents the very essence of their being.

חֶרְפָּתָם אֲשֶׁר חֵרְפוּךָ אֲדֹנָי — *Their disgrace with which they have disgraced You, O Lord.*

They disgraced and degraded the righteous men of Israel, which was tantamount to disgracing the Lord Himself *(Orchos HaTzaddikim).*

Or, as *Alshich* renders, It is *to their disgrace* and to their shame that they dared to disgrace You, O Lord.

13. וַאֲנַחְנוּ עַמְּךָ וְצֹאן מַרְעִיתֶךָ — *Then*

12 *Repay our neighbors sevenfold —*
into their bosom —
Their disgrace with which
they have disgraced You, O Lord.
13 *Then we, Your nation*
and the sheep of Your pasture,
shall thank You forever,
For generation after generation
we shall relate Your praise.

we, Your nation and the sheep of Your pasture.

When justice is meted out to the heathens, then we who are Your nation will offer You praise *(Metzudas David)*. [Then we will feel that You are protecting us like the helpless sheep of Your pasture.]

נוֹדֶה לְּךָ לְעוֹלָם לְדוֹר וָדֹר נְסַפֵּר תְּהִלָּתֶךָ — [*Shall thank You forever, for generation after generation we shall relate Your praise.*

[At the conclusion of this fervent plea for redemption, the psalmist makes it clear that we will praise God regardless of His actions. Whether or not God redeems us, forever, for generation after generation, we shall relate His praise (see *Radak*).]

מזמור פ
80

Hirsch *explains that this psalm is dedicated to the generations of exiled Jews who have called upon God to end the agonies of captivity and exile. Their suffering, he maintains, is described in three degrees of intensity corresponding to the circumstances and significance of three distinct eras of exile.*

Hirsch's *analysis is structured around three similar verses (verses 4, 8, and 20) all of which are pleas for God to lead us back to the Holy Land. He notes that the three verses are almost identical, except that in each successive verse an additional Divine Name is invoked. In verse 4, God is addressed as* אֱלֹהִים, *(God); in verse 8, He is called* אֱלֹהִים צְבָאוֹת, *(God of Legions); finally in verse 20, He is beseeched as* ה׳ אֱלֹהִים צְבָאוֹת *(HASHEM, God of Legions). He contends that verse 4 alludes to the exile of the Ten Tribes of Israel, verse 8 refers to the Babylonian exile, and verse 20 alludes to the present Roman exile.*

Thus, Hirsch's *interpretation speaks of the three physical exiles from the Land. This should not be confused with the Four Monarchies — Babylon, Persia, Greece and Rome — which subjugated Israel from the time when the Monarchy of Judah first fell into decline (see Overview and comm., ArtScroll* Daniel*). The exile of the Ten Tribes is not commonly reckoned among the exiles because they are regarded as a rebellious offshoot, rather than as the essential part of the nation. Our psalm, however, as the commentary will show, clearly alludes to them.* Rashi *however, sees our psalm as three pleas for salvation as referring to the Babylonian Exile, the Greek subjugation, and the Roman Exile.*

Hirsch *divides the psalm into three sections. Verses 2-4 constitute the pleas which the Ten Tribes direct to God. (When they were dispersed and lost, a major portion of the Jewish people vanished from history. Nevertheless, the Temple still stood.) Verses 5-8 contain the Babylonian exiles' petition for Divine salvation. The Babylonians destroyed the First Temple and exiled the remaining tribes of Judah and Benjamin, leaving the land a desolate ruin. Nevertheless, the exiles returned after seventy years, and the Temple was rebuilt. Verses 9-20 express the cry of those exiled by the Romans, who destroyed the Second Temple and scattered Israel to the four corners of the earth. This exile has been the longest of all — it continues today and its end is unknown. In each of these tragic eras, Israel beseeches God,* Return us, and set Your face aglow that we may be saved!

פ
א־ד

א לַמְנַצֵּחַ אֶל־שֹׁשַׁנִּים עֵדוּת לְאָסָף מִזְמוֹר:
ב רֹעֵה יִשְׂרָאֵל | הַאֲזִינָה נֹהֵג כַּצֹּאן יוֹסֵף
ג יֹשֵׁב הַכְּרוּבִים הוֹפִיעָה: לִפְנֵי אֶפְרַיִם |
וּבִנְיָמִן וּמְנַשֶּׁה עוֹרְרָה אֶת־גְּבוּרָתֶךָ
ד וּלְכָה לִישֻׁעָתָה לָּנוּ: אֱלֹהִים הֲשִׁיבֵנוּ

1. לַמְנַצֵּחַ אֶל שֹׁשַׁנִּים — *For the Conductor, to the* Shoshanim.

[Psalms 45 and 69 bear a similar superscription: אֶל שֹׁשַׁנִּים, *upon* Shoshanim.

In all three places, *Targum* interprets *Shoshanim* as the members of the *Sanhedrin,* the High Court, for they are as fragrantly 'perfumed' with good deeds and wisdom, as the שׁוֹשַׁנָּה, *rose.*

Here and in *Psalms* 69:1, *Rashi* comments that this name refers to Israel, which resembles a fragile rose surrounded by menacing thorns, and which desperately needs a prayer beseeching Divine protection].

עֵדוּת לְאָסָף מִזְמוֹר — *A testimony, a song of Assaf.*

According to *Targum,* this means that this psalm was composed by the justices of the *Sanhedrin,* who carefully study the עֵדוּת, *testimony,* of the Torah.

This psalm bears עֵדוּת, *witness,* to the three calamitous periods in our history when Jews languished in exile *(Rashi).*

[Only one steeped in the *testimony* of Torah can truly *witness* the hand of God controlling every phase of Jewish history.]

Ibn Ezra suggests that עֵדוּת is related to עֲדִי, *ornament,* implying that this unique composition is a rare gem among the psalms.

☙ The Exile of the Ten Tribes

2. רֹעֵה יִשְׂרָאֵל הַאֲזִינָה — *O Shepherd of Israel, give ear.*

[Here the psalmist speaks of the Ten Tribes of Israel, who were led by the tribe of Ephraim, the son of Joseph.] When Jacob blessed Joseph on his deathbead (*Genesis* 49:24), we find that the patriarch referred to God as רֹעֶה אֶבֶן יִשְׂרָאֵל, *the Shepherd, the rock of Israel (Ibn Ezra).*

The Rabbis of the *Talmud (Yoma* 69b) stress that the existence of Israel in exile, surrounded by seventy hostile nations, is truly miraculous. Israel resembles a lonely, lost sheep hounded by a pack of hungry, vicious wolves. Surely Israel must be protected by a supernatural Guardian, the Divine *Shepherd of Israel (Chazah Zion).*

נֹהֵג כַּצֹּאן יוֹסֵף — *You Who leads Joseph like a flock!*

Since Joseph provided for his brethren and their families throughout the years of the Egyptian famine, all of Jacob's descendants, who survived by virtue of Joseph's benevolence may be called by his name *(Rashi).*

In particular, the Ten Tribes of Israel, who seceded from the rule of Judah and Benjamin, are called *Joseph* because they were led by the tribe of Joseph's preeminent son, Ephraim *(Radak).*

Rabbi Tanchuma taught that these words exhort God to remember the merit of Joseph, who cared for his brethren despite the harm which they had inflicted upon him. Here, the beaten exiles implore God to overlook their evil deeds and disobedience and to remain beneficient *(Midrash Shocher Tov).*

יֹשֵׁב הַכְּרֻבִים הוֹפִיעָה — *He Who is enthroned upon the Cheruvim appear!*

The *Zohar* teaches that whenever Israel goes into exile, God's Holy Spirit accompanies them. This spirit always chooses a specific vehicle which is worthy of transporting God's sanctity. At first, God chose Joseph to carry the Divine Presence to foreign soil. In later

For the Conductor, to the Shoshanim,
a testimony, a song of Assaf.
2 O Shepherd of Israel, give ear,
You Who leads Joseph like a flock!
He Who is enthroned upon the
Cheruvim, appear!
3 Before Ephraim and Benjamin and Manasseh,
arouse Your might,
And for You it is seemly to help us.
4 O God, return us,

exiles, God caused His spirit to rest upon the תִּינוֹקוֹת שֶׁל בֵּית רַבָּן, *the pure young children who study Torah.* [In their angelic purity, these innocent students resemble the *Cheruvim.*]

Here the psalmist offers a fervent prayer for God's spirit to return to its true home in the Holy of Holies, on top of the Ark of the Covenant, where the golden *Cheruvim* spread out their wings to soar heavenward *(Alshich).*

3. לִפְנֵי אֶפְרַיִם וּבִנְיָמִן וּמְנַשֶּׁה עוֹרְרָה אֶת גְּבוּרָתֶךָ — *Before Ephraim and Benjamin and Manasseh, arouse Your might.*

Mention is made of Ephraim and Menasseh because they are the sons of Joseph, mentioned in the preceding verse. Benjamin was Joseph's dearest brother, the only other son of his mother Rachel. Together these important tribes represent the glory of the Israelite nation *(Radak).*

Hirsch points out that in the wilderness, these three tribes traveled under the same banner as one cohesive unit (*Numbers* 2:18-24). Later, Ephraim and Manasseh led the Ten Tribes which broke away from Benjamin and Judah. A prayer is offered here that these three tribes be reunited to form a nucleus around which the entire camp of Israel may reassemble under the guidance of God.

Rashi cites numerous instances in which God helped these tribes to overcome their adversaries, although the tribes did not merit such Divine assistance. In particular, God showed His *might* by saving Israel through Mordechai, a descendant of Benjamin, and enabling him to triumph over Haman.

וּלְכָה לִישֻׁעָתָה לָּנוּ — *And for You it is seemly to help us.*

The translation follows *Rashi,* and *Minchas Shai,* who base their opinion on the tradition that לְכָה is a more emphatic form of לְךָ, *to You.* It alludes to the fact that Israel's salvation depends on *You* and *You* alone. Furthermore, the salvation will be לְכָה, *for You,* i.e., for Your sake as well as for ours. Our redemption will afford us the opportunity to be free to study Your Torah and to fulfill Your precepts without hindrance *(Alshich).*

Radak, however, maintains that לְכָה is related to הָלַךְ, *to go.* He translates: *O God, go toward a salvation for us.*

4. אֱלֹהִים הֲשִׁיבֵנוּ — *O God, return us.*

Hirsch notes that the Ten Tribes address God with the Name associated with the Divine Attribute of Justice. He explains that the tribes had become assimilated and ceased to relate to God as fully-commited Jews who could address Him as His Own uniquely chosen nation. Nevertheless they continued to be human beings who could appeal to God the Creator and Judge to stamp out oppression in His universe. Since the

ה וְהָאֵר פָּנֶיךָ וְנִוָּשֵׁעָה: יהוה אֱלֹהִים
צְבָאוֹת עַד־מָתַי עָשַׁנְתָּ בִּתְפִלַּת עַמֶּךָ:
ו הֶאֱכַלְתָּם לֶחֶם דִּמְעָה וַתַּשְׁקֵמוֹ בִּדְמָעוֹת
ז שָׁלִישׁ: תְּשִׂימֵנוּ מָדוֹן לִשְׁכֵנֵינוּ וְאֹיְבֵינוּ
ח יִלְעֲגוּ־לָמוֹ: אֱלֹהִים צְבָאוֹת הֲשִׁיבֵנוּ

tribes had been the victims of injustice, they appealed to God as their Judge.

[This is the first of three parallel verses (4, 8, and 20) which beseech God to lead us back to our homeland. The verses are almost identical except that in each successive verse an additional Divine name is invoked. See *Prefatory Remarks.*]

The exiles cry out: 'Inspire us to repentance so that we may return to You' *(Radak; Ibn Ezra).* 'In the merit of our penitence, *lead us back* to our homeland' *(Metzudas David; Malbim).*

Rashi interprets this verse as a reference to the last days of the Babylonian exile. Then our leader, Mordechai the Benjaminite, prayed for Israel's redemption.

וְהָאֵר פָּנֶיךָ וְנִוָּשֵׁעָה — *And set Your face aglow* [lit., *cause Your face to shine*] *that we may be saved.*

When You are angered, Your countenance is hidden from view. Please reveal Yourself as a loving Father, whose face shines upon us *(Radak),* and redeem us *(Ibn Ezra).*

◆§ The Babylonian Exile

5. ה' אֱלֹהִים צְבָאוֹת — *HASHEM, God of Legions.*

Hirsch explains that this verse begins the description of the Babylonian exile. Although the exiled Jews had been guilty of idolatry, the lapse was temporary. They repented their sin and viewed themselves as one of God's legions, one of the many groups and forces which function in order to do His will. This Divine Name, יהו״ה, is composed of the letters of הָיָה הֹוֶה יִהְיֶה, *He was, He is, He will be,* and represents His eternal aspect as the God of the entire development of history, from its genesis until the most distant future. צְבָאוֹת, which designates God as the ruler of *legions,* is also a Divine Name. It refers to One Who controls all the forces of creation as a general controls his many *legions,* to make them all act in harmony toward a single goal. Even though the function of one soldier is far different and even seemingly contradictory to that of another, all direct themselves toward fulfillment of the general's strategy and objective.

Ibn Yachya contends that this designation refers to God in His role of Master of all celestial powers. (These are the angels and spiritual forces through which God controls the world.)

At present, God seems to have limited His sphere of influence exclusively to the heavenly heights; His presence is not evident on earth, which abounds with injustice against Israel, and where discrimination is rampant.

The psalmist calls upon God to command His legions of angels to fulfill the destiny of this earth so that Israel will triumph.

עַד מָתַי עָשַׁנְתָּ בִּתְפִלַּת עַמֶּךָ — *How long will You fume* [lit., *smoke*] *at the prayers of Your nation.*

When God is angered, Scripture states that עָלָה עָשָׁן בְּאַפּוֹ, *smoke arose from His nostrils (Psalms* 18:9), for it seems as if a barrier of smoke bars the path of Israel's prayers, as they struggle to ascend heavenward *(Ibn Ezra; Alshich).*

6. הֶאֱכַלְתָּם לֶחֶם דִּמְעָה — *You fed them bread of tears.*

Bread made of grain is the daily fare of the ordinary person. However, when Israel is in exile, they are sustained by

and set Your face aglow
that we may be saved.
5 *HASHEM, God of Legions,*
how long will You fume at the prayers
of Your nation?
6 *You fed them bread of tears,*
You made them drink tears in great measure;
7 *You made us a source of strife*
for our neighbors, and our enemies mock You.
8 *O God of Legions,*

tears of sorrow. Scripture states (*Psalms* 42:4), *For me my tears were bread* (sustenance) *day and night, as they taunt me all day long, 'Where is Your God' (Radak).*

Metzudas David observes that tears and sorrow rob a person of his appetite. Melancholy stills a man's hunger just as bread does.

וַתַּשְׁקֵמוֹ בִּדְמָעוֹת שָׁלִישׁ — *You made them drink tears in great measure.*

The translation of שָׁלִישׁ follows *Menachem* (quoted in *Rashi*) and *Metzudas Zion.* They cite a similar usage וְכָל בַּשָּׁלִשׁ, *and everything in measure (Isaiah* 40:12).

Rashi offers other interpretations which render שָׁלִישׁ as cognate with שְׁלִישׁ, *one third* or שָׁלֹשׁ, *three.*

According to *Rashi's* first interpretation, this describes the seventy years of the Babylonian exile which lasted only one third as long as the Jews' two hundred-ten year bondage in Egypt.

According to his second interpretation, this refers to the conquest of Israel by the Syrian Greeks, which occurred as number *three,* after two preceding national exiles.

A third interpretation maintains that this refers to the exile imposed by the Romans, who were descendants of Esau. When Esau realized that Jacob had received Isaac's blessings and nothing was left for him, *he raised his voice and wept (Genesis* 27:38). At that time, three tears came to Esau's eyes. One teardrop fell from each eye, however, the שָׁלִישׁ, *the third one,* formed on the edge of Esau's eye, but never was shed, for it was only שָׁלִישׁ, *one-third* the size of a normal tear.

The Congregation of Israel exclaimed, 'Sovereign of the Universe, because Esau cried but three tears, Your compassion was aroused and You granted him affluence and mastery over the world. Therefore, please heed the miserable plight of Your sons of Israel, who shed tears incessantly!' (based on *Midrash Shocher Tov).*

7. תְּשִׂימֵנוּ מָדוֹן לִשְׁכֵנֵינוּ — *You made us a source of strife for our neighbors.*

All neighboring nations quarrel with us without pause *(Radak).* Every one of them makes some false claim on our territory *(Ibn Ezra).*

[And when we languish in exile, our gentile neighbors spread libels about us, accusing us of fomenting revolution and unrest. They accuse the Jews of agitating all international *strife* and war.]

וְאֹיְבֵינוּ יִלְעֲגוּ לָמוֹ — *And our enemies mock You* [lit., *themselves*].

They yell, 'Your God is helpless' *(Radak).*

The psalmist employs a euphemism, saying that they mock לָמוֹ, *themselves,* in order to avoid speaking openly of the insults which they hurl against God *(Ibn Ezra; Radak).*

פ ט וְהָאֵר פָּנֶיךָ וְנִוָּשֵׁעָה: גֶּפֶן מִמִּצְרַיִם תַּסִּיעַ
ט־יב י תְּגָרֵשׁ גּוֹיִם וַתִּטָּעֶהָ: פִּנִּיתָ לְפָנֶיהָ
יא וַתַּשְׁרֵשׁ שָׁרָשֶׁיהָ וַתְּמַלֵּא־אָרֶץ: כָּסּוּ
יב הָרִים צִלָּהּ וַעֲנָפֶיהָ אַרְזֵי־אֵל: תְּשַׁלַּח

8. אֱלֹהִים צְבָאוֹת הֲשִׁיבֵנוּ – *O God of Legions, return us.*

With this request, Israel ends its plea for redemption from the second (Babylonian) exile. In this second plea for Divine Salvation, God's Name is more elaborate than it is in the first plea (*v.* 4). Here He is אֱלֹהִים צְבָאוֹת, *God of Legions,* whereas in verse 4 He is אֱלֹהִים, *God.*

Hirsch explains that the Jews' conduct during the Babylonian Exile demonstrated that they remained the special *legion* of God. Therefore they address this plea to God as if to say, 'We have remained Your loyal *legion,* O God; therefore we ask that You return us to the homeland You have chosen for us!'

וְהָאֵר פָּנֶיךָ וְנִוָּשֵׁעָה – *And set Your face aglow that we may be saved.*

Rashi maintains that this plea for redemption refers specifically גָּלוּת יָוָן, *the Greek oppression,* when Israel was subjugated within its land. [The plea for the illumination of God's 'shining face' is uniquely suited to this period. The Sages refer to the Greek oppression as a time of extreme spiritual darkness, finding it alluded to in the verse, *and darkness covered the face of the watery deep (Genesis* 1:2). In that bleak era, Israel desperately needed the illumination of God's countenance.]

☙ The Roman Exile

9. גֶּפֶן מִמִּצְרַיִם תַּסִּיעַ – *A vine You caused to journey out of Egypt.*

[From here until the end of this psalm, we read of the anguish of the third exile. For the sake of contrast and emphasis, the psalmist first describes the glory of the exodus from the Egyptian exile and compares our present misery with our former triumph.]

The prophet Isaiah (5:1-7) devotes a number of passages to an allegory comparing Israel to a vineyard *(Radak),* as does the prophet Ezekiel (*Ezekiel* 15).[1]

The vine is only valuable when it produces its succulent fruit. The unproductive wood of the vine is worthless. Similarly, Israel's existence is meaningful only so long as the Jews fulfill their responsiblities to God. If they become unfaithful to their Divinely assigned mission, Israel's survival is without any purpose *(Sforno; Hirsch).*

[God did not liberate the Jews from Egypt merely to grant them physical or political freedom. Rather, He freed them so that they would be capable of receiving the Torah at Sinai and fulfilling its precepts.]

Hirsch notes also that of all fruits, only the grape is so crushed and extensively altered from its natural state. But this very abuse serves to transform the grape into something far above what it had been — from an ordinary fruit into valuable, and treasured wine. Ultimately, the finished product, wine, intoxicates and overpowers the one who mangled the grape.

Similarly, Israel is improved by the beatings of the gentiles and eventually

1. The Sages compare Israel to a vine in three respects: 1) The vine is alive, yet it is supported by posts of dead wood. Similarly, Israel is bolstered by the merit of its forefathers, who are long dead (*Shemos Rabbah* 44); 2) If the vine fails to thrive on a given plot of soil, the farmer will uproot it and replant it elsewhere. Similarly, if Israel sins in one land, God will uproot them and replant them on foreign soil *(ibid.);* 3) The grapes of the vine produce both sweet-

return us and set Your face aglow
that we may be saved.
9 *A vine You caused to journey out of Egypt,*
You expelled nations and implanted it,
10 *You cleared a space for it,*
it struck roots and filled the land.
11 *They covered the mountains with its shadow,*
and its branches became mighty cedars.

the Jews will overcome their captors and tormentors.

תְּגָרֵשׁ גּוֹיִם וַתִּטָּעֶהָ — *You expelled nations and implanted it.*

[Even the sturdiest of vines cannot flourish if it lacks the proper soil. Similarly, Israel requires the soil of the Holy Land in order to 'blossom' in Torah and *mitzvos.*] God chased the seven nations out of the land of Canaan so that Israel could settle and develop there *(Rashi; Ibn Ezra; Metzudas David).*

10. פִּנִּיתָ לְפָנֶיהָ — *You cleared a space for it.*

No man of Canaan dared to stand in their way *(Radak).* Thus You provided ample room for the people of Israel to flourish *(Malbim).*

וַתַּשְׁרֵשׁ שָׁרָשֶׁיהָ — *It struck roots.*

The translation follows *Rashi* and *Metzudas David* who understand the verse to mean that Israel became firmly established in the land.

According to *Radak* and *Ibn Ezra,* תַּשְׁרֵשׁ means, *You uprooted.* This describes the manner in which God *cleared a space* for Israel: He did so by completely *uprooting the roots* of the Canaanites.

[But even when HASHEM uprooted the Canaanites He did so in a manner which would bring no harm to the land, as we read, *And HASHEM Your God will chase away these nations before You little by little, You will not be able to destroy them swiftly, lest the wild beasts of the field overwhelm You* [as a result of the desolation] *(Deuteronomy* 7:22).]

וַתְּמַלֵּא אָרֶץ — *And filled the land.*

[The arduous forty-year journey in the wilderness sapped Israel's strength and hindered procreation. But after they settled in *Eretz Yisrael,* God invested them with new strength to populate the land.]

11. כָּסּוּ הָרִים צִלָּהּ — *They covered the mountains with its shadow.*

[The psalmist continues the allegory in which he compares Israel to a lush vine.]

The fruits of the vine which left Egypt [Israel] grew until they covered the mountains *(Malbim).*

God inspired Israel to build a towering Temple and lofty houses of study, which covered the Holy City of Jerusalem with a protective shadow resembling the shade of the vine *(Targum).*

וַעֲנָפֶיהָ אַרְזֵי אֵל — *And its branches became mighty cedars* [lit., *cedars of God*].

In this sacred environment, Torah scholarship flourished and the students became mighty authorities of the law *(Targum).*

wine and sour vinegar. Similarly, the fate of Israel may be sweet or it may be bitter. Under all circumstances, however, Israel blesses God for doing as He sees best (*Vayikra Rabbah* 36).

יג קְצִירֶהָ עַד־יָם וְאֶל־נָהָר יוֹנְקוֹתֶיהָ: לָמָּה
פָּרַצְתָּ גְדֵרֶיהָ וְאָרוּהָ כָּל־עֹבְרֵי דָרֶךְ:
יד יְכַרְסְמֶנָּה חֲזִיר מִיָּעַר וְזִיז שָׂדַי יִרְעֶנָּה:
טו אֱלֹהִים צְבָאוֹת שׁוּב נָא הַבֵּט מִשָּׁמַיִם
טז וּרְאֵה וּפְקֹד גֶּפֶן זֹאת: וְכַנָּה אֲשֶׁר־נָטְעָה

12. תְּשַׁלַּח קְצִירֶהָ עַד יָם — *It stretched its boughs until the sea.*

The settlements of Israel spread through the length of the land *(Radak; Metzudas David)* from the Sea of Reeds in the south to the Sea of Philistia in the north *(Ibn Ezra).*

[At the same time, the spiritual and intellectual sphere of Israel's influence spread. Jewish scholars were acclaimed far and wide.]

וְאֶל נָהָר יוֹנְקוֹתֶיהָ — *And to the river its tender shoots.*

The יוֹנְקוֹת are the *tender shoots* and leaves [which spread out in search of moisture] *(Radak).*

The settlements also expanded along the width of the land *(Radak; Metzudas David)* from the wilderness [of Judah] in the east to the Euphrates in the west *(Rashi).*

13. לָמָּה פָּרַצְתָּ גְדֵרֶיהָ — *Why have You breached its fences?*

[Having completed his brief survey of Israel's former glory, the psalmist now turns to the grim reality of the present (third) exile.]

The psalmist laments, 'Suddenly, You stripped this privileged, protected nation of all its defenses. You withdrew Your Divine Presence *(Radak),* leaving Israel at the mercy of Babylon, Media, Greece and Rome' *(Midrash Shocher Tov).*

וְאָרוּהָ כָּל עֹבְרֵי דָרֶךְ — *So that all wayfarers pluck its fruit.*

The governor passes through and robs us, the general marches by and plunders us *(Midrash Shocher Tov).* No one fears any retaliation, for God warned *(Deuteronomy* 31:17): *And I will forsake them, and I will hide my face from them, and they shall be devoured, and many evils and troubles shall befall them (Radak).*

14. יְכַרְסְמֶנָּה חֲזִיר מִיָּעַר — *The boar of the forest ravages it.*

The root כרסם is unique in Scripture. In the *Mishnah (Peah* 2:7), קרסם refers to the breaking of stalks of grain by insects *(Rashi).*

According to the *Masorah,* the letter ע in יָעַר is raised above the other letters to indicate that the word may be read יַר, which is identified with יְאֹר, *river. Rashi* (based on *Midrash Shocher Tov)* comments that if Israel is virtuous, then its enemies are restrained like the wild creatures of the יְאֹר, *river,* and *sea.* (These creatures lack the ability to attack the people who dwell on dry land). But if Israel sins, then their enemies will overwhelm them with savage fury, like that of the *boar* which storms out of a thick forest.

The *Midrash (Bereishis Rabbah* 65) identifies the *boar* which terrorizes Israel as Esau [the ancestor of אֱדוֹם, *Rome*] who resembles a wild swine. Esau's identity is alluded to by the raised ע, *ayin,* since the name עֵשָׂו, *Esau,* also begins with the letter *ayin.*

The Sages see a swine as the symbol of deception and hypocrisy. Of the two signs of a kosher animal, the swine has only one — a split hoof. Typically, it rests with its hooves extended as if to say, 'Look at my hooves, they prove I am kosher!' Similarly, Esau was thoroughly wicked, yet he attempted to erect a facade of integrity and piety

12 *It stretched its boughs until the sea,*
and to the river its tender shoots.
13 *Why have You breached its fences,*
so that all wayfarers pluck its fruit?
14 *The boar of the forest ravages it,*
and the prowlers of the field feed on it.
15 *O God of Legions please return,*
look down from heaven and see,
and show concern for this vine.
16 *And its support which Your right hand has planted*

around himself by posing to Isaac as a scrupulously religious person.[1]

The *Talmud (Kiddushin* 30a) points out that the raised ע of יָעַר is exactly in the middle of the *Book of Tehillim. Maharsha (Kiddushin* 30a) explains that this symbolizes the essential purpose of the *Book of Psalms*, which is to engulf and nullify the forces of evil (which are personified by Esau). [When the heretical influence of those who rebel against God threatens, a person should immerse himself in these rapturous songs of God's praises. Then all heresies will be dispelled by reinforced faith.]

וְזִיז שָׂדַי יִרְעֶנָּה – *And prowlers of the fields feed on it.*

The root of זִיז is זָז, *to move (Rashi).* The belligerent enemy is likened to the swift bird of prey which is constantly on the move as it hunts its quarry *(Ibn Ezra). Targum* observes that this description most aptly describes the wild cock.

15. אֱלֹהִים צְבָאוֹת שׁוּב נָא – *O God of Legions, please return.*

[Instead of drawing away from us, please return to our side and witness our degradation.]

הַבֵּט מִשָּׁמַיִם וּרְאֵה – *Look down from heaven and see.*

Although You are high and mighty and we are despicable and low, pay attention to our mundane needs *(Radak).*

וּפְקֹד גֶּפֶן זֹאת – *And show concern for this vine.*

Here, the psalmist beseeches God to take notice of the fate of His 'plant', which had been created by special Divine Providence *(Hirsch).*

Care for it, so that no one should ever trample it again *(Radak).*

16. וְכַנָּה אֲשֶׁר נָטְעָה יְמִינֶךָ – *And its support which Your right hand has planted.*

The כֵּן is the *base* or *foundation* which supports the structure built above it. Here it refers to the vine which is too weak and fragile to thrive unless it is supported by posts and trellises *(Malbim).*

This allegorically describes the support and basis upon which Israel's survival depends: the Holy City of

1. Scripture relates: *And when Esau was forty years old, he took a wife (Genesis* 26:34). *Rashi (Genesis* 26:34) comments that *Psalms* 80:14 compares Esau to the swine, which shows off its split hooves in an attempt to pose as a kosher animal. Esau was steeped in violence and robbery. He spent the first forty years of his life snatching wives from their husbands and raping them. When he reached the age of forty, he represented himself to his father Isaac as an obedient and pious son, and declared: 'Father was wed at forty (to fulfill the commandment properly); I, too, wish to follow this righteous approach.'

יז יְמִינֶךָ וְעַל־בֵּן אִמַּצְתָּה לָּךְ: שְׂרֻפָה בָאֵשׁ
יח כְּסוּחָה מִגַּעֲרַת פָּנֶיךָ יֹאבֵדוּ: תְּהִי־יָדְךָ
עַל־אִישׁ יְמִינֶךָ עַל־בֶּן־אָדָם אִמַּצְתָּ לָּךְ:
יט וְלֹא־נָסוֹג מִמֶּךָּ תְּחַיֵּנוּ וּבְשִׁמְךָ נִקְרָא:
כ יהוה אֱלֹהִים צְבָאוֹת הֲשִׁיבֵנוּ הָאֵר פָּנֶיךָ
וְנִוָּשֵׁעָה:

Jerusalem and the Holy Temple *(Radak).*

[The initial letter כ, *chaf*, of כַּנָּה is enlarged. This suggests that although the foundation of an edifice normally possesses no intrinsic significance, but becomes important because it supports the structure above it, the foundation of Israel, the Holy Temple, is of major significance in its own right.]

וְעַל בֵּן אִמַּצְתָּה לָּךְ – *And the son whom You strengthened for Yourself.*

Malbim observes that as the vine spreads and grows, it becomes necessary to prop it up with a more elaborate בִּנְיָן, *structure*, called a בֵּן.

Allegorically, this refers to Messiah, the בֵּן, *son*, of David whom God *made strong* – both physically and intellectually – so that he might reinforce the flagging spirits of the exiled people *(Ibn Yachya).*

When the son of David triumphs, then the ancient blessing *(Genesis* 27:40) will be fulfilled. Although Isaac loved Esau and held him exceptionally dear, God preferred Jacob and *made* him *strong*. Esau was to be subservient to his brother, as Isaac told Esau *(Genesis* 27:40): וְאֶת אָחִיךָ תַּעֲבֹד, *and you shall serve your brother (Rashi).*

[In modern usage, אימוץ means *adopt* an orphan. Jacob resembled an orphan, since his father preferred Esau, and since only one of the sons was to inherit the blessings of Abraham and the privilege of receiving the Torah, the preference for Esau was tantamount to removing Jacob from the Patriarchal lineage. But God 'adopted' Jacob and brought him the paternal blessings.]

17. שְׂרֻפָה בָאֵשׁ כְּסוּחָה – *Consumed by fire, razed* [lit. *cut down*].

Look at the dismal fate of Jacob, Your chosen son. No traces of Messianic triumph can be detected. We see only downtrodden people, burnt and slaughtered *(Rashi).*

מִגַּעֲרַת פָּנֶיךָ יֹאבֵדוּ – *Before Your angry shout they perish.*

You have withdrawn from Israel and hidden Your countenance from them *(Radak).* Their numbers have dwindled to the point that they are threatened with extinction *(Rashi).*

According to *Sforno*, these last words are a plea for the extinction of Rome: Since they burnt us and cut us down, cause them to perish!

18. תְּהִי יָדְךָ עַל אִישׁ יְמִינֶךָ – *Let Your strong hand rest upon the man at Your right.*

Rashi interprets this as a call for punishment against Esau. It is Esau whom You originally strengthened with Your right hand of mercy. Now smite him with Your left hand of wrath and strict justice *(Malbim).*

Radak and *Ibn Ezra* see this as a plea for protection: Israel is the vine which *Your right hand has planted (v.* 16). Safeguard this precious creation of Your hands.

עַל בֶּן אָדָם אִמַּצְתָּ לָּךְ – *Upon the son of man whom You strengthened for Yourself.*

Rashi says that this refers to Esau, who was strengthened by Isaac's blessing, *Behold, your dwelling shall be of the fatness of the earth (Genesis* 27:39).

and the son whom You strengthened
for Yourself.

17 *Consumed by fire, razed;*
before Your angry shout they perish.
18 *Let Your strong hand rest*
upon the man at Your right,
Upon the son of man whom You strengthened
for Yourself.
19 *Then we shall not draw back from You,*
revive us and we shall invoke Your Name.
20 *HASHEM, God of Legions, return us;*
set Your face aglow that we may be saved.

Now God is begged to strike Esau down.

Sforno interpets this entire verse as a reference to Messiah, the son of David, of whom the psalmist writes *(Psalms* 110:1): *HASHEM says to my master, sit at my right hand.* The psalmist begs God to strengthen Messiah.

The Messiah is truly בֶּן אָדָם, *son of Adam (man),* for David received the seventy years of his life from *Adam* and owed his existence to him *(Chazah Zion;* see *Overview Tehillim,* Vol. I, part 1,5).

19. וְלֹא נָסוֹג מִמֶּךָּ – *Then we shall not draw back from You.*

We will not abandon You, since You will not abandon us, as the prophet promised *(I Samuel* 12:22): כִּי לֹא יִטֹּשׁ ה' אֶת עַמּוֹ בַּעֲבוּר שְׁמוֹ הַגָּדוֹל, *For HASHEM will not forsake His nation for the sake of His great Name (Midrash Shocher Tov).*

תְּחַיֵּינוּ וּבְשִׁמְךָ נִקְרָא – *Revive us and we shall invoke Your Name.*

Revive us from the mortal danger of exile *(Rashi).* Revive us with Torah, which is the very breath of life *(Sforno).* Then we shall vigorously proclaim to all that You are our Redeemer *(Radak).*

20. ה' אֱלֹהִים צְבָאוֹת הֲשִׁיבֵנוּ – *HASHEM, God of Legions, return us.*

In this plea for deliverance God is addressed by three Names. [See *Prefatory Remarks* and *comm.* to *vs.* 4 and 8].

As *Hirsch* explains (see *comm.* to *v.* 5) the Name ה', *HASHEM*, signifies that God controls and molds the entire panorama of past, present, and future history to suit His will. Thus, He creates the conditions necessary for the redemption to occur despite the progressively worsening exile.

As the gloom of the exile deepens, a greater revelation of God's Name is required to bring about the redemption *(Rashi).*

In verse 19, Israel pledged *and we will invoke Your Name.* This promise will be fulfilled when we address God by these three titles *(Ibn Ezra).*

Then all will see that He is ה' אֱלֹהִים, *the Dispenser of Justice* to the hostile nations, and צְבָאוֹת, *God of Legions*, the sovereign of all the legions of the universe *(Sforno).*

הָאֵר פָּנֶיךָ וְנִוָּשֵׁעָה – *Set Your face aglow that we may be saved.*

The final salvation will be permanent only if it is accompanied by intellectual enlightenment, which results from Torah study. The prophet teaches *(Jeremiah* 31:32): *'This will be the covenant that I will make with the House of Israel after those days,' says HASHEM, 'I will put my Torah into their innards and write it in their hearts and I will be their God and they will be My nation'* *(Sforno).*

The psalm concludes with this fundamental lesson: the gloom and suffering of exile will never extinguish the pure light and glow of Torah.

מזמור פא 81

In Psalm 80, Israel beseeched God to redeem His people from exile. Psalm 81 celebrates the Divine salvation which ended our servitude in Egypt. The climax of the redemption from bondage in Egypt occurred when the Jews actually left the land on the fifteenth of Nissan, *a day which is commemorated by the Passover festival. However, the process of redemption began six months earlier, on the first of* Tishrei, Rosh Hashanah, *when the Israelites stopped working as slaves for their Egyptian taskmasters (*Rosh Hashanah *11a).*

This composition commemorates that event: From the burden I removed his shoulder, I let his hands pass from the kettle (v. *7). This psalm also speaks of the shofar blast (*v. *4), a powerful call to celebrate new found freedom and a new year.*

*This psalm was designated to accompany the Temple sacrifices on Rosh Hashanah (*Rosh Hashanah *30b). It is also* שִׁיר שֶׁל יוֹם, the Song of the Day, *for* יוֹם חֲמִישִׁי, the fifth day *of the week, as will be explained in the commentary to verse 2.*

פא א־ה

א־ב לַמְנַצֵּחַ | עַל־הַגִּתִּית לְאָסָף: הַרְנִינוּ
לֵאלֹהִים עוּזֵּנוּ הָרִיעוּ לֵאלֹהֵי יַעֲקֹב:
ג שְׂאוּ־זִמְרָה וּתְנוּ־תֹף כִּנּוֹר נָעִים עִם־
ד נָבֶל: תִּקְעוּ בַחֹדֶשׁ שׁוֹפָר בַּכֶּסֶה לְיוֹם
ה חַגֵּנוּ: כִּי חֹק לְיִשְׂרָאֵל הוּא מִשְׁפָּט

1. עַל הַגִּתִּית – *On the* Gittis.

[See *comm.* to 8:1.] *Targum* and *Rashi* explain that this instrument was manufactured in the town of *Gat.*

Rashi [*comm.* to 8:1] cites the Rabbis of the *Midrash* who say that גִּתִּית is related to גַּת, *the winepress.*

Hirsch translates: To Him Who grants victory over the wine pressing. He explains that psalm 80 depicts Israel as a grapevine and describes the exile and persecution of God's 'plant,' whereas psalm 81 portrays the glory which the vine will receive if it submits to being purified by the winepress. [Psalm 80 depicts Israel as a גֶּפֶן, *grapevine* taken out of Egyptian bondage (*v.* 9). Servitude is likened to a winepress, which crushes its contents. This psalm celebrates Israel's release from that crushing toil and physical oppression on *Rosh Hashanah* (see *Prefatory Remarks).*]

לְאָסָף – *By Assaf.*

Literally אָסָף means *to gather in,* alluding to the ingathering of Israel from tyranny and exile *(Chazah Zion).*

2. הַרְנִינוּ לֵאלֹהִים עוּזֵּנוּ – *Arouse joyous song a to the God of our might.*

On Rosh Hashanah, God showed that He was *our might* because He no longer allowed the Egyptians to enslave us. This event was a cause for *joyous song (Radak).*

Meiri points out that הַרְנִינוּ is the causative form. It implies: Do not celebrate in seclusion; let your ecstasy also bring joyous melodies to the lips of others.

The *Talmud* designates this psalm as the Song of the Day for יוֹם חֲמִישִׁי, *the fifth day,* of the week. On the fifth day of creation, God made the birds and the fish, which bring joy to the world. When people observe the vast variety of colorful birds and fish, they are awed by the tremendous scope of God's creative ability, and they are stirred to praise Him with song (*Rashi, Rosh Hashanah* 31a).[1]

הָרִיעוּ לֵאלֹהֵי יַעֲקֹב – *Call out to the God of Jacob.*

The Patriarch Jacob is singled out because he went down to Egypt with his sons and their families. From the moment Jacob arrived in Egypt, the 210 years of bondage [רְדוּ] began. During this period the children of Jacob called out to God in their distress *(Radak).*

Meiri associates הָרִיעוּ with תְּרוּעָה, *blast of the shofar.* Thus: Proclaim your liberation from Egypt with triumphant fanfare.

The theme of the *shofar* also pertains to Rosh Hashanah, the יוֹם הַדִּין, *Day of Judgment.* God sits on His throne as אֱלֹהִים, *the strict Dispenser of Justice,* but Israel begs for mercy through the wailing *shofar* sound. The call of the *shofar* changes God's anger to compassion (*Pesikta Rabbosi* 40:1).

3. שְׂאוּ זִמְרָה וּתְנוּ תֹף – *Strike* [lit. *lift*] *up a song and sound the timbrel.*

Make music to God in every possible

1. The *Talmud (Shabbos* 156a) says that anyone born on the fifth day of the week will be a kind person who shares joy and goodness with others, because the fish and the birds were formed on the fifth day of creation. *Rashi (Shabbos* 156a) explains that these creatures exemplify a carefree existence because God provided them with ample, readily accessible food supplies. The availability of sufficiency frees one from the compulsion toward selfishness for the sake of survival.

81
1-5

For the Conductor,
upon the Gittis, by Assaf.
2 Arouse a joyous song to the God of our might,
call out to the God of Jacob.
3 Strike up a song and sound the timbrel,
the sweet Kinnor with the Neivel.
4 Blow the Shofar at the moon's renewal,
at the time appointed for our festive day.
5 Because it is a decree for Israel,

way [both with words and with instruments] *(Radak).*

Raise your voice so high that even the [loud] noise of the timbrel will not drown it out *(Alshich).*

כִּנּוֹר נָעִים עִם נָבֶל — *The sweet* Kinnor *with* Neivel.

[See *comm.* to 33:2 for lengthy discussion of the *Kinnor* and *Neivel.*]

Rashi cites a Talmudic debate (*Arachin* 13b) as to whether the names describe the same instrument or two different ones.

The *Midrash* explains that the נֶבֶל, *Neivel,* is unique; its exquisite music makes all other instruments seem to be נָבֵל, *worn out; disgraced.*

4. תִּקְעוּ בַחֹדֶשׁ שׁוֹפָר — *Blow the* shofar *at the moon's renewal.*

Radak explains that the first day of the month is called חֹדֶשׁ [related to חָדָשׁ, *new*] because the moon which waned and disappeared at the end of the previous month then reappears and begins a new cycle. Rosh Hashanah, which occurs on the first day of *Tishrei,* also coincides with the renewal of the moon. It is the only one of all the Jewish festivals which occurs at this time of the month.

The *shofar* is blown on Rosh HaShanah to commemorate the cessation of the Israelites' slavery on that day.

Similarly, the *shofar* blast is blown on Yom Kippur of the יוֹבֵל, *Jubilee,* year as a summons to liberate slaves (*Leviticus* 25:9).

Midrash Shocher Tov adds that Rosh Hashanah is a time for חִדּוּשׁ, *renewal,* of one's deeds and שׁוֹפָר [cognate with שִׁיפּוּר, *beauty*] *improvement,* of one's deeds.

בַּכֶּסֶה לְיוֹם חַגֵּנוּ — *At the time appointed for our festive day.*

The translation of כֶּסֶה follows *Rashi, Radak,* and *Ibn Ezra.*

Others relate כֶּסֶה to כִּסָּה, *covered.* All other Jewish holidays occur later in the month, when the major part of the moon is visible. Only Rosh Hashanah occurs at the very beginning of the month, when the moon is still *covered (Rosh Hashanah* 8a).

Furthermore, God judges Israel on this day and mercifully *covers* and forgives their sins *(Midrash Shocher Tov).*

Sforno translates כֶּסֶה as cognate with כִּסֵּא, *throne.* Rosh Hashanah is *our festive day* despite the fact that the Almighty then sits on His *throne* of strict Justice.

5. כִּי חֹק לְיִשְׂרָאֵל הוּא — *Because it is a decree for Israel.*

The *shofar* is sounded on Rosh Hashanah not because of mere custom, but because God has commanded this as a חֹק, *decree,* for Israel on this day of *Judgment for the God of Jacob (Rashi).*

The *Talmud (Beitzah* 16a) translates חֹק as *a fixed ration.* On Rosh Hashanah, the heavenly tribunal fixes each man's sustenance for the coming year. However, if one spends extra to

ו לֵאלֹהֵי יַעֲקֹב: עֵדוּת | בִּיהוֹסֵף שָׂמוֹ
בְּצֵאתוֹ עַל־אֶרֶץ מִצְרָיִם שְׂפַת לֹא־
ז יָדַעְתִּי אֶשְׁמָע: הֲסִירוֹתִי מִסֵּבֶל שִׁכְמוֹ
ח כַּפָּיו מִדּוּד תַּעֲבֹרְנָה: בַּצָּרָה קָרָאתָ
וָאֲחַלְּצֶךָּ אֶעֶנְךָ בְּסֵתֶר רַעַם אֶבְחָנְךָ עַל־

honor the Sabbath and festivals and to teach his children Torah, then God returns the money to him generously. If he spends little, then God decreases his allotment.

מִשְׁפָּט לֵאלֹהֵי יַעֲקֹב — *A judgment for the God of Jacob.*

The *Yerushalmi (Rosh Hashanah* 1:3) stresses that if the Jewish people display confidence in God's mercy, Rosh Hashanah will be transformed from a day of *judgment* to one of forgiveness.[1]

Meiri points out that a חֹק is a *statute* for which there is no apparent reason, whereas the purpose of a מִשְׁפָּט, *judgment* is self-evident.

The psalmist means that the Torah laws or the historical events which appear to be unfathomable statutes *for Israel* are incomprehensible only because of the limitations of the human mind. But to the Divine intellect, these same matters have clear and profound meaning: *for the God of Jacob*, they are not statutes, but *judgments.*

6. עֵדוּת בִּיהוֹסֵף שָׂמוֹ בְּצֵאתוֹ עַל אֶרֶץ מִצְרָיִם — *As a testimony for Joseph He imposed it when he went out over the land of Egypt.*

On *Rosh Hashanah,* Joseph was released from prison and brought before Pharaoh to interpret his dreams and to warn him of the future *(Rashi).*

[Similarly, if a man is found worthy on Rosh Hashanah, the Day of Judgment, he will be absolved from a harsh sentence and he will stand in the presence of the King of Kings. If a man is truly righteous, he will gain insight and prophetic vision which will allow him to comprehend what the Heavenly Tribunal has ordained for him for the year.]

יְהוֹסֵף — *Joseph.*

When the wife of Potiphar attempted to seduce יוֹסֵף, *Joseph,* in the privacy of her home, Joseph feared God and refused to give in to temptation. Because he sanctified God's Name, he merited that the letter ה׳, *hey,* from God's Name should be added to his own, making it יְהוֹסֵף *(Sotah* 10a).

שְׂפַת לֹא יָדַעְתִּי אֶשְׁמָע — *A language unknown to me I heard.*

The *Talmud (Sotah* 36b) offers yet another reason why the letter ה׳, *hey,* was inserted in Joseph's name: Pharaoh was deeply impressed by Joseph's wisdom when Joseph interpreted his dream, and he wished to elevate Joseph to the post of viceroy. However, Pharaoh's counselors reminded him that an Egyptain statute stipulated that appointees to royal position must know the seventy languages of the world. That night, the angel Gabriel attempted to teach Joseph all seventy languages. The angel's efforts were unsuccessful until he added the letter ה׳ from God's Name to Joseph's name. As a result, Joseph became inspired and grasped the

1. The *Yerushalmi* [*Rosh Hashanah* ch. 1] states: Which people can compare to the Jewish people? It is the way of the world that if a person has a judgment pending against him, he dresses in black, wraps himself in black, and lets his beard grow because of anxiety and uncertainty of the outcome. Israel however, is different. They dress in white, they eat, drink and rejoice in the knowledge that God will perform miracles on their behalf [and favor them with forgiveness.]

a judgment for the God of Jacob.
6 *As a testimony for Joseph*
He imposed it,
When He went out over the land of Egypt,
a language unknown to me I heard.
7 *From the burden I removed his shoulder,*
I let his hands pass from the kettle.
8 *In distress you called out,*
and I released you,
I answered you with thunder
when you hid,
I tested you Mei Merivah, *Selah.*

spiritual content of each language. Soon he knew all seventy tongues and was fit for the royal post.

Yalkut Shimoni (831) points out that this verse begins and ends with the letter ע, *ayin,*which has a numerical value of seventy. This alludes to Joseph's initial ignorance of ע, *seventy*, languages and his ultimate comprehension of these ע, *seventy*, tongues.

Radak interprets this verse as a reference to the entire congregation of Israel. The Jews assumed the name of Joseph because he sustained them in Egypt [see *comm.* 80:2]. At the time of the exodus, they *went out over* [i.e., from] *the land of Egypt* because they had struggled to maintain their national identity. *A languague unknown to me I heard,* suggests that the Israelites took pains to speak only the holy language, Hebrew. They considered Egyptian to be a foreign tongue of which they had no knowledge.

7. הֲסִירוֹתִי מִסֵּבֶל שִׁכְמוֹ — *From the burden I removed his shoulder.*

On Rosh Hashanah the Jews were released from the back-breaking task of building Pharoah's treasure cities *(Radak).*

כַּפָּיו מִדּוּד תַּעֲבֹרְנָה — *I let his hands pass from the kettle.*

Rashi says that this refers to the cooking and menial kitchen work which the Jewish slaves were forced to do for their Egyptian taskmasters.

According to *Radak,* this refers to the pots in which the Jews hauled mortar and lime to the construction sites.

8. בַּצָּרָה קָרָאתָ וָאֲחַלְּצֶךָּ — *In distress you called out and I released you.*

Scripture states *(Exodus* 2:23): And the children of Israel groaned because of the bondage, and they cried out, and their cry rose up to God by reason of their bondage *(Radak).*

אֶעֶנְךָ בְּסֵתֶר רַעַם — *I answered you with thunder when you hid.*

You, Israel, cried out to Me in privacy, in the lonely recesses of your hearts. But I responded to Your plea publicly, with a thunderous display of might which demonstrated My concern for you *(Rashi; Radak).*

[This corresponds to the *shofar* of Rosh Hashanah. The mouth of the *shofar* is very narrow yet the other opening is wide. Similarly, when Israel makes a small request of God, He amplifies the whispered plea into a thunderous prayer which demands a Divine response.]

אֶבְחָנְךָ עַל מֵי מְרִיבָה סֶלָה — *I tested you at* Mei Merivah [lit. *waters of strife*], *Selah.*

The Lord says, 'Although I knew that

ט מֵי מְרִיבָה סֶלָה: שְׁמַע עַמִּי וְאָעִידָה בָּךְ
י יִשְׂרָאֵל אִם־תִּשְׁמַע־לִי: לֹא־יִהְיֶה בְךָ אֵל
יא זָר וְלֹא תִשְׁתַּחֲוֶה לְאֵל נֵכָר: אָנֹכִי | יהוה
אֱלֹהֶיךָ הַמַּעַלְךָ מֵאֶרֶץ מִצְרָיִם הַרְחֶב־
יב פִּיךָ וַאֲמַלְאֵהוּ: וְלֹא־שָׁמַע עַמִּי לְקוֹלִי

Israel was destined to sin at מֵי מְרִיבָה, *Mei Merivah*, I overlooked this future transgression and saved Israel from the dangers which confronted them in Egypt' *(Rashi).*

9. שְׁמַע עַמִּי וְאָעִידָה בָּךְ – *Listen My nation and I will attest to you.*

After you come to the realization that it is I, God, who performed these acts of kindness [recounted in the previous verses], you should certainly pay attention to what I say *(Rashi).*

I can attest that if you listen to Me, all will be well *(Radak).* [However, since history bears evidence that you failed to heed My warnings אָעִידָה בָּךְ, *I testify against you, and I will say: My people did not heed My voice and Israel did not desire Me (v.* 12).]

יִשְׂרָאֵל אִם תִּשְׁמַע לִי – *O Israel, if you would but listen to Me.*

When God issued the Ten Commandments at Sinai, Israel heard only the first two commandments from the mouth of God Himself. They heard God say, *'I am HASHEM, your God'* and *'You shall have no other God besides Me' (Exodus* 20:23).

The *Midrash (Shir HaShirim* 1) says that God's commanding voice made such a profound impression on them that the Evil Inclination was purged from their hearts. After hearing these two commandments, however, Israel grew weak. They panicked and refused to listen to God's awesome voice. They demanded that Moses become their intermediary and transmit the remaining eight commandments to them. At that moment, they ceased to be spellbound by God's holy words, and the Evil Inclination returned to their hearts.

Therefore, God says, *'O, Israel, if you had listened to Me* [directly then] (*v.* 10) *there would be no strange god* [i.e., Evil Inclination] *within you' (Shevet M'Yisroel;* see *comm.* of *Dorash Moshe* to *v.* 12).

10. לֹא יִהְיֶה בְךָ אֵל זָר – *There shall be no strange god within you.*

Malbim explains that a נֵכָר is a complete *alien* whereas the זָר is someone or something relatively near which has become estranged.

The Sages (*Shabbos* 105b) teach that the אֵל זָר, *strange god,* is the Evil Inclination which is found בָּךְ, *within you* (i.e., in your heart), and which is not completely נֵכָר, *alien*, to man's proper mission.

[This inclination can also be harnessed constructively. Even seemingly negative character traits can be disciplined and utilized in the service of God. For example, anger can be used to combat evil. Avarice can be channeled into a desire to collect funds for charity, and so on.

If the Evil Inclination is left undisciplined, however, it becomes זָר, *a stranger,* to its possessor. Instead of being man's tool, it becomes his master.

Therefore,the *Talmud (Shabbos* 105b) teaches that a person who tears his clothes, smashes pots, or throws coins around in anger, is akin to an idol-worshiper. This is the strategy of the Evil Inclination: today it drives you toward one transgression, tomorrow it leads you to commit another, and ultimately it influences you to worship idols.][1]

וְלֹא תִשְׁתַּחֲוֶה לְאֵל נֵכָר – *Nor shall you bow before an alien god.*

[9] *Listen, My nation,*
and I will attest to you;
O Israel, if you would but listen to Me.
[10] *There shall be no strange god within you,*
nor shall you bow before an alien god.
[11] *I am HASHEM, your God, who raised you*
from the land of Egypt,
Open wide your mouth
and I will fill it.
[12] *But My people did not heed My voice*

If the אֵל זָר, *strange god,* gains internal control over you, eventually it will influence your external actions as well, and you will worship *alien gods* (*Yerushalmi, Nedarim* 9:1).

[Since the Israelites did not listen to God at Sinai, the Evil Inclination controlled them and led them to worship an *alien god* — the Golden Calf.]

11. אָנֹכִי ה׳ אֱלֹהֶיךָ הַמַּעַלְךָ מֵאֶרֶץ מִצְרָיִם — *I am HASHEM, your God, who raised you from the land of Egypt.*

Remember that I am a benevolent God who seeks your welfare. Just as I redeemed you from Egypt in order to improve your lot, so do I continually search for ways to make your existence more wholesome and pleasant (*Ibn Ezra*).

I did not merely *take you* out of Egypt [i.e., מוֹצִיא] rather, I *raised you* [i.e., הַמַּעַלְךָ] to a higher plane of existence and of spiritual achievement (*Hirsch*).

[Because of my goodness and generosity, it is certainly foolish for you to follow *strange* and *alien gods* (*v.* 10).]

הַרְחֶב פִּיךָ וַאֲמַלְאֵהוּ — *Open wide your mouth and I will fill it.*

Ask of me all that your heart desires, and I will fulfill every request (*Ibn Ezra*), on the condition that you hearken to me. Then you will never know want, hunger, or thirst [just as you were completely provided for when I brought you from Egypt] (*Radak*).

From these words, the *Yerushalmi* (*Taanis* 3:6) derives the halachic principle that the worshiper should supplicate God for *all* his needs, thereby demonstrating his complete faith in God's omnipotence and benevolence. The more one asks for God's help, the wider he opens his mouth, the more he shows that he believes in God's ability to provide *all* of man's needs.

12. וְלֹא שָׁמַע עַמִּי לְקוֹלִי — *But My people did not heed My voice.*

Unfortunately, the dramatic exodus did not leave a lasting impression upon the people. Immediately afterwards, in

1. Listening to the *shofar* on *Rosh Hashanah* serves to subdue the evil forces within man. In the words of the *Talmud* (*Rosh Hashanah* 16b), the repeated blasts of the ram's horn are כְּדֵי לְעַרְבֵּב אֶת הַשָּׂטָן, *in order to confound and frustrate Satan.*

Rabbeinu Nissim (*Rosh Hashanah* 16b) explains the *Talmud's* (*Bava Basra* 16a) teaching that the Evil Inclination and Satan are actually the same force. The vicious cycle begins when the sinister force descends to earth as the Evil Inclination and seduces man to sin. Then this very same force assumes the role of Satan, the prosecuting angel and ascends before the heavenly tribunal to accuse and condemn the sinner.

On *Rosh Hashanah*, the terrifying call of the *shofar* intimidates man and subdues his Evil Inclination. Thus the evil force cannot assume the role of Satan. In this way, Satan is confounded and frustrated.

יג וְיִשְׂרָאֵל לֹא־אָבָה לִי: וָאֲשַׁלְּחֵהוּ
יד בִּשְׁרִירוּת לִבָּם יֵלְכוּ בְּמוֹעֲצוֹתֵיהֶם: לוּ
עַמִּי שֹׁמֵעַ לִי יִשְׂרָאֵל בִּדְרָכַי יְהַלֵּכוּ:
טו כִּמְעַט אוֹיְבֵיהֶם אַכְנִיעַ וְעַל־צָרֵיהֶם
טז אָשִׁיב יָדִי: מְשַׂנְאֵי יהוה יְכַחֲשׁוּ־לוֹ וִיהִי
יז עִתָּם לְעוֹלָם: וַיַּאֲכִילֵהוּ מֵחֵלֶב חִטָּה
וּמִצּוּר דְּבַשׁ אַשְׂבִּיעֶךָ:

the wilderness, they refused to obey God. They continued to neglect God in the days of the judges and during the reign of the kings *(Radak)*.

Dorash Moshe notes that the psalmist once again laments Israel's failure to hear all of the Ten Commandments from the lips of God (see *comm. v.* 9). Because *My people did not heed My voice* at Sinai, the Evil Inclination corrupted Israel so that *they had no desire for Me* [and followed strange gods].

וְיִשְׂרָאֵל לֹא אָבָה לִי – *And Israel did not desire Me.*

They even despised the messages I sent them through My chosen prophets *(Sforno)*. This situation continued until finally I no longer desired them (Israel); then I drove them into exile and destroyed their Temple *(Radak)*.

13. וָאֲשַׁלְּחֵהוּ בִּשְׁרִירוּת לִבָּם – *So I let them follow their heart's fantasies.*

The translation follows *Rashi*, who traces the root of שְׁרִירוּת to שׁוֹרְרַי, *those who watch me*, (see *comm.* to *Psalms* 5:9). Literally, שְׁרִירוּת means the *visions* or *imagination* of the heart. [Those who follow the path of sin entertain a distorted image of reality and fantasize that evil succeeds and that sins go unpunished.]

Radak and *Ibn Ezra* identify שְׁרִירוּת with שָׁרִיר, *strong, impervious.*

Thus, the hearts of the sinners were hard and remorseless. Since they refused to repent, I stopped protecting them. I abandoned them to the whims of the gentiles

יֵלְכוּ בְּמוֹעֲצוֹתֵיהֶם – *I let them follow their own counsels.*

They imagined that their corrupt schemes and *counsels* would assure them success, but I knew that by following their own crooked *counsel*, they would seal their doom *(Radak)*.

14. לוּ עַמִּי שֹׁמֵעַ לִי – *If only My nation would heed Me.*

God yearns for Israel to heed His words saying, 'If only they would listen and improve their ways, I would eagerly accept their repentance' *(Rashi)*.

יִשְׂרָאֵל בִּדְרָכַי יְהַלֵּכוּ – *If Israel would walk in My ways.*

The commentaries explain that עַמִּי, *my nation*, refers to the common people (see *Alshich*) who are relatively uncultured. God would be satisfied if the general population would simply *heed* Him. However, יִשְׂרָאֵל, *Israel*, refers to the scholars. God expects them to immerse themselves in the study of His word and to toil incessantly in Torah study (*Sifra, Bechukosai* 26:1). Only thus will they become elevated and walk in God's ways. This refers to entry into the Divine Presence *(Nefutzos Yehudah)*.

Dorash Moshe cites the *Talmud's* statement (*Sanhedrin* 11a) that a heavenly voice once proclaimed, 'Shmuel Hakattan is truly worthy of being granted the holy spirit of prophecy, but he shall not receive it because the rest of his generation is unworthy.' This teaches that the spiritual level of the general population determines the limits of the achievements of the scholars, for

and Israel did not desire Me.
13 *So I let them follow their heart's fantasies,*
I let them follow their own counsels.
14 *If only My nation would heed Me,*
if Israel would walk in My ways.
15 *In an instant I would subdue*
their foes,
And against their tormentors
turn My hand.
16 *Those who hate* HASHEM *lie to Him —*
so their destiny is eternal.
17 *But He would feed him*
with the cream of the wheat,
And from a rock
sate you with honey.

scholars cannot divorce themselves from their environment.

Thus, the psalmist says in God's Name, *'If only My nation* [the masses] *would heed Me,* [then] *Israel* [the elite scholars] *would walk My ways* [and achieve the highest levels of prophecy and wisdom].'

15. כִּמְעַט אוֹיְבֵיהֶם אַכְנִיעַ — *In an instant I would subdue their foes.*

God continues, 'If Israel had hearkened to My words in the wilderness, then they would have had no difficulty in subduing the seven Canaanite nations who opposed their entry into the Holy Land' *(Alshich).*

וְעַל צָרֵיהֶם אָשִׁיב יָדִי — *And against their tormentors turn My hand.*

Had Israel been faithful and obedient, I would have restrained My hand from beating them. I would have turned My blows upon their tormentors instead *(Rashi).*

16. מְשַׂנְאֵי ה׳ יְכַחֲשׁוּ לוֹ — *Those who hate* HASHEM *lie to Him.*

[If Israel would listen to God, their tormentors would be considered as those who torment and hate God]. Those tormentors would be condemned to terrible suffering. Then they would lie in an effort to deny their guilt. Deceitfully, they would protest to God that they never had done Israel any harm *(Rashi).*

וִיהִי עִתָּם לְעוֹלָם — *So their destiny is eternal.*

Rashi explains that this refers to the gentile tormentors who are condemned to everlasting suffering: עִתָּם, *their time* of punishment, לְעוֹלָם, *endures forever.*

Radak however, maintains that this refers to Israel. God continues to muse, 'If only Israel obeyed Me, then their period of blessing and prosperity would endure forever.'

17. וַיַּאֲכִילֵהוּ מֵחֵלֶב חִטָּה — *But He would feed him with the cream* [lit. *the fat*] *of the wheat.*

Whenever Israel obeys God, He provides for them handsomely. In the wilderness, for example, God fed them manna, which was more succulent and nutritious than *the cream of the wheat* *(Ibn Ezra).*

וּמִצּוּר דְּבַשׁ אַשְׂבִּיעֶךָ — *And from a rock sate you with honey.*

In the wilderness, God also gave them water from the well of Miriam, whose waters were sweeter than honey (*Ibn Ezra*). [Miriam's well was in the form of a צוּר, *rock*, which rolled along with the camp as it traveled. When they stopped, sweet waters gushed from the rock and refreshed the nation.]

Rashi, Ibn Ezra, and *Radak* all note that the Torah itself describes Israel's fortunes in similar terms: וַיֵּנִקֵהוּ דְבַשׁ מִסֶּלַע וְשֶׁמֶן מֵחַלְמִישׁ צוּר, *He made him suck honey out of the stone, and oil out of the hard rock (Deuteronomy* 32:13).

Rokeach observes that this verse is a most appropriate conclusion, since this psalm is so intimately related to Rosh Hashanah. On Rosh Hashanah we pray for a sweet and pleasant New Year. It is customary to dip an apple in honey on that day and to offer a prayer for a sweet year.

מזמור פב
82

T his composition presents a vigorous affirmation of the Torah judicial system and a forceful condemnation of those who corrupt and falsify God's law.

The Talmud (Rosh Hashanah *31a) designates this psalm as the* שִׁיר שֶׁל יוֹם, Song of the Day, *for the third day of the week, because on the third day of creation God 'uncovered the earth with His wisdom and prepared the world for His chosen assembly,' alluding to* Genesis 1:9: *where we read:* God said, 'Let the waters beneath the heaven be gathered into one area, that the dry land may appear.'

Maharsha (Rosh Hashanah *31a) explains that the continued existence of the earth depends on the maintenance of equity and justice. When men discipline themselves to remain within the strict confines of the law, God reciprocates by keeping the forces of nature within their proper boundaries. But when men disregard moral values, God reciprocates by unleashing the destructive forces of nature. At the time of the* מַבּוּל, flood, *for example,* the earth became corrupt before God and the earth became filled with robbery (Genesis *6:11). As a result, the seas ignored their boundaries and filled the land with flood waters.*

Furthermore, on the third day of Creation, the earth brought forth דֶּשֶׁא, vegetation (Genesis *1:12). In* Pirkei Avos *(1:18) we learn that the world endures because of three things:* אֱמֶת, truth, דִּין, justice *and* שָׁלוֹם, peace. *Some commentators note that the three letters of the word* דֶּשֶׁא *are also the initial letters of* דִּין, שָׁלוֹם *and* אֱמֶת. *This suggests that the presence of these three social virtues is indicative of the goodness and fruitfulness of human civilization, just as vegetation represents fertility in the physical world. When truth, justice, and peace prevail, the entire earth flourishes. Indeed, the* Talmud (Shabbos *10a) states that every judge who renders true justice becomes, so to speak, a partner of God in the work of creation* (Ethics from Sinai).

פב
א־ד

א מִזְמוֹר לְאָסָף אֱלֹהִים נִצָּב בַּעֲדַת־אֵל
ב בְּקֶרֶב אֱלֹהִים יִשְׁפֹּט: עַד־מָתַי תִּשְׁפְּטוּ־
ג עָוֶל וּפְנֵי רְשָׁעִים תִּשְׂאוּ־סֶלָה: שִׁפְטוּ־דָל
ד וְיָתוֹם עָנִי וָרָשׁ הַצְדִּיקוּ: פַּלְּטוּ־דַל

1. מִזְמוֹר לְאָסָף — *A song of Assaf.*

Radak and *Malbim* suggest that this psalm was composed during the reign of King Jehoshafat [whose name literally means 'HASHEM Judges'].

This king of Judea, a descendant of King David, was basically a righteous ruler. However, he erred when he allied himself with the wicked King Achav of Israel. These two monarchs were defeated by the host of Aram at Ramos Gilad. Achav was killed, and Jehoshafat barely escaped with his life. Terribly shaken, Jehoshafat returned to Jerusalem determined to arouse a wave of repentance among the people. He understood that without an honest judicial system, there was no hope of inspiring the populace with a sincere respect for the law.

And he appointed judges in the land throughout all of the fortified cities of Judea, city by city, and he said to the judges, 'Pay heed to that which you are doing for you are not judging for men, rather for HASHEM, Who is with You in the judgment. And now let the fear of HASHEM be upon you, take heed and do it for there is no iniquity with HASHEM, our God, and no granting of favors, nor acceptance of bribes (II Kings 19:5-7).

[It is most appropriate that a מִזְמוֹר, *song,* was composed in recognition of Jehoshafat's efforts, because Jehoshafat considered *song* to be his most effective weapon. The Rabbis relate (*Pesichta, Eichah Rabbosi* 30) that there were four kings who made different demands of God. David, Assa, Chizkiyahu and Jehoshafat — Jehoshafat arose and proclaimed, 'I have no strength to kill or to pursue my enemies. Rather, I will recite songs of praise, and You, O God, will make war!']

אֱלֹהִים נִצָּב בַּעֲדַת אֵל — *God stands in the assembly of God.*

Targum understands *the assembly of God* to be the pious scholars who are אֵל, *powerful,* [see *Psalms* 22:1] in their knowledge of Torah law.

When the magistrates assemble to sit in judgment, God pays very close attention to their decisions *(Radak)* in order to determine if the judges are inspired by a quest for truth and equity *(Rashi).* [These men represent Divine justice on earth; therefore, they deserve the title *the assembly of God.*]

The proximity of God is a boon for the righteous judge because God grants him Divine perception which helps him to discover the truth *(Sforno).*

Indeed, the *Talmud (Sanhedrin* 7a) says that the totally honest judge causes the spirit of God to descend upon the entire congregation of Israel.

In addition any quorum [*Minyan*] of ten Israelites is called an עֵדָה, *assembly.* When a *minyan* gathers to study Torah or to pray, God's spirit pervades their *assembly (Avos* 3:6).

בְּקֶרֶב אֱלֹהִים יִשְׁפֹּט — *In the midst of the judges, shall He judge.*

God's spirit penetrates deep into the קֶרֶב, *midst* — i.e., into the heart — of the judge and endows him with the wisdom and insight needed to issue just sentences *(Alshich).*

If the magistrate proves to be corrupt, he himself will be judged and punished by the wrath of God *(Radak; Sforno).*

2. עַד מָתַי תִּשְׁפְּטוּ עָוֶל — *How long* [lit., *until when*] *will you judge lawlessly?*

Will you persist in your pursuit of iniquity until you are trapped in a web of crime and punishment? *(Sforno).*

וּפְנֵי רְשָׁעִים תִּשְׂאוּ סֶלָה — *And favor the*

82
1-4

A song of Assaf,
God stands in the assembly of God,
in the midst of the judges,
shall He judge.
2 How long will you judge lawlessly
and favor the presence of the wicked?
3 Judge fairly the needy and the orphan,
vindicate the poor and impoverished.
4 Rescue the needy and destitute,

presence [lit. *uplift the faces*] *of the wicked?*

You accord them unwarranted privileges due to their wealth and influence *(Radak)*. You refuse to take them to task for their maltreatment of poor and defenseless litigants *(Sforno)*.[1]

3. שִׁפְטוּ דָל וְיָתוֹם — *Judge fairly the needy and the orphan.*

[At the very outset of his reign, King Jehoshafat recognized that the protection of the poor and of the orphan was his prime responsibility. In his days, the people of Israel were scattered throughout the mountains, like straying sheep without a shepherd *(Sifri Nitzavim* 304).

Once Jehoshafat established his rule, he refrained from advancing his royal powers and he gave no thought to amassing wealth and glory. He gave his full attention to assuring justice by appointing judges *(Tanchumah, Shoftim* 1).]

עָנִי וָרָשׁ הַצְדִּיקוּ — *Vindicate the poor and impoverished.*

If the poor man is in the right, pass judgment in his favor, and pay no heed to the ire of the rich man who is found to be in the wrong *(Rashi)*.

Alshich renders הַצְדִּיקוּ as *execute charity* (צְדָקָה), toward *the poor.*

The magistrates are exhorted to follow the example of King David, of whom Scripture says: וַיְהִי דָוִד עֹשֶׂה מִשְׁפָּט וּצְדָקָה לְכָל עַמּוֹ, *And David executed justice and charity for all his people (II Samuel* 8:15).

The *Talmud (Sanhedrin* 6b) explains that if a rich man and a poor man came before David, he would first execute strict justice and render an honest decision, even if that went against the pauper. Afterwards, David would consider the dire straits of the poor man and supply him with charity so that he might meet his obligations.

The psalmist here advises that judges first *pass* [precise and unbiased] *judgment for the needy and the orphan* [even if they are found guilty]. Later, the judges should *execute charity towards them,* if they are too impoverished to make the payments ordered by the court *(Alshich)*.

4. פַּלְּטוּ דַל וְאֶבְיוֹן — *Rescue the needy and destitute.*

The sphere of the judge's responsibility is not restricted to the confines of the courtroom. He is obligated to go out to investigate all injustices which are perpetrated in the

1. King Jehoshafat showed no favor to the wicked but displayed utmost respect for the righteous and scholarly. The *Talmud (Kesubos* 103b) relates that whenever Jehoshafat saw a Torah sage, he would rise from his throne and embrace him, exclaiming, 'My teacher, My teacher! My Master, My Master!'

In addition, Jehoshafat never flaunted his royalty in the presence of those who excelled him in piety. The *Midrash (Bamidbar Rabah* 21:6) relates that this king never appeared before a prophet of God in his royal raiment, but only in the clothes of a simple commoner.

ה וְאֶבְיוֹן מִיַּד רְשָׁעִים הַצִּילוּ: לֹא יָדְעוּ |
וְלֹא יָבִינוּ בַּחֲשֵׁכָה יִתְהַלָּכוּ יִמּוֹטוּ כָּל־
ו מוֹסְדֵי אָרֶץ: אֲנִי־אָמַרְתִּי אֱלֹהִים אַתֶּם
ז וּבְנֵי עֶלְיוֹן כֻּלְּכֶם: אָכֵן כְּאָדָם תְּמוּתוּן
ח וּכְאַחַד הַשָּׂרִים תִּפֹּלוּ: קוּמָה אֱלֹהִים
שָׁפְטָה הָאָרֶץ כִּי־אַתָּה תִנְחַל בְּכָל־
הַגּוֹיִם:

community, so that he may rescue the poor, defenseless victims *(Sforno).*

מִיַּד רְשָׁעִים הַצִּילוּ — *From the hand of the wicked deliver them.*

The most tragic aspect of the pauper's life is that he must submit to the authority of his employers and benefactors. The conscientious judge should take pains to deliver the poor man from those who might intimidate him or exploit him in their selfish schemes *(Hirsch).*

5. לֹא יָדְעוּ וְלֹא יָבִינוּ — *They neither know nor understand.*

The psalmist laments that, despite the tremendous responsibility given the judges of Israel, they remain ignorant of the fundamentals of justice *(Rashi).*

They do not realize that God Himself sits in judgment on the magistrates and punishes those who are corrupt. Neither do the magistrates understand that their unfair decisions cause the entire nation tremendous damage *(Radak).*

בַּחֲשֵׁכָה יִתְהַלָּכוּ — *In darkness they walk along.*

The eyes of the judges are blinded by bribes [*Exodus* 23:8], prejudice, and selfish interests *(Radak).*

Therefore, they shall enter the dark pit of eternal punishment *(Sforno).*

יִמּוֹטוּ כָּל מוֹסְדֵי אָרֶץ — *All foundations of the earth collapse.*

Justice is one of the three pillars upon which the earth rests *(Avos* 1:18). It is the basis for all stability, as King Solomon said *(Proverbs* 29:4): מֶלֶךְ בְּמִשְׁפָּט יַעֲמִיד אָרֶץ, *The king, through justice, upholds the world (Akeidas Yitzchok).*

[The corrupt judge shakes the confidence of the populace and upsets their faith in the public institutions charged with upholding law and order.][1]

6. אֲנִי אָמַרְתִּי אֱלֹהִים אַתֶּם — *I said, 'You are angelic.'*

In this manner the Holy Spirit of God addresses itself to the judges of the realm *(Alshich):*

You, the honest judge who represents the Will of God on earth, are called אֱלֹהִים *(Exodus* 22:8), just as the angels and celestial bodies who perform God's Will are called אֱלֹהִים. All of you are selfless agents of the Almighty. Your sole concern is to ensure that God's world runs smoothly *(Radak).*

1. The *Talmud (Sukkah* 55a) says that because of this verse, Psalm 82 was chosen as the Temple song for *Hoshanah Rabbah,* the seventh day of the Festival of Tabernacles [*Sukkos*].

Rashi (Sukkah 55a) explains that at the end of Sukkos, the festival of the autumn harvest, all of the required gifts to the poor were supposed to have been delivered in full. Therefore, the populace is encouraged to *judge fairly the needy and the orphan, vindicate the poor and impoverished (v.* 3), by paying them their due tithes and gifts.

But there are many misers, who are oblivious to their obligations; *they neither know nor understand (v.* 5). Their punishment will be death: *in darkness they walk along.* Even worse, they cause *the foundations of the earth to collapse (v.* 5). *Avos* (5:9) teaches that those who rob the poor of their due, cause plagues and pestilence to descend upon the land.

from the hand of the wicked deliver them.

5 *They neither know nor understand,*
in darkness they walk along.
All foundations
of the earth collapse.
6 *I said: 'You are angelic,*
sons of the Most High are you all.'
7 *But just like men*
shall you perish,
and like one of the princes
shall you fall
8 *Arise O God,*
Judge the earth.
For You allot the heritage
among all the nations.

וּבְנֵי עֶלְיוֹן כֻּלְּכֶם — *Sons of the Most High are you all.*

Although all men are fashioned in God's image, the honest judge bears the closest semblance to the Divine. All men are related to the Almighty, but the judge is as close as a *son*, because when he dispenses justice he is performing the function of the Lord Himself *(Sforno).*

The chief desire of the Creator is to perpetuate His Creation. Since strife can tear the whole world apart, the judge who settles disputes is called a *son of the Most High,* because he is the guardian of that which God has set as His 'highest priority' *(Malbim).*

7. אָכֵן כְּאָדָם תְּמוּתוּן — *But just like men* [lit. *like Adam*] *shall you perish.*

If the judge is an honest representative of God, he may aspire to God-like immortality. But if he betrays his sacred calling, then he is as vulnerable as the frailest of men. The judge resembles Adam: he almost achieved the stature of an angel, but his sin forced him to suffer human decay *(Metzudas David).*

וּכְאַחַד הַשָּׂרִים תִּפֹּלוּ — *And like one of the princes shall you fall.*

Rashi interprets this as a reference to the celestial angels, which are described by the prophet *(Isaiah* 24:21) as צְבָא הַמָּרוֹם בַּמָּרוֹם, *the highest of legions on high.*

[Every sovereign prince on earth is controlled by a Divine force above. When a heavenly force is reduced, the corresponding prince is toppled from his temporal power (see *Berachos* 17a; *Rashi, s.v.* בְּפַמַלְיָא שֶׁל מַעְלָה).][1]

1. At Sinai, Israel returned to the purity of Adam before the sin. Once again the sanctity of man rivalled that of the angels. The *Talmud (Shabbos* 146a) states, בְּסִינַי פָּסְקָה זוּהֲמָתָן, *At Sinai the defilement* [which the serpent injected into man] *disappeared.*

R' Yose taught *(Avodah Zarah* 5a) that Israel accepted the Torah at Sinai so that the Angel of Death should have no power over them, as Scripture states, *I said: 'You are angelic, sons of the Most High are you all'.*

However, after Israel sinned by following the Golden Calf, they forfeited their immortality and Divine stature: *But just like men shall you perish, and like one of the princes shall you fall* (82:6). [See *Vol. I, Overview* part 1).

8. קוּמָה אֱלֹהִים שָׁפְטָה הָאָרֶץ – *Arise O God, judge the earth.*

Assaf concludes the psalm with a vigorous effort to arouse God to take action against the wicked *(Rashi)*.

Alshich interprets this as a final effort to shift God's wrath away from the judges of Israel whose practices were subject to criticism.

The psalmist pleads: 'O God, do not focus on the shortcomings of the Jewish judges alone. *Arise, judge the earth.'* The earth refers to the corrupt judicial systems of all nations. In comparison to their injustice and evil, the errors of Israel will appear insignificant.

כִּי אַתָּה תִנְחַל בְּכָל הַגּוֹיִם – *For You allot the heritage among all the nations.*

[When You created the world, You took steps to prevent dissension which might jeopardize the survival of human society. You sought to satisfy everyone by dividing the earth fairly among all the nations. You took pains to assure that every people received a portion commensurate with its needs.

That world order can only be permanent it if is protected by the principles of law and order. Therefore, O God, we beg You to recognize human frailty which makes it almost impossible for man to judge with perfect fairness and precision. Therefore, involve Yourself in the dispensation of justice, so that truth and integrity will enable Your Creation to flourish.]

מזמור פג 83

The preceding psalm was based on King Jehoshafat's accomplishments which Scripture recounts in II Chronicles, *chapter 19. This psalm is related to the period of Jehoshafat's reign recorded in* II Chronicles, *chapter 20* (Radak; Malbim).

After Jehoshafat completed his renovation of the judicial system, the land of Judea was attacked by the armies of Ammon, Moab, Aram and Seir (Edom). Malbim (II Chronicles *20:23) proves from this psalm that these nations were bent on annihilating Israel. They hired mercenaries from every prominent nation in the area, so that Israel would be completely overwhelmed by their vast legions.*

The psalmist here reveals the deeper intentions of these marauding nations. Their ultimate desire was not merely to destory Israel, but to obliterate the name of God from the face of the earth. Therefore, Jehoshafat employed the power of song as his chief weapon against his foes. Through song he declared that God does indeed reign supreme over the universe.

פג
א־ו

א־ב שִׁיר מִזְמוֹר לְאָסָף: אֱלֹהִים אַל־דֳּמִי־לָךְ
ג אַל־תֶּחֱרַשׁ וְאַל־תִּשְׁקֹט אֵל: כִּי־הִנֵּה
אוֹיְבֶיךָ יֶהֱמָיוּן וּמְשַׂנְאֶיךָ נָשְׂאוּ רֹאשׁ:
ד עַל־עַמְּךָ יַעֲרִימוּ סוֹד וְיִתְיָעֲצוּ עַל־
ה צְפוּנֶיךָ: אָמְרוּ לְכוּ וְנַכְחִידֵם מִגּוֹי וְלֹא־
ו יִזָּכֵר שֵׁם־יִשְׂרָאֵל עוֹד: כִּי נוֹעֲצוּ לֵב יַחְדָּו

1. שִׁיר מִזְמוֹר — *A song with musical accompaniment.*

See *commentary* to *Psalms* 30:1 which cites the *Siddur Baal haTanya,* who explains that שִׁיר refers to the lyrics of the composition and מִזְמוֹר describes the accompaniment of כְּלֵי זֶמֶר, *musical instruments.*

When the enemy armies gathered at the border of Israel to attack Jehoshafat's legions, the prophet informed the people that God would fight for them. Israel's sole role in the battle was to offer songs of praise to God. Scripture states, *And there arose from amongst the Levites, from the sons of Kehos and from the sons of Korach those who offered praise to HASHEM the God of Israel,* בְּקוֹל גָּדוֹל לְמָעְלָה, *with an overwhelmingly loud voice (II Chronicles* 20:19). This means that the words of שִׁיר, *song,* drowned out the accompanying כְּלֵי זֶמֶר, *musical instruments,* because the time for total rejoicing had not yet arrived. While the threat of the foe still loomed, the Jews engaged in prayer and praise of God. Only after the enemy was completely destroyed did the nation celebrate wholeheartedly. Revelry and joyous music pervaded the festive atmosphere: *And they came to Jerusalem with* neivels *and* kinnors *and with trumpets; to the House of HASHEM (II Chronicles* 20:28).

Therefore, in the superscription to this composition the psalmist mentions שִׁיר, *song,* (lyrics) before מִזְמוֹר, *instrumental accompaniment.*]

לְאָסָף — *By Assaf.*

Malbim points out that this psalm has a special relationship to *Assaf* because one of Assaf's descendants played a key role in Jehoshafat's victory: *And Yachaziel, the son of Zecharya, the son of Benaya, the son of Ye'iel, the son of Matanyah the Levite, from the family of Assaf, was possessed by the spirit of HASHEM in the midst of the congregation (II Chronicles* 20:14).

Yachaziel told the populace that God would wage war for them and that there was no cause for fear. This prophecy inspired the people to recite songs of praise.

2. אֱלֹהִים אַל דֳּמִי לָךְ — *O God, do not hold Yourself silent.*

Do not remain silent [and seemingly indifferent] at a time when Israel is in such peril and distress *(Rashi; Radak).*

Sforno notes that דום also means to *delay* [see *commentary* to *Psalms* 37:7]. Thus, 'O God, do not be forbearing toward our enemies. Destroy them without delay!'

אַל תֶּחֱרַשׁ וְאַל תִּשְׁקֹט אֵל — *Be not deaf and be not still, O God.*

Do not behave like a deaf man, who does not respond to an entreaty, or like a cripple, who does not react to a crisis *(Malbim).*

3. כִּי הִנֵּה אוֹיְבֶיךָ יֶהֱמָיוּן — *For behold, Your foes are in uproar.*

The translation follows *Radak,* who perceives the root of יֶהֱמָיוּן as הָמָה, *to make noise.*

Ibn Ezra identifies יֶהֱמָיוּן with the הָמוֹן, *multitude,* who gather in noisy hordes to threaten Israel.

וּמְשַׂנְאֶיךָ נָשְׂאוּ רֹאשׁ — *And those who hate You have raised their head.*

A song with musical accompaniment,
by Assaf.
2 O God, do not hold Yourself silent;
be not deaf and be not still, O God;
3 For behold,
Your foes are in uproar
And those who hate You
have raised their head.
4 Against Your nation
they plot deviously,
They take counsel
against those whom You protect
5 They said, 'Come,
let us cut them off from nationhood,
So Israel's name
will be remembered no more!'
6 For they take counsel together unanimously,

Your detractors and enemies have become רֹאשׁ, *leaders*, in world affairs. The *Talmud (Gittin* 56b) states that any nation which oppresses Israel becomes a leader amongst the nations (*Chazah Zion*).

4. עַל עַמְּךָ יַעֲרִימוּ סוֹד — *Against Your nation they plot deviously* [lit. *they make devious secrets*].

Secretly, the nations plot their alliance against Israel *(Radak)*. They use deceit to convince any hesitant nations to join their cause *(Sforno)*.

Their most heinous deception is that they claim to be fighting Israel, without acknowledging that their main purpose is to challenge God *(Norah Tehillos)*, and the authenticity of His Torah. They seek to undermine and distort the Torah through deliberate and deceptive misinterpretation *(Eretz Hachaim)*.

וְיִתְיָעֲצוּ עַל צְפוּנֶיךָ — *They take counsel against those whom You protect.*

[Their animosity for Israel was aroused by the Jew's privileged status as God's protected people. The things which God safeguards most they hate with the greatest passion.] Thus, the Torah scholar — who is sheltered in the House of Study — is a prime target of their hatred. They also attack the Torah itself, which is the repository of God's concealed wisdom, which remains 'protected' against all attempts to eradicate its study *(Sforno; Norah Tehillos)*.

5. אָמְרוּ לְכוּ וְנַכְחִידֵם מִגּוֹי — *They said 'Come, let us cut them off from nationhood.'*

The nations reasoned that as long as Israel survives, the Almighty will be called אֱלֹהֵי יִשְׂרָאֵל, *the God of Israel*. By destroying His people, they thought they would obliterate God's Name, as well! *(Midrash Shocher Tov)*.

וְלֹא יִזָּכֵר שֵׁם יִשְׂרָאֵל עוֹד — *So Israel's name will be remembered no more!*

The nations continue their argument: 'The very name of Israel must be eradicated, for this nation contradicts the goals and ideals of the rest of the peoples. This one group defies the rest

ז עָלֶיךָ בְּרִית יִכְרֹתוּ: אָהֳלֵי אֱדוֹם
ח וְיִשְׁמְעֵאלִים מוֹאָב וְהַגְרִים: גְּבָל וְעַמּוֹן
ט וַעֲמָלֵק פְּלֶשֶׁת עִם־יֹשְׁבֵי צוֹר: גַּם־אַשּׁוּר
נִלְוָה עִמָּם הָיוּ זְרוֹעַ לִבְנֵי־לוֹט סֶלָה:
י עֲשֵׂה־לָהֶם כְּמִדְיָן כְּסִיסְרָא כְיָבִין בְּנַחַל

of the world and obstructs global unity *(Sforno).*

6. כִּי נוֹעֲצוּ לֵב יַחְדָּו — *For they take counsel together unanimously* [lit. *with hearts all together*].

These nations had been sworn enemies, locked in murderous hostility for generations. Suddenly they became mutual allies in their intense animosity of Israel *(Radak).*

עָלֶיךָ בְּרִית יִכְרֹתוּ — *Against You they strike a covenant.*

They have singled out Israel as their universal enemy because Israel represents Your Name. The nations are in total agreement that the Name of God must be erased from the minds of men *(Rashi).*

7. אָהֳלֵי אֱדוֹם וְיִשְׁמְעֵאלִים — *The tents of Edom and Ishmaelites.*

Ishmael was the son of Abraham; Edom (Esau) was the son of Isaac. The descendants of these rebellious sons gathered to destroy the God of their forefathers *(Ibn Yachya).*

These nations did not intend to limit themselves to a single attack on Israel; rather, they came fully equipped for a prolonged campaign against the Jews. Therefore, *Edom* and *Ishmael* brought *tents* fit to provide long-term shelter *(Radak).*

מוֹאָב וְהַגְרִים — *Of Moab and Hagarites.*

The *Hagarites* are the descendants of Hagar, who was once Abraham's concubine. These hostile gentiles are her children from a marriage to another man *(Ibn Ezra; Radak).*

If Hagar is identified as Keturah [cf. *Genesis* 22:1 and *Rashi, ibid.*], *the Hagarites* may be the sons which Abraham sired with this woman. but who [like Ishmael] were not accorded the status of Jews *(Radak).*

8. גְּבָל וְעַמּוֹן וַעֲמָלֵק — *Gevol and Ammon and Amalek.*

[In *II Chronicles* 20:1, we read that Ammon and Moab were Israel's principal attackers. These two nations were joined, by a detachment *of the Ammonites. Rashi (II Chronicles* 20:1) explains that this extra contingent consisted of Amalekites who disguised themselves as Ammonites so that the Jews would not be able to identify their attackers in their prayers. They changed their clothing and their language in order to blend homogenously into the main Ammonite force.]

פְּלֶשֶׁת עִם יֹשְׁבֵי צוֹר — *Philistia and the inhabitants of Tzor.*

Shem M'Shmuel (Parshas B'Shalach) points out that Philistia is situated between Egypt and Canaan; it adopted the worst characteristics of both nations. The Egyptians were lewd and lecherous, the Canaanites were corrupted by idolatry, and Philistia was contaminated by both sins. The very name פְּלֶשֶׁת is related to מְפוּלָשׁ, *open from both sides,* for Philistia was a thoroughfare through which both perverted cultures passed.

9. גַּם אַשּׁוּר נִלְוָה עִמָּם — *Even Assyria joined with them.*

Assyria's association with this wicked alliance of nations represents an abrupt departure from its historic role as an *adversary* of evil. In earlier times, Nimrod united all the nations in a universal alliance which defied the authority of God. Of all the peoples,

against You they strike a covenant.
7 The tents of Edom and Ishmaelites,
of Moab and Hagarites,
8 Gevol and Ammon and Amalek,
Philistia and the inhabitants of Tzur;
9 Even Assyria joined with them,
they became the strong arm of Lot's sons,
Selah.
10 Do to them as to Midian,
as to Sisera and as to Yavin at Nachal Kishon,

Assyria alone refused to join, as Scripture states, (Genesis 10:11) *Out of that land* [i.e., Shinor, the land of Nimrod] *Assyria went forth and built Nineveh (Rashi).*

[In *Jonah* (3:2), we read that the Assyrian capital, Nineveh, was עִיר גְּדוֹלָה לֵאלֹהִים, *a great city of God,* which means a 'city founded for the sake of serving God'. This explains why God was so concerned about the spiritual level of this city. When the inhabitants sinned, He manifested this concern by sending Jonah to chastise them, so that they would repent.

However, when the nations amassed to destroy Israel in Jehoshafat's time, even Assyria could not withstand the worldwide spirit of contempt for God and His chosen people. Even this formerly righteous nation joined Israel's enemies.]

Rav Yosef Kimchi (quoted by his son *Radak)* emphasizes another reason why Assyria's participation was surprising. Not long before, in the days of King Chizkiyahu, the entire host of Assyria, 185,000 strong, had been annihilated by the angel of God as they were beseiging Jerusalem [*II Kings* 19:35]. This tremendous defeat should have taught Assyria an indelible lesson.

הָיוּ זְרוֹעַ לִבְנֵי לוֹט סֶלָה – *They became the [strong] arm of Lot's sons, Selah.*

[Ammon and Moab were the offspring of Lot (*Genesis* 19:37-38), born out of his incestuous relationships with his daughters. They had previously been second-class nations because of this stigma. But now the most prominent peoples gathered around these two degraded nations in order to defy God.]

10. עֲשֵׂה לָהֶם כְּמִדְיָן – *Do to them as to Midian.*

Alshich comments that when the myriads of Midian amassed against Israel, Gideon attacked them with a handful of men. With Divine assistance, this small force sent a wave of terror and panic through the vast Midianite host, *And HASHEM caused every man's sword to be against his fellow throughout the camp (Judges 7:22).*

Similarly, the prophet told Jehoshafat that he would not have to defend himself, because the enemy armies would destroy each other: *For the children of Ammon and Moab rose against the inhabitants of Mount Seir [Edom] to utterly slay and destroy them and when they had annihilated the inhabitants of Seir they all helped to destroy one another (II Chronicles 20:23).*

כְּסִיסְרָא כְיָבִין בְּנַחַל קִישׁוֹן – *As to Sisera and as to Yavin at Nachal Kishon.*

Yavin was the king of Canaan, and Sisera was the commander of his army (*Judges* 4:2). Inspired by the prophetess

יא קִישׁוֹן: נִשְׁמְדוּ בְעֵין־דֹּאר הָיוּ דֹּמֶן
יב לָאֲדָמָה: שִׁיתֵמוֹ נְדִיבֵמוֹ כְּעֹרֵב וְכִזְאֵב
יג וּכְזֶבַח וּכְצַלְמֻנָּע כָּל־נְסִיכֵמוֹ: אֲשֶׁר
אָמְרוּ נִירְשָׁה לָּנוּ אֵת נְאוֹת אֱלֹהִים:
יד אֱלֹהַי שִׁיתֵמוֹ כַגַּלְגַּל כְּקַשׁ לִפְנֵי־רוּחַ:
טו כְּאֵשׁ תִּבְעַר־יָעַר וּכְלֶהָבָה תְּלַהֵט הָרִים:
טז כֵּן תִּרְדְּפֵם בְּסַעֲרֶךָ וּבְסוּפָתְךָ תְבַהֲלֵם:
יז מַלֵּא פְנֵיהֶם קָלוֹן וִיבַקְשׁוּ שִׁמְךָ יְהוָה:

Devorah, Barak ben Avinoam and his men destroyed the invading army of Sisera at the river *Nachal Kishon*. There God performed many miracles and wonders. The entire enemy host was swallowed up by this river *(Rashi)*.

11. נִשְׁמְדוּ בְעֵין דֹּאר — *Who perished at Ein-dor.*

Scripture never mentions this location in connection with any military victory. Therefore, it is unclear whether this was the site of the Jewish victory over Midian or over Sisera *(Rashi; Radak)*.

הָיוּ דֹמֶן לָאֲדָמָה — *They became dung on the earth.*

When the enemies of God were slain, they were trampled underfoot like discarded refuse *(Radak)*.

12. שִׁיתֵמוֹ נְדִיבֵמוֹ — *Make their nobles.*

This refers to the officers of the present enemy: Let their fate resemble the disastrous defeat of Israel's previous enemies *(Radak)*.

כְּעֹרֵב וְכִזְאֵב וּכְזֶבַח וּכְצַלְמֻנָּע — *Like Orev and Ze'ev, like Zevach and Tzalmuna.*

[These were the generals who led the Midianite army which Gideon destroyed (see *Judges*, 8).]

13. אֲשֶׁר אָמְרוּ נִירְשָׁה לָּנוּ — *Who said, 'We will conquer for ourselves.*

The ten marauding nations enumerated above entertained thoughts of annexing portions of Jehoshafat's kingdom, just as the Midianite host which invaded Israel in Gideon's time desired to seize Jewish territory *(Radak)*.

אֵת נְאוֹת אֱלֹהִים — *The pleasant habitations of God.*

[The nations sought the land of Israel not because of its physical attractions but because of its designation as the spiritual center of God's universe. They sought to disturb the exquisite atmosphere of sanctity which everyone enjoyed in the presence of God.]

14. אֱלֹהַי שִׁיתֵמוֹ כַגַּלְגַּל — *O, my God, make them like the whirling chaff.*

The גַּלְגַּל, *wheel*, refers to a fine growth at the tip of a thorny plant. When winter comes, this thorn dries up and shrivels. Then the growth blows into the wind in whirling balls which resemble flying wheels *(Rashi)*.

The nations sought to secure a firm foothold in the land of Israel. Here the psalmist asks God to foil their plans by making them as insecure and as transient as *whirling chaff (Alshich)*.

כְּקַשׁ לִפְנֵי רוּחַ — *Like stubble before the wind.*

Alshich explains that the גַּלְגַּל mentioned here is a mechanical device, a rotating water*wheel* or cart*wheel*]. These wheels require relatively large amounts of energy to move them; the windmill, however does not. Therefore, the psalmist prays: 'Let the enemy be kept

11 *Who perished at Ein-dor;*
they became dung on the earth
12 *Make their nobles like Orev and Ze'ev,*
and all their princes like Zevach and Tzalmuna;
13 *Who said, 'We will conquer for ourselves*
the pleasant habitations of God.'
14 *O my God, make them like the whirling chaff,*
like stubble before the wind.
15 *Like a fire burning the forest,*
and a flame igniting mountains.
16 *So pursue them with Your tempest*
and terrify them with Your storm.
17 *Fill their faces with shame,*
then they will seek Your Name, HASHEM.

on the run; let him be moved as readily as the windmill wheel which turns swiftly in the slightest breeze and blows the stubble in the field.'

15. כְּאֵשׁ תִּבְעַר יָעַר — *Like a fire burning the forest.*

The mighty kings of the gentile nations are likened to majestically tall trees *(Sforno).*

When these towering trees are clustered in a forest, the fire which begins in one tree swiftly spreads to one and then to another, until the conflagration consumes the entire area. Similarly, the monarchs who attacked Jehoshafat were destroyed by one another *(Radak).*

וּכְלֶהָבָה תְּלַהֵט הָרִים — *And a flame igniting mountains.*

When fire attacks the thickly wooded mountains, the danger is most intense because gusts of wind whip the flames into a blazing inferno which swiftly turns the mountaintop into a barren ruin. Similarly, the enemy kings will be annihilated with utmost haste *(Radak).*

[Indeed, the decimation of Jehoshafat's enemies was swift and sure. Just a short while after the armies began to slay each other, Scripture states, *And when Judah (Jehoshafat's army) came to the watchtower in the wilderness, they looked upon the multitude and behold they were dead bodies fallen to the earth and none had escaped (II Chronicles* 20:24).]

16. כֵּן תִּרְדְּפֵם בְּסַעֲרֶךָ — *So pursue them with Your tempest.*

God struck the enemy with panic and madness causing them to turn against each other in tempestuous self-destruction *(Radak).*

וּבְסוּפָתְךָ תְבַהֲלֵם — *And terrify them with Your storm.*

Hirsch (comm. to *Exodus* 2:3) explains that סְעָרָה, *tempest,* is derived from סחר, *to go round in a circle,* and refers to a whirlwind which whips around madly.

The word סוּפָה is a violent *storm* which has exceeded its normal סוף, *boundary* or *limit,* and rages out of control.

17. מַלֵּא פְנֵיהֶם קָלוֹן — *Fill their faces with shame.*

They sought to shame God by devastating *His pleasant habitations (v.* 13). Therefore, let them be shamed, measure for measure *(Ibn Ezra).*

יח יֵבֹשׁוּ וְיִבָּהֲלוּ עֲדֵי־עַד וְיַחְפְּרוּ וְיֹאבֵדוּ׃
יט וְיֵדְעוּ כִּי־אַתָּה שִׁמְךָ יהוה לְבַדֶּךָ עֶלְיוֹן
עַל־כָּל־הָאָרֶץ׃

Rav Yosef Kimchi (quoted by his son, *Radak)* identifies the root of קָלוֹן as קָלוּי, *burnt.* The person who is disgraced 'burns' with shame and his face reddens.

וְיבַקְשׁוּ שִׁמְךָ ה׳ — *Then they will seek Your Name, HASHEM.*

Let them come to realize that only You deserve to be called by the name God *(Radak).*

Only You can give assistance to those in need *(Chomos Anoch).*

18. יֵבֹשׁוּ וְיִבָּהֲלוּ עֲדֵי עַד — *Let them be shamed and terrified forever.*

Let the kings who dare to attack You be [violently] overthrown. Ensure that they never regain their thrones *(Sforno).*

וְיַחְפְּרוּ וְיֹאבֵדוּ — *Then they will be disgraced and doomed.*

When the kings come to realize the sheer folly of their attempts to obliterate God's presence from the earth, they will suffer the most intense feelings of disgrace. Eventually they will meet their doom *(Alshich).*

[Actually the bodies of the kings and their armies were disgraced when they lay unburied on the battlefield. Then they were stripped of their precious garments and ornaments, as Scripture states: *And when Jehoshafat and his people came to take away their spoil, they found among them an abundance of riches with the dead bodies; the precious jewels which they stripped off for themselves were more than they could carry away. They were engaged in gathering the spoil three days, there was so much* (II Chronicles 20:25).]

18 *Let them be shamed and terrified forever,*
then they will be disgraced and doomed;
19 *Then they will know that You,*
Whose Name is HASHEM, are alone,
Most High over all the earth.

19. וְיֵדְעוּ כִּי אַתָּה שִׁמְךָ ה׳ לְבַדֶּךָ — *Then they will know that You, Whose Name is HASHEM, are alone.*

The translation follows *Ibn Ezra. Alshich* explains that the nations will realize that God differs from human kings who depend on their officers and nobles for support. God can stand alone and defeat all the nobles and princes on earth.

עֶלְיוֹן עַל כָּל הָאָרֶץ — *Most High over all the earth.*

The allied nations which sought to destroy Jehoshafat believed that HASHEM dwelled in the heavens and paid no heed to His devoted servants (such as Jehoshafat) on earth. The downfall of these nations will teach them that God is *Most High* and mighty *over all of the earth* as well as over the heavens *(Tehillos Hashem).*

[Jehoshafat and his people certainly learned of God's omnipotence from this victory. Scripture vividly describes their triumphant celebration: *And on the fourth day, they assembled in the Valley of Berachah [blessing], for there they blessed HASHEM. Therefore the name of that place was called the Valley of Berachah unto this day. Then they returned every man of Judah and Jerusalem with joy, for HASHEM had made them rejoice over their enemies. And they came to Jerusalem with* Neivels *and* Kinnors *and trumpets to the House of HASHEM. And the fear of God was over all of the kingdoms of those countries when they heard that HASHEM fought against the enemies of Israel. So the realm of Jehoshafat was quiet, for his God gave him rest from all of his surroundings (II Chronicles* 20:26-30).]

מזמור פד 84

The preceding psalm concludes the series of compositions attributed to Assaf. Psalm 84 is the first in a second group of psalms (84, 85, 87 and 88) ascribed to the sons of Korach. (The sons of Korach also composed Psalms 42-49).

Radak comments that this psalm was inspired by David's experiences when he fled from Saul and sought refuge in the land of Philistia. There, on foreign soil, far removed from the spiritual centers of Israel, David yearned to return to the Holy Ark and to the sacrificial altar. With this psalm, David captured the innermost longing of all the lonely exiles in future generations.

The psalmist stresses that many living creatures possess a powerful homing instinct which binds them to a specific location, where they reproduce and shelter their young.

Similarly, the nest of Israel can only be in the holy environs of God's dwelling place. Only there is Israel strong and secure enough to develop its future, as the psalmist proclaims (v.8): They advance from strength to strength and appear before God in Zion.

א לַמְנַצֵּחַ עַל־הַגִּתִּית לִבְנֵי־קֹרַח מִזְמוֹר:
ב מַה־יְּדִידוֹת מִשְׁכְּנוֹתֶיךָ יהוה צְבָאוֹת:
ג נִכְסְפָה וְגַם־כָּלְתָה | נַפְשִׁי לְחַצְרוֹת יהוה
ד לִבִּי וּבְשָׂרִי יְרַנְּנוּ אֶל אֵל־חָי: גַּם־צִפּוֹר |
מָצְאָה בַיִת וּדְרוֹר | קֵן | לָהּ אֲשֶׁר־שָׁתָה

1. לַמְנַצֵּחַ עַל הַגִּתִּית — *For the Conductor, upon the* Gittis.

[See *commentary* to 8:1 for definition of גִּתִּית.] *Zera Yaakov* explains that this psalm echoes the cries of the exiled Jews who are crushed like grapes in a גַּת, *winepress.*

The psalmist assures the exiles that those gentiles who dared to destroy the Holy Temple are themselves destined to be crushed in the גַּת, *winepress,* on the future day of Divine retribution *(Midrash Shocher Tov).*

לִבְנֵי קֹרַח מִזְמוֹר — *By the sons of Korach, a song.*

[The sons of Korach initially joined their father's mutiny against Moses. They too were swallowed in the bowels of the earth. At the last moment, however, their yearning for truth and sanctity surpassed their loyalty to their rebellious father. Then they repented and were released.

Psalm 42 provides an eloquent example of the fiery thirst for God which the sons of Korach experienced: *My soul thirsts for God the living God. When shall I come and appear before God?* (42:3). This psalm is another passionate expression of that intense yearning to dwell in the presence of the Almighty.]

2. מַה יְּדִידוֹת מִשְׁכְּנוֹתֶיךָ ה׳ צְבָאוֹת — *How beloved are Your dwelling places, HASHEM of Legions.*

O, how dear these places are to me *(Rashi).* How intense is my yearning to be in Your dwelling place once again *(Radak).*

The *Talmud (Menachos* 53a) points out that anyone who had any relationship with the construction of the *beloved dwelling place* of God is also called יְדִיד, *beloved.* Abraham, the founder of our nation, is called יְדִיד *(Jeremiah* 11:15). The children of Israel are called יְדִידִים *(Jeremiah* 12:7). The Holy Temple was built mainly on the territory of Benjamin, who is called יְדִיד: *The beloved of HASHEM he shall dwell securely by Him (Deuteronomy* 33:12). King Solomon, who built the *Beis Hamikdosh,* was named יְדִידְיָה [lit., *beloved of God*], *because HASHEM loved him (II Samuel* 12:24,25).

From the first moment when God began His creation, His prime desire was to establish a place which would allow Him to dwell in the midst of His creatures on earth. The Temple is His *beloved,* therefore, because it is, so to speak, the culmination of God's aspirations *(Alshich).*

Furthermore, the atmosphere of the *Beis HaMikdash* fostered a spirit of יְדִידוּת, *love* and *comradery,* among the Jewish people. Even if they were embroiled in strife, when they entered the Temple, they were united by a spirit of peace and brotherhood *(Battei Nefesh).*

3. נִכְסְפָה וְגַם כָּלְתָה נַפְשִׁי — *My soul yearns, indeed it pines.*

Radak notes that כָּלְתָה is a much stronger emotion than נִכְסְפָה; it describes a person about to כָּלָה, *expire,* because of his uncontrollable desire.

לְחַצְרוֹת ה׳ — *For the courtyards of HASHEM.*

The psalmist yearns for the Temple *courtyard,* where the masses assembled to display their devotion. The הֵיכָל, *inner sanctuary,* in contrast, was inaccessible to all but the priests *(Radak).*

For the Conductor, upon the Gittis,
by the sons of Korach, a song.
2 How beloved are Your dwelling places,
HASHEM of Legions!
3 My soul yearns, indeed it pines
for the courtyards of HASHEM,
My heart and my flesh will sing
joyously to the Living God.
4 Even the bird found a home
and the free one, a nest for herself

לִבִּי וּבְשָׂרִי יְרַנְּנוּ אֶל אֵל חָי – *My heart and my flesh will sing joyously to the Living God.*

Ibn Ezra comments that לִבִּי, *my heart,* refers to the intellectual and intuitive faculties which are the essence of the human soul.

The term בְּשָׂרִי, *my flesh,* refers to the physical powers which are completely overwhelmed by a longing for God, as stated in 35:10: *All my limbs will say, 'HASHEM who is like You?' (Radak).*

When a person is far from the presence of God, his body becomes coarse and profane, and does not coexist in harmony with his soul. But when man draws near to the Divine, his body is steadily refined until it becomes pure enough to merge with the spirit. At that moment, says the psalmist, *my heart and my flesh will sing joyously* [together, as a single entity] *(Baalei Bris Avrohom).*

גַּם צִפּוֹר מָצְאָה בַיִת – *Even the bird found a home.*

According to the *Midrash (Shemos Rabbah* 20:6), the congregation of Israel is likened to a *bird.* First, Israel wandered from place to place like a migrating bird, but finally Israel *found a home* in the Holy Land.

Midrash Shocher Tov notes a difference between the יוֹנָה, *dove,* and the צִפּוֹר, *bird.* If predators remove the dove's chicks from its nest, the dove nevertheless returns to the very same nest to continue to breed. When the nest of another צִפּוֹר, *bird,* is raided, however, it never returns to that place.[1]

The enemies of Israel taunt the Jews by likening them to the molested bird which is frightened from its nest forever. But the psalmist refutes this jibe and reaffirms his belief in God's promise to return Israel to its homeland: *Even the bird* (Israel) *will find its* [original] *home,* after being chased away.

Rashi perceives in these words a lament over the destruction of the Temple: See how desolate the holy environs have become! Stray birds now dare to build their nests where the Holy of Holies once stood! *(Radak).*

The psalmist here draws our attention to the tragic irony that while the smallest and most insignificant bird has the opportunity to establish a home for

1. The Torah relates that Noah's ark housed כֹּל צִפּוֹר כָּל כָּנָף, *Every bird of any king of wing (Genesis* 7:14). According to the *Talmud (Chullin* 139b), צִפּוֹר, *bird,* refers only to clean birds which a Jew is permitted to eat, and כָּנָף, *winged creatures,* includes both unclean birds and locusts.

Ramban comments on *Leviticus* 14:4 that the term צִפּוֹר is a generic term for *small* birds that rise early in the morning to chirp and sing. This term is associated with the Aramaic word צַפְרָא *[tzafra], morning.* [See ArtScroll *Bereishis,* Vol. I, *commentary to 7:14.*]

אֶפְרֹחֶיהָ אֶת־מִזְבְּחוֹתֶיךָ יהוה צְבָאוֹת
ה מַלְכִּי וֵאלֹהָי: אַשְׁרֵי יוֹשְׁבֵי בֵיתֶךָ עוֹד
ו יְהַלְלוּךָ סֶּלָה: אַשְׁרֵי אָדָם עוֹז־לוֹ בָךְ
ז מְסִלּוֹת בִּלְבָבָם: עֹבְרֵי | בְּעֵמֶק הַבָּכָא

itself, the nation Israel wanders aimlessly, with no country to call its own *(Ibn Ezra).*

וּדְרוֹר קֵן לָהּ — *And the free one, a nest for herself.*

Ibn Ezra describes the דְּרוֹר [*dror*], *free one,* as a songbird, well-known in Spain, which never sings in captivity. [Israel is depicted as a bird which longs to be free to sing to God unhindered.]

This bird is free of fear and dares to make its nest in inhabited dwellings *(Radak).* [Israel also yearns to be free of fear.]

According to Masoretic notes, the ק of קֵן is enlarged. *Rabbeinu Bachya* explains that David prepared immense treasures of silver and gold to finance the construction of the Temple. In a prophetic vision David glimpsed the exact dimensions and design of the Temple. He saw that the main הֵיכָל, *sanctuary,* (which was so to speak, the קֵן, *nesting place,* of the Divine presence), was to be ק (the numerical equivalent of 100) cubits in height. David prayed fervently that he be granted the privilege of building this lofty Temple [see *Baal HaTurim, Genesis* 27:46].

אֲשֶׁר שָׁתָה אֶפְרֹחֶיהָ אֶת מִזְבְּחוֹתֶיךָ — *Where she laid her young by Your altars.*

All birds are extremely protective of their young. Nevertheless, the clean birds were eager to hatch their young near the altar, to insure that their chicks would be readily accessible for offerings in the Temple. This phenomenon illustrates the instinctive desire of all creatures to sanctify their existence in the presence of their Creator *(Alshich).*

Meiri notes that parents must be willing to dedicate their youngsters to the holy altar of Torah, so that they sanctify God's Name through their studies.

Radak points out that it was impossible for birds to nest in the Temple's altar. All birds were chased away for fear that they might be carrying something unclean, which might be dropped on the Holy Site. There was even a special scarecrow on the roof of the Temple to chase away the birds [see *Menachos* 107a and *Arachin* 6a, *Rashi* and *Tosafos s.v.* כְּגוֹן אַמָּה כַּלְיָא עוֹרֵב].

David, whose experiences inspired the psalm, does not refer here to the Temple's altar, but to the בָּמוֹת, *high places,* which were situated all over the land before the construction of the Holy Temple. Since these altars were not as sacred as those of the Temple, birds *could* nest there.

ה׳ צְבָאוֹת מַלְכִּי וֵאלֹהָי — *HASHEM of Legions; my King and my God.*

I long to be near You because You are מַלְכִּי, *my king,* for a servant finds security with his master; and because You are אֱלֹהָי, *my God,* for a creature belongs near his Creator *(Toras Chacham).*

5. אַשְׁרֵי יוֹשְׁבֵי בֵיתֶךָ — *Praiseworthy are those who dwell in Your House.*

This refers to the Priests and the Levites who serve there *(Rashi)* and to the scholars and devout men who meditate there in solitude. Indeed, anyone who merely laid eyes upon the Temple was most fortunate *(Radak).*

This also refers to those pious men who dwell in the house of prayer. The *Talmud (Berachos* 32a) relates that the devout men of old would meditate for a full hour in preparation for their prayers.

Rabbeinu Yonah (Berachos 32a) explains that the supplicant should feel that he is presenting his petition before God's heavenly throne. It takes an hour

Where she laid her young by Your altars,
HASHEM of Legions; my King and my God.
5 *Praiseworthy are those who dwell in Your house,*
continually they will praise You, Selah.
6 *Praiseworthy is the man whose strength is in You,*
like the highways of his heart.
7 *Those who pass through the Valley of Weeping*

for the supplicant to succeed in arousing within himself this sense of being in God's House.

עוֹד יְהַלְלוּךָ סֶּלָה — *Continually they will praise You, Selah.*

Although dwelling in the House of God is a privilege, it is an even greater privilege to go out to publicize God's praises to the masses *(Rashbam).*

From this verse, the *Talmud* (*Sanhedrin* 91a) teaches that one who recites songs of praise to God in this world will be permitted to *continue to praise You* (God) in the World to Come.

[Psalm 145, which begins תְּהִלָּה לְדָוִד, *A praise, by David,* is one of the most important works in *Tehillim.* The *Talmud* (*Berachos* 4b) states that one who recites the psalm תְּהִלָּה לְדָוִד three times a day is surely destined to share in the World to Come.

Psalm 145 has become a focal point of Jewish liturgy. It appears twice in the morning service and once as the prelude to the afternoon service. Psalm 145 is always introduced with the present verse because this verse also assures those who sing God's praises of a share in the World to Come. This verse is so closely identified with Psalm 145 that the psalm תְּהִלָּה לְדָוִד is commonly referred to as אַשְׁרֵי. (See commentary of *Rosh, Berachos* 4b).]

6. אַשְׁרֵי אָדָם עוֹז לוֹ בָךְ — *Praiseworthy is the man whose strength is in You.*

The praiseworthy man who dwells in the House of God (*v.* 5) draws great strength from his faith in God *(Radak).*

In particular, this man derives strength from the study of Torah, for Torah study gives him the power of a king; as Solomon says (*Proverbs* 8:15), *Through me* [Torah], *kings rule (Sforno).*

מְסִלּוֹת בִּלְבָבָם — [*Like*] *highways in his* [lit. *their*] *heart.*

Praiseworthy is the man who scrutinizes his actions so that his way in life will be upright *(Rashi),* leading him on a straight path towards the presence of God *(Ibn Ezra).*

This man follows the smooth road of pure logic *(Radak).* Since his teachings are readily understandable, his words appeal to the masses, who then follow on the *highway* upon which he treads *(Sforno).*

7. עֹבְרֵי בְּעֵמֶק הַבָּכָא — *Those who pass through the Valley of Weeping.*

Rashi (based on *Eruvin* 19a) interprets עֹבְרֵי as those who commit עֲבֵירוֹת, *transgressions.* These sinners will descend to the עֵמֶק, *depths,* of Hell, where suffering will cause them to weep. [This is in sharp contrast to the lot of the *praiseworthy* servants of God, described in the preceding verses.]

According to *Radak,* this verse is actually a continuation of the previous verse: Those who yearn to fathom God's wisdom delve into the very depths, where the wellsprings of knowledge are found. In his view, the word בָּכָא is related to נִבְכֵי יָם, *the springs of the sea (Job* 38:15).

Radak offers another interpretation. The בָּכָא, *bacha,* is a type of tree which grows where there is no water. The psalmist yearns for the groups of pilgrims who journeyed to Jerusalem to

מַעְיָן יְשִׁיתוּהוּ גַּם־בְּרָכוֹת יַעְטֶה מוֹרֶה:
ח יֵלְכוּ מֵחַיִל אֶל־חָיִל יֵרָאֶה אֶל־אֱלֹהִים
ט בְּצִיּוֹן: יהוה אֱלֹהִים צְבָאוֹת שִׁמְעָה
י תְפִלָּתִי הַאֲזִינָה אֱלֹהֵי יַעֲקֹב סֶלָה: מָגִנֵּנוּ
יא רְאֵה אֱלֹהִים וְהַבֵּט פְּנֵי מְשִׁיחֶךָ: כִּי טוֹב־
יוֹם בַּחֲצֵרֶיךָ מֵאָלֶף בָּחַרְתִּי הִסְתּוֹפֵף

be near God. These pilgrims passed through dry valleys filled with sand where the בָּכָא, *bacha*, trees grew. But they would not let drought deter them. They dug deep until they struck water and turned the desert valley *into a waterspring*. In addition, God soaked the thirsty pilgrims with a מוֹרֶה, *first rainfall*, which filled the terrain with בְּרֵיכוֹת, *rivulets and streams*.

Finally, *Rashbam* offers a homiletic explanation in which the word בָּכָא is related to נָבוֹךְ, *confused*. After being shrouded in darkness, man can truly appreciate light. After stumbling through the morass of בָּכָא, *confusion*, a man can arrive at clear, unfettered thought. The *Talmud (Gittin* 43b) teaches that a man truly understands a subject only after he misinterprets it and then struggles to fully comprehend it.

Therefore, the בָּכָא, *confusion*, may be transformed into a מַעְיָן, *waterspring*, of crystal-clear logic.

מַעְיָן יְשִׁיתוּהוּ — *Transform it into a wellspring.*

Those who burn in *Gehinnom* shed a constant flow of tears which transforms the parched, fiery floor of purgatory into a watery sea of sorrow *(Rashi)*. This penitential flood drowns out the terrible fires which consume the wicked *(Shemos Rabbah* 7:4).

According to *Radak*, the dedicated scholars [who long to comprehend God's wisdom] prove to be a מַעְיָן, *wellspring*, of inspiration for their disciples.

גַּם בְּרָכוֹת יַעְטֶה מוֹרֶה — *Even with blessings they enwrap their Guide.*

Those who burn in Hell ultimately see the truth of the Torah and the justice of God's ways. Instead of cursing God, they shower Him with blessings in gratitude for His guidance *(Rashi; Eruvin* 19a).

Indeed, the praises of God which ascend from Hell surpass those issued from Paradise (the Garden of Eden), for suffering etches the truth on man's heart as no other experience can *(Midrash Shocher Tov)*.

In the opinion of *Radak*, the *guide* and mentor *envelops* his fortunate students with the *blessings* of spiritual enlightenment.

8. יֵלְכוּ מֵחַיִל אֶל חָיִל — *They advance* [lit. *go*] *from strength to strength.*

Those who expend their strength in Your service find that their strength has not diminished, but doubled *(Rashi)*.

The performance of a *mitzvah* does not leave them exhausted, but invigorates them to fulfill more precepts. After praying in the בֵּית הַכְּנֶסֶת, *synagogue*, they do not stop to rest, but go on to study in the בֵּית הַמִּדְרָשׁ, *the House of Study*.

יֵרָאֶה אֶל אֱלֹהִים בְּצִיּוֹן — *And appear before God in Zion.*

The *Talmud (Berachos* 64a) states that Torah scholars [and all intensely dedicated Jews] have no rest in this world or in the next, for *they advance from strength to strength* (i.e., they continue their spiritual development even after death) until finally they *appear before God in Zion* (i.e., they reach the loftiest level of Paradise). [Spiritual development should be a continuous

transform it into a wellspring,
Even with blessings
they enwrap their Guide.
8 *They advance from strength to strength*
and appear before God in Zion.
9 *HASHEM, God of Legions, hear my prayer,*
give ear, O God of Jacob, Selah.
10 *Our shield behold, O God,*
and gaze at Your anointed one's face.
11 *For better a day in Your courtyards*
than a thousand,
I prefer to stand upon

process. In life, the soul must overcome the encumbrance of animal urges and material distractions. After death, the soul is able to continue its spiritual rise without the hindrances of physical existence. This continues the ultimate goal of 'appearing before God.']

9. ה׳ אֱלֹהִים צְבָאוֹת שִׁמְעָה תְפִלָּתִי – *HASHEM, God of Legions, hear my prayer.*

[See *commentary* to 80:5.]

Redeem us swiftly *(Ibn Ezra)* and rebuild our Holy Temple *(Rashi).*

Listen to David of the tribe of Judah and thereby fulfill Moses' request, *Hear, HASHEM the voice of Judah (Deuteronomy* 33:7; *Midrash Shocher Tov).*

הַאֲזִינָה אֱלֹהֵי יַעֲקֹב סֶלָה – *Give ear, O God of Jacob, Selah.*

Respond to our prayers as You responded to the pleas of our father Jacob, whom You promised (Genesis 28:15), *Behold I am with you, and I will protect you wherever you go; and I will bring you back to this land, for I will not abandon you until I fulfill all that I promised you (Alshich).*

10. מָגִנֵּנוּ רְאֵה אֱלֹהִים – *Our shield behold, O God.*

Targum identifies *our shield* as the merits of our forefathers, which still protect us. *Rashi* says that *our shield* refers to the Temple.

Ibn Ezra interprets this as a prayer for the king, who is the protector of his subjects. *Radak* and *Sforno* perceive this as a reference to God Himself, for He is Israel's Guardian and Defender.

וְהַבֵּט פְּנֵי מְשִׁיחֶךָ – *And gaze at Your anointed one's face.*

Send the Messiah soon and guide him closely to insure his success *(Radak).*

Rebuild the Holy Temple, so that the monumental efforts which David, *Your anointed,* expended in preparing for its construction, should not be in vain *(Metzudas David).*

11. כִּי טוֹב יוֹם בַּחֲצֵרֶיךָ מֵאָלֶף – *For better a day in Your courtyards than a thousand.*

It is far better to dwell in Your presence [i.e., in the Temple] today and to die tomorrow than to live elsewhere [in exile] for one thousand years *(Targum; Rashi; Radak).*

[For in Your presence, my spirit flourishes, but estranged from You, it withers.][1]

Indeed, even one day of life in this

1. The *Talmud (Makkos* 10a) relates that David said to the Holy One, Blessed be He, 'Sovereign of the Universe, I overheard people saying, 'When will this old man [i.e. David]

יב בְּבֵית אֱלֹהַי מִדּוּר בְּאָהֳלֵי־רֶשַׁע: כִּי
שֶׁמֶשׁ | וּמָגֵן יהוה אֱלֹהִים חֵן וְכָבוֹד יִתֵּן
יהוה לֹא יִמְנַע־טוֹב לַהֹלְכִים בְּתָמִים:
יג יהוה צְבָאוֹת אַשְׁרֵי אָדָם בֹּטֵחַ בָּךְ:

world surpasses all of the existence in the World to Come [*Avos* 4:17], for this world is a *courtyard*, i.e., a corridor, where one prepares himself before entering the main hall, i.e., the World to Come [*Avos* 4:16]. Only in this world can a man fulfill God's commandments and gain merits which will enrich his future reward. In the World to Come, it is too late, for that is the time for reaping, and this world is the time for planting *(Alshich; Meir Tehillos).*

בָּחַרְתִּי הִסְתּוֹפֵף בְּבֵית אֱלֹהַי — *I prefer to stand upon the threshold of my God's house.*

The root of הִסְתּוֹפֵף is סַף, *threshold,* [which marks the סוֹף, *limit,* of the house]. David proclaimed: 'I prefer living uncomfortably on the *threshold* of a home in the land of Israel, to dwelling in the most splendid palaces on foreign soil' *(Radak; Tanchumah Re'eh* 8).

מִדּוּר בְּאָהֳלֵי רֶשַׁע — *than to dwell in the tents of wickedness.*

The faithless ones seek security in their fortified palaces and shun the company of God, but I know that these massive structures are impermanent. Only the abode of God will endure for eternity *(Malbim).*

[The verse teaches that although the fortresses of the wicked appear indestructible, this is an illusion. Actually, they are like flimsy *tents,* for their existence is temporary and they offer no permanent protection to their evil inhabitants. Man's sole true refuge lies in the fulfillment of God's will.]

12. כִּי שֶׁמֶשׁ וּמָגֵן ה׳ אֱלֹהִים — *For sun and shield is HASHEM, God.*

According to *Radak,* this refers to the status of Israel in exile. The exile is dark and forbidding, yet God is like a *sun* illuminating Israel's way. Also, He is a *shield* protecting them from the attacks of the gentiles.

Ibn Ezra understands this verse as a reference to the devoted pilgrims who make the long, difficult journey to Jerusalem. God mercifully provides the pilgrims with perfect weather and sunny skies. However, since overexposure to sun can be harmful, God acts as a *shield* to protect the pilgrims from the potentially injurious effects of the sun.

Sforno adds that when a pilgrim arrives in the courtyards of God, the Almighty rewards him with an unprecedented wave of intellectual il-

die, so that his son Solomon may build the Temple and enable us to make the festival pilgrimage to that Holy Place?' David rejoiced when he heard this [because it demonstrated how intensely the people yearned to serve God].

But God was not pleased. He said, '*Far better a day in your courtyard than a thousand*', i.e., a single day of David's devoted Torah study in My Presence surpasses the one thousand burnt-offerings which Solomon is destined to sacrifice before me on the Temple altar. [See footnote to *Psalms* 39:5, which cites *Shabbos* 30a.]

the threshold of my God's house
Than to dwell in the tents of wickedness.
12 *For sun and shield is HASHEM, God.*
Favor and glory does HASHEM bestow
He withholds no goodness
from those who walk in wholesomeness.
13 *HASHEM of Legions,*
praiseworthy is the man who trusts in You.

lumination which is as dazzling as the *sun.* At the same time, God acts as a *shield* against the pitfalls of intellectual error and misunderstanding.

Rashi, based on the *Targum,* renders שֶׁמֶשׁ as *a high, fortifed wall,* a term which describes God's protection.

[See commentary to *Psalms* 35:2 for a lengthy description of the מָגֵן *shield.*]

חֵן וְכָבוֹד יִתֵּן ה׳ — *Favor and glory does HASHEM bestow.*

Radak comments that the exile will come to an end when Israel returns to God. Then God will cause the gentiles to alter their maliciousness toward the Jews. Then the nations will no longer revile and harm the Jews, but will honor and aid them.

Ibn Ezra explains: As the pilgrims make their way to Jerusalem they will be greeted warmly in all the cities and towns they pass through. The pilgrims will find favor (חֵן) in the eys of their hosts who will be honored (כָּבוֹד) to extend them the warmest hospitality.

לֹא יִמְנַע טוֹב לַהֹלְכִים בְּתָמִים — *He withholds no goodness* [lit. *will not withhold good*] *from those who walk in wholesomeness.*

When the devout are redeemed from exile, they will lack no amenity, for the entire world will be at their service. The prophet *(Isaiah* 49:21-23) foretells: *Thus says the Lord, HASHEM, 'Behold, I will lift up my hand to the nations and will set up my standard to the peoples and they shall bring your sons in their arms and your daughters shall be carried on their shoulders. And kings shall be your mentors and their queens your nursemaids' (Radak).*

According to *Ibn Ezra,* this verse teaches that all the pilgrims' needs will be met, as they journey to Jerusalem.

13. ה׳ צְבָאוֹת אַשְׁרֵי אָדָם בֹּטֵחַ בָּךְ — *HASHEM of Legions, praiseworthy is the man who trusts in You.*

It is the man who trusts in HASHEM, who is assured [in the preceding verse] that God *will withhold no goodness* from him *(Ibn Ezra).*

This is the man who refuses to give up hope, despite the terrible length of the exile. He retains the firm belief that ultimately the Temple will be rebuilt and Israel will return to the home for which their soul yearns *(Radak).*

The Rabbis taught (*Yerushalmi, Berachos* 5:1), 'Speak these words forever and never forget them: *HASHEM of legions! Praiseworthy is the man who trusts in You.'*

מזמור פה 85

*T*his psalm describes Israel's return from the Babylonian exile to build the Second Temple. This return was not enduring because the Second Temple was eventually destroyed. Therefore, the long suffering nation yearns for a permanent redemption in which God will be completely reconciled to His land.*

One very significant sign of God's favor is the renewal of abundant precipitation and fertility in the land. Pesikta Zutrasa (Parshas Ki Tavo) *observes that a day of great rains is as significant as the day of* קִבּוּץ גָּלֻיּוֹת, Ingathering of Exiles. *Reflecting this concept, the sons of Korach juxtaposed these two themes in this psalm. First they plead (v. 7):* Will You not revive us again so Your nation will be glad in You? *Then the psalmist prophetically foretells (v. 13):* HASHEM, too, will provide good, and our land will yield its produce.

The fertility of the earth is the most accurate indication of God's favorable attitude towards Israel, because when Israel, God's chosen people, fulfills its mission on earth, God allows the earth to flourish so that Israel's way is eased and its efforts rewarded. As the psalmist declares (v. 12): Truth will sprout from earth. *This verse teaches that the 'redemption' of the soil will truly prove that Israel has returned to God's favor.*

א־ב לַמְנַצֵּחַ לִבְנֵי־קֹרַח מִזְמוֹר: רָצִיתָ יהוה
°שְׁבִית ג אַרְצֶךָ שַׁבְתָּ °שבות יַעֲקֹב: נָשָׂאתָ עֲוֹן
ד עַמֶּךָ כִּסִּיתָ כָל־חַטָּאתָם סֶלָה: אָסַפְתָּ
ה כָּל־עֶבְרָתֶךָ הֱשִׁיבוֹתָ מֵחֲרוֹן אַפֶּךָ: שׁוּבֵנוּ

2. רָצִיתָ ה׳ אַרְצֶךָ — *HASHEM, You have favored Your land.*

Rashi and *Radak* interpret this psalm as a prophecy describing our eventual redemption from the present exile. The psalmist declares, 'O God, when *You have returned the captivity of Jacob* (*v.* 2), and when *You have forgiven the iniquity of Your nation* (*v.* 3) and when *You have withheld Your entire wrath* (*v.* 4), then it will be evident that You are favorably inclined towards the Holy Land and towards the world at large. But until that time arrives, Israel and the world will not enjoy Your approval.'

Ibn Ezra and *Radak* in an alternative interpretation, perceive this psalm as a reference to Israel's return from the Babylonian Exile. The psalmist recounts how Israel merited God's favor and how He granted them the right to rebuild the Holy Temple.

Malbim contends that this psalm also alludes to the period of Ezra and Nechemiah, who returned from Babylon to establish the Second Commonwealth. The psalmist prayed that the redemption would be a permanent one.

Maharam Markado points out that in the seventh year, called שְׁמִיטָה, *shemitah,* the land of Israel is supposed to remain fallow as a testimony that the land belongs to the Almighty, Who rested on the seventh day of Creation. During the era of the First Commonwealth, the Jewish people ignored this precept and desecrated the sanctity of seventy *shemitah* years. For this reason, God devastated their land and exiled them for exactly seventy years.

The Torah warned Israel of this calamity long in advance; *Leviticus* 26:34 states: *Then shall the land find favor in her Sabbaths, as long as it lies desolate and you are in your enemies' land, then shall the land rest and find favor in her Sabbaths.*

Therefore, in describing this era, the psalmist states, *You favored Your land* [see *Midrash Shocher Tov*].

שַׁבְתָּ שְׁבוּת יַעֲקֹב — *You have returned the captivity of Jacob.*

[Similar expressions occur frequently in Scripture. Examples include בְּשׁוּב ה׳ אֶת שְׁבוּת עַמּוֹ, *When HASHEM brings back the captivity of His nation* (14:7), and בְּשׁוּב ה׳ אֱלֹהֶיךָ אֶת שְׁבוּתְךָ, *When HASHEM your God will bring back your captivity* (*Deut.* 30:3). See also *Jeremiah* 30:3, 18 and *Ezekiel* 29:14].

Malbim points out that the word is spelled שְׁבוּת, *the return,* but pronounced שְׁבִית, *the captivity.* This alludes to the fact that even when the Jews returned from Babylon, they still were not independent, but remained under Persian rule. [In the year 3390, they were permitted to return to the land only at the behest of King Cyrus. In 3408 they required the permission of King Darius II, who allowed them to begin reconstruction of the Holy Temple.

The *Talmud* (*Avodah Zarah* 9a) teaches that Persian rule of Israel lasted until [the year 3342] thirty-four years after the construction of the Second Temple began. One hundred and eighty years of Greek subjugation followed.[1]

יַעֲקֹב — *Jacob.*

1. The *Mishnah* (*Middos* 1:3) relates that the eastern gate of the Second Temple was decorated with a picture of Shushan, the capital of the Persian Empire. The *Talmud*

85
1-4

For the Conductor,
by the sons of Korach, a song.
2 HASHEM, You have favored Your land,
You have returned the captivity of Jacob.
3 You have forgiven the iniquity of Your nation,
and concealed their entire sin, Selah.
4 You have withheld Your entire wrath,
You have retreated from the fierceness of Your anger.

[Since those who return from exile will still be downtrodden captives, the psalmist refer to them as יַעֲקֹב, *Jacob* (the name reserved for the general masses) and not as יִשְׂרָאֵל, *Israel* (the name which denotes the aristocracy). See *comm.* to 14:7.]

3. נָשָׂאתָ עֲוֹן עַמֶּךָ – *You have forgiven the iniquity of Your nation.*

Israel was sent into exile only because of its sins. Once those iniquities were forgiven, You returned them to their land *(Ibn Ezra).*

כִּסִּיתָ כָל חַטָּאתָם סֶלָה – *And have concealed their entire sin, Selah.*

Although God forgets nothing, because of [His love for] the children of Israel, God makes Himself overlook and conceal their sins *(Yerushalmi Kiddushin* 1:9; *Sanhedrin* 10:1).

[The Babylonian Exile had not completely purged the Jewish people of their sins. However, because God was especially magnanimous and forgiving, He redeemed Israel because of His oath to the Patriarchs rather than the merit of Israel.][2]

4. אָסַפְתָּ כָל עֶבְרָתֶךָ – *You have withheld* [lit. *gathered in*] *Your entire wrath.*

[God's restraint and mercy at the time of redemption represented a dramatic turnabout from His unbridled anger at the time of the destruction of the First Temple. In *Lamentations* 2:1-3, we read: *Alas, the Lord in His anger has clouded the daughter of Zion. He cast down from heaven to earth the glory of Israel. He did not remember His footstool on the day of His wrath. The Lord consumed without pity all the dwellings of Jacob; in His anger He razed the fortresses of the daughter of Judah... He cut down in fierce anger all the dignity of Israel...*].

הֱשִׁיבוֹתָ מֵחֲרוֹן אַפֶּךָ – *You have retreated from the fierceness of Your anger.*

[At the time of destruction, God's anger was so fierce that the desolation was astounding. The *Talmud (Shabbos* 145b) relates that for fifty-two years no human being entered the barren land of Judea. (*Rashi* explains that this period lasted from the exile of King Tzidkiyahu in 3338 until King Cyrus

(Menachos 98a) offers two reasons for this strange decoration, which would have seemed inappropriate for such sacred environs.

Some sages maintain that this served to remind the people of their great indebtedness to the Persian kings who granted them the right to return home.

Others contend that the picture of the fortified capital was mandated by the Persian government to instill fear and awe in the hearts of the Jews, so that they would remain subservient to their Persian overlords.

2. *Ramban (comm.* to *Leviticus* 26:16) explains that the curses recorded in *Leviticus* refer to the destruction of the First Temple. There God assures Israel only that He will remember the covenant of their fathers (*Leviticus* 26:42) and the promise of their sacred land (*Leviticus*

ו אֱלֹהֵי יִשְׁעֵנוּ וְהָפֵר כַּעַסְךָ עִמָּנוּ: הַלְעוֹלָם
ז תֶּאֱנַף־בָּנוּ תִּמְשֹׁךְ אַפְּךָ לְדֹר וָדֹר: הֲלֹא־
אַתָּה תָּשׁוּב תְּחַיֵּנוּ וְעַמְּךָ יִשְׂמְחוּ־בָךְ:
ח הַרְאֵנוּ יהוה חַסְדֶּךָ וְיֶשְׁעֲךָ תִּתֶּן־לָנוּ:
ט אֶשְׁמְעָה מַה־יְדַבֵּר הָאֵל | יהוה כִּי | יְדַבֵּר

the Persian allowed the Jews to return in 3390). So scorched were the earth and the atmosphere that no animal passed through and no bird flew over the land. Even the fish abandoned the streams and followed the Jews into exile in Babylon. When God's anger abated and Israel returned, the wildlife returned with them.]

5. שׁוּבֵנוּ אֱלֹהֵי יִשְׁעֵנוּ — *Return us, O God of our salvation.*

In the preceding verses, the psalmist described how God favored Israel when He redeemed them from the Babylonian exile. Now the psalmist addresses himself to their present situation, the Roman exile, which appears to be endless. Israel implores God: *Return to us* (now) and be gracious, just as You were when You acted as the *God of our salvation,* when You terminated the first exile *(Ibn Ezra).*

וְהָפֵר כַּעַסְךָ עִמָּנוּ — *And annul Your anger with us.*

If You have taken an oath to be angry with us, please nullify it *(Tehillos Hashem),* and henceforth take a new oath to refrain from all hostility *(Sforno).* [*Thus, You will certainly be* עִמָּנוּ, *with us,* from now on, rather than against us.]

6. הַלְעוֹלָם תֶּאֱנַף בָּנוּ — *Will You forever be angry with us?*

The Babylonian Exile was confined to a preordained period of seventy years, but the present exile stretches on from generation to generation, with no end in sight *(Ibn Ezra).*

O God, You are infinite and Your punishment is infinite. How can we finite mortals endure Your endless punishment? *(Divrei Shlomo).*

תִּמְשֹׁךְ אַפְּךָ לְדֹר וָדֹר — *Draw out Your wrath for ages* [lit. *for generation and generation*].

[The psalmist echoes *Lamentations* 5:19,20: *You HASHEM are enthroned forever, Your throne is ageless. Why do You ignore us eternally, forsake us for so long?*]

Malbim points out the difference between אַף and אֲנָף. אַף refers to *wrath* which is dissipated slowly over a long period of time. It is even drawn out לְדֹר וָדֹר, *for generation upon generation.*

However, אֲנָף, *anger,* denotes a burst of anger in which the entire punishment is administered in a single dose. If God were to punish Israel with overwhelm-

26:4). God does not say, however, that He will forgive their iniquity or that He will love them as in the past or that He will gather in all the exiled Jews.

Indeed, only the tribes of Judah and Benjamin returned from the exile in Babylon, accompanied by a small group of Levites and a few members of the other tribes. They returned in poverty and in servitude to the kings of Persia.

Leviticus does not say that the people will repent completely and sincerely, but only that *they shall confess their iniquity and the iniquity of their fathers (Leviticus* 26:40). This prophecy was fulfilled by the people of the Babylonian exile in the confessions of Daniel (*Daniel* 9:5, 8, 16) and *Nehemiah (Nehemiah* 1:6-7).

This covenant of the *Book of Deuteronomy* (28:1-69) however, does not mention the duration or the end of the exile. There Scripture refers to our present captivity, which will only be terminated by our complete repentance.

5 *Return us, O God of our salvation,*
and annul Your anger with us.
6 *Will You forever be angry with us;*
draw out Your wrath for ages?
7 *Will You not revive us again*
so Your nation will rejoice in You?
8 *Show us Your kindness, HASHEM*
and grant us Your salvation.
9 *Let me hear what the God,*
HASHEM, will speak,

ing אַפְּךָ, *anger*, then we would be annihilated לְעוֹלָם, *forever.*

7. הֲלֹא אַתָּה תָּשׁוּב תְּחַיֵּינוּ – *Will You not revive us again* [lit. *return, revive us*].

In exile, we are like dead men who cannot be brought back to life by anyone but You, O God *(Ibn Ezra).*

We know that You are destined to bring about a national revival, for You have made this promise to us through Your prophets *(Rashi). Ezekiel* (37:12) prophesied: *Thus said my Lord, HASHEM, 'Behold, I am opening up your graves and I will lift you from your graves and I will bring you to the soil of Israel' (Malbim).*

[Therefore, why wait forever to honor Your solemn pledge, since it since inevitably be fulfilled?]

וְעַמְּךָ יִשְׂמְחוּ בָךְ – *So* [lit. *and*] *Your nation will rejoice in You.*

The long-awaited revival of the nation will come about by the hand of God Himself, not through an angel or an agent. Therefore, at that time, *Your nation will rejoice in You* and in no other force *(Chazah Zion).*

8. הַרְאֵנוּ ה׳ חַסְדֶּךָ – *Show us Your kindness, HASHEM.*

We hope to be worthy of redemption in accordance with the strict letter of the law. But if we are found wanting, then *show us Your kindness* and overlook our deficiencies *(Radak).*

Furthermore, let that demonstration of kindness come immediately, in our days, so that we may witness it *(Sforno).*

וְיֶשְׁעֲךָ תִּתֶּן לָנוּ – *And grant us Your salvation.*

The redemption from the first (Babylonian) exile was only a temporary salvation [which lasted through the 420 years of the Second Temple]. May the salvation from this (Roman) exile be permanent, for it is the result of Your חֶסֶד, *kindness,* which is endless; as *Isaiah* 54:8 states: וּבְחֶסֶד עוֹלָם רִחַמְתִּיךְ, *I had mercy on you with eternal kindness.*

Furthermore, may it be יֶשְׁעֲךָ, *Your salvation*, i.e., the result of Divine intervention rather than the result of human effort, for man and his accomplishments are temporary; only the achievements of God endure *(Malbim).*

9. אֶשְׁמְעָה מַה יְדַבֵּר הָאֵל ה׳ – *Let me hear what the God, HASHEM, will speak.*

The psalmist experiences a prophetic vision in which he foresees a utopian future. Inspired, he begs to witness the time when God Himself *will speak of peace to His nation (Ibn Ezra).* [Then He will be completely satisfied with their actions and by their devotion to Him.]

At Sinai, Israel heard only the first two commandments from the mouth of God. They were overwhelmed by fright, and refused to hear God's awesome

שָׁלוֹם אֶל־עַמּוֹ וְאֶל־חֲסִידָיו וְאַל־יָשׁוּבוּ
י לְכִסְלָה: אַךְ קָרוֹב לִירֵאָיו יִשְׁעוֹ לִשְׁכֹּן
יא כָּבוֹד בְּאַרְצֵנוּ: חֶסֶד־וֶאֱמֶת נִפְגָּשׁוּ צֶדֶק
יב וְשָׁלוֹם נָשָׁקוּ: אֱמֶת מֵאֶרֶץ תִּצְמָח וְצֶדֶק

voice any longer. The remaining commandments were conveyed to them through Moses.

The *Midrash* says that the voice of God purged their souls of the Evil Inclination. However, when they spurned the voice of God in favor of the words of Moses, this Evil Inclination returned to them [see *comm.* to 81:9,12,14].

In the future, the Jews will elevate themselves to a level of devotion surpassing that of Sinai. Then they will demand to *hear what the God, HASHEM, will speak.* Thus the Evil Inclination will be uprooted from their hearts forever, and Israel will never be exiled again *(Zerah Yaakov).*

כִּי יְדַבֵּר שָׁלוֹם אֶל עַמּוֹ וְאֶל חֲסִידָיו — *For He will speak of peace to His nation and to His devout ones.*

When God is reconciled with His nation, He will deliver them from the bondage of exile. All of the חֲסִידֵי אוּמוֹת הָעוֹלָם, *the devout people of the gentile nations,* who accepted God's sovereignty (even before He manifested His glory by redeeming Israel) will accompany the Jews to the Holy Land *(Radak).*

וְאַל יָשׁוּבוּ לְכִסְלָה — *That they may revert not to folly.*

Those who returned from the Babylonian Exile stumbled and returned to the path of *folly.* Therefore, they were condemned to destruction and to exile once again *(Radak).*

10. אַךְ קָרוֹב לִירֵאָיו יִשְׁעוֹ — *Surely His salvation is close for those who fear Him.*

Now the psalmist comforts the bereaved nation in exile: Do not be distraught by the length of the exile, for it can easily be brought to a swift end. The moment Israel fears HASHEM, HASHEM's anger will immediately subside *(Ibn Ezra).*

As *Deuteronomy* 30:2, 3 states: *And You will return to HASHEM, your God, and you will listen to His voice...And HASHEM, your God will return your captives and have mercy on you (Radak).*

לִשְׁכֹּן כָּבוֹד בְּאַרְצֵנוּ — *To settle glory in the land.*

In the future, God's glory will return to the land and to the Holy Temple. In the Second Temple, however, this glory was absent. The *Talmud (Yoma* 21b) relates that five Divine manifestations which were present in the First Temple were absent in the Second Temple. These were: 1) The holy Ark, along with its cover, and the *cheruvim;* 2) the heavenly fire which descended upon the altar; 3) the *Shechinah* [manifestation of the Divine Presence]; 4) *Ruach HaKodesh* [the Divine Spirit of prophecy]; and 5) *Urim V'Tumim* [the breastplate of the High Priest, which relayed prophetic messages].

All of these phenomena will be present when the Third Temple is built *(Radak; Meiri).*

11. חֶסֶד וֶאֱמֶת נִפְגָּשׁוּ — *Kindness and truth met.*

The redemption will take place when Israel becomes the universally recognized spokesman for אֱמֶת, *truth.* At that time, God will reciprocate and send forth from heaven a stream of חֶסֶד, *kindness,* to 'meet' Israel's אֱמֶת, *truth.* The *Divine kindness* will correspond to Israel's *truth* both in its extent and in its intensity *(Rashi).*

The prophet *Zephaniah* (3:13) de-

For He will speak of peace to His nation
and to His devout ones,
That they may not revert to folly.
10 *Surely His salvation is close*
for those who fear Him,
To settle glory in the land.
11 *Kindness and truth met,*
righteousness and peace kissed.
12 *Truth will sprout from earth,*
and righteousness will peer from heaven.

scribes the future role of Israel as the paragon of truth: *The remnant of Israel shall do no iniquity, nor speak lies, neither shall deceitful language be found in their mouth (Radak).*

צֶדֶק וְשָׁלוֹם נָשָׁקוּ — *Righteousness and peace kissed.*

When Israel lives by the tenets of justice and *righteousness*, it is inevitable that *peace* and harmony will ensue. *Deuteronomy* 16:20 teaches: *Righteousness, only righteousness shall you pursue so that you may live* [peacefully] *and inherit the land which HASHEM your God gives you (Sforno).*

Similarly, the prophet *Isaiah* (32:17) said, וְהָיָה מַעֲשֵׂה הַצְּדָקָה שָׁלוֹם, *And the accomplishment of righteousness will be peace (Rashi).*

[Because these two virtues are so intimately intertwined, their bond is described as a *kiss*.][1]

12. אֱמֶת מֵאֶרֶץ תִּצְמָח — *Truth will sprout from earth.*

When Israel strives to maintain *truth*, and integrity on earth, God will respond by generating a flow of *righteousness* and kindness *from heaven (Rashi; Radak).*

Sforno observes that the pious leaders of Israel can only perpetuate *truth* on earth by establishing centers of Torah study where dedicated students strive to preserve the word of God.

The *Talmud (Taanis* 8a) determines that in the merit of those who have unswerving faith in the אֱמֶת, *truth*, of God's word, the אֶרֶץ, *earth*, becomes productive, and rich crops *sprout* from the soil.

Many commentators interpret this homiletically: A person cannot percieve *truth* until he has achieved humility. Only after a person has engaged in self-criticism, ignoring pride (by figuratively lowering himself to the *earth*), can the *truth sprout (Bris Avraham; Degel Machneh Ephraim).*

וְצֶדֶק מִשָּׁמַיִם נִשְׁקָף — *And righteousness will peer from heaven.*

In response to the *truth* which

1. The *Midrash (Shemos Rabbah* 5:10) perceives this verse as an allusion to the meeting of Moses and his brother Aaron, after a long period of separation. Each brother developed differently, and represented a unique character trait. Aaron represented חֶסֶד, *kindness*, which connotes flexibility and compassion, whereas Moses embodied אֱמֶת, *truth*, which connotes firm standards and values. Aaron strove for שָׁלוֹם, *peace*, and compromised; while Moses stood for צֶדֶק, *righteousness*, and strict adherence to the law, without concessions.

Nevertheless, these brothers, who were ostensibly complete opposites, met and kissed each other *(Exodus* 4:27) to signify that they would complement one another by blending their diverse talents into a unified leadership unit.

יג מִשָּׁמַיִם נִשְׁקָף: גַּם־יהוה יִתֵּן הַטּוֹב
יד וְאַרְצֵנוּ תִּתֵּן יְבוּלָהּ: צֶדֶק לְפָנָיו יְהַלֵּךְ
וְיָשֵׂם לְדֶרֶךְ פְּעָמָיו:

sprouts from the earth, God acts with kindness and *righteousness* and sends the rains down from heaven *(Taanis* 8a).[1]

13. גַּם ה׳ יִתֵּן הַטּוֹב – *HASHEM, too, will provide good.*

The rains which HASHEM will send as a reward for אֱמֶת, *truth*, will not be ordinary precipitation; these rains will come from a special cache of טוֹב, *good*, as Scripture promises *(Deuteronomy* 28:12): יִפְתַּח ה׳ לְךָ אֶת אוֹצָרוֹ הַטּוֹב אֶת הַשָּׁמַיִם..., *HASHEM shall open up to you His good treasure, the heaven, to give the rain to your land in its season and to bless the work of your hand (Radak).*

[Ordinary rain can sometimes

1. The *Talmud (Bava Basra* 11a; *Yerushalmi Peah* 1:1) relates the story of King Munbaz who converted to Judaism. Once, in a year of famine, he spent his entire fortune in an attempt to feed the poor. His brothers and relatives criticized him severely for dissipating the wealth which his royal forebears had accumulated over many generations.

Munbaz explained to his relatives that the dissipation of this fortune was decidely more advantageous to him than the hoarding practiced by his royal ancestors. He said: 'My forebears gathered riches for This World, but I gather riches for the World to Come. My forebears left their fortunes to others; they never enjoyed what they greedily amassed. My fortune [i.e., my reward] is preserved for me eternally. My forebears stored their wealth here on earth, where it is vulnerable to theft and loss, but I stored my wealth in heaven above, where it is safe from all harm. Scripture states: *When truth* [i.e., fulfillment of Torah] *will sprout from* [good deeds performed on] *the earth,* [this truth will be transformed into spiritual wealth], *and righteousness will peer from heaven* [where this wealth is stored].'

13 *HASHEM, too, will provide good,*
and our land will yield its produce.
14 *Righteousness will precede him,*
and he will set his footsteps on the path.

produce undesirable or harmful effects, and storms can devastate the land. But the benign rains which descend from *the good treasure* bring only prosperity and blessing.]

וְאַרְצֵנוּ תִּתֵּן יְבוּלָהּ — *And our land will yield its produce.*

[God suffuses the Holy Land with sanctity by saturating the earth with the rains which are stored in the sacred *good treasure* in heaven.

The fruits and produce of the Holy Land absorb this unique spiritual power, and become a source of nutrition not only for the body, but also for the soul (see commentary of *Bayis Chadash* to *Tur Orach Chaim* 208).]

14. צֶדֶק לְפָנָיו יְהַלֵּךְ — *Righteousness will precede him* [lit. *go before him*].

[When *righteousness will peer from heaven* — i.e., when it will fill the earth (*v.* 12), men will always recognize God's righteousness (see *Radak*).]

וְיָשֵׂם לְדֶרֶךְ פְּעָמָיו — *And he will set his footsteps on the path.*

[When God's righteousness becomes clearly evident, men will strive to emulate His ways by acting righteously. They will make this their life's goal, and they will train their *footsteps* in that direction (see *Radak*).]

Dorash Moshe comments that the righteous deeds which a person performs in his lifetime pave his *path* to heaven. [If the deeds were perfect, the pathway will be smooth. If the deeds were not performed wholeheartedly, the highway heavenward will be tortuous and cracked.] When the time comes for a man's soul to depart from This World, he *will set his footsteps on the path* of good deeds which he prepared in his lifetime.

[Similarly, if Israel yearns to return from exile, the only path open to them is the highway which they themselves will pave with their own righteousness.]

APPENDIX:
The Menorah

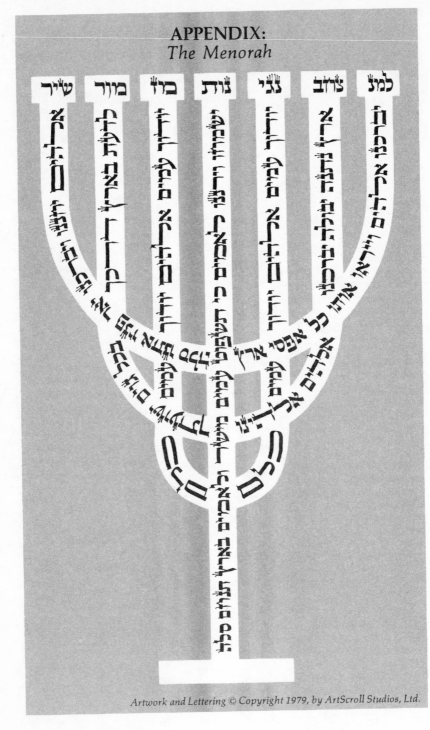

למנ צחב נגי נות מז מור שיר

יברכנו אלהים וייראו אותו כל אפסי ארץ

ארץ נתנה יבולה יברכנו אלהים אלהינו

יודוך עמים אלהים יודוך עמים כלם

ישמחו וירננו לאמים כי תשפט עמים מישור ולאמים בארץ תנחם סלה

יודוך עמים אלהים יודוך עמים כלם

לדעת בארץ דרכך בכל גוים ישועתך

אלהים יחננו ויברכנו יאר פניו אתנו סלה